RESIDENCE OF THE LATE CAPT. JOSEPH J. WHITING.

A HISTORICAL SKETCH OF THE TOWN OF HANOVER, MASS., WITH FAMILY GENEALOGIES.

BY JOHN S. BARRY,

AUTHOR OF "RECORDS OF THE STETSON FAMILY."

BOSTON:

PUBLISHED FOR THE AUTHOR BY SAMUEL G. DRAKE, 15 BRATTLE ST.

BAZIN & CHANDLER, PRINTERS, 37 CORNHILL.

ENGRAVINGS BY BAKER, SMITH AND ANDREW, 46 COURT ST.

1853.

TABLE OF CONTENTS.

CHAPTER I.

Early settlement of the territory, in connection with that of Scituate — Incorporation of the Town, and present boundaries — Remonstrance of Abington — Acquiescence of Scituate — Ancient boundaries — Family locations previous to the Revolution. 9–27

CHAPTER II.

NATURAL HISTORY.

Geology of the Town — Forests, ancient and modern, with their products, value and uses — Herbaceous Plants — Birds, &c. — Laws for their destruction, and argument for their preservation — Wild and Domestic Fruits — Ancient Sheep Husbandry, and the Culture of Flax, Wheat, &c. Materials for improving the soil — Indications of progress. 28–41

CHAPTER III.

INDIANS.

Names of the seven principal tribes — Chikatabut's possessions — Indian Deed of Scituate — Manners and customs of the natives — Stature, clothing, money, weapons, dwellings, food, &c. — Dishes at the first meeting of the Old Colony Club — Philip's War — Reminiscenses of the Indians of Hanover — Changes which have taken place since those days. 42–53

CHAPTER IV.

ECCLESIASTICAL HISTORY.

Provisions for the support of Public worship — Erection of the *first meeting house* in Hanover — Its appearance — Gathering of the worshippers — Settlement of Mr. Bass — Seating the house — Communion service — Insubordination of the youth — Sternhold and Hopkins' Hymns — Decease of Mr. Bass — His character — Settlement of Mr. Baldwin — Gift of a parsonage — Erection of the *second meeting house* — Its appearance — Decease of Mr. Baldwin — Sketch of his life — Attempt to settle Mr. Litchfield — Settlement of Mr. Mellen — First *Bell* — Painting the house, and other repairs — Withdrawal of Mr. Mellen — His decease — Sketch of his life, and list of his publications — Settlement of Mr. Chaddock — Withdrawal — Sketch of his life — Settlement of Mr. Chapin — Sketch of his life — Settlement of Mr. Smith — His life and writings — Erection of the *third meeting house* — Settlement of Mr. Duncan. 54–74

CHAPTER V.

ECCLESIASTICAL HISTORY CONTINUED.

Establishment of St. Andrew's Church in Scituate — First meeting house — Mr. Davenport's ministry — Mr. Brockwell's — Mr. Thompson's — Sketch of his descendants — Mr. Wheeler's ministry — Removal of the Church to Hanover — Erection of a New Meeting House — Rectorship of Messrs. Cooper, Wolcott, Appleton, Greenleaf, and Cutler — Establishment of a Society in the Northerly part of Hanover, and Westerly part of Scituate — Incorporation as a Universalist Society — Sketch of its history — History of the Baptist Society. 75–84

CHAPTER VI.

EDUCATION.

Early laws for the support of education — Our Common School System — Schoolmasters — Schools established in Hanover — Mr. Fitzgerald — Joseph Cushing — Luke Stetson — Sketch from 1750 to 1840 — Table of appropriations — Academy, Mr. Chaddock's — Removal to the Four Corners — Second building — New Edifice, built in 1852 — Proprietors — Lawyers — Physicians — Graduates. 85–101

CHAPTER VII.

MILITARY HISTORY.

Military training of our ancestors — Town's stock of powder &c. — Expedition to the Spanish West Indies — Expedition to Cape Breton — French Neutrals — French War, with extracts from the Muster Rolls. 102–107

CHAPTER VIII.

INCIDENTS OF THE REVOLUTION.

Causes of the Revolution — Stamp Act — Convention in Boston — Plymouth County Convention — Provincial Congresses — Preparations for defence — Minute men — Provincial Treasurer chosen — Committees of Safety — Boston Port Bill — Tories, and the Ruggles Covenant — Balfour's troops — Commencement of hostilities — Sea coast guards — General Washington assumes the command of the Army — Station of the army — Operations for 1776 — Entrenchment on Dorchester heights — Evacuation of Boston — Alarm at Cohasset — Declaration of Independence — Operations around Boston — Men for Ticonderoga and for Rhode Island — Operations for 1777 — Committee of Safety — Prices for labor — Town's quota — Expedition to Rhode Island — Other military movements — Operations for 1778 — Quota of Shirts, &c. — State Constitution rejected — Enlistments for this year — Extracts from the Pay Rolls — Operations for 1779 — Committee of Safety, &c. — Enlistments — Committee of Safety for 1780 — Military movements for the year — Depreciation of Currency — The dark hour — Movements for 1781 — Incidents subsequent to the War. 108–130

CHAPTER IX.

MILITARY HISTORY CONTINUED.

Military Companies subsequent to the Revolution — Hanover Artillery Company — Hanover Light Infantry — Hanover Rifle Company — War of 1812 — List of Soldiers. 131–136

CHAPTER X.

MANUFACTURES AND TRADE.

History of Manufactures in the town — Forges and Furnaces — Bardin's, now the Curtis Forge — Barstow's, now Sylvester's Forge — Dyer's, now Perry's Tack Factory — Sketch of the Life of Col. Jesse Reed — The Drinkwater Works, now Bates and Holmes — Barker's Foundry — Salmond's Tack Works — Tolman's Mills — Saw and Grist Mills — Plough Manufacture, and Sketch of the Life of David Prouty — Other branches of Industry. 137–155

CHAPTER XI.

SHIP BUILDING.

Former and present state of the art of Ship-building in America — Materials for the construction of vessels — Massachusetts Enterprise — Ship-building on the North River — Yards in Pembroke — Yards in Hanover — The Barstows, Sylvesters, Sampsons, Clarks, Perrys, Eells, Paiges, Baileys, Smiths, Kingmans, Wings, Stockbridges, &c. — Obstructions in the River — Petitions to Congress for their removal — Decline of the business — Present condition of the village. 156–165

CHAPTER XII.

PROVISIONS FOR THE POOR — TEMPERANCE CAUSE — SLAVERY — RESTING PLACES FOR THE DEAD — LONGEVITY.

Provisions for the Poor — Poor kept by Friends — Selectmen to provide for them — Put out at Auction — Establishment of an Alms-House — Temperance Cause — Excise Bill of 1751 — Rum Trade at that date — Extracts from the Church Records Relative to the Excise Bill — Temperance Society formed in 1816 — Later History of the Cause — Slavery in New England — Owners of Slaves, from the Church and Town Records — Touching Incident — Burial Ground near the Centre of the Town — Gifts of Land by David Stockbridge, Esq., and by John Barstow, Esq., — Burial Ground at Snappet — Table of Longevity. 166–180

CHAPTER XIII.

Highways — Streets — Bridges — Ponds — Streams — and Landmarks. 181–192

PART II.

FAMILY GENEALOGIES. - - - - - 193

LIST OF ILLUSTRATIONS.

1. Residence of the late Capt. Joseph J. Whiting. (Frontispiece)
2. First Central Meeting House - - - - - - - 57
3. Second, and Present Central Meeting Houses - - - 65
4. Old, and Present Episcopal Churches - - - - - 77
5. Old, and Present Universalist Meeting Houses - - - 81
6. Baptist Meeting House - - - - - - - - 83
7. Academy, at the Four Corners - - - - - - 93
8. The Curtis Forge - - - - - - - - 139

9 and 10. Ancient and Modern Ploughs - - - - 148 and 149

11. Ancient Ship, of the days of the Pilgrims - - - - 156
12. Plan of the Ship yards - - - - - - - 158
13. Bailey Coat of Arms, and Autographs - - - - - 199
14. The Baldwin House - - - - - - - - 206
15. Residence of Capt. Seth Barker - - - - - - 207
16. Barstow Coat of Arms - - - - - - - - 208
17. Residence of Col. John B. Barstow - - - - - 227
18. Residence of Mr. Elisha Bass - - - - - - 244
19. Bates Coat of Arms - - - - - - - - 245
20. Curtis Coat of Arms - - - - - - - - 272
21. Residence of Mr. George Curtis - - - - - - 286
22. The Judge Cushing House - - - - - - - 290
23. Residence of Rev. Samuel Cutler - - - - - - 291
24. Residence of Capt. Nathan Dwelley - - - - - 299
25. Residence of Mr. Charles Dyer - - - - - - 300
26. Residence of J. T. Gardner, Esq. - - - - - 312
27. Residence of Dr. A. C. Garratt - - - - - - 313
28. Jacobs Coat of Arms - - - - - - - - 319
29. Josselyn Coat of Arms - - - - - - - - 335
30. Residence of Rev. R. L. Killam - - - - - - 348
31. Likeness of Col. Jesse Reed - - - - - - - 363
32. Stetson Coat of Arms - - - - - - - - 378
33. Residence of Martin W. Stetson - - - - - - 380
34. Stockbridge Coat of Arms - - - - - - - 384
35. Studley Coat of Arms - - - - - - - - 392
36. Sylvester Coat of Arms - - - - - - - - 400
37. Residence of Mr. John Sylvester - - - - - - 404
38. " " " Michael Sylvester - - - - - 406
39. " " " Robert Sylvester - - - - - 407
40. Whiton Coat of Arms - - - - - - - - 419

INTRODUCTION.

In sending forth the following work, to be subjected to the inspection and criticism of the public, the author is aware, that he assumes a great responsibility, inasmuch as every historical work, is to effect, for good or ill, the reputation of those who are named in its pages. For the manner in which this difficult task has been executed in the present instance, it is hoped that but little cause of complaint will be found. Many thanks are due to those who have kindly aided my labors, and strenghtened my purposes.

Valuable assistance has been derived from the Library of the Mass., and New England Historical Societies, and that of the State, the Records of Plymouth and Suffolk Counties, and from many published histories, and private manuscripts. If the work meets the approbation of the public, and if it is found to contain a faithful and impartial record of facts, the author will feel that his labor has not been in vain. Every attempt, however humble, to rescue from oblivion the fast fading mementos of the past, is laudable, and valuable; and local histories, furnish the materials from which, hereafter, works of a more general character, will be written. That this work, imperfect as it is, may fill some niche in the "gallery of history," is all that the author can ask.

ERRATA.

A few errors have been discovered, in carrying the work through the press, the most important of which are here noted, for correction.

Page 10. The date of the incorporation of Scit., should be 1636, not 1642, and it was strictly the 2nd town *incorporated*, as well as the 2nd *settled*, in Plymouth Colony.

P. 14, line 7, read 42° 7', instead of 40° 7',

P. 18, line 3, read *son* of William, instead of *grandson*.

P. 19, line 16, read 1660, instead of 1690.

P. 27, last line, read *gleanings* instead of *gleamings*.

P. 33, *note*, read 20 ft., instead of thirty.

P. 50, line 21, read *Winslow*, instead of *Winston*.

P. 56, line 35, read Isaac *Buck*, instead of *Bush*.

P. 73, last line of the quotation, read *frondes* instead of *fondes*.

P. 264, last line, read *records* , instead of *readers*.

P. 271, last line but one, note, read 1648 instead of 1748.

P. 328, line 27, read p. 32, instead of 34.

P. 311. The dates of birth, &c., in the family of Mr. Hiram Gardner, should be as follows: (by 2nd,) *Charlotte S.*, May 17, 1842; *Anne R.*, Feb. 8, 1844; *George*, May 12, 1845; *Curtis*, Nov. 2, 1846, d. Sept. 24, 1848; and *Sarah C.*, Mar. 29, 1852. So says the wife of Mr. G.

P. 374 The w. of Mr. Eben'r. Simmons, was of Little Compton, R. I., instead of Prov.; and Mr. S. was a Lt., in the war of 1812, under the U. S. Gov't. His son Perez, was a member of the "Suffrage Convention,' as it is called, whilst in R. I., and in consequence of difficulties growing out of his sympathy with Mr. Dorr, he left the State, and settled in his native town.

HISTORY OF HANOVER, MASS.

CHAPTER I.

"O dark the scene and dreary,
When here they set them down,
Of storms and billows weary,
And chilled with winter's frown.
Deep moaned the forests to the wind,
Loud howled the savage foe,
While here their evening prayer arose,
Two hundred years ago." FLINT.

Early settlement of the territory, in connexion with that of Scituate — Incorporation of the Town, and present boundaries — Remonstrance of Abington — Acquiescence of Scituate — Ancient boundaries — Family locations previous to the Revolution.

THE TOWN OF HANOVER, whose history we propose to sketch in the following pages, was incorporated as late as 1727, or more than one hundred years after the landing of the Pilgrims; but its territory was actually settled as early as 1649, or less than thirty years after the landing. Although its municipal age, therefore, may not be so great as that of many other towns in the county, yet its history may properly date back a century at least previous to its incorporation.

The landing of the Pilgrims took place on Monday, December 11th, 1620, *Old Style*, or December 21st, *New Style*, on the ever memorable Rock at Plymouth: and this was the first successful settlement made in Massachusetts.[1] It was not till twelve

1 Thacher's History of Plymouth, p. 24.

years after, or in 1632, that the first settlements were made in Duxbury,[1] and this town, which was incorporated in 1637, then embraced within its limits the present towns of Marshfield, incorporated in 1640; Bridgewater, incorporated in 1656, and covering the territory included in North, East, West, and South Bridgewater, or Bridgewater proper;[2] Abington, incorporated in 1712;[3] and Pembroke, also incorporated in 1712, from which, in 1820, the present town of Hanson was set off.

Less than eight years after the landing of the Pilgrims, however, or in 1628, settlements were made in Scituate; and although this town was not incorporated until 1642, or five years after Duxbury, and two after Marshfield, yet it properly ranks next to Plymouth in age, it having been the second town settled in the Plymouth Colony.

The greater part of the present territory of Hanover originally belonged to Scituate, and so remained, until its erection into a township by itself. The early history of the town, therefore, is identified with, and strictly belongs to, that of Scituate. But it will not be necessary to enter into many details relating to the latter town. The history of Scituate has been published to the world; and had we the disposition, it is doubtful if we could add much to Deane's excellent narrative.

We shall content ourselves with a few brief notes; and present these, more for the purpose of showing how, when, and by whom the territory and town of Hanover were first settled, than to rewrite what has been once so ably written.

As we just remarked, the first settlements were made in Scituate eight years after the landing of the Pilgrims, or in 1628; and the names of these early settlers were William Gilson, Anthony Annable, Thomas Bird, Nathaniel Tilden, Edward Foster, Henry Rowley, and others, called "Men of Kent," probably from their having come from the County of Kent in England.[4]

The first lots on record, granted in Scituate in 1633, were in

1 Winsor's Duxbury, p. 9.
2 Mitchell's Bridgewater, p. 10.
3 Hobart's Abington, p. 35.
4 The name of this ancient town is found on the map in "Wood's New England's Prospect," published in 1633, a copy of which is annexed to "Fowle's Outline Map of Massachusetts," hanging upon the walls of most of our school-rooms. Also in Young's Chronicles of Massachusetts, p. 389.

that part of the town called *The Harbor*, and on the *second cliff*. The *third cliff* had been previously appropriated and occupied. In August, 1633, the inhabitants proceeded to lay out a regular *village*, allowing to no man more than *four acres* for a house lot, the proposition being "to build a compact street for purpose of mutual defence."[1] This was called *Kent Street*, and led from the bridge at the harbor, easterly to the third cliff. Here houses were built; and when, in 1634, the Rev. Mr. Lothrop, with thirty of his church, arrived from London, who were joined the same winter by others, some of whom were "Men of Kent," additional house lots were granted, and additional tenements reared. Deane suggests that these primitive houses were built of logs, and covered with thatch cut from the sedges which grew profusely upon the neighboring marshes. But as it was "agreed upon by the whole Court, held the sixth of January, 1627, that from henceforward no dwelling-house was to be covered with any kind of thache, as straw, reed, &c., but with either board or pale, and the like to wit of all that were to be new built in the towne," we think it probable that most of the houses were covered with "board or pale."[2] True, the law applied to Plymouth only, when passed, but would be likely to be observed throughout the colony. And as the settlers of Scituate were many of them men of substance, they were not compelled by poverty to build their dwellings in the rudest form, though those of the poorer class may have been covered with thatch. Houses were built, however; and here, for a series of years, dwelt in comparative seclusion, in their wilderness home, a race of men, many of whom had lived in far costlier habitations in the land of their nativity, and enjoyed advantages, for literary culture and social intercourse, far superior to what could be immediately expected in their new abode.

But though the act of their coming here was to some extent voluntary, yet it must have been with feelings of loneliness and depression, in their thoughtful moods, that they looked out upon that broad ocean, stretching before them, not whitened as now with the sails of every clime, but expanding, a gulf of three thousand miles between them and their

1 Deane's Scituate, p. 8. 2 Plymouth Colony Laws, p. 29.

former home; its waves, in the storm, lashing with fury the rock-bound coast, and striking terror to the mother's heart; or in its milder moods, laving the shore with quiet murmurings, the more calculated to awaken in the saddened spirit emotions which find vent chiefly in sighs. Or as they looked behind, upon that broad forest, clothing plain and hill, where wild beasts prowled, and the Indian roamed, and not a sign or a token of civilized life appeared, and as they felt their exposure to the deadly incursions of these hostile foes, iron wills must have been possessed by the men, and iron nerves have braced the gentler sex, else could they never have passed through the perils which surrounded them, and the dangers of their earlier days, with that calm composure and unwavering trust which they ever displayed.

But a life of privation, and hardship and toil, was encountered with cheerfulness, and endured without murmuring, for the praiseworthy object of permanently securing for themselves and their posterity, what they had never fully enjoyed on English soil,—a diffusive civil, and an enlightened religious liberty. Animated by this purpose, they moved steadily on, "fainting not for weakness, faltering not for pain," their tears and their blood watering the soil, and their lives yielded a willing sacrifice to the cause of freedom!

The boundaries of Scituate remained unsettled for some years. It was the practice of the Colony Court to make grants, from time to time, to new planters, as they requested it; waiting until each settlement should become of sufficient magnitude to require corporate powers, before conferring the same. The "Conihasset Grant" was made in 1633, to four gentlemen, usually called "Merchant Adventurers of London;"[1] and in 1637, the tract called "The Two Miles," now a part of Marshfield, was granted on the application of Mr. Timothy Hatherly, and the Rev. Mr. Lothrop, accompanied by a Committee of fifteen of the principal planters.[2]

Finally, in 1642, by order of the Court, the general bounds of the town were fixed "on the westerly side up the Indian Head River, to the Pond, which is the head of said River; and from

1 Deane's Scituate, p. 4. 2 Ibid, p. 7.

thence to Accord Pond; and from thence to the sea, by the line that is the bound between Massachusetts and Plymouth." [1]

Upon this territory, which included the most of Hanover, the first settlers, with their descendants, and those who subsequently joined them, took up their abode, and spent their days, in the peaceful pursuit of agriculture, manufactures, and commerce, interrupted only by occasional periods of Indian warfare, during which, and especially in that bloody and protracted campaign which signalized Philip's war in 1676, much suffering was endured, many of their houses were destroyed, and many precious and valuable lives were lost. But of these matters we shall have occasion to speak more at large hereafter.

As we have already observed, the first settlements in Scituate proper, were at the *harbor*. But as years rolled on, and the country around was explored, and the population continued to increase, by internal growth and external additions, lands farther back from the shore began to be improved, and settlers pushed their way along up the windings of the North River, dotting its banks here and there with their simple dwellings, and spacious farms; — occasionally varying the scene by the establishment of a ship-yard; — and thence up the Indian Head, where forges and furnaces were erected from 1704 to 1710; and so back towards the colony line, and in the vicinity of the third Herring Brook, where were saw and grist-mills, and farms of considerable extent; until eventually, towards the close of the seventeenth century, a respectable number of busy and enterprising men were resident upon the territory now included in Hanover; and during the first quarter of the eighteenth century, that number was so much enlarged, (the population amounting to nearly three hundred souls,) that the inhabitants began to think of petitioning to be incorporated into a town by themselves; and in 1727, their petition having been presented and carefully considered, their wishes were gratified, the new town took its place among the municipalities of the county, and received its name of HANOVER, probably in compliment to the DUKE OF HANOVER, who had lately been called to the English throne under the title of GEORGE THE FIRST.

At present, the town is bounded on the North by Abington and

1 Deane's Scituate, p. 1.

South Scituate; on the East by South Scituate; on the South by Pembroke and Hanson; and on the West by Abington. Its area is fifteen and one half square miles, or nearly ten thousand acres. The latitude of the centre-meeting house, from the State Trigonometrical Survey, is 42° 06′ 49″, and lon. 70° 49′ 13″, and of the Town Hall, as laid down on the map published by Mr. Whiting, the lat. is 40° 7′, and the lon. 70° 50′ 58″. Distance from Boston to the Four Corners, twenty-two miles; from thence to Plymouth, fourteen miles. This was the *thirteenth* town established within the limits of the county; and according to the census of 1850, is the *fourteenth* in point of population, and the *fifteenth* on the valuation list. Being principally a farming town, and possessing but few external advantages, its growth has not been so rapid as that of some other towns, perhaps more recently incorporated. Still, industry and frugality have ever characterized the people; and steadiness in business, and general intelligence, have proved the sure elements of rational prosperity.

As might well be supposed, the new town was not incorporated without some opposition on the part of its neighbors. Scituate, which was to be most seriously affected, sent no remonstrance to the General Court which remains on file, and voted at a meeting held in 1726 not to oppose its incorporation; but Abington, which was then less thickly settled than Scituate, though now having nearly double the population, and which was struggling to maintain its own existence, complained that the change contemplated would not only considerably diminish its territory, but seriously weaken and cripple its resources.

In the latter town, in September, 1726, Lieutenant William Reed, Matthew Pratt, Edward Bates, and Samuel Noyes, were chosen a committee "to draw up objections in answer to the Drinkwater people's petition to draw off from them," and it was voted, "that Matthew Pratt and Samuel Noyes should carry the answer to the Court."[1] This remonstrance was presented April 19, 1727, and the reasons assigned in it why the inhabitants of Abington opposed the petitioners prayer are,—"1. Because of the fewness of our families in number, which is but about fifty-

[1] Hobart's History of Abington, p. 131.

three, including the eight desiring to be set off; and of these five are newly married, and have neither house nor home, but as they sojourn under the roofs of others; and of the rest, six are widows, whose husbands have of late deceased, leaving their families much broken, and under low circumstances; which nineteen, taken from fifty-three, leaves but thirty-four; — and even of these some are so poor that they are left out of the rates, and have need of support from the town; — so that there will be but thirty families left to bear the public charges. 2. The part of the town petitioning to be set off, contains eleven polls, and above one-fifth of the rateable estate; and although there will still be left to Abington a considerable tract of land, yet but little part of it is capable of settlement, except the easterly part, which is chiefly in gentlemen proprietors hands, who do neither sell nor settle their lands, they living in other towns, and improving the same only as timber lots; and the inhabitants petitioning to be set off dwell on the easterly part of these great lots, which run westerly nearly to the centre of Abington, which will hence be exempt from taxation here for the support of the ministry. And, 3. That the eight petitioners for the separation, viz.: Elijah Cushing, Jeremiah Hatch, Nathaniel Davis, Joseph Bryant, Nehemiah Cushing, Benjamin Loring, and Isaac Hatch, though they urged their distance from public worship, were but four miles from the meeting house, and that if it was objected that the way was difficult and impassable, yet several responsible men had offered to make it good and passable, for man and horse, for £5 charge."[1]

The Court, on the reception of this remonstrance, appointed a Committee, consisting of Lieut.-Governor Tailor, and Elisha Cook, Esq., of the Council, and Ezra Bourne, Esq., Major Tileston, and Edward Arnold, Esq., of the House, to view the territory, and they reported in favor of its incorporation, although they allowed that it would "put the inhabitants of Abington under some difficulties, respecting the supporting the public worship of God, for that several large tracts of land within the town did not pay towards the maintenance of the ministry."

To remedy this evil, however, at a subsequent date, by petition

1 State files, "Towns," 113, pp. 684, 694.

presented June 20, 1727, the Court authorized Abington to levy a tax of one half-penny per acre, for three years, on all dormant or non-resident lands within their limits, for the support of the ministry, and also granted them as a compensation for what they had lost, a tract of land lying to the North-east of that commonly called Waldo's farm.[1]

Scituate, the town most deeply interested in this decision, seems to have acquiesced in it, without any serious complaints, and so far as we can learn from an examination of the records of that town, cheerfully extended to the inhabitants of the newly incorporated district the hand of fellowship, and continued to live with them on terms of friendship, and reciprocal good will.

And now that the new town is fairly started upon a career of its own, it may be well to pause for a moment, and glance at the *territory* it embraced, and at the *men* who settled that territory; picturing to ourselves, as well as we can, the appearance which it would have presented, had we been permitted, from some appropriate eminence, to survey the scene, and note its features.

First and foremost stands the *Town itself*. Its *ancient boundaries* are described in the Act of Incorporation, as "beginning at the Third Herring Brook, at David Jacobs' Saw Mill Dam, and from thence running near West about two hundred and fifty six rods, to the Northeast corner of Isaac Turner's Great Lot, then near west with the north side line of said Great Lot, one mile to the *share line*,[2] and then continuing the same course three quarters of a mile; then turning and running near South, two miles to the South west corner of Nehemiah Cushing's lot, then South five degrees and forty minutes West to the Southerly bounds of Abington and Pembrook, and on Indian Head River, and South easterly by the North River, and easterly by the aforesaid Third Herring Brook, from the said North River, to the Dam before mentioned."[3]

The territory here described, is substantially that now constituting the town, — only a small gore having been annexed to Pembroke; — and valuable as it is to the present proprietors,

1 State Files, "Towns," 113, p. 708.
2. This *share line* was the original easterly boundary of Abington.
3. State Files, "Towns," 113, pp. 704 and 707.

and pleasant as is the home it affords to nearly sixteen hundred free and industrious people, it was still more highly prized, because obtained at greater sacrifices, by the *original settlers;* and the *location* of these early residents we propose briefly to notice, according to the best information we have been able to obtain, derived from the Records of the Town and Church, from wills and deeds, and from family tradition; and should any mistakes occur in this, which has proved a difficult part of our task, we can confidently affirm that our list of *names* is correct, so far as it extends, and errors of *location* it is impossible always to avoid, inasmuch as the ways travelled then were not, in every case, precisely the same as the highways of our own days, and many families have removed from the town, leaving few traces of their existence behind them.

At the Four Corners, and along the North, and Indian Head Rivers, the earliest settlements were made. Near the North River, and N. 18° W. 125 rods from the Four Corners, the respectable and enterprising family of *Barstows* settled, as early as 1649. The house of William, the ancestor, who was a carpenter or shipwright by trade, stood in the pasture a few rods North of Back, and East of Washington Street. How it was constructed, or when it was torn down, we have no means of determining with certainty. It had a *cellar*, the outlines of which are still visible, partially filled with stones and rubbish; and a few scattering trees, the remnants of an old orchard, known as the Benjamin Barstow orchard, are standing near the spot. Whether these trees constituted a part of the original orchard of Mr. Barstow, we cannot say, but it is certain that he had an orchard, as in the volume of "Actions," in the Records of the Old Colony, p. 69, William Barstow complains of John Palmer, Sen. and John Palmer, jr. in an action of £10 damage, "for setting of trapps and caching of swine, whereby the said Barstow is damnified;" and on the same page, is the entry of another action instituted against John Palmer, damage £10, "for pulling down fence, and *damnifying his apple trees*, and for stroying his corn, English and Indian, with his hoggs." In the old family mansion, William, the youngest son of William, Senr. resided, and after him, his son Benjamin, with his numerous family of *twenty-one children.*

Farther east, or 41 rods N. E. of the Corners, and opposite the residence of Joseph S. Bates, on Broadway, stood the house of Joseph Barstow, grandson of William, which was used as a block-house or garrison house in the Indian War of 1676. This structure was removed many years ago, but its foundation is still visible, and the outlines of the same may be traced even from the road.

In March 1672, liberty was "graunted and allowed to Joseph Barstow to keep an ordinary at the place where he now lives, and that he be provided always with necessaries for the entertainment of travellers, and keep good order in his house, that there be no just cause of complaint against him in that behalfe."[1]

Across the North River, in Oct. 1656, William, Senr. was authorised to build a bridge, "above the third herring brook, at stoney reache, being the place where now passengers goe frequently over; the said bridge to bee made sufficient for horse and foot; and to cleare and marke a way to Hughes cross, and to open and clear and make a way along beyand Hughes Crosse toward the bay, soe as to avoid a certain Rocky hill and swamp; — he to have £12 current countrey pay for so doing."[2]

July 27. 1662, Mr. Barstow agreed with Mr. Constant Southworth, and Major Josias Winslow, in behalf of the Colony of New Plymouth, to keep in repair and maintain the bridge called Barstow's bridge, upon the North River, in consideration of £20 in hand paid, for 20 years, to serve for transportation of passengers, horses, chattle, and all such use as they shall ordinarily put it to," and pledged for the fulfilment of this contract, the house and land in and on which he dwelt, a small tract already disposed of to his son (in law) Moses Simmons, only excepted.[3]

This bridge, the first built on the stream, stood above the present bridge, and the old piers, which are still visible, and which belonged to the second bridge, are probably near, if not on the spot where Mr. Barstow built.

In 1657, Mr. Barstow was "allowed by the Court to draw and sell wine, beer, and strong waters for passengers that come and goe

1 Col. Rec. 3. 78.
2 Ibid. 3. 107.
3 Col. Rec. 4. 76.

over the bridge he hath lately made, or others that shall have occation, unless any just exception shall come in against him."[1] He had been previously licensed to keep an ordinary;[2] so that we think it probable that near his bridge he had a small building as a kind of toll-house, and here his refreshments were kept.

About 1662, a grant of land was made to William Barstow, "lying westward of Cornett Studsons graunt, in reference to satisfaction for his paines &c. in the countreys business;"[3] and the commissioners were instructed to lay out for him not less than 40, nor more than 50 acres of arable land.

Benjamin, Capt. Joseph, and Samuel Barstow, were the representatives of the family in Hanover, at the date of the incorporation of the town.

Benjamin, who occupied his grandfather's house, was engaged principally in ship-building, at the yard established by the family on the North River, as early as 1690, and this business is still followed by his descendants. Some of his sons moved to Rochester, and established ship-yards, yet improved by their descendants, who are among the most active and enterprising men in Mattapoisett.

Capt. Joseph, in connexion with Benjamin Stetson, received in 1720, a grant of two acres of land on the Indian Head River, between Pine Hill and Rocky Run, for the accommodation of a forge and finery, and erected the forge subsequently known as Barstow's forge, but now as Sylvester's, and which was improved by his descendants for nearly a century, or until about the year 1800.

Samuel Barstow resided in the Drinkwater district, and owned land in the Central and Westerly parts of the town. He was engaged principally in farming, having an estate of nearly one thousand acres, and was somewhat interested in commercial pursuits as a ship owner, and in manufactures as proprietor of a mill.

The descendants of these families, and of the common ancestor, are widely scattered over the Northern and Western States, and wherever known are men of respectable standing, and several have risen to eminence and honor, in the councils of States, and the Congress of the nation.

1 Col. Rec. 3. 115. 2 Ibid. 4. 126. 3 Ibid. 4. 160 and 186.

Of the Eells family, which has also furnished to the town useful and enterprising men, who served it faithfully in the French War, and were commanders of Companies in the War of the Revolution, Samuel, a descendant of Revd. Nathaniel, fourth pastor of the Second Church in Scituate, dwelt at the Four Corners, on the spot where the house of Joseph C. Stockbridge stands, and in the building erected and occupied by his father-in-law, Mr. Witherell. He was a blacksmith by trade, and his *shop* is spoken of in the laying out of a highway in 1730. His career was short, but distinguished. In 1740, a company was enlisted in the county of Plymouth, by Capt. Winslow, to serve in the expedition against the Spanish West Indies, under Admiral Vernon, whose original muster-roll, on parchment, is still in existence, and in the possession of Revd. Benjamin Kent, of Roxbury. Of the 500 men sent in the expedition by Massachusetts, not more than 50 returned, many having fallen victims to the prevailing tropical fevers.[1] Samuel Eells enlisted in this company as an Ensign, and died, either on the passage from Carthagena to Jamaica, or at Jamaica, May 9, 1741, in the 35th year of his age. His widow, Hannah, who survived him for many years, and occupied his homestead, obtained a pension from the British Government, through the friendly aid of the Revd. Ebenezer Thompson, Rector of St. Andrew's Church, which, we understand, was punctually remitted to her to the close of her life.[2]

Abner Dwelley, a descendant of Richard, of Scituate, was in Hanover in 1727, but died soon after, and his descendants left the town. He lived on Elm St. not far from Col. J. B. Barstow's, and an old orchard, known as the "Abner Orchard," marks the spot. The cellar and well are yet visible. His brothers settled in Pembroke, and some of their descendants are now in Hanover. Dr. Melzar, Dwelley, also a descendant of Richard, of Scituate, came to Hanover in the latter part of the last century, and remained until his death in 1828. His descendants are in Ashburnham, and South Boston. One of his sons yet resides in Hanover.

Melatiah and John Dillingham seem to have lived near the Corners, and tradition says that the former was a blacksmith, and

1 Winsor's Duxbury, p. 116. 2 Letter of J. Barstow, Esq.

built the house at present occupied by the widow Eells. Joshua, the Quaker, a descendant of Melatiah, was also a blacksmith, and his shop stood at the corner, near Wood & Torrey's store. He moved to New York. A few descendants of these brothers, in the male line, lived in Hanover until the close of the last century, but the name is now extinct. There were several intermarriages in this family with the Este's, of Hanover.

Below the Corners, and on the old Scituate road, near the third Herring brook, called by some the smelt brook, lived the Palmer's. John, supposed to be the same who came with the first settlers of Hingham, in 1635, and who was a freeman in Massachusetts in 1638, was freeman in Plymouth in 1657, with his sons John and Elnathan. His house lot was near the junction of the road S. E. of Church Hill.[1] He is the one referred to in our account of the Barstows. In 1660, he built a log-bridge over the third Herring brook, "from firm upland to firm upland," which is still known as Palmer's bridge. Ezekiel and Josiah, his descendants, were citizens of Hanover for a time, and others of his descendants have resided in the town, though there is but one of the name now living here.

Not far from the residence of the Palmers, lived the Stockbridges, descendants of Charles, of Scituate, who was son of John, the *wheelwright*. To Charles was granted, in 1673, "30 acres of land on the third Herring brook, on condition that he erect a corn mill on that brook, and keep and tend the mill fourteen years."[1] This mill, subsequently known as Jonah's mill, and the Tiffany mill, stood near the tack factory of Mr. Samuel Salmond, and was built in 1677. In the division of the estate of the father, in 1684, there was given "to Charles, the oldest son, land at third Herring brook, and half the corn-mill and three fourths of the saw-mill there ; To Thomas, land on third Herring brook, half the corn-mill, and one fourth of the saw-mill ; To Joseph 50 acres of land in Duxbury, near Indian-head river."

The first of these, Charles, lived near the Herring brook, and also Thomas.[3] Joseph, the third son, became a citizen of Pembroke

1 Deane's Scitnate, p. 319. 2 Deane, p. 343.
3 In the house occupied by Ephraim Stetson.

in 1735, but continued to be a member of the Church in Hanover until his death, in 1773, at the advanced age of 100 years. His farm, which was his father's grant, was in what is now Pembroke, and where Haviland, son of the late Capt. William Torrey resides, —the first house in Pembroke, after crossing the bridge at the Curtis Forge. His son David, who married Deborah, daughter of Judge John Cushing, built the house near North River bridge, where the new house of Edmund Q. Sylvester stands, and was Town Clerk for many years, Representative, &c. and *his* son David was Senator, &c.

Within a half-mile of the Corners, Northward, dwelt the Sylvesters, descendants of Richard, who was of Weymouth in 1633, and of Scituate in 1642. Capt. Joseph, the father of Amos and Benjamin, of Hanover, had, according to Deane,[1] a farm north of the Church Hill, which in part he purchased of John Whiston in 1664, and his house stood where that of Samuel Waterman stands, not far from the third Herring brook. He was Capt. under Col. Benjamin Church, the famous Indian warrior, in the Eastern expedition in 1689, and in 1690, was Captain with 16 men from Scituate, many of whom never returned, in Phips' expedition to Canada, and died in the service. His will, which was verbal, was proved in the Court by three of his soldiers, Benjamin Stetson, and John and William Perry, and gives "all my land at Hugh's cross to son Joseph; the three younger sons (Amos, Benjamin, and David,) to be provided for by their mother (Mary,) out of the remainder of my estate."

On Broadway, and on Elm and Spring Streets, dwelt the Josselynns, descendants of Thomas, who came from London in 1635, through Abraham, his oldest son, and Henry, his grandson, who settled in Scituate in 1669. Nathaniel, Jabez, Joseph, and Dea. Thomas, were living in Hanover at the date of the incorporation of the town. The descendants of this family are very numerous, and widely scattered.

The Burdens or *Bardins*, Isaac and Thomas, probably descendants of Abraham of Scotland,[2] also resided on Broadway, and tradition says the latter built the house now occupied by David Her-

1 Deane, p. 349. 2 Deane, p. 215.

sey. He was likewise proprietor of the First Forge, erected on the Indian Head river, about 1704, where the Curtis Forge now stands, whose dam stretched across the stream from shore to shore, and near which the then highly important alewife fishery, subsequently a matter of controversy, and now of no consequence to the town, was carried on in its season.

Farther up the stream, and on the gore which was annexed to Pembroke, dwelt the Cushings, Lt. Elijah and Lt. Nehemiah, descendants of John of Scituate, who came from Hingham in 1662, and who was son of Matthew, born in England in 1588.[1] Both these men were useful in the town, the former serving as Moderator, Representative, &c. The latter, Nehemiah, became a citizen of Pembroke before 1750, and also Elijah; and their descendants are principally in Hanson.

Few families in the country have been more celebrated than the Cushings, and probably no other one has furnished more Judges for our Probate, Municipal and Supreme Courts. In all its branches, it has been highly respectable, and it still maintains its ancient standing.

In the vicinity of the Cushings, and on the gore annexed to Pembroke, so far as I can learn, dwelt a few other families, whose descendants are now in Hanson; as Richard Bowker, Richard Hill, and perhaps Edmund Bowker, William Cocks (Cook, now *Coxe*,) and Israel Smith.

In the Westerly part of the town, on Torrey's lane, now Winter Street, the Tilden house, a portion of which is still standing, was erected over 130 years ago, and was occupied by a brother of Lt. Job, when the town was incorporated. On the same lane dwelt the Torreys, David and Stephen,—and James and Nathaniel lived more towards the centre of the town. Farther on, and on the same street, the Wings,—Bachelor, Sylvanus, and Ebenezer,—were settled. In the male line, all these names are extinct here. A few of the female descendants still survive, among whom we may name the wife of Thomas M. Bates, who was a Wing.

Around Circuit Street, and in other parts of the Drinkwater district, were settled Robert Young, Thomas Jones, and John

1 Deane, p. 254.

Cobb, who left no descendants in Hanover; Joseph and Samuel Ramsdell, whose descendants are in the western part of the State; Job Otis, who returned to Scituate; and near Abington line, Samuel Staples, who occupied the old Wanton House, and John Bray and Thomas Wilkes, the latter of whom has descendants in Abington. William Ford may have lived in the same neighborhood, though of this we cannot speak with confidence.

On and near what is now Plain Street, lived Caleb Barker, the Quaker, whose descendants are in Pembroke and New York; and Matthew, William, and Edward Estes, a few of whose descendants are in Hanover, but who mostly removed to the Western States.

On Center Street, and near the present residence of Albert White, Esq., the Hatch family settled, on land bought before 1680, by Jeremiah and Walter Hatch, of John Hanmer, being a portion of Hanmer's Hook. Jeremiah, Isaac, and Dea. James, were in Hanover in 1727, and all lived in the Westerly part of the town, James owning the saw-mill near Teague's bridge, then Hatch's bridge, and which stood where stood the mill of Cobb & Cushing, burnt in 1852. The Hatch estate, improved as a farm, and on which was a family burial ground, is said to have been sold in 1743, to Cornelius White, then of Marshfield, and a descendant of Peregrine White, *the first male child born in Plymouth Colony* — and it has since been in the possession of, and is yet improved by his descendants.

Benjamin Hanmer, a descendant of John, who was of Scituate in 1639, seems to have lived on some part of the hook, and I infer, from scattered notes, that he was settled not far from the old Meeting House.

In the vicinity of this Meeting House, lived the Stetsons, descendants of Cornet Robert, of Scituate, a noted and valuable man in the Colony. Matthew, Benjamin, Seth, Robert, and Samuel, were heads of families when the town was incorporated. Tradition says that Isaac Buck lived in the same neighborhood; but none of his descendants remain in the town. Probably the venerable schoolmaster, Richard Fitzgerald, lived in the same section of the town; and Thomas and John Rogers, a few of whose descendants yet remain.

The Bates family settled in the Westerly and Southerly parts of the town, and descended from Clement, who was of Hingham in 1636. Joseph, Solomon, Amos, and Clement were in Hanover in 1727, and a large number of their descendants still reside in the town.

The Baileys, descendants of John, of Scituate, 1670, settled first on Curtis Street, and afterwards principally on King Street. Col. John and Major Luther, of Revolutionary memory, belonged to this family, — also Dr. David, of Scituate, and others.

The Curtis family lived on Washington Street, where many of the descendants still reside, and on Curtis, now Main Street. Benjamin, Benjamin, jr., William, John, Elisha, Richard, Jesse, David, Ebenezer, Samuel, Thomas, and Bezaleel, were in Hanover before 1727.

The Turners, descendants of Humphrey, of Scituate, and Thomas, of Hingham, settled on Curtis Street, and in the North part of the town, in the "Snappet" neighborhood.

Joseph House lived on Curtis Street, and David, the hatter, near T. J. Gardner's mill, on the third Herring brook.

John, Uriah, and Isaac Lambert, lived in the Northerly part of the town. This name is extinct in Hanover.

Of the Manns, descendants of Richard the planter, who came over in the *Mayflower* in 1620, Benjamin was in Hanover in 1723, and owned part of a mill on Curtis Street, where he resided.

Eliab Studley, a descendant of Benjamin, of Hingham, settled on Pleasant Street; and Benoni, who was of another family, from Sandwich, lived on Hanover Street, and his house, one of the oldest in the town, is still standing, not far from the residence of the late Dr. Joshua Studley.

Benjamin Bass, the first minister of the town, also lived on Hanover Street, and his house stood near the house of William Church.

Joseph Cornish resided near him, but no descendants are left in the town.

Jonathan and Othniel Pratt resided on Washington Street, near where Martin and Samuel S. Church now reside. A few of their descendants yet live in the town.

Thomas Rose, a descendant of Thomas, who was in the "Two mile" in 1660, seems to have lived near where Edwin Rose now resides, on Hanover Street; and Edward Brisco lived in the same neighborhood, the plain on which his house stood being known on old records as Brisco's Plain. If I am not mistaken, he moved to North Carolina over a hundred years ago.

Of the Perrys,—Samuel and Joseph were early in Hanover, and have descendants here, and in Pembroke, and other towns in the vicinity.

William Witherell, the First Town Clerk, lived at the Four Corners, and perhaps Samuel and Daniel also. John Woodwarth, or Woodward, lived beyond William Church's, on Hanover Street, near Woodward hill, so called. Both these names are now extinct in the town.

Capt. Joseph Soper, lived on what is now Union Street, back of the house occupied by Josiah Bonney, on the hill. His descendants are in Hanson.

A few other names occur on the early records, but most of them are extinct. Of these are Henry Merritt, Ezekiel Vinal, John Warren, Benjamin and John Taylor, Nathan Bourne, Samuel Harlow, Hugh Vickery, Daniel Foster, John Stoddard, and Recompense Tiffany; the last of whom lived near Palmer's Bridge.

The families of Briggs, Brooks, Barrell, Clark, Church, Chamberlin, Gardner, Ellis, Jacobs, Munroe, Robbins, Simmons, and Whiting, appear on the records from 1740 to 1775. The other names in the town are of a more recent date. Sketches of all these families will be found in our Second Part.

In the foregoing pages, our aim has been to give a picture of the town before the Revolution, and especially in the earlier days of its settlement. We do not claim that our sketch is perfect; on the contrary, we think it highly probable that some errors will be detected in it; but we have sought to make it correct and reliable. Should errors be discovered, however, we hope they will be noted, and that those who have it in their power to correct them, will take the liberty so to do.

The records on which we have been obliged to rely, are scattered and fragmentary. The *elders* of the town are fast disappearing; and many from whom much that is valuable might have been learned, have departed to the spirit-land. Those that remain have been diligently consulted, and the gleamings of their memories faithfully recorded.

CHAPTER II.

NATURAL HISTORY.

"To me be Nature's volume broad displayed,
And to peruse its all-instructing page,
Or, haply catching inspiration thence,
Some easy passage, raptured to translate;
My sole delight, as through the falling glooms
Pensive I stray, or with the rising dawn,
On fancy's eagle-wing excursive soar."

THOMSON.

Geology of the Town—Forests, ancient and modern, with their products, value and uses — Herbaceous Plants — Birds, &c. — Laws for their destruction, and argument for their preservation — Wild and Domestic Fruits — Ancient Sheep Husbandry, and the Culture of Flax, Wheat, &c. — Materials for improving the soil —Indications of progress.

It is an interesting fact, and one calculated to impress us with an exalted sense of the Infinite Wisdom of our Heavenly Father, that every square mile of the earth's surface has an aspect of its own, and presents to us features which, though resembling in some respects what may be elsewhere seen, are so different in others as to give to it a distinctive character, sufficient to render it worthy of a separate notice. Hence every town has its own natural history. The contour of its surface, with its hills and plains; the quantity of its arable land, with the proportion unfit for cultivation, and covered with rocks or water; the extent of its forests, with the comparative abundance, age, and size of the trees of which they are composed; — these, and other minuter details, which we need not specify, give to every spot on our globe a peculiar interest in the eyes of those most familiar with its scenery, and encircle it with that mysterious charm which hovers around the place of our nativity, or the home of our adoption.

Of the town of Hanover, we may briefly say that its surface is comparatively level, — undulating in some parts, — and with a few scattered hills, but none of any great elevation. There are spots of highland, here and there, from which beautiful views may be obtained of the country around, stretching away to the distance of from twelve to twenty miles, with the Blue Hills to the North, and Manomet to the South. On Walnut Hill is one of these "look outs," and on a beautiful summer's day, or even in October, when the leaves are changing, and the forests are clothed in their rich autumnal drapery, it is worth one's while to take a seat in the top of a majestic pine, very easy of ascent, which stands near the summit, and from thence to survey the attractive picture, of God's own painting, spread out before the eye; attractive, not only for its own diversity and beauty, but for the associations connected with it, as compassing the home of the Pilgrims, — the ground pressed by their feet, and watered by their blood, and hallowed by their spirits which seem as if gazing, with a rapture full equal to our own, on what was to them a consecrated soil!

Of the geology of the town, traces of diluvial action are everywhere visible, not only in the range and shape of our hills, but in the numerous boulders of granite and greenstone, with which its surface is covered; some of which were evidently transported from Hingham, and correspond with the ledges of that town, especially with the granite ledge, intersected by veins of trap, through which the South Shore Rail Road is cut in West Hingham; — others from Cohasset, corresponding with the rocks *in situ* there; — and others from Weymouth, from the vicinity of the Old Spain Meeting House, and the Depot at Back River.

The largest, however, are from the extensive granite beds which underlie all but that part of the town bordering on the North River, and which outcrop on Walnut Street, and along the third Herring brook, and in the vicinity of Brooks's upper mill, and on Centre Street, as may be seen by the references on the map of the town, placed there by Mr. Whiting at the author's suggestion. Of these boulders, some, of great size, are still nicely poised upon the parent rock, and have been moved but a few feet at the most. An example may be seen in the pasture land of Rev. Robert L. Killam, on Walnut Street.

Along the North River, a grauwacke formation occurs, which extends North-westerly through Hanson and Abington; and in the latter town, near the residence of Benjamin Hobart, Esq., explorations have been made for coal, but not with sufficient success, in the estimation of Mr. Hobart, to warrant a continuance of the enterprise. Undoubtedly coal exists in the whole of this formation, but at such a depth, and mixed, especially in its upper beds, with so large a per centage of the carburet of iron, that it will not for a long time, if ever, be wrought with profit. Even in the grauwacke of Rhode Island, where explorations for coal are now in progress, near the Blackstone river, and about three miles from Pawtucket, and where an article of much better quality than formerly, is being raised, the depth of the shafts is over 300 feet, and the expense of conducting the work is so great, that it absorbs nearly if not quite all the *materiel* which is sold.

Specimens of *crystallised quartz*, though not of great beauty, are frequently found in the Westerly and Southerly parts of the town, where quartz boulders occur. The author has one lump of considerable size, in which the crystals radiate from a central nucleus, apparently of grey quartz, in a stellar form, — the crystals themselves being white or cream colored, and slightly tinged with the oxide of iron. Specimens of *earthy chlorite*, the *granules* of which are green, and often of a triangular form when seen through a magnifier, occur in the same localities. A peculiar kind of *ferruginous asbestiform quartz*, called by the people "*petrified chips*," also occurs somewhat abundantly near the North River, with *bituminous shale*; and in the rock near Perry's Tack Factory, is a vein of *ochrey brown oxide of iron*, nearly a foot wide; and there are traces of the *earthy oxide* of *manganese*, on the bank of the river.

Micaceous oxide of iron, in small quantity, is found in the granite region, and sometimes handsome specimens of *porphyry* may be obtained, in which the crystals of feldspar are white, large, and quite numerous. The *hydrate* or *bog iron*, of fair quality, and yielding a considerable per centage when smelted, may be found in most of our low grounds, especially near the water courses, as at Iron Mine Brook, and in alluvial tracts.[1] *Hydrate of Silica* is also common in the low grounds, with peat.

1 Bog iron was formerly carted from near the "Cricket Hole," to the Drinkwater works.

Clay occurs on Walnut Hill, and bricks were made there sixty years ago, by Dea. Benjamin Mann. In this clay are rarely disseminated crystals of *selenite*, and specimens of *nodular argillaceous iron ore*. Some years since, and in the days when less was known of geology than now, a search for the *precious metals* was made in one part of the town, and quite a California fever raged for a season. A few crystals of quartz were obtained; and when the little cubical blocks of *sulphuret of iron*, which have deceived so many, made their appearance, glittering in the sun, and of a golden yellow, they were seized with avidity, and the miners thought their fortune was made.

At a still earlier period, when physical science was rarely studied even by the learned, divining by the *hazel rod*, and by the *stone in the hat*, which made the universe transparent, taught sapient divines, as well as astute laymen, that beneath the surface treasures vast were within their grasp, and could be easily obtained! But the only *treasure* that has thus far been dug from our soil, is the *plentiful crop* which the *plough* and the *hoe* have brought forth.

The forests of Hanover, which cover a large part of its territory, are extensive and valuable; and here are found trees of the kinds most common in our State, as the white, swamp white, grey, red, scarlet, yellow bark, and bear or "ragged plain" Oak; the upland and swamp Elm; the crabbed Hornbeam; the pignut and shellbark Hickory; the white, the black, and the yellow Birch; the fragrant Sassafras, an article of commerce two centuries ago; the common white maple; the tremulous Poplar; the majestic Beech; the white and the black Ash; the spine-leaved Holly; the Wych-Elm, or Iron Wood, as some term it; the verdant Hemlock; the tall Spruce; the white and the red Cedar; and the white, yellow, and pitch Pine.

White Birch is a wood of rapid growth, and is fit to cut once in twelve or fifteen years. Oak, Maple, Birch, and Walnut, may be cut once in from twenty-five to thirty-five years. Pines attain to a considerable size in thirty years, and some trees, with that growth upon them, are large enough for board logs. The Cedar, the Hemlock, and the Spruce, are of a slower growth and cannot usually be cut oftener than once in about sixty years.

There are large tracts of Cedar Swamp in the Westerly part of the town, the wood from which is valuable for posts and rails, and if of good quality, for the manufacture of tubs, piggins, pails and churns.

Several hundred cords of pine, called *rare-ripes*, are annually carted to Hingham, for the use of the *coopers*, to be made into the pails, firkins, dumbetty tubs, and other articles of wooden ware for which that place is so famous. Crocker Wilder & Co., are the most extensive purchasers, and the largest manufacturers, though the business is carried on, more or less, all over that town.

Nearly a half million feet of boards are also sawed annually, — mostly pine, —the *half-inch stuff* being used chiefly for the manufacture of shoe-boxes, and trunks;—a business extensively carried on at Shepherd's Factory, in Pembroke, at the steam mill of Mr. John Jones, in South Scituate, at the workshop of Mr. John Gross, in the same town, and at several establishments in Hanover, especially on Whiting Street.

Cedar and pine shingles are sawed at Brooks's upper mill, and at the mill owned by Mr. Nahum Stetson, on Pleasant Street.

There is a ready market for from two to three hundred cords of pine wood, annually, at the brick-yard of Mr. Edward Jacobs, in South Scituate. Oak, maple, and other kinds of hard wood, find a market principally in Hingham, Abington, and Weymouth. Charcoal is manufactured to a considerable extent every year by Mr. Ethan Perry, on Main Street. Ship-timber is saleable at Scituate harbor, and at the yards on the North River, though the quantity cut is not very large. Oak and maple butts are sold to the coopers, at Hingham, and plank to the wheelwrights of Hanover and Scituate. Our farmers engage in the lumbering business more or less every winter; and it not only furnishes steady employment for their teams, but a fertile field for the exercise of their own industry, and a by no means unfruitful source of addition to their income.

It is sometimes asserted that the quantity of wood in the town is not so great as it was fifty or seventy five years ago; and it may be, and doubtless is true, that trees of great size, and of an old growth are diminishing, though there are still "not a few" left. But as much, if not more territory is now covered with forests, —

many fields and pastures having been left to grow to wood, and pieces which were planted within the memory of the living, and on which the *indian hills* are yet visible, are covered with trees from fifteen to eighteen inches in diameter. Indeed, we think we may safely say, that there is a supply left sufficient for home consumption for several generations ; and at least for one century, even if the demand is as brisk as now, no apprehensions of an entire failure in this supply need be entertained.

It was probably the custom of the early settlers of New England, as it is of the emigrants of different nations who are peopling the Western States, to make clearings by cutting the trees upon those tracts designed for cultivation, and heaping the trunks and limbs into one vast pile, which was set on fire, and burned to ashes ; and this process as at present conducted, is termed "*burning the fallow.*"

It is quite certain that the forest trees which stood on our soil two hundred years ago, were much larger than any that are seen in our day, and doubtless approximated in size the monarchs of the Mississippi valley. The author has seen, in the State of Illinois, red oaks four feet in diameter, and black walnuts five feet through ; and in the low, rich bottom lands, the cotton-wood trees grow to a great height and size, their tops appearing to pierce the clouds. But farther west, on the borders of the Pacific, in California and Oregon, travellers, upon whose veracity we can rely, inform us that the trees are of a still larger growth, and that pines are found there three hundred feet high ![1] It is not uncommon to find pine trees in Hanover, one hundred feet high, and from three and one half to four feet in diameter. These are old trees ; — but our old men tell me that in their boyhood, the trees were still larger, and Cedars and Oaks were found from three to four feet through !

We are not to infer, however, that the fertility of the soil, or its capacity for the production of such trees is exhausted ; for were the forests now standing left undisturbed for two centuries to come, and could we then look upon the scene which they would present to our view, we should have a picture of New England as it was

1 I have heard of one Pine thirty feet in diameter, and one hundred feet from the ground to the first limb.

seen by the Pilgrims, and the primeval aspect of our hills and plains would be restored, and the deer and the wolf be once more seen in the land.

The Indians disturbed not often the vegetation of the country they inhabited. Their axes of stone, were not so well fitted as our keen-edged tools of steel for felling trees. Hence the forests continued to grow, from age to age, furnishing lairs for the wild beasts, and favorite resorts for herds of deer, and countless multitudes of wild fowls which lodged in their branches.

Of the *herbaceous* plants described by Bigelow, in his Plants of Boston, the author has found over three hundred species in the town of Hanover, and probably more might be discovered were the whole of its territory explored. Of the *flowerless* plants, as the mosses, the lichens, the ferns, and the fungi, we have also a large number of species, some of which are not only rare, but exceedingly beautiful. Indeed, our little municipality is by no means an uninteresting field for botanical researches, and several plants are common here, and in Scituate, which are less frequently met with in other towns in the State; as the *Kalmia latifolia*, or *Mountain Laurel*, which in June is covered with a multitude of rich and fragrant blossoms; — the *Epigæa repens*, or *Mayflower*, a sweet-scented, and modest little plant, blossoming early in April, and which was probably the first plant seen in bloom by the pilgrims the spring after they landed, — whence its name; — and the *Pyrola maculata*, or *spotted pyrola*, with its zebra-striped leaves, peeping out from the dry and mouldering vegetation scattered every fall around in the forest.

The author has taken great pleasure in rambling through woods and swamps, and over pastures and meadows, at all seasons of the year, in quest of flowers; and seldom has he made an excursion without learning something new; either discovering fresh localities, or returning laden with more beautiful specimens, or with plants of a different species from any that had been previously met with in his walks. But wo to the luckless wight who, in such strolls, comes in contact, all unconsciously perhaps, with the *poisonous ivy*, in scaling stone walls, or the *malignant dogwood*, in threading his way through the swamps; for swollen features, and days of pain will be the portion of those who imbibe the venom of these plants through the pores of the skin, or inhale it through the lungs! And blessed are they who can handle with impunity these usually annoying "subjects of the vegetable kingdom."

In the earlier days of our Country's history, deer and wild cats, and even bears and wolves were found in all our forests, and ducks, and geese, and crows, and blue jays, and other birds, were far more numerous than now; —so much so that laws were passed, and bounties offered, to aid in extirpating those which were most destructive, or from which danger was apprehended. Deer were protected, however; and December 13, 1739, in Hanover, Dea. James Hatch and William Curtis were chosen "to look after the Deer that none are killed and destroyed contrary to law." But wild-cats, and many birds were doomed. Thus, March 1, 1732–3, there was paid to Joseph Bates, Solomon Bates, Stephen Torrey, John Woodworth, Benjamin Curtis, Ebenezer Curtis, and others, each 20s. for "killing wild cats;" and in 1738, 40s. a head were voted for killing them, and in 1744, £3 each was voted to be paid for every one killed in Hanover or Abington.

In 1736–7, £6, 18s. were voted to different persons for killing "birds and squirals;" and in 1740, 3d. a head was voted for "killing black birds, squirals, jay birds, chuits, read thrashers and wood-peckers."

In 1773, a bounty of 1s. a head was granted for killing crows, and 2d. a head for crow blackbirds, and ground or red squirrels, the head to be shown as proof of the killing. The bounty on crows continued to be paid so late as 1837.

In 1836, the Legislature of the State offered a bounty on killing foxes, and throughout the State a destructive warfare was waged against them. In Hanover, 13 were killed, for which a bounty was received.[1]

Of the policy of such regulations, every one must judge for himself. For our own part, whilst we admit the propriety of destroying wolves, wild cats, racoons, skunks, and beasts of the like nature, we are free to own that in our opinion, the jay, and the wood-pecker, and the red thrasher, and the blackbird, and even the crow, though they do much mischief, and are less melodious

1 Sen. Doc. No. 32, 1837, and No. 45, 1838.

singers than some others, pay their way, and deserve to be protected, for preserving our trees and vegetables, from the ravages of insects and field mice, which increase just in the ratio that birds diminish.

The crow is by no means an uninteresting bird. True he is a rogue, and wants watching, — but he will devour scores of grubs in a day, and save more corn for the *harvest*, than he steals in the *seed*. Let all the birds live, to enliven our forests! Let the robin come to our door-yards, and pick up the crumbs; and if he does steal a *few* cherries, *we* take *more* from the trees!

To rise at break of day, and hear these sweet warblers breathing forth their morning hymn; — the prelude by the robin, and the chorus swelled by the trill of the oriole, the scream of the jay, the hawk, and the wood-pecker, and the distant cawing of the crow, with the solo of the bobolink, and the symphony of the peewit, or chickadee; and at mid-day, to hear in the stillness of noon, the chant of the cuckoo, or the plaintive call of the cat-bird, and the chattering of the striped, red, grey, and flying squirrels, as they skip from tree to tree; and at night, to hear the whippoorwills complaint: — all these to me, are sweet and pleasant sounds; — and even the flight of the butterfly, the note of the bee, and the hum of the locust, with at eventide the chirp of the cricket, the radiance of the glow-worm, or that mimic lightning, flashing out with incessant scintillations from the multitude of fire flies hovering over field and meadow; — all have charms for my spirit, and lead me to adore the wisdom and goodness of Him who has made everything beautiful in its time, and who is good unto all, and whose tender mercies are over all his works.

Of the *agricultural* interests of Hanover, we think we may truly say that the farmers of this section are beginning to manifest a commendable spirit of progress and improvement, and fine crops of corn, rye, potatoes and hay, are raised in favorable seasons. Of wild fruits, we have the usual variety. Grapes are abundant in the woods, and cranberries in the meadows. Whortleberries, strawberries, blueberries, and blackberries, too, are abundant; and in the summer months, when a vacation is given to our school children, they may be seen daily in groups wending their way to the pastures and woods, with *baskets*, or tin *kettles*, or *barks* on their arms, their merry voices striking like sweet music on the parent's ear, and returning with their luscious offerings to the domestic shrine, which, served with baked apples and milk, furnish a dish so luxurious that we doubt whether Queen Victoria, or the Emperor Nicholas, or any other monarch or prince, of ancient or modern times, ever tasted a better, or ate one more palatable, nourishing, and innocent.

Considerable attention is beginning to be paid to the raising of *domestic* fruits, and plantations of the apple, and peach are becoming quite common; and even the pear, the quince, and the cherry, with the smaller fruits, including the currant and gooseberry, are not wholly neglected; though much remains to be done before public attention will be thoroughly awakened to these matters, and every farm will be supplied with fruit of all kinds, in rich abundance, both for summer and winter use.

The famous *high-top-sweeting*, an apple which is a native of Plymouth County, ripe in September, of a medium size, golden yellow, and mellow and juicy, is not so common as it was when our fathers were young. Orchards of these trees were then quite numerous. But the crabbed, sour apples with which they were accompanied, and which caused the cider press to shriek in agony as the teeth of the cog-wheels met and crunched them, and whose juice was vinegar almost as soon as expressed, have given place to the Baldwin, the Greening, the Roxbury Russet, the Spitzenberg, the Early Harvest, the Yellow Bough, and the many other varieties of far more palatable fruits, which characterise the present age. Nurseries, too, are being established here, and in adjoining towns, which are doing an increasing business, in the sale of trees to our own citizens and others.

The Pratt Rare Ripe, is an excellent seedling peach, a native of this town, raised by Mr. B. C. Pratt, who resides about one half a mile from the Four Corners; and it is not only hardy and prolific, but seems to be almost entirely exempt from that common scourge,—the yellows,—which destroys so many of our finest trees.

There was a time in the history of the town, when all our farmers kept their flocks of sheep, and raised, and spun their own wool, and made their own cloth; and the hum of the wheel, and the clatter of the loom, tended by the *goodwife*, were heard in about every dwelling. Indeed, such was the esteem in which this branch of industry was held, that in 1732, the town "made choyce of Caleb Barker and Thomas Josselyun as agents to draw up a Town act for the Regulation of *Rames*," to prevent them from running at large, to the injury of the flocks.

It is to be borne in mind, that farms of from two to four hundred acres, and even more, were owned by many of our townsmen then, and hence the range of pasturage was such that sheep could be kept to good advantage. But it is now rare to find farms containing even one hundred acres. Hence sheep are kept by but few; and the loom and the spinning wheel, with but rare exceptions are mouldering in the garret, or have long since been cut up into fire wood to heat the oven on baking days; — and the daughters of our farmers, and even the mothers, for the most part, spend their time either in fitting shoes, or in the manufacture of coarse garments for the ready made clothing establishments of Boston.— The *flocks* have gone to the hills of New Hampshire and Vermont, or to the prairies of the West, and the *wool* is sent to our extensive factories, at Lowell and elsewhere, to be converted into carpets and rugs for our floors, or shawls and de-laines for the ladies wear, or broad cloths and cassimeres for the men.

Flax was also an article to whose cultivation considerable attention was once paid; and the smaller wheels, upon which linen thread was spun, of which the snow white table cloths, and sheetings and shirtings were made, which constituted, so important a part of the outfit of the new housekeeper, have not been laid aside over thirty years. The *hatchel*, and *swingling-knife*, alas! are numbered, forever, we fear, with the things that were but are not!

Doubtless these changes are all for the best, when rightly viewed. Occasionally we hear lamentable jeremiads upon the degeneracy of the times, and complaints that the simplicity of former days has entirely vanished, and that strength, and vigor, and power of endurance, are likewise departing from our sons and daughters, who are rising up around us a puny race, wholly unfit for the storms and tempests of life.

But we long since learned to look at the world, not from the deceptive position with which the imagination is ever inclined to invest the past, but from that broader stand-point which looks at man, not as a beast of burden alone, having a body to feed and a back to clothe, but as an intellectual and a moral being, capable of unlimited advancement in that exalted career which God has marked out for him, and of making continued improvements, tending not only to increase his physical comforts, but to open the way for nobler pursuits and purer joys, in the expansion of the mind, and the cultivation of the heart.

About fourteen years ago, or in 1838, the Committee on Agriculture made a report to the Legislature, in favor of "allowing a bounty on the production of Wheat,"[1] which led to the passage of a law granting such bounty, and to the publication, by order of the Legislature, of a valuable report "on the cultivation of Spring Wheat," from the pen of the lamented Henry Colman.[2] In 1839, from the "Abstract of the returns of the bounties paid for Wheat,"[3] Hanover is represented by six claimants, who raised 101 bushels, and received a bounty of $12.55. Mr. Colman, the Commissioner, in his return for 1840, states that these six claimants sowed 11¼ acres, and that the average yield was 9 bushels per acre. The several crops were 14 bushels, 10 6/7 bushels, and four of 7½ bushels. Samuel House was one of the claimants, and his certificate is the only one I find on file in the Town Clerk's office. The largest crop was obtained by the application of 12 loads of compost from the yard. The crop is said to have suffered from the drought.[4] In 1840, there were two claimants from Hanover, who raised 38½ bushels, and received $4.43.[5] But this experiment was not attended with all the results which its sanguine friends desired. Perhaps it was too soon abandoned.— At all events, it developed important facts, and taught us clearly, as the returns show, that there are sections of the State, and especially the Western Counties, in the limestone region of Berkshire and Franklin, where wheat can be raised successfully and profitably.

The materials for improving the soil in Hanover, and increas-

1 House Doc. No. 12. 1838.
2 Senate Doc. No. 77. 1838.
3 House Doc. No. 40. 1839.
4 Senate Doc. No. 36. 1840.
5 Senate Doc. No. 25. 1841.

ing our crops, are probably as abundant, and can be as easily obtained, as in any of the adjoining towns; and the natural resources are as great and as available. In our low grounds are vast deposites of decaying vegetable matter, the accumulation of ages, in the form of peat, and muck, and beds of leaves, all of which are useful as manures, and of excellent quality and incalculable value when judiciously composted, and liberally applied.

By the drainage of our meadows, too, and more skill on the upland, the produce of the soil might be easily doubled in a very few years, and the wealth of our citizens proportionably increased. We need a more enlightened industry in all our towns, to secure the highest results. Intelligent labor is as applicable in farming and quite as advantageous, as in any branch of human enterprise. And when it is borne in mind by our citizens, that we have no rail road, with its freight trains, running through the place; that the old line of Plymouth stages which daily passed the Four Corners is discontinued; and that ship-building has shifted its quarters to the vicinity of Boston; it will be at once apparent, that our chief dependance for the future must be upon the soil and its productions. And though our Mills, and Forges, and Tack Factories, and Boot and Shoe Establishments, may do much to develope our industry, and increase our wealth, yet the earth is our great nursing-mother, and from her prolific bosom must we draw our nourishment, and our means of support.

Assiduous labor in this direction, accompanied by persevering effort, and enlightened skill, will enable us to keep pace with the towns around us; so that Hanover will continue to be, as in the past, respectable for the industry, the enterprise, and the intelligence of its citizens. And what has been accomplished within the past twenty five years, should be an encouragement to us to continue to progress. Houses were then unpainted, and the walls, for the most part covered with shingles; — and many were but half-finished within, and but few were carpeted. Barns were mere hovels, without cellars, with the wind whistling through every crack. Now, almost every house is neatly finished and painted, and well furnished within; and our barns are being rebuilt, of fair proportions, with the walls shingled, and with large cellars. Improved implements of husbandry have been introduced, and land, though divided into small fields, is much better tilled and the produce of hundreds of acres has been greatly increased. The smallness of our fields, however, is partly a matter of necessity, to make room in the walls, for the stones which are cleared from the surface.

To complete our sketch, we should perhaps add, that several of our townsmen are engaged in driving cattle, sheep, and swine, every spring and fall, for the supply of this and other towns; and the size and power of our oxen, the milking quality of our cows, the fattening properties of our hogs, and the speed of our horses, have all partaken of the changes which have been made in other respects.

Onward seems to be New England's motto, and the spirit of improvement, now so generally diffused, will eventually bless every home, and will tend, in the Providence of God, to make the future richer in comfort, and a scene of higher advancement, than any thing we have dreamed of, or which we have even thought it possible to attain.

3

CHAPTER III.

INDIANS.

"Indulge, my native land, indulge the tear
That steals, impassioned o'er a nation's doom,
To me, each twig from Adam's stock is near,
And sorrows fall upon an Indian's tomb." DWIGHT.

Names of the seven principal tribes — Chikatabut's possessions — Indian Deed of Scituate — Manners and customs of the natives — Stature, clothing, money, weapons, dwellings, food, &c. — Dishes at the first meeting of the Old Colony Club — Philip's War — Reminiscenses of the Indians of Hanover — Changes which have taken place since those days.

Previous to the settlement of New England by the white race, the whole country was in the possession of the Indians, who were very numerous, until reduced by a great war, and by a devastating sickness, which some have supposed was the plague, others the small pox, and others the yellow fever, and which took place about the year 1617. Early voyagers speak of "countless multitudes" seen by them when they visited the country. Smith, who took his survey in 1614, says,—"the seacoast as you pass, shows you all along, large cornfields and great troupes of well proportioned people." Gookin enumerates 18,000 warriors, in five nations, and some have computed that, in all, there were at least 25,000 warriors, and 100,000 people.

According to Lechford, they were governed by Sachems, Kings, and Sagamores, or petty lords, and were divided into several great nations, each of which consisted of many tribes. Seven of these nations are named in New England, viz.:—1, the warlike Tarantines, under Nultonanit, who were in the Eastern part of Maine, beyond the Penobscot river;—2, the Chur-churs, under Bashaba, from the Penobscot to the Piscataqua;—3, the Pawtuckets, numbering 3000 warriors, under Nanapashemet, whose dominion reached from the Piscataqua to the river Charles, and extended north, as far as Concord, on the Merrimac; — 4, the Wampanoags, divided into 32 tribes, and numbering 3000 warriors, who were ruled by Massasoit, a sachem of great power, but who was ever a friend to the English, and whose dominion was in the Southeastern part of Massachusetts, from Cape Cod, to Narraganset Bay; — 5, the Narragansets, numbering 5000 warriors, and governed by Canonicus and Miantonimo, who lived in Rhode Island on the west of Narraganset Bay; — 6, the Pequots, numbering 4000 fighting men, under Sassacus, a name of terror, who dwelt in Connecticut; — and 7, the Massachusetts, so named from the Blue Hills at Milton, numbering 3000 warriors, under Chikatabut, whose territory extended from Nishamagoguanett, near Duxbury mill, to Titicut, near Taunton, and to Nuckatateset, now Nippenicket, a pond in the Southwest part of Bridgwater, adjoining Raynham, — and from thence in a straight line to Wanamampuke, or Whiting's Pond in Wrentham.[1]

The latter tribe owned the land around Hanover, and their sachem, Chikatabut, was one of the nine who, on the 13th September, 1621, subscribed at Plymouth, the Articles of Submission to King James,[2] and he, with many of his people, died of the small pox, in 1633, and was succeeded by his son Josias Wampatuck.

The Pilgrims were well aware of the diminution of the Indians, by war and sickness, before their arrival. Their charter from King James states "that he had been given certainly to knowe, that within these late years there hath, by God's visitation, raigned a wonderfule plague, together with many horrible slaughters and murthers, committed amongst the savages and brutish people there heertofore inhabiting, in a manner to the utter destruction, devastacion and depopulacion of that whole territorye, so that there is not left, for many leagues together in a manner, any that doe claime or challenge any kind of interests therein."[1]

This circumstance, — the death of the savages, — was doubtless favorable to the Pilgrim band, and contributed greatly to their peaceful and permanent settlement. Our fathers, however, ac-

1 Lewis's Hist. Lynn, p. 45. Drake's Indians, Book II. Thacher's Plymouth, p. 363. N. E. Gen. Reg. 3, 332. Hobart's Abington, p. 23, &c.

2 Morton's Memorial, Ed. 1772, p. 33.

1 Hazard's Hist. Coll. 1, 105, quoted in Drake's Book of the Indians, p. 11, Book II. Also Plym. Col. Laws, p. 3.

knowledged an Indian title to the soil, which consisted chiefly in a privilege of free fishing, trapping, and hunting; and this title, they considered themselves bound lawfully to extinguish, by purchase or otherwise.

They did not, therefore, seize with violence the possessions of the red race. Their rights were generally respected. And the Indian deeds which have descended to us, are not only valuable to the antiquary, but are living mementos of our father's honor, and convincing proofs that they were willing to render some equivalent for whatever they received.

The land comprised within the limits of Scituate and Hanover, together with the tract called the "Two Miles," was purchased of Josias Wampatuck, and the deed, which bears date "Plymouth, June 1653," reads as follows:

"I Josias Wampatuck do acknowledge and confess that I have sold two tracts of land unto Mr. Timothy Hatherly, Mr. James Cudworth, Mr. Joseph Tilden, Humphrey Turner, William Hatch, John Hoar, and James Torrey, for the proper use and behoof of the Town of Scituate, to be enjoyed by them according to the true intents of the English grants: The one parsel of such land is bounded from the mouth of the North River as that River goeth to the Indian head River, from thence as that River goeth unto the Pond at the head of that River, and from the pond at the head of the Indian head River upon a straight line unto the middle of Accord Pond: from Accord Pond, by the line set by the Commissioners as the bounds betwixt the two jurisdictions, untill it meet with the line of the land sold by me unto the sharers of Conihasset, and as that line runs between the Town and the shores, untill it cometh unto the sea: and so along by the sea unto the mouth of the North River aforesaid. The other parcell of land lying on the easterly side of the North River, begins at a lot which was sometime the land of John Ford, and so to run two miles southerly as the River runs, and a mile in breadth towards the east, for which parcell of land, I do acknowledge to have received of the men whose names are before mentioned, fourteen pounds in full satisfaction, in behalf of the inhabitants of the town of Scituate as aforesaid; and I do hereby promise and engage to give such further evidence before the Governor as the Town of Scituate shall think meet, when I am thereunto required; in witness whereof, I have hereunto set my hand in presence of

NATHANIEL MORTON, EDWARD HAWES, SAMUEL NASH,	JOSIAS WAMPATUCK his ⋈ mark

At the same time when Josias made acknowledgment as above mentioned, there was a Deed brought into Court which he owned to be the Deed which he gave to them whose names are above specified for the said lands, and that he had not given them another; which deed was burnt in presence of the Court.

NATHANIEL MORTON, Secretary." [1]

The manners and customs of the Indians have been painted by some writers in glowing colors; but, viewing their condition as sober reason presents it to our view, it cannot be regarded as enviable or desirable. True, they were free; roamed the land at will; ate of its fruits as spontaneously produced, spending but little time in the cultivation of their maize and roots; and lived chiefly by hunting and fishing. But this, though usually a fertile supply, often failed, through indolence, and other causes, so that they knew the gnawings of hunger, and the distress of famine. The different tribes, too, were freqently at war with each other; and the amenities of life, and the kindlier feelings of the heart were but little cultivated, and were even lightly esteemed. Stern endurance, and unshrinking submission to the fiercest tortures, were regarded as the principal virtues, and he was the greatest hero, who had taken the most scalps, and slain the most enemies in battle.

In their persons, the Indians were not taller than the white race. Wood, in his New England's Prospect, published in 1633, describes them as "black haired, out nosed, broad shouldered, brawny armed, long and slender handed, out breasted, small waisted, lank bellied, well thighed, flat kneed, handsome grown legs, and small feet."

Josselynn, also, in his New England's Rarities, says of the women, "many of them have very good features, seldom without a come-to-me in their countenance, all of them black eyed, having

1 Deane's Scituate, p. 144.

even, short teeth, and very white, their hair black, thick and long, broad breasted, handsome straight bodies and slender, their limbs cleanly straight, generally plump as a partridge, and saving now and then one, of a modest deportment."[1]

It was their constant practice to oil their bodies and face with fat of bears and eagles, and to paint the face with various fantastic colors, as red, black, and white; — and though this smearing of the person may have seemed beautiful in their eyes, yet it must have given to them any thing but an agreeable odor, in a warm day, or in a close apartment![2] The dress of the men was the skin of a deer or wolf, though generally they were naked, except a slight covering around the waist. The women wore robes of beaver skin, with sleeves of deer skin, dressed, and drawn with lines of different colors into ornamental figures. Some wore a short mantle of trading cloth,—blue, or red,—fastened with a knot under the chin, and girt around the waist with a zone; their buskins fringed with feathers, and a fillet around their heads, which were often adorned with plumes. The moccasins, worn by both sexes, were made of skins, and their snow-shoes were ingeniously constructed for winter's use. The men considered labor as degrading to them, and maintained that "squaws and hedge hogs were made to scratch the ground," and called the white people "much fool to spoil their women by keeping them from out door labor and making them lazy squaws." The women, therefore, were held in abject servitude, and compelled to do all the drudgery, — as planting, harvesting, and carrying burdens, — while their lords lolled listlessly around, smoking, or recounting their warlike exploits.

Their money was made of shells, and was of two kinds, the *wampum peag*, or white, and the *suckauhoc*, or black; the latter being twice as valuable as the former. Roger Williams, in his Key, says "one fathom of this, their stringed money, is worth five shillings." Josselynn, speaking of these beads, which were their money, says, the one is their gold, and the other their silver. "These they work out of certain shells, so cunningly that neither

1 Lewis's Lynn, p. 53.

2 It has been suggested to me, that a custom similar to the above, prevails in Eastern nations, and that the practice of oiling the body, is considered conducive to health.

Jew nor Devil can counterfeit. They drill and string them, and make curious works with them, to adorn the persons of their Sagamores and principal men, and young women, as belts, girdles, tablets, borders for their women's hair, bracelets, necklaces, and links to hang in their ears. Prince Philip, a little before I came away for England, (1671,) coming to Boston, had a coat on and buskins set thick with these beads, in pleasant wild works, and a broad belt of the same; his accoutrements were valued at £20."

Their war weapons, were bows, arrows, and tomahawks. The bows, which were strong and elastic, were made of walnut or ash, and strung with sinews of deer or moose. With these they could throw an arrow to a great distance, and strike any object desired with remarkable precision.

Their arrows were made of elder, feathered with the quills of eagles, and pointed with sharp stones wrought for the purpose, or with bones, or eagle's claws. Their tomahawks, were of an oblong form, sharpened to an edge, and fixed to the handle by a withe, passed around the groove, formed at the head, or blunt part of the weapon.

Their houses, or wigwams, were rude structures, made of poles or young saplings, set round in the form of a cone, and covered with bark or mats, the smoke passing out at the top. In winter, one great house, built with more care, served for the accommodation of many.

They had two kinds of boats, called canoes; the one made of a pine log, twenty to sixty feet in length, burnt and scraped out with shells; the other of birch bark, very light, and very pretty. Their fishing lines were made of wild hemp, equal to the finest twine, and fish bones were used for hooks.

Their chief objects of cultivation were corn, beans, pumpkins, squashes, and melons,—all of which are indigenous plants,—which were tended by the women. Their fields were cleared by burning the trees and brush in the autumn. Their season for planting, was when the leaves of the oak were as large as the ear of a mouse; and from this arose the rule of the first settlers,

"When the white oak trees look goslin grey,
Plant then, be it April, June or May."

The corn was hoed with large clam shells, or the shoulder-bone of a moose or deer, fixed to a handle, and harvested in cellars dug in the ground, and covered with mats.

Their food, says Gookin, in his Historical Collections of the Indians in New England, " is generally boiled maize, or Indian corn, mixed with kidney beans, or sometimes without. Also they frequently boil in this pottage fish and flesh of all sorts, either new taken or dried, as shads, eels, alewives, or a kind of herring, or any other sort of fish. But they dry mostly those sorts before mentioned. These they cut in pieces, bones and all, and boil them in the aforesaid pottage. Also they boil in this fermenty all sorts of flesh they take in hunting, as venison, beaver, bear's flesh, moose, otters, rackoons, or any kind that they take in hunting, cutting their flesh in small pieces, and boiling it as aforesaid. Also they mix with the said pottage several sorts of roots, as Jerusalem artichokes, and ground nuts, and other roots, and pompions, and squashes, and also several sorts of nuts or masts, as oak-acorns, chestnuts, walnuts; these, husked and dried, and powdered, they thicken their pottage therewith. Also sometimes they beat their maize into meal, and sift it through a basket, made for that purpose. With this meal they make bread, baking it in the ashes, covering the dough with leaves. Sometimes they make of their meal a small sort of cakes and boil them. They make also a certain sort of meal of parched maize; this meal they call *nokake*. It is so sweet, toothsome, and hearty, that an Indian will travel many days with no other food but this meal, which he eateth as he needs, and after it drinketh water. And for this end, when they travel a journey or go a hunting, they carry this *nokake* in a basket or bag for their use."

Many of the old Indian dishes are still well known, and in common use in the country; as for instance, *samp*, made of whole corn, boiled with ashes to remove the hull, and eaten with milk; — *hominy*, made of corn coarsely pounded and boiled; — and *hasty pudding*, made of corn ground fine and boiled; — *succatash*, made of corn and beans boiled together; — *baked pumpkins*, eaten with milk; — *boiled* and *roasted ears* of green corn; — *parched corn*, — and were this ground and made into a pudding and eaten with

1 Thacher's Plymouth, p. 182 and his Sketch of the Indians. See also Lewis's History of Lynn, Drake's Book of the Indians, &c.

milk, it would be luscious;—and last, not least, *whortleberry cakes*. To this, if we add, a cake made of strawberries and parched corn, we have quite a variety of dishes, all of which are good and palatable.

The Old Colony Club, at its first celebration of the Landing of the Forefathers, held Dec. 22, 1769, in remembrance of the simplicity of early days, provided for their entertainment on the occasion, "1, a large baked Indian whortleberry pudding; 2, a dish of sauquetash, (succatash, corn and beans boiled together); 3, a dish of clams; 4, a dish of oysters and a dish of cod fish; 5, a haunch of venison, roasted by the first Jack brought to the Colony; 6, a dish of sea-fowl; 7, a dish of frost fish and eels; 8, an apple pie; and 9, a course of cranberry tarts, and cheese made in the Old Colony."[1]

That the early settlers of our State experienced much trouble from the Indian tribes, every one knows who is acquainted with the history of those times. The bloodiest contest, was that known as Philip's War, which commenced in 1676. In this, the inhabitants of the territory of Hanover, then inhabitants of Scituate, suffered their part, in common with the rest of the people in the vicinity.

We do not propose to enter at large into the events of this war, as we have nothing new to add to what is already known. We shall present a few details, pertaining principally to the immediate subject of our sketch.

In was in 1674, that the Colony Court began to make serious preparations for the rumored war with Philip, which was soon expected to break out; and as one of these preparations, in 1675, a garrison of twelve men was ordered to be established at the house of Mr. Joseph Barstow, which, as we have elsewhere remarked, stood on what is now Broadway, and opposite the residence of Mr. Joseph S. Bates. Other garrison houses were fitted up at the same time, in Scituate, but this was the only one which stood on the present territory of Hanover.

In the spring of 1676, the Narragansetts, having committed ravages in Rhode Island, and penetrated even to Plymouth, in which neighbourhood they had killed a number of inhabitants,

Capt. Michael Pierce, of Scituate, with a company of 50 or 63[1] Englishmen, and 20 friendly Indians, from Cape Cod, were ordered in his pursuit, and proceeded, without being molested, as far as Seekonk, where he arrived on Saturday, March 25 Hearing of Indians in the vicinity, he went immediately in their pursuit, and a bloody battle was fought, in which the Captain, and 18 of his men, from Scituate, were slain or wounded. Among this number was Jeremiah Barstow, a descendant of William, the earliest settler on the territory of Hanover.[2]

On the 20th of May, the Indians made an attack upon Scituate. They came from Hingham, where the day previous they had burnt several houses,[3] and entered the town by the Plymouth Road, now Washington Street. Striking down the "Indian path," which led to the Mattakeeset settlements at Indian-head ponds, they burnt the saw mill near Ellis's bridge, and Cornet Stetson's mill, near what is now Winslow's bridge; also the house of Capt. Joseph Sylvester, on the easterly side of the Third Herring brook, which stood where Mr. Samuel Waterman now resides. The garrison house at Joseph Barstow's, which was well fortified, was carefully avoided by the invaders; and, according to Gov. Winston's letter to Mr. Hinckley, a company of 14 men, which had marched up from Marshfield as far as Mr. Barstow's, saw the enemy, and put them to flight, thus, doubtless, preserving other houses in the neighborhood, which would have been destroyed had it not been for their presence.

Those who desire to know more of the events of this day, must read the graphic account of Deane, in which he enumerates the houses destroyed in Scituate proper.[4]

We have no other notices which connect the events of this war directly with the history of Hanover, though casual traditions speak of damages sustained at different periods, from the ravages of the Indians; and it is a matter of satisfaction to know, that the war was prosecuted with such vigor, on the part of the Col-

1 The number is 50, in Deane, but 63, in Bliss's Hist. of Rehoboth, p. 88.

2 The names are given in Deane's Scituate, p. 123, and in Bliss's Hist. of Reheboth, p. 92

3 Hobart's Journal.

4 Hist. Scit. p. 126, &c.

onists, and with such success, that Philip was slain, his warriors routed, and from that time forth the people lived in comparative security.

At the date of the incorporation of Hanover, no *hostile* Indians lived in its vicinity. It is said that the last tribe, from which the citizens had trouble, congregrated on an island in Drinkwater Swamp, in the westerly part of the town, from whence they issued, and committed their depredations. They were discovered early one morning, by the smoke of their fire, seen rising from amidst the trees, and were attacked and routed.

Friendly Indians resided in the town for a long time, and the last of the race has not been dead many years. Some of these lived on the Bank land, so called, which is near Oren Josselynn's, or west of King Street; and old samp mortars, pestles, tomahawks, or axes, and spear, or arrow heads, have been frequently found on the spot. Others resided on Curtis, now Main Street, and their wigwams stood on Joseph Dwelly's land. Here, too, relics have been occasionally found, turned up by the plough.

On the land of Capt. Elisha Barrell, in the north-easterly part of the town, and but a few rods distant from his barn, on the knoll, stood the wigwam of George Toto, probably a son of Mercy Toto, and sister of Rhoda, and perhaps of Sarah, who married James Still, in 1764. George's wife was Mary. He had no children. The old well dug by him, in the low ground near his hut, is still visible, in the midst of the bushes which surround it, and even the children of the neighborhood know it as Toto's well.

King Dick and Queen Daphne lived on Pine Island, so called, situated on what is now Hanover Street. Dick requested Col. John Bailey to write a letter for him to his friends, on the Cape, and on being asked *what* he should write, replied, "King Dick and Queen Daphne, ebery ting, ebery ting."

It is said that there was an old Indian burial ground on this island, and that, before the violent September gale of 1815, known as the *hurricane*, the mounds covering the graves of those who had been buried on the spot could be distinctly seen. Since then, all traces of them have disappeared.

There was another Indian burial ground, back of Assinippi Hall, in the north-easterly part of the town, on land owned by Capt.

Thomas Simmons. This was used, if we have been rightly informed, so late as the former part of the present century, and some of our old people remember when the last burial took place on the spot.

It is said that there was another burial ground, not far from Rocky Swamp; and perhaps there were others, in other parts of the town.

Old Peter, an Indian, lived on land owned by Turner Stetson, and married a black woman, who gave the name to the tract known as Peg's Swamp. She resided, the latter part of her life, in a house which stood where that of Albert Stetson stands, not far from the Town House, and d. May 1, 1815, æ. 87.

One John Fredericks, a Hessian, deserted from the British Army, during the Revolution, came to Hanover, and married an Indian woman named Joanna. A bounty being offered for the detection and return of deserters, he was obliged to secrete himself for a time in Plymouth woods, and on being asked by the father of the present Zaccheus Estes, how he fared while there, he replied, "*if turkentine had been molasses, I should have done very well.*"

The author has in his possession several relics of the Indians of Hanover, and other parts of Plymouth County; among which are a *pipe*, of clay, hard baked, and of a brownish color, a present from Mr. David Mann; — *arrow* and *spear* heads, the gifts of different friends; an *axe or tomahawk*, of a greenish color, and fine finish, from Mr. John Gross, of South Scituate, and others from other friends; a *pestle*, 9 or 10 inches long, and about 2 inches in diameter, a present from Mr. Seth Jones, of Pembroke; and a stone *ball*, perfectly round, and about the size of a four pound cannon ball, which was picked up near the residence of Cornet Stetson, on the North River, on the occasion of a pilgrimage made to the spot a few years since, when the author drank water from the spring from whence his ancestor, more than two hundred years ago, slaked his thirst, and gave his children to drink!

What changes have taken place since those days! No longer is the war-whoop heard, breaking upon the stillness of the night, arousing the father to arms, and causing the mother to clasp her trembling little ones closer in her embrace. Neither is the light canoe seen gliding down the Indian Head, or the North River, to the sea. The deer and the wolf are gone. The ponds of Pembroke, where Hobomok dwelt, no longer reflect upon their placid bosoms the graceful forms of the Indian maidens, who came there to bathe, and to sport in the waters.

Even the rude dwellings of our ancestors are gone. Their fortresses have long since perished. And every building, erected two hundred years ago, has fallen to decay, and returned to the dust. Yet the same sun shines brightly upon us, by day, as upon them. The same moon sheds down its clear and silvery light upon our fields and homes. And the same stars sparkle above us! Even the *forests* have changed. Here and there may be a scattering tree which saw the light when the pilgrims landed. The brave old white oak, by Jacob's saw-mill dam,

> "Oft in moonlight by whose side
> The Indian wooed his dusky bride,"

is one of these; — also the two white oaks at Barstow's yard, on the North River. But the mighty cedars, the giant pines, the tall walnuts, with the spreading beech, the waving poplar, and the graceful elm, all are gone. Trees of a recent growth alone occupy the soil. One hundred and thirty summers, will probably number the years of our most aged forest trees.

The hum of our grist mills, the clatter of our tack-machines, or the louder reverberations of the descending trip-hammer; with the noise of the saw, cutting its way through the log; the ring of the blacksmith's hammer, upon the anvil; the cheerful call of the farmer, to his team, and the rumble of our wagons, along the road to market, laden with boxes, and shoes, and the produce of the farm; — these are the sounds which now strike the ear; — and the spire of the church pointing to heaven, the village school-house, and our neatly painted dwellings, dotting the sides of our streets; these are the signs of advancing civilization, and a manifest token that man is subduing the earth to his dominion, and making the elements his ministers; and though monuments of the past are occasionally seen among us, connecting by visible links what *has been* with what *is*, yet these are only incentives to greater exertions, and stimuli to prouder achievements!

CHAPTER IV.

ECCLESIASTICAL HISTORY.

FIRST CHURCH.

"Before the loftier throne of Heaven,
The hand is raised, the pledge is given,
One monarch to obey, one creed to own —
That monarch, God, that creed, his word alone."

SPRAGUE.

Provisions for the support of Public worship — Erection of the *first meeting house* in Hanover—Its appearance — Gathering of the worshippers — Settlement of Mr. Bass — Seating the house — Communion service — Insubordination of the youth — Sternhold and Hopkins' Hymns — Decease of Mr. Bass — His character—Settlement of Mr. Baldwin — Gift of a parsonage — Erection of the *second meeting house* — Its appearance — Decease of Mr. Baldwin—Sketch of his life — Attempt to settle Mr. Litchfield — Settlement of Mr. Mellen — First *Bell* — Painting the house, and other repairs — Withdrawal of Mr. Mellen —His decease — Sketch of his life, and list of his publications — Settlement of Mr. Chaddock— Withdrawal — Sketch of his life—Settlement of Mr. Chapin — Sketch of his life — Settlement of Mr. Smith — His life and writings — Erection of the *third meeting house* — Settlement of Mr. Duncan.

A portion of the Preamble to the "General Laws and Liberties of New Plimouth Colony, published in 1671," sets forth, that "Whereas the great and known end of the first comers, in the year of our Lord 1620, leaving their dear Native Country, and all that was dear to them there; transporting themselves over the vast Ocean into this remote waste wilderness, and therein willingly conflicting with Dangers, Losses, Hardships, and Distresses sore, and not a few, WAS, that without offence, they under the protection of their Native Prince, together with the enlargement of his Majesties Dominions, might, with the liberty of a good conscience, enjoy the pure Scriptural Worship of God, without the mixture of Humane Inventions and Impositions, And that there children after them might walke in the Holy wayes of the Lord; And for which end they obtained leave from King James of happy memory, and his Honourable Council, with further Graunts from his Gracious Majesty Charles the first and his Honourable Council, by Letters Patent, for sundry Tracts of land, with many Priviledges therein contained for their better incouragement to proceed on in so Pious a Work, which may especially tend to the propagation of Religion, &c., as by Letters Patents more at large appeareth, and with further assurance also of the continuance of our Liberties and Priviledges, both Civil and Religious, under the Royal Hand and Seal of our Sovereign Lord King Charles the Second; And whereas by the good Hand of our God upon us many others since the first comers are for the same pious end come unto us, and sundry others rise up amongst us, desirous with all good conscience to walk in the faith and order of the Gospel; whereby there are many churches gathered amongst us walking according thereunto: And whereas (by the Grace of God) we have now had near about Fifty Years Experience, of the good consistency of these Churches, with Civil Peace and Order, and also with Spiritual Edification, together with the welfare and tranquility of this Government. It is therefore for the Honour of God and the propagation of Religion, and the continued welfare of this Colony, Ordered by this Court and the Authority thereof, That the said Churches already gathered, or that shall hereafter be orderly gathered, may and shall from time to time by this Government be protected and encouraged, in their peaceable and orderly walking, and the Faithful, Able, Orthodox, Teaching Ministry thereof, duly encouraged and provided for; together with such other Orthodox able Dispensers of the Gospel which shall or may be placed in any Township in this Government where there is or may be a defect of Church Order."

From this, we see the views of our Pilgrim Fathers, and their reverence for religion led to the enactment of many laws for its regulation and support. Provisions were made for the support of the ministry in every town of the Colony; and no act of incorporation was granted, without containing a clause especially enjoining the erection of a meeting house, and the settlement of a "learned, pious, and orthodox minister."

After the junction of the two Colonies, Plymouth and Massachusetts, in 1692, the laws for the maintenance of the ministry, and the erection of meeting-houses continued in force; and accordingly, in the act incorporating the town of Hanover, it is stipulated as one of the conditions of the grant, "that the Inhabitants of the said Town of Hannover do within the space of Two years from the Publication of this act erect and finish a suitable house for the Public Worship of God, and as soon as may be procure and settle a learned Orthodox Minister of good conversation, and make Provision for his comfortable and honourable support, and that thereupon they be discharged from any Further Payment for the maintenance of the ministry, &c., in the Towns of Scituate or Abington, for any estate lying within the said Town of Hannover."

In pursuance of this proviso, one of the first steps taken by the town, was to provide for the support of Public Worship; and July 17, 1727, "Mr. Daniel Dwight was chosen to dispense the word of God for three months,"[1] Amos Sylvester, and Thomas Josselynn being chosen to treat with him for that purpose; and £7 19s. were subsequently voted him as a remuneration for his services. Meetings were held at this time in private dwellings; and that of Mr. Samuel Stetson, being nearest to the centre of the town, and most convenient for the public accomodation, was principally used, for which he was liberally paid.

August 29, £60 were voted for the support of a minister, and Isaac Buck, Elijah Cushing, and Joseph House were chosen to provide one. Nov. 13, It was agreed "to erect a meeting-house at the most convenient place, by the road called the Drink water road," and Elijah Bisbee, Joshua Turner, and Aaron Soule, who were probably of Pembroke, were chosen to select the site, and Job Otis was appointed to inform them of the town's desire. Dec. 13, "Voted that the size of the house be as follows: Length 48 feet; width 38 feet; and height between joints 19 feet; — to be completed by Oct. 1, 1728;" and Elijah Cushing, Joseph House, and Abner Dwelley were chosen a building committee, they to have the house done in a workmanlike manner, but as cheap as possible.

January 22, 1728, Isaac Bush was chosen agent to apply to the town of Scituate for aid in erecting the new meeting-house; a

1 Mr. D. seems to have preached in the town a few Sabbaths before its incorporation.

FIRST CENTRAL MEETING HOUSE.

subscription paper was circulated by him, on which the sum of £90 was subscribed, but of which only £66 1s. 6d., were realised; and it was agreed that the money thus obtained, should be proportioned on the polls and estates, towards defraying the charges. Mr. Buck was also agent to apply to citizens of Hanover for aid. Gifts of land were made, by John Cushing, James Cushing, Job Otis, Nicholas Litchfield, Stephen Clapp, Senr., and others, of Scituate; Rev. Thomas Clapp, of Taunton; and Joseph Barstow, and Samuel Barstow, of Hanover; the lots being laid out for the town by Caleb Torrey, and Stephen Clapp, of Scituate. The land on which the house was built, is said to have been given by Thomas Buck. Isaac Buck was the agent of the town to receive the deeds of the above lots.

March 3, 1728, the town voted to take their part of the Government loan of £60,000, "now in the Treasury at Boston," and Joseph Barstow, Benjamin Curtis, and Samuel Barstow, were chosen to receive the same, and to let it out towards paying the carpenters. Gifts of lumber were made by several persons, and what was left, after the house was finished, was sold for the use of the ministry. The whole cost of the house appears to have been about £300.

This first meeting-house, stood on the same spot as the present house, and continued in use until 1765, under the ministry of Mr. Baldwin, when the second house was built. No records exist from which a correct idea of its appearance can be gained. An old lady, Mrs. Perry, yet lives in Pembroke, born in 1755, who is now in her 98th year, and who was ten years of age when the second house was erected, who has a distinct recollection of that event, but not of the looks of the original edifice. From the best information I can gain, I learn that it was a plain structure, in accordance with the simplicity of the times, facing the South; without steeple or chimney; the windows glazed with diamond-shaped glass; the walls unplastered; and unwarmed by stove or furnace; and here, for about forty years, the fathers of the town, with their wives and little ones, gathered together, from Sabbath to Sabbath, in summer's heat and winter's cold, listening devoutly to the ministrations of the Word of God, and chanting, to the quaint, old fashioned tunes of the day, Sternhold and Hopkins' hymns, deaconed off to them line by line.

I seem to see them now; — the fathers, with broad-brimmed hats, turned up into three corners, with loops at the sides; long coats, with large pocket folds and cuffs, and without collars, — the buttons, either plated, or of pure silver, and of the size of a half-dollar; shirts, with bosoms and wrist ruffles, and with gold or silver buttons at the wrist, united by a link;[1] the neckcloth, or scarf, of fine white linen, or figured stuff, broidered, with the ends hanging loosely on the breast; the breeches close, with silver buckles at the knee, of goodly size; the legs covered with grey stockings; boots, with broad, white tops, or shoes, with straps and silver buckles; — the mothers, with black silk or satin bonnets; gowns, extremely long-waisted, with tight sleeves, or else very short sleeves, with an immense frill at the elbow; and high-heeled shoes;—these mounted upon the "family horse,"—for carriages were unknown in those days,—the father in front, and the "gude wife" seated on a pillion behind; the children, either on foot, or in the "horse cart," with a goodly store of bread and cheese, or doughnuts and apple pie, for the noon lunch; all moving sedately along, with becoming gravity, and decorous deportment, towards the "ancient temple;" and on arriving at the house, the husband, assisting the wife to dismount upon the bank-wall, in the rear of the building; and she, with the children, passing quietly in at the door; whilst the horse is hitched to the post, and the father also walks in, and sits near the door of the pew, in accordance with the custom established in times of danger, when sudden attacks from the Indians were feared; and over the house stillness reigns, until the minister, with ample gown, and powdered wig, walks up the aisle, and mounts the long flight of stairs leading to his desk, from which, as from a tower, high above his hearers, with the sounding board over his head, to convey the sonorous tones of his voice to his flock, he dispenses to them the word of life, and bears up their prayers to the throne of God!

The first minister settled in the town, was the Rev. Benjamin

[1] Mr. Samuel Brooks, on Main Street, has in his possession, specimens of the buttons here referred to, and also of the knee buckles.

Bass, son of Joseph and Mary Bass, of Braintree, and a descendant of Samuel Bass, who, with his wife Anne, and one or two young children, came to New England in 1630, and settled first in Roxbury, and afterwards in that part of Braintree now Quincy.[1] Benjamin was born in 1694, graduated at Harvard College in 1715, and settled in Hanover in 1728.

August 27, 1728, Benjamin Curtis, Elijah Cushing, William Witherell, Thomas Josselynn, and Benjamin Curtis, Jr., were chosen "to advise with the neighboring ordained ministers as the law directs, in order for the settlement of the Rev. Benjamin Bass in the work of the ministry;" and subsequently the sum of £130 per annum, after the rate of silver money, at 16s. per oz., was voted as his salary.

Nov. 23, 1728, it was voted to ordain Mr. Bass to the work of the ministry; and Amos Sylvester was chosen to provide entertainment for the council.

The ordination took place Dec. 11th; the 4th of the month having been observed as a day of Fasting and Prayer, and the Church, consisting of 10 (male?) members, besides the pastor, being formed on the 5th. Rev. Mr. Eells, of Scituate, and Rev. Mr. Lewis, of Pembroke, were present and assisted in the services on the day of Fasting.

The ceremonies of the Ordination are thus given on the Church Records: "Dec. 11, 1728, Benjamin Bass, A. M., was, by prayer and fasting, with imposition of the hands of the Presbytery, ordained a pastor of the Church, the Rev. Mr. Eells, of Scituate, Mr. Lewis, of Pembroke, Messrs. Hobart and Gay, of Hingham, and Mr. Checkley, of Boston, laid on hands; Mr. Gay began with prayer; Mr. Checkley preached; Mr. Eells gave the charge; and Mr. Lewis the right hand of fellowship."

The *house* being completed, and a *minister* settled, next in importance was the "*seating the worshippers.*" From a report made Nov. 31, 1728, it appears that there was room in the house for 31 pews, valued at £10 each, or £310 in all. But, the record proceeds to say, "as it is usual and commendable that there should be *dignities*, we generally vote and allow for the same; that therefore we vote that the highest pew in dignity should be

[1] Thayer's Family Memorial, p. 53.

valued at £15, and the next £14 10s., and so proportionally lower, until we come down to those pews which are of no difference in dignity, and then proportionable to each man's rates, either by a general vote, or lots, to take in the more people into each pew so valued or prized, as shall amount to the money;" and Joseph Stockbridge, John Hatch, and William Witherell, were chosen to proportion the pews according to these votes. Their action not being entirely satisfactory, June 29, 1730, votes were passed anew "to proportion the pews to make all persons easy, and to take in those that were left out;" a committee of seven was chosen to attend to this duty, and their doings were confirmed Aug. 31.

Although the mention of *dignities* may cause some to smile, yet substantially the same custom prevails in our own day, certain seats, in all our churches, being deemed more fashionable, and more valuable, than others.

January 10, 1728–9. At a church meeting, it was "voted to raise money by contribution to provide utensils for the Lord's table;" and by the 30th of the month, were bought, and brought to town, "three Pewter Tankards, marked C. T., of 10s. price each; five Pewter Beakers, costing 3s. 3d. each, and marked C. B.; two Pewter Platters, marked C. P.; a Pewter Basin for baptisms; and a Cloth for the communion table." The communion was celebrated, for the first time, March 2, 1729, and the first service plate continued in use until 1768, and Oct. 30th of that year, the Church received a present of "four silver cups for the communion table, by order, and at the expense of Deacon Stockbridge, the cost of each cup at £25, old tenor, and each having this inscription, THE GIFT OF DEACON JOSEPH STOCKBRIDGE TO THE CHURCH OF CHRIST IN HANOVER, 1768." For this present, the thanks of the Church were voted.

January 8, 1786. Two silver cups for the communion table were received, "a Legacy from Deacon Thomas Josselynn, cost £7 4s., and recorded as a token of gratitude, and to perpetuate the memory of the Benefaction."

The tankards and flagons are still in the possession, and these, with the silver cups above referred to, constitute the present communion service, of the church.

Not long after the erection of the meeting-house, the juvenile portion of the town, not having the fear of the law before their eyes, began to manifest a disposition to violate the fourth commandment, by congregating in the school-house, and other acts of insubordination; and March 1, 1734, it was "voted that the schoolmaster should lock up the school-house on Saturday's, to keep people out Lord's day;" and March 1, 1741, it was "voted that David Curtis look after the boys and negroes in the school-house on Sabbath days;" also, "voted Thomas Wilkes and Joshua Studley to look after the meeting-house Sabbath days, to keep the boys in order." Oct. 29, 1746, "Appointed Jacob Bailey to take care of the school-house for four months next coming, and to have full power to prosecute any person that shall presume forcibly to break into the school-house on the Lord's day."

This propensity to mischief, however, was not confined simply to tumultuous gatherings in the school-house, and disorderly conduct in the meeting-house; for other demonstrations, in the shape of broken windows, and shattered doors, attested their skill in the old-fashioned sport of casting stones; and votes for re-setting glass, and repairing locks, duly recorded, still bear testimony to these deeds of wantonness. But we are not to suppose that the youth of Hanover were more given to such proceedings than those of other towns. Public records, generally, show more or less of such outbreaks and damages in all towns. Nor need we be surprised at the *character* of these offences, for even in our own days, the school-house, and the meeting-house, are not exempt from such visitations, and the winds shrieking mournfully through shattered panes, seem like ghosts, lamenting the desolations of Zion, and the desecration of the Sanctuary. This Vandal spirit should ever be deprecated; for not only is it irreverent, but a sure sign of ill-breeding, and a state of semi-civilization.

1742, May 7. "The church took a vote to see if the Society would sing in the *new way*, and it passed in the affirmative, *nem. con.* Then being desired to bring in their votes for a TUNER, Mr. Ezekiel TURNER was chosen by a considerable majority." Previous to this, singing, in most, if not all the New England churches, had been strictly *congregational*, the lines of the hymns being read off by the *Deacon*, who usually pitched the tune, and all, who could

sing, joined in the performance. By this vote, Sternhold and Hopkins' version of the Psalms was rejected, and Tate and Brady's adopted.

1748, April 8. £14 15s. were collected, "to buy good books with, to lend to such of the Society as stand in need of them, and would be glad to read them." With the above money, says Mr. Bass, "I bought in less than a week, a parcel of books, whose Titles, Authors, and Price in Old Tenor, may be met with in a book which is an exposition of the Epistle to the Colossians, by Nicholas Byfield."

The ministry of Mr. Bass, which was quiet and undisturbed, passed peacefully on, until terminated by his death, which took place May 23, 1756, in the 63d year of his age, after a settlement of 27 years, 5 months, and 15 days, during which period 83 persons joined the church, and 588 were baptised.

The remains of Mr. Bass, with those of his wife, who died Feb. 25, 1772, lie in the south-east corner of the old burying ground; and the grave stones, which mark the spot, are still in a state of tolerable preservation, though that of Mr. Bass appears to have been broken, and re-set. The inscriptions on the same are simple, and can be easily deciphered.

Our materials, for a sketch of the life of this first servant of the Church, are quite scanty. In vain have we sought for some notice of his career in the papers of that day. From his writings, he appears to have been a man marked more by common sense, than by brilliancy of diction, withal a little inclined to facetiousness, yet open-hearted, and frank, and laboring diligently for the welfare of his people. He was often consulted by neighboring Churches, and acted as Moderator in Ecclesiastical Councils;[1] and, in the midst of the excitement which prevailed, during the latter years of his ministry, occasioned by the preaching of Whitefield, and the rise of the "New Lights," as they were termed, he preserved his own hold on the good-will of his Society, and left his people in a state of as great prosperity as was enjoyed in any of the adjoining towns. His habits were simple, and his manner of living frugal and unostentatious; yet his was ever a hospitable board, to which his parishioners and friends were cordially wel-

[1] Winsor, Hist. Duxbury, 196, and 199.

comed. He took great interest in the children of his parish, and never passed a child, in the road, without noticing it. And the children so loved him, that whenever they saw him approaching, they would arrange themselves in a row, and, as he drew near, greet him, with bows, and curtesies, while smiles of joy illumined their faces. His grandson, Elisha, has, at his house, the *wedding dress* of Mrs. Bass, which was a cream colored, brocade silk, of considerable beauty, — also a silk apron, of a sage color. A lady, whom I saw there, Oct. 18, 1852, informs me, as an illustration of Mr. B's facetiousness, that having received an invitation to settle at Eel River, Plymouth, and on being asked if he should accept, he replied, "No, Eel River may do for small fish, but it is not large enough for a Bass."

After the decease of Mr. Bass, Ezekiel Turner, Esq., Joseph House, and Michael Sylvester, were chosen a committee by the town, June 14, 1756, to join a committee chosen by the Church, "to supply the pulpit with preaching;" and Aug. 30th, the Church having laid before the town their choice of Mr. Samuel Baldwin for their pastor, the town concurred in the choice, and voted as his salary £73 6s. 8d., lawful money. Mr. B. declining to settle for this sum, it was voted, Oct. 11th, to give him £80 lawful money, and to build him, within the space of 18 months, "a dwelling-house 40 feet long, 30 feet wide, and 17 feet between joints, with two stacks of chimneys, a plain roof, with a suitable number of windows with crown glass, and to be painted inside and outside, such a color or colors as shall be agreeable to his mind, and to build and finish under the house a cellar 30 feet long, and 14 feet wide, pointed, &c., and every thing, both inside and outside, both wood work, iron work, and joiners' work, with two *Bofatts* (cupboards) and as many closets in said house as may be convenient, all to be done to the turning of a key, and to be underpinned in a suitable manner, to the acceptance of the said Mr. Baldwin, and this to be a free gift as a settlement, to which proposal Mr. B. gave his answer in the affirmative." Feb. 7, the dimensions of the house were altered to 38 by 32 feet; and it was voted to pay for the building in money, and to give Joseph Curtis £160, lawful money, for building and completing it. March 5, 1759, Mr. Baldwin acknowledged the receipt of the house as his settlement gift.

October 18, 1756, "Voted that Mr. Baldwin be ordained Dec. 1, if the Thanksgiving be not on that week, but if it is, the ordination to be on the second Wednesday of said December." Also, "Voted to give Captain Joseph Josselynn £16, in lawful money, to provide handsome and suitable entertainment for the ordination, and he agreed to do it for that sum."

The ordination took place Dec. 1; "the Rev. Messrs. Gay, of Hingham, Cook, of Sudbury, Storer, of Watertown, Smith, of Pembroke, and Swift, of Acton, laying on hands. Mr. Smith prayed, Mr. Cook preached, Mr. Gay gave the charge, Mr. Storer the right hand of fellowship, and Mr. Swift offered the last prayer. The churches or pastors sent to besides the above, were Wales, of Marshfield, Hitchcock, of Pembroke, Woodward, of Weston, Dodge, of Abington, and Barnes, of Scituate."

Under the ministration of Mr. Baldwin, the meeting-house was soon filled; and accordingly, June 25, 1764, it was voted, to open the same "in two parts, and to put in a new piece in the middle of 13 or 14 feet in length." This vote was reconsidered, October 22, and it was then voted to build a new house, of the following dimensions: — "62 feet in length, 43 in width, and 22 feet between joints, according to the plan in the office of the Town Clerk."

At the same time, it was voted, that "each person enjoy their pews as heretofore, only giving way for the new additional pews to be built;" and the Committee was empowered to "dispose of the old meeting-house, and the new additional pew room, to the undertaker or undertakers of the meeting-house aforesaid, or to any other person or persons, in part of pay for the work aforesaid." Mr. Joseph Tolman, was the contractor for the erection of the new house; and May 20, 1765, it was voted "to have a steeple to the meeting-house, provided the money for the same can or shall be raised by subscription."

This steeple was built; and the new house was erected on the site of the old one. It stood facing the South, and the roof pitched North and South. At the East end, was the women's porch, extending from the ground, to the eaves, and projecting from the building, a few feet; in the entry, was the stairway leading to the gallery, and overhead, the *powder room*, in which the town's

SECOND CENTRAL MEETING HOUSE.

PRESENT CENTRAL MEETING HOUSE,

stock of powder was kept, during the Revolution. The men's porch, was at the West end, also projecting from the building, and rising above the eaves, with a long, tapering spire, or steeple, surmounted with a vane. This spire was removed about 1784, when a bell was presented to the society by Mr. Josselynn, and a new steeple, with a suitable belfry, was erected.

Within, the walls were plastered, the pews square, the galleries spacious, and the accommodations for the worshippers comfortable and decent. The author does not know of any house now standing, from which a perfect idea of this ancient tabernacle could be obtained. Perhaps in *internal* arrangement, the old meeting house in Carver, near the residence of John Savary, Esq., may be considered as an approximation to that of the second house in Hanover, though *externally*, the porches and steeple are wanting. It is said, that, while this house was being erected, meetings were held in a pine grove, near by, and here, Mr. Baldwin's daughter Hannah was baptised.

The affairs of the society, from this time forward, until the war of the Revolution commenced, continued in a state of quiet prosperity, and the salary of Mr. Baldwin was paid regularly and promptly ; but the derangement in the finances of the country introduced by that struggle, led to difficulties in many religious societies, and, finally, to a dissolution of the connexion, which had so long and so happily subsisted, between Mr. Baldwin, and the society in Hanover. On the Church records, under date of Nov. 28, 1779, is the following entry by Mr. Baldwin himself: "I preached a farewell sermon to the people of Hanover for the want ot support, and on the 8th March following, I asked a dismission for the want of support, which they granted, and it was confirmed by a vote of the town."

Mr. Baldwin remained with the society 23 years, 3 months, and 3 days, during which period, 107 persons joined the Church, and 632 were baptised. As a pastor, his services gave general satisfaction, and as a preacher, his talents were not only highly respectable, but his manuscripts evince that he was a ready and eloquent writer, and his discourses display good judgment, keen perceptions, and strong common sense.

Mr. Baldwin early espoused the cause of America, in the struggle with Great Britain, and, throughout the continuance of the war of the Revolution, took a deep and anxious interest in his country's success.

He officiated as a Chaplain in the Army, and gave eloquent exhortations to his own flock at home, and to the minute men of the town; and, so completely was he absorbed in this work, that the intensity of his devotion, joined with other causes, affected his mind, and for a period of four years, previous to his decease, he was partially deranged, and under the faithful care of his devoted wife.

It is said that on one occasion, during this period, a neighbor, Miss Studley, called at the parsonage, to converse with Mrs. Baldwin, upon the events of the war, not then wholly closed. Mr. B. lay on his bed, apparently unmindful of what they were saying, in his usual state of apathy and indifference. Suddenly he arose, left the room, went to his study, and returned with the manuscript of a discourse which he had delivered to the minute men, and, standing in the doorway, he deliberately read it from beginning to end. Mrs. B. was rejoiced, thinking the balance of his mind was about to be restored. But when he had finished his reading, he carried the manuscript back, returned, and laid himself on the bed in silence.

His death took place December 1, 1784, about one year after peace was declared; and his remains, with those of his wife, lie in the old burial-ground; grave stones having been erected to their memory, by vote of the town, March 9, 1796.

I have been able to learn of but one of his productions that was printed,—his address before the Pilgrim Society, delivered in 1775.

The house in which Mr. Baldwin lived is still standing, on Hanover Street, not far from the residence of the late Dr. Joshua Studley; and it is a fair specimen of the style of building here one hundred years ago. It is still in decent repair, and promises yet to stand for many years, a memorial of the past, and one of the few relics of olden time, becoming rarer every year.

After the withdrawal of Mr. Baldwin, several candidates for the pastorship of the society were heard, and some time elapsed before a settlement was effected.

Rev. Joseph Litchfield, subsequently of York, Maine, a descendant of Lawrence Litchfield, of Barnstable, Massachusetts, was one of these candidates; and a call was given him, with a salary of "£90 per annum, in silver money, at 6s. per dollar, or gold equivalent, or in paper bills at the rate or value the General Court or Assembly shall settle the same, and 12 cords of firewood at his door, within a mile from the meeting-house;" and December 27, 1780, was fixed upon as the day for his ordination; Capt. Joseph Soper to provide entertainment for the Council. The Council met, and, it is said, were in session two or three days; but Mr. L. was not ordained, many of the society being opposed to his settlement. Tradition says, that the objections urged against him were of the most trifling character;—one being, that he wore stockings, "footed up" with yarn of a different color from that in the "tops;" and this was "beneath the dignity of the clerical office;" — and the second, and perhaps the most frivolous of the two, affirming, that, on a certain occasion, in making a call, instead of entering the yard by the *gate*, as a clergyman should have done, he "clambered over the rails of the fence, much to the lowering of the dignity of his profession."

We suspect, however, that political, or other differences, were the real grounds of objection against him.

But though not settled when first called, a second attempt was made to effect that object; which resulted as before, in his rejection and withdrawal.

Finally, after hearing several other candidates, to some of whom a call was given, a more unanimous request was sent, in 1783, to the Rev. John Mellen, of Sterling, to come and labor among them; and this call was successful. He was settled in Hanover, February 11, 1784; Capt. Joseph Soper making the entertainment for the Council. "Six churches were sent to on the occasion, but Cambridge failed by reason of the aged and Reverend Dr. Appleton's death on the same week. Rev. Mr. Hitchcock, of Pembroke, gave the charge; Rev. Mr. Barnes, of Scituate, the right hand of fellowship; his son, Rev. Mr. Mellen, of Barnstable, preached the sermon; Rev. Mr. Prentiss, of Reading, began with prayer; and Rev. Mr. Niles, of Abington, concluded. *Anthems* were sung by the choir, on entering and leaving the Meeting house."

In 1785, the Society received, of Col. Joseph Josselynn, a donation of $100, which they agreed " should go towards buying a *bell*, if there can be enough subscribed to make up the rest; " and November 29, 1785, the bell was purchased, of Col. Aaron Hobart, of Abington, and a committee of twenty, " with all the rest of the town that see cause to assist," were chosen to "hang it."

This bell was broken, not long after, through want of skill on the part of the person appointed to ring it; was re-cast, and when re-hung, December 18, 1788, Dea. Bass, Dea. Robbins, and Benjamin Stetson were chosen to " give the sexton directions how to ring the bell. "

In 1789, it was voted to *paint* the meeting-house; " the walls to be stone yellow, the roof spanish brown, and the corner boards and window frames and sashes white." May 30, 1791, "Voted to give Capt. Timothy Rose, £3, to take care of, and sweep and *sand* the meeting house, and ring the bell the present year."

October 14, 1793, a Committee chosen " to get the meeting-house underpinned, and to procure a stock lock for the door. " June 9, 1797, a Committee was chosen to *seat the singers;* and alterations were made in the house to provide for their accommodation. The same year, $300 were voted as the salary of Mr. Mellen, and from that time forward, his salary was paid in *Federal*, instead of *Sterling*, currency. In 1802, the bell was re-hung; and in 1803, Capt. Albert Smith presented to the town a number of Lombardy poplar trees, which were set out near the meeting house. Not one of these is now standing. The last was cut down, a few years since, by Mr. Samuel Stetson.

The ministry of Mr. Mellen was terminated, by the infirmities of age, in 1805, and he removed to Reading, Massachusetts, where he closed his long and useful life, in the house of his daughter, the relict of Caleb Prentiss, July 4, 1807, aged 85.

His life was an eventful one. He was born in Hopkinton, March 14, 1722, and graduated at Harvard College, in 1741, teaching school the same year for £85, at Sudbury.[1] He was ordained the first pastor of the church in Sterling, December 19, 1744, where he continued, probably at the head of the clergy of Worcester County, until November 14, 1774. His connexion with this society, which had continued for thirty years, was dis-

[1]Barry's History of Framingham, p. 328.

solved, in consequence of disputes, occasioned by his endeavors to maintain what he considered the true discipline of the churches, and by his adoption of doctrinal sentiments, not wholly in accordance with those generally prevailing at the time. "He with others, as tradition says, had sensibly departed from the standard of faith that had been generally received in the New England Churches, and had extended his speculations in such a manner, as to give great offence to some who had not pursued the same course of reasoning. In 1756, he delivered an eloquent series of discourses addressed to parents, children, and youth, which contained sentiments highly obnoxious to many of his brethren in the ministry. These were published, and were extremely well received by his people. In the unguarded hours of social conversation, too, he, as was well understood, rejected many of the articles of the popular faith. Nor were his people dissatisfied with him on this account, but rather for publicly co-operating in the censure of those doctrines which it was supposed he embraced as the truth of the gospel. It was now understood by some of the most intelligent of the parish, that their minister was verging towards doctrines that he had publicly disclaimed. In 1765, he published a volume of sermons on the doctrines of Christianity. These contained a learned system of scholastic theology, maintaining a middle course between the two extremes of Calvinism and Arminianism. Upon some of the controverted points it is not easy to understand which side his speculations favor most. The volume is highly creditable to his memory as a scholar and a theologian, and when published was considered an acquisition to the literature of the country. When his people produced their allegations against him in 1773, they urged but few instances of false doctrines, and of these he fully exculpated himself before a council. The principal charge of this character was, that he had said that God was the author of sin. The sermon was produced where it was said to be contained. He stated that he had never held this doctrine in its gross sense, but only that sin was by permission, &c. The council cleared him, as his church had previously." He is described, in the work from which we have just quoted, as a man "liberally endowed by nature with a strong and energetic mind, which was

[1]See an elaborate article in the Worcester Magazine, Vol. 2. p. 213, &c.

highly improved by diligent and successful cultivation, and he obtained a high rank as a preacher and scholar."

Besides the volume of doctrinal Sermons, to which we have already referred, and his sermons to parents, &c., his other published works, were, a Sermon at the Ordination of Rev. J. Palmer, 1753 ; — a Discourse at a General Muster, 1756 ; — on the Mortal Sickness among his People, 1756 ; — on the Conquest of Canada, 1760; — on the Death of Sebastian Smith, 1763 ; — Religion productive of Music, at Marlboro', 1773 ; — a Sermon at the Ordination of Rev. Levi Whitman, 1785 ; — a Discourse before a Lodge of Freemasons, 1793 ; — and a Thanksgiving Sermon, 1795. [1]

A few of these, as will be seen by the dates, were delivered after his settlement in Hanover. He is spoken of here, with much affection, by his old parishioners ; and was a man of sociable habits, lively in conversation, fond of a jest, and of ardent feelings. Many anecdotes are related of his ministry ; but we have already extended our sketch as far as will be generally interesting, or we should be happy to introduce them.

October 21, 1805, "Voted to repair the *bass viol*, and *the singers' seats.*"

July 23, 1806, Rev. Calvin Chaddock, late of Rochester, was installed as pastor of the Society ; the entertainment being provided by Lemuel Dwelly, at an expense of $125. Seven churches were sent to on the occasion ; five only attended. Rev. Mr. Strong, of Randolph, offered the Installing Prayer ; Rev. Mr. Niles, of Abington, preached the sermon, and offered the consecrating prayer ; Rev. Mr. Barker, of Middleboro', delivered the charge ; Rev. Mr. Norton, of Weymouth, the right hand of fellowship ; and Rev. Mr. Richards, of Halifax, offered the concluding prayer." During the ministry of Mr. Chaddock, the Academy was built, of which we shall speak in our Chapter on Education ; and of this Academy, Mr. C. had the charge, until his removal from the place, in 1818, after a settlement of 12 years. He is spoken of as a ready preacher, a man of great natural eloquence, fluent in speech, and one whose discourses were generally popular. In the possession of his son, Mr. Ebenezer N. Chaddock, of Boston, is a large sized painting, containing a likeness of Mr. C.,

[1] Allen's Biographical Dictionary, and Worcester Magazine.

and of his wife, and three of his children, executed nearly 50 years since, by Arad Thompson, and representing him in the attitude of imparting instruction to the children.

Mr. Alden, one of the pupils at his school, says of him, that, "with a mind richly gifted by the Father of Spirits, he possessed a native, simple, and truly genuine eloquence. His bosom, a fountain of the tenderest sympathies spontaneously gushing forth, moved him often and copiously "to weep with them that weep." To the afflicted — to the mourner in Zion — his words of consolation were the breathings of angelic sweetness; while the truth of God heard from his lips in tones of deepest solemnity, thrilled the hearts of assembled multitudes. "Of like passions with others — by no means faultless — yea, even specially "compassed with infirmity," — yet in conflict with his spiritual foes "he was more than a conqueror." The peaceful close of his useful life was passed on the sunny plains of Western Virginia. While passing up the beautiful Ohio, of a pleasant summer's morning, many years since, I was providentially thrown in company with some of those who enjoyed his last ministrations; and thus, from the lips of his personal friends, I received the animating account of his final exit from earth, in the triumph of the Christian faith."[1]

Rev. Seth Chapin, the sixth Pastor, was the son of Seth and Eunice Chapin, of Mendon, Mass.; and was born June 25, 1783. His father was an officer in the Revolutionary Army, and was stationed, a portion of the time, in Rhode Island; being engaged in Sullivan's celebrated expedition. The son pursued his studies, preparatory for College, under the Rev. Dr. Crane, of Uxbridge, entered Brown University, in 1804, graduated in 1808, studied Theology at Andover, which place he left in 1811; and in November of that year, was installed as pastor of the Church in Hillsboro', N. H. Here he remained until 1816; and the following three years were spent in Rowley, Mass., Mansfield, Conn., and elsewhere. In 1819, he was settled in Hanover, and remained until 1824, after which he preached in East Haddam, Conn., Hunter, N. Y., Attleboro', Mass., and Granville, Mass. In 1845, he relinquished the duties of his profession, and engaged in agricul-

[1] Letter, in the Pamphlet giving an account of the Exercises at the Dedication of the New Academy, p. 12.

tural pursuits, with such ardor, and success, in the language of his son, as to "have the pleasure of matching the wonderful Georgic transformation, and saw,

> "Ingens
> Exiit ad coelum ramis felicibus arbos
> Miraturque novas fondes et non sua poma."

He married Mary Bicknell, second daughter of the Hon. Joshua Bicknell, of Barrington, May 28, 1810, — her father having been, "for more than 50 years, prominent in the councils of the State; and a man of such unflinching political integrity as to have received the title of "old Aristides." By this marriage he had two sons, the elder of whom, Henry, graduated at Brown University, in 1835, received the degree of L.L.B., at Harvard College, in 1838, and is settled as a Physician, in Providence, Rhode Island. The younger son, read law with the Hon. A. C. Greene, of Rhode Island, and settled in Alabama, where he died September 11, 1836, at the early age of 21. Mr. Chapin, the father, died in Providence, Rhode Island, April 19, 1850, æ 67. His widow survives, and is residing with her son, in Providence. As a preacher, Mr. Chapin was earnest, and faithful; his discourses being instructive, and copiously illustrated. As a scholar, he was diligent, and studious; and several of his occasional productions were published. He was successful in his calling; a man of usefulness, and indomitable perseverance; and he left behind him a good name, as an inheritance for his surviving son.

Rev. Ethan Smith, the 7th pastor, "was born in Belchertown, Mass., Dec. 16, 1762, and while young, was a soldier for one summer in the Revolutionary War, and was at West Point when the traitor Arnold sold that fortress to the British. Having attended to the preparatory studies, he entered Dartmouth College in 1785, and graduated in 1790. Soon after taking his degree, he was licensed to preach, and spent the first Sabbath of October, 1790, at Haverhill, N. H., where he was first settled in the ministry. In about a year from that time, he was married to Bathsheba Sandford, second daughter of Rev. David Sandford, of Medway, Mass. He remained at Haverhill nine years, and was then dismissed for want of support. He was installed in the ministry at Hopkinton, N. H., March 12, 1800, and continued there about eighteen years, during sixteen of which he was Secretary of the New Hampshire Missionary Society. He was afterwards settled at Hebron, N. Y., about four years; at Poultney, Vermont, about five years; at Hanover, Mass., five years; and then spent a season as a city missionary in Boston. His publications were, 1. A Dissertation on the Prophecies, two editions; 2. A View of the Trinity, two editions; 3. A View of the Hebrews, two editions; 4. Lectures on the Subjects and Mode of Baptism, two editions; 5. A Key to the figurative Language of the Bible; 6. Memoirs of Mrs. Abigail Bailey; 7. A Key to the Revelation, 2 editions; 8. Prophetic Catechism; 9. Two Sermons on Episcopacy; 10. Farewell Sermon at Haverhill, N. H.; 11. First Sermon after installation at Hopkinton; 12. Two Sermons on the Vain Excuses of Sinners, preached at Washington, N. H.; 13. Sermon on the Moral Perfection of God, preached at Newburyport, Mass.; 14. Sermon on the daughters of Zion excelling, preached before a Female Cent Society; 15. Sermon on the happy Transition of Saints, preached at the funeral of Mrs. Jemima, consort of Rev. Dr. Harris, of Dunbarton; 16. Sermon at the ordination of Rev. Stephen Martindale, at Tinmouth, Vermont; and 17. Sermon at the ordination of Rev. Harvey Smith, at Weybridge, Vermont. His children were Myron, born at Haverhill, N. H., 1794, and died 1818, aged 24; Lyndon Arnold, born at Haverhill, 1795, graduated at Dartmouth College, married a daughter of Rev. Dr. Griffin, and settled as a physician, in Newark, N. J.; Stephen Sanford, born at Haverhill, 1797, and settled as pastor of the Congregational Church, Westminster, Mass.; Laura, who died in infancy; Carlos, born in Hopkinton, 1801, graduated at Union College, and settled as pastor of the Presbyterian Church in Massillon, Ohio; Grace Fletcher, wife of Rev. Job H. Martin, died in Haverhill, Mass., 1840; Sarah Towne, second wife of Rev. J. H. Martin, of New York; Harriet, wife of William H. Sanford, of Boylston, Mass.; and Ellen, wife of C. B. Sedgwick, Esq., of Syracuse, died May 23, 1846, aged 33. The wife of Mr. Smith, died in Pompey, N. Y., April 5, 1835, aged 64. He was living, in 1847, in Boylston, Mass.," but has since deceased.[1]

1 See a communication in the N. E. Gen. Reg., for 1847, p. 182 et seq.

During the ministry of Mr. Smith, the second meeting-house was torn down, and the third, or present house erected; which stands in the centre of the town, facing the East, and is a modest structure, surmounted by a steeple, and in the belfry hangs the old bell, given by Mr. Josselynn, in 1785, and re-cast in 1788.

Rev. Abel G. Duncan, the present pastor of the Society, graduated at the Bangor Theological Seminary, in 1828, was settled for four years at Jackson and Brooks, Maine, and was installed in Hanover, August 22, 1833. He has proved himself a faithful minister, and an excellent citizen; having had the honor to Represent the town, for six years, in the State Legislature, and having been, for many years, Chairman of the School Committee.

The Central Society, like all others that have been long established, has seen its days of prosperity, and its days of adversity. As the oldest society in the town, it has enjoyed great advantages, and has done much to maintain the ordinances of the gospel. We are happy to say that the annals of the Town are but little stained with the records of protracted controversies, and bitter animosities. A few such unpleasant memorials occur, but we have chosen to leave them unnoticed, rather than to make our pages the vehicle of perpetuating events of so little consequence in themselves, and so unprofitable to the present, or to future generations. The *virtues* of our fathers, should ever be remembered. And among these, by no means the least conspicuous, are their reverence for God, their zeal for his worship, and their devotion to the interests of learning and piety. May we, their children, endeavor to follow them in everything good, and may we transmit, to our children, blessings as great as have descended to us from them.

CHAPTER V.

ECCLESIASTICAL HISTORY CONTINUED.

"In vestment white, the minister of God
Opens the book, and reverentially
The stated portion reads." GRAHAME.

"I cannot go,
Where UNIVERSAL LOVE not smiles around."
THOMSON.

"To his great baptism flocked,
With awe the regions round." MILTON.

Establishment of St. Andrews Church in Scituate—First Meeting house—Mr. Davenport's ministry—Mr. Brockwell's—Mr. Thompson's—Sketch of his descendants—Mr. Wheeler's ministry — Removal of the Church to Hanover—Erection of a New Meeting House—Rectorship of Messrs Cooper, Wolcott, Appleton, Greenleaf, and Cutler—Establishment of a Society in the Northerly part of Hanover, and Westerly part of Scituate—Incorporation as a Universalist Society—Sketch of its history—History of the Baptist Society.

ST. ANDREWS CHURCH.

About the year 1725, Episcopal service was first performed in the town of Scituate, by Rev. Timothy Cutler, D. D., Rector of Christ Church, in Boston. According to Deane, [1] the statement if made in Nichols's collection of anecdotes, that "Mr. Cutler, withs several attendants, came to Scituate, during the absence of Mr. Bourne, minister of the north parish, by the invitation of Lieut. Damon, (then at variance with Mr. Bourne,) and another gentleman of large estate, and performed divine service in the Church form, in the north Meeting-house."

This statement, in its leading features, is copied by Mr. Cutler, into his "Sermon on the origin, progress, and present condition of St. Andrews Church, Hanover, Massachusetts," which was published in 1848 ; [2] to which he adds, "Whether any minister of the Church of England had previously visited or resided as a missionary," in Scituate, "does not appear. The Society for Propa-

1 History of Scituate, p. 45. 2 Sermon, p. 4.

gating the Gospel in Foreign Parts, which is connected with the Church of England, and to whose assistance this Church was subsequently indebted for aid, had missionaries located in New England, some years prior to this visit of Dr. Cutler, in 1725, and it is not impossible that their labors may have been held in this region."

In a communication, received from John Barstow, Esq., of Providence, R. I., he speaks of the Rev. Mr. Miller, of Braintree, Mass., as one of these Missionaries, and says, that, in his annual Report to the Society, in 1731, he observes that "he had preached from time to time to the people of the Church of England, in Scituate, and the neighboring towns, that the services were held in a private house, and that the auditory was so large that the house could not contain them."

The first meeting-house belonging to this Church, was erected in 1731, on the central part of Church hill, in Scituate, and enlarged in 1753;[1] and, though not entirely finished at the time, it "was opened for divine service, October 11, 1731, when Mr. Miller preached a sermon, and baptised eight children. More people were present than the church could contain. Mr. Miller preached again, on the last day of November, being St. Andrew's day, from which the Church takes its name. The members of the Church sent an earnest request, to the Society in England, to provide them a missionary, and the Rev. Mr. Davenport was sent them, with an allowance, from the Society, of £60 per annum, and an allowance of Books, for Libraries, and devotional books, for distribution among the poorer members. Mr. Davenport continued their Rector, from 1733, to 1736, inclusive."[2]

Deane states, that Mr. Davenport, who graduated at Harvard University, in 1719, and also received a degree at Oxford, England, gave, in 1743, "his house and land in Scituate, to the Society for propagating the gospel in foreign parts, in trust, towards the support of the ministers of St. Andrew's Church in Scituate, in perpetuity; and in this conveyance, he adverts to the fact of his

[1] It was struck by lightning many years ago, but experienced no material injury. It had a steeple, and bell.

[2] Letter of John Barstow, Esq.

OLD EPISCOPAL CHURCH.

PRESENT EPISCOPAL CHURCH.

having been *their first rector*."[1] We shall have occasion to refer to this gift hereafter.

Rev. Mr. Brockwell, the next Rector, had charge of the society "from 1737, to the early part of 1739. He then left Scituate, and accepted a call from a Church in Salem. While he preached at St. Andrews, he received £60 per annum, from the Society in England."[2]

From the time Mr. Brockwell left Scituate, the church was destitute of a regularly appointed minister, until 1743, when the mission was re-established, by the appointment of Rev. Ebenezer Thompson, of New Haven, as Rector, with a yearly allowance from the society, in England, of £40 per annum; and he continued in his office until his death, November 28, 1775, aged 64.[3] The request for this renewal of the mission, came not only from Scituate, but from citizens of *Hanover*, Pembroke, and Marshfield.

During the settlement of Mr. Thompson, he resided, for about thirty years, on the glebe which had been given by Mr. Davenport; but for a year or two before his death, he purchased and occupied the house now owned and occupied by Mr. John Gardner, in Scituate, and there resided at the date of his decease. He is spoken of as a prudent, worthy minister, pleasing and interesting in his conversation and general deportment. He was buried in the burial-ground connected with the church, on the hill, in Scituate. His widow died, July 27, 1813, in the 99th year of her age,[4] and her remains are deposited by his side.

According to Mr. Barstow, Mr. Thompson was the son of Ebenezer Thompson, of New Haven, Connecticut, and was born in 1711, and married Esther Stephens, of New Haven. His children, born in New Haven, were Esther, who died young, and Ebenezer, born January 15, 1735. After his removal to Scituate, he had John, Amey, Anna, Lucy, Lois, Mary, and Jane. *John*, died in early life, at Bilboa, in Spain. *Amey*, married Benjamin Palmer, of Scituate, and died, May 16, 1813, aged 73. Her daughter

[1] Hist. Scituate, p. 46.
[2] Letter of John Barstow, Esq.
[3] Letter of J. Barstow, and Mr. Cutler's Sermon, p. 7.
[4] Mr. Cutler's Sermon, p. 8.

married Dr. Freeman Foster, of Scituate. *Anna*, died May 2, 1816, aged 71. *Lucy*, died December 3, 1819, aged 72. *Lois*, died November 14, 1826, aged 76. *Mary*, married Lemuel Ransom, and died July 9, 1833, aged 81. *Jane*, married Rev. William W. Wheeler, and died July 30, 1821, aged 64. All the above lie in the burial ground on Church hill.

Ebenezer, the surviving son, settled in Providence, Rhode Island, in 1764, having previously married Lydia Kennicott, by whom he had Sarah, 1760; — Edward K., 1762; — and Mary, 1764. His wife, Lydia, died in 1770, and he married her sister Elizabeth, by whom he had five sons, and one daughter, viz: Ebenezer, John, Thomas, Joseph, Lydia, and Stephen.

Edward Kennicott, the son of Ebenezer and Lydia, went to Alexandria, Virginia, to engage in commercial pursuits, and there married Sarah Kuhn Swoope, daughter of Col. Michael Swoope, and removed soon after to Providence, Rhode Island, where he had five children, Mary Ann, 1789; — Elizabeth K., 1791; — Sarah Swoope, March, 1794, married John Barstow, Esq., 1828, now of Providence; —Edward K., 1797;— and Esther L., 1802.

After the death of Mr. Thompson, the services of the Church, in Scituate, were suspended for a season, during the War with Great Britain, popular sentiment in New England then setting very strongly against the form of worship prescribed by the Church of England; and, except the occasional services of Rev. Samuel Parker, from 1780, to 1782, the Church remained without a Rector, until the appointment of Rev. William W. Wheeler, May 15, 1783. During the time that Mr. Parker served the Church, Joseph Donnell, of Hanover, and Benjamin James, Jr., of Scituate, were Wardens, and Dr. Charles Stockbridge, and Benjamin Jacobs, of Scituate, and Elijah Curtis, Thomas Stockbridge, Jr., Mordecai Ellis, Stephen Bailey, and Benjamin Mann, of Hanover, were vestrymen.

We should have remarked, that Job Otis, Thomas Bardin, Jacob Bailey, Joseph House, Isaac Buck, Isaac Hatch, Henry Merritt, and John Lane, all of Hanover, are spoken of as "Churchmen," on the town records, in 1736; so that citizens of Hanover have been connected with the Society, from about the date of its first formation.

Mr. Wheeler officiated as Rector, in Hanover, and elsewhere a portion of the time, until his death, which took place, January 14, 1810, at the age of 75. It was during his Rectorship, in 1797, that the church was incorporated, Charles Bailey, and Thomas Barstow, Jr. being wardens.

About the year 1810, owing to difficulties in the First Parish in Hanover, some of the members left, and joined the Episcopal Church.[1] This led to the proposition, for the erection of a new Church, in a more favorable location; and, at a meeting of the parish, held April 24, 1810, it was "Voted, that the Society are willing to attend public worship in Hanover, provided individuals will build a new Church in said Hanover.[2] This house was built in 1811, at an expense of $5,000,—the building committee consisting of Horatio Cushing, Esq., Reuben Curtis, and Edward Eells; Capt. Albert Smith, and Melzar Curtis, Esq., being the contractors for its erection; and it was consecrated to the worship of God, according to the usage of the Protestant Episcopal Church, June 13, 1811, by Bishop Griswold, being the first church in Massachusetts consecrated by him.

In the same year, 1811, a subscription for the endowment of a perpetual fund for the Church was made, amounting to $1236. 75, to which was afterwards added the sum of $188. 82, from the proceeds of the old church, and other items.[3] The Trustees of this fund were incorporated, in 1815, and in 1848, it consisted of 22 shares in the State Bank, Boston, valued at $1,320. This is now invested in the Parsonage, occupied by Mr. Cutler.

After the erection of the Church, in Hanover, which stands near the Four Corners, Rev. Joab G. Cooper, was elected Rector, and held that office until 1816, when he retired. According to Deane, he was from Long Island.[4] Rev. Calvin Wolcott, the next Rector, was chosen in 1818, and continued to serve until 1834, when he resigned. He is now settled as colleague, with the Rev. Dr. Tyng, in New York, and during his settlement in Hanover, the affairs of his Society were in a prosperous condition. An account of his family will be found in our Genealogical Sketches.

In 1835, Rev. Samuel G. Appleton, took charge of the parish,

1 Cutler's Sermon, p. 14.
2 Ibid, p. 6.
3 Cutler's Sermon, p. 14.
4 Hist. Scituate, p. 47.

and continued with it until November, 1838; and during his Rectorship, a new organ was purchased, at an expense of $450. Eleazer A. Greenleaf, the next Rector, took charge of the Parish in 1839, and remained until 1841, in which year the present Rector, Rev. Samuel Cutler, came to the place, and here he has since remained, now residing in the fine parsonage house, built for him in 1849, which stands on Washington street, near the Four Corners.

It is remarked, by Deane, that the Episcopal Church in Marshfield, established as early as 1745, was for many years connected with St. Andrews, the rector of the latter officiating there one Sabbath in four; — also the Church in Taunton, where the rector of St. Andrews likewise officiated one Sabbath in four.[1]

For a fuller account of this Society than our limits permit us to give, we must refer our readers to the valuable discourse of Mr. Cutler, from which we have largely quoted, and to which we have been greatly indebted for many of the facts herewith presented.

We are happy to say, in concluding this sketch, that the Church at the Corners, is in a prosperous condition, under their present Rector, and as an indication of their outward progress, we may remark, that their temple has lately changed its appearance somewhat, by the removal of the old steeple, and the erection of a new one; and this Society, like that in the centre of the town, numbers among its members many of our most valuable and enterprising citizens.

UNIVERSALISTS.

There is no Universalist Society properly within the limits of Hanover, although one has existed, for many years, in the westerly part of Scituate, whose house of Worship stands within less than three rods of the boundary line of Hanover.

This parish was commenced as early as 1766, and is referred to, not only on the records of Scituate, of that date, but also of *Hanover*; and many items relating to its history, are found on the books of the latter town. Besides, as quite a number of our citizens are connected with the Universalist Society, and as *three* of its pastors have resided in Hanover, — two of the number being

[1] History of Scituate, p. 47.

OLD UNIVERSALIST MEETING HOUSE.

PRESENT UNIVERSALIST MEETING HOUSE.

still citizens of the town, of whom the Author is one, — he feels that if full sketches of the First Parish, and of St. Andrew's Church, have been given, a few words, with reference to the denomination with which he is personally connected, may be permitted him.

The petition of the inhabitants of the northerly part of Hanover, praying to be set off as a separate district, or parish, which was presented in 1766, did not ask that the new parish should be of a different faith from the old; although, doubtless, there was not an entire sympathy between the views of the petitioners, and those of the rest of the inhabitants. The town, however, refused to grant the request. In 1767, the signers of the first petition, with others, from Hanover, and Scituate, petitioned the General Court to be set off as a Parish by themselves; and the Town chose a Committee to oppose them. In 1771, this petition to the General Court was renewed, but without success.

In 1792, the Town voted to permit Mr. Mellen to preach a few Sabbaths in the house which the petitioners had erected in Scituate, as early as the date of their first movement towards being set off.

December 12, 1796. A new petition was presented to the town "for a parish in the North part of Hanover," which was signed by David Jacobs, Elisha Barrell, Jesse Curtis, Nathaniel Jacobs, Eells Damon, Elisha Simmons, David Jacobs, Jr., Ezra Damon, Thomas Hatch, Curtis Brooks, Amos Curtis, Ezra Briggs, Jr., Benjamin Mann, Jr., Peres Jacobs, Joshua Simmons, and Ebenezer Curtis; — but this petition met with the same fate as those which had preceded it, being rejected.

Finally, in 1812, petitioners, from Scituate, and Hanover, were incorporated as a "Universalist Society," and from that day to this, the Society has continued in existence, and is still in good standing with the denomination.

This Society was one of the first of the Universalist order, established in Plymouth County; its members being residents of Scituate, Hanover, Abington, Halifax, Duxbury, and other towns; and Rev. John Murray, an early apostle of Universalism, preached in the old meeting-house 60 years ago. The present neat and commodious edifice, was erected during the pastorship of Rev. Robert L. Killam, in 1832, and stands on a beautiful eminence, near Barstow's hill, just on the line between South Scituate and Hanover, — the Church itself being in South Scituate.

The old meeting house, which stood on the same site as the present house, was two stories high; the roof pitching East and West; with a porch on the East, extending from the ground to the eaves, having doors, in front, and on each side of the same, with stairways within, leading to the galleries. There were doors on the North and South ends of the house, about the centre of the same; and two rows of windows, the lower row lighting the body of the house, and the upper the galleries. There were pews in th floor, but the galleries were furnished with long seats, or benches, as was the custom in those days. The house had neither steeple nor bell, was unplastered for a long time; nor had it a chimney, until after the commencement of the present century. It was a venerable structure, and beneath its roof, the members of the Society enjoyed, for many years, the ministrations of the gospel, according io their own views of its teachings, though at first the parish was in a measure an off-shoot from the older parishes, in Scituate and Hanover.

The names of those who have preached to the Society, from time to time, are, David Pickering; Samuel Baker; Elias Smith; Joshua Flagg; Benjamin Whittemore; Robert L. Killam, from 1829 to 1838; H. W. Morse, 1838; John F. Dyer, 1839; J. E. Burnham, 1840; John S. Barry, 1841—1844; M. E. Hawes, 1844 & 5; Horace P. Stevens, 1846 & 7; and Robinson Breare, the present pastor, settled in 1849.

The names of the original members of the Society, appended to the Act of Incorporation, granted June 18, 1812, are, *Enoch Collamore, *Loring Jacobs, Ichabod R. Jacobs, John Jones, Jr., Calvin Wilder, *James H. Jacobs, *Charles Totman, Charles Jones, (in Illinois,) *Isaac N. Damon, Joshua Bowker, *James Jacobs, Abel Silvester, *Charles Simmons, *William Hyland, *David Turner, *Samuel Randall, Jr., *Samuel Randall, *Joshua Damon, Ebenezer Totman, *Jonathan Turner, *Enoch Collamore, Jr., *Benjamin Bowker, John Gross, *Josiah Witherell, *Samuel Simmons, *John Jones, *Peleg Simmons, Jr., *Seth Stoddard, *George Litchfield, *Elisha Gross, *Reuben Sutton, Theophilus Cortherell, Edward F. Jacobs, *Elisha Barrell, Elisha Barrell, Jr., Stephen Jacobs, and *Edward Curtis.

BAPTIST MEETING HOUSE.

Those to whose names an asterisk is prefixed, have since deceased; some have removed; and of the original number, but ten remain, all of whom still "hold fast to the profession of their faith without wavering."

This Society is in a prosperous condition, and free from debt; and though many of its older members have deceased within a few years, whose familiar faces are seen no more, yet those who remain can be relied upon, we think, for its future and permanent support.

BAPTIST SOCIETY.

The First Baptist Church, in Hanover, was constituted Feb. 11, 1806, and was composed of members from the First Church, in Marshfield, residing in Hanover, and Scituate, favorable to the religious opinions held by that denomination. Rev. Barnabas Perkins, was the first pastor; and from 1807, to 1809, William Curtis served the infant Society. In 1810, Rev. John Butler was settled, and ordained to the work of the Gospel Ministry, in December of the same year. Mr. Butler continued to labor with this Church about 14 years, serving them with much ability, and with good success. During his ministry, their house of worship was erected, in 1812, which stands on Main Street, and is a small, but neat edifice, in good repair, and of fair proportions.

From 1824, to 1832, the Church passed through seasons of trial and discouragement, and did not enjoy, for much of the time, a stated ministry. Mr. Darius Dunbar, was ordained to the pastoral office, in 1833, remained about two years, and was succeeded by Rev. Robert B. Dickie, from Nova Scotia, who entered upon his duties, July 1, 1834, and remained until Sept. 3, 1836. Rev. Horace Seaver, of Maine, was the next pastor, preached about two years, and was followed by Rev. Nathan Stetson, whose name appears on the Minutes of 1839.

From 1840, to 1842, Rev. Thomas Conant, now of Scituate, served the Society; and after his removal, for a period of between two and three years, the Society was destitute of a pastor. In 1845, Rev. Nathan Chapman entered upon its charge, but remained only one year, and was followed, in 1846–7, by Rev. B. N. Harris. In June, 1849, Rev. William N. Slason, the present pastor, took charge of the Society, and his services, we believe, have been acceptable and profitable.

This Society, though small, is highly respectable in its character; its members are zealous; and the earnestness with which they have engaged in the cause of religion, is worthy of all praise. Its officers, have been men of excellent standing in the community; and to their energy, is doubtless to be attributed much of the Society's success. The present Deacons,—Col. John Collamore, of South Scituate, and John Brooks, of Hanover, (the former of whom was long and favorably known as one of the Board of County Commissioners,) have long held the office which they now sustain, and are men never weary in well doing.

CHAPTER VI.

EDUCATION.

" From education as the leading cause,
The public character its color draws;
Thence the prevailing manners take their cast,
Extravagant or sober, loose or chaste." COWPER.

Early laws for the support of education — Our Common School System — Schoolmasters — Schools established in Hanover — Mr. Fitzgerald — Joseph Cushing — Luke Stetson — Sketch from 1750 to 1840 — Table of appropriations — Academy, Mr. Chaddock's — Removal to the Four Corners — Second building — New Edifice, built in 1852 — Proprietors.

Very early in the history of the Plymouth Colony, it was " proposed by the Court unto the severall Townshipes of this Jurisdiction as a thinge they ought to take into theire serious consideration That some course may be taken that in every towne there may be a Scoolmaster sett up to traine up children to reading and writing ; "[1] and in 1677, we read, that " Forasmuch as the maintainance of good literature doth much tend to the advancement of the weale and flourishing estate of societies and Republiques— This Court doth therefor order ; That in whatsoever township in this Govrment consisting of fifty families or upwards ; any meet man shall be obtained to teach a Gramer Scoole such townshipp shall allow at least twelve pounds in currant marchantable pay to be raised by rate on all the Inhabitants of such Towne, and those that have the more emediate benefitt thereof by theere Childrens good and general good shall make up the resedue necessarie to maintain the same, and that the profitts ariseing of the Cape Fishing, heretofore ordered to maintaine a Gramer Scoole in this Collonie, be destributed to such Townes as have such Gramer Scooles for the maintainance thereof ; not exceeding five pounds per annum to any such Towne, unless the Court Treasurer or

1 Laws, p. 143.

other apointed to manage that affaire see good cause to adde therunto to any respective Towne not exceeding five pounds more pr anum; and further this Court orders that every such Towne as consists of seaventy families or upwards and hath not a gramer scoole therein shall allow and pay unto the next towne which hath such Gramar scoole kept up amongst them, the sum of five pounds p annum in current merchantable pay, to be levied on the Inhabitants of such defective townes by rate, and gathered and delivered by the Constables of such Townes as by warrant from any Majestrate of this Jurisdiction shalbe required." [1]

In 1672, it was ordered, that "every County Town shall have and maintain a Latine School; which if they do and the Master (be) judged by the major part of the ministers of the County a Person capable to bring up Youth fitt for the Colledge; then such Town for their encouragement shall have one third part annually of the money raised on the account of the Cape Fishery, &c." [2] Those who enjoyed the benefit of this school, by sending their children, were "to pay three pence a week for Writing and Reading, and six pence a week for a Schollar after he comes to his Grammar;" and every such schoolmaster was "to be capable to teach to Write and Cypher," and was "to receive children after they are fit to begin in their Psalter," &c.[3]

This was the foundation of our justly celebrated system of MASSACHUSETTS COMMON SCHOOL INSTRUCTION; — and from this policy, the people have never departed. One of the bright spots in our history is, that through all reverses of fortune, and in all times of danger and peril, the education of the young has always been properly attended to. It is this that has given success to our enterprise, prosperity to our commerce, and stability to our institutions.

In early days, we are told, "the only schoolmasters were the clergy of the towns, who exercised this office in many instances in addition to the arduous duties of their peculiar avocation. Youths were received into their families to receive a preparation for college, and over the whole body of the younger portion of the inhabitants they extended their care." [4]

1 Colony Laws, p. 185.
2 Ibid, p. 300.
3 Colony Laws, p. 300.
4 Winsor's Duxbury, p. 71.

Many of the first settlers of Scituate, according to Deane,[1] were men of intelligence and education. "It was an object of high emulation," he remarks, "as well as of religious principle with the early Congregational Churches, to be supplied with a thoroughly educated ministry; and such, without exception, were those pastors who, having been silenced in England, came hither to minister to the little flocks in the wilderness: nay, men of education and talents were selected for the subordinate offices in the Churches. . . . . . . Professional school-masters were few, and there was no publick provision for their remuneration. Not only the pastors, but other men of learning must have given instructions, and almost gratuitously, in their own houses. It is known that Mr. Chauncy prepared his own sons, and others, for college, and also several young men for the ministry, between 1640 and 1650. Mr. Witherell had been a Grammar school-master by profession, before leaving England, and many proofs are left of his skill in the languages."

By the enactment of the Colony Laws, to which we have referred, school-teachers, as a class, were encouraged; and many men, of learning, and virtue, attached themselves to this profession.

In the Act incorporating the Town of Hanover, the customary stipulation, of the establishment and support of a *school* was inserted; and accordingly, March 2, 1727–8, it was "voted to keep a school this year at *three places*, where the selectmen shall think best;" and £27 10s. *old tenor*, were assessed for its support. Who the teacher was at this time, does not appear. The school was kept in *private houses*, and those of Joseph Cornish, and John Bailey, were used for the purpose.

1729, May 29, it was "voted to have a school at or near the meeting-house."

1730, April 17, a *standing school* was voted, "at or near the meeting house;" and May 18, provisions were made for building a school house of wood. This first school house stood near the centre of the town, and tradition says it was opposite the present gun-house.

1734, May 14, Richard Fitzgerald was voted "school-master;" and he continued to teach in the town until his death,

1 Hist. Scituate, p. 92.

in 1746. From whence Mr. F. originated, I have been unable to learn. He seems to have been a man of talent, well skilled in the languages, especially the Latin, and to have taught with good success. He was an instructor in Scituate, before his settlement in Hanover, and had the honor of preparing for the University the Hon. William Cushing, LL. D., who graduated at Harvard College, in 1751, and was educated for the bar under the care of the celebrated Jeremy Gridley, of Boston, for many years Attorney General of the Province of Massachusetts.[1] We consider the town highly favored, in securing the services of so valuable a man, early in their municipal career; and under his judicious training, many were reared, who afterwards became distinguished, in the Town and the State.

1746, March 16, a *moveable school* voted, "to be kept the first three months at the school-house by the meeting-house; the next three, at or near the house of John Studley (who lived near the Four Corners) ; the third term at or near the house of David Jenkins (probably in the Salmond District,) ; and the last term, at or near the house of Isaac Hatch, (in the Westerly part of the town, or what is now the King Street District.) "

1748, June 27, a moveable school voted, to be kept from December 16, to March 16, at the *new school house near Silvanus Wing's* (on Circuit Street,) ; from October 1, to December 16, at or near the dwelling house of Benjamin Stetson, the residents of that quarter to provide the place; from August 1, to October 1, at or near William Dwelley's, the residents of that quarter to provide the place ; and the remainder of the year at the school-house by the meeting-house. October 31, £6 10s. were voted to John Barker, for boarding the school-master in 1747, and £4 10s. to Silvanus Wing, and £6, to John House, for the like purpose.

1750, A moving school voted for this year. Nov. 27th, Voted to Margaret Fitzgerald 18s. 8d, "for boarding JOSEPH CUSHING school master, last winter." This is the first time Mr. Cushing's name appears on the records, as a teacher; and he continued to serve the town in that capacity, a part of the time, for several years. He is the gentleman, who afterwards became distin-

1 Deane's Scituate, 256-7.

guished in the history of the State, and whose services we shall sketch in our Chapter on the Revolution.

1752. LUKE STETSON, is named as one of the masters for this year; bills of board, for twenty-six weeks, being audited and allowed, and his own bill of services; and he continued to teach for several years. Mr. Stetson was a native of Hanover; and he, with Mr. Cushing, were both, probably, pupils of Mr. Fitzgerald, and received from him valuable aid, qualifying them for the posts they held.

It would seem, from our records, that a school was taught throughout the year, both summer and winter. The attendance of girls, was greatest in the summer season; that of boys, in the winter; many being kept at home, by their parents, a portion of the time, to assist in the labors of the farm. In this respect, boys in the city then, and always have, enjoyed advantages far superior to those in our country towns.

1763. The selectmen were authorised to hire a school-master for one year, "to keep the school in each quarter of the town, three months at a place."

1772, March 9. A committee was chosen to divide the town into four quarters, and to determine where each school-house should stand; and they reported, "First, that the school-house by the meeting-house, in the middle quarter, so called, stands as conveniently to accommodate said quarter as we can place it. Second, the school-house in the East quarter is equally convenient in location. Thirdly, in the North quarter, or on Curtis Street, we recommend the removal of the house Northward, between the dwelling houses of Joseph Bates and Caleb Sylvester. Fourthly, in the Westerly quarter we recommend either the removal of the present school-house to a spot of plain ground between the dwelling-houses of Isaac Hatch and Stephen Randall, or the erection of an additional house between the dwelling-houses of Eliab and Benjamin Studley, the time to be equally divided between said two school-houses."

1773, October 26. Voted to Isaiah Josselynn £3 15s., for keeping school one month, from December 9, 1772, to January 16, 1773.

1774. March 14. £11 were voted to support a Grammar school

this year. Also, "voted to give the old school-house by the meeting-house, to the middle quarter of the Town, they repairing the same, or building a new one on the same spot."

1777, May 19. The Selectmen instructed to provide a school for the town as usual.

1778, March 20. Voted to postpone the school till October next.

1781, April 2. £600 in *continental bills*, voted for the use of a school; and October 29, the selectmen were instructed to "hire a school-master as soon as may be."

1784, March 15. The selectmen were instructed to hire a *grammar* school-master for three months; and Mr. THOMAS, is named as one of the teachers for this year. At the same meeting, Joseph Brooks, Joseph Ramsdell, Jr., Robert L. Eells, and Timothy Robbins, with the three selectmen, were chosen to divide the town into four quarters; and it was voted "that one quarter shall not send their children into another school." For some years before this, it had been a custom, with those parents most anxious for the instruction of their children, to keep them at school as much as possible; and hence they travelled from quarter to quarter, as the school was moved, to enjoy this advantage. Complaints having been made against this course, by the above vote it was stopped.

1800, January 6. The School money to be divided into four parts, "according to the number of scholars in each quarter of the town."

1801, April 6. A Committee chosen to number the scholars in each school district.

1802, March 8. A Committee of two from each district chosen to report how the money should be divided in the several districts, and they recommended to district the town anew, and divide the money equally in the districts, and their report was accepted.

1804. Capt. Daniel Barstow, Calvin Bailey, Snow Curtis, Robert Eells, Elisha Barrell, Jr., Joshua Mann, and Clement Bates, were chosen to divide the school money; — from which it appears that there were then seven districts in the town.

1808. The school districts were numbered as follows: — The Meeting-house District, No. 1; Broad Oak District, No. 2; Upper Forge District, No. 3; Drinkwater District, No. 4; Beech

Woods District, No. 5; Curtis Street District, No. 6; Snappet District, No. 7. The Curtis street District was divided in 1831--2, the Southerly part being called No 8; and this is the number into which the town is now divided.

1812. The three selectmen, and the three ministers were chosen a School Committee. Petitions were presented this year for aid to the small districts, and the town voted that "no district should draw a larger sum than $105, nor any less than $45, or in that proportion according to the sum raised."

1819, March 8. A School Committee was chosen, consisting of "the three selectmen, and all the ministers in the town, together with Ebenezer Curtis, John B. Barstow, Robert Salmon, Caleb Whiting, Elisha Barrell, Jr., and Elijah Wing." November 1:—This Committee was discharged, and a new one chosen, consisting of Rev. John Butler, Rev. Calvin Wolcott, Rev. Seth Chapin, Aaron Hobart, Esq., and Dr. Joshua Studley.

1822, November 4. The Committee chosen to divide the school money were instructed to make out a list of the scholars from four to sixteen years of age, with the names of their parents or guardians.

1827. A general Committee of seven chosen, and seven persons as a prudential Committee, one for each district.

1836. Voted to divide the school money, one half on the districts, and the other half on the scholars; and this course, with but few exceptions, has been pursued to the present time.

1837. Voted to apply $200 of the *surplus revenue* to schools this year.

We have no means at hand, for ascertaining the names of the school books used in the town one hundred years ago. From our oldest citizens we learn that the Psalter, the New England Primer, and the Testament, were the principal reading books in their school days, and the Young Man's Companion, and Pike's were the most common Arithmetics. There was one spelling book before Noah Webster's; this last was introduced nearly seventy years ago. There was also a small Geography used in some of the schools. Text books were not so numerous as now.

Among the female teachers "Ma'am Mann," as she is called, was one of the most celebrated, and taught, in Hanover and Scituate, seventy years ago. Girls carried their "samplers" to be wrought, and their "knitting and sewing." It sometimes taxed the patience of our worthy pedagogues severely, to have little misses come up and ask questions about their knitting. Luke Stetson, it is said, told one of his pupils to "widen,—widen,"— until she had knit her stocking "as wide as a meal bag."

Considerable improvement has been made of late in our school-houses. The old, dilapidated structures, which were visible in all the districts a few years since, are gradually giving way to more commodious and tasteful edifices. The houses in Districts No. 2, 3, and 4, are quite neat. In 1847, the question of the town's purchasing the existing school houses, and erecting new ones in the several districts, began to be agitated, and eventually the course was adopted, and is now being carried out.

The following table exhibits the amount appropriated for the support of schools at different periods.

1728.	Old Tenor.	£27 10s.	1782–'91.	In Silver.	£60 00s.
1729–'35.	"	50 00s.	1792–'93.	"	75 00s.
1736.	"	55 00s.	1798–1802.	"	$300 00
1738–'40.	"	60 00s.	1802–'03.	"	450 00
1741–'42.	"	80 00s.	1804–'05.	"	550 00
1743–'45.	"	100 00s.	1806–'32.	"	600 00
1747.	"	145 00s.	1833–'38.	"	800 00
1762.	In Silver.	26 13s	1838–'47.	"	1000 00
1763–'69.	"	30 13s.	1848.	"	1200 00
1770–'77.	"	27 16s.8d	1849–'50.	"	1250 00
1779.	In Bills.	200 00s.	1851–'52.	"	1300 00
1781.	"	600 00s.			

From the foregoing table, it appears that the amount, appropriated by the Town for the support of Schools, has been doubled within the last 20 years. This fact, we think, speaks well for our citizens, and shows a commendable interest in the cause of Education.

Our schools, we think, will not suffer in comparison with those of equal size in the neighboring towns. A desire is felt to procure good teachers, and to pay them liberally for their services. We hope this interest, in so vital a cause, will continue to increase; and that the amount appropriated, will keep pace with the wants of our children, and the ability of the people.

ACADEMY.

In 1792, the State of Massachusetts encouraged the establishment of Academies within its limits, by grants of tracts of land in the District of Maine. In consequence of these grants, many such institutions sprung into existence, and contributed greatly to aid the cause of education, by giving more thorough instruction in the different branches taught in the public schools. In 1798, the attention of the citizens of Hanover was turned to this subject, and March 7, a Committee was appointed to draw up a petition to the General Court, probably for an Act of Incorporation. We hear no more of the matter, however, until after the settlement of Rev. Calvin Chaddock, in 1806, and he, having been for some years preceptor of an Academy in Rochester, Massachusetts, which he built at his own expense, and where, in the short space of six years, nearly 1300 different pupils were taught by him, soon took measures for establishing one in Hanover; and so well was he seconded in his efforts, that before 1808, a building was erected for that purpose, and was ready for occupancy. It stood on the common, a little West of the Centre Meeting House, and was two stories high, of fair proportions, neatly painted, furnished with venetian blinds, and crowned with a cupola and bell. A respectable number of pupils of both sexes attended the school, from towns both of Plymouth and Norfolk counties. Beside the common English branches, instruction was given in the Latin and Greek languages, the higher mathematics, navigation, surveying, &c.; and in the female department, under the charge of Mrs. C., considerable attention was given to embroidery, and painting in water colors; and all the pupils took part in weekly declamations, on Wednesday afternoons, in the hall above the school-room. Many young men were fitted for college here, some of whom were subsequently distinguished for eminence in their professions; and of the "honorable women not a few," Mrs. Almira Little Torrey, is named, as one "whose amiable disposition, high intelligence, and devoted piety, have embalmed her memory in the hearts of a numerous circle of friends; and who, by means of her interesting and published memoirs, being dead, yet speaketh."[1]

"The venerable founder of Hanover Academy," says Mr. A., "will not be forgotten, either by those 'who sat at his feet,' as pupils, or were his hearers as a preacher of the Gospel." The town has reason to remember him with gratitude, for his patient and earnest efforts for the improvement of the young.

This school continued in a flourishing condition, throughout the period of the settlement of Mr. C.; but soon after his departure, it began visibly to decline, and was finally suspended for a season. The first Sabbath School was held in this building, during the ministry of Mr. Chapin,—the Assembly's Catechism being the instruction book placed in the children's hands. At length, about the year 1822, the building was sold, moved to the Four Corners, and is now occupied as a store, and shoe-manufactory, by Mr. Stephen Josselynn.

The second Academy, was erected in 1828, and stood on Broadway, not far from the Episcopal Church. It was built, in shares of $25 each, at an expense of about $1200;—the Trustees were Incorporated in 1829; and the names of the original shareholders were, Alexander Wood, Esq., Capt. Haviland Torrey, Joseph Eells, Ephraim Stetson, Dr. Ezekiel D. Cushing, Rev. Calvin Wolcott, Sarah Gardner, Robert Eells, Asaph Magoun, Horace Collamore, Esq., Gen. A. W. Oldham, Capt. Tilden Crooker, Benjamin C. Pratt, Ethan A. Stetson, Capt.

[1] Letter of Lucius Alden.

William Josselynn, Eli Stetson, Joseph S. Bates, Horatio Cushing, Esq., Isaac Magoun, Col. John B. Barstow, Capt. Thomas Waterman, Capt. Nathaniel Barstow, John C. Stockbridge, George Bailey, Dr. Joshua Studley, Justus Whiting, Thomas Damon, Benjamin Mann, Esq., Lemuel Dwelley, Samuel Tolman, Jr., Elias W. Pratt, Luther Howland, James Waterman, Samuel Waterman, Samuel Stetson, Elias Magoun, John Barstow, Esq., Albert Clapp, and John Wilder.

The preceptors at this Academy, from its erection in 1828, were, Zephaniah Bass, 1828; Horace H. Rolfe, 1829; Rev. Cyrus Holmes, 1830; Ethan Allen, 1830; Rev. Calvin Wolcott, 1831; John P. Washburn, 1832; Dr. Ira Warren, 1833; Thomas F. White, 1834, and 1835; Herman Bourn, 1837; Josiah Fuller, 1838, and 1839; and Rev. Cyrus Holmes, 1840, to the year previous to his death.

Since then, the Instructors have been Charles Hitchcock, who taught two terms; George Wolcott, who taught one term; and M. P. McLauthlin, Esq., the present Principal. There have been female teachers connected with the Academy, a portion of the time; and the number of pupils, in 1832, was 56; in 1833, 34; and in 1834, 66.

In 1843, the Dorcas Society held meetings in the upper hall, and the Episcopal Society also held evening prayer meetings in the hall, once a week, during the same year.

Finally, in 1851, the friends of Education in the vicinity, thinking a better building was needed, endeavored to raise, in shares of $25, each, a sum sufficient for that purpose; and in a short time $2,750 were subscribed, including a liberal donation of $1,000 from Mr. Samuel Salmond, to which was added $375 received for the old house; and the present beautiful edifice, which stands a few rods south of the old one, was built at an expense of about $3,500, including the bell, which was a gift from Miss Salmond, — and was dedicated, by appropriate services, March 2, 1852; the address being delivered by Rev. E. Porter Dyer, of Hingham, the invocatory prayer by Rev. A. G. Duncan, the dedicatory prayer by Rev. Samuel Cutler, and hymns, composed by Miss Lucy S. Delano, Rev. E. Porter Dyer, and Rev. A. G. Duncan, being sung, under the direction of Mr. Benjamin Frost.

Other impromptu addresses were delivered, by Rev. H. D.

Walker, of East Abington, Rev. Mr. White, of North Abington, Rev. W. N. Slason, of Hanover, and M. P. McLauthlin, the Principal of the Academy.

The board of Trustees consists of Rev. Samuel Cutler, President, Alfred C. Garratt, M. D., Secretary, Rev. Abel G. Duncan, Samuel Salmond, Seth Barker, Elijah Barstow, Treasurer, and M. Parris McLauthlin, ex officio.*

Mr. McLauthlin has had charge of the Academy for a few years past, and his services have given general satisfaction, and have been attended with a good degree of success. The institution has no *fund* invested for its support, but its income is derived from

* Proprietors of Hanover Academy with the number of shares owned by each in 1852. Par value $25 per share. Erected 1851–52. Dedicated March 2, 1852.

	shares.
Samuel Salmond, Hanover,	42
Robert Sylvester, "	7
Seth Barker, "	4
Elijah Barstow, South Scituate,	3
Isaac H. Harding, "	2
Abner Stetson, "	1
Thomas Waterman, "	1
Young Ladies Society of St. Andrews Church, Hanover, by *the Rector*,	2
Dorcas Society of St. Andrews Church, Hanover, by the Rec.	2
Samuel Cutler, Hanover,	1
Miss Frances Baldwin, Hanover,	1
Alexander Wood, "	1
Gustavus Percival, "	1
Stephen Josselynn, "	2
Thos. B. Donnell, "	1
Haviland Torrey, Pembroke,	3
Hannah Barstow, Hanover,	1
Levi Sturtevant, Jr., Pembroke,	1
Adams Billings, "	1
Charles Dyer, Hanover,	1
Luther Howland, Hanson,	1
Robert Hersey, Hanover,	1
Martin W. Stetson, "	1
Hannah Stetson, "	1
John P. Eells, "	1
Benjamin Whitwell "	1
John Sylvester, "	2
Nathaniel Barstow, "	1
Benj. F. Burgess, "	1
M. P. McLauthlin, "	2
Michael Sylvester, "	2
George Curtis, Hanover,	1
Sam'l Tolman, Jr., South Scituate,	1
Lemuel C. Waterman, So. Scit.	1
J. M. Smith, and G. P. Clapp, South Scituate,	1
Warren Wright, Hanover,	1
Jos. B. Fobes, "	1
Edmund Q. Sylvester, Hanover,	3
Robert E. Dwelley, "	1
William Church, "	1
Nathan Dwelley, "	1
John B. Barstow, "	2
Thos. H. C. Barstow, "	1
Alfred C. Garratt, "	1
Abel G. Duncan, "	1
Melzar Hatch, "	1
	110

Cost of Academy.

Total amount for land, building, and fixtures,	$3,488 52
The expense was defrayed by proceeds of 110 shares at $25 per share,	$2,750 00
Sale of Old Academy,	375 00
Donation of a Bell,	138 03
Donation from Young Ladies Societies,	51 75
Subscription of Sundry persons,	50 00
Balance provided for by subscription,	123 74
	$3,488 52

the quarterly fee paid by the pupils, and the number of scholars of both sexes in attendance, averages about 50.

LAWYERS.

Previous to the Revolution, and for some years afterwards, there was no regularly educated lawyer settled in Hanover; the business usually transacted by the members of this profession, being attended to by Elijah Cushing, Esq., Joseph Cushing, Esq., David Stockbridge, Esq., and a few other enterprising and educated Justices of the Peace, and by the Selectmen of the Town.

The first lawyer who settled in the town, so far as our records show, was Benjamin Whitman, Esq., son of Zachariah Whitman, of South Bridgwater, who was born in 1768, graduated at Brown University, in 1788, and resided in Pembroke, and then in Hanover, to which town he moved about the year 1792. He lived on Broadway, for a season, in the house now occupied by Samuel Eells, but afterwards purchased the Nathaniel Sylvester house, near North River Bridge, which is now occupied by Rufus Farnum. In 1799, he built the house in which Seth Barker, Esq., resides, — on a spot of elevated ground, commanding a fine view of the river, and of the ship-yards, which were then in active operation. His office, was on the opposite side of the road, and is still standing, near the house of Mr. Sylvanus Percival. He was Post Master for several years. He left the town about the year 1806, moving to Boston, of which city he was subsequently one of the Representatives, and of whose Police Court he was for many years Chief Justice. He was an able lawyer; a man of great business enterprise; an active politician; and his services were of great value to the town during the period of his residence in it. John Holmes, of Kingston, was one of his students while in Hanover, who subsequently settled in Maine, while that State was part of Massachusetts, and from which he was a Representative to the General Court of Massachusetts, and afterwards a Member of Congress. Barker Curtis, a native of Hanover, and a son of Simeon Curtis, Esq., was also one of his students, and had an office, for a time, in the North Easterly part of the town, where Hiram Curtis resides, but finally settled in Maine. Wm.

G. Curtis, a native of Hanover, was also a student with Mr. Whitman, but died before entering upon his professional career.

The next lawyer settled in Hanover, was John Winslow, Esq., only son of Dr. Isaac Winslow, of Marshfield, grandson of Gen. John Winslow, of Marshfield, and great grandson of Col. Isaac, who was the only surviving son of Governor Josiah Winslow. John, son of Dr. Isaac, graduated at Brown University, in 1795, and settled in Hanover about the year 1810. He lived first in the house now occupied by Stephen Josselynn, but soon after built the house recently occupied by Capt. John Cushing, near St. Andrew's Church, at the Four Corners. He was a thorough lawyer; gentlemanly in his manners; and one whose professional practice was very extensive. He died at Natchez, Mississippi, about the year 1830, and his widow and children moved to Hingham, where she died. He has sons in Boston.

Isaiah Wing, a native of Hanover, was, it is said, a pupil at the Academy of Mr. Chaddock, after he was a married man; and he subsequently studied law with Mr. Winslow, and practiced for a time in Hanover; but finally moved to Cincinnati, Ohio, where he died.

Jotham Cushman, Esq., was in Hanover, about the same time as Mr. Winslow, and built and occupied the *long house* at the Four Corners, now owned by the widow of Thomas Turner. Jabez Crooker was one of his students, and went into the Army during the war of 1812.

Aaron Hobart, Esq., son of Aaron, Esq.; and grandson of Col. Aaron, of Abington, graduated at Brown University, in 1805, and settled in Hanover about the year 1812, residing at the Four Corners. Whilst in Hanover, he was chosen to the Senate of Massachusetts, from Plymouth County, in 1820, and was a member of Congress in 1826–7. He moved to East Bridgewater, and was soon after appointed Judge of Probate for Plymouth County, which office he now holds. His public services have at all times been of great value to the community; upon his judgment great reliance is placed; and his demeanor as a citizen, and in the walks of private life, have gained for him the confidence and esteem of all who have the pleasure of his personal acquaintance.

Alexander Wood, Esq., of Middleboro', studied law with Judge Wood, of Middleboro', and practiced in Hanover for a short time; but afterwards relinquished the duties of his profession, and for some years past has been engaged in trade, at the Four Corners, with Capt. Haviland Torrey.

Perez Simmons, Esq., a native of Hanover, graduated at Brown University, in 1833, and settled first in Providence, Rhode Island, but came to Hanover, in 1843, and has since resided in the town, in the practice of his profession. He has been for some years past a member of the board of Selectmen, and was chosen to represent the town in the State Legislature, in 1851–2.

PHYSICIANS.

For about twenty years after the incorporation of the town, no physician resided within its limits; but Drs. Joseph Jacobs, and Charles Stockbridge, who were both of Scituate, extended their practice into Hanover, and the former resided quite near the Northerly bounds of the town.

Dr. Jeremiah Hall, settled in Hanover, about the year 1749, married Keziah Bailey, and remained until 1764, when he moved to Pembroke, of which town he was chosen delegate to the Provincial Congresses of 1774–5. He was a valuable citizen; a man well qualified for the duties of his calling; and he left behind him the memorials of a life of usefulness and virtue.

Dr. Lemuel Cushing, was a resident of Hanover, about the time of the Revolution, and was appointed by the Provincial Congress, a surgeon in the army. The precise time when he came to town is unknown, as also the date of his leaving.

Dr. Peter Hobart, of Hingham, came to Hanover in 1783, and here resided until his death, in 1793. His house was on Main Street, not far from the residence of the late Gideon Studley. His widow moved to New York State, and there died.

Dr. Marsh, of Hingham, was in Hanover for a few years, about the same time as Dr. Hobart.

Dr. Melzar Dwelley, previously of Ashburnham, came to Hanover, about the year 1798, and resided here, until his death, in 1828. He lived on Hanover Street, in the house now occupied by Norman Chamberlin. As a Physician, his abilities were highly respectable, and his professional services were in great demand. His descendants are in South Boston, and in Ashburnham.

Dr. Cartier, a Frenchman, from the island of Martinique, came to Plymouth, where he remained for a period; and about the time of the last war, he settled in Hanover, remained seven years, and boarded at the house of Mr. Reuben Curtis. He was subsequently of Hanson, and finally, it is said, returned to Martinique, where he died. He was a man thoroughly educated, but eccentric in his manners.

Dr. Joshua Studley, a native of Hanover, practiced medicine from 1808, until 1848.

Dr. Ezekiel D. Cushing, was in Hanover from 1827 to 1828, when he deceased. He lived at the Four Corners. He was a man of eminent abilities; had practiced in the best hospitals in France; and was every way qualified to prosecute with distinguished success the brilliant career which opened before him. His early death was a melancholy event to his friends; and in him, the public lost one who, had he lived, would doubtless have made himself conspicuous, and have ranked among the greatest and best physicians and surgeons of the age.

Dr. Henry Wade, was in Hanover, in 1829, and died in 1830.

Dr. Jacob Richards, now of Braintree, practiced in Hanover from 1834 to 1836. An account of his family will be found in our genealogical sketches.

Dr. Calvin B. Pratt, now of Bridgewater, was in Hanover, from 1836 to 1838.

Dr. Joseph B. Fobes, his successor, remained in the town until 1851. His practice was very extensive, and very successful.

Drs. Benjamin Whitwell, and Alfred C. Garratt, are at present settled in Hanover, and both reside at the Four Corners.

GRADUATES.

The town of Hanover has not furnished a large number of students to our colleges; nor can we present so long a list of graduates, as many other towns in the State. The following are all whose names we have learned:—

Joseph Cushimg,	Harvard College,	1752.
Joseph Stockbridge	"	1755.
Prentiss Mellen,	"	1784.
Henry Mellen,	"	1784.
William Simmons,	"	1804.
Nathaniel Jacobs,	"	1806.
Zachariah G. Whitman,	"	1807.
Benjamin Whitman,	Brown University,	1815.
Albert Smith,	Dartmouth "	1825.
Perez Simmons,	Brown University,	1833.
Frederick O. Barstow,	"	1852.
William P. Duncan,	At Amherst.	

Horatio Stockbridge, was at Harvard College, two years.

Joseph B. Damon, and Franklin Damon, graduated at the Newton Theological Institute.

There have been many graduates in families that have moved from Hanover; but these do not properly come within our scope.

CHAPTER VII.

MILITARY HISTORY.

"After years the tale shall tell,
In words of light revealed,
Who bravely fought, who nobly fell"
Mrs. E. T. DANIELS.

Military training of our ancestors—Town's stock of powder, &c.—Expedition to the Spanish West Indies—Expedition to Cape Breton—French Neutrals—French War, with extracts from the Muster Rolls.

The circumstances in which the early settlers of New England were placed, rather than their inclination, or natural desire, led them to engage, more or less, in military pursuits, and the study of the art of war. Not only were they exposed, from the outset, to deadly encounters with the Indians who surrounded them; but after these foes were vanquished and subdued, others sprung up, in the neighboring provinces, of their own color, though not of their own nation; and the French and Spanish wars, called into active service the able-bodied citizens of Massachusetts, and perhaps contributed, in a measure, to prepare the way for that successful resistance to the encroachments of the mother country, which led to the establishment of our National Independence. Had it not been for these wars, and for the discipline which our troops received in them, and the military experience gained by our officers, it is doubtful if the war of the Revolution would have been so successfully prosecuted, had our fathers dared even to engage in it. We do not, however, appear as the advocate of war. It is a great calamity;—a frightful evil;—and under the influence of Christian truth, we hope the time may soon arrive, when swords shall be beaten into ploughshares, and spears into pruning hooks, and PEACE shall reign over all the earth.

But, as a faithful historian, it becomes our duty briefly to chronicle those events, which, when transpiring, were of so much consequence to the welfare of the people, and to their national existence. We give, therefore, not an extended account, but the simple incidents, alluded to on the records of the town, and contemporary papers, in the Archives of the State, and the possession of individuals.

1734, Sep. 9. £35 were voted for a " town stock of ammunition." Such a stock, every town was required by *law* to keep on hand.

1740, Mar. 2. It was voted that the Town's stock of powder and shot, should be kept " in the meeting-house chamber ;"—a small room, over the womens' gallery ;—and the Treasurer of the Town was authorised " to take out of the lease of the *flats* as much money as will purchase said stock, agreeable to the Law, with what Thomas Josselynn already has."

It was during this, and the following year, that the expedition to the Spanish West Indies, to which we have alluded on p. 20, was undertaken ; but the only references to this expedition, which we find on the Town records, are the following under date of Dec. 28, 1741.—" Voted Dea. Thos. Josselynn, £13 16s. 4d. for mens rates gone to *Cuba and elsewhere.*" Six other similar votes occur under the same date. The names of those who went from Hanover, are not given, nor are the tax bills in existence, from which to learn whose rates were remitted ; but, from scattered hints, we think we may venture to name, besides Samuel Eells, who was an Ensign, and who died in the service, John Stoddard, Joshua Turner, John Whitcomb, and Ezekiel Ladd, alluded to on Town records as having had their taxes remitted ; and perhaps Robert Young, whose widow Margaret received aid from the town this year. There must have been quite a number from Hanover, the whole sum remitted in taxes, being about £50, and not less than seven allusions being made to those " gone to Cuba."

The manuscript in the possession of Rev. Benj. Kent, of Roxbury, gives the names of only the 55, who survived in May, 1741. Over 400 men died in the expedition.

1744, Oct. 30. Capt. Elijah Cushing was instructed " to inform his Excellency concerning Dea. Thos. Josselynn's making way with the Town stock of gunpowder ;" and Nov. 5, Capt. Cushing was appointed " to take care of the Town's powder and bullets."

In 1745, the expedition to Cape Breton, was undertaken, at the instance of Gov. Shirley; the forces from Massachusetts, consisting of upwards of 3,200 men, aided by 500 from Connecticut, and 300 from New Hampshire.[1] This may be considered as the commencement of the French war, which with various fortune, was carried on until the peace of 1763, and the reduction of the provinces to the dominion of Great Britain.

We have been at some pains to examine the huge folios of Muster Rolls, relating to this war, which are deposited in the State House, at Boston; and though our gleanings from this source are not very extensive, and may not embrace the names of all who enlisted from Hanover, yet such as they are, we present them as an attempt towards collecting facts, which, owing to the want of more thorough information, can only be regarded as an approximation to the truth.

In 1755, preparations were made for dislodging the French from Nova Scotia; and the Massachusetts forces, formed into a regiment of two battalions, of which Gov. Shirley was the Colonel, were commanded by Lt. Col. John Winslow, of Marshfield, who raised 2000 men, for one year, or longer, if required.[2] The *French Neutrals* were taken prisoners in this expedition, and torn from their country, and sent into banishment, being scattered over Massachusetts, and other provinces. In all, 1923 suffered this fate; viz: 483 men, and 337 women, heads of families, and their sons and daughters, 527 of the former, and 576 of the latter. Their stock was upwards of 5000 horned cattle, 493 horses, and 12,887 sheep and swine.[3]

The history of this unfortunate race, is one of melancholy interest, but we cannot pursue it to any extent. In Abington, there were a few settled, and in other towns of Plymouth county. We have heard of one or more in Hanover, who settled somewhere on Broadway, but cannot give their names.

The following notices of enlistments from Hanover, during the progress of this war, are all we have been able to find. A few of the names given, were residents of Scituate, referred to in other places of this work.

In 1755, Col Ezekiel Turner served in the expedition to Crown

1 Minot's History of Mass. Vol. 1, p. 75.
2 Minot's Hist. Mass. Vol. 1, p. 217.
3 Minot's Hist. Mass., Vol. 1, p. 225.

Point; and in Capt. Samuel Clarke's Co. (of Braintree,) for 13 weeks, from Dec. 16, 1755, were Barnabas Perry, of Scituate, and Richard Bowker, Stephen Hatch, Joseph Palmer, Gideon Stetson, and Theophilus Witherell, of the same town.

Reuben Bates, set down as of Scituate, was a corporal in Elisha Hersey's Co. (of Abington); and Nehemiah Silvester was sergeant, and Thomas Stetson, sentinel.

James House, of Hanover, was Captain of a Company in the expedition to Crown Point, from Mar. 29, to Sep. 8. 1756. On the back of the instrument, he is called Major James House. Cooms House, Seth Witherell, and Daniel Garnett, of Hanover, were in his Company.

In the same expedition, Joseph Nowit,[1] born in Pembroke, but living in Hanover, was in Capt. Loring's Co.; and John B. Worrin, a native of England, enlisted from Hanover in Capt. Abel Keen's Co.

James House was Major of a Company at Fort William Henry, from Nov. 27, 1755, to Mar. 24, 1756.

In the muster roll of Capt. John Loring's company, encamped at Fort Edward, July 25, 1756, occur the names of Lawrence Ekins, a native of Ireland, but a resident of Hanover; Jeremiah Rogers, of Hanover; and Bezaleel Palmer, Thomas Cook, Samuel Witherell, and Nathaniel Palmer, the latter of whom was a shipwright by trade.

In the Roll of Capt. Abel Keen's Company, in Col. Joseph Thacher's Regiment, occur the names of Luke Bowker, blacksmith, and John B. Worrin.

In the return of Thomas Clapp's Regiment, (of Scituate,) July 20, 1756, in the expedition to Crown Point, occur the names of Peter B. Warren, Samuel Witherell, Joseph Turner, Joshua Dwelley, John Perry, Thomas Barstow, Jeremiah Dillingham, Nathaniel Stetson, William Gray, Thomas Cornish, John Hanmer, Joseph Stetson, Jr., John Ramsdell, Bezaleel Palmer, Thomas Cook, Elisha Palmer, and Benjamin Estes, all of whom are set down as of Hanover.

James House was Captain in Thomas Clapp's Regiment, which marched for the relief of Fort William Henry, in August, 1757;

[1] An Indian.

and Job Crooker, and Henry Perry, of Pembroke, were in his Company.

Dr. Jeremiah Hall, of Hanover, was Surgeon in Joseph Thacher's Company, in 1757.

Elisha House, of Hanover, was in the expedition to Canada, in 1759; and Seth Joyce, and David House, also of Hanover, served in the same campaign.

Nathaniel Josselynn, æ. 37, went to Canada in 1758, in Thomas Clapp's regiment; also Edward Peters, æ. 19, who was in the employ of Joseph Curtis; Seth Woodworth, æ. 22; James Silvester, æ. 39; John Hunt, æ. 17, in the employ of Peleg Curtis; and Joshua Remington, æ. 37.

April 12, 1759. There were mustered in Capt. Abel Keen's Company, for the invasion of Canada, by Lt. Col. Elijah Cushing, Henry, son of John Bray, æ. 18; Lemuel, son of Joseph Bates, æ. 18; and Mark, son of Jeremiah Rogers, æ. 18.

At the same date, in Col. Thomas Clapp's Regiment, for Canada, were Elisha Palmer, æ. 41; Prince Osgood, æ. 18, in the employ of Joseph Josselynn; and Mark, son of Jeremiah Rogers, æ. 18.

In Abel Keen's Company, of which Thomas Doty was Colonel, for Canada, in 1759, were Jeremiah Rogers; Abraham Cato, who was discharged; Abner French; Nathaniel Josselynn, who was discharged; Amos Love; Dennis Morrison; Prince Osgood, in the employ of Joseph Josselynn, discharged; Jonathan Pratt; Jonathan Peters, who died in the service; Edward Peters; Thomas Rogers; Aaron Rowell, employed by Jeremiah Rogers; Joshua Staples; Jesse, Abner, and Jonathan Torrey; and Zephaniah and Samuel Witherell. All these are named as of Hanover.

In Abel Keen's Company, at Lunenburg, from March 31, to November 1, 1759, were Jeremiah Rogers; Henry, son of John Bray; Lemuel, son of Joseph Bates; Samuel Bowker; Leonard, son of Richard Hill; Prince Osgood; Elisha Palmer; and Mark, son of Jeremiah Rogers.

Isaac Nowett, was in Col. John Thomas' Company, for Canada in 1760.

In Daniel Reed's Company, which was at Ticonderago in 1760,

were Gideon Studley, who was out 46 weeks; Timothy Church, out 40 weeks; Isaac Nowett, in the employ of Col. Thomas; Edward Peters, in the employ of Thomas Wilkes; and Thomas Rogers.

In 1762, the town was divided into two districts, and a military company was raised in each district. Of the North Company, David Stockbridge, was Captain; Joseph Cushing, 1st Lieutenant; John Bailey, Jr., 2nd Lieutenant; and David Jacobs, Ensign. Of the South Company, Joseph Josselynn, was Captain; Simeon Curtis, 1st Lieutenant; Joseph House, 2d Lieutenant; and John Josselynn, Ensign. Of the Division to which these companies belonged, David Stockbridge, was Lieutenant Colonel, and Joseph Josselynn, was Major. Robert L. Eells was second Quarter Master in the Troop of Horse.

In the same year, 1761–2, Edward Peters, of Hanover, was in Capt. Lemuel Dunbar's Company, from April 18, 1761, to January 4, 1762. Stephen Curtis was out in 1762. Benjamin, son of Daniel Teague, was in Abel Keen's Company; also John Bates, and Henry Dillingham. In Job Williams' Company, from November 18, 1761, to July 29, 1762, were John Bates, William Bradley, and Stephen Curtis, in the employ of Benjamin Curtis.

Elisha Barrell, who died in Hanover, in 1829, æ. 96, was out in the French War; also Samuel Brooks, who died in Hanover, in 1830, æ. 95, and Jedediah Dwelley, William Perry, and Oliver Winslow, — the latter of whom died near Crown Point, in 1759. These men were of Scituate, though their names occur on the Hanover Records; and at a subsequent date, or after the close of the war, some of them resided in the town.

1768, November 7. "Voted to Samuel Barstow 6s. for making a door to the powder room, and for moving the powder."

1771, March 11. "Capt. John Bailey, and Capt. Simeon Curtis chosen to take care of the Town's Gun Powder in the best way and manner they can."

1774, November 21. Paid Capt. John Bailey for four quarter barrels of Powder, £9 8s.

These are all the minutes which occur previous to the Revolution. Of the incidents of this war, we shall make a separate Chapter; as also of the War of 1812, in which we shall include a sketch of the Hanover Artillery Company.

CHAPTER VIII.

INCIDENTS OF THE REVOLUTION.

> " By their pious shades we swear,
> By their toils and perils here,
> We will guard with jealous care,
> Law and Liberty." LUNT.

Causes of the Revolution—Stamp Act—Convention in Boston—Plymouth County Convention—Provincial Congresses—Preparations for defence—Minute men—Provincial Treasurer chosen—Committees of Safety—Boston Port Bill—Tories, and the Ruggles Covenant—Balfour's troops—Commencement of hostilities—Sea coast guards—General Washington assumes the command of the Army—Station of the army—Operations for 1776—Entrenchment on Dorchester heights—Evacuation of Boston—Alarm at Cohasset—Declaration of Independence—Operations around Boston—Men for Ticonderoga, and for Rhode Island—Operations for 1777—Committee of Safety—Prices for labor—Town's quota—Expedition to Rhode Island—Other military movements—Operations for 1778—Quota of Shirts, &c.,—State Constitution rejected—Enlistments for this year—Extracts from the Pay Rolls—Operations for 1779—Committee of Safety &c.,—Enlistments—Committee of Safety for 1780—Military movements for the year—Depreciation of Currency—The dark hour—Movements for 1781—Incidents subsequent to the War.

The story of the Revolution, will ever be read with interest by the citizens of this growing republic. The simple recital of our father's wrongs; of their peaceful remonstrance against those wrongs, until forbearance ceased longer to be a virtue; of their calm deliberation upon the course next to be pursued; of their reluctant, but firm conviction, that an appeal to arms was their only alternative; of their solemn consecration of their lives, and fortunes, and sacred honor, upon the altar of liberty; and of their accompanying deeds of heroism, until their INDEPENDENCE was acknowledged; if these events, which, viewed in their broadest light, are calculated to make every heart glow, ever become to us as a "thrice told tale," or cease to arouse us to emulate their virtues, then may we be assured that the day of our downfall is approaching, and that we are becoming unworthy of the continued enjoyment of those inestimable blessings, now so freely and widely diffused throughout our land.

In a work like the present, however, which is local in its character, it will not be expected that we should give an extended notice of these events. We shall confine ourselves to the part which the citizens of Hanover took in the great drama then performed, only giving such general details, as may serve to render our sketch intelligible, and complete.

The principal causes which led to the War of the Revolution, were the adoption of measures, and the enactment of laws, by the Parliament of the mother country, which were deemed oppressive in their character, and an invasion of the rights of the people of the colonies.

Indeed, quite early in the history of our country, we find the right of England to Legislate for the colonies, questioned by many. We could bring abundant proofs to sustain this position, were it necessary. Not only do the laws of Plymouth and Massachusetts show this, but the writings of the most eminent men of those days, furnish clear and decisive evidence of the fact.[1] Hence when, in the reign of George the II, an act of Parliament was passed, imposing a duty on sugars, &c., which, in the reign of George the III, in 1764, was continued and enforced, and the duty increased, and an impost also laid on molasses, brought to the colonies from any other than British plantations in the West Indies, and the jurisdiction of vice-admiralty courts was enlarged, by which the people were deprived of trial by juries, in all cases relating to revenue arising from these duties, and made liable to unreasonable and oppressive suits; — these acts were all resisted, and all tended to foster a feeling of injury, and a spirit of resentment, among the people.

But the famous Stamp Act, passed in 1765, awakened the most general indignation; and as soon as it arrived at Boston, the bells were muffled, and rung a funeral peal, and the act itself was hawked about the streets, with a Death's head affixed to it, and styled the *Folly of England, and the ruin of America*, and afterwards publicly burnt by the enraged populace;[2] and throughout

[1] Massachusetts State Papers, p. 13, et seq.
[2] Low's American Encyclopedia, Vol. 1, p. 288.

the province, meetings were held, and the act denounced. The new act of 1768, imposing a duty on tea, papers, painters' colors, and glass, caused, if possible, a ferment greater than that caused by the Stamp Act; and so thoroughly were the people aroused, that it was finally resolved to call a Convention, to meet in Boston, September 21, "to consult upon measures for the safety of the Province." Delegates to this Convention were sent from a large number of towns. Hanover deputed Joseph Cushing, Esq., to act as its Representative; a gentleman who had been long and favorably known to his townsmen, and who was distinguished for his unbending integrity, and affable deportment; — who afterwards held an honorable rank in the Conventions of the County, and the Congresses of the Province; and who, at a still later period, when peace had been declared, and order restored to our disturbed civil institutions, as a token of gratitude, and esteem for his services, was elevated to the office of Judge of Probate for the County of Plymouth, and received a military commission, with the rank of Brigadier General.

But the oppressions of England did not cease with the Act of 1768. Farther encroachments were made upon the rights of the Colonies; and the public mind was kept in a constant state of feverish excitement; until, all over the land, the necessity for an appeal to arms was beginning to be felt, and even to be advocated, by the most bold and resolute. Monday, September 26, 1774, a meeting of delegates from every town in Plymouth County, was held at Plympton, and by adjournment, at the court house in Plymouth, on Tuesday the 27th; and Hanover sent as its Representatives, Capt. Joseph Cushing, Joseph Ramsdell, Joshua Simmons, Capt. Robert L. Eells, and Dr. Lemuel Cushing; and the first named gentleman was chosen one of the committee of nine, to prepare an address expressive of their feelings in view of the aggressions of the British Government. The proceedings of this Convention are given in full in the Journal of the Provincial Congress, pp. 621–625, but are too long to be inserted here.

On the 7th, of October 1774, the First Provincial Congress was convened at Salem; on the 11th, at Concord; on the 17th, at Cambridge, and again at Cambridge, November 23d, and dissolved, December 10th. The Second Congress was convened at

Cambridge, February 1, 1775; at Concord, March 22d, and April 22d; and at Watertown April 22d, and dissolved May 29th. The Third Congress convened at Watertown, Wednesday, May 31st, 1775, and was dissolved Wednesday, July 19th, 1775. To all these, Col. Cushing, as he is called on the Journals, was sent as a delegate from Hanover, and in all he took an active and prominent part. We could enumerate many instances, in which he was appointed on important committees; and that his services were held in the highest esteem, may be inferred from the fact that his associates were ever ready to assign to him new trusts.[1]

During the session of the First Congress, the importance of the improvement of the *militia* was urged, and the several towns and districts in the colony were advised "to see that each of the *minute men* not already provided therewith, should be immediately equipped with an effective fire-arm, bayonet, pouch, knapsack, and thirty rounds of cartridge and balls, and be disciplined three times a week, and oftener as opportunity may offer;" and in the Second Congress, where any deficiency in arms or accoutrements was found, the Selectmen were instructed to supply the same "out of the town stock, and in case of a deficiency there, to apply to such inhabitants as can best spare their arms or accoutrements, and to borrow or purchase the same for the use of the inhabitants so enlisting;"[2]

In accordance with these votes, companies of minute men were formed in all the towns in the province, — indeed this work had commenced as early as 1773, — and these companies furnished efficient aid in procuring recruits for the Army, communicating intelligence on sudden emergencies, and forwarding the war. According to Col. J. B. Barstow, Hanover was divided into two districts, by the road running from the North River bridge past the Four Corners, to what is now Hanover Street, and thence to the Meeting House, and on West to the Drinkwater Forge, and to Abington. The inhabitants of the Southerly part of the town were in one district, and the company formed here was commanded by Colonel, then Capt. Amos Turner, and Lt. Samuel

1 See the Journals, pp. 55, 66, 85, 95, 97, 118, 130, 148, 255, 284, 291, 298, 300, 310, 363, 374, 377, and 479.

2 Jour. Prov. Cong. pp. 71, and 209–10

Barstow; and those to the North, were in the Second District, and their Company was commanded by Capt. Joseph Soper, and probably Lt. Lemuel Curtis. In the County, a regiment was formed of companies of minute men, and Theophilus Cotton, of Plymouth, was chosen Colonel; Ichabod Allen, of Duxbury, Lt. Colonel; and Ebenezer Sprout, of Middleboro', Major.[1] January 16, 1775, The town procured a stock of thirty-five fire arms, as a public supply, to be furnished to those who had not the means, or were not able to provide for themselves.

One of the earliest acts of the Provincial Congress was to provide funds for the expenses of Government, and the conduct of the war. Harrison Gray, Esq., was the treasurer appointed by the old authorities; but as funds in his hands were not available to the public, the Congress advised all constables and collectors of taxes "who have or shall have any money in their hands collected on province assessments," not to pay the same to Mr. Gray, but to retain them in their own hands until otherwise instructed; and they soon made choice of Henry Gardner, Esq., as Treasurer, and directed all monies to be paid to him.[2] Accordingly the town of Hanover, having voted, Jan. 16, 1775, to raise £43 15s. 2d. "for purposes of defence," instructed Israel Perry, collector for 1773-4, to pay over the same to Mr. Gardner, "with the remainder of the Province tax in his bills not then collected," and agreed to "indemnify and hold him harmless in so doing."

Another of these preliminary steps, was the appointment of Committees of Correspondence and Safety; and the committee of Hanover, for the year 1775, consisted of David Jacobs, Lieut. Whiting, Joshua Simmons, Abner Curtis, Ezra Briggs, Dr. Cushing, Seth Bates, Lemuel Curtis, Capt. Curtis, Capt. Eells, Joseph Ramsdell, Amos Turner, Michael Silvester, Lieut. Barstow, Bezaleel Curtis, Benjamin Bass, Israel Perry, Benjamin Studley, John House, jr., and Seth Josselynn; and they were instructed "to see that the resolves of the Continental Congress relative to trade, &c., are strictly adhered to."

By the operation of the Boston Port Bill, the inhabitants of that town were thrown into great distress, and provisions for their

[1] Winsor's Duxbury, p. 123.
[2] Jour. Prov. Cong. pp. 19, 38, and 45.

relief were made, not only throughout Massachusetts, but in several of the other Colonies. In Hanover, Dea. Barstow, and Thomas Rose, were chosen to receive donations, and forward them to the proper authorities, to be distributed.

In the winter of 1774, the tories of Massachusetts, were active in forwarding their schemes; and the Hon. Timothy Ruggles, of Hardwick, one of the most conspicuous, drew up a document, called the Ruggles Covenant, intended for the signature of all favorable to the royalist cause. This paper found its way to Hanover, and suspicions of its presence being entertained, the town instructed the Committee of Correspondence, "to inquire into the ground and foundation of a report that a covenant called the Ruggles Covenant is signed and circulated among some of the inhabitants." This incendiary document is given at large on the Journals of the Provincial Congress, p. 68.

It will hardly be necessary to say that such a compact found but few signers in Hanover. Indeed, in a town so loyal to *freedom*, tories were rare. When, in 1777, Israel Perry was chosen to collect "the evidence relative to those persons supposed to be inimical to their country," after the most diligent search, he reported but seven names, and these were either peaceable members of the Society of Friends, whose principles caused them to look upon all war as wrong, or members of the Episcopal Church, who, from that fact alone, were supposed to be friendly to the King. The names reported were Charles Bailey, Peleg Ewell, Mordecai Ellis John Bailey 3d., Joseph Donnell, and William and Jane Stockbridge.

All who did favor the royalists, were everywhere treated with a severity proportioned to the magnitude of their offence. They were ingloriously tipped from the cart's tail, and commanded forthwith to depart from the limits of the town, under the threat of heavier penalties, should they dare to appear within its borders again. Of all crimes, that of aiding and abetting the enemies of America, was most heartily despised, and treated with the sternest rebuke.

Previous to the commencement of the hostilities of the 19th of April, 1775, which may be regarded as the opening scene of the war of the Revolution, there were found, in Marshfield, a large number of friends of England, and signers of the Ruggles Covenant; and these, as appears by a letter dated Jan. 26, 1775, sent an express to Gen. Gage, acquainting him with their situation, and begging support.[1] This led to the forwarding of a body of one hundred troops, under the command of Capt. Balfour, and three subalterns, with two field pieces, and three hundred stands of arms, to be put into the hands of the loyalists. The troops were detached on board two small vessels, and landed quietly, and without disturbance. But the presence of such a body of men could not fail to be attended with some murmurings, and dissatisfaction, on the part of the people of the adjoining towns, although the signers of the covenant made their boast that "every faithful subject to his King dare fully utter his thoughts, and drink his tea, and kill his sheep as profusely as he pleases."[2]

Accordingly, in the Boston Evening Post, of Feb. 27, 1775, there was published an address to Gen. Gage, signed by the selectmen of Plymouth, Kingston, Duxbury, Pembroke, *Hanover*, and Scituate, protesting against the course he had pursued, in which, after declaring that the fears and intimidations of the people of Marshfield were entirely groundless, they proceed to say, "It appears as evident as if written with a sunbeam, from the general tenor of the testimony, which we are willing to lay before your excellency, if desired, that their expressions of fear, were a fallacious pretext, dictated by the inveterate enemies of our constitution, to induce your excellency to send troops into our country, to augment the difficulties of our situation, already very distressing; and what confirms this truth, if it needs any confirmation, is, the assiduity and pains which we have taken to investigate it. We have industriously scrutinized into the cause of this alarm, and cannot find that it has the least foundation in reality."[3]

The Congress, on the reception of the above—a copy of which was forwarded to them — passed a vote highly approving the vigilance of the selectmen and committees of correspondence of the towns named in the address, and recommended to them "steadily to persevere in the same line of conduct, which has, in this instance,

[1] Winsor's Duxbury, p. 128.
[2] Winsor's Duxbury, p. 127.
[3] Jour. Prov. Cong. p. 104.

so justly entitled them to the esteem of their fellow countrymen, and to keep a watchful eye upon the behavior of those who are aiming at the destruction of our liberties." [1]

The troops under Balfour, however, did not remain long in the county. On the 21st of April they departed, as they came,—in their hurry leaving behind them most of their camp equipage and stores, — and being engaged in the battle at Bunker Hill, on the 17th of June, all but their commander, and five of the soldiers, perished, although they entered the field "with as fine a com pany as was in his Majesty's service."[2]

Before their departure, the military companies in the vicinity were on the alert, and were contemplating an attack. Col. John Bailey ordered his troops to march to the spot, but they did not arrive until the enemy had left. Mr. Jabez Studley was among the soldiers engaged in this expedition, according to his son, the present Mr. Jabez Studley, of Hanover.

We have now reached that period when actual hostilities commenced, and the struggle for liberty, at the point of the bayonet, began in earnest.

April 8, 1775. The Provincial Congress resolved "that the present dangers, and alarming situation of our public affairs, renders it necessary for this colony to make preparations for their security and defence, by raising and establishing an army." [3] This army, as appears by a subsequent report, was raised, and consisted of twenty-two regiments complete, of ten companies each, containing sixty men; and three regiments incomplete. But all the privates were not properly equipped, and of military stores, of some descriptions, the supply was very small. [4] John Bailey, of Hanover, was Lieut. Col. in the regiment of Gen. Thomas.

On the first of May, 1775, or about two weeks after the battle of Lexington, according to Winsor, four companies were ordered to Plymouth "to guard the sea-coast," where they were stationed until the first of September. [5] Of this order I find no

[1] Jour. Prov. Cong. p. 103-4.
[2] Winsor's Duxbury, p. 120.
[3] Jour. Prov. Cong. p. 135.
[4] Bradford's Hist. Mass. Vol. 1. p. 382.
[5] Winsor's Duxbury, p. 120.

record ; but on the first of July, a memorial having been presented from Plymouth, stating that the people in that neighhorhood were "in danger of being attacked by the enemy," it was resolved by the Congress "that General Ward be and hereby is directed, immediately to issue his orders that two full Companies from Col. Cotton's regiment, under proper officers, march without delay, to Plymouth, and there remain for the guard and defence of the inhabitants, until they can be relieved by such Companies as are to be raised for the defence and protection of the sea-coast, and to be stationed there for that purpose."[1]

Among those who thus guarded the sea-coast, "Samuel Eells and others" are spoken of, on the records of the town, and Oct. 30th, there was paid to him, and to Nathaniel Torrey, for their services, £1 12s. 8d. ; and in the "Pay Roll of the Company stationed on the sea-coast in the Massachusetts service till the last of December, 1775, occur the names of "Samuel Eells, jr., Fifer ; and Eliab Studley, Benjamin Studley, Ezra Briggs, Solomon Bates, Jabez Studley, Henchman Silvester, Clement Bates, and Seth Curtis, Privates," — all of whom were citizens of Hanover.[2]

On the third of July, 1775, General Washington, by appointment of the Continental Congress of June 14th, took command of the American troops in the vicinity of Boston, which were then estimated at 15,000. Of these, more than 9,000 belonged to Massachusetts, — the rest having been furnished by Connecticut, New Hampshire, and Rhode Island.[3]

These troops were in a comparatively undisciplined state, and almost destitnte of clothing, and ammunition. But a few days after Washington's arrival, the alarming discovery was made, that the actual quantity of powder on hand, was not more than sufficient to furnish each man with nine cartridges.[4] The main body of the British army, at this time, under the immediate command of Gen. Howe, was entrenching itself strongly on Bunker Hill. Three floating batteries lay in Mystic river, near the camp, and a twenty gun ship below the ferry, between Boston and Charles-

[1] Jour. Prov. Cong. 433.
[2] Revolutionary Rolls, 36, 226.
[3] Bradford's Massachusetts, Vol. 2. p. 18.
[4] Marshall's Washington, Vol. 1. p. 30.

town. A strong battery on the Boston side of the water, on Copp's hill, served to cover and strengthen the post on Bunker Hill. Another division was entrenched on the Neck. The light horse, and a small body of infantry, were stationed in Boston. The American army lay on both sides of Charles river. The right occupied the high grounds about Roxbury; whence it extended towards Dorchester; and the left was covered by Mystic or Medford river, a space of at least twelve miles. A change was afterwards made in the position of the American troops, and Washington himself took up his head quarters at Cambridge.[1] A rigorous blockade was thus kept up over the British army, and Boston itself was in a state of siege, and so continued until the spring of 1776.

1776. The Committee of Safety for this year consisted of Joseph Cushing, Joshua Simmons, Capt. Robert L. Eells, Joseph Ramsdell, Lemuel Curtis, David Jacobs, Benjamin Bass, Benjamin Studley, Capt. Amos Turner, Capt. Joseph Soper, Samuel Barstow, jr., Michael Silvester, Calvin Curtis, Lt. John Hatch, Ezra Briggs, Seth Stetson, John Curtis, jr., Joshua Barstow, and Thos. Whiting.

Feb. 12, 1776. Capt. Nathaniel Winslow's Company marched to Roxbury, and other troops from Hanover had joined the army at that place, in preparation for the contemplated attempt to dislodge the British army from Boston. This was in accordance with a resolution of the Provincial Congress of the previous January, "that a vigorous attempt ought to be made on the ministerial troops in Boston, before they can be reinforced in the spring; and that thirteen regiments of militia should be asked for from Massachusetts and the neighboring colonies, in order to put the army in a condition to make the attempt."[2] To effect this object, it was determined that entrenchments should be thrown up on Dorchester heights; and Major General Thomas had the command of the troops detached for this arduous service; and Col. John Bailey, and the troops from Hanover were among the number. They passed from the camp at Roxbury, to the place of their destination, with great caution, under cover of the night; and

[1] Marshall's Washington, Vol. 1. p. 29 et seq.
[2] Marshall's Washington, Vol. 1. p. 29.

when the light of day exposed them to the view of the British in Boston, they had thrown up a sufficient breastwork for protection and security in prosecuting the object of their enterprise.[1] Gen. Howe, in order to frustrate the intentions of the Americans, sent a picked body of 3,000 men, commanded by Lord Percy, to assault the works which had been thus commenced; and they embarked, and fell down to the castle, to proceed to the intended scene of action, but were scattered by a furious storm, which disabled them from immediately prosecuting the enterprise, and before they could be again in readiness for the attack, the works were made so strong, that the attempt to storm them was thought unadvisable, and the evacuation of the town soon afterward took place.[2]

A part of the glory of this enterprise belongs to Hanover; and among those who were thus engaged, from the Pay Roll of Capt. Nathaniel Winslow's company, which marched for Roxbury Feb. 12, 1776, we gather the names of Benjamin Studley, 1st Lieut.; Joseph House, 2d Lieut.; Timothy Rose, Sergeant; David Torrey, Drummer; and Stephen Torrey, Job Tilden, Robert White, Elijah Silvester, Elisha Palmer, Seth House, Samuel Eells, Samuel Gross, Nathaniel Torrey, Jonathan Pratt, Benjamin Bates, Joseph Bates, Benjamin Silvester, Adam Perry. James Whiting, Nathaniel Josselynn, Seth Bates, Nathaniel Stetson, Isaac Turner, Seth Bates, Jr., Joseph Brooks, Gideon Studley, Benjamin White, James Torrey, Benjamin Stetson, Laban Rose, and Ebenezer Eddy, Privates.[3] Tradition says that Clement Bates was also at Dorchester heights, and aided in fillling with sand, the barrels which were to be used for the defence of the breastwork. As all Col. Cotton's regiment, which had been stationed at Plymouth, moved to Roxbury, and formed part of the detachment which threw up these entrenchments,[4] there were probably other citizens of Hanover engaged in the enterprise, but the foregoing are all the names we are able to give authentically.

In March, 1776, there was an alarm of "danger at Cohasset," probably arising from the British vessels which were hovering

1 Bradford's Massachusetts, Vol. 2. p. 85.
2 Marshall's Washington, Vol. 1. p. 43.
3 Rev. Rolls, 24. 38.
4 Winsor's Duxbury, 131.

upon the coast, and troops were ordered to the spot to aid in its defence. From Hanover, the whole company under the command of Capt. Lemuel Curtis was detached; and in the Pay Roll of the same, which was sworn to before Joseph Cushing, Esq., Jan. 20, 1777,[1] occur the names of Lemuel Curtis, Captain; John Hatch, 1st Lieut.; Abner Curtis, 2d Lieut.; Calvin Curtis, Michael Silvester, James Curtis, and Israel Perry, Sergeants; and Elijah Curtis, Jabez Studley, Joseph Curtis, Prince Curtis, Thomas Hatch, David House, Snow Curtis, Joshua Dwelley Jesse Curtis, John Totman, Eliab Studley, Marlboro' Turner, Joseph Randall, Abel Curtis, Seth Bailey, Ezra Briggs, Elisha Simmons, Abner Curtis, jr., Robert Corthrell, Gershom Curtis, Job Curtis, Isaac Hatch, Simeon Curtis, Seth Curtis, William Gilbert, Elijah Stetson, Melzar Curtis, Ebenezer Curtis, Job Barstow, Solomon Bryant, Benjamin Bass, Seth Josselynn, Lemuel Bates, and Gamaliel Bates.

Whilst these events were transpiring, the Continental Congress was in session, and the declaration of Independence was under discussion; and June 30, at a meeting in Hanover "held to take into consideration a resolve of the Honorable House of Representatives of the Massachusetts Bay, relative to advising the person or persons chosen to represent them in the General Court, whether, if the Honorable American Congress should for the safety of the American Colonies, declare them Independent of the Kingdom of Great Britain, they the said inhabitants, will solemnly engage, with their lives and fortunes, to support them in the measure, Voted, to instruct their Representative, that if said Congress, should think it safest to declare them Independent of the Kingdom of Great Britain, they the inhabitants will support them in the measure."

During the summer of 1776, the soldiers from Hanover were mostly stationed in the vicinity of Boston, and fortifications were erected at Noddle's island, and at other places in the harbor; twenty British vessels were driven from the coast; and two regiments, and the battalion of artillery were kept in the service of the province throughout the season.[2]

[1] Rev. Rolls, 18. 10.

[2] Bradford's Massachusetts, p. 111 et. al.

The references to the enlistments from Hanover, during this period, are quite numerous. In the Pay Roll of Capt. Nathaniel Winslow's Company, in Col. Whitney's Regiment, for one month's advance pay, &c.,[1] are the names of Calvin Curtis, 2d Lieut.; Joseph Curtis, Corporal; and Stephen Torrey, Sergeant. The same men were paid for services in August and November, 1776,[2] and Clement Bates was in their company.

In the Rolls for September and October, besides the foregoing, are the names of Abner Dwelley, Abner Curtis, Seth Bates, Joel Silvester, Nathaniel Torrey, Isaac Turner, Samuel Eells, Edward Ramsdell, Benjamin Studley, Elijah Silvester, and Reuben Curtis.[3]

In the roll of Capt. Stetson's Company, in Col. Dike's Regiment, for three months service, are the names of Benjamin Studley, 1st Lieut.; Solomon Bates, Corporal; and Benjamin Studley, Jr., Warren Torrey, Amos Berry, Cornelius Silvester, and Seth Bates; and in the pay roll of Capt. Stetson's Company, for three months, to Nov. 1776, are the additional names of James Whiting, Stephen Randall, Dowty Bates, Thomas Gross, Francis Josselynn, and Adam Perry.[4]

On the town records, under date of Oct. 1, 1776, *five men* are spoken of, as having been engaged for the expedition to Ticonderoga this year, and £13 bounty per man was voted them. *Fifteen men* were also hired to go to New York to reinforce the Continental Army, and a bounty of £5 15s. was voted to each. *Sixteen men* also went to Rhode Island for two months, to whom a bounty of 20s. each per month, was voted: and a like bounty to *fifteen men* who went to Bristol for three months.

Of the first named expedition,—that to Ticonderoga,—the only record I find, is in the "Pay Roll of Capt. Christopher Bannister's Company, which went to Ticonderoga for two months and seven days," where may be found the names of David Studley, Corporal, and Abner Dwelley, Private.

The names of the *fifteen*, who went to New York, I have not been able to learn.

Of the *sixteen*, who went to Rhode Island for 2 months, and the

[1] Rev. Rolls, 24. 11.
[2] Rev. Rolls, 24. 37, and 24. 35.
[3] Rolls, 24. 40.
[4] Rolls, 26. 420, et al.

fifteen who went to Bristol, I find the following minutes. In the Pay Roll of Capt. Amos Turner's Co., in Col. John Cushing's Regiment, which marched to Rhode Island in 1776, for two months, dated at Newport, R. I., Nov. 17, 1776,[1] occur the names of Michael Silvester, Snow Curtis, Nathl. Josselynn, Joseph Ramsdell, Samuel Brooks, Benj. Stetson, Simeon Curtis, Prince Curtis, Benj. White, and Benj. Bass, Privates; and Israel Perry, Drummer.

In the Field and Staff Officers Roll, upon the Bristol Alarm, in 1776, are the names of Samuel Baldwin, Chaplain; John Cushing, Colonel; Benj. Bass, Quarter Master; and Melzar Turner, Adjutant.

In the Muster Roll of Capt. Amos Turner's Co., &c., which marched to Rhode Island in 1776, are the names of[2] Amos Turner, Captain; Seth Josselynn, Lt.; Benj. Stetson, Benj. White, and Belcher Clark, Sergeants; Phillip Josselynn, and Clement Bates, Corporals; David Torrey, Drummer; Samuel Eells, jr., Fifer; Isaac Josselynn, Clerk; and Elijah Garnett, Wm. W. Eells, Abner House, Nathl. Josselynn, Robt. Cushman, Cornelius White, Oliver Bonney, Nathl. Clark, Joseph Carrel, Benj. Bates, Nathl. Josselynn, jr., Sam. Eells, Seth Bates, Stephen Torrey, Joseph Ramsdell, Robt. Eells, Theoph. Witherell, Luther Torrey, Thos. Oldham, Abner Studley, and Simeon Witherell, Privates.

In the Pay Roll of Capt. Joseph Soper's Co. to Bristol, 1776, are the names of Joseph Soper, Captain; John Hatch, 1st. Lt.; Joshua Dwelley, 2d Lt.; Wm. Curtis, Timothy Rose, and Michael Silvester, Sergeants; Snow Curtis, Corporal; and Asa Whiting, Caleb Silvester, Benj. Clark, Elisha Palmer, Isaac Perry, Jona. Pratt, Abel Whiting, Seth Curtis, jr., Jas. Whiting, Thos. Hatch, Gideon Studley, Seth Curtis, Henchman Silvester, Job Curtis, Elijah Gilbert, Benj. Mann, Josh. Mann, Joseph Brooks, Elisha Simmons, Jesse Curtis, Prince Curtis, Melzar Curtis, Eliab Studley, Jabez Studley, Thos. Stetson, Israel Perry, Abel Curtis, and Elijah Curtis, Privates.

1777. March 10, Committee of Safety, &c., Joshua Simmons, Joseph Cushing, Timothy Rose, Benj. Bass, Lemuel Curtis, Capt.

[1] Rev. Rolls, 3, 178. [2] Rev. Rolls, 3, 132.

Prince Stetson, Israel Perry, Capt. Robert L. Eells, Michael Silvester, David Jacobs, Calvin Curtis, Lt. Benjamin Studley, Jesse Curtis, Joseph Ramsdell, Abner Curtis, Seth Stetson, jr. Melzar Curtis, Timothy Robbins, and Samuel Barstow, jr.

By an Act of the Province, called an " Act to prevent monopolies and oppression," the following scale of prices for labor and goods was fixed this year.

Day labor, for reaping and mowing, 3s. 6d. From April 1, to last of September, 2s. 8d. For March, October, and November, 2s. 4d. For the three winter months, 2s. 6d. Good wheat, per bu., 6s. 8d. Rye, 4s. 4d. Indian corn, 3s. 8d. Spanish potatoes, in the field, 1s. ; out of the cellar 1s. 4d. Good men's shoes, 7s. 6d. Good tried tallow, 8d. Good veal, mutton, and lamb, 3d. Horsekeeping, 1s. 4d. per 24 hours. A yoke of oxen, 1s. 4d. Teaming work at 1s. 6d. per mile. Turkeys, ducks, dunghill fowls, and goese, 4d. per lb. Milk, 2d. per qt. Good English hay 3s. per hund., and in proportion for a meaner quality. Good merchantable boards, 40s. per M. at the mill. Good turnips, 1s. 4d. per bu. Cider at the mill, 6d. per bbl. Summer apples, 6 1-2d. per bu. Winter apples, 8d. A middling sized yoke of oxen, 2s. per day. For a common plow, in common business, 1s. 6d. White oak bark, at the tannery, 20s. per cord. Black oak, 18s. Hemlock, 13s. 4d. Hog's fat, 7 1-2d. per lb. Womens' shoes, 5s. 8d. per pair. Making mens' shoes, 2s. 6d. Womens' shoes, the same, the shoemaker finding the heels. Other shoes, in proportion. Hemlock boards, 32s. per M. Pine shingles, without sap, 13s. 4d. Hemlock shingles, 12s. good and clear, and with the grain. Tobacco, 5s. per. lb. Smith's coal, at the pit, 13s. 4d. per load. Horse shoeing, steeled, toed, and corked, fixed for the winter, 6s. 8d. Wood, at the E. end of the town, from Oldham's to Benj. Clark's, and so to the old forge, walnut, 13s. ; oak, 11s. ; swamp-wood 9s. The other parts of the town, walnut, 9s. 6d. ; oak, 8s. ; swamp wood, 7s. An ox cart and wheels, 1s. 4d. per day, and all other tools and implements, and all other labor and business, according to former wages and customs.

In March of this year, the town's quota of every seventh man was called for, and it was voted to give those that enlisted £14 each, in addition to the Continental and State bounties; and a committee of twenty was chosen, to hire the money and the men. This measure, of offering *bounty* to soldiers, was adopted at the urgent solicitation of Washington, and was deemed by him of great importance, to encourage enlistments, and to secure their permanence.[1]

In the early part of this year, there was another expedition to R. I.; and in the muster roll of Capt. Amos Turner's company, are the names of[2] Amos Turner, captain; Reuben Rose, lieutenant; William Eells, sergeant; Leonard Hill, corporal; and Ezra Briggs, Elisha House, John Hatch, John Bates, Solomon Bryant, Samuel Brooks, Samuel Eells, Jr., Luther Torrey, Shuble Munroe, Jr., Joseph Robbins, Samuel Torrey, Melzar Stoddard, Reuben Curtis, and Henry Dillingham, privates. Of this number, Shuble Munroe died in Hanover, in 1851, at the age of 90.

In Hayward Pierce's company, which marched on a secret expedition to Tiverton, in Rhode Island, occur the names of[3] William Curtis, sergeant; Laban Rose, corporal; and Simeon Curtis, Elijah Sylvester, Joshua Dwelley, James Barstow, Elisha Stetson, Elisha Simmons, Seth Curtis, Jr., Jesse Curtis, Elijah Curtis, Samuel Brooks, Joseph Brooks, Seth Curtis, Elisha Silvester, Elisha Palmer, Lemuel Bates, Seth Bates, Nathaniel Josselynn, Nathaniel Torrey, Isaac Stetson, James Whiting, Joseph Nickerson, Josiah Mann, Elijah Gilbert, Zachariah Lambert, Benjamin Bowker, Japhet Crooker, Josiah Damon, Nathaniel Magoun, and others.

In the pay roll of the four independent companies, stationed at Hull, March 1, 1777, are the names of Caleb Silvester, sergeant; and Henchman Silvester, Levi Mann, Joshua Mann, and Cuffy Tilden, privates.[4]

In the roll of bounty due Capt. Seth Stower's company, in 1777, are Calvin Curtis, Luther Robbins, Elisha Curtis, Reuben Curtis, Cornelius Silvester, and Ezra Briggs.[5]

There were doubtless others out during this year, but the names given, are all we have found.

Oct. 20, 1777, £490 were voted for the pay of the soldiers already enlisted; and it was voted to purchase 105 lbs. of powder for a town's stock, "if it can be had for 5s. per lb." A

[1] See Marshall's Washington, vol. 1, p. 106, &c.
[2] Rev. Rolls, 3, 302 [3] Ib. 21, 266. [4] Ib. 37, 4. [5] Ib. 23, 25.

committee of three was also chosen, agreeable to the orders of the Provincial Congress, to supply the families of soldiers absent on service.

The operations for 1778, were quite extensive. Jan. 26, a new quota was called for, and arrangements were made to obtain the men. April 6. £200 were voted to supply the soldiers' families.

A quota of *shirts* being called for, to supply the army, the town voted that the selectmen should purchase the same, also the "shoes and stockings called for by the Hon. Court of this State, as cheap as they can"; which was accordingly done, and the supply forwarded.

In April, meetings were held throughout the State, to act upon the draft of the CONSTITUTION which had been prepared; but this draft was so objectionable, that few towns voted in its favor. In Hanover, a committee of fifteen was chosen to take the subject into consideration, and report; and at a meeting held June 8, at which seventy-three persons were present, they "voted the plan null and void to a man."

The enlistments for this year were as follows:—The Records of the town speak of eleven men, as engaged April 11, to whom a bounty of £27 each per month was voted; of men who went to Hull the 3d of March last, to whom £88 bounty were voted; of sixteen men raised, June 22, to guard the New England States, to whom it was voted to give £15 each, per month, in addition to the State's pay,—these being for the *secret expedition* to Rhode Island;—of eleven men raised June 29th, for six months, "to join General Sullivan at Providence," to whom $4 per day were voted, "with the publick's pay"; and October 26th, the sum of £3317 12s. 6d. was voted, "to pay the men that are and have been raised since October last, in the different services of the Commonwealth."

From the Revolutionary Rolls, we gather the following particulars, relating to the service this year. In the "Pay Roll of Captain Calvin Curtis' company, in Colonel John Jacobs Regiment, of Massachusetts, from Jan. 1, 1778, to Jan. 1, 1779,"[1] are the following Hanover names, viz: Calvin Curtis, captain; and

[1] Rev. Rolls, 1-147

Jabez Studley, Clement Bates, Neal Bates, Nathaniel Josselynn, and Abner Studley, privates. In the "Pay Roll of Captain Abraham Washburn's company, which did duty near Boston, six months, from July 1, 1778," [1] are the names of Caleb Silvester, Seth Perry, Henchman Silvester, Thomas Torrey, Abner Curtis, Elijah Turner, John Turner, Asa Turner, and Job Curtis.

In the "Pay Roll of Capt. Ichabod Bonney's company, that did duty on Castle Island, agreeable to an order of Sept 7, 1778, discharged Dec. 11, and allowed four days to return home,"[2] are the names of Nathaniel Chamberlin, sergeant; Isaac Turner, corporal; Joseph Barstow, fifer; and Albert Smith, Elijah Silvester, Caleb Rogers, Luther Robbins, Nathaniel Torrey, Benjamin Studley, Job Curtis, Samuel Garnet, Josiah Mann, and John Bosworth, privates.

In Capt. Joseph Clift's company, in Col. Whitney's regiment, which went to Rhode Island, in July 1778,[3] occur the names of Joshua Dwelley, lieutenant; Snow Curtis, sergeant; and Benjamin Studley, Simeon Curtis, Job Tilden, Seth Curtis, Lemuel Bates, Jacob Silvester, Luther Robbins, Seth Bates, Job Barstow and Eells Damon, privates.

In the Pay Roll of Capt. John Turner's company, in Colonel Eleazer Brook's regiment, which was at Cambridge, from Feb. 8, to April 4, 1778,[4] are the names of Asa Whiting, Benjamin Bates, Seth Bates, Jonathan Pratt, Simeon Curtis, James Whiting, Henry Perry, Samuel Ramsdell, and Job Silvester. The same names are on the Rolls from Feb. 18, 1777, to June 2, 1777.

In the Rolls for eight months service in 1778[5] are the names of Calvin Curtis, captain; and Reuben Rose, lieutenant.

Finally, in the Muster Roll of Militia to serve in Gate's regiment, until January 1, 1779,[6] are the names of Amos Turner, and Joseph Soper, captains; and Nathaniel Josselynn, jr., Abner Studley, Joseph Neal Bates, Clement Bates, and Jabez Studley, privates.

On the Town Records, the names of the *eleven men*, raised April 12, are thus given:—Joseph Turner, Solomon Bryant, Gershom Curtis, Elijah Stetson, William W. Eells, Lot Ramsdell,

1 Rev.Rolls, 24-94. 2 Ibid 25, 17. 3 Ibid 1, 171.
4 Ibid, 23, 155. 5 Ibid, 1, 62.

Thomas Gross, Ezra Briggs, jr., Francis Josselynn, Nathaniel House, and Melzar Lindsey.

1779. The Committee of Correspondence for this year, consisted of Joseph Cushing, Esq., Benjamin Studley, John Curtis, Samuel Stetson, Timothy Robbins, John Hatch, Prince Stetson, and Marlboro' Turner. On the 9th of August, the Town voted to "stand by the doings of the State Convention that met at Concord, July 14;" and Joseph Cushing, Esq., was chosen, to "meet at Cambridge the 1st of September next, to draw a form of Government." On the 30th of August, the town voted to "stand by the report of the County Committee for two weeks;" and Sept. 13, it was voted "to abide by the regulations of the County Committee until further orders." The convention alluded to in the last two votes, was held at Mr. Caleb Loring's, in Plympton, Aug. 24.[1] The references to enlistments for this year, on the *town* records, are the following: March 23.—A committee was appointed to settle "with the eight and nine months' men, that went to the North River." July 5.—"Three men were raised for an expedition of nine months to Springfield, and £3 per month, in the old way, and the Continental wages," were voted them. Sept. 20.—"Five men" were raised for "two months, to go to Rhode Island, and £50 per man, were voted them." Oct. 4.—The officers of the companies in the town were instructed to hire two men "to go to Rhode Island, the first of January." Oct. 19.—"Voted to pay the four men that went to North River, and the three that went to Rhode Island."

From the Revolutionary Rolls, our gleanings for this year are but few. In the "Pay Roll of Lieut. Abner Dwelley's company, in an expedition to Manchester, in the Northern Department,"[2] are the names of Abner Dwelley, lieutenant; and John Skiffe, sergeant. In the "Abstract of pay due Captain Calvin Curtis' company, &c., July, 1779,[3] for two months after arrival in camp, &c., are the names of Calvin Curtis, captain; Reuben Curtis, corporal; and Leonard Hill, Jabez Studley, and Joshua Palmer, privates.

It is to be regretted, that the names of all who served in the

[1] Winsor, Hist. Dux. [2] Rev. Rolls, 18, 222. [3] Ibid. 31, 163.

army, were not entered on the records of the town. Had this course been adopted, it would have been easy to ascertain who were out, and the time they were absent. But to the confusion incident to the general disturbance of the ordinary functions of government, we are to attribute this neglect; and when we consider the highly excited state of the public mind, and the anxiety which prevailed as to the result of the war, we should be thankful for the few items we may be able to glean.

1780. Committee of Correspondence: Joseph Cushing, Esq., Calvin Curtis, Joseph Soper, jr., Israel Perry, Benjamin Bass, David Jacobs, John Hatch, Robert L. Eells, and Snow Curtis.

March 9. Voted, to give the five men that went to Rhode Island, last Fall, for two months, £189, each.

April 10. £5,000 were raised for the use of the town, and the pay of soldiers.

June 16. A meeting held, to raise fifteen men for six months, to go to Springfield, and a Committee was chosen to engage them.

June 26. "Agreed to give the soldiers thirty silver dollars, per month, and the Continent's pay."

June 27. £1,000, hard money, voted, to pay the six months' men with; and a Committee chosen, to settle with the three men that went to North River, last Summer.

July 3. Voted, to give the three months' men, being eighteen in number, "one silver dollar, or one bushel of corn, per day, which ever they may choose." July 6. Voted, the eighteen men, called for June 22, the same that the six months' men had." July 21. £500, in silver, raised to pay the soldiers with. Oct. 23. A meeting held, to get a quantity of *beef*, for the use of the State; and it was voted to raise $35,320, to purchase the same. Oct. 30. £3,160, voted, "to supply the soldier's families."

A glance at the foregoing votes, shows the confusion and distress which prevailed at this period.

The war had lasted over four years. The private business of the soldiers had been neglected. And though their *families* were comfortably supported, yet the prospect for the future was gloomy and threatening.

It was the country's *dark hour*. The *currency* was *depreciated*. The *army* was *suffering*. The most *sanguine* were becoming *discouraged*. Had it not been for the noble generosity of a few, and the determined energy of George Washington, the Commander-in-Chief, all would have been lost. Enlistments proceeded slowly. Patriotism, if not flagging, was beginning to despair. But, by desperate efforts, by earnest entreaties, and by liberal promises, the army was recruited, funds were procured, and the movements of the troops successfully conducted.

It is probable, that many of the soldiers named in the foregoing lists, served in the army this year, and, perhaps, to the close of the war. The policy of three years' enlistments had been adopted; and many were entered "during the war." Our extracts from the Rolls, for this year, are few.

In the Pay Roll of Capt. Amos Turner's Company, in Col. John Jacobs' Regiment,[1] &c., are the names of Amos Turner, Captain; Benjamin Stetson, first Lieutenant; Luther Robbins, Sergeant; and Amos Berry, Levi Bates, Job Tilden, Dowty Bates, Theophilus Witherell, Benjamin Bates, jr., Nathaniel Barstow, James Woodward, Elisha Palmer, and Samuel Baldwin, Privates.

1781, Jan. 8. A meeting held to raise eighteen men, for three years, or during the war, and a Committee chosen "to petition the General Court to lessen the number called for from this town." The sum of $100, in hard money, was voted to each man that shall engage, and Capt. Luther Bailey was directed "to get the men, if he could, for that encouragement."

March 5. Men raised for Rhode Island, for forty days. Committee of Safety: Capt. Joseph Soper, John Hatch, David Jacobs, Benjamin Studley, Timothy Rose, Jesse Curtis, Thomas Whiting, jr., Seth Bailey, Abner Curtis, Marlboro' Turner, John Stetson, Joseph Brooks, and Simeon Curtis.

July 9. A meeting held to raise two men, for Rhode Island, for five months, and a bounty of five shillings per day was voted to each, with a like allowance for every twenty miles' travel home, when discharged, — the same to be paid in *silver money*.

July 30. Voted, to raise £116. 7s., in silver, for the purchase of *beef*, and a Committee having reported that beef could be had for four pence per pound, it was voted, "that all those that turn

[1] Rev. Rolls, 3, 164.

in four silver dollars to the Committee, be allowed one hundred pounds of beef for the same."

August 8. Men raised for West Point, for three months, and six shillings per day were voted them, and ten dollars each, before marching.

The only entry I have found on the Revolutionary Rolls, for this year, is the following:

In the Pay Roll of Capt. Joseph Soper's Company, in Col. Theophilus Cotton's Regiment, for service done in the State of Rhode Island, in March, 1781,[1] are the names of Joseph Soper, Captain; John Hatch, and Michael Silvester, Lieutenants; Comfort Bates, Sergeant; Neal Bates, and Josiah Chamberlain, Corporals; Reuben Curtis, Drummer; Joseph Turner, Fifer; and Samuel Perry, Nathaniel Clarke, Cornelius Turner, Benjamin Bates, Jabez Studley, Ezra Briggs, Clement Bates, Gershom Curtis, Benjamin Bates, jr., and Edmund Silvester, Privates.

In the foregoing sketch, we do not claim to have presented the names of all who enlisted in the war from Hanover. We have, however, given as full a list as our means permitted. And what we have furnished, is sufficient to show, that the citizens of this town failed not of their duty in the great struggle for freedom, but performed their part with fidelity and zeal.

Our limits do not allow us to enter more at large into the gen eral details of the war; neither can we narrate all the incidents of a traditionary character, which exist in the town. Many of these are of interest; but the fund of anecdotes already in existence, and published to the world, is such as not to require enlargement by us.

Of the incidents subsequent to the war, we have but little to say. In 1784, a Committee of nine was chosen to consider the offer of five years pay to the officers of the Revolution, and report; and February 9, the Committee reported, that "Scituate, Marshfield, Pembroke, and Abington, be invited to send a man or men from their town to meet a man or men from this town, at such time and place as they shall think proper, to consult what is best to be done, concerning the pay of the Continental Officers."

[1] Rev. Rolls, 3, 134.

March 15, Lt. Benj. Studley, and Mr. Melzar Curtis were chosen to meet at the Widow Loring's, with the County Convention, to consult about the "officers pay."

1794, July 28. "Voted, that the town will take into consideration the law of the Congress of the United States, particularly as it respects the raising the men ordered to be procured in this town."

August 9. Chose a Committee to procure the men when called for into actual service. "Voted, that the town will give those men who are returned by the officers, six shillings per day, or three shillings for each half day, they shall be called upon for service. Voted, that the town will indemnify the Committee, they procuring the men as cheap as they can."

1795, November 9. A meeting was held to "take into consideration the loss of the Town's stock of powder, — the same having been stolen, — and to adopt such measures as may be thought best calculated to recover the same or the value thereof," and a Committee was chosen to "prosecute such person or persons as may appear to them expedient."

1797, October 23. Voted to give the men who shall be detached by the Commanding Officers of the two Companies, by order of Goverment, or such as shall voluntarily enlist, $1 per day, for each day they shall be called upon for service. Chose a Committee to procure men when called for, into actual service, to serve in their stead, and voted to indemnify them for all expenses accruing.

1799. Voted to allow the training band nine shillings compensation, for two days at the Brigade muster at Halifax, — the officers to send a list of the same to the assessors.

The foregoing notes bring us to the time when the Hanover Artillery Company was formed; and the History of this Company, and the sketch of the war of 1812, will form the subject of the ensuing chapter.

CHAPTER IX

MILITARY HISTORY CONTINUED.

Military Companies subsequent to the Revolution — Hanover Artillery Company — Hanover Light Infantry Company — Hanover Rifle, Company — War of 1812 — List of Soldiers.

Although it has never been the policy of the American people, to encourage the formation of a standing army, for national defence, yet the military spirit, awakened by the Revolution, continued to animate the public mind for many years; and for some time after the war of 1812, military offices were held in much greater esteem than now, and military parades were frequent, and attracted considerable attention. Hence military companies have existed in almost every town, in New England, down to a comparatively recent period; but the Legislation of Massachusetts, for the past twenty years, has done little to revive or encourage the war spirit, and its concomitants.

From 1783 to 1794, we find but one regularly organized company in Hanover, which was commonly known as the "old militia company," and which was commanded by Col. John B. Barstow, prior to the year 1800.

During the administration of the elder Adams, a second company was formed, which was commanded by Capt. Timothy Rose; but this continued in existence for a few years only, and was eventually merged into the Hanover Artillery Company—the only company now in existence in the town.

This last company was established about the year 1798, under the auspices of Benj. Whitman, Esq., then settled as a lawyer in Hanover, of whose history we have elsewhere spoken. Mr. Whitman was the first Captain; his subalterns being, Dr. Melzar Dwelley, 1st Lieut., and Dr. Charles Turner, 2d Lieut.

The equipments of the members were, to each a white leather belt, with a brass breast-plate; coats of blue cloth faced with red, with brass buttons, and cord; pants and vest of a buff color; and the old fashioned *chapeaux des bras*, or cocked hats, of fur, surmounted with a black plume, tipped with red.

The Company, at its parades, is said to have made a fine appearance; its officers were gentlemen of high respectability; and no company, at the annual gatherings, on the muster field, attracted to itself more notice, or elicited warmer applause for the skillfulness of its manœuvres. A fine band of music usually attended it; and everything connected with the Company was such, that the few survivors, who were among its earliest members, speak of it with an enthusiasm, which age has not damped, nor time abated.

The Armory stood, in the first instance, on the rising ground, still known as "Gun-house Hill," near the residence of Mr. Robert Silvester; and during the Captaincy of Mr. Whitman, the Company often marched to the Four Corners, for review. Here, too, in the hall, over the store of Mr. Silas Morton, the festivities of election and parade days, were celebrated; — the collations served, and the "suppers" eaten. It is said, that, on one occasion, the Company was marched to the Corners for parade, and a large number of spectators were present at the review,— among others, Kilborn Whitman, Esq., a brother of the Captain, from the adjoining town of Pembroke. When seated at the dinner table, their guest was called upon for a "toast," as the glasses circulated; and, rising with much dignity and impressiveness, he gave, "The Hanover Artillery Company; may their pieces be loaded with true New England principles, wadded with Jacobinism, and pointed against every aspiring demagogue," — a toast, which, however exceptionable to some, and gratifying to others was drank with the usual cheers, perhaps for the sake of the *New England in the glasses.*

In 1806, Albert Smith was chosen Captain of the Company and, at his request, the town voted that "the Artillery Company may move the Gun-house on the Town's land near the meeting house," and Capt. John B. Barstow, Capt. Daniel Barstow, Israel Perry, Capt. Joshua Mann, and Capt. Clement Bates, were appointed a Committee to select a site for the same. The site chosen, was in the rear of the meeting house, on one corner of the old burial ground; and here the house stood until a new one was erected.

In October, 1806, the Selectmen were instructed to purchase "what *powder* is wanted for the company;" in Oct. 1808, they were instructed to purchase "four camp kettles for the company;" and in 1811, they were instructed to "complete the town's stock of military equipments."

In 1819, Elisha Barrell, jr., being chosen Captain, it was deemed advisable to erect a new Gun-house; and Captain Barrell applied to the Adjutant General, for aid from the State, and in November of that year, the Selectmen were appointed "agents to convey to the Commonwealth, land whereon to set a Gun-house," and the same was erected, being that now occupied by the Company, and standing near the centre of the town.

We do not know that we can give a complete list of the officers of this Company; but the names of the Captains, so far as we have learned, were as follows: Benj. Whitman, Esq.; Albert Smith, Esq.; Hon. E. F. Jacobs, of Scituate; Elisha Barrell, jr.; Edward Curtis; Levi Curtis; Elias W. Pratt; William Morse; Isaac H. Haskins; Wm. Thomas; Joseph Brooks, jr.; James House; Daniel Barstow, jr.; James Brooks; Benjamin N. Curtis; Charles Brooks; and Duncan T. Stoddard, the present Captain.

During the residence of Col. Jesse Reed, in Hanover, an Independent Infantry Company was formed, under his auspices, of which he was commander, which lasted for some years, but was finally disbanded.

About the year 1816, the Hanover Rifle Company was formed, of which Elijah Hayward, was the first captain; and after him, Hosea Whitman, William Josselynn, Nathan Dwelley, Samuel Bennett, and others, commanded it, until its removal to Hanson. It was annexed to the 2nd Regiment, 1st Brigade, 5th Division, of the Massachusetts Militia, and the Commissions of Captain Dwelley we have seen. The members of the Company were from Hanover, Scituate, Marshfield, Pembroke, Hanson, &c. Their uniform and equipments, consisted of green pants and coat; a felt cap, with a long green plume; and to each a rifle, knapsack,

&c. The arms were kept at their own houses. The company met at the Four Corners, for review, near the Episcopal Church. Their band consisted of two fifers, two tenor drummers, one bass drummer, and sometimes performers on the clarionet and bugle. There was no practice of "target shooting," by the company; but it attended the musters held at Church-hill, in Scituate; in Pembroke, near Horace Collamore's; and elsewhere.

Mr. Dwelley was chosen Ensign in 1820; on which occasion, a standard was presented, and an address delivered, by one of the young ladies of the town. The clergy of the neighborhood were present on the occasion; and an assemblage of from two to three hundred spectators, among whom were the ladies, dressed in white, each with a green ribbon encircling the waist; and Miss Eliza Stetson, who delivered the address, was accompanied by Miss Eells, now the wife of Capt. Dwelley, and Miss Ruth Stockbridge. The standard being presented, and waved, the music cheered, and the company, with their guests, marched to the hall, opened right and left, the ladies entered, the refreshments were served, and the remainder of the day was passed in partaking of cake, tea, lemonade, and *strong drinks*, which, in some cases, proved a little *too strong* for those who partook too freely.

Having a copy of the address delivered by Miss Stetson, we present it as a memorial connected with the history of the company.

"Sir,—The Ladies of Hanover and its vicinity, impressed with a high sense of the merits of the Rifle Company, in their behalf, I present you this Standard, in full confidence that you will not suffer it to be wrested from you, nor its reputation sullied. To be a lover of peace while prepared for war, is a characteristic of the American soldier; but though peace is our anxious wish, we would not have it purchased or preserved by the surrender of any of those rights and privileges procured and transmitted to us by our Fathers. Should any insolent foe attempt to deprive us of these dear-bought, and invaluable blessings, then, Sir, think of this banner! Think of our ancestors! and you must be brave! Remember your *friends*, and you *will conquer!*"

WAR OF 1812.

Of the causes which led to the war of 1812, we need not speak at large here. Its history is so recent, that the materials for its investigation are ample and complete. We shall only notice the proceedings of the citizens of Hanover, and this but briefly, as many other matters yet remain to be treated, and our space is limited.

June 2, 1812. The town voted, "to make soldiers up $15 per month, with what the Government pay, when called upon for actual service." Also, "voted, to give them $1 per day, for every day they are called out of town to do duty."

Aug. 3. A committee was appointed to draft resolutions, expressing the views of the town concerning the war; and these resolves were recorded, and copies sent "for publication in the Republican newspapers in Boston."

The Committee of *Safety* for this year, consisted of Turner Stetson, Albert Smith, Aaron Hobart, jr., Joshua Mann, and Snow Curtis. The Selectmen were likewise instructed to purchase a town's stock of powder, and $50 were voted to pay for the same.

In 1814, the Selectmen were instructed to "hire such sums of money as may be necessary for the safety of the town during the war." Also, "voted, to make up the soldier's pay to $20 per month, until October 1, and those that have been called out before, and the non-commissioned officers to receive the same pay." The selectmen were likewise instructed, to "furnish the militia with a suitable number of cartridges."

The Committee of Safety for this year, consisted of Aaron Hobart, jr., Esq., Isaiah Wing, Esq., Elijah Hayward, John B. Barstow, and Benjamin Stockbridge.

A detachment of the Artillery Company of the town, under Lieut. Elisha Barrell, jr., was at Scituate harbor, for sixty-eight days, from July 1, to September 6, 1814; and the whole company, under Captain Edward F. Jacobs, was at Plymouth, from September 19 to October 19, 1814.

The following, from the pay roll of the company, is a list of the officers and matrosses, who went to Plymouth.

Capt. E. F. Jacobs,
Lieut. Elisha Barrell, jr.,
" Edward Curtis,
Sergt. Amos Dunbar,
" Stephen Jacobs,
" Levi Curtis,
" Stephen Curtis,
Corpl. Calvin D. Wilder,
" Reuben Curtis,
" Oren Josselynn,
" Elias Barrell,

Luther Turner, Eleazer Josselynn, Gideon Perry, Levi Perry, } *Musicians.*

Matrosses.

John Clapp,
Luther Curtis,
Robert Curtis,
Elisha Magoun,
Nathaniel Curtis,
Elias Magoun,
Nathaniel Farrow,
Lewis Gross,
Ozias Whiting,
Charles Bailey, jr.,
Benjamin S. Munroe,
Joseph Brooks, jr.,
Joseph Sylvester,
Benjamin C. Pratt,
Justus Whiting,
Barker Wing,
John Jones, jr.,
Piam Damon,
Cyrus White,
John Curtis,
Melzar Curtis,
Joshua Stetson,
Job Curtis,
David T. Joyce,
John Gross,
Benjamin Bowker.
Gideon Studley, jr.,
Lemuel Curtis,
Joseph Damon,
Gad Bailey,
Benjamin H. Clark,
Allen Clapp.

CHAPTER X.

MANUFACTURES AND TRADE.

" Yet I exult,
Casting reserve away, exult to see
An intellectual mastery exercised
O'er the blind elements: a purpose given,
A perseverance fed, almost a soul
Imparted, to brute matter."

WORDSWORTH.

History of Manufactures in the town — Forges and Furnaces — Bardin's, now the Curtis Forge—Barstow's, now Sylvester's Forge—Dyer's, now Perry's Tack Factory — Sketch of the Life of Col. Jesse Reed — The Drinkwater Works, now Bates and Holmes — Barker's Foundry — Salmond's Tack Works — Tolman's Mills — Saw and Grist Mills — Plough Manufacture, and Sketch of the Life of David Prouty — Other branches of Industry.

To attempt to give a full sketch of the history of manufactures and trade, in this town, would require far more space than we can spare for the subject;—nor would such a sketch, which must necessarily be principally statistical, be generally interesting. We should be happy to give a list of the names of all, who have, at different periods, been owners of the forges, furnaces, saw-mills, grist-mills, &c., which have been erected; as well as of those who have engaged in trade, and other branches of industry; but, apart from the fact that authentic records are wanting, from which to draw these names, and the difficulty of obtaining them only from tradition, such a list, however gratifying as a memorial of family enterprise, could only be regarded as a sort of muster-roll, telling who *had* served, it is true, but not much of what they had *accomplished*.

We do not propose, however, to pass the subject by in silence. On the contrary, in itself, it is of far too much importance, to be treated with neglect, and the place which it occupies in our history is too conspicuous to be entirely overlooked. The town of Hanover has done *something*, in the line of manufacturing enterprise, as the statistics of the State show; and considering the many disadvantages under which our population have labored, from many sources, we think that what has been done, is highly creditable to their industry and perseverance.

9

The petition for the incorporation of the town, states that there were, then within its limits, "five saw-mills, and three iron-mills, and others," probably grist-mills.

As the *names* of these mills, and of the *owners*, are not given, we are left to learn them from the few hints scattered over our records.

FORGES, TACK WORKS, ETC.

As early as 1704, according to Deane, Bardin's Iron Works were erected on the Indian Head River; and these are called, on the records of the town, in 1730, the "old iron works." Thomas and Joseph Josselynn, were owners of the same, before 1743, and they were afterwards improved by Seth, Philip, Isaac, and John R. Josselynn, and others. They are now in the possession of Mr. George Curtis, who is engaged principally in the manufacture of Anchors, and other heavy forge work. On the Pembroke side of the stream, and opposite these works, stands an old saw-mill, now owned by Messrs. George Curtis, and Capt. Haviland Torrey; also a carding-mill, first built by Jesse Reed, at a spot farther up the stream, and moved from thence to its present locality. This, too, is owned by Mr. Curtis. A small furnace stood on the same side of the stream some years ago, but it is now gone.

The Curtis family has been connected with these works at least sixty years, or since 1790, though Seth Josselynn continued to be an owner until 1803, and Lemuel Dwelley, as late as 1839. Benj. Studley, and John R. Josselynn, were part owners in 1791, at which date they disposed of their interest to Lemuel Curtis. The year previous, or in 1790, Lemuel Curtis sold one fourth of the forge, &c. to Reuben and Consider Curtis, and Reuben disposed of his fourth to George Curtis, in 1831.

In 1839, Lemuel Dwelley, sold his half to George Curtis, and since that period, the last named gentleman has conducted the works individually.

The first works owned by the Curtis family, as also the building erected for a *corn-mill* in 1832, were destroyed by fire in 1848, and new buildings have been since erected. The old saw-mill, on the Pembroke side, yet remains, and is used some every winter; — also the old carding-mill, though the wool carding business, which was once very good, is now comparatively worthless. This mill was leased to Mr. Edward Y. Perry, for two years, from 1836–38, for running tack machines.

Mr. Curtis employs, in his anchor works, about sixteen hands, and manufactures from 200 to 250 tons of anchors per year. Business has always been active at this place; and, for nearly one hundred and fifty years, from amidst the charming and romantic scenery around, has ascended the smoke of the furnace, and the loud din of the descending hammer may be heard daily.

It is said that, from twenty-five to thirty years ago, anchors were made for the United States Government at this Forge, some of which were of great size, weighing five tons! Since the erection of the works at Washington, private contracts have been discontinued.

Formerly ship-knees, of iron, were made here; but at present, wooden knees are considered quite as serviceable, and are generally preferred.

The anchors made by Mr. Curtis, are for merchant ships and other vessels, and range in weight from 100 to 5000 lbs.

We annex a view of the "Old Forge."

Barstow's Forge, to which we have alluded on p. 19, was erected in 1720, and was occupied by the Barstow family, until the removal of Joshua, to Exeter, N. H., in 1795, when it was purchased by the Salmonds, and was improved by them, and by Nathaniel Cushing, and Charles Josselynn, for about thirty years.

In 1828, Mr. Salmond disposed of his interest in the works to Thomas Hobart, of Abington, who had been part owner for several years; and at that time there were, on the premises, one forge for the manufacture of bar iron, one anchor shop, one tack factory, and a corn mill. Mr. John Silvester, who is still connected with the works, entered them at about this date. About one hundred tons of bar iron were made per year, and one hundred tons of anchors. Of tack machines, from twelve to fourteen were run, and from two to three tons of tacks were made a week.

About the year 1825, Messrs. Hobart & Salmond had a contract from the United States Government for the manufacture of anchors for the Navy, and several were made for seventy-four gun-ships, of the largest size ever forged probably.

As far back as the period of the *Revolution*, quite a business is said to have been done at this forge, in the manufacture of *cannon balls* by Mr. Barstow, and he is spoken of as one of the most enterprising men ever in the town. He melted his iron at an ordinary forge fire, and moulded his balls in the bottom of the forge.

At present, the works, which are conducted by Mr. Silvester, are adapted principally to forging anchors, shaftings, locomotive cranks, and wagon axles. Mr. Silvester commenced the manufacture of locomotive cranks as early as 1830, and was one of the pioneers in this branch of business.

Many tack machines are built here yearly, though the tack business is not conducted at the place as formerly. About one hundred and fifty tons of iron are used at this forge.

Between the Curtis Forge, and that of Mr. Silvester, and at a place called "Project Dale," stands the tack factory of Mr. Edward Y. Perry, moved to this spot by Mr. Charles Dyer, about the year 1830, from Col. Reed's dam, of which we shall soon speak. There was an old dam, a grist mill, and carding mill, on the premises.

From papers, in the possession of Mr. Dyer, we learn that James Torrey had a fulling-mill at this spot, in 1737, at which date the place was called Project Dale. Mr. Torrey had bought fifty-two acres of land of Wm. Clift, deceased; and five acres, with a dwelling house, of Joseph Smith, in 1730. This mill privilege was sold to Thomas Josselynn, in 1737, and, for some time, the plac was known as "Josselynn's Corn-mill," and the lane leading to it, as "Mill Lane."

During the latter part of the 18th century, Joseph Stetson was proprietor of this mill, at which date it was known as "Stetson's mill;" and at his decease, it was sold by his administrators, to Lemuel Curtis, who gave it to Nathaniel Curtis, and by him it was sold to Mr. Elisha Hobart. It is now owned by the heirs of Mr. Curtis, and is occupied by Mr. Perry.

Mr. Dyer conducted the works for ten years, from 1829 to 1839, as agent for Mr. Hobart, after which he formed a partnership with Mr. Perry, which continued until 1850, when Mr. Perry took the sole charge of the works.

An idea of the extent to which the business is conducted by Mr. Perry, may be gathered from the following statistics. He employs sixteen hands, twelve of whom are males, and four females; — manufactures three hundred pounds of shoe nails per day, and about eight hundred thousand of tacks; — uses from two to three tons of copper, twenty-five tons of zinc, and seventy-five tons of iron per year; runs three shoe nail, and seven tack machines, and one machine for three-penny nails, of which about one hundred pounds per day are made.

The location of these works is very pleasant, especially in the summer season, being in a quiet dale, environed by hills, clothed with evergreen, and deciduous trees; and both here, and at the place next named, at an early period, the business of tack making was commenced, and has since been continued.

A short distance farther up the stream, Col. Jesse Reed, now of Marshfield, was located for a time. He came to Hanover about the year 1812, and lived on what is called the Smith farm, which he purchased of Mr. Robert Salmond, and which is now owned by Mr. Nathan Dwelley. The privilege which he improved, was purchased of Mr. Enos Bates, where Mr. Bates contemplated the erection of a dam and grist mill. Col. Reed built the dam, and put up a grist mill, and nail factory and machine shop. He remained in the town several years, and thence moved to Marshfield, where he yet resides.

The career of this gentleman, is worthy of notice, as an instance of the manifold blessings which a genius like his confers upon the public.

His father was a clock maker by trade, and, at the date of the birth of Jesse, in 1778, resided in North Bridgewater, Mass. At the age of nine years, the son went to Easton, to reside with Mr. Dean, with whom he remained three years, during which time his mechanical taste was displayed in the construction of a *trip hammer*, put in operation by a wheel and cam shaft, propelled by water. At the age of twelve, he returned to his father, and soon after constructed the main part of a wooden clock. At the age of fifteen, he was apprenticed to a joiner in Randolph, Mass., where he served a regular apprenticeship at that business.

During this period, he tried his skill on *perpetual motion*; and the result of his labors is thus given in his own words: "I worked two days and three nights without sleep. The last night, a little before day light, I got it ready to put into operation; and to avoid notice, I went into a little pine grove, with a friend, to put it together and set it in motion. I found that as soon as it was put together, it would go as well one way as the other, and that it would not go either way without help. I was then fully convinced that it was out of the power of *man* to put machinery together so as to produce perpetual motion, and that nothing short of the power to *create* could do it. To this belief I have ever since adhered."

At the age of twenty-two, or thereabouts, he invented and constructed a *rotary pump*, which worked well, but which was soon laid aside. His mind was next drawn to improvements in the manufacture of cut nails, and his first machine, for making nails from rods, was patented in 1802. One third of his interest in this right was sold to Rev. Jonathan Strong, of Randolph, and another third to Thomas Ordiorne, of Boston; they to have two-thirds of all improvements Mr. Reed should make in the businesss. But the experiment of manufacturing from rods, proved a failure, in a pecuniary point of view; and the next plan was to roll the iron to a suitable thickness, and slit it into pieces of the right size for the body of the nail, and flatten the point,—but this plan also failed.

The third step was the construction of a machine for cutting and heading at one operation. On this machine a patent was obtained, but it was soon laid aside. A heading machine was next constructed, into which, after the nails were cut, they were fed by hand; but this was also laid aside.

The partners of Mr. Reed now leaving him, he located in North Bridgewater, and built a small house by a waterfall, as a family residence, using the lower part of the building as a machine shop. Here he built two or three nail machines of different kinds, but pecuniary embarrassments caused him to lose his all, and he left his home, and went to Boston, where he worked at his trade, of a joiner, and was employed in constructing the first lock on the canal through Medway. Thence he went to Providence R. I. There he made the model of a nail machine known as the "Odiorne Tool." Leaving Providence, he moved to West Bridgewater, Mass., and there commenced making patterns for a machine for four-penny nails, to be propelled by the foot, which made sixty-two nails per minute. This was in 1803. His old partners now joining him again, machines for four-penny and six-penny nails were made, and set up in Plymouth.

In 1805 or 1806, the machine known as the "Odiorne Tool," was patented, which was sold to the Messrs. Odiorne in 1806, and Mr. Reed moved to Kingston.

It was about this time, that his machine for pulverizing dye-woods was invented, for Messrs. Barrett & Shattuck, of Malden, Silk Dyers. Letters patent for this invention were obtained in 1807.

Soon after this, the machine known as the "Reed Tool," for the manufacture of *nails*, was invented; and whilst in Hanover, his *tack machines* were invented, and put into operation. He likewise worked, for a time, on a *high pressure steam engine*, but soon abandoned it.

Disposing of his first privilege, in Hanover, he moved to one near Rocky Run, where he erected works, and conveyed water to his wheel through a trough one third of a mile long; but the difficulties encountered here were such, that he finally sold out entirely, and moved to Marshfield, where he has since resided.

His later inventions, are machines for steering vessels; different patterns of pumps; cotton gins; treenail machines, &c. In all, he has obtained patents on from twenty to thirty different machines in his day, many of which are of great importance to the community; and every house builder has the benefit of his ingenuity.

Mr. Reed is a man of indefatigable industry, and of indomitable perseverance. He has made and lost several fortunes in his day. Free and generous in his manners, he is not one who hoards all his gains, to increase his own stores; but considers himself as a public servant, and expends, on new inventions, the fruits of his previous toils. Thus, in his old age, not a *millionaire*, resting from his labors, he is still at work, with a mind as active and vigorous as ever.

On King-street, the "Drinkwater Iron Works," or "Mighill's Works," were erected, about the year 1710. The early history of these works is involved in some obscurity. Tradition says, that during the Revolution, *cannon* were cast here, and carried down by the old fulling mill, near where Barker's foundry now stands, for trial; and Tilson Gould was killed by the bursting of one of the guns, the pieces of which are said to be yet lying on the bottom of the old furnace pond.

About the year 1816, Charles Josselynn, Oren Josselynn, Timothy Rose, Calvin Bates, and others, erected a forge on the dam, and the works are now owned and improved by Messrs. Bates and Holmes,—the latter gentleman being the agent. Besides the forge, there are on the dam a saw mill, a grist mill, a box board mill, and a shingle mill, owned by the same company.

We learn from Mr. Bates, that five hands are usually employed in the forge, and from fifty to sixty tons of anchors, with wrought iron bars, &c., are made at the works.

The three forges above-named,—viz: those of George Curtis, John Silvester, and Messrs. Bates and Holmes, are old establishments,—among the oldest in Plymouth County;—and, by a glance at the dates given, it will be seen that the town of Hanover may justly claim to have borne its part in this highly useful branch of industry; and these works have not only added to the wealth, but to the prosperity of the town, and the promotion of its outward interests.

To the eastward of the works of Messrs. Bates and Holmes stands the foundry of Mr. Joshua Barker, erected about the year 1830, at which stoves, hollow-ware, and machinery of different kinds are cast.

An old fulling mill formerly stood near this spot, improved, many years ago, by Messrs. Bailey, Hatch, and others.

The tack works of Mr. Samuel Salmond, are on the Third Herring Brook, and at the spot where the "Stockbridge mill" formerly stood. This mill was erected as early as 1677, by Charles Stockbridge; it descended to his sons; and, in 1692, Thomas Stockbridge sold one-half of the mill to John Bryant, and Samuel Stetson. In 1729, Thomas Stockbridge, son of the first Thomas, sold "one-fourth of the saw-mill" to *Jonah* Stetson, whence the name of *Jonah's Mill;* Samuel Stetson having sold his fourth of the "corn mill," to the said Jonah Stetson, in 1726.

The mill was afterwards the property of Recompense Tiffany, and was called the Tiffany mill.

Tack works were erected on the premises about 1830, and were conducted, for some years, by Capt. Zephaniah Talbot, and by John, and William, brothers of Mr. Samuel Salmond. The latter gentleman has conducted the works since 1838, uses about sixty tons of tack plates per year, employs fifteen male hands, and five females, and runs from twenty to twenty-five machines.

Tolman's mills are near Winslow's bridge, on the Third Herring Brook, but the proprietor is a resident of Scituate.

The tack business was commenced in Hanover at an early date, and tack machines were invented here by Col. Reed; so that we feel as if our town could claim some credit on the score of useful inventions, and the successful prosecution of the branch of industry opened by these inventions.

SAW AND GRIST MILLS.

We cannot devote much space to the history of the saw and grist mills in the town.

Eliab's mill, so called, or the Studley mill, stood on Pleasant street, and the site is now occupied by the shingle mill of Mr. Nahum Stetson. The privilege has been improved since the middle of the last century.

Tradition says, that an old saw mill formerly stood near Ellis' bridge, which was burnt by the Indians in 1676, and the erection of a new mill on the spot, at whose raising *cold water*, instead of *spirituous liquors*, was furnished as a beverage, gave rise to to the term "Drinkwater," so frequently occurring on the Town records.

As early as 1723, a saw mill was erected on Curtis street, where the mill of Deacon John Brooks now stands. The latter mill was erected in 1851, and is the third which has stood on the dam. Mr. Brooks has been connected with this mill for seventeen years, and saws, on an average, from eighty to one hundred thousand feet of inch and half-inch pine boards, annually, besides pine and oak plank, joist, and timber.

In the woods, west of the mill of Mr. John Brooks, stands the shingle and box board mill, built by Joseph Brooks, about 1820, and which was occupied as a grist mill until 1833. Here, the iron work of Mr. Prouty's ploughs was polished. Cedar and pine shingles are now sawed,—the material being obtained from the forests of Hanover, and the adjoining towns.

An old grist mill formerly stood on North street, where the *brook* crosses the street, at the bridge, and was owned, many years ago, by Caleb Mann. It was built by his father, Benjamin Mann, and was an old-fashioned mill, with a large wheel, requiring a great quantity of water to turn it.

The mill of the Messrs. Jacobs, stands on the Third Herring Brook, and is on the bounds of Hanover and South Scituate,—the saw mill being in South Scituate. This was erected, probably, about the year 1700.

The old Curtis mill, also on the Third Herring Brook, is now in the possession of T. J. Gardner, Esq., and was erected about the year 1692.

The Clapp mills, are also on the Third Herring Brook, not far from Mr. Gardner's, but belong to South Scituate, as does the mill of Mr. Gardner. Large quantities of lumber are sawed at all these mills, annually, for the trunk and box factories in South Scituate and Hanover, and for building purposes.

A small grist mill was early erected by the Curtis family, on Hugh's Cross, now Silver Brook, and is yet standing, though but little used.

The late saw mill of Messrs. Cobb & Cushing, burnt in 1852, stood near Teague's Bridge, in Hanson, and was formerly known as Hatch's mill.

PLOUGH BUSINESS.

About the year 1811, Mr. David Prouty, a native of Scituate, came to Hanover, settled on the place which had been owned by Mr. Thomas Hatch, and lived in the house built by Mr. H. Here he found a farm, rough, and hard to cultivate, especially to one in his feeble health. In connexion with his farm, he opened a store, and, with his trading, joined the business of weaving cotton cloth. This cloth was made from yarn obtained at the factories in Dedham, Dorchester, and Marshfield, and was put out by Mr. Prouty to females in his neighborhood; furnishing, to a large number, a source of steady, and, for a season, profitable income. This business was continued, until the system of weaving by power-looms was introduced, which caused hand-weaving to be soon abandoned.

Mr. P. was then, for about two years, engaged in manufacturing black morocco shoes, with Major Wm. Morse; which he pursued with his usual zeal and earnestness. The business, however, was not conducted by him very extensively,—but six hands being employed in the shop;—and, on its relinquishment, we find him contemplating a visit to New York State, with a view to a permanent settlement. Whilst in that State, his attention was called to the ploughs used by agriculturists at that date; and though we cannot confidently say, that he was the *first inventor* of the cast iron ploughs, which have since given to his name a world-wide celebrity, yet patents were early obtained by him for their manufacture, on principles whose discovery must be attributed to him;—he was a *pioneer* in the business;—and, to the close of his useful life, he gave all his energies to its prosecution, and his efforts were crowned with a success, not only gratifying to him personally, but eminently beneficial to the community, reflecting honor upon his genius, and attesting the fertility of his resources.

At the time Mr. Prouty commenced the manufacture of the ploughs which still bear his name, the implements then in use by farmers, were of a far different stamp from those seen at the present day, as may be seen from the annexed cuts. That part of the instrument which performs the labor, was of wood, strapped with iron bars; and the form and durability were far below the

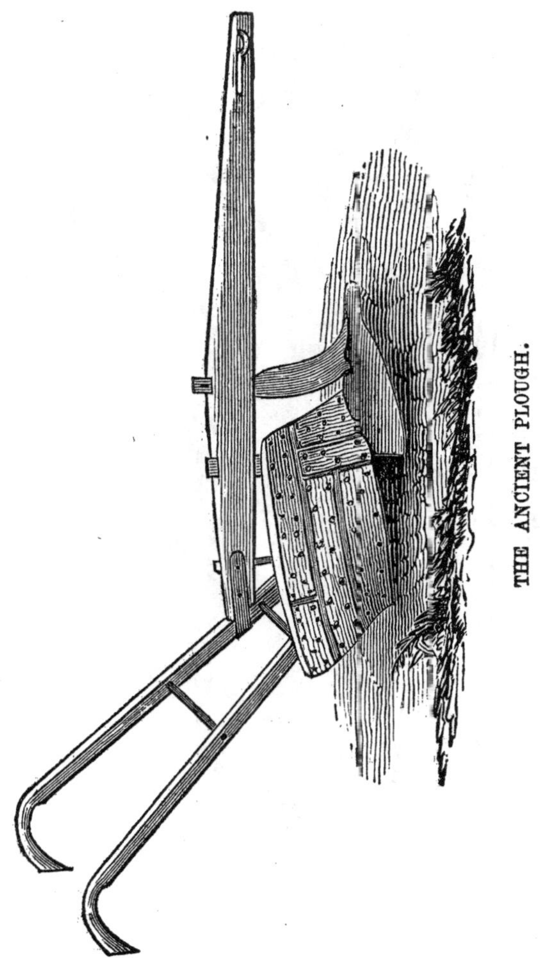

THE ANCIENT PLOUGH.

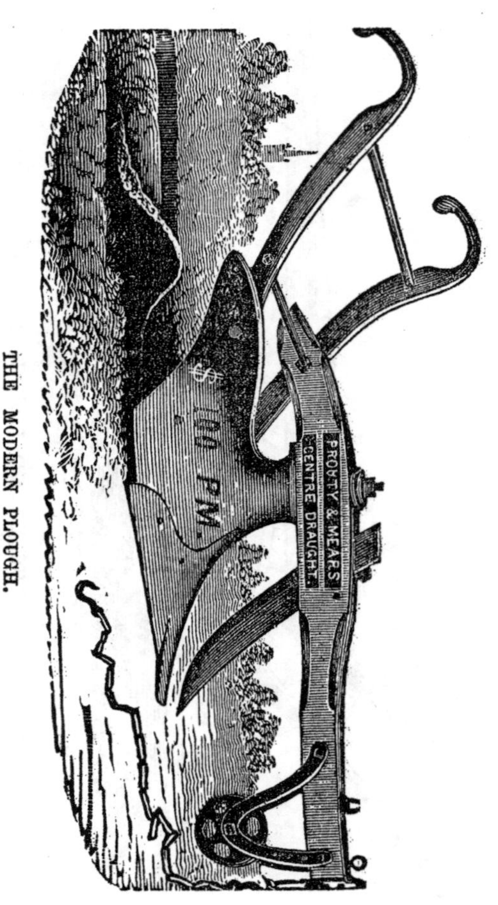

THE MODERN PLOUGH.

ploughs of Mr. Prouty's construction. But it was no easy matter for him, at the outset, to convince the public of the superior value of his invention. He had not only hereditary prejudices to encounter ;—that spirit of conservatism, too much of which still exists among the yeomanry of New England,—but also the idea which prevailed, that *pot metal,* as it was termed, was too brittle a substance to stand the rough use to which the plough is subjected. But, by practical demonstrations of the strength of his implements, he silenced this objection, and vanquished those prejudices.

Deacon John Brooks, of Hanover, well recollects when the first plough made by Mr. P. was put in operation. It was taken to a gravel knoll, on the highway, near the present residence of Mr. Samuel Brooks, Main Street, and many were the prophecies, that as soon as the oxen were attached, and an attempt was made to break up the almost impenetrable surface, it would at once be shattered, and found worthless. But Mr. P., who had all confidence in his success, held the plough himself, guided its operations, and, as the team moved on, and the furrows were turned, the prophecies of failure, vanished as the dew before the morning sun.

Not long after, as a farther test of their strength, Mr. P. caused one of his ploughs to be taken to a piece of land on Walnut street, almost covered with rocks; and here, it was freely prophesied, that his instrument would be broken ;—but here, as before, it worked admirably, and the triumph of Mr. P. was final and complete.

The establishment of Mr. Prouty, in Hanover, was not on so extensive a scale, as was that conducted by him subsequent to his removal from the town. About one thousand ploughs, per year, were made, and from three to four hands employed in the shop. There was a blacksmith's shop attached to his premises, also a building in which was machinery for sawing plough beams, &c., by horse-power.

Mr. Prouty left Hanover about the year 1838, and established himself in Boston, where, in company, with Mr. John Mears, and Mr. Lorenzo Prouty, and under the firm of Prouty and Mears, the business of manufacturing ploughs, and other agricultural implements, was carried on until the decease of Mr. Prouty, and is now conducted by Mr. Lorenzo Prouty, and Mr. John Mears, jr., at their extensive warehouses, on North Market, and Clinton streets.

It would be agreeable to us, did our limits permit, to quote a few of the many testimonials which have been published, in favor of the value and excellence of Mr. Prouty's ploughs, and the importance of his invention to the agricultural community. Not only at most of the Fairs in the different Counties of Massachusetts, have premiums been awarded, but similiar premiums have been bestowed at the Fairs of other States, and even at the World's Fair. Indeed, the fame of the inventor has spread farther than that of many a warrior, and many a statesman; and it will endure so long as the community can appreciate the worth of those who have been the benefactors of the laboring classes.

The light in which his invention has been viewed by practical farmers, may be seen from the following note, from the pen of the lamented Elias Phinney.

LEXINGTON, Mass., February 25th, 1846.

To Mr. James Pedder,

Dear Sir: — You ask my opinion of the "CENTRE DRAUGHT PLOUGH." I give it freely, and in few words. If my opinion of its merits, will, in any measure induce my brother Farmers to adopt this, in preference to any other plough now in use, I shall feel that I have rendered an important service to the public, and, at the same time, contributed my share toward the discharge of the debt of gratitude due to the Inven tor of this invaluable improvement, in an implement of so great importance to Agriculture.

I have, for twenty-five years past, personally superintended my own estate, part of which I have annually had under the plough. I have tried English, Scotch, and every variety of American ploughs, and presume I shall be excused for saying, that I consider myself a competent judge of their relative value in the hands of farmers. The application of the "Centre-Draught" principle to the plough, by Messrs. Prouty & Mears, is, unquestionably, the greatest improvement that has been made in the Implement since its first invention. The remedy for the long existing evil of having the whole resistance *on one side* of the line of draught, and the necessity of placing the centre of resistance exactly *on the line of draught*, first suggested itself to the philosophical mind of DAVID PROUTY.

Mr. Prouty was a practical farmer. He saw the objections to the old-fashioned plough—his ingenious mind set about devising means, whereby the power of draught might be greatly lessened, the liability to wear, in certain parts more than others obviated, the labor of managing greatly diminished, and, at the same time, doing the work infinitely better; and well has he done it. And when his improvement shall be generally adopted by farmers, and its merits justly appreciated, Mr. Prouty will be ranked among the greatest benefactors of his age. And although some of his contemporaries may injure him by unjustly interfering with his rights, and appropriating to themselves some of the fruits of his ingenuity—they can never rob him of his well-earned fame—Posterity will do justice to his memory. And the approbation and magnificent testimonial of one of the most powerful and enlightened Monarchs of Europe, is but a foretaste of what he may expect from his own countrymen, when the merits of his invention shall be rightly appreciated.

I am aware that my strong convictions of the vast utility to farmers of this improvement in the Plough, may lead me—in the minds of some—to speak in extravagant terms of the merits of the Inventor. But you have known Mr. Prouty; you have been familiar with the operations, and can fully appreciate the benefits of his invention; and by you, I presume, I shall not be charged with bestowing unmerited praise, in saying, that if the farmers of his own state should appropriate to that object, but a *single tithe* of what this improvement in the Plough has saved them, in the cultivation and better condition of their farms, it would raise a monument to his memory, which would not be transcended in beauty, in grandeur and durability, by any that have been erected to the memory of the greatest benefactors of mankind.

With great respect,

I am, my dear sir,

Very truly and sincerly yours,

E. PHINNEY.

Mr. Prouty is remembered, in Hanover, with much respect, by those best acquainted with him; and probably few have done more for the prosperity of the town, and the advancement of its interest, than did that gentleman, whilst he resided here.

OTHER BRANCHES OF INDUSTRY.

Of the other branches of industry in the town, we shall be obliged to speak briefly.

The carriage manufactory of Mr. Thomas Turner, is on Broadway, who conducts this business in all its branches; the wood work, iron work, painting, trimming, and even harness-making, being all done on his premises. His buildings were erected in 1850, at which date Mr. Turner came to Hanover from South Boston, where he had been previously engaged in the same calling. He employs ten hands, and builds about forty carriages per year.

On Washington street, stands the wheelwright shop of Mr. Robert Eells, and near it, the blacksmith shop of Mr. Warren Wright.

On the easterly side of the street, is the shop of Mr. John P. Eells, who is a painter by trade.

At the corner of Broadway and Washington streets, is the carriage trimming shop of Mr. Henry Chandler.

In this vicinity, there were formerly several blacksmiths shops, when ship building was in its prime, conducted by Robert L., Robert, and Joseph Eells, and by the Dillinghams, and others.

Mr. Haynes, a few years since, had a harness manufactory, in Wood & Torrey's store.

In the days when there were no *carriages* owned here, the *saddle* business was a prominent branch of enterprise, and was conducted by Benjamin Stockbridge, at the Four Corners, and by the family of Estes, on what is now Plain street, and perhaps by others.

There have been many blacksmiths shops scattered around in the town, at different periods, on Washington street, Centre street, Broadway, Main street, &c. The only ones now in operation, besides Mr. Wright's, are Mr. McFarland's, at Snappet, and Mr. Judson Bates', on Centre street.

We have heard John Jacobs, Walter Rogers, Lemuel Curtis, Joshua and Elisha Simmons, Benjamin Stetson, Bela Mann, Charles Mann, Ezekiel Hatch, and Richard Estes, named as blacksmiths in years past; and there were probably many others, whose names we have not learned.

Of traders, we have had many; and we dare not attempt to give the names of all who have engaged in trade. The principal establishments, at present in the town, are the Messrs. Blanchards, at Snappet; and John B. Bates, Isaac M. Wilder, and Stephen Josselynn, at the Four Corners. Messrs. Wood & Torrey, have just relinquished the business conducted by them for many years.

Mr. Josselynn, and the Messrs. Blanchards, are extensively engaged in the manufacture of shoes, and this is one of the prominent branches of industry in the town; a large number of males being engaged in making boots and shoes.

Mr. Edward Y. Perry recently had a store on Broadway, near Silvester's Forge, which is now occupied by Mr. Howland.

Formerly, the clock and watch making business was conducted by John Bailey, and Calvin Bailey, on Curtis, now Main street, and at the Four Corners;—also by David Studley, and by Benjamin D. Torrey. There is now nothing done here at this business. The Messrs. Bailey, as well as the others, were ingenious workmen; and there are still to be found, in several houses, the large, old-fashioned, eight-day clocks, with a "full moon" on the face, made by "John Bailey."

The town has had the usual complement of carpenters, masons, &c., and there are several yet engaged in these branches.

The tannery of Messrs. Seth and Edwin Rose, is on Hanover street; and that of Mr. William Church is on the same street;—the former at the westerly, and the latter at the easterly part of the street. Mr. Simeon Curtis had tan-works some years ago, on Silver street, the old *pits* being yet visible.

Messrs. Daly & Co. have a tailor's shop at the Four Corners; and there is a stove shop on Broadway, in the old Academy building.

The only tavern now in operation, is that that of Mr. Joseph Pocorny, at the Four Corners.

In former years, when spirituous liquors were freely used and sold, taverns were common; so much so, that as early as 1747, the town "voted not to set up any more taverns"; and also "voted that there is too many taverns in town already"; and "voted that one tavern is sufficient for this town." We have never heard of *breweries* or *distilleries* in the town.

Bricks were made sixty years ago, at Walnut Hill. Mr. Joseph Sylvester is engaged in the manufacture of soap, on Broadway.

We dare not affirm that the foregoing sketch is complete. On the contrary, we doubt not some omissions will be discovered; but these, we trust, will be attributed, not to intentional neglect on the author's part, but to his limited knowledge, and the difficulty of obtaining information concerning the past.

CHAPTER XI.

SHIP BUILDING.

"To mark the ship in floating balance held,
By earth attracted and by seas repelled;
Or point her devious track thro' climes unknown,
That leads to every shore and every zone." FALCONER.

Former and present state of the art of Ship-building in America — Materials for the construction of vessels — Massachusetts Enterprise — Ship-building on the North River — Yards in Pembroke — Yards in Hanover — The Barstows, Sylvesters, Sampsons, Clarks, Perrys, Eells, Paiges, Baileys, Smiths, Kingmans, Wings, Stockbridges, &c. — Obstructions in the River — Petitions to Congress for their removal — Decline of the business — Present condition of the village.

The history of ship-building in New England, could it be faithfully written, would present to us memorable instances of the triumphs of genius over contending obstacles, and striking proofs of the degree of perfection to which this art, which, two centuries ago, was but in its infancy, has been carried by the persevering skill, and industrious application, of the Anglo-Saxon race.

Compare the pictures of the small, ill-shaped, and clumsily-rigged vessels, which bore the Pilgrim Fathers to this land in 1620,[1] with those sumptuously furnished, and palace-like "ocean monarchs,"—faultless models of beauty and elegance,—of from sixteen hundred to two thousand tons burthen, which may be seen in all the great harbors of our country, spreading their sails to every breeze, and conveying our hardy sailors to the Polar Circle, in pursuit of the whale, or to the East Indies, and the ports of Europe, swelling our commerce, increasing our comforts, and augmenting our wealth.

If OLD ENGLAND is "mistress of the seas," in the weight of her armament, and the amount of her shipping, she must yield the palm to NEW ENGLAND, in excellence of structure, beauty of finish, exquisiteness of proportion, and those fast sailing properties which have already borne off the prize for NEW YORK on the theatre of the WORLD'S FAIR, held in her own metropolis, and on the waters of the seas washing her own shores!

The facilitiés for procuring materials for the construction of vessels of the largest class, from the forests of this State, are not so great as formerly. The giant oaks, which once spread their shadows over the land, have almost entirely disappeared. In the western counties they are most abundant.

Yet, for centuries to come, so extended is our republic, and so expansive are its resources, American skill will continue to compete with the most enterprising of the Old World, and the superiority of our naval architecture, already acknowledged and felt, will not soon be cast into the shade, or suffered to diminish.

The oaks and pines in the forests of Michigan, and all over the Western States, and even upon the Pacific Coast, will furnish a supply for generations to come; and when our iron-arms, Briareus-like, shall be spread out to embrace the whole of those now distant regions, the rich harvest, which has been accumulating for ages, will pour in its treasures upon us, to stimulate to higher attainments and prouder triumphs.

Massachusetts, one of the earliest settled of the New England States, has ever borne her part in the promotion of our country's prosperity. Her citizens, some of whom are in the ship yards of

1. See the Wood-cut annexed.

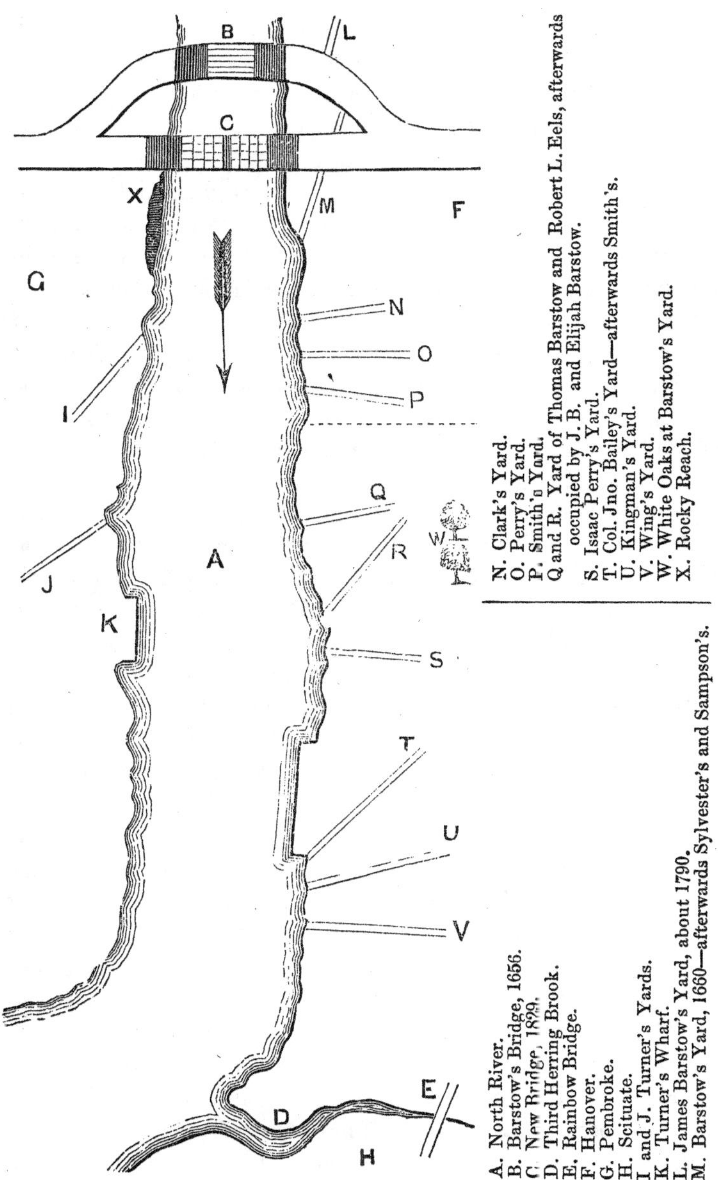
B
L
C
X
M
F
G
N
O
P
I
Q
W
R
A
J
K
S
T
U
V
E
D
H
A. North River.
B. Barstow's Bridge, 1656.
C. New Bridge, 1829.
D. Third Herring Brook.
E. Rainbow Bridge.
F. Hanover.
G. Pembroke.
H. Scituate.
I and J. Turner's Yards.
K. Turner's Wharf.
L. James Barstow's Yard, about 1790.
M. Barstow's Yard, 1660—afterwards Sylvester's and Sampson's.
N. Clark's Yard.
O. Perry's Yard.
P. Smith's Yard.
Q and R. Yard of Thomas Barstow and Robert L. Eels, afterwards occupied by J. B. and Elijah Barstow.
S. Isaac Perry's Yard.
T. Col. Jno. Bailey's Yard—afterwards Smith's.
U. Kingman's Yard.
V. Wing's Yard.
W. White Oaks at Barstow's Yard.
X. Rocky Reach.

Maine, and New Hampshire, and others peopling the prairies of the Mississippi Valley, and the shores of the Pacific, carry with them those habits of industry and thrift, for which she has ever been famed, and maintain her ancient power, and present dignity, unstained, wherever they are found.

Here has been educated an army of shipwrights; and, when business has been wanting at home, they have scattered abroad, and are the principal mechanics at many of the yards where shipbuilding is largely conducted, along the Atlantic sea-board.

The North River, in Plymouth County, which forms the boundary between Hanover and Scituate, on the one side, and Pembroke and Marshfield, on the other, is a comparatively small stream, not over twenty miles in length, never with a great depth of water, but a few rods in breadth, and very tortuous in its course, with shoals at the bends, and sand bars at its mouth. Standing on the bridge, beyond the Four Corners, and looking first above, and then below, as far as the eye can reach, and noting the quietness which seems usually to reign over the spot; or walking along the banks of the stream, across the fairy-like bridge of plank, worn by the tread of human feet for many years, and spanning the Third Herring Brook, which, from its shape, is expressively called the RAINBOW BRIDGE;—and thence over Fox Hill, and past where Seabury's point stretches off to the right, until the old Brick-kilns appear in sight; one, who did not know what busy scenes had been enacted here in past times, would hardly imagine that, from 1660 to 1835, or for more than a century and a half, the business of ship-building was carried on, probably to a greater extent, than on any other river, of the same size, anywhere in the State! Not only on the Hanover side, were the yards compacted together, in close proximity one to another, but on the Pembroke side, below Rocky Reach, and at Seabury's point, yards were established by George and Thomas Turner, and Nathaniel Cushing; and, on the banks of the stream, near the "reach," by the bridge, the indentation, or hollow, where the *saw pit* stood, is distinctly visible, and the old wharf yet projects its rocky piers into the stream below.

On the Hanover side, before the present bridge was built, shipyards existed, above and below the old bridge. The banks of the stream here, for some distance, present peculiar facilities for this business, being sloping, and somewhat abrupt, though not precipitous; so that, whilst the *bows* of the vessels were near the water, the *sterns* were on the hill sides, and easy of access by the aid of a few plank, without the necessity for those lofty stagings which are indispensable in many yards.

From the top of these banks, stretches back a large tract of rough, rocky, pasture land, also easy of access from the travelled ways, where timber was landed, brought from the surrounding country, in such quantity, that the whole surface of the tract was covered at times.

Above the old bridge, on the Hanover side, is a small ravine, or gorge, on the land of Seth Barker, Esq., just wide enough to admit the hulk of one of the small craft built in those days, and sloping towards the river, at such an angle as to afford a fine opportunity for launching, were it not for the bridge. The site is visible from the present bridge, being but a few rods above; and the scenery around has that wildness of aspect, which renders it quite romantic. Here, James Barstow built one vessel, previous to the Revolution, which, it is said, was launched directly across the road. But the existence of the bridge presented too formidable an obstacle, to encourage the building of many vessels at this spot; and the yard, accordingly, was soon abandoned.

Just below the old bridge, and in the space intervening between its piers, and the piers of the present bridge, was another ship yard, first improved by William Barstow, and his descendants for two generations. It was, probably, established near the year 1660. The vessels built at this yard, by the Barstows, were mostly small ones, and their sides rose higher than the piers of the present bridge, their bows reaching up the bank into the door yard of the present residence of Mr. Barker. It is said that the Barstows abandoned this yard, because of the difficulty experienced in launching their vessels, in consequence of their impinging frequently against the rocky ledge, on the opposite shore.

After they left the yard, about 1745, it was improved for a period of from twenty to thirty years, by Nathaniel Silvester, familiarly known as "builder Silvester," who was born in 1718, and died in 1781, at the age of sixty-three. He built the house occupied by Rufus Farnum, on Washington street, just above Mr. Barker's, and nearly opposite Mr. Sylvanus Percival's.

His son, Nathaniel, afterwards occupied the house, and improved the ship yard, until his removal to Winchendon. The vessels built, both by father and son, were small, seldom exceeding two hundred tons burthen, and were mostly schooners.

After the Silvesters, the yard was improved by Jonathan Sampson, from 1795 to 1820, he residing in Pembroke, just over the bridge, on the hill, in the house now occupied by Sumner Stetson, which has been a tavern stand.

Mr. Sampson built many vessels for the Cod Fishery at the Grand Banks; and some ships, of from two hundred and fifty to three hundred tons burthen, for residents of Duxbury and Cape Cod, for citizens of Boston, and for Nathaniel Cushing, of Hanson. These ships were for the Southern trade, for the West Indies, and for different ports in Europe; and their stern-posts, it is said, stood quite up to the old road, and some of the staging, for building the projecting part of the stern, was actually over the road, which, at this place, was but about two and one-half rods wide.

The yard next below, and close by the present bridge, was improved by the Clarks,—Nathaniel and Belcher,—sons of John Clark, of Scituate. The former, Nathaniel, lived on Washington street, in the low and ancient building now occupied by Mr. Henry Bates, and died in 1814, aged seventy-three. The latter, Belcher, lived in a house which stood where stands that of Mr. Samuel Salmond, and died in 1826, aged eighty-four. The yard improved by these brothers, is said to have been occupied by their father before them. It was probably established as early as 1736, but no vessels were built there after the year 1800. Zebulon, the son of Belcher, born in 1780, recollects when his father built, while he was a lad.

The next yard, a small one, was mproved for a time by Dea. Isaac Perry; but seems not to have been occupied by him long, as we subsequently find him building at a yard farther down the stream.

Mr. Perry is spoken of as a man of unblemished integrity, and of high moral excellence. He was born in 1736, and died in 1825, at the age of eighty-nine. He lived on Washington street, and his house stood where stands that of Mr. Josiah Winslow, near the corner of Hanover street.

The next yard was at a little distance farther down, and its site is marked by a work-house, yet standing, and by two gigantic oaks, of venerable appearance, at least three centuries old, which were, of course, of goodly size when the Pilgrims landed! Against these trees, still lean the logs, forming the frame work of the old saw pit, and around the spot is a vast deposite of decaying vegetable matter, accumulated in the yard, black, spongy, and apparently valuable for the compost-heap, which might be profitably carried off to add its enriching materials to the stercorary of the owner of the land.

This yard was improved by Thomas Barstow, the father of Col. John B. Barstow, of this town; and by Capt. Robert Lenthal Eells, who was an extensive landholder; one of the wealthiest citizens of his day; a man whose chief greatness consisted in the greatness of his soul; of unbounded hospitality; charitable; kind to the poor and the suffering; devoted to every thing public spirited; eminently patriotic; an able officer in the war of the Revolution; who opened his doors cheerfully and widely to all who were engaged in that struggle; and whose daughters, evinced their zeal for Liberty, in ministering to the wants of the soldiers, and in manufacturing cartridges for the use of the companies enrolled in the town.

This yard, which was established about the year 1755, was improved by Messrs. Barstow and Eells, for about thirty years; the former having the superintendence of the wood work, and the latter furnishing the iron work,—his blacksmith shop standing near the hay scales, by the Four Corners.

No very large vessels were built by this firm, as previous to the Revolution, the burthen seldom exceeded two hundred tons; but after that period, and especially after the opening of the present century, by their descendants, and by others, vessels of from three hundred to four hundred tons burthen were built, from 1810 to 1834.

Mr. Barstow died in 1797, aged sixty-five; and Mr. Eells in 1800, aged sixty-eight;—both being born in the same year, 1732; and in the same month, Februray;—the former on the 27th, and the latter the 17th! Companions in life, and cousins, they dwelt in harmony, and their business was conducted successfully and prosperously.

A few years previous to the death of Mr. Barstow, his son, John B., was concerned in ship-building at this yard, with his father; in which business he was afterwards joined by his brother Elijah, and they, together, improved the yard, until 1817, when they went to a site still farther below, which presented greater facilities for launching. This firm built many ships for Nantucket and New Bedford, for the whaling business, of from 300 to 350 tons burthen; also many merchant ships, among which were five, built for the sons of John B. Barstow, who were at that time in business in the city of New York.

Next to the yard of the Barstow's, was one called Paige's yard, which was afterwards occupied by Dea. Isaac Perry, and occasionally by Albert and Josiah Smith, when they had a small vessel to build, and when their other yard was occupied.

Next below, was the yard of Col. John Bailey, whose master workman was Joseph House. This yard was not long improved by Mr. B., he being personally engaged in other business; and it was afterwards occupied by Albert and Josiah Smith, sons of Josiah Smith, of Pembroke, who married sisters, — daughters of Capt. Robert L. Eells, himself a blacksmith by trade, but a ship-builder in connection with Thomas Barstow.

Capt. Albert Smith, in early life, followed the seas, as a ship-master, being in the Baltimore trade for some time, and making several voyages to Russia, during the reign of the Emperor Paul.

About the year 1790, he settled in Hanover, residing on Broadway, in the house now occupied by Martin Stetson, which he bought of Joseph Josselynn; and, forming a partnership with his brother Josiah, he carried on the business of ship-building for about ten years, from 1798 to 1808, fitting for sea, on an average, three vessels a year, of from 300 to 400 tons burthen, for himself and others, for Liverpool and other European ports. The descendants of Capt. Smith are now in the service of the United States; his oldest son, Joseph, being a Commodore in the United States Navy, and Chief of the Bureau of Docks and Yards; and Albert, Esq., being an eminent lawyer in Washington city.

After the Smiths, Edward and Samuel Eells built a few vessels at this yard; and subsequently, it was improved by John B. and Elijah Barstow, from 1817 to 1835; and then by Elijah Barstow, Jr.; the latter of whom, in connection with Capt. Thomas Waterman, is still engaged in the business, at their yard in Scituate, below Fox hill.

The last yard, on the Hanover side, was that of David Kingman, who built the tavern stand at the Four Corners, now occupied by Mr. Joseph Pocorny. Isaiah Wing built one vessel, very near this yard, about the time of the last war; and also Benjamin and Martin Stockbridge. Dea. Perry built one vessel at this yard, about 55 years ago; — a ship of some 300 tons burthen.

Nearly all the above yards were on the land of Mr. Benjamin Stockbridge, and were comprised within the space of *one third of a mile* from the bridge; from which their compactness and juxtaposition, may be easily judged.

Previous to the year 1795, the business demand was principally for vessels of a small size, such as could be easily launched on the river, and taken down the stream without much difficulty, from the bars. During the Revolution, Mr. Thomas Barstow built several small privateers,—some for Mr. Derby, of Salem. Towards the close of the last century, vessels of a larger size were in demand, besides the small fishing and coasting vessels; and this call continued, until business was suspended by the war with Great Britain, in 1812.

The occurrence of that war, just as the business was in its most prosperous state, was a serious shock to those who were engaged in it; but they re-commenced in 1815, after peace was declared; though the growing scarcity of timber, and the obstruction of the channel of the river with rocks and sand bars, which rendered it tedious and expensive to get large ships down the stream, and over the bar at the mouth, caused the business to decline, until now, in Hanover, it has entirely ceased. The process of moving large ships, was by attaching the scows called *gundaloes*, (a corruption of gondolas ?) two to the stern, and two to the stem; which were lashed down at low water, so as to lift the ship as the tide flowed.

Several attempts have been made to obtain aid from the National Government, for the improvement of the navigation of the North River; but hitherto, with but little success. In 1839, Col. J. B. Barstow, Joseph S. Bates, and Elijah Barstow, jr., were chosen a committee to petition for the appropriation of a small sum "for the purpose of removing sand-bars, and cutting a channel for the North River into Massachusetts Bay;" but their prayer was not favorably answered.

During the great storm of April 16th and 17th, 1851, the sea broke completely over the narrow strip of beach between the third and fourth cliffs, near Scituate harbor, at the very point where the cutting of a canal has been thought feasible.

A new petition for aid has been circulated within the past year; but we fear its fate will be like that of its predecessors.

The palmy days of ship-building, in Hanover, were from 1800, to 1808. Then, five or six yards were in active operation, and at least ten vessels were annually fitted for sea. The scene on the North River, was one of animation and industry. Every morning, the carpenters might be seen, crossing the pastures, or walking along the river bank, or over the tiny "Rainbow Bridge," to the place of their daily toil; and the stroke of the axe, the thump of the maul, the cheerful calls, and the various other sounds always heard in the ship-yard, constantly saluted the ears of the passers by.

The pasture, too, was strewed with timber; and teams of "fat oxen," daily brought in, from the forests around, their loads of round, or rough-hewn, white oak, beech, maple, and other timber; and oak and pine plank, for sheathing, and for the decks, &c. Then, business was stirring. All were active. And never since, has the village, at the corners, presented so cheering a spectacle of thrift and prosperity. That village is beginning to rise again; and though the character of its business has changed, yet the promise is fair, that ere long, if a liberal policy prevails, it will become, once more, a place of activity, and the number of its buildings, and the advantanges of its citizens, be greatly increased.

CHAPTER XII.

PROVISIONS FOR THE POOR — TEMPERANCE CAUSE — SLAVERY — RESTING PLACES FOR THE DEAD — LONGEVITY.

"Epitomise the life; pronounce, you can,
Authentic epitaphs on some of these,
Who, from their lowly mansions hither brought,
Beneath this turf lie mouldering at our feet.
So by your records, may our doubts be solved;
And so, not searching higher, we may learn
To prize the breath we share with human kind,
And look upon the dust of man with awe."

WORDSWORTH.

Provisions for the Poor — Poor kept by Friends — Selectmen to provide for them — Put out at Auction — Establishment of an Alms-House — Temperance Cause — Excise Bill of 1754 — Rum Trade at that Date — Extracts from the Church Records Relative to the Excise Bill — Temperance Society formed in 1816 — Later History of the Cause — Slavery in New England — Owners of Slaves, from the Church and Town Records — Touching Incident — Burial Ground near the Centre of the Town — Gifts of Land by David Stockbridge, Esq., and by John Barstow, Esq. — Burial Ground at Snappet — Table of Longevity.

WE group together, in this chapter, a few subjects, each of which merits some notice in a work like the present.

PROVISIONS FOR THE POOR.

For many years after the incorporation of the town, the *poor* were kept in the families of their friends, an annual appropriation being made for their maintenance. The number thus aided was small, so that no further provisions in their behalf were necessary, and no other arrangement could have been more generally acceptable to those whom misfortune had reduced to a state of dependence.

Oct. 29, 1736, "Voted to the widow Frances Josselynn £5 old tenor, to keep Jean Barron from Nov. 18, 1746, to Nov. 18, 1747, but if she should have any extraordinary sickness in that time, to be further allowed what is reasonable."

Mar. 5, 1750, "Voted to give Thomas Curtis 31s., old tenor, per week, for boarding Margaret Young one year in sickness and health, the town finding clothes, and paying Doctor's bills, if any there be; and he agreed to keep her at that price."

At the same date, "Voted £15 to Benjamin Woodworth, for bringing up John Loud's (or Ladd's) daughter to the age of 18 years; and £24 for bringing up the said Loud's youngest son to the age of 21 years."

This course continued to be followed even after the Revolution, and so late as the beginning of the present century; and to the selectmen was entrusted the general oversight of those thus aided, to see that they were properly cared for.

Thus, in 1782, the selectmen were instructed to provide for the poor, and to supply Job Long's family with the necessaries of life. March 13, 1786 :—The selectmen and Dea. Timothy Robbins were chosen a committee "to agree with Mr. Samuel Witherell, to maintain his father during his natural life, by the lump or by the week, as they shall agree, and pay him out of the town's money."

Oct. 17, 1796. The selectmen were instructed "to provide for the poor under their care, and call on the Treasurer for money as they shall want it."

About the year 1803, we find the first notice of a change in this mode of proceedure. The selectmen were then chosen a committee, to meet a committee of the town of Pembroke, "to consult on the expediency of building a work-house."

In 1809, a donation of $278, having been made to the town by Maj. John B. Barstow for the poor, he, with the selectmen, were chosen to distribute the same.

In 1814, it was "voted to raise $110, to purchase Mary Peterson's house and land for a poor house;" and the purchase was made,—but the town being dissatisfied, in 1816 the building was sold, and for the first time on the records, it was voted to put out the poor *at auction* to the lowest bidder; the auction to be at the Central Meeting House, on Wednesday, Jan. 31, at 4 P. M.; and the person bidding off the same was "to give good and sufficient security to the overseers of the poor that he will support them well, in sickness and in health, and furnish them with good and comfortable clothing, and pay all expenses for physicians, and to receive pay for the same at the end of the year."

But this policy, though adopted by many towns in Massachusetts, and quite common twenty-five years ago, was soon found to be exceedingly defective, and liable to serious evils. Enough allowance was not made for that principle or maxim, which prompts men, in business affairs, to trade sharply, and to make the most of their bargains, of whatever character they may be. We do not deem it necessary to revive the controversies which grew out of this system, which, notwithstanding its exceptionable features, continued to be followed for twenty years. We need only say that in 1836, it was voted to establish a Poor House, and a Committee of five, consisting of Ebenezer Simmons, Turner Stetson, Benjamin Mann, Levi Curtis, and William Morse, were chosen to look up a suitable farm; and in a very short time, the present establishment, located on Washington street, in the North-easterly part of the town, was purchased, which was formerly Nathaniel Jacobs' place,—and here the poor have since been kept in a manner creditable to the liberality and humanity of the Town. The expense of maintaining the poor is about $600 per annum, and the number supported for some years past, has been from eight to ten.

TEMPERANCE CAUSE.

It is well known to all conversant with the history of our country, that, until within a comparatively recent period, spirituous liquors were a common beverage of all classes in the community, and were freely sold and freely used in every town in this State. True, the evils attendant upon intemperance have been always felt, and always acknowledged; and efforts have been made, from time to time, to check the tide which threatened to overwhelm. But it is only within the past twenty or thirty years, that these efforts have been attended with any signal success. And even now, such is the selfishness of avarice on the one hand, and such are the cravings of appetite, on the other, that the temperance cause has attained but a measurable triumph, and much remains to be done, before every mind will be actuated by right motives, and brought under the influence of the laws of moral rectitude.

That great good has been accomplished, however, only those interested to perpetuate evil can deny. The evidences of improvement are too palpable to be mistaken. The thriftiness of our villages; the decrease of *native* pauperism; the general sobriety of the people; the absence of loungers at the bar-room of the tavern, or at the grocery on rainy days; and the rareness of the sight, especially in the country, and in the open highway, of men lying under the walls, sleeping away the effects of their deep potations; — all these are *tangible* proofs that *something* has been done; — proofs which none can gainsay; — and we trust the time is not far distant, when it will be deemed, throughout our land, beneath the dignity of any one claiming the attributes of humanity, to taste of the intoxicating cup; and when *reason* shall sit firmly on its throne, and all who are made in the image of God, shall stand erect in their manhood, not victims of passion, or slaves of appetite; but walking the earth in the exercise of those nobler qualities, which distinguish us from the brutes, and which ally us to angels.

Were we writing a treatise on temperance, much that is valuable in the history of the cause might be gathered from the Laws of Plymouth Colony, and from those of the Massachusetts Colony. But however interesting these extracts might be, we shall be obliged to omit them, inasmuch as we have enough from the records of our own town, and contemporary annals, to fill the space we propose to devote to this subject.

Although the law passed by the Legislature of Massachusetts, and called "the Maine Law," is regarded by some as a novel eature in human legislation, and an encroachment upon the *rights and liberties* of the people, yet laws embodying similar principles, or partaking of a similar character, were passed long ago, in this country.

In 1754, a bill called the "Excise bill," for "granting to his Majesty an excise upon wines and spirits distilled, &c.," was introduced, and taken into consideration by the people; and the town of Hanover, after debating it for some time, "Voted, that the said bill is disagreeable to the minds of the town, and Voted, that David Stockbridge, Esq., representative of said town, be desired to use his endeavors to prevent the said Bills passing into an Act."

The extent and character of the traffic in spirits at this time, and the course of argument by which the business was sustained, may be gathered from the following luminous and curious statement from Minot's History of Massachusetts, vol. 1, pp. 155–161.

"A great part of the inhabitants of Massachusetts Bay live chiefly by the sea, and are employed in

1. Fisheries. 2. Navigation. 3. Building and providing materials for ships.

By these employments, they depend upon Great Britain for

1. Clothes. 2. Materials for furnishing their houses of many kinds. 3. Cordage and sail cloth for equipment of their vessels. 4. Lines, hooks and cables, &c., for the fishery.

They are dependent on the northern Colonies for bread corn.

RUM is their chief manufacture; there being upwards of 15,000 hogsheads of rum manufactured in the Province annually.

This, with what they get from the English islands, is the grand support of all their trades and fishery; *and without which they can no longer subsist.*

Rum is a standing article in the Indian trade, and the common drink of all the

1. Laborers. 2. Timber-men. 3. Mast-men. 4. Loggers. 5. Fishermen in the Province.

These men could not endure the hardships of their employments nor the rigor of the seasons without it.

Rum is the merchandize principally made use of to procure

1. Corn. 2. Pork for, 1. Their fishermen, and 2. Other navigation.

The best and cheapest provision in this way of life!

This is done in winter, when there is no catching fish, nor any other employment for the fishermen.

Then, a great number of fishing vessels with their men, go to North Carolina, Virginia, Maryland, &c. These trade with rum and molasses for corn and pork, which serves for a supply for the next season.

Newfoundland has large annual supplies from Massachusetts Bay of rum, molasses, pork, &c., without which they could not carry on the fishery to so much advantage.

Halifax at present, and for some years at least, must depend on New England for a supply of those articles in order to carry on the fishery; which can only be done by coming at those commodities at a moderate price.

The rum carried from Massachusetts Bay, and the other northern Colonies to the coast of Guinea, is exchanged for *gold and slaves*. The gold is sent to London, to help pay for their annual supplies; and the slaves are carried to the English Sugar Colonies, and exchanged for their commodities, or sold for bills of exchange on Great Britain.

So that rum is useful in all their traffic, especially in supporting the fishery; not only as it is the common drink of persons in that business, but in being a means of employing the vessels and men at a season, when no other business can be carried on by them; and procuring provisions for their supplies, which otherwise they could not have but by their labor at the season proper for fishing.

From evidence in the cause, when before the lords of trade, it appeared that Jamaica at this time produced about 12,000 puncheons of rum, of 110 gallons each, per annum; Barbadoes 12,000; Antigua from 10,000 to 12,000; St. Christophers 6,000; Monsterrat 1,500; amounting in the whole to at least 41,500 puncheons, or 4,565,000 gallons ! ! !

But the excise bill was passed; and on the Church Records of Hanover for 1755, we find the following curious documents relating to the Act: —

" Hanover, Dec. 26, 1755. The following persons gave in their accounts, as follows, viz.: —

These may certify that we the subscribers have not expended in our families or business, any spirituous liquors but only what we bought of Innholders or Retailers in this Province, in less quantities than 30 gallons, since December 26, 1754, as witness our hands: —

Joshua Barstow,
Benj. Mann, jr.,
Ebenezer Wing,
Nathaniel Josselynn,
Wm. Whiting,
Uriah Lambert,
Thomas Palmer,
Samuel House,
Benjamin Curtis,
John Torrey,
Joshua Staples,
Isaac Lambert,
Edmund Silvester,
Ralph Chapman,
John Barker,
Othniel Pratt,
Marlboro' Turner,
Thomas Bardin,
Ezekiel Palmer,
Jeremiah Rogers,
Isaac Gross,
Thos. Barstow,
Joseph House, jr.,
Thos. Silvester,
Job Tilden,
Lemuel Curtis,
Samuel Harlow,
Ebenezer Right,
Jesse Torrey,
Joseph Soper,
Melatiah Dillingham,
Edward Dillingham,
Benjamin Mann,
Seth Stetson,
Seth Woodworth,
Benj. Stetson,
Joseph House,
Thos. Whiting,
Caleb Church,
Sam. Curtis,
Nathaniel Robbins,
Joseph Cornish,
Benj. White,
Josiah Curtis,
Thos. Rose,
Amos Silvester,
Ezekiel Turner,
Benj. Studley,
Taylor Brooks,
Elisha Palmer,
Joseph Curtis,
Jere. Stetson,
John House,
Mordecai Ellis,
Isaac Hatch,
Thos. Wilkes,
Jacob Silvester,
Sam. Barstow,

Hanover, Dec. 26, 1755. The following persons gave in as follows: To David Stockbridge, Town Clerk. These may certify that I have not expended any spirituous liquors in my family for this year past, but I have had of the retailers, as witness my hand.

Adam Prouty,
John Bray,
Silvanus Wing,
Robt. Barker,
Caleb Barker,
Matt. Estes,

Dec. 26, 1755. I have had no rum, wine, or other spirits, in the year past.
ABNER CURTIS.

Dec. 26, 1755. All the rum I have had, I have it of a retailer this year.
JEREMIAH HATCH.

Dec. 26, 1755. Inform the Farmer of Excise that I have not expended any spirituous liquors in my family or business, from the 4th Dec. 1754, to the 26 Dec. 1755.
ELIHAB STUDLEY.

These lines are to inform you that I have not bought nor sold no strong drink since this famous act hath been made, nor consumed any in my house contrary to said act.
CALEB ROGERS.

Dec. 27, 1755. Esq. Stockbridge, These may certify you that I have bought no rum these two years only of retailers and inn holders. RECOMPENCE TIFFANY.

Hanover, Dec. 26, 1755. These may certify that I, the subscriber, have consumed, in my private capacity, trade and business, from the 26 Dec. 1754, *forty-two gallons and three pints* of rum, &c., except what I have purchased of taverners and retailers. THOS. JOSSELYNN.

Hanover, Dec. 26, 1755. These may certify that I, the subscriber, have expended only thirty gallons and one quarter of spirituous liquors, taken in the middle of Oct. last past, the rest I expended in my family, business, &c., I bought of tavern-keepers and retailers in this province in less quantities than thirty gallons, within one year past. As witness my hand.

JACOB BAILEY.

Hanover, Dec. 26, 1755. These may certify that I, the subscriber, have expended in my family, business, &c., in one year past, one gallon and three quarts of rum only, except what I bought of a retailer or innholder in this province, in less quantities than thirty gallons. As witness my hand.

JOSEPH RAMSDELL.

Jan. 6, 1756. Clement Bates gave in his account, that he had expended two gallons of rum only, except what he bought of tavern-keepers and retailers in this province, since Dec. 26, 1754, to Dec. 26, 1755.

And at the same time, Shuble Munroe gave in his account of two gallons, as said Bates did."

We presume the foregoing extracts give us the names of nearly, if not quite all, the legal voters, or heads of families in the town.

From another source,—the old Justice Records of David Stockbridge, Esq., we learn that all who violated the law, were prosecuted and fined for the same; and actions against Adam Rogers of Marshfield, Bezaleel Palmer, Stephen Otis, Jr. of Scituate, David Allen, of Middleboro', Jesse Thomas, of Pembroke, Ebenezer Mann, of Pembroke, are recorded, the fines being generally 40s. for eacho ffence.

About the year 1816, a society for the suppression of intemperance was formed in Hanover, and at a meeting of the Association, held April 28, 1817, an address was delivered by the Rev. John Butler, pastor of the Baptist Society, which was printed,—a copy of which is in our possession. It is a plain and sensible document, its reasoning being straight-forward and cogent, and its array of arguments clear and convincing.

We take from it the following extract:—

"By the exertions of this Association, the prevailing practice of intemperance has been brought into *public view*. It has been taken under serious consideration by many, and made a subject of conversation by all classes of people among us. The object of this society has been proposed for consideration to the selectmen of the adjacent towns, with whom it has been favorably received. The respectable inhabitants of the town of Scituate have felt the importance of the subject, and united in an association for the suppression of this public vice. The several *retailers* in the town of Hanover have been *respectfully addressed* upon the importance of observing the wise and good laws of this Commonwealth, made expressly for the regulation of their conduct; and measures have recently been taken, which we have good reason to hope, will secure obedience to these laws."

In 1830, May 3, the town voted, "that the selectmen be requested not to license any retailer or innholder, who shall, between this and August, permit spirituous liquors to be sold and drank in and about their premises, and engage not to sell after that time to be drank in like manner."

For several years past, a temperance committee has been annually appointed by the town, to take cognizance of all violations of the laws; and though we do not affirm that no ardent spirits have been brought into the place, or sold, or used by the people, yet no one can doubt, that there is more sobriety, more order, and a better state of moral feeling in the community, than existed twenty-five or thirty years since.

May the blessing of God continue to rest upon this, and every other cause which has for its object the moral elevation of our race, and the deliverance of the soul from the dominion of lust and destructive appetites.

SLAVERY.

It may seem to some singular to find anything in a town history in Massachusetts, relative to the subject of human slavery. And yet, it is a well known and undeniable fact, that, previous to the Revolution, slavery existed in all the colonies, not even excepting our own, and slaves were held in almost every family wealthy enough to own them. The minister, the deacon, and even quiet members of the Society of Friends, if we mistake not, held slaves; and justices of the peace, innholders, proprietors of forges, &c., all sinned after the similitude of the same transgression!

The following items, which we have gleaned from various sources, may be interesting in this connection, and present as full a sketch of the history of slavery in this town, as we are able to furnish.

In 1754 there were eight male and nine female slaves held in Hanover.[1]

In 1764–5, the number of slaves held in Scituate was 107![2] The number in Hanover is not given. At the same date there were thirteen Indians in Scituate;[3] but the number in Hanover is not given.

Not only were *blacks*, but *Indians*, were held as slaves; and intermarriages between the black and red race were not infrequent.

We do not know that we can give the names of all who held slaves in Hanover; we are only able to present the scattered notices of marriages, births and deaths, which occur on the records of the town and church.

These are as follows:

Dick, James Bailey's negro, and Daphne, Col. Barker's negro, were married Dec. 25, 1741, and Boston and Margaret, slaves of Elijah Cushing, were married in the same year. Windsor Jonas, and Mercy Red, an Indian, were married March 9, 1749. Jack and Bilhah, Job Tilden's servants, were married Feb. 8, 1751. Tradition says, that Mr. T. raised slaves for the market! Newport and Kate, slaves of Nathaniel Silvester, were married

[1] Annals of the Am. Stat. Ass. Vol. 1.
[2] Ibid. Vol. 1.
[3] Ibid. Vol. 1.

May 25, 1760. Cæsar, child of Deacon Stockbridge's slave, died June 14, 1728. Joseph Ramsdell's negro child died April 25, 1733. Deacon Stockbridge's negro, Cuffy, died Jan. 18, 1736. Elijah Cushing, Esq.'s negro child died March 5, 1736. A negro of Mr. Dillingham, died Feb., 1738. Fred, a negro of Matthew Estes, died Feb. 13, 1739. Phillis, Captain Josselynn's negro, died Feb. 9, 1742. Captain Cushing's negro child died July 30, 1744. A negro child of Uriah Lambert's, died Sept., 1746. A negro child of Elijah Cushing, Esq., died Feb., 1747. Jupiter, Mr. John Curtis's negro, died Dec. 1747. Briton, negro child of John Studley, died January 23, 1749. This child belonged to Edward Jenkins, of Scituate, and was given by him to Mr. S. soon after its birth. A negro child of Ensign John Bailey, died August 7, 1751. A negro child of Lieutenant Job Tilden, died Dec. 25, 1754, and another February 12, 1760. Dinah, negro servant to Mr. Amos Sylvester, died Feb. 1756. Ben, an Indian slave of John Bailey, died May, 1756. Bilhah, Joshua Barstow's negro woman, died May 21, 1757. Jeffrey, negro of Colonel Turner, was drowned in the furnace pond, Aug. 29, 1765. Dick, slave of Rev. Samuel Baldwin, died Feb. 3, 1762. Phebe, negro slave to David Jacobs, died Jan. 8, 1769,—also Jane, a negro servant of David Jacobs, died Feb. 28, 1775. Jesse Boos, negro slave of Rev. Samuel Baldwin, died Oct. 5, 1775. Daphne, an old negro, probably Col. Barker's slave, died March 10, 1779. London, negro of the widow Turner, died Jan. 15, 1786. Dick, negro of Col. Bailey, and husband of Daphne, died Jan. 20, 1786, aged 90. Mingo, negro of Capt. Simeon Curtis, died April 7, 1791, aged 70. He lived on Silver street, with his wife and child, and gave the name to Mingo's field. Susannah, negro of Deacon Bass, died May 2, 1791, aged 73. Bess, negro of Rev. John Mellen, died Sept. 20, 1793, aged 36. Mary, negro of Robert Estes, died March 20, 1794, aged 76. Cuba, a negro woman of Deacon Brooks, died March 25, 1795, aged 84. Cuffee Josselynn, a slave of Col. Joseph Josselynn, died in the almshouse, at the advanced age of 103, in 1831. He was out in the Revolution as a soldier, as the rolls show.

It is related of one slave, held at the Four Corners, that he earnestly desired to be free, and often asked his master to give him his liberty, who put him off with the promise that he should be made free, as soon as all the water in the North river had run by; and the simple-hearted creature was frequently seen looking wistfully at the stream, doubtless hoping daily that it would become dry!—but alas! for him, slavery knew no end but *death.* Heartily do we rejoice that our State no longer labors under this terrible curse!—and would to God it were abolished in *all* our land, that in *truth*, as we'll as on *parchment*, all were free and equal,—possessing and enjoying their inalienable rights,—and that the banner of *freedom* might wave triumphantly over every mile of our territory.

BURIAL GROUNDS.

Of our burial grounds, the oldest in the town is that near the centre meeting house. In 1727, the town of Scituate made a grant of ten acres of land to Hanover, for a " training field and burial ground;" and on the records of Hanover, under date of June 17, 1727, Benjamin Curtis and Samuel Barstow were chosen agents to attend the Surveyors in laying out the same, and in case they could not agree where it should be laid out, it was voted that the two surveyors should lay it out at their discretion.

This land was divided into two lots, one of seven and a half acres, for the training field, and the other of two and a half acres, for the burial ground; but we find no record which fixes the original bounds of either lot. The former, the training field, seems to have been exchanged with John Rogers, in 1730, as June 15th of that year, Isaac Buck was chosen agent to give John Rogers a deed of seven and a half acres of land in the town's behalf, and to take in return, a deed for three acres; and at the same time it was voted to pay Isaac Buck £3 for one acre of land. We incline to the opinion that Buck's acre was that on which the meeting-house was built, and that the three acre lot of Rogers constituted the burial ground. In 1769, we find on the Scituate records, the minutes of the laying out of the ten acres granted in 1727; — one of the pieces, containing nearly eight acres, being near the residence of Mr. Baldwin; and the other, of two acres and a little over, is described as "lying near Captain John Bailey's new house, in the East of the way that leads to Deacon Thomas Roses's, &c."

In 1788, David Stockbridge, Esq., "for and in consideration of his good will and affection to the town, presented a piece of land containing one acre, one quarter and twenty-five rods, to enlage the present burial ground; said lot lying westerly of the former lot."

In 1792, £6 were voted for the purchase of a Pall, and in 1804, $103,55, for fencing the ground. In 1808, it was voted "to purchase a *hearse*, and build a house for the same on the burying ground," where it still stands.

A gift of land for the enlargement of the burial ground, has just been received from John Barstow, Esq., of Providence, son of Col. J. B. Barstow, of Hanover, on which occasion the following votes were passed:

"Whereas John Barstow, Esq., of Providence, Rhode Island, a native of Hanover, in consideration of his "respect to the birthplace of his ancestors for six successive generations," has been pleased to present to the Town, as a token of his good-will and regard, a Deed of Two Lots of Land in Hanover, adjoining the present burial-place, near the centre meeting house, for the enlargement of said burial ground, which lots are fully described in the Deed and Plan forwarded by him; therefore Voted, that the Town accept said lots, with the Proviso attached, in reference to driftways, and agree to improve the same according to the intents of the Donor.

"Voted, that the Deed of said lots be entered at large upon the records of the Town, in token of our acceptance of the same, and to perpetuate the remembrance of the liberality of the Grantor.

"Voted, that the Town duly appreciate the generous motives which have prompted this gift; and that the filial reverence therein displayed for the resting place of the Dead, meets our cordial approbation, and our hearty sympathy.

"Voted, as a token of our respect for the memory of the departed, and of our desire to co-operate with the generous Grantor, in the laudable object which he had in view in said gift, that the Town will, at their earliest opportunity, take such measures to cause said burial-ground to be suitably fenced, and otherwise improved, as may render the spot more attractive in its appearance, and more in accordance with the genial spirit of our holy religion.

Voted, that the Town Clerk be requested to forward a copy of these proceedings to Mr. Barstow, at his earliest convenience; and that the minutes of this meeting be entered on the records of the Town."

We trust these votes will soon be carried into effect; that our *ancient burial ground*, will be cleared of stones and bushes; that trees and shrubbery will be set out to adorn it; and that the whole will be enclosed with a good and substantial fence.

To beautify and adorn the "place of the dead," is one step towards embalming their memories more effectually in the hearts of the living, and tends to cherish a purer regard for the spot where our fathers sleep in peace.

In the extreme North-easterly part of the town, or in the *Snappet* neighborhood, is another burial ground, owned by proprietors, who reside in Hanover and South Scituate. This was established about the year 1789; but, like the lot in the centre of the town, it needs attention, as the fences are fallen, and the ground is bare, and destitute of shubbery.

We present the following table of longevity, to show that a fair share of the citizens of Hanover have lived to a "good old age," and passed the bounds of three score years and ten, and even four score years, allotted to man as the term of his earthly pilgrimage. We give the date of death, and the age, so far as they can be learned:—

1730. Henry Josselynn, 90.
1743. Robert Stetson, 90.
1744. Widow Turner, 86.
1748. Elnathan Palmer, 86.
1761. Widow Joanna Wing, 100.
1773. Widow Sarah Ramsdell, 91.
1773. Dea. Joseph Stockbridge, 100.
1775. Elijah Stetson, 89.
1786. Dick, a negro, 90.
1787. Joseph Josselynn, 88.
1787. Sarah Hatch, 86.
1788. Ezekiel Palmer, 87.
1788. Joseph Ramsdell, 86.
1788. Wid. Hannah Stockbridge, 95.
1789. Wid. Abigail Clark, 85.
1790. Capt. Joseph Soper, 87.
1794. Samuel Curtis, 86.
1794. Wid. Sarah Church, 91.
1795. Wid. Mary Stetson, 90.
1796. Benjamin Sylvester, 87.
1796. David House, 87.
1797. Mrs. John Curtis, 86.
1797. Widow Magoun, 90.
1797. Wid. Eliab Studley, 90.

1798. Wid. Hannah Ford, 88.
1798. Michael Silvester, 85.
1799. John Curtis, 90.
1801. Deacon Samuel Barstow, 94.
1801, Wid. Alice Mann, 88.
1803. John Torrey, 88.
1805. Caleb Rogers, 88.
1805. Wid. Ruth Turner, 86.
1807. Wid. Hannah Robbins, 86.
1807. Wid. Lucy Ramsdell, 89.
1807. Joshua Simmons, 88.
1808. Rhoda Rose, 90.
1809. Mary Heyford, 92.
1810. Mordecai Ellis, 93.
1811. John Chapman, 105.
1811. Abigail Hanmer, 93.
1811. Wid. Molly Silvester, 86.
1812. Wid. Mary Rogers, 89.
1812. Capt. Joseph Chaddock, 88.
1813. Lydia Wright, 94.
1814. Peg Peters, 87.
1814. Waitstill Turner, 92.
1814. Wid. Hannah White, 94.
1814. Wid. Mary Munroe, 91.
1816. Joseph, Bates, 88.
1816. Benjamin Mann, 89.
1820. Isaiah Wing, 89.
1821. Wid. John Bailey, 91.
1823. Mary Wing, 86.
1823. Wid. Beulah Estes, 88.
1825. Jabez Studley, 86.
1826. Samuel Barstow, 92.
1826. Wid. Mary Whiting, 95.
1828. Orpha Hatch, 85.
1829. Samuel Brooks, 87.
1829. Elisha Barrell, 94.
1829. Capt. Timothy Rose, 86.
1830. Wid. Samuel Brooks, 89.
1830. Ruth Bates, 92.
1831. Wid. Elisha Barrell, 95.
1831. George Bailey, 90.
1821. Wid. Joshua Dwelley, 90.
1831. Wid. Ruth Eells, 94.
1831. Cuffee Josselynn, 103.
1831. Ruth Wing. 86.
1832. Wid. Rosamond Studley, 92.
1834. Hannah Wing, 95.
1839. Clement Bates, 88.
1842. Japhet Studley. 85.
1842. Daniel Barstow, 97.
1842. Experience Curtis, 87.
1843. David Stockbridge, 88.
1848. Mrs. Benjamin Bates, 87.
1848. Caleb Whiting, 87.
1849. Molly Whiting, 94.
1851. Mrs. Sarah E. Barstow, 92.
1851. Shuble Munroe, 90.
1852. John Curtis, 90.

CHAPTER XIII.

HIGHWAYS — STREETS — BRIDGES — PONDS — STREAMS — AND LANDMARKS.

The details of the laying out of highways are usually of but little interest to readers in general. They have, however, a local value, and are often of great assistance, in fixing the residence of some, of whom we could otherwise obtain but little information. We shall make our sketch as brief as possible, consistent with the omission of nothing of importance. There were some roads laid out before the incorporation of the town, and whilst it formed a part of Scituate. The "Drinkwater road," so called, was one of these, also the "country road," from Boston to Plymouth, that from the Four Corners towards Scituate harbor, and others. The following are from the town records: —

Mar. 29, 1729. A highway laid out near the road from James Hatch's to the saw-mill, thence to the S. E. corner of Amasa Turner's ten acre lot; thence to a marked tree in James Hatch's range; thence to John Cobb's corner; thence to the corner between John Cobb and Bachelor Wing; and thence to Drinkwater road, near where the old gate stood by the widow Deborah Hatch's. Vol. 1, p. 375.

Mar. 29, 1729. A private way laid out, from Ebenezer Curtis's barn, to the W. end of Joseph House's house; thence to Joseph Curtis's lot; thence to Benj. Curtis's lot; thence to Timothy White's great lot; thence to Josiah Curtis's ten acre lot; thence to the N. W. corner of Joseph Randall's 10 acre lot; thence to a tree at the corner of John Rogers's land, which the town bought of the said Rogers; and thence to the road near the new meeting house. Vol. 1, p. 375. This was part of Curtis street.

Mar. 29, 1729. A private way laid out, from Abington line, near Michael Wanton's house, where Samuel Staples lives, thence to the top of a dug hill; and thence to the county road beyond Elijah Cushing's. Vol. 1, p. 375.

Mar. 16, 1730. A driftway laid out, beginning at the gate near the widow Deborah Hatch's, as the way goes down the dug hill; thence to Caleb Barker's line, between his land and that of Isaac Hatch; and so on to the way to the furnace, and thence to the furnace mill dam. Vol. 1, p. 374.

Mar. 16, 1730. A driftway laid out, beginning at the N. side of the road leading to the furnace, on the W. division of widow Deborah Hatch's garden to her son; thence to Caleb Barker's corner; thence to Drinkwater dam; and thence, being a private way, running to the line of the 8th Pond Lot; thence to Otis's corner; thence to House's corner; thence to the corner of Otis's pond lots; thence to the W. end of Edward Estes's dam; thence to the corner of Thomas Rogers's and Charles William's lot; and thence to a stake in the line between Joseph Ramsdell and Thomas Wilkes. Vol. 1, p. 374.

Feb. 25, 1730. A private way laid out, from the way from Barstow's to the New Forge, in the range between James and Nathaniel Torrey's; thence to the N. E. corner of Benjamin Hanmer's field; thence to the upper end of Nathaniel Torrey's lot; thence to the corner of Benjamin Stetson's lot; and thence in his range and Matthew Stetson's range, to Drinkwater road. Vol. 1, p. 272.

Feb. 27, 1737. A private way laid out, from a corner of the lands belonging to the heirs of Capt. Joseph Barstow, deceased, near Matthew Stetson's shop, to the highway, from Samuel Eell's shop to Capt. Joseph Josselynn's house. Vol. 1, p. 27.

Oct. 24 1774. A highway laid out, at the request of Matthew and William Estes, beginning at the top of the hill above William Estes's shop, and turning N. to the E. side of said Estes's fence, to Matt. Estes's line, and thence to Caleb Barker's fence on said Estes's land, till it comes to Matt. Estes's orchard fence. Vol. 1, p. 370. Now Plain street.

Mar. 21, 1749. A way laid out, from the end of the lane

leading by Capt. Ezekiel Turner's house; thence to the W. side of a brook in Dea. George King's land; thence to Ridge hill; thence as the said hill goes, to the most convenient place of coming off the same into the way that goes from Ezekiel Turner's to the county road; and thence as the cartway goes to said county road. Vol. 2, p. 7.

Mar. 5, 1750. Accepted the highway laid out from Ezekiel Turner's, to the way leading from Elijah Cushing, Esq.'s to Hatch's mill. Vol. 1, p. 57.

June 29, 1751. A way laid out, from the way from David Jenkins's to Abijah Stetson's, near the S. E. corner of said Stetson's cornfield, and thence by a cartway cleared out by said Stetson, till it comes to the way at the foot of the great lots, &c. Vol. 1, p. 369.

1756. A highway laid out to Abington, through land of John Bray and Benjamin Studley.

Feb. 27, 1758. A way laid out, from the Beech woods saw mill dam, as the way now goes, till it comes to the W. side of the cedar swamp, thence to John Bray's barn; and thence to the S. E. of Abington way. Vol 2, p. 207.

Feb. 27, 1764. A way laid out from the land of Marlboro' Turner, and the heirs of Joseph Curtis, late of Hanover, deceased; thence N. as the way now lies to Samuel Whiting's and James White's land; thence to a beech tree on Joshua Jacobs's land; thence to the S. end of the lane between the land of Thomas and William Whiting; and thence N. as the way now lies, till it comes to the N. bounds of the town of Hanover. Vol. 2, p. 208. Whiting street.

Mar. 26, 1764. A way laid out, from the S. W. corner of Gideon Randall's land, on the N. side of the way that leads from the furnace to the meeting house; thence to Isaac Hatch's fence; thence turning W. and running straight to the way that leads from Mordecai Ellis's to the meeting house. Vol. 2, p. 208.

April 17, 1782. A way laid out, beginning at Scituate line, at the South end of the highway from Captain Thomas Collamore's to Hanover meeting-house; thence to Job Curtis's corner; thence to Oles's lot; thence to the head of a wall between Benjamin

Mann's and Thomas Hatch's; thence to the head of a wall between Thomas Hatch's and Job Curtis's; thence by Lemuel Curtis, jr.'s house; and thence to the highway heretofore laid out. Vol. 1, p. 357. Part of Curtis street.

April 25, 1791. A highway laid out across the land of Richard Estes, from the highway leading from said Estes's dwelling house to the old furnace, beginning at the South-west corner of his farm, and running North to the highway opposite the dwelling house of Isaac Hatch. Vol. 1, p. 368.

Dec. 1, 1792. Main street laid out, the details corresponding generally to those already given, under date of March 29, 1729, and April 17, 1782. Vol. 1, p. 351.

May 16, 1796. A way laid out, from the North-east corner of William Stockbridge's land, by the highway near Charles Bailey's, and thence West to the highway near John Bailey, jr's. Vol. 1, p. 355.

Aug. 9, 1798. A new road petitioned for at the North-west part of the town, and laid out, being that passing through Walnut and North streets.

Oct. 20, 1800. The town voted against the road from Lemuel Curtis's to the meeting-house, and not to accept the road turned out by Joshua Dwelley near his house.

Oct. 12, 1801. A way laid out across Birch bottom.

1807. The road widened on the East side of the burying ground.

Nov. 1819. The highway near Eleazer Joselynn's, past David Studley's shop, widened and straightened.

June 1820. A new way laid out from Zaccheus Estes's to Paul Perry's being part of Plain street.

May 5, 1823. The road over the furnace dam repaired, as per agreement between the town, and the owners of the works.

Nov. 1832. Alteration of the road over land of Lewis Litchfield and Joshua Gates, near Ellis's bridge.

June 1834. A road laid out below Studley's mill, from near the house of Gridley Studley, over his land to the mill privilege, and thence to land of Charles Lane, and to the highway, &c.

April 7, 1835. The road past the house of George Curtis altered, and that portion of the old road between the termini discontinued.

May 5, 1835. A road laid out from Charles Dyer's over the driftway to the old forge, across land of Elisha Bass, John B. Barstow, and Reuben Rogers, out to the road to Pembroke.

June 17, 1837. A road laid out from Charles Dyer's house, to the road near Nathan Dwelley's, on the road from Hanson to the Four Corners. At the same date, the road from Hiram Gardner's to Scituate line was widened.

June 9, 1840. The road from Joseph W. and Zebulon Clark's, to School-house No 2, widened and straightened.

June 10, 1842. Road from David Mann's to Abington widened.

The roads laid out since the last date, are Pine street; that part of Hanover street called the Pine Island road; and a road from London bridge to Benjamin Mann's. Several alterations have likewise been made in existing roads, and new locations of portions of the old roads. The sum expended on highways, for a few years past, has been quite large, considering the population of the town, and the extent of its territory; but though the taxes have been high, they have been paid with commendable promptitude, and usually with but little complaint. One thing we think can be said of the town of Hanover with truth;—that whatever differences of opinion may have temporarily arisen, and however warmly party feelings may have been enlisted for or against certain measures; these feelings have never resulted in any violent outbreaks, as in some towns, nor have they produced alienations in families or neighborhoods, which have been lasting. We do not claim that our citizens are void of the common passions of humanity; but a spirit of forbearance has been usually exercised, worthy of all praise.

STREETS.

All the streets in the town were named by a Committee of eight, one from each School district, in 1848, and are as follows:

Back Street: from Thomas Barstow's, to the widow Magoun's.
Birch Street: from John Dwelley's, to Gideon Studley's.
Broadway; from Teague's Bridge, to the Four Corners.
Cedar Street: from Main Street, near Benj. Bailey's to Whiting Street.
Centre Street: from the Meeting House to Capt. Tribou's corner.
Church Street: from the Old Academy, past the Episcopal Church.
Circuit Street: from Edwin Rose's, past Thos. M. Bates,' to Hanover Street.
Cross Street: from Abner Wood's to Silvester's works.
East Street: from Joseph Silvester's to Scituate line.
Elm Street: from Col. J. B. Barstow's to Pembroke line.
Grove Street: from Timothy Robbins' to Main Street.
Hanover Street: from Washington Street to Abington Line, past the Centre Meeting House.
King Street: from Hanson Line, past the Forge, to Lewis Litchfield's.
Main Street: from the Centre Meeting House, past the Baptist Church, to South Scituate Line.
Mill Street: from Hiram Gardner's to South Scituate Line.
North Street: from David Mann's to Joseph Vining's.
Pine Street: from Washington Street to Union Street.
Plain Street: from Ethan Perry's to John Hatch's.
Pleasant Street: from Studley's Mill to J. W. Estes'.
School Street: from David Corthell's to King Street.
Silver Street: from the Centre Meeting House to John Curtis'.
Spring Street: from Elisha Bass' to near Studley's corner.
Summer Street: from Circuit Street to Abington Line
Union Street: from Joseph Briggs, jr's. to Josiah Bonney's.
Water Street: from Curtis's Forge, past Dyer's Works to Broadway.
Walnut Street: from the Baptist Meeting House to Assinippi Hall.
Washington Street: from North River Bridge to South Scituate Line, being the old Plymouth Stage Road.
Webster Street: from Ezekiel Turner's to Abington Line.
Whiting Street: from J. W. Estes' to Abington Line, past Benj. Mann's.
Winter Street: from Circuit Street, past Ozias Perkins', to Broadway.

New Guide Boards, with substantial red cedar posts, are placed at the corners of all these streets, with the names, and suitable directions to the neighboring towns. In this respect, the town of Hanover has not only fulfilled its legal obligations, but has set an example which, were it followed by every town, would be of great assistance to the stranger and traveller.

It is bad enough to journey over unknown roads *with* guide boards, but where there are *none*, or only defaced and illegible ones, it not only occasions great perplexity, but is often a serious detriment, in the loss of time and distance, besides causing additional fatigue to both man and beast.

BRIDGES.

The principal bridge in the town, is that over North River, below the Four Corners, and on the old stage road from Boston to Plymouth. The *first* bridge was erected here in 1656, by Wm. Barstow, of which we have already given an account.

In 1682, the Colony Court ordered the *second*, or a *cart bridge*, to be built over the North River at Barstow's bridge, at the expense of three towns; Scituate to pay £10, Duxbury £5, and Marshfield £5.[1] The place where this bridge stood is still visible, and its old piers, built of loose stones, yet remain.

The present bridge, with split stone abutments, was built, by order of the County Commissioners, in 1829, and is a substantial structure, which promises to last for many generations.

At the Curtis forge is a small bridge, across the Indian Head River, which was probably built as early as 1704, the date of the erection of Bardin's Iron Works. Ludden's Ford, so called, is near here, over which Gov. Winthrop was carried upon a man's back, on his visit to Plymouth in 1632.[2]

Above this, and in the neighborhood of Dyer's, now Perry's Tack Factory, there was formerly a bridge, over the Indian Head; but it has been gone for some years.

Still farther up, at Silvester's, formerly Barstow's Forge, is another bridge, built as early as 1720, when the "new forge" spoken of on the town records, was set up.

Teague's bridge, the next above, which unites Hanover with Hanson, was built before 1740, at which time it was known as Hatch's bridge.

[1] Deane's Scituate, p. 15.   [2] Ibid, pp. 13 and 162.

Following the stream up, which now has the name of Drinkwater river, we come to the old Furnace Dam, near Daniel Barstow's, where Mighill's works were erected in 1710.

Ellis's bridge, is near Abner Magoun's, and was built as early as 1676,as an old saw mill then stood on the spot, which was burnt by the Indians in that year.

On the third Herring Brook, and below the Four Corners, is Palmer's bridge, named on the town records in 1742, and built by John Palmer, of Scituate, in 1660, who covenanted with John Bryant and Humphrey Johnson, to build a logway and bridge, and cover it with gravel, from firm upland to firm upland.[1] A permanent bridge of stone was built here, by vote of the town, in 1835.

Above this is Winslow's bridge, named on the records in 1765, and probably built as early as 1676, at which date the mill of Cornet Stetson, which was burnt by the Indians, stood near this spot.

Still farther north, is the bridge covering the stream between the mills of T. J. Gardner (formerly the Curtis mill,) and that of John Clapp. This was built as early as 1690.

At South Scituate line, is the dam connected with Jacobs' mills.

There are other small bridges over our brooks, which have local names.

PONDS AND STREAMS.

There are no natural ponds of any size in Hanover. Almost all the mill privileges, however, have formed artificial ponds, some of which are of considerable extent. The largest is at the forge near Daniel Barstow's, covering a portion of Drinkwater swamp.

North River, the principal stream, received its name before 1633, probably from the circumstance that its general course is from North to South.[2] It is very winding,—its length, from North River bridge to the mouth, being over eighteen miles, and the tide rises at the bridge from three to five feet,—there being a perceptible tide some distance higher up.

Its three chief sources are the Namatakeese, and Indian Head,

[1] Deane, p. 15. [1] Deane, p. 15.

which flow from the Mattakeesett Ponds in Pembroke; and the Drinkwater, which has its source chiefly in Abington, flows into the Pond by Bates & Holmes' Anchor Works, thence by a general southerly course, being a stream of some size, into Cobb & Cushing's Pond at Hanson, and thence easterly, forming the boundary line between Hanover and Hanson, past Silvester's Works, and Perry's Tack Factory, into Indian Head River.

Though hardly within our scope to describe this river throughout its course, its *mouth* being in another town, yet the views which it presents are often so beautiful and picturesque, that we can scarce resist the temptation to give them a passing glance, at the risk of being accused of deviating slightly from the beaten path in which historians usually tread. Suppose, then, we go down to the "landing" at the bridge, and step on board one of these "*gundaloes*," or flat barges, used by our farmers for transporting their salt hay from the marshes below. Shall ours be a moonlight excursion, with the workmen, starting thus early to be in season for the morrow? or shall we choose rather to glide down the stream by daylight? The former is certainly the time which the poet would choose; the silvery beams of "night's chaste queen," then shimmering upon the waters, and reflecting upon their placid bosom the trees which border its banks, flitting like shadows by as we move on, without oar, without sail, impelled only by the silent current;—anon passing a ship yard, where, in silent grandeur, looms up the hulk of some half-finished bark, which will soon be sailing upon the mighty deep, perhaps to distant climes;—and then opening upon an expanse of meadow, winding through which, like a thread of silver, the stream may be seen, far beyond us. What stillness reigns! How quiet! Not a sound of life is heard around us! Who can resist the feelings of reverence which such a scene is calculated to inspire!

The trip by day, though not possessing all the enchantment of that by night, is still beautiful, especially if taken when the leaves are changing, and our forests are robed in their autumn hues! It is certainly delightful, on a clear October morning, when the air is just cool enough to brace the nerves, and invigorate the lungs, to move noiselessly down with the tide, viewing the scenery on either bank, with the landings, and ship yards, the old "brickilns," "Cornet's rocks," and "gravelly beach," and noting the meanderings of the stream, sometimes almost doubling upon itself, and the fine farms which are passed, and the broad meadows, with the hills at a distance, and the sloping plains, until we arrive at the "New harbor marshes." Here, as Deane truly observes, "the scenery is on a sublime scale, when viewed from Colman's hill, or from the fourth cliff. The broad marshes are surrounded by a distant theatre of hills, and the river expands, and embraces many islands in its bosom. Here it approaches the sea, as if to burst through the beach, but turns almost at right angles to the East, and runs parallel with the sea shore, for nearly three miles before it finds its outlet, leaving a beach next the sea of twenty rods in width, composed chiefly of round and polished pebbles, excepting only the fourth cliff, a half mile in length, which comprises many acres of excellent arable land."[1]

The author has looked upon this broad, marshy tract, from Coleman's hill, after a severe storm, and seen the whole covered with water, like a mimic sea, with Will's Island standing out in the midst, like an oasis in the desert. The contrast between the smooth expanse here spread to view, and the turbulent waves, fretting the beach beyond, is exceedingly grand.

The town owns, near the mouth of the river, a body of flats, formerly quite valuable, the produce of which was annually rented for a considerable sum; but the depreciation in value of all fresh and salt meadow land within the last fifty years, renders these now comparatively worthless.

Deane asserts[2] that *salmon* were formerly taken in the North river, and that bass were once abundant in the winter season. Shad and alewives are still taken; and in the early history of the town, the alewive fishery was a subject of interest and contention, but has latterly ceased to attract much notice. Pembroke, Scituate, and Marshfield derive the most profit from this fishery.

The principal brooks are the following: —

1. The Third Herring Brook, which forms the boundary line between South Scituate and Hanover, rises in Valley Swamp,

[1] Deane, p. 20. [2] Scituate, p. 21.

towards Hingham, and empties into the North river. This is a valuable water privilege, which was early improved for saw and grist mills, and to which have since been added tack factories. Alewives formerly passed up this brook as far as Valley Swamp.

2. Silver, formerly Hughs' Cross brook, rises near the central meeting house, and runs parallel to Silver street throughout its course, forming a small pond at the Curtis family mill, and emptying into the Third Herring brook.

3. Trout brook, rises in Randall Swamp, west of Washington street, and flows southerly past Church's Tannery, emptying into North river.

4. Torrey's brook, rises near Rose's Tannery, on Circuit street, and runs in a south-westerly direction, emptying into Drinkwater river.

5. Beaver dam brook, rises in the low ground east of the house of Zaccheus Estes, on Plain street, and runs westerly, emptying into Longwater brook.

6. Stetson's brook, rises in Hell swamp, back of Church's Hill, and west of Washington street, crosses Union, Main, and Cedar streets, and empties into Bailey's brook.

7. Bailey's brook, rises in the low ground east of Main street, which it crosses, flowing Southerly until it receives Stetson's brook, and then westerly, emptying into Longwater brook.

8. Longwater brook, rises in South Scituate, near Accord Pond, and flows south-easterly, crossing North street beyond David Mann's, at a spot where formerly stood an old grist mill, thence forming the pond by Brooks' lower mill, and thence flowing southerly, crossing Cedar, Hanover, and Circuit streets, and emptying into Drinkwater river.

9. Studley mill brook, rises in Abington, and flows South-easterly, crossing Webster and Pleasant streets, forming near the latter a pond of considerable extent in the winter season, and emptying into Long-water brook.

10. Iron-mine brook, rises in the low ground near Broadway, and flows south-westerly, emptying into Drinkwater river.

There are other small streams in the town, dry in the summer season. Those that we have named are permanent, and some of them copious.

LANDMARKS.

The locations of many of the ancient landmarks are given, in different parts of our work, and these we do not deem it necessary to repeat. The following have not been alluded to.

Bank Land—In the woods, near Oren Josselynn's. Said to have been so called, because paid for in *bank bills.*

Beech Woods—West of King Street, towards Abington. A famous place for early whortleberries.

Brisco's Plain—Near Gideon Studley's.

Candlewood Plain—Near the Centre Meeting House.

Chapman's Landing—On Wampum's Swamp, near Rose's Tannery. There is another place of the same name on North River, where hay is landed.

Cuffs Field—At the corner of Grove Street.

Cushing Lot Dam By Brooks' upper mill.

Dug Hill—On Silver Street.

Hayden Hill—On land of Col. J. B. Barstow.

Halifax Road—From Brook's upper mill towards Abington.

King Stone Hill—North of Richmond Winslow's.

Little Cedar Swamp—Near Indian Head River.

London Bridge—On North Street.

Mingo Field—On Silver Street.

Oles' Lot—Between Washington and Main Streets.

Park—On Broadway, near David Hersey's.

Peg's Swamp—Back of Charles Winslow's.

Pond Lots—Near the Widow Joshua Dwelley's.

Project Dale—Near Charles Dyer's.

Purr Cat Lane—Now Spring Street.

Ridge Hill—From Main to Grove Street.

Strawberry Hill—West of Spooner Ellis's.

Shuble's Ridge—Crosses Centre Street, near E. Thayer's.

Share Lots—From the old highway on Walnut Hill, towards Abington.

Tumble-down Hill—Near John Hatch, jr's.

Turkey Plain—Near Indian Head River.

Wolf Trap, or Wolf Rock.—On land of Col. J. B. Barstow.

Walnut Hill.—South of Walnut, and West of Washington Street.

Woodward Hill—Between the Four Corners, and the Centre Meeting House.

FAMILY GENEALOGIES.

PART II.

FAMILY GENEALOGIES.

In the following pages, we have endeavored to give notices of all the families at present settled in the town, so far as records could be obtained, with extended sketches of several of those early settled on its territory, and now widely scattered abroad, throughout the country. We do not claim that these notices are perfect or complete. Every one who has had any experience in such matters, knows the difficulty, and even the impossibility, of attaining to absolute perfection. The author expects some errors will be discovered, but he trusts none of great consequenee. No pains have been spared to obtain reliable information; authentic records have been consulted wherever they could be found; and traditions have never been given as authority, without first endeavoring to verify them from different sources.

The author ventures to hope that a little indulgence will be extended to him, when the variety and multiplicity of details and dates here presented are considered. It may be that some of these sketches are not so extensive as the families themselves might desire. But all that has been learned of these families is published; and want of *materials*, not of *inclination*, is the reason why more has not been said. The author has endeavored to do as equal justice as possible to all whose names are presented. He has published as cheerfully minutes of one family as of another. And according to the interest the parties themselves have taken, and the fulness of the information they have furnished, will the sketches be found.

The brief memoirs of individuals scattered throughout this part, are such as have been obtained from letters, and the recollections of those who knew the persons alluded to; and it is believed they will be found to be courteous and respectful, at least. The names of all who have ever lived in the town are not entered. Some were but transient residents. Others, who had descendants for two or three generations, finally removed, and are settled in different places. To have recorded all of these, would have enlarged the *size* of the volume, but probably not its *interest*. Enough, however, is given here to satisfy reasonable minds. Liberal criticism will never be deprecated. A candid judgment is all that is asked.

Trusting that this part of the work will prove acceptable to those for whom it was prepared, and not lacking in value as a family memorial, and a contribution to the general fund of genealogical knowledge, it is sent forth, in the belief, that though not free from errors, it contains much that is correct, and perhaps as few inaccuracies as most books of the kind.

PLAN OF THIS PART.

The plan adopted in the following pages, is simple, and will be easily understood by all familiar with genealogical tables. But for the information of such as have not this acquaintance, we deem it necessary to remark, that the *figures* which *precede* the names of individuals, denote their place in the series, and the figures which *follow*, point back to the place in the series where the *paternal* ancestor is to be found. For instance, in the first family, the Bailey's, we read, "21. Benjamin, s. Charles 14." The figure 21, denotes that this is the twenty-first family described; and the figure 14 refers back to the fourteenth family, in examining which we find that Benjamin was born Feb. 24, 1797. By observing this rule, it will be easy to trace any family back to the first ancestor.

ABBREVIATIONS.

The following table explains the meaning of most of the abbreviations used in this part.

ab. about.
Abn. Abington.
Adm. Administration.
ae. aged.
acc't. account.
acs. acres.
Am. Tr. Ass. American Tract Association.
A. M. Master of Arts.
Acad. Academy.
Asst. Assistant.
b. born.
bap. baptised.
betw. between.
Brigd'r. Bridgewater.
bro. brother.
B. U. Brown University.
Bos n. Boston.
Camb. Cambridge.
ch. children.
Ch. Church.
Chasn. Charlestown.
Co. Company.
Ct. Connecticut.
Col. Colony or Colonel.
Cong. Congregational.
Cont. Estab. Continental Establishment.
Cant'y. Canterbury.
Capt. Captain.
Clk. Clerk.
Const'n. Constitution.
Cal. California.
d. died.
das. daughters.
decsd. deceased.
descts. descendants.
Dux. Duxbury.
Dea. Deacon.
denom. denomination.
ea. each.
Eng. English.
Est. Estate.
fa. father.
freem. freeman.
grad. graduated.
gr. s. grandson.
gr. gr. s. great grandson.
gent. gentleman.
H. Hanover.
H. C. Harvard College.
Hm. Hingham.
Hn. Hanson.
Ham. Coll. Hamilton College.
husb. husband.
Inv'y. Inventory
Ills. Illinois.
inf. infant.
Ky. Kentucky.
Letts. Letters.
m. married.
Me. Maine.
Mfd. Marshfield.
mos. months.
mfr. manufacture.
Matt't. Mattapoisett.
mo. mother.
Md. Maryland.
Meth. Methodist.
Misso. Missouri
M. D. Physician.
Miss. Mississippi,
Mass. Massachusetts.
memb. member.
N. H. New Hampshire.
N. Bed. New Bedford.
ord. ordained.
off. office.
p. page.
Pass. Passenger
Past. Pastor.
Pemb. Pembroke.
Plym'h. Plymouth.
prob. probably.
Prob. Rec. Probate Records.
Prov. Cong. Provincial Congress.
Philad. Philadelphia.
Pa. Pennsylvania.
Ports'h. Portsmouth.
pub. published.
Prov. Providence.
Rec. Records.
recom. recommended.
Rev'n. Revolution.
Rox'y. Roxbury.
R. I. Rhode Island.
Regt. Regiment.
Roch'r. Rochester.
Rep. Representative.
rec'd. received.
s. son.
Scit. Scituate.
Sen. Senior.
Sett. Settled.
Scot'd. Scotland.
Sab'h. Sabbath.
Supt. Superintendent,
Stud. Studied.
Theol. Theology.
unm. unmarried
Va. Virginia.
w. wife.
Wat'n. Watertown.
Wey'h. Weymouth.
wid. widow.
wks. weeks.

BAILEY FAMILY.

Arms: Az., nine estoiles, three, three, two, and one, ar.

Crest: A morning Star, ppr.

John Bailey See No. 6.

John Bailey Jun See No. 11.

Luther Bailey See No. 12.

Calvin Bailey See No. 13.

R. C. Bailey See No. 20.

FAMILY GENEALOGIES.

BAILEY, an ancient, and common English name, represented in this country by the descendants of several persons, who came early to N. Eng. and left posterity. Thomas was of Bos'n., 1643, and with his w. Ruth, was prob. of Wey'h., 1661, and was prob. fa. of John, of Scit.

1. John, according to Deane, came from Wey'h. to Scit. in 1670, and was tenant to Capt. Jno. Williams, at Farm Neck. He m. 1. Sarah White, Jan. 25, 1672, and 2. Ruth Clothier, Dec. 9, 1699, and d. 1718, leaving a will, (Deane.) ch.: 1. John, Nov. 5, 1673. 2. Sarah, Oct. 1675. 3. Mary, Dec. 1677, m. Jas. Perry, Jan. 1, 1701. 4. Joseph, Oct. 1679, m. and left descts. in Scit. 5. Benjamin, Ap. 1682. Moved to Marlboro', Mass., ab. 1712, m. and left descts. 6. William, Feb, 1685, m. Judith Booth, Jan. 1714, and left descts. in Scit. 7. Hannah, Jan. 1687–8, m. Jas. Briggs, Dec. 24, 1716. 8. Samuel, Aug. 1690. Supposed by Deane to have moved after his father's decease. Was there another da. Elizabeth ? who m. Wm. Barrell, July 2, 1706.

2. John, s. John 1, m. Abigail, da. Dea. Saml. Clapp, Feb. 19, 1700, and d. in H. in June, 1752, and his wid. Mar. 2, 1753. He was Selectman from 1735–37, and a man of influence in the town. ch.: 1. Jane, June 30, 1700. 2. John, May 23, 1703. 3. Jacob, Dec. 13, 1706. 4. Capt. Israel, May 13, 1708, m. Keziah Perry, Nov. 12, 1730, and left descts. in Brigd'r. and Scit. 5. Timothy, March 20, 1709. 6. Abigail, Feb. 4, 1712–3, m.

John Bates, May 21, 1733. 7. Sarah, 1714, m. Thos. Jenkins, Mar. 4, 1731. 8. Deborah, 1717, m. Jere. Rogers, 1738. 9. Hannah, 1719. 10. Rachel, 1719. m. Jas. Rogers, 1741. 11. Naomi, 1722. m. Benj. Curtis 1741.

3. John, s. John 2, m. Elizabeth Cowen, Ap. 11, 1723, and lived on what is now Main st., nearly oppo. the present residence of Lebbeus Stockbridge. His w. d. Ap. 12, and he Sept. 28, 1778. He was Selectman in 1744, and a man of business talents, and considerable enterprise. ch.: 1. Elizabeth, Aug. 15, 1727, m. Dr. Jere. Hall, Dec. 22, 1748, first of H., who sett. in Pemb. ab. 1764, was a distinguished physician, and a member of the Prov. Cong. in 1775. 2. John, Oct. 30, 1730. 3. Joan or *Jane*, Jan. 20, 1732, m. Thos. Hubbard, or *Hobart*, of Abn., July 5, 1750. 4. Seth, July 5, 1739.

4. Jacob, s. John 2, m. 1. Ruth Palmer, June 10, 1728, and 2. a Hatch, and had 1. Jacob, Jan. 20, 1729. Moved to Me., m. a Tinkham ? and had ch. 2. Ruth, Jan. 10, 1731 ,m. Geo. Sterling, of Eng'd, May 13, 1788, who d. Dec. 24, 1791, and she June 12, 1804. His grave-stone, a curiosity in its way, stands in the old burial ground, near the Centre Meeting-house. 3. Charles, Ap. 26, 1734. 4. Stephen, Feb. 27, 1737. 5. Hannah, June 29, 1739, m. Saml. House of Pemb. 6. George, Aug. 2, 1741.

5. Timothy, s. John 2, m. 1. Sarah Buck, May 27, 1731, who d. Oct. 9, 1740, and 2. Hannah Curtis, June 7, 1742, and with his w., was recom. to the Church in N. Yarmouth, Me., whither he moved. ch.: 1. Olive, May, 1735, d. May 26, 1736. 2. Tim'y., June, 1737, d. young. 3. Sarah, Mar. 13, 1739. (By 2d.) 4. Delight, June 12, 1745. 5. Olive, bap. May 15, 1748. 6. Tim'y., bap. Oct. 13, 1751.

6. John, s. John 3, m. Ruth Randall, Oct. 18, 1750, and d. Oct. 27, 1810, and his wid. June 3, 1820, ae. 90. He was Lt. Col. of the Regt. of Col. John Thomas, of Kgsn., which marched to Rox'y. in Ap. 1775, and when Col. T. was commis. as a genl. off. in May, Mr. B. had charge of the Regt., and the next year was chief Col. of a Regt. in the Cont. Estab., and held that rank during the war, having the reputation of a brave and attentive officer. Towards the close of his life, he kept a Tavern, on Curtis

st., near where Abisha Soule resides. He was Selectman from 1768–71. ch.: 1. John, May 6, 1751. 2. Luther, Sept. 14, 1752. 3. Ruth, Nov. 8, 1754, m. Wm. Stockbridge, Oct. 9, 1774. 4. Lucinda, Feb. 20, 1757, m. Jas. Lincoln, of Taunton, June 29, 1774. 5. Calvin, 1760? 6. Lebbeus, moved to N. Yar'h., Me., m. a Myrick, and left ch., of whom the *Rev. Rufus W.* is in Va. 7. Sage, m. Dr. Gad Hitchcock, of Pemb., July 9. 1778. 8. Betsey, m. 1. Rev. Eben'r. Dawes, June 25, 1789, who grad. H. C. 1785, was ord. at Scit. 1787, and d. Sep. 29, 1791; 2. Jno. Lucas, Esq., of Brookline, Mass.; and 3. the venerable Dr. Williams, of Deerfield, Ct., where she d. She is spoken of as a "lady of pleasing personal accomplishments."

7. Seth, s. John 3, m. 1. Lydia Barstow, Feb. 11, 1762, who d. Sep. 17, 1767; and 2. Alice Neal, July 28, 1768, and d. Oct, 12, 1796, and his wid. was recom. to the Church in Freeport, Me., 1800, and moved there with her family. Mr. B. lived first on Curtis st., in his father's house, and then on Union st. where John Dwelley now resides, and there d. He was Selectman in 1781–82. ch.: 1. Seth, bap. Dec. 12, d. Dec. 14, 1762. 2. Marg't., bap. Ap. 8, 1764. 3. Seth, bap. Dec. 8, 1765. (By 2d.) 4. Alice, bap. May 27, 1770, and d. the same year. 5. Alice, bap. Nov. 18, 1770, d. Mar. 1, 1796. 6. Lydia. 1772? d. Jan. 13. 1794, ae. 22. 7. Joseph, bap. Sept. 5, d. Oct. 9, 1773. 8. Joseph, bap. Oct. 2, 1774. 9. Rebecca, bap. Mar. 10, 1776, d. July 15, 1778. 10. Abigail, bap. June 1, 1776, d. July 11, 1778. 11. James; 12. Israel; 13. Rebecca; 14. Abigail; and 15. Lucy;—all bap. Oct. 24, 1790. *Lucy and Israel* are now in H.

8. Charles, s. Jacob 4, m. Betsey Palmer, ab. 1768, and d. in Boston, Oct. 27, 1810, being killed by the fall of a chimney, as he was passing through the street. Lived on Curtis st., near Benj. Bailey's. ch.: 1. Charles, 1769? 2. Ezekiel, m. Hannah, da. Stephen Bailey, and wid. of Ezek'l. T. Hatch, and moved to the West, leaving a da. *Sarah*, in H., who m. Capt. Thos. B. Donnell, Jan. 13, 1850. 3. Rebecca, m. Isa. Wing, July 4, 1802, and moved to Ohio. 4. Sally, m. Eliph't. Smart, of Me., Sept. 20, 1795. 5. Betsey, m. a Gilbert? of Me. 6. Polly, m. a

Whiting? of Me. 7. Martha, m. Saml. Gilbert, of Me., Mar. 6 1785.

9. Stephen, s. Jacob 4, m. Abigail Turner, and d. in H. Aug. 10, 1806. He was Selectman from 1790–93, and lived on King st. ch.: 1. Abigail, m. Reuben Curtis, Nov. 23, 1801. 2. Hannah, m. 1. Ezek'l. T. Hatch, May 8, 1788, and 2. Ezk'l. Bailey, Mar. 28, 1802, and d. at the West. 3. Ruth, d. Dec. 3, 1795, ae 20. 4. Deborah, m. Robt. Barker, Feb. 4, 1798. 5. Stephen, 1780.

10. George, s. Jacob 4, m. Rebecca Ellis, and lived on King st. His w. d. May 30, 1820, and he Nov. 12, 1831. He was Selectman in 1787–88. ch.: 1. Geo. W., Nov. 22, 1777. 2. David, Nov. 1779. 3. Lucy, 1781? m. Robt. Silvester, Nov. 8, 1796. 4. Gad, July 29, 1784.

11. John, s. John 6, m. 1. Ruth Ellis; 2. Mary Hill, who d. Oct. 29, 1792; and 3. Tabitha Olney, of R. I.; and d. Jan. 23, 1823, and his wid. Dec. 30, 1827, ae. 77. Mr. B. was a natural mechanic, a man of great ingenuity, and a successful inventor. He was a clockmaker by trade, and a manufacturer of compasses. Many of his clocks still exist in the town, and are creditable specimens of his skill. He was an upright and zealous member of the Society of Friends, and a minister among them, travelling into different States to speak as the spirit moved. He was an honest man; of great simplicity of character; a worthy citizen; and eminently a peace maker. He resided, the latter part of his life, near the Four Corners, in the house occupied by Wm. Dawes, and built by Robert Silvester. ch.: 1. Joseph, went off, and d. unm. 2. Mary, m. Danl. Newell, of Lynn, and is d. 3. John, Mar. 13, 1787. 4. Ruth, m. Horatio Cushing, Esq., May 10, 1811. He died, and she moved, with her ch., to Hartford, Ct. (By 2d.) 5. Amy, m. 1. Edward, s. Col. J. B. Barstow, Sept. 2, 1821, and 2. Wm. Dawes, and lives in H.

12. Luther, s. John 6, m. Silvester Little, Oct. 21, 1784, who d. June 27, 1788, ae. 35, and an inf. da. Aug. 15, ae. 7 weeks. An older ch., Sylvia, d. May 17, 1792, ae. 6. Mr. B. d. in H. May 12, 1820, ae. 68. He served, with his fa., in the Rev. as

Adjt., was aft. made Capt., and finally Major. He was a man of good education, ranked high as an officer, and was generally esteemed as a citizen.

13. Calvin, s. John 6, m. Sarah, da. Col. John Jacobs, of Scit., and d. in Bath, Me., in 1835, and his wid. in H. Nov. 24, 1846, ae. 82. He was a clockmaker by trade, and an ingenious workman, like his brother John. He was also upright in his dealings with others, and a man of integrity and honesty. ch.: 1. Lucinda, July 11, 1794, m. Stephen Curtis, of Scit. June 16, 1816, and d. in 1818. 2. Calvin B., May 17, 1796. 3. Capt. Edwin, May 7 1798, m. Ann T. Ingraham, of Port'd., Me., in May, 1825, had 1 ch., wh. d. in 1828, and he in Aug. 1828. 4. Luther, and 5. Martin, Aug. 29, d. Sep. and Nov., 1798. 6. Capt. Henry, Aug. 2, 1801, m. Sarah Gardner, of Hm., Jan. 16, 1832, and lives in Quincy. 7. Eliza, July 5, 1803. 8. Sarah, Aug. 20, 1805, m. Lemuel Dwelley, jr., of H., and lives on Union st.

14. Chas., s. Chas. 8, m. Chloe Mann, Oct. 28, 1792, and lived on Main st., in his father's house, where he d. June 11, 1820, and his wid. Feb. 2, 1844, ae. 73. He, and his bro. Ezk'l., were owners, for a time, of the fulling, saw, and grist mills, on King st ch.: 1. Chas., May 25, 1793. Moved to Indiana, and m. there. 2. Chloe, Feb. 23, 1795, m. Paul Perry, Sept. 23, 1813. 3. Benj., Feb. 24, 1797. 4. Betsey, Feb. 6, 1799, m. Josh. Dwelley, Nov. 30, 1823. 5. Barker, Jan. 22, 1801. 6. Luther, Dec. 23, 1803, d. Aug. 27, 1804. 7. Martin, May 4, 1807, d. Mar. 20, 1844. 8. Mary, May 24, 1809, m. Ensign Crocker, Dec. 24, 1828, and is d. 9. Marcia, m. Albert Holbrook, Nov. 3, 1830.

15. Stephen, s. Stephen 9, m. Ruth Hatch, June 9, 1803, lives on King st., and is a Farmer. ch.: 1. Ruth, Jan 8, 1804, m. Julius House, Jan. 13, 1825. 2. Lucy, Dec. 17, 1805. 3. Stephen, Mar. 8, 1810, m. Sylvia W. Bates, May 6, 1834, lives on King st., is a shoemaker, and has *Edwin*, Ap. 4, 1835 ; *Laura A.*, March 20, 1838 ; *Stephen W.*, Dec. 1840 ; and *Albert W.*, Dec. 22, 1844. 4. Amos H., Mar. 6, 1815, not m.

16. Geo. W., s. Geo. 10, m. Asenath Curtis, Jan. 1, 1801, lives on King st., and is a Farmer. ch.: 1. George, Sep. 13, 1802. 2. Asenath, Dec. 2, 1804, m. Thos. Stetson, of Hn., Dec. 10, 1827,

and d. July 21, 1849. 3. Kezia, Jan. 15, 1807, m. Josh. Dwelley, Jan. 16, 1827. 4. Melzar C., m. Charlotte C. Waterman, Aug. 1, 1833, and d. Sept. 29, 1843, having had *Melzar C.*, Aug. 17, 1839, and *Saml. W.*, Dec. 31, 1841, d. Nov. 5, 1843. 5. Priscilla, May 18, 1813, m. Joseph Wilder, and lives with her fa. 6. Lucinda, May 19, 1816, m. Hiram Gardner, of H. 7. Sally E., June 3, 1819, d. Feb. 7, 1851.

17. Dr. David, s. Geo. 10, m. Joanna Curtis, Nov. 7, 1801, settled as a Physician in Scit., and there d. Jan. 13, 1836, ae. 56, and his wid. Ap. 4, 1846, ae. 61. Mr. B. was successful in his practice, and esteemed as a citizen. ch.: 1. David, Nov. 16, 1802, m. Debo., da. Amos Dunbar, Ap. 24, 1833, lives in So. Scit., is a shoemaker, and had 1 ch. wh. d. young. 2. Joanna, Dec. 13, 1804, d. July 14, 1813. 3. Rebecca, Nov. 27, 1807, m. Hiram Gardner, June 5, 1831, and is d. 4. Elizabeth, June 12, 1810, m. Alfred Loring, of Hm., Nov. 15, 1827, no ch. 5. Joanna, June 1, 1813, m. Albert Loring of Hm., Mar. 19, 1837, and has ch. 6 Luther, Feb. 18, 1816, not m. 7. Lucy, Sept. 11, 1818, m. Edward Stowell, Jan. 29, 1848, and has *Lucy E.*, and *Helen M.* 8. Jeremiah, Aug. 12, 1822, a Carpenter, of Wey'h., m. Elizabeth G. Dunbar, and has *Helen C.*, Ap. 1846; *Chas. H.*, Nov. 1847, d. ae. 2 mos; and *Geo. A.*, Oct. 1850.

18. Gad, s. Geo. 10, m. Thankful Loring, of Hm., and lives on King st. ch.: 1. Maria, Aug. 20, 1810, m. Nahum Stetson, of Hn., Mar. 3, 1831. 2. Sarah A., Jan. 21, 1813, m. Ira Josselynn, of H. 3. Lydia L., Nov. 11, 1814, m. Jno. S. Fogg, of S. Wey'h. Oct. 28, 1838. 4. Gad J., Ap. 13, 1817, m. Lydia B. Clark, June 1841, lives on King st., is a shoemaker, and had *Helen E.*, Oct. 30, 1844, d. Nov. 1849. 5. Eliza J., Mar. 24, 1819, m. John Waterman, of Carver, Nov. 26, 1846.

19. John, s. John 11, m. Ann, da. of John Taber, of Port'd. Me., 29 d. 11 mo. 1810, is a clockmaker by trade, and resides in Lynn, Mass. ch: 1. Catherine, 9 d. 11 mo. 1811, d. 3 d. 8 mo. 1817. 2. Miriam H., 5 d. 12 mo. 1813, m. Wm. Gifford, jr., of Falmouth, in 1834, and resides in Peoria, Ills. 3. John T., 17 d. 12 mo. 1815, sailed fr. N. Bed. in 1831, in the ship Mentor, Capt. Barnard, on a whaling voyage, was wrecked in the Straits of Ti-

mou, and he, with 9 others, who took to a boat to escape, were dashed upon the rocks, and all perished within 50 yds. of the ship. 4. Ann M., 24 d. 12 mo. 1817. 5. Joseph, 23 d. 12 mo. 1819, m. Abby, da. Jas. Ingraham, of N. Bed., in 1844, had a da. *Caroline A.*, and sailed fr. N. B., in 1850, as Master of the Ship Champion, and d. in 1852, in Hong Kong, China. 6. Wm., 27 d. 8 mo. 1821, d. 22 d. 10 mo. 1822. 7. Wm., 2 d. 8 mo. 1823, m. Frances Kelley, in 1846, and has *Geo. R. F.*, 1850. The fa. sailed fr. N. Yk. in 1852, in the ship Red Rover, for Cala. and thence to Canton, &c. 8. Mary N., 9 d. 7 mo. 1825, m. Chas. C. Folger, in 1845, and has 2 sons, *Chas.*, and *John B.* 9. Catherine, 10 d. 8 mo. 1828. 10. Elizabeth, 15 d. 8 mo. 1830, d. 9d. 9 mo. 1830. 11. Geo. H., 18 d. 6 mo. 1832, d. 27 d. 1 mo. 1834. 12. George, 21 d. 11 mo. 1833, d. 31 d. 8 mo. 1834.

20. Calvin B., s. Calvin 13, moved to Bath, Me., in 1815, m. Jane B. Donnell, May 21, 1820, and yet lives in B., being a man of successful business enterprise, and a somewhat extensive ship-owner. ch.: 1. Sarah J., Feb. 1821, m. George Davis, in 1841. 2. Col. Samuel D., July 1825. 3. Lucinda, May 1829.

21. Benja., s. Chas. 14, m. Rachel Dwelley, Ap. 4, 1822, lives on Main st., and is a farmer. ch.: 1. Benj. W., Feb. 11, 1823, m. Ruth Thomas, in Jan. 1850, lives on Main st., in the house built by himself in 1849, and has *Ada M.*, Jan. 15, 1851. 2. Joshua D., Aug. 20, 1824. 3. John Q., m. Lydia A. Curtis, and has *Wm. E.*, Oct. 1850, and a *son* b. 1852, and his w. d. in 1852. 4. Rachel J. D., d. May 15, 1839. 5. Maria E., May 20, 1833. 6. Rachel, d. Sep. 24, 1848.

22. Barker, s. Chas. 14, m. Alice Ayres, Feb. 20, 1825, lives in Chas'n., Mass, is a shipwright by trade, and has 1. Alice B., b. June 29, 1826, m. Jno. Viall, June 4, 1846, Leather dealer, Bos'n., and has *John B.*, May 10, 1849. 2. Charles, b. Mar. 29, 1828, unm. 3. Ellen J., Dec. 24, 1838. 4. Andrew J., July 18, 1840.

23. George, s. Geo. W. 16, m. Olive Bates, June 20, 1824, and d. Mar. 29, 1835. His wid. survives, and lives on King st. ch: 1, Geo. C., Oct. 25, 1824, m. Julia A. Thomas, lives in Hn.,

and had 1 ch., wh. d. 2. Olive W., Aug. 24, 1826. 3. Calvin S., July 27, 1828, m. Lucy F. Stetson, June 1852, and lives in Hn., shoemaker. 4. Elbridge, Aug. 28, 1829. 5. Reuben C., June 24, 1831. 6. Horatio N., July 17, 1833, d. Jan. 1834. 7. Horatio N., July 23, 1834.

THE BALDWIN HOUSE.

BALDWIN, Rev. Saml., 2d Pastor of the 1st Church in H., (s. David, of Sud'y., gr. s. of Henry, and gr. gr. s. of Henry, of Devonshire, Eng'd.,, who sett. at Woburn, in 1650,) grad. H. C. 1752, m. Hannah, da. Judge John Cushing, Jan. 4, 1759, and d. Dec. 1, 1784, and his wid. May 8, 1790. ch.: 1. Abigail, Nov. 13, 1759, d. Dec. 22, 1831. 2. Saml., Ap. 19, 1761, d. May 7, 1762. 3. Saml., Feb. 18, 1763, d. in N. Y., æ. ab. 20. 4. Hannah, July 13, 1765, d. Nov. 2, 1789. 5. Mary, Nov. 25, 1768, m. Robert Salmond, Nov. 1, 1787, and d. Aug. 12, 1847. 6. Bethia C., May 19, 1771, m. Thos. Young, of E. Bridg'r., Jan. 5, 1792, and had 7 ch. 7. Wm., bap. Mar. 20, 1774, d. unm. in Bridg'r., ae. ab. 70, a hatter by trade. 8. Lucy, Oct. 3, 1776, m. Barzillai Allen, of E. Bridg'r., and had 5 ch. 9. Fanny, June 8, 1780, living unm. with Mr. Saml. Salmond.

BARKER, Caleb, a Quaker, s. Lt. Robt., of Dux., was in H. in 1727, and lived on Plain st., near Zaccheus Estes'. He was Selectman in 1735. His son, Robert, m. Hannah Turner, and had

Robert, whose descts. are in Pemb., and *Gideon* and *Joshua*, who were furnacemen, and whose descts. are in N. Y. The das. m. and sett. in Pemb.

NOTE. Two bros., Robert and John, were of Dux., ab. 1632, and were the ancestors of most of this name in Plymouth Co. John s. John, was of Scit., and was the ancestor of most of the Barkers in that town.

2. Joshua, s. Benj., of Hn., and gr. s. of Joshua, of Scit., m. Debo. Sturtevant, and lives on King st. His w. is dead. Mr. B. is the enterprising conductor of the Iron Foundry on King st., known as Barker's Foundry, and is a man of energy, and industry. ch.: 1. Deborah, May 22, 1834, d. Mar. 2, 1842. Sarah J., June 24, 1836. 3. Joshua, Dec. 6, 1837. 4. Eveline, Nov. 8, 1840. 5. Jas. M., May 25, 1843. 6. Alfred, Dec. 20, 1847. 7. Mary, July 15, d. Sept. 14, 1849.

RESIDENCE OF CAPT. SETH BARKER.

3. Capt. Seth, s. Josiah, of Pemb., m. Harriet S., da. of Isaac Mead, of Chas'n., Mass., in 1840, and lives near N. River bridge, in the Judge Whitman house. Has one da., Alice, b. June 19, 1848. Mr. B. was a shipmaster for many years, sailing from Boston to the Sandwich Islands, and to the N. W. Coast, in the Fur Trade. In 1838, he left the Seas, and in 1848, sett. in H. His fa. was for many years a Naval Constructor, at Chas'n., in the employ of the U. S. We give a view of Capt. B.'s residence above.

BARREL, Elisha, b. 1735, s. Wm., gr.s. Wm., and gr.gr. s. of Wm., who d. in Bos'n., 1639, (Deane.) m. Mary, da. Jno. Collamore, and d. in H., Mar. 21, 1829, ae. 94, and his wid. Jan. 8, 1831, ae. 95. He was a soldier in the Fr. war, and built the house now occupied by his son Elisha. ch.: 1. Mary, Sep. 21, 1774, m. Levi Burr, of Hm., who is d., and she is living in H., on Walnut st. 2. Elisha, Mar. 7, 1777. 3. Sarah, Feb. 4, 1779, m. Calvin D. Wilder, Jan. 15, 1815, and d. in 1845.

2. Elisha, s. Elisha, Lt. in the war of 1812, and Capt. of the H. Artil. Co., in 1819, m. Lydia Clapp, of Scit., June 11, 1806, who d. Oct. 17, 1849, ae. 71. He yet survives. ch.: 1. Harriet, June 28, 1808, m. Israel H. Gardner, of H. 2. John, Oct. 19, 1811, d. Dec. 1817. 3. Lydia S., Dec. 13, 1818, m. Capt. Benj. N. Curtis, Dec. 25, 1836, and d. Mar. 24, 1840.

BARRY, John S., s. Wm. and Esther, of Boston, b. March 26, 1819, m. Louisa, da. Lott and Kezia Young, of Rox'y., Ap. 8, 1840, and sett. in H. in 1841. ch.: 1. Caroline L., Ap. 12, 1841. 2. Eliza B., June 6, 1843. 3. Henrietta M., Jan. 1, 1848.

"BARSTOW,
Naburn Hall, York.
Ermine, on a fesse sable, three crescents, or.
Crest, a horse's head, couped ar."

BARSTOW. This family is of English origin, and from the West Riding of Yorkshire, where the name still occurs. According to Whittaker's Ed. of Thoresby's Hist. of Leeds, "Edmond Barstow, Esq., J. P., for the North Riding of Yorkshire, was in

1816, possessed of Hingerskil, formerly the seat of the Hoptons, being the second husband of Ellinor Hopton, of the ancient and eminent family of Hopton of Hopton, by whom he had Edward, Thomas, Mary, Eleanor, and Henrietta. He was the son of Edward, the son of Thos. Barstow, of N. Allerton, whose da. Elizabeth, m. Darcy Conyers, Esq.; and his bro. Walter, was fa. of Mr. Jeremiah Barstow, of Leeds, who, by Alice, da. of Mr. John Douglass, of Anstrop Hall, had issue Jere., Esq., Mayor of Leeds, 1706, Michael of Wakefield, and Wm. of Leeds. The oldest son, by Elizabeth, da. of Mr. Wm. Brook, of Killingbrook, had issue Jere., d. unm., Wm., and Hannah."[1] We find in London, at the present date, James, and Thos. I. Barstow, Esqr's., barristers, in the Temple, who were of Yorkshire. The fa. of the latter is also a lawyer, in Yorkshire. We have likewise heard of the Rev. Francis Barstow, of Scalesboro' Park, who d. ab. 1830; of Mr. Barstow, of Green Gate House, near Leeds; and of Mr. Barstow, of Headingly, near Leeds, — a man of property.[2]

Four brothers of this name came early to N. Eng., and settled at Cambridge, Watertown, and Dedham. These were George, Michael, John, and William. Of but two, George and William, have we been able to learn when and how they came. We find that, on the 20th Sept. 1635, William Barstow, ae. 23, and Geo., ae. 21, embarked for N. Eng., in the Truelove, John Gibbs, Master. The place from which they came is not given, but they were probably of Yorkshire.

The following are the principal minutes which we have obtained of the history of these brothers.

1. George, one of the brothers, according to the Mids'x. Prob. Rec., m. Susan, da. Thos. Marrit; had land granted him in Dedham, in 1642;[3] was a member of the An. and Hon. Art. Co., in 1644;[4] a householder in Scit. in 1652, and a member of the second Church;[5] and d. in Camb. 18d. 6m., 1652, his will being on file, and his estate being appraised at £85 14s. 6d.[6] His wid.

[1] The above is varied slightly from the original, to embrace more facts in less compass.

[2] Letter of Mr. Henry Barstow, and communication from Rev. R. Breare.

[3] Worthington's Hist. Dedham.

[4] Hist. An. & Hon. Art. Co.

[5] Scit. Town and Church Recs.

[6] Prob. Rec. Mid.

Susan, d. at Camb. in 1654, and in the Invt. of her Est., allusion is made to a "steere and cow at *Dedham*, and two young heffers at *Scituate*," and Thos. Marrit is called her father, and was appointed guardian to her two ch.[1] This Invt. is signed by John Bridge and *Michael Barstow*. The names of the ch. were, 1., Margaret, bap. in Scit., Feb. 24, 1649–'50, and 2., George, bap. in Scit., June 12, 1652, his father being then decs'd. These ch. are alluded to in the will of Michael, of Watn., in 1674, and to each he left a legacy. Of their history we know nothing with certainty. We think it highly probable, however, that the Barstows of *Rehoboth*, descended from the son *George*. There we find that Saml., s. *George* and *Mary*, was b. May 1, 1705, and m. Mary Mason, Mar. 29, 1733; and this *Geo.*, seems to have had a son Geo., b. at a previous date, prob. as early as 1690, before the fa. sett. in R. *Geo., senr.*, d. Ap. 6, 1726, but his age is not given. Geo., jr., m. Martha Mason, Sep. 29, 1715, and d. May 11, 1733. His ch. were, 1. Martha, b. Ap. 16, 1716; 2. Jno., b. June 14, 1718, m. Susanna Carpenter, Mar. 15, 1743, and is prob. the one alluded to in letter of Eben'r. B., of Scot'd. Ct., who, he says, was "killed in the famous battle at the heights of Abraham, in Quebec, Canada, (1759,) leaving 3 ch., one of whom was Wm. (of Prov., m. Bethiah Bourn? June 10., 1773,) whose s. John? now resides in Killingly, Ct., and *his* son John is in Scot'd., Ct., and was previously of Prov., R.I."; 3. Hannah, Ap. 2, 1721, d. young; 4. Geo., Mar. 19, 1724, m. Abigail Mason? Mar. 14, 1753; 5. Hannah, Feb. 7, 1726–7.

NOTE.—Another John, called John the 3d., m. Judith Carpenter, Feb. 18, 1756? and had, 1. Lucy, Mar. 26, 1757? d. young. 2. Danl., July 25, 1759. 3. Abel, Oct. 20, 1760. 4. Huldah, Jan. 26, 1762. 5. Lucy, Jan. 26? 1762, 6. John, Mar. 6, 1765. "Joseph Munroe, of Rehoboth, m. Sarah Barstow, June 9, 1782."

2. Mich. Barstow brother of George, was made freeman of Mass. Mar. 3, 1635-6, and possessed in Wat., as per Rec., "1.—a homestead of 14 acs. 2.—2 acs. of meadow at beere brook. 3.—2 acs. of meadow in Plain Meadow. 4.—7 acs. of Plowland, being the 10th lot in the further plain. 5.—7 acs. of meadow, being the 10th lot in the remote meadow. 6.—12 acs. of upland beyond the

[1] Prob. Rec., vol. 1, p. 73.

further plain, being the 29th lot. 7.—a Farm of 129 acs. of upland, in the 5th division, and 8.—50 acs. of land, being a great dividend in the 4th div. and 9th lot." He was a man of note in the hist. of the town, his name often occurring on its records, and he being Selectman in 1652, Rep. in 1653, and often on the Jury of trials.[1] From the disposition made of his property, we infor that he left no family. He was prob. m., and his w. Grace, d. July 20, 1671,—3 years before his own decease. No ch. are named. His will is dated June 23, 1674, and in it, he gives legacies to Rev. Jno. Sherman, of Wat.; to the Church of Christ in Wat.; and to Dea. Thos. Hastings, and Dea. Henry Bright, whom he names as his executors. The bulk of his property was disposed of as follows:—"To Hannah Barstow, alias *Prince*, one great bible, and the debt due to me in my booke, which her first husband, Wm. Barstow was indebted, &c.; to Elizabeth, w. of Wm. Randall, of Scit., £5; the same to Susan, w. of Wm. Perry, of Mfd.; to Michael, son of *John Barstow, deceased*, a lot of upland, &c. in Wat.; and to John and Jeremiah, ch. of the aforesaid *John Barstow, decs'd.*, to ea. £15. The rest of the est., after paying debts, &c. to be divided into 10 shares, 2 of wh. parts or shares were given to the ch. of his bro. Geo. B. decs'd., and 8 to the ch. of his bro. Wm. decs'd." His est. was appraised at £273 18s. 3d.[2]

3. John, although not expressly called so, was, we have no doubt, bro. of George and Michael, and resided in Camb., where he died in 1657, the Inv. of his Est. being entered the 20 d. 12 mo. 1657,[3] and consisting chiefly of farming utensils. In this Inv., mention is made of a *widow*, who appeared before the governor, Feb. 25, 1657-8 and testified to that being a true Inv. of the Est. of her husb. &c As no *will* exists, we find no ch. named; but if he be the one alluded to in the will of Michael, above, he had 3 sons, *Michael, John*, and *Jeremiah*;—and if this *Michael* be the one who testified in the case of a complaint vs. Susanna Woodward et. al. 1671, 3, 6,[4] where he is called *Michael, jr.*, and said to be ae. ab. 17, he was b. ab. 1654. We find that John, the father, instituted a suit vs.

1 Middlesex Court Files, passim.
2 Mid. Prob. Rec. 4. 168.
3 Mid. Prob. Rec. 1, 143.
4 Mid. Court Rec., An. 1671.

Ann Hibbins, Relict and Exec. of Wm.Hibbins, desc'd., in 1656, 3, 29,[1] which was but about a year before his decease. The name of his wid. we have not learned. *Michael*, the son, m. Rebecca Thaire or *Thayer*, Jan. 12, 1676, and d. Dec. 2, 1698, leaving an only da. Hannah.[2] He owned "a homestall containing 6 acres of upland and meadow, with a mantion house, and barn, orchards, and cyder mill, &c."

The history of the other sons,—John and Jeremiah,—is involved in a little obscurity. There was a *John* Barstow in Scit. in 1678, who is called by Deane a son of *Wm.*, formerly of Dedham, and who, he says, was *prob. b. in Dedham*. There was also a *Jeremiah* in Scit., who was "killed by the Indians in 1676," and whose wid. Lydia m. Richard Standlake, 1677. This *Jeremiah* is also called by Deane a son of *Wm.* of Dedham. But as there is *no actual record of the birth of such sons to Wm.*, we think there is room to doubt the correctness of Deane's suggestion. It is *certain* that John of Camb., had sons Jno. and Jere., but *not* certain that Wm. had such. We think it most probable, therefore, that John and Jeremiah settled in Scituate, and were sons of John, who d. at Camb., and not of Wm. of Dedham.

Of their history, and descendants, we shall speak hereafter.

4. William, the fourth bro., was in Dedham in 1636, and signed the Pet'n. for the incorp'n. of that town under the name of Contentment.[3] The 16 d. 12 mo. 1642, grants of "upland ground fit for improvement with the plough," were made to him, and to his bro. George. He was a freem. in Scit. 1649, and the first settler, of whom we have record, on the present territory of H. He was prob. m. to his w. Anne, after he came to N. Eng. but we have found no record of this marriage, and cannot, therefore, give her maiden name in full. Mr. B. was a noted man in his day, as will be seen from what we have already said of him. He was also an extensive landholder, a man of high respectability, and a worthy and enterprising citizen. He d. in Scit. in 1668, ae. 56, leaving no will, and his wid. Anne, admin. on his Est.[4] In the will

[1] Mid. Court Rec. an. 1656.
[2] Mid. Prob. Rec. Vol. 9, pp. 225–7.
[3] Worthington's Hist. Ded.
[4] Col. Rec., 3, 56.

of Michael, his bro., mention is made of "8 ch. of his bro. Wm." We have succeeded in learning the names and dates of birth of but 5 of these. There seem to have been but 2 sons; the rest were probably daughters. Their names were, 1. Joseph, b. in Dedham, 6 d. 4 mo., 1639. 2. Patience, b. in Dedham, 3 d. 10 mo., 1643, m. Moses Simmons, of Scit., 1662. 3. Deborah b. in Scit. in Aug. 1650. 4. Wm. b. in Scit., in Sep. 1652. 5. Martha b. in Scit., 1655, m. Sam'l., eldest son of Sam'l. Prince, 1674, who d. bef. 1686. (N. E. Gen. Reg. 1851 p. 379.)

NOTE.—It would appear, from the will of Michael, of Watn., that the w. of Mr. B. m. a *Prince*.

5. John, s. John 3, is prob. the one who was a householder in Scit. in 1678. According to Deane, "a consid. tract of land was laid out to him W. of the So. Meeting-house common, extending to Jordan Lane. His house was 50 rods south of the present road, and was afterwards the house of John Ruggles," &c. He m. Lydia Hatch, Jan. 16, 1678, da. of Wm. Hatch, who moved to Swansey, and had 1. Job, Mar. 8, 1679. 2. Jeremiah, Aug. 28, 1682. 3. John, Feb. 15, 1684, bap. an adult, July 18, 1708, and prob. d. unm. 4. Jerusha, Nov. 21, d. Dec. 18, 1687. 5. Susanna, May 5, 1689. 6. Abigail, Mar. 8, 1692. 7. Lydia, Mar. 26, 1696.

6. Jeremiah, s. John 3, is prob. the one who was killed by the Indians, with Capt. Michael Pierce, of Scit., at Rehoboth, in 1676. He m. Lydia ———, and she, after his decease, m. Richard Standlake, in 1677. The ch. of Mr. B. were, 1. John, and 2. Jeremiah, and of these the wid. Lydia was appointed guardian, "to demand and recover a legacy given unto each of them by their *great uncle*, Michael Barstow, late of Watn. decsd., as by his will."[1] Lett's. of Adm. were granted to John, bro. of "Jeremiah, deceased, so he keep a faire accompt thereof, and be reddy to shew it before said Court, when by them required."[2] According to Deane, Jeremiah, the youngest of these sons, was a captive, for a time, amongst the Indians.[3] We have no knowledge of the subsequent history of this family.

[1] Col. Rec., 6, 15. [2] Ibid. [3] Hist. Scit., 218.

7. Joseph, s. Wm. 4, m. Susanna Lincoln of Hm., May 16, 1666, (Hm. Rec.) and d. Ap. 17, 1712, and his wid. Jan. 31, 1730, being very aged. For some acc't of his life, see p. 18. That he was an extensive landholder, is evident from the large grants made to him by the Col. Court, which embraced many hundred acres,[1] now lying chiefly in Abington. These grants were in the vicinity of the grants made to Cornet Stetson, with whom Mr. B. seems to have been on terms of intimate friendship, and whose will he witnessed. ch.: 1. Susanna, June 3, 1667, m. Isaac Randall, Nov. 19, 1684. 2. Joseph, Jan. 22, 1675. 3. Benjamin, Mar. 1, 1679, prob. d. young, as he is not named in his father's will. 4. Deborah, Dec. 26, 1681, m. John Bryant, jr., Jan. 1, 1707. 5. Samuel, Jan 1, 1683.

8. William Barstow s. Wm. 4, m. Sarah ——, and is called a *husbandman*.[2] He occupied his father's house, and probably, also, to some extent, followed the business of ship-building. He was owner of a saw-mill, and of other property, which he bequeathed to 2 sons and 5 das., and his will bears date 1711. ch.: 1. Rebecca, Mar. 12, 1676. 2. Martha, 1678, m. John McFarland ? Dec. 25, 1705. 3. Anna, June 26, 1681, m. Saml. Curtis, Sep. 11, 1707. 4. Wm., Nov. 23, 1684. 5. Mary, Feb. 21, 1687, m. Saml. Harlow, Plym'h., Jan. 3, 1715–6. 6. Benj., July 22, 1690. 7. Susanna, Nov. 8, 1693, m. Benj. Taylor, Nov. 19, 1724.

NOTE.—A son of Wm. bap. Nov. 7, 1680, prob. d. young.

9. Job, s. John 5, sett. in Norwich, Ct., and m. Rebecca, da. Joseph and Mary Bushnell, (formerly a Saffingwell,) Mar. 2, 1707–8, she being 19 yrs. of age. He d. Sept. 14, 1767, ae. 84, and his wid., May 7, 1782, ae, 94, (as per records from Ct.) The fa. is spoken of as a man of strong intellect, sound judgment, unbending integrity, gentlemanly deportment, and manners peculiarly bland and conciliatory. His advice and counsel were often sought, and he was eminently a peace-maker, and a healer of

[1] Hobart's Abington, pp. 18 and 19. [2] Prob. Rec., Plym.

divisions among his neighbors and friends. The mother was also intelligent and pious. Ch.: 1. Rebecca, Dec. 18, 1708, d. Oct. 1709. 2. Jerusha, Sept. 1, 1710, m. John Gager, of Frank'n., Ct., had 6 sons and 2 da's., and d. July 7, 1775. 3. Jonathan, Dec. 26, 1712. 4. Lydia, May 27, 1715, m. 1, an Edgerton, ? and 2, Bradford Peck, and d. May 7, 1767. 5. Mary, Dec. 16, 1717, m. Alpheus Wickwire, had 2 da's. and 1 son, and d. Sep 25, 1799. 6. Ebenezer, June 16, 1720. A baker by trade, lived in Norwich, and d. unm., Sep. 30, 1755. 7. Yetonce, July 17, 1722, m. Esther Wood, had 2 das., and d. Dec. 28, 1799. 8. John, Dec. 31, 1724. 9. Abigail, Feb. 17, 1727, m. 1, Danl. Kingsbury, and had 3 das., and 1 son; and 2, David Bottom, and had 1 son, and d. ae. 83.

10. Jeremiah, s. John 5, was prob. of Marlboro', Mass., and with his w. Elizabeth, ? were members of the Church in 1704. He m. Sarah Howe, perhaps a 2d w., "ye 6 d. 10 mo., 1711," and had ch. bap. in M., 1. Jeremiah, and 2. Elizabeth bap. 26 d. 8 mo., 1712. The former prob. d. 3. Dorothy, 25 d. 2 mo., 1714. 4. John, 18 d. 1 mo., 1716. 5. Abigail, 10 d. —mo., 1718. 6. Wm., 21 d. —mo., 1719. 7. Sarah, 3 d. 7 mo., 1721. 8. Lydia, 19 d. 7 mo., 1725. 9. Jeremiah, 9 d. 5 mo., 1727. See Church Rec. Marlb. This is all the information I can obtain of the family.

11. Joseph, s. Joseph 7, called Capt. Joseph, on the H. Rec., m. Mary ——— and d., in H., July 25, 1728. The Inv. of his Est. speaks of $\frac{1}{4}$ of a sloop; his farm of 70 acs.; the farm of 40 acs. on which Wm. Stetson lived, in Scit.; the farm of the wid. Amy Dwelly, of Scit., 24 acs.; 328 acs. called the Court Grant, between land of Dea. Stockbridge and Saml. Barstow; 32 acs. of cedar swamp, partly in said grant; 70 acs. joining the N. side of Elij. Cushing's farm; 45 acs. on the S. of sd. C's. farm; 6 acs. fresh meadow; $\frac{1}{4}$ of the new forge; 5 $\frac{1}{3}$ acs. by Gershom Stetson's; 6 acs. adjoining Chas. Stockbridge's; 1$\frac{1}{4}$ acs. on the N. side of the road to Benj. Perry's; $\frac{1}{9}$ of a saw-mill; 184 acs. of land in Pemb., adjoining the new Forge; 14 acs. in Pemb., near the Major'sPurchase; $\frac{1}{4}$ grist mill at new Forge; $\frac{1}{2}$ ac. by N. River bridge; and a negro woman named

Rose. The whole was appraised at £6,926, — a large sum for those days. (Prob. Rec. Plym. 5, 846–8.) Mr. B. lived on Broadway, built the Barstow Forge, and it is said, built the house now known as the *Salmond House*. His wid. m. Thos. Bryant, of Scit., May 14, 1735. Ch.: 1. Elizab., Aug. 23, 1699, m. 1, Isaac Barker, of Newport, R. I., Jan. 25, 1719, and 2, Elijah Cushing, Esq., —— 1724. (See her father's will.) 2. Joseph, Sep. 6, 1701, d. Ap. 4, 1703. 3. Joseph, Jan. 10, 1704. 4. Joshua, Sep. 8, 1706, d. young. 5. Mary, Feb. 21, 1709, d. young. 6. James, Ap. 20, 1711, d. Jan. 16, 1733, leaving a will. (Prob. Rec. Plym.) 7. Mary, May 20, 1717. 8. Joshua, Sep. 8, 1720. 9. Abigail, bap. May 9, 1723.

NOTE,—An inf. da. bap. Oct. 12, 1719, prob, d. soon after.

12. Samuel, s. Joseph 7, m. Lydia Randall, Mar. 17, 1708, d. Oct. 23, 1730, ae. 47, and his wid. m. Thos. Tracy, of Pemb. May 28, 1733, and moved to P. with her ch. Mr. B. prob. lived near the centre meeting-house, in which vicinity, and in the westerly part of the town, he was the owner of a large body of land, and other property. His est. was appraised at £3,700,[1] and was divided into 9 shares, 2 of wh. were left to his son Saml., 1 to Debo., 1 to Lydia, 1 to Job, 1 to Michael, 1 to Elizab., and 1 to Priscilla. Lett. of Adm. were granted to Lydia, relict, &c., 1731, and in 1741, she is called Lydia *Tracy*, Adm'x. on Est. Saml. B. &c., and rendered her final acc't. Mr. B. was Selectman, in 1729. ch.: 1. Samuel, Feb. 7, 1709. 2. Deborah, bap. Oct. 5, 1712, m. Sam'l. Hatch ? Dec. 25, 1732. 3. Lydia, Ap. 1, 1717, m. Ichabod Brewster,[2] of Dux., June 3, 1735, and settled in Lebanon, Ct. 4. Job, bap. Ap. 3, 1720. 5. Michael, Jan. 9, 1723. 6. Joseph, bap. June 13, 1725. 7. Elizab., May 8, 1727, prob. m. Job Young, June 6, 1762. 8. Priscilla, Oct. 5, 1729.

13. William, s. Wm. 8, m. Sarah Randall, Dec. 20, 1709, and d. previous to 1734, in wh. year his Est. was sett. His wid. Sarah, is named, and Han'h., w. Wm. Ford, and a da. Sarah, and an only

[1] Prob. Rec. Plym. 5, 814–16.

[2] Winsor's Dux. He says Ichabod B. m. Lydia *Brewster*, of Pemb. It should be *Barstow*.

son Wm. The wid. d. May 13, 1738.? ch.: 1. Hannah, Aug. 10, 1710, m. Wm. Ford, of Mfd., Oct. 30, 1728, (N. E. Gen. Rec., 1752.) 2. Sarah, Oct. 2, 1712, m. Ezekiel Lad, of H. (See old deeds, &c.) 3. Wm., Ap. 10, 1715.

14. Benjamin Barstow Benjamin, s. Wm. 8, m. 1, Mercy Randall, Dec. 20, 1709, (Scit. Rec.,) who d. in H., Dec. 17, 1728;—2. Sarah Barden, or Burden, ? of Mid'o., May 15, 1729–30, who d. ab. 1738;—and 3. Wid. Ruth Winslow, Nov. 22, 1738. Mr. B. occupied his father's house, being that of his gr. fa. Wm., and seems to have followed their trade, being a shipwright, and having his yard near the N. River Bridge. (See the chap. on Ship-building.) Tradition says that he had 21 ch. in all. From a diligent search of the Town and Church Records, of Scit., Pemb., and Hanover, I find the following 19. The other 2 prob. d. young. 1. Benjamin, Oct. 9, 1710, prob. d. 1715. 2. Martha, Jan. 20, 1712, prob. d. young. 3. Martha, bap. Aug. 14, 1715, m. Eliab Turner, May 12, 1731. 4. Benjamin, bap. Sep. 2, 1716. 5. Nath'l. bap. Aug. 11, 1717. 6. Caleb, bap. Mar. 20, 1719, prob. d. young. 7. Mercy, bap. Aug. 19, 1722, m. Joshua Thomas, 1747, (Pemb. Rec.) 8. Margaret, bap. June 27, 1725. 9. Rebecca, bap. June 11, 1727. 10. A da., bap. July 10, 1728, being sick; prob. d. 11. Gideon, Feb. 14, 1728–9, prob. d. young. (By 2d.) 12. Geo., bap. Jan. 10, 1731. 13. Thomas, Feb. 27, 1732. 14. James, Feb. 22, 1734. 15. Jacob, Feb. 15, 1736. 16. Gideon, Jan., 1738. (By 3d.) 17. Caleb, 18. Sarah, May 5, 1741, m. Silvanus Cook, of Kgs'n, Mar. 22, 1764. 19. Content, m. — Barlow, of Rochester.

15. Jonathan, s. Job 9, m. Abigail Hyde, and d. Nov. 28, 1747, ae. 35. ch.: 1. Abigail, m. Ebenezer Hartshorn, of Franklin, Ct., and had 9 ch. 2. Betsey, m. Phinehas Peck, and had several children. 3. Jonathan, m. Mary Pettes, lived in Tolland, Ct., and had *Mary, Jonathan, Nancy, Alvin, and Royal.*

16. John, s. Job 9, m. Jerusha or Elizabeth ? Newcomb, of Franklin, Ct., ab. 1746, and sett. in Cant'y., Ct., ab. 1750, where he d. Feb. 9, 1796, ae. 71, and his remains, with those of his w.,

lie "in the old grave yard in Westminister parish."—"They were loved and respected in their lives, and mourned, not only by a large family, but by the community among whom they lived." ch.: 1. Alpheus, 1748. 2. Samuel, Jan. 1749. 3. John, Oct. 2, 1751, d. young. 4. John, Dec. 21, 1752. 5. Hezekiah, Feb. 28, 1755. 6. Ebenezer, Sep. 7, 1756. 7. Anne, July 31, 1759, d. ae. 14. 8. Job, Mar. 5, 1760. 9. Rebecca E., June 11, 1763, m. 1, Nath'l Annable, and 2, Col. Pierce. 10. Wm. A., Feb. 21, 1765. 11. Jerusha, Mar. 2, 1767, m. Nathan Palmer, Esq., of Wilkesbarre, Pa., a lawyer, and a memb. of the Senate of Pa., for 4 yrs. &c. Their ch. were: 1. *Sterne*, of Mt. Holly, Pa., Chief Cl'k. Farmer's Bank, m. Mary, da. Jno. Palmer, of Monmouth Co., N. J., and has a son, Theodore, in Cala. 2. *Strange N.*, Ed. of the Pottsville Emporium, and fomerly Judge of the C. C. P., m. Jane Moffat, and his da. m. Rev. Abel C. Thomas, of Philad.; a da., m. a Potts, of Pottsville; and his son *Robert*, is Dist. Att'y, &c. 3. *Volney Barstow*, the distinguished and enterprising ADVERTISING AGENT, whose offices are in Boston, N. York, and Philad.,—m. Eliza B., da. Joseph Boyd, of Philad., and has *M. Julia*, *Ella V. B.*, *Mary R.*, and *C. Lillie.* 4. *John*, of Rye, N. Y., farmer, m. Harriet Barker, and has 3 ch. 5. *Eliza*, not m. 6. *George.*

17. Joshua, s. Joseph 11, m. Elizab. Foster, of Scit., Ap. 21, 1741, and, according to an inscrip'n. in the H. grave yard, "was drowned at the Eastward, Oct. 3, 1763, ae. 44." It has been said that he owned, for a time, the Gad Bailey place, on King-st. He was proprietor of the Forge built by his father in 1720, (see p. 20 ?) which he improved until his decease, and probably occupied his father's house. ch.: 1. Joseph, Nov. 13, 1742, d. May 2, 1759. 2. Mary, June 6, 1743, m. a Curtis, ? resided at Harpswell Neck, Me., and had a large family, mostly sons. 3. James, Oct. 8, 1744. 4. Barshaway, Feb. 20, 1745, m. a Merrill. ? 5. Abigail, Sep. 26, 1747, d. Oct. 24, 1749. 6. Joshua, June 26, (T. Rec.,) or July 7, (Fam. Rec.,) 1749. 7. Calvin, Oct. 7, 1750, was m., and d. in Preston, Ct., in 1826, leaving a son, *Jedediah*, of Jewett City, Ct., who was m., and d. in E. Hampton, Ct., in 1846; and a son, *Joshua*, of Preston, b. Feb., 1776, who m., and had 6 ch.,—4 are living, viz: a son in Mich'n, a son in N.

York., a da. m., in Preston, and the youngest son, with his fa 8. Ezekiel, June 7, (T. Rec.,) or July 7., (Fam. Rec.,) 1752. 9. Abigail, Sep. 29, (T. Rec.,) or Dec. 7, (Fam. Rec.,) 1753, m. an Ainsworth, of Portland, Me. 10. (Timothy ?) Hatherly, Feb. 22, 1755, sett. in Port'd., Me. 11. Foster, Ap. 2, 1757. 12. Elizabeth, Feb. 5, 1760. 13. Joseph, ? sett. in N. Yarmouth, Me., was first a blacksmith, and afterwards a saddler.

18.  Samuel, s. Sam'l. 12, is called Dea. Sam'l. on the H. Rec., and was for many years Dea. of First Ch. He m. Margaret., da. Dea. Joseph Stockbridge, ? Nov. 26, 1731, who d. Ap. 12, 1788, ae. 80, and he d. Nov. 19, 1801, ae. 93. He was Selectman in 1745 and 6. ch.: 1. Lusannah, Oct. 9, 1732, m. John Ruggles, jr., Scit., Mar. 11, 1755. 2. Samuel, July 28, 1734. 3. Lydia, Mar. 14, 1736, m. Seth Bailey, Feb. 11, 1762. 4. Marg't, Feb. 20, 1738, d. June 1, 1739. 5. Charles, May 3, 1740. 6. Seth, June 15, 1742. 7. Daniel, July 1, 1744. 8. Marg't, June 1, 1746, d. Jan. 24, 1757. 9. Grace, May 27, 1748, m. Elisha Foster, jr., Scit., Oct. 19, 1769.

19. Joseph, s. Sam'l 12, with his sister Lydia, moved to Lebanon, Ct., ab. 1735, and m. wid. Mary Webster, formerly a Bliss, May 6, 1752, who d. Mar. 4, 1770. ch.: 1. Job, Mar. 17, 1753. 2. Michael, May 24, 1754. 3. Joseph, Nov. 16, 1755. 4. Molly, Jan. 12, 1757. 5. Lydia, Dec. 15, 1758, m. Jesse Loomis, of Lebanon, Ct., and sett. in Bennington, Vt., where she is yet living, ae. 94! 6. Samuel, Ap. 8, 1760. 7. Elizab. or Betsey, Jan 31, 1762, m. Chas. Wright, of Columbia, Ct., "was left a wid. many years ago, and now resides in Canton, Bradford Co., Pa., with her ch., retains to a remarkable degree her faculties of body and mind, and is able to walk from house to house with a quick step, while her tongue is loosed on the great subject of religion." 8. Mehitabel, Dec. 14, 1764. 9. Charles, Ap. 15, 1766. 10. Elias, Sep. 5, 1768.

20. George, s. Benj. 14, m. Asenath Taylor, Jan. 10, 1750-1.

It is said that he lived, for a time, where Col. J. B. Barstow resides, and finally moved to Me., where he d. His ch. bap. in H., were 1. Isaac, Sep. 20, 1761, and 2. Asenath, Aug. 5, 1764.

21. Thomas, s. Benj. 14, m. Sarah, da. John Studley, and lived in Scit., his farm lying near Palmer's bridge, by the third Herring brook, and his house being the same as that now occupied by his grandson, Elijah. He was a ship-builder by trade, as were his ancestors before him, and occupied the yard whose site is marked by the two venerable white oaks. He d. Mar. 27, 1797, ae. 65, and his wid. Feb. 2, 1805, ae. 74. A man of capable business habits, and of excellent moral character. Ch.: 1. Sarah, b. 1754, bap. Mar. 16, 1755, m. Sam'l Woodward, moved to Me., and has desc'ts. there. 2. Thos., b. 1756, bap. May 22, 1757. 3. Rebecca, b. 1759, bap. Sep. 13, 1761, m. Nath'l Church, of Scit., and moved to Me., where she d. in 1812. 4. Nath'l. b. 1761, bap. June 13, 1764. 5. John Burden, b. 1764, bap. June 17, 1764. Jane D., b. 1766, bap. Aug. 31., m. Sam'l Donnell, of H. 7. Mary, or Molly, b. 1768, bap. Oct. 2, d. unm., June 1, 1850. 8. Elijah, b. 1771.

22. James, s. Benj. 14, m. Rhoda House, Feb. 23, 1758, was a ship-builder for a time in H., and moved to Dux'y., where he engaged in the same business, and where he d. in 1808, and his wid. in Pemb., Sep. 5, 1819, ae. 84. ch.: 1. James. 2. Joseph. 3. Nabby, m. Asa Keen, of Pemb., and had 12 ch. 4. William. 5. George, Ap. 7, 1775. 6. Ruth, m. Wm. Standish, of P., and had 10 ch.

23. Jacob, s. Benj. 14, m. Kezia or *Desire* Brattles, Mar. 13, 1760, who d. in Pemb., Sep. 28, 1793, ae. 52. His death was caused in a singular manner. He was riding on the beach, by the Brant Rock, in Mfd., not far from the farm of the Hon. Daniel Webster, when his horse, being either frightened, or too suddenly checked, threw him into the surf, and stepped on his breast, killing him instantly. ch:. 1. Huldah, Jan. 23, 1760–1, m. Alanson Carver, of Mfd., and had sev'l. ch., of whom Barstow Carver is yet living in M. 2. Jacob, Nov. 7, 1762. 3. Burden, June 11, 1768, d. unm. 4. Charles, Sep. 1, 1771. 5. Kezia, Jan. 1, 1775., m. Sylvanus Lapham, of Mfd., Ap. 12, 1795. 6. Deborah, m. John Jones, of Mfd.

24. Gideon, s. Benj., 14, m. 1. Jane Wilson, of Chatham, Mass., in 1759, who d. April 1, 1816, ae. 84, and 2. Tamar Cushing, of Pemb., Oct. 28, 1816, and d. in Mattapoisett, Mar. 9, 1826, ae. 88. He was a ship-builder by trade; a man of enterprise and integrity; one who stood high in the esteem of the people among whom he lived; and who gave to the place an impetus which it yet feels, and did much to promote its prosperity. ch.: 1. Gideon, Sep. 11, 1760. 2. Mary, Nov. 15, 1762, m. Capt. Nath'l. Pope, of Fairhaven, and d. in June, 1851, ae. 89. 3. Wilson, June 3, 1765. 4. Benj., Aug., 26, 1767, d. unm., in Ap., 1847, ae. 80. 5. Caleb, and 6. Sarah, Feb. 1, 1770. The former d. Aug. 7, 1794, and the latter Aug. 4, 1774. 7. Lucy, Mar. 25, 1772, m. Nath'l. Hammond, Esq., of Matt., and d. Oct. 20, 1802. 8. Sarah, July 1, 1777, m. Rev. Geo. Barstow, Nov. 26, 1801, and is yet living in S. Bridg'r.

25. Caleb, s. Benj. 14, m. Sylvina Magoun, of Pemb., Nov. 23, 1770, and d. in Windsor, Ct., Mar. 17, 1800, and his wid. in Matt., May, 1816, ae. 67. ch.: 1. Caleb, Sept. 1771, m. Alice McDaniell, of Johnston, R. I., moved to Marietta, Ohio, in 1807, and d. ab. 1835, leaving ch. He had 12 in all, of whom 4 survive; viz.: *Lydia*, *Salvinia*, *Maria*, and *Isaac*. 2. Benj., d. young. 3. Sylvia, Mar., 1775, d. Oct., 1791. 4. Benj., and 5, Sarah, Aug. 22, 1776. The latter d. Oct., 1791. 6. Elias, July 3, 1779. 7. Achsa, Mar. 17, 1781, m. Saml. Snow, of Prov., R. I., Oct. 17, 1798, and has *Richard M.*, 1799, *Caleb B.*, 1801, and *Sylvina*, 1803. 8. Isaac, Oct. 1783, m. a Walker, and lives in Ohio. 9. Wm., Dec., 1785. 10. Nath'l., Ap. 28, 1788.

26. Alpheus, s. John 16, m. Content Carter, and lived in Leyden, Mass. Had 5 das. and 2 sons, of whom a son John lives in L.

27. Samuel, s. John 16, m. 1, Mary Adams; ? 2, Hannah Spaulding, Ap. 11, 1779, who d, Mar. 9, 1788, ae. 33, and 3, Amy Fitch, of Lisbon. Ct., Ap. 16, 1790, and d. in Cant'y, Ct., July 17, 1822, ae. 72, and his wid. Dec. 24, 1845, ae. 92. ch.: 1. Curtis, Sep. 5, 1782. 2. Simon, Ap. 12, 1784. 3. Orra, Mar. 24, 1786, m. Gad Bulkley, Esq., of Canterbury, (Merchant, of the firm of Tainter and Bulkley,) in 1805, and has 4 ch., *Adaline*,

Jno. W., Sam'l. B., and Simon S. The first 3 are m. and have children. 4. Spaulding, Feb. 27, 1788. (By 2d.) 5. Benj. F., Jan 10. 1792, d. at S. Amboy, N. J., Mar. 7, 1852, from injuries rec'd. as he was stepping into the cars, on his way to Md. His home had been in Misso., where, at the time of his death, he held the off. of U. S. Marshall. He was intelligent and gentlemanly. Not m. 6. Elisha P., Aug. 15, 1793. 7. John, Nov. 2, 1795. 8. Susan P., Oct. 5, 1797, m. Isaac Backus, Esq., of Cant'y., Ct., Ap. 30, 1817, the sen'r part'r of the firm of Backus & Barstow, dealers in Hardware, Ag'l. Imp'ts., &c., in Norwich and Cant'y., Ct. They have a large Foundry and Machine-shop in Cant'y.

28. John, s John 16, m. Susannah Smith, of Cant'y., Ct., was Dea. of the Church there, and "for ab. 50 y'rs. was never absent from meeting but one Sabbath. His minister said, "I can set my watch correctly when I see Dea. B. coming to meeting." For ab. 20 y'rs. he was Selectman of Cant'y. He d. Dec. 9, 1838, ae. 86, and his w. Sep. 14, 1829, ae. 73. ch.: 1. Bethiah, m. Eph'm. Palmer, of Scot'd, Ct., had 3 ch. who are m. and have ch., and she lives a wid. with her only s. Alfred. 2. Septimus, Dec. 16, 1781. 3. Luther, 1785, ? grad. B. U., 1807, sett. as a lawyer, in Homer, N. Y., and d. Aug. 12, 1817, ae. 33, on a visit to his father's. 4. Calvin. 5. Ebenezer, Sep. 12, 1788. 6. Zedekiah S.

29. Hezekiah, s. John 16, m. Olive Bradford, and lived in Ct., on the old homestead, where he d. ch.: 1. Olive, m. a Robinson. 2. Susan, m. a Park. 3. Sophia, m. Russell Park, and sett. in Pa. 4. Elizab., m. Samuel Henry. 5. Jerusha, m. Judge Lyon, of Cant'y. 6. Hezekiah, of Cant'y, lives on his father's place. 7. Polly m. a Palmer. 8. Anne, m. a Morse, of Cant'y.

30. Ebenezer, s. John 16, lived in Shelburne, Vt, near Lake Champlain, m. Esther Owen, of Colchester, and d. Mar. 30, 1834, having had ch.: 1. Anna, m. Theodore Catlin, of Burlington, Vt., and has 8 ch. 2. Elisha, m. Betsy Hollabird ? and had *Martha, Mary*, and an inf. son, d. 3. Herman, m. Laura Lyon, of Shelburne, Vt., and has *Matilda, Homer, Laura, Hiram, Marietta, Les-*

ter, and *Rollin*. 4. John, m. Matilda Crossman, of Burlington, Vt., and has *Rufus*, *Fayette*, *George*, *Matilda*, and others. 5. Sophia, m, Ed. Irish, and has 8 ch. 6. Laura, m. Benj. Irish, and has 2 ch. 7. Jarvis, m. Pamelia Blin, and has *Cordelia*, *Lemira*, and *Samuel*. 8. Lucy, m. Dan'l P. Adams, of Colchester, Vt., and has 2 ch., of whom the son grad. at the Univ'y. of Vt. 9. Jerusha, not m. 10, Ira, is m., has ch., and lives in Colchester, Vt. 11. George,. is m., and lives in Burlington, Vt.

31. Job, s. John 16, m. Lurania Curtis, lived in ——, and had 1. Fred'k. of Hinsdale, Mass., has *Andrew*, *John*, and *Henry*, all in Ohio. 2. Job, of Williamsville, Erie Co., N. Y., has *Samuel L.* 3. John C., Mar. 1797, Judge of Chester, Meigs Co., Ohio, is m. and has *Levi S.*, *Joseph D.*, and *Henry P.* Lost 3, d. young. 4. Sam'l. L., d. ae. 12. 5. Marcus L., at Coolville, Athens Co., Ohio, has *Marcus P.* —— There were 4 das., but their names have not been sent.

32. Wm. A., s. John 16, m. 1, Katharine Spaulding, and 2, Sally Hall, and sett. first in Plainfield, Ct., and then in Ohio, where he d., leaving ch., among whom was a son, who was drowned some years since, while acting as Agent for removing the Indians beyond the Miss'i. We understand that there were 12 ch. in all, viz: 7 sons and 5 das.

33. Joshua, s. Josh. 17, m. Marg't. Bonney, of Pemb., Sep. 23, 1773, and conducted the Forge known as Barstow's Forge, until his removal to Exeter, N. H., ab. 1795, where he d. Dec. 22, 1821, ae. 73, and his wid. Oct. 26, 1825, ae. 80. ch.: b. in H. 1. Ezek'l., July 23, 1774. 2. Betsey, Dec. 12, 1776, m. Simon Magoun, Esq., of E. Kgs'n., N. H., and d. in 1840, having had 9 ch., of whom *Josh. B.*, was an eminent M. D., at Woodville, Miss., where he d. in 1838, and *Cyrus S.* is also an M. D., and Sup't. of the State Hosp'l. at Natchez, Miss. 3. Marg't., Sep. 5, 1780, m. Wm. Graves, and d. at Gilmanton, N. H., 1817, leaving 3 ch. 4. Joshua, Ap, 6, 1782, m. Hannah Webster, of E. Kgs'n. and d. in 1811, leaving 2 das. 5. Calvin, June 10, 1784, d. ae. 12. 6. Charles C., Jan. 25, 1786. 7. Sophia, bap. Sep. 18, 1788, m. Brackett Johnson, of Ports'h., N. H., and d. in 1814, leaving an inf. son.

34. Lt. Sam'l., s. Dea. Sam'l. 18, m. 1, Huldah House, Jan. 27, 1759, and 2, Sibyl Hatch, Jan. 15, 1792, who d. Mar. 25, 1820, ae. 79, and he May 4, 1826, ae. 92. Lived in H., on King st., and is described as " a man of infinite jest; spry as a boy, even at the age of 70, and as full of his jokes." He was Selectman from 1765–'67—in 1772, and in 1776, and '77. ch.: 1. Sam'l., July 15, 1757, d. in the Rev. Army, at Rox'y, Jan. 31. 1776. 2. Job, Oct., 17, 1758, d. unm., in Sharon, Ct., in 1790. 3. Joseph, July 10, 1760. 4. Huldah, July 29, 1763, m. Asa Townsend, Dec. 7, 1796. 5. Philip, Feb. 29, d. Dec. 28, 1765. 6. House, Aug. 16, 1767, d. young.

35. Charles, s. Dea. Sam'l. 18, m. Sally Stockbridge? and lived and d. in Taunton, Mass., over 50 yrs. ago. ch.: 1. Charles, d. unm. 2. Stockbridge, m. a Carver, and left a son Charles, now living in T. 3. Sally, m. a Carver. 4. Lydia, not m.

36. Seth, s. Dea. Sam'l. 18, m. Ruth Allen, of Martha's Vineyard, where he lived for a time, and thence moved to Mattapoisett, and thence to Sharon, Ct., in 1777, where he d. in 1822, and his wife in 1816. He was a shipwright by trade. ch.: 1. Allen, Sep. 2, 1767. 2. Peggy, Sep. 1769, m. Dan'l Lindsley, ab. 1793, and d. ab. 1822, leaving ch. 3. Olive, Nov., 1771, m. Silas St. John, in 1795, and is living in Sharon, Ct. 4. Mary, Feb., 1775, m. Reuben Calkins, and d. ab. 1837, leaving ch. 5. Samuel, May, 1777. 6. Seth T., Oct. 30, 1779. 7. Betsey, Dec., 1781, m. Thos. B. Beebe, and d. ab. 1847, leaving ch. 8. Gamaliel H., 1783? 9. Charles, 1787, was m., and d. in 1816, leaving 1 daughter.

37. Capt. Daniel, s. Dea. Sam'l. 18, m. Betsey Tilden, July 4, 1771, who d. Mar. 8, 1826, ae. 77, and he Feb. 25, 1842, ae. 98. Lived on King st., where his son Daniel resides. He is described by Hon. G. H. Barstow, as " a gent. of the old school, dressed in cocked hat, long blue coat, breeches, and long boots fastened at the knee by a strap and buckle." This was in 1809. He was Selectman in 1786, and Capt. of one of the old Military Companies prior to 1800. ch.: 1. Betty, Aug. 1, 1772, m. Walter Rogers, Mf'd., Oct. 21, 1794. 2. Dan'l., Ap. 28, 1774. 3. Lucy, Aug. 21, 1777, m. Barnab. Stetson, Ab'n., Oct. 10, 1802.

4. Sally, and 5. Grace, July 30, 1780. The latter d. May 12, 1849. 6. Lydia, Oct. 17, 1786, d. May 12, 1822. 7. Nabby, June 27, 1791, m. Eph'm Stetson, Ab'n., Dec. 21, 1813.

38. Michael, s. Joseph 19, according to letters received from Geo. Barstow, Esq., of N.Y., was a gunner in the Rev. Army, and was at the battle of Bunker Hill, in the Regt. of Col. Trott, of Hebron, Ct., and afterwards was at Trenton and Monmouth, also at Princeton and White Plains. He was in the army 6 yrs., and was in the celebrated winter encampment at Valley Forge. Leaving "the tented field," he m. Ruth, only da. of Capt. Abbot, of "Lebanon Crank, Ct.," (a *shipmaster*, who was shot on the deck of his own vessel in an engagement,) and bro. of Dr. Walter Abbot, of Salem, Mass. Her mo., after her husband's decease, lived in Thetford, Vt., m. Dea. Avery, and moved to Orford, N. H., where they "kept about the first public house in that town," She d. in Thetford, ae. 92. Mr. Barstow, after his m., moved first to Campton, N. H., and thence to Haverhill, N. H., where he d. June 28, 1837, ae. 85, and his wid. 3 mos. after, ae. 84. In person, he was of a medium size, with a "Roman face and nose;" a large, high, broad forehead; a head of fine brown hair, which flowed down and curled around his neck; and at the age of 60 he had not one *grey hair*. He was exceedingly athletic and nimble; and at the age of 70, stood upon a level piece of ground, and sprang upon the back of a wild colt that had never been ridden. At the age of 84, he mowed in the field all the forenoon, with his hired man. He received a pension from Gov't., for many years previous to his decease. "The prominent traits in his character were courage and piety; and he died as he had lived, a Christian soldier, and an honest man." ch.: 1. Wm.; 2. Henry; 3. Chas. 4. Thomas; 5. Nancy, d.; 6. Ruth, d.

39. Dea. Samuel, s. Joseph 19, m. Lucina Wright, of Columbia, Ct., Dec. 13, 1781, and sett. on a sterile tract of land, in the outskirts of the town of C., where he spent his days, in frugality and industry, and accumulated, by his own labor, an estate of $30,000. He d. Feb. 27, 1846, ae. 86, and his widow still survives, at the age of 88; her descendants being so numerous, that she is able to say, "arise daughter, and go to thy daughter, for

thy daughter's daughter hath a daughter." She is bright, and intelligent, and takes the charge of her own household, and of her invalid son, doing much of the labor herself, and is a highly worthy and respectable lady. She was m. at the early age of 16. Her husband was chosen Dea. of the Ch., in C., in 1802, and his religious character is ably set forth in the interesting Tract, No. 112, pub. by the Am. Tr. Ass'n. He was of a cheerful disposition, liberal to the poor, upright in all his conduct, and a "consistent Christian." His death was peaceful, and the consolations of Christian hope attended him to the last. ch.: 1. Lydia, Dec. 13, 1782, m. Dea. Benj. Lyman, of Columbia. 2. Elvira, Nov. 4, 1784, m. Oliver Payne, of Lebanon, Ct. 3. Randall, Oct. 13, 1786. 4. Sally, Sep. 19, 1788. 5. Hubbard, July 5, 1791. 6. Lucian, July 10, 1793, m. a da. of Chester Hunt, of Windham, Ct., and d. in 1819, leaving 1 da. 7. Sam'l., July 15, 1797, an invalid. 8. George, d. in 1819, ae. 21.

40. Thomas, s. Thos 21, sett. in Scit., on the farm known as the Fox Hill Farm, adjoining the North River, where some of his descendants still reside. Like his ancestors, he was engaged principally in shipbuilding, at the family yards on the North River. He m. Lydia Sylvester, and d. Sep. 1, 1834, and his wid. Jan. 19, 1840. ch.: 1. Thos., Jan. 2, 1783. 2. Lydia, Aug. 29, 1785, m. Thos. Green, of N. Bed., Mass., who d. She yet lives in N. B., and her son, Thos. Barstow Green, in S. Scit. 3. Ellinor, Feb. 27, 1788, d. in Scit., Dec. 17, 1846. 4. Rebecca, Oct. 24, 1790, m. Gideon Richmond, of N. Bed., and has 1 son in N. B. 5. Barker, May 12, 1793, d. Oct. 1, 1811. 6. Olive S., Aug. 3, 1795, m. Capt. Thos. Waterman, of S. Scituate.

41. Nath'l., s. Thos. 21, m. Elizab., da. Hon. Joseph Cushing, of H., Aug. 31, 1786, and sett. in Me., where he d. in 1798. He was engaged in ship-building, on the Damariscotta river. ch.: 1. Betsy C., bap. Sep. 14, 1788, m. Gilbert Brooks, of Scit., and d. in Medford, no ch. 2. Deborah, bap. July 11, 1790, d. unm., in Camden, Me. 3. Mary, bap. May 22, 1791, m. 1, Rev. Thos. Cochran, of Camden, Oct. 10, 1808, and had ch.; and 2

BROAD OAK FARM.

RESIDENCE OF COL. JOHN B. BARSTOW.

Ralph Conway, and lives in C. 4. Joseph C., lived and d. in Litchfield, Me.; was m., and had ch. 5. Nath'l. ? in Me. 6. Ruth.

42. *John, B. Barstow* (Col. John Burden,) s. Thos. 21, m. Betsey, da. of Capt. Robt. L. Eells, and is yet living in H, in the 90th year of his age, ab. $\frac{1}{3}$ of a mile S.W. of the Four Corners, on his farm, known as the "Broad Oak Farm," and in the house built by himself, in 1799. He has been a valuable citizen; an enterprising shipbuilder; was Selectman in 1797 and '98; Representative from 1808 to 1810; and has held the military offices of Lieut., Capt., Major, and Col.; and though now the frosts of 90 winters have gathered upon his brow, and the infirmities of age are upon him, his mind retains, to a remarkable degree, the power of memory, and we have derived from him valuable aid in the preparation of some portion of this work. His w. d. in 1851, in the 91st year of her age. ch.: 1. Sarah, May 21, 1788, m. Joseph S. Bates, Oct. 2, 1820, and lives on Broadway. 2. Betsey E., Sep. 22, 1789, living with her fa. 3. John, Feb. 17, 1791. 4. Jane, July 24, 1792, m. David Hersey, of H., Nov. 12, 1816, and d. Ap. 4, 1847. 5. Hannah, Jan. 27, 1794, living with her fa. 6. Edward, Aug. 27, 1795. 7. Robert, Feb. 1, 1797, d. unm., in Falmouth, Eng'd., in 1818. Mariner. 8. Capt. Benjamin, Dec. 15, 1799. Has been sett. as a merchant, at the South, but is now a shipmaster, in N. Y. Not. m. 9. Salome, July 24, 1801, m. Capt. Haviland Torrey, of Pemb., Oct. 1, 1826, and has had 5 ch., of whom are living 2 sons, *Benj. Barstow*, and *Herbert*.

43. Dea. Elijah, s. Thos. 21, m. 1, Lucy, da. Capt. Robt. L. Eells, Nov. 8, 1798, who d., and 2, Diana Everson, of Kigs'n. Lived in Scit., on his father's place; was a shipbuilder, and farmer; and for many years Dea. of the central Church in H. He d. in 1842, and his wid. returned to Kigs'n. ch.: 1. Nath'l., Aug. 16, 1799. 2. Lucy E., bap. June 6, 1801, m. Ozen Josselyn, now of Bos'n. 3. Elijah, bap. Sep., 28, 1806. 4. Edwin. 5. Abby, m. Capt. Thos. H. C. Barstow, of H. 6. Andrew.

44. James, s. James 22, m. Sarah Leavitt, of Pemb., and was killed during the great gale of Sep. 23, 1815, at Kigs'n., by the fall of a plank from the staging of a ship, on which he was at work. ch.: 1. James, Nov. 25, 1786. 2. Calvin, July 26, 1791. 3. John. 4. Solomon, d. unm. 5. Sally, m. 1, a Gibbs; 2, a Freeman; and 3, a Bryant. 6. Rhoda, d. ae. 15. 7. Betsey, m. 1, Elisha C. Stetson, of H., Jan. 14, 1816, who d.; and 2, Lewis Litchfield, and lives in H. 8. Ruth K., m. Elijah S. Ewell, Oct. 29, 1815. 9. Charlotte, m. Marcus Robinson, of E. Bridg'r., Ap. 29, 1820. 10. Joanna, m. Stephen Faunce, of Pemb.

45. Joseph, s. James 22, m. Lydia Soule, of Dux'y, July 16, 1786, and d. in D., July 15, 1834, and his wife Jan. 31, 1812. ch: 1. Joseph, Aug. 14, 1787, m. Nancy, da. Capt. Eden Wadsworth, of D., Ap. 22, 1812, and d. in Prov., R. I., Ap. 22, 1813, leaving a da., *Beulah W.*, who m. Francis Barstow, of Mattapoisett. 2. Peleg, Oct. 22, 1788, m. Mary Robbins, of Va., in 1810, and his w. is d. No ch. 3. Samuel, Nov. 8, 1791. 4. Mehitable, Jan. 17, 1793, m. Joseph Howland, of Hanson, Ap. 9, 1815. 5. Ichabod, Mar. 15, 1794. 6. Richard, Mar. 26. 1796. 7. George, Sep. 28, 1798. 8. Susan, Jan. 9, 1801, m. John Washburn, of Kigs'n., Sep. 18, 1817, and lives in Matt't. 9. Wilson, Feb. 11, 1803. 10. Briggs, May 11, 1805. 11. Daniel, July 23, 1807, d. in 1834. Left no ch. 12. Thos. Sep. 12, 1809, is m., and lives in Hudson, N. Y. 13. Lydia S., Jan. 4, 1812, m. Chas. Curtis, of E. Ab'n.

46. Wm., s. Jas. 22, m. Lydia Simmons, and lived in Pemb. ch.: 1. Benj. 2. Wm. 3. Jehiel, is m., and lives in Provincetown, Mass. 4. Lewis. 5. Lydia, m. Levi Washburn, E. Bridg'r. 6. Ruth, d. ae. 23. 7. Rogers L., July 15, 1811.

47. Rev. George, s. James, 22, grad. at B. U., in 1801, "holding a high and respectable standing in his class;" studied Theol. with Rev. Perez Forbes, of Raynham; and sett., in 1803, in that part of Pemb. now H'n., where he was devoted to his profession, and discharged its duties to the acceptance of his people, until his death, which took place, Feb. 11, 1826, ae. 51. He m. Sarah, da. Gideon Barstow, of Rochester, Nov. 26, 1801, and

she survives, and resides in Bridg'r. ch.: 1. George W., Aug. 13, 1802. Fitted for Coll., was afterwards Cl'k., in Bos'n., and there d. July 23, 1834. 2. Sarah W., Sep. 2, 1805, m. Nahum Stetson, Esq., s. Capt. Abisha Stetson, Nov. 13, 1828, and d. Aug. 17, 1842, having had *George B.*, Oct. 10, 1830. *Sarah L.*. June 7, 1834. *Nahum*, jr., Dec. 14, 1836, and *Wm. B.*, Mar. 20, 1839. 3. Jane W., Dec. 8, 1810, m. Capt. Edwin W. Barstow, Sep. 11, 1834. 4. Lucy A. F., Jan. 4, 1818, m. Nahum Stetson Esq., July 4, 1823, and has *Lucy A.*, Oct. 12, 1848, and *Helen F.*, Dec. 16, 1850.

NOTE.—Mr. S. is the intelligent, and gentlemanly Agent of the Iron Works, at S. Bridg'r. and also of the Wey'h. Works, and as a man of business enterprise, has few equals in the State. He was Rep. to the State Leg., from 1837–39; Director of the F. R. R. R.; President of the Bristol Co. Bank; and Director of the Cape Cod R. R.; and in the walks of private life, for integrity, courtesy, affability, hospitality, and all the qualities which make up the true gentleman, he is well known to all who have the pleasure of his acquaintance.

48. Jacob, s. Jacob 23, m. a Young, of Scit., lived in Bos'n. and was prob. owner, with Alex. Vannevar, of a tomb in Copp's hill burial ground, in 1819. ch.: 1. Jacob, m., lived in Boston, and was Inspector of Fish, of the firm of Barstow and Vinton, and d. in B., leaving ch. 2. Alice, m. a Pierce. 3. Abigail, m. Calvin Lewis, of Mf'd.

49. Charles, s. Jacob 23, m. Abigail, or Nabby Perry, of Pemb., Ap. 10, 1796, and d. May 4, 1829, and his wid. yet survives. ch.: 1. Burden, Dec. 15, 1797, d. unm., in N. Orleans, in 1830. 2. Wm. C., May 9, 1801. 3. Abigail, or Nabby, Sep. 20, 1803, m. Wm. Josselyn, of Pemb., Oct. 10, 1822. 4. Charles, Aug. 13, 1805. 5. Thos. H. C. 6. Caroline, m. John O. Hudson, of E. Bridg'r., Feb. 4, 1833.

50. Gideon, s. Gideon 24, m. 1, Ann Mead, Oct., 1782, who d. Sep. 12, 1798; and 2, Deborah Loring, May, 1800, and d. in Matt't., Feb. 3, 1849, ae. 88, and his wid. in June, 1851, ae. 79. Lived in Mattapoisett, was a shipbuilder by trade, and was a member of the Convention for revising the Const'n. of Mass., in 1820. ch.: 1. Gideon, Sep. 7, 1783. 2. Jane, Oct. 31, 1785, m. Dan'l. B. Loring, in 1805, and d. in Aug., 1813, leaving *Mary*, who m. Western G. Robinson, of Fairhaven, and *Ann*, who m.

James Robinson, of F. 3. Samuel, Dec. 15, 1787, d. May 27, 1803. 4. Zaccheus M., Jan. 1, 1790. Living in M., unm. 5. Anne, Mar. 25, d. Dec. 5, 1792. 6. Mary, Sep. 28, 1793, d. Oct. 6, 1801. 7. Benjamin, Feb. 18, 1796. 8. Wilson, Feb. 17, 1798.

51. Wilson, s. Gideon, 24, m. Susanna P., da. Rev. Jona. Moore, of Roch'r, Mass., Oct. 30, 1791, and lived first in Matt't, and then in N. Y., where he d. Jan. 20, 1850, ae. 84, and his wife Ap. 3, 1848, ae. 78. Mr. B. was for some years a ship-master, and for about 20 years, an extensive ship-builder, in the place of his nativity;—in private life, distinguished for his benevolent character, and the activity of his mind; and publicly, for his energy in business, and his integrity. Like many others, who were engaged in active affairs from 1800 to 1805, he suffered severely from the check in business which followed the Embargo Act of 1807, and from the reverses incident to that event, he never after fully recovered. ch.: 1. Susanna P., May 22, 1793, d. 1798. 2. Caleb, Mar. 8, 1795. 3. Lucy, Mar. 3, 1797, d. ae. 7. 4. Jona. M., Mar. 25, 1799, d, in N. Or's., Jan. 19, 1826, being Cl'k. of a Count'g. House, in N. O. 5. Henry W. Mar. 7, 1801. 6. Wm. P., Ap. 20, 1803. Drowned, Dec. 28, 1829, on his passage from Trieste to N. Y'k. He was a ship-master. 7. Sam'l., June 9, 1805. 8. Anna S., Oct. 23. 1810, m. Joshua L. Pope, Merch't., of N. Y'k., and has 3 sons and 2 daughters.

52. Benja., s. Caleb 25, m. Rebecca Hammond, Ap. 25, 1800, and lives in Matt't., where, and in N. Bedf'd., he has been distinguished as a master shipbuilder. He has been Rep. from Roch'r to the Gen. Court. ch.: 1. Benj. F. Mar. 28, 1801. 2. Caroline, Jan. 24, 1803, d. Sep. 3, 1804. 3. Edwin, June 15, 1805, d. Mar. 26, 1824. 4. Nathan H., Oct. 5, 1807. 5. Caroline, Dec. 19, 1812, d. Sep. 25, 1813. 6. Elizab. P., Nov. 28, 1814, d. Dec. 13, 1816. 7. Henry, Dec. 3, 1817. 8. Susan C., May 29, 1820, m. David H. Cannon, of Matt't., and has *Mary H.*, May 18, 1852.

53. Elias, s. Caleb 25, m. Mary, da. John and Rebecca Wood, Sep. 14, 1800, and d. in Prov. R. I., Oct. 28, 1840, and his w.

who was b. Dec. 21, 1778, d. May 25, 1834. He was a shipwright by trade, and built a number of vessels in Prov. He was a strictly *temperate* man through life, and a Trustee of the Meth. Ch., to which office he was elected in 1821. ch.: 1. Ann E. Aug. 9, 1801, m. Thos. Hathaway, Dec. 25, 1821, lives in Prov., and has *Ann E.*, 1822, *Thos. Z.*, 1824, *Sarah A*, 1826, *Elias B.*, 1829, *Wm. H*,, 1835, and *Achsah B.*, 1838. 2. Edwin, Ap. 14, 1803. 4. Elias, Feb. 26, 1805. 4. Thos. Oct. 16, 1807. 5. Rebecca W., Ap. 4, 1810. 6. Wm., July 10, 1812. 7. Sarah B., July 6, 1814, m. Allen F. Manchester, of Prov., Feb. 2, 1834, and has *Mary B.*, 1834, *Sarah F*, 1837, *Geo. F.*, '39, *Julia G.*, '41, *Abby E.*, '43, *Thos. A.*, '45, *Emma M.*, '49, and *Albert C.*, '50. 8. Achsa, Dec. 22, 1816.

54. Wm., s. Caleb 25, m. Waity Reynolds, of Wickford, R. I., ab. 1809, and has been a clergyman of the Meth. denom., but owing to the loss of his voice, has been unable, for some years, to attend to the duties of his profession. He lives in Philad. ch.: 1. Elizab., d. young. 2. Wm., d. young. 3. Sarah, m. Rev. Josiah Litch, in 1836, and has 2 ch. living, *Wilbur F.*, and *Josiah L.* 4. Joseph S., d. young. 5. Joseph M., Mar., 1824. A dentist by profession, and is living in Philad., unm.

55. Nath'l., s. Caleb 25, m. 1, Sophia Chaffee, Dec. 2, 1810, who was b. Nov. 25, 1792, and d. July 6, 1817; and 2, Martha Randall, May 4, 1818, who was b. Nov. 6, 1791. Mr. B. d. in Providence, Nov. 3, 1849, and his wid. survives. He was a man of respectability. ch.: 1. Nathan C., Feb. 16, d. June 1, 1812. 3. Hon'l. Amos C., Ap. 30, 1813. 3. Paris, Nov. 25, 1815. Lost at sea, Dec. 15, 1830,—a bright and promising youth. (By 2d.) 4. Eph'm. R., Sep. 21, 1819.

56, Curtis, s. Sam'l 27, m. Eliza, da. Jno. Parker, of Cant'y. Ct., in 1812, and d. July 4, 1826, ae. 44. ch.: 1. Hannah, 1813, d. in Norwich. 2. George, 1815, d. in N., July 20, 1852, leaving a wid. and 2 ch. 3. Eunice, 1818, d. Dec. 5, 1834, 4. Katharine, 1819, d. young. 5. Martha, 1821. Living in Norwich. 6. Orra, 1823. Living in N. 7. Charles, 1825. Living in N.

57. Simon, s. Sam'l, 27, grad. B. U., 1808, but having the misfortune to lose the sight of one eye, he relinquished his design of stud. Theol, and sett. in Delaware, as a Teacher; m. Hannah Frazier, of D., Aug. 24, 1818, and d. at Wilmington, Oct. 24, and his wid. at Newcastle, Del., Aug. 26, 1829, ae. 40. ch.: 1. Sam'l., Sep. 8, 1819. Lives in Woonsocket, R. I. 2. Hannah S., May 23, 1821, m. A. J. Bulkley, and lives in Louisville, K'y. 3. Elizab. V., May 11, 1824, d. Feb. 3, 1828.

58. Spaulding, s. Sam'l. 27, m. Temperance E. Holmes, da. Dr. H., of Woodstock, Ct., who d. June 14, 1823, ae. 25. ch.: 1. Sarah S., m. Col. Geo. Saltonstall Stoddard, of W. 2. Emma, m. Rev. Geo. Langdon, A. M., of Hartford, Ct., and has 3 ch. 3. Mary E.. d.

59. Elisha P., s. Sam'l. 30, m. Mary P., da. Andrew and Mary Rogers, of Augusta, Me., and d. in Cant'y., Ct., Sep. 28, 1850, ae. 57. ch.: 1. John P., of Norwich, Ct., m. Abig. T. da. Geo. and Lucretia R. Sharpe, of Pomfret, Ct., Aug. 28, 1850, and is engaged in the mf. and sale of Hardware, being of the firm of Backus and Barstow, of N. 2. Susan B., m. Arthur F. Drinkwater, Esq., lawyer, of Ellsworth, Me, Sep. 18, 1848. 3. Mary F., m. John Backus, of Norwich, Ct., Aug. 21, 1851. 4. Elizab. R., 1841. Lives with her mother, in Ct.

60. John, s. Sam'l. 27, m. 1, Harriet, da. Josiah and Sarah Parkes, of Cant'y., Ct., Mar. 1818, who d. Sep. 27, 1822, ae. 23; 2, Eliza S., da. Dr. Jno. Fitch, of Clinton, N. Y., who d. at Bridgeport, Ct., June 3, 1840; and 3, Jane. da. Dr. John Fitch, in 1841. Mr. B. lives in Bridgeport, Ct. ch.: 1. Josiah P., July 6, 1821, d. July 7, 1822. (By 2d.) 2. John F., in Cal'a. 3. Samuel. F., at Williamstown Coll., Mass. 4. Isaac B., d. 5. Charles. 6. Simon, printer, at Jamestown, N. Y. (By 3d.) 7. Kate. 8. Harriet E. 9. Susan B. 10. Wm. F.

61. Septimus, s. John 28, m. and lived in Hadley, Mass., where he d. Dec. 16, 1843, ae. 42. ch.: 1. Luther. 2. Elias B. 3. Olive C. 4. Orrelia. 5. Harriet. 6. Susan, d. 1851.

62. Calvin, s. John 28, m. Orra Herrick, of Cant'y., Ct. ch.: 1. Luther. 2. Olive. 3. John. 4. Harriet. 5. Emma.

63. Ebenezer, s. John 28, m. Lucy Learned, of New Braintree, Mass., Sep. 12, 1811, and lives in Scotland, Ct. ch.: 1. Fidelia, m. Jno. A. Kellogg, of Vt., who d. in 1846, and she is a wid. with 4 ch., in Miss'o. 2. Sarah L., m. Homer Thayer, of Thompson, Ct., lives in E. Douglass, Mass., and had 1 ch., wh. d. 3. Timo. D., was a merchant, at St. Louis, Mo., where he d. May 23, 1852, ae. 31. 4. Martin Luther, 1833, with his fa.

64. Rev. Zedekiah S., s. John 28, grad. at Yale, 1813., stud. Theol. at N. Haven, under Rev. Pres. Dwight, and taught Hopkins Acad., in N. Haven, until licensed to preach. Thence went to N. Y'k., and was Ass't. in the High School, under the care of Jno. Griscom, LL.D., and in 1816 and '17, was Tutor at Ham. Coll., N. Y., during which period, a second A. M. degree was conferred upon him. During his last year at Ham. Coll., Pres't. Backus, decs'd., and Mr. B. preached in the chapel to the students, until Pres't. Davis was chosen, in Aug., 1817. In Feb. 1818, he rec'd. a call to sett. at Keene, N. H., and July 1, was ord. as Pastor of the Ch. in that place, where he yet remains, having enjoyed such health as to be prevented from preaching but four Sabbaths in 34 years! He has been, for twenty years, a memb. of the Board of Kimball Acad'y.; of the Board of Dart. Coll., since 1834, at which Coll. the degree of D.D., was conferred upon him, in 1849; Trustee and Sec'y. of Keene Acad., since its inst'n.; many years Sec'y. of the Gen'l. Ass'n. of Cong. and Presb. Min's., of N. H.; Cl'k of the Cheshire Conf. of Ch's., for 20 years; a Corp. Memb. of the A. B. C. F. M.; and one of the Sup. Com. of the Pub. Schools of Keene, for 30 years. He m. Elizab. F. Blake, of Westboro'. Mass., Aug. 19, 1818, and has 1. Timo. D., July 17, d. Dec. 22, 1820. 2. Wm., Sept. 8, 1822. Grad. A. B., in 1842, A. M., 1845, and M. D., 1848, and is in Cal'a. 3. Elizab. W., July 24, 1824, d. Jan. 3, 1832. 4. Josiah W., June 21, 1826. Grad. A. B., 1846, and M. D., 1852, and is Ass't. Phys'n. of the Hosp'l. at Blackwell's Island, N. Y. 5. John, Feb. 21, 1828, lived but 1 hour.

65. Ezekiel, s. Joshua 33, m. Mary Conner, of Exeter, N. H., Nov. 28, 1799, and returned to Hanover, his native place, in 1805, and there d. Jan. 10, 1815, and his wid. and ch. returned

to Exeter, where she d. Oct. 4, 1845, ae. 67. ch.: 1. Almira, Sep. 27, 1800, m. a Collins, of New Lond'n., Ct. No ch. 2. Mary J., Feb. 10, 1803, m. a Nichols, of Haverhill, Mass., and has 7 ch. 3. John C., Feb. 6, 1805, m. Lucretia Moore, of Danvers, Mass., and is sett. as a farmer, in Groton, N. H. No ch. 4. Joshua, Mar. 6, 1808, d. in Oroquimbo, Texas, in 1836. 5. Marg't. F., Mar. 27, 1810. An instructress, in Alabama. 6. Ezekiel Hale, May 17, 1815.

66. Chas. C., s. Joshua 33, m. Sophia, da. Chas. Fanning, Esq., of Griswold, Ct., Jan. 1, 1809, and d. in Dover, N. H., Jan. 31, 1828, and his wid. in Kgs'n., N. H., Dec. 23, 1833, ae. 52. ch.: 1. Catherine, Sep. 18, 1810, m. Benj. Magoun, of Kgs'n., in 1830, and d. Oct. 29, 1838. No ch. 2. Mariah, May 3, 1812, d. June 4, 1814. 3. Charles, Ap. 28, 1814, m. Martha M. Taylor, of Bangor, Me., is Cl'k. in Bos'n., and has *Annie D.*, and another ch. 4. Frederick, Mar. 7, 1816, d. in Chas'n., S. C., Sep. 12, 1838. 5. Henry H., Mar. 6, 1819, d. June 21, 1822. 6. Ariannah, Feb. 20, 1821, m. Aaron Whittemore, Esq., of Pemb., N. H., Dec. 13, 1840, and has *Sophia F.*, '42, *Ariannah B.*, '44, *Aaron B.*, '46, d. '49, *Aaron*, '49, *Adaline*, '50, and *Jno. C.*, '52. 7. Henry H., Sep. 23, 1823, m. a Holloway, of Eng'd., resides in Palermo, Sicily, and has 2 ch. 8. Marg't. A., Mar. 20, 1825, m. J. M. Turner, in 1842, lives in Warren, Pa., and has 3 ch.

67. Joseph, s. Lt. Samuel 34, m. 1, Mary Hatch, of Pemb.? Ap. 11, 1782, and 2, wid. Tufts, and lived in Cornish, Vt., where he and his w. d. ch.: 1. Anne, Aug. 5, 1785. 2. Capt. Sam'l., Feb. 27, 1788, m. Elenor Jewell, and, with his w., d. in N. Y'k., leaving no ch. 3. Job, May 19, 1790. 4. Joseph, May 13, 1795. Drowned in the W. Indies. 5. Jas. H., July 5, 1798. 6. Nancy, m. a Chamberlin. 7. Polly, m. a Chace.

68. Allen, s. Seth 36, m. Olive Foster, of Sharon, Ct., in 1794, and lives in Canaan, N. Y. His wid. d. ab. 1845. ch.: Two da's., who d. in infancy, and of the sons, 1. David F., Esq., lawyer, of Towanda, Pa., b. Nov. 1795, m. Amelia Mix, and has a son *Henry*, and a daughter, both young. 2. Sam'l., b. ab. 1801, is of

Canaan, N. Y., m. Betsey Douglass, of C., and has *Allen*, *Samuel*, *Henry*, *David*, *Charles*, *Elizabeth*, and *Olive*.

69. Samuel, s. Seth 36, stud. Med., and sett. first in W. Stockbridge, Mass., of which town he was Rep., in 1808; and thence moved to Gr. Barrington, was Senator in 1812, and d. in 1813. He m. Lavinia Wilson, of Alford, Mass., who d. ab. 1843, in Nichols, N. Y. ch.: 1. Pluma A., m. Increase Sumner, Esq., lawyer, of Gr. Bar'n., and d. ab. 1849, leaving ch. 2. Charles R., lawyer; sometime Sheriff of Tioga Co., N. Y.; memb. of the Assemb., and P. M. at Oswego; m. Charlotte Coburn. ab. 1827, and has *Henry*, d. ae. 18; *Sumner*, b. ab. 1832; *Edward*, *Samuel*, *Charles*, and 2 daughters. 3. Oliver A., merchant in Tioga Co., N. Y., m. Frances Palmer, ab. 1837, and has *Edmund*, *Charles*, *Amelia*, and others.

70. Seth T., s. Seth 36, m. Clarissa Woodruff, of Litchf'd., Ct., June 4, 1806, and resided in Bradford Co., Pa., where he d. Sep. 13, 1852, ae. 73. His wid. survives, though in feeble health. Mr. B. was a favorite pupil of the celebrated Dr. Rush, of Philad.; a grad. of the Med. Coll. of that city, and a thoroughly educated Physician, though he followed that profession but a short time, devoting the principal part of his life to trading and farming. He was an early settler in the valley of the Susquehanna, nearly 50 years ago, and was a man of strong intellect, great energy, and gentlemanly deportment. ch.: 1. Ellen C., Feb. 17, 1808, d. Feb. 17, 1833. 2. Erasmus D., Dec. 30, 1809, d. Ap. 19, 1812. 3. Marguerite St. Leon, the distinguished poetess, and authoress of "Wayside Flowers," &c., b. Ap. 17, 1812, m. John Loud, Esq., Nov. 17, 1833, lives in Philad., and has *Caroline M. St. L.*, 1834, *Clara E.*, 1837, and *Darwina F.*, 1841. 4. Darwina F., Jan. 4, 1815, m. Richard Catlin, May 7, 1834, and lives in Wisconsin. 5 Julius R., Ap. 9, 1817, d. Sep. 21, 1852. Not m. 6. Henry H., Feb. 5, 1819, m. Jane Calkins, May 1842, had *Darwina F.* May 1843, and *Marguerite St. L.*, July 21, 1837, d. Oct. 16, 1841, and the fa. d. in Oct. 1847.

71. Hon'l. Gamaliel H., s. Seth 36, resided with his father in Sharon, Ct., until 25 years of age, working at farming in the summer season, and teaching school in the winter. In 1809, he com-

menced the study of Medicine, with his bro. Sam'l., in Gr. Bar'n., and in Jan. 1812, sett. in the beautiful valley of the Susquehanna, in Tioga Co., N. Y., where he practised Med. successfully, until the fall of 1823, since which time he has given his attention chiefly to trading and farming. He was a memb. of the Assemb. of N. Y., in 1816, '17, '18, '23, and 26; in the Senate from 1819—'22; memb. Cong., from 1830—'32; Treas'r. of the State of N. Y., in 1825, and 1838; and First Judge of Tioga Co., from 1818—1823. He m. Nancy, da. Emanuel Coryell, formerly of N. Jersey. in Jan. 1813, and has 1. Sam'l., b. ab. 1813, of the firm of Barstow and Lockwood, Atty's., Detroit, Mich'n. He is U. S. Dist. Att'y., and Pres't. of the Farmers and Mechanics Bank; m. 1, Miss Spofford, who d., and 2, Frederica Williams, and has one son, *Sam'l. F.*, a few months old. 2. Frances, Jan. 28, 1815, m. Wm. H. Baird, of N. Y'k., and has 2 sons, *Walter*, and *Gamaliel.* 3. Mary, Feb. 27, 1820. Not m. 4. John C., Feb. 28, 1822. Lives with his fa., and is unm. 5. Ellen, d. young. 6. Juliet, Oct. 10, 1829, m. John S. Williston, of Wellsboro', Pa., and has an inf. da.

72. Daniel, s. Capt. Dan'l. 37, m. 1, Ruth Estes, Jan. 15, 1801, and 2, Lydia Stetson, and lives in Hanover, on King-st. Farmer. ch.: 1. Daniel, m. Betsey Estes, Dec. 30, 1830, and lives on King-st. No ch. 2. Samuel, m. Saba D. Estes, Oct. 28, 1830, and lives with his fa. No. ch.

73. Wm., s. Michael 38, m. Abigail, da. Eben'r. Townsend, of Chester, N. H., and lived and d. in Haverhill, N. H., where his wid. yet resides. ch.: 1. Julia A., d. 2. George, Esq., counsellor-at-law, 74 Wall st., N. Y'k., author of the History of New Hampshire, and of an Eulogy on General Jackson; and Aide-de-Camp of Maj.-Gen. John McNeil, with the rank of Major, in the Militia of N. H.; m. Emily E., da. Hon. John Shepley, of Saco, Me., June 11, 1844. No ch. 3. Wm. H., b. 1812, m. at the age of 19, Marg't., da. of the Rev. Wm. Woodward, of Norwich, Vt., and d. of the cholera, at Auburn, N. Y., in 1832, ae. 20. 4. Abigail, d. 5. Jas T., town clerk of Hav'l., N. H., m. 1, Maria Loring, and 2, Jane, da. Richard N. Buren. 6. Abigail. Not m. 7. Mary A., at Columbia, Texas. Not m. 8. Charles, Mora-

vian Missionary at Catesville, Ia. 9. Mary, m. Edwin S. Thayer, of S. Milford, Mass. 10. Ebenezer T., merch't., Columbia, Texas. Not m. 11. Catherine, unm.

74. Henry, s. Michael 38, m. 1, Harriet Webster, of Plym'h., N. H., and 2, Frances Pierce, of Woodstock, Vt. Lived first at Hav'l., N. H., and 2d. at Lowell, Mass., where he d. ch.: 1. Lydia, m. Merrill Pearson, and lives in Ill's. 2. Harriet, d. 3. Henry, in Cal'a. 4. Horace, d. 5. Frances. 6. David. 7. Alfred, in Cal'a. 8. Anson, in Cal'a. 9. Ellen.

75. Charles, s. Michael 38, m. and lived in Campton, N. H., where he d. ch: 1. Charles, in Canada. 2. Hannah, is m., and lives in Canada.

76. Thomas, s. Michael 38, m. Sarah Hale, of Wells River, Vt. and lives in Piermont, N. H. ch.: 1. Sarah A. 2. Harriet, is m., and lives in Derby, Vt. 3. Nancy, is m., and lives in Thetford, Vt. 4. Michael H., of Boston, Mass. 5. Thos, A., in Cal'a. 6. Arthur C., in Cal'a. 7. Louisa. 8. Ruth A. 9. Wm. H.

77. Thos., s. Thos. 40, m. Alice Thomas, Sep. 28, 1806, and d. in N. Bedford, in Nov. 1850, having had ch.: 1. Julia A., m. Philip Smith of N. Bedford. 2. George. Drowned, ae. 7. 3. Mary, m. Jared Parkhurst, and d. in Balt. Md., ab. 1846. 4. Lydia S., m. Gen. Thomas, of N. Bedford.

Note.—Two ch., Rebecca and Elizab., d. young.

78. John, s. Col. John B. 42, m. Sarah Swoope Thompson, da. Edward K. Thompson, of Providence, R. I., and gr. gr. da. of Rev. Ebenezer Thompson, Rector of St. Andrew's Church, Scituate, Mass. ch.: 1. Lydia K. 2. Elizabeth T. 3. Hannah, d. He resided principally in New York, where he was extensively engaged in commerce. In 1838 he withdrew from commercial pursuits, and removed to Providence, where he now resides.

79. Capt. Edward, s. Col. John B., 42, m. Amy, da. John Baily, Sep. 2, 1821, and d. Jan. 27, 1833, and his wid. m. Wm. Dawes, of H., and resides near the Four Corners, in the house formerly of John Bailey, and now owned by the heirs of Mr. Barstow. Mr. B. was a shipmaster for some years previous to his decease, and sailed from N. Y'k. ch. 1. John E., June 11, 1822, m. Eliza Crary, resides in N. Y., and has *John*, d., and *Eliza C.* 2. Rob-

ert, June 24, 1824, m. Ann Josselynn, Dec. 24, 1845, is in Cal'a., and has *Amy*. 3. Elizab., June 17, 1826, m. Capt. Nath'l. Cushing, of H., Dec. 18, 1845. 4. Joseph B., Feb. 3, 1828, machinist, in Bos'n. 5. Frederic O., 1830 ? grad B. U , 1852. 6. Edward, Jan. 27, 1833, mechanic in Bos'n.

80. Capt. Nath'l, s. Dea. Elijah 43, m. 1, Grace Foster, in 1833, and 2, Abby Hammett, in July 1837, and resides in H., at the Four Corners. A shipmaster. ch.: 1. Grace F., Ap., 1834. (By 2d.) 2. Lucy A., June 25, 1840. 3. Mary E., Feb. 13, 1842. 4. Sarah R., Dec. 29, 1845. 5. Marietta H., June 15, 1850.

81. Elijah, s. Dea. Elijah 43, m. Caroline Briggs, lives in So. Scit., on his father's place, and is a shipbuilder, in connexion with Capt. Thos. Waterman. ch.: 1. Albert. 2. Henry.

82. Capt. Edwin, s. Dea. Elijah 43, m. Jane W., da. Rev. Geo. Barstow, and lives in Bridg'r. A shipmaster. ch.: 1. Jane W., Aug. 7, 1835. 2. Jacob P., June 29, 1839. 3. Sarah W., June 6, 1842. 4. Edwin W., Dec. 5, 1844. 5. Walter J., Aug. 14, 1847. 6. Salome T., Sep. 28, 1850.

83. Andrew, s. Dea. Elijah 43, m. Mary Abernethy, and lives in Bridg'r. ch.: 1. Andrew. 2. Henrietta W. 3. Rachel.

84. James, s. James 44, m. 1, Abby Hyde, of Lebanon, Ct., Oct. 1. 1812, who was b. Sep. 15, 1787, and d. Ap. 11, 1815 ; and 2, Sarah Munroe, Aug. 12, 1819, who was b. Mar. 2, 1798. Lives in Mattapoissett, and is a shipwright. ch.: 1. Abby H., Feb. 14, 1815, is m. and lives in Buffalo, N. Y. (By 2d.) 2. James M., June 1, 1820, d. Oct. 5, 1821. 3. Sarah T., May 12, 1822, d. Dec. 11, 1840. 4. Caroline, Oct. 30, 1824, m. F. W. Russell, of Matt't. 5. Mary M., Mar. 5, 1828. 6. Debo. L., June 27, 1830, m. James M. Washburn, of Matt't.

85. Calvin, s. James 44, m. Betsey Josselynn, of Pemb.. Aug. 7, 1814, and lives in Matt't. Shipwright. ch.: 1. Betsey J., July 30, 1815, m. Benj. R. Gifford, of Fairhaven, Jan. 10, 1832. 2. Joanna, Sep. 15, 1817, m. Elisha B. Handy, Oct. 1, 1841. 3. Calvin J., Jan. 15, 1820, d. Mar. 16, 1826. 4. Henry W., Ap. 7, 1823. Shipjoiner, in M. 5. Sarah L., Aug. 23, d. Nov. 26, 1825. 6. Calvin, Oct. 4, 1827. In Cal'a. 7. Charles

B., Ap. 20, 1830. A mariner. 8. James, Oct. 3, 1834. 9. A son, b. and d., 1839.

86. John, s. James 44, m. Dian Bolles, and lives in Matt't. ch.: 1. Sarah, m. John Mendell, of M. 2. Dian, m. Andrew Dunham, of M. 3. Jedida, m. Walter Gammon, of M. 4. John. A mariner. 5. Abby. 6. Solomon. Two ch. d. young.

87. Samuel, s. Joseph 45, m. and lives in Hingham, where his w. d., Mar. 9, 1851. ch.: 1. Samuel. 2. George. 3. Benja. 4. Joseph.

88. Ichabod, s. Joseph 45, m. 1, Sally R., da. John Clark, of Plym'h., Oct. 4, 1818, and 2, Sally, da. Reuben Peterson, of Dux'y., Sep. 8, 1833, and lives in D. Has one son, Henry.

89. Richard, s. Joseph 45, m. Mary Munroe, May 1822, who was b. June 16, 1798. Resides in Matt't., and is a trader. Formerly a shipwright. ch.: 1. Josiah M., Ap. 30, 1822, d. Sep. 15, 1823. 2. Francis H., Feb. 23, 1824, m. Beulah, da. Joseph Barstow, lives in M., and has a da. *Hope*. 3. Josiah M., Feb. 14, 1825. Mariner. 4. Richard, Feb. 12, 1828. In Cal'a. 5. George B., Nov. 16, 1829, d. July 28, 1830. 6. Mary M., Feb. 19, d. May 2, 1832. 7. Georgiana, Jan. 8, 1835.

90. George, s. Joseph 45, m. Dorcas, da. Capt. Cyrus Brewster, in 1822, and d. Aug. 11, 1835, leaving a son George.

91. Wilson, s. Joseph 45, m. —— Pettengill, and lives in Fairhaven. ch. 1: Henry B. 2. Joseph. 3. Serena. 4. Wilson. 5. Emeline. 6. Sarah. 7. Maria. 8. Edward.

92. Benj., s. Wm. 46, m. Sarah Little, of Pemb., Dec. 31, 1820, and lives in W. Dux'y. A mason. ch.: 1. Charles L., June 1824, m. Jane Ford, lives in W. Dux'y., is a mason, and had *Ada J.*, d. ae. 2 mo's. 2. Henry W., Oct. 1827. 3. Debo. L., Nov. 1830.

93. Wm., s. Wm. 46, m. Mary Weston, and lives in Dux'y. Shipwright. ch.: 1. Mary J. 2. Hiram. 3. Wm. 4. Dan'l.

94. Lewis, s. Wm. 46, m. Lydia Lowden, of Dux'y., and lives in Dux'y. ch.: 1. Lewis B., Nov. 1831. 2. Agustus P., Jan. 1839.

95. Rogers L., s. Wm. 46, is a merchant, ship owner, and a man of great business enterprise; resides in Matt't.; m. Abby H., da. Elijah Willis, Esq., Jan. 7, 1837, who was b. *Aug.* 6, 1811.

ch.: 1. Wm. M., Ap. 21, 1838, d. Mar. 30, 1839. 2. Eliza A. W., Aug. 13, 1840. 3. Elijah W., Aug. 12, 1843. 4. Rogers L., Nov. 9, 1845. 5. George W., June 23, 1848, d. Aug. 29, 1849. 6. Charles H., Ap. 29, 1850.

96. Capt. Wm. C., s. Charles 49, m. Sarah F., da. Capt. Silas Morton, of Pemb., May 4, 1825, (who was b. Dec. 27, 1800,) and lives in E. Bos'n. From the age of 15 to 46, Mr. B. followed the seas,—a portion of the time as shipmaster. He is now Treas'r. of the E. Bos'n. Co., and is a gentleman of great kindness of heart,—prompt and efficient in business, and of a sociable temperament. ch.: 1. Sarah E., Mar. 16, 1826, m. Henry T. Jenkins, of N. Y'k., Sep. 14, 1846, and has ch. 2. Amelia, July 22, 1828, m. Henry Bowers, jr., Sep. 14, 1846, and lives in N. Y'k. 3. Harriet M., June 22, 1831. 4. Francis T., June 5, 1833, d. Aug. 17, 1834. 5. Maria L., Ap. 26, 1837. 6. Wm. H., June 16, 1838. 7. Eloise K., Aug. 1, 1840. 8. Francis D., Ap. 28, 1843.

NOTE.—The last 4 were b, in H.; the first 2 in Pemb.; the third in Brooklyn, N. Y.; and the fourth in Roxbury, Mass.

97. Charles, s. Charles 49, m. Sarah A., da. Dan'l. Hudson, of E. Bridg'r., May 4, 1833, who was b. in Bridg'r., Mar. 28, 1812. He lives in Bos'n., and is a shipwright by trade. ch.: 1. Sarah A., June 23, 1834, d. Feb. 23, 1845. 2. Charles W., Feb. 24, 1837. 3. Fanny H., Feb. 28, 1851.

98. Capt. Thos. H. C., s. Charles 49, m. Abby, da. Dea. Elijah Barstow, in 1836, and lives in H., at the Four Corners. ch.: 1. Emma. 2. Haviland. 3. Sidney.

99. Hon. Gideon, s. Gideon 50, grad. B. U., 1801, stud. Med. with Dr. Kittredge, of Salem, and sett. as Phys'n., in S., where he enjoyed the reputation of being skilful in his profession, and attentive to its duties. In 1820, he was a member of the Conv'n. for revising the Const'n. of Mass.; and from 1821—'23, was a memb. of Cong., from Mass. He d. at St. Augustine, Fla., in 1852, whither he had gone for the benefit of his health. He is spoken of as possessing fine talents, and being gentlemanly in his manners. He m. Nancy, da. Simon Forester, of Salem, who survives. ch.: 1. Haley F., grad. H. C., 1832, and is sett. as a lawyer, in

Syracuse, N. Y. Is m. 2. Charlotte F., d. in Detroit, Mich'n., in 1849. 3. Gideon F., grad. H. C., 1834, and is Assist. Engineer of the Hartford, Prov., and Fishkill R. R., in Ct. 4. Simon F., Dec. 1818, grad. H. C., 1841, at the Law School, and is a counsellor, in Bos'n. Not m. 5. Anne M., m. Samuel Ashburnham, Chief Eng'r. of the Hartford, Prov., and Fishkill, R. R., in Ct. 6. Capt. Dan'l. H. Shipmaster, in the E. Indies. 7. John S. Merchant, in Calcutta. 8. Elinor. 9. Katharine F. 10. Francis. 11. Nath'l. S.

100. Capt. Benj., s. Gideon 50, m. Anstiss S., da. Jas. Dunlap, of Salem, June 18, 1822, and d. in S., May 21, 1823, ae. 27, leaving an only son, Benj., b. May 2, 1823, who grad. H. C., 1842, and is sett. as a lawyer, in Salem. The fa. was engaged in business with the Hon. Gideon, his bro., for a time, and the fa.-in-law, Mr. Dunlap, was of a Scotch family, came to Am'a. in 1790, m. Sarah, da. Robert Stone, of Salem, and was fa. of Andrew Dunlap, Esq., Dist. Att'y., during the Presidency of Gen. Jackson, and of Anstiss S., who m. Mr. Barstow.

101. Wilson, s. Gideon 50, m. Betsey S. Drew, Ap. 12, 1820, resides in Mattapoisett, and is extensively engaged in ship building, at his yards, in M., where several vessels are annually fitted by him for whaling voyages. He is J. P.; P. M.; and a man of enterprise and ability,—respected by the people of Rochester, and a valuable citizen. His w. d. Jan. 10, 1849. ch: 1. Jane L., June 1, 1821, d. Aug. 26, 1823. 2. Elizabeth D., May 6, 1823. 3. Samuel, Ap. 26, 1825, d. July 28, 1826. 4. Jane W., Jan. 23, 1827, d. Oct. 19, 1848. 5. Samuel, Ap. 11, 1829. 6. Wilson, Mar. 13, 1831. 7. Zaccheus M., Sep. 1, 1833. 8. Altol O., Oct. 25, 1835. 9. Gideon, Ap. 1, 1838, d. Nov. 23, 1840.

102. Caleb, s. Wilson 51, m. Frances S., da. Pliny Brewer, of Norwich, Ct., in 1836, and resides in Brooklyn, N. Y. No ch. Mr. B. has been for 31 years, a merchant of the highest respectability, in N. Y. city, and his business has been attended with signal success. He was first in partnership with John H. Howland & Co.,—then, for ten years, with John Barstow, Esq., now of Prov. R. I., during which period, several vessels were built for

them, in Hanover, for foreign and coastwise voyages. Subsequently, he was of the firm of Barstow, Pope & Co.; but has latterly withdrawn from active pursuits. He is Dea. of the Church of the Restoration, under the charge of the Rev. H. R. Nye, and is spoken of, in terms of the highest commendation, as a man of unblemished integrity, judicious liberality, and sterling moral worth.

103. Henry W., s. Wilson 51, m. Mary Louisa Brewer, of Norwich, Ct., Sep. 27, 1827, and is an active merchant in the city of N. York; prompt and efficient in business, and energetic and successful in its pursuit. ch.: 1. Wm. P., Mar. 17, 1829. 2. Louisa B., Feb. 12, 1833. 3. Caleb, Feb. 28, 1835. 4. Samuel, Ap. 26, 1836. 5. Mary E., Nov. 2, 1838. 6. Christopher A., Mar. 31, 1841. 7. Frances R., July 27, 1845. 8. Anna S., Mar. 15, 1847.

104. Samuel, s. Wilson 51, m. Mary T. Blossom, of N. York, and is a wholesale grocer, and commission merchant, in that city. ch.: 1. Ann M., June 26, 1831. 2. Susanna M., May 9, 1836. 3. Elisha B., Feb. 18, 1840, d. Mar. 7, 1845. 4. Mary B., Aug. 17, 1842, d. Mar. 15, 1845.

105. Benj. F., s. Benj. 52, m. wid. Sarah S. Leach, formerly a Drew, who was b. Sep. 26, 1806. He resides in Mattapoisett, is Ass't. P. M.; J. P.; Not. Pub.; and a gentleman of general intelligence, and much repected by the community in which he lives. ch.: 1. Benjamin, Dec. 11, 1834, d. Aug. 12, 1836. 2. Benj., Jan. 24, 1827. Killed instantly, by a falling spar, on board schooner Lamartine, lying at the port of M., July 8, 1850. He was a bright and promising youth, and his loss was a severe blow to his parents. 3. Elisabeth S., Sep. 27, 1839. 4. Sophia, May 28, 1842. 5. Edwin, and 6. Frank, Sep. 20, 1845, d. the same day. 7. Edwin Franklin, Oct. 7, 1846.

106. Nathan H., s. Benj. 52, m. Mary Dexter, lives in Matt't., and is a shipwright by trade. ch.: 1. Helen, Ap. 29, 1831. 2. Caroline, Nov. 12, 1832. 3. Elizab. P., Dec. 10, 1833. 4. Mary T., Nov. 13, 1835, d. July 9, 1838. 5. Mary T., Dec. 8, 1838. 6. Nathan H., July 6, 1842, d. Sep. 10, 1843.

107. Henry, s. Benj. 52, m. Mary Southworth, and lives in Matt't. ch.; 1. Sarah, Aug. 1, 1842. 2. Henry, Oct. 16, 1847.

108. Edwin, s. Elias 53, is a shipwright by trade; m. Harriet

Albro, Sep. 28, 1828, and lives in Prov., R. I. ch.: 1. Harriet E., Aug. 15, 1829. 2. Abby F., July 4, 1833. 3. Amelia A., July 8, 1838. 4. Edwin, Sep. 1, 1846.

109. Elias, s. Elias 53, is a tailor by trade, and lives in Prov., R. I.; m. 1, Margaret Downing, of Green Co., Ga., Nov. 15, 1826, who d. in Prov., Jan. 6, 1831, leaving a da., Mary J., b. Aug. 22, 1827, who resides in Lex'n., K'y. The fa. m. 2, Abby P. Tompkins, July 28, 1836, by whom he has no ch.

110. Thos., s. Elias 53, is a grocer, in Prov., R. I.; m. Abby G. Albro, Jan. 27, 1833, and has 1. Benj. T., Nov. 28, 1833, and 2. Wm. U., June 12, 1842.

111. Wm., s. Elias 53, is a merchant, in Prov.,—dealer in carpets, &c.; m. Julia G. Hodges, July 18, 1839, and has Martha P., Oct. 1, 1841.

112. Hon. Amos C., s. Nath'l. 55, the present gentlemanly and intelligent Mayor of Prov., R. I., is of the firm of A. C. Barstow & Co., and is extensively engaged in the iron business. He has been for several years a memb. of the Assemb. of R. I.; is a man of correct moral habits, repected by the community, a friend of temperance, liberal in his disposition, and successful in business. He m. Emeline M., da. Jas. and Sally Eames, May 28, 1834, (who was b. Feb. 20, 1813,) and has 1, Sarah S., June 3, 1839. 2. Emeline E., Nov. 13, 1840. 3. Mary L., Dec. 13, 1842. 4. Martha M., Aug. 31, 1844. 5. Anne J., Jan. 1, 1846. 6. Amos C., Nov. 2, 1848. 7. George E., Nov. 19, 1849.

113. Ephriam R., s. Nath'l. 55, lives in Prov., R. I., and is engaged in the iron trade. He m. Joanna Eames, June 10, 1847, and has Laura E., Jan. 4, 1851.

114. Rev. Ezekiel H., s. Ezekiel 65, grad. Dart. Coll., 1839, and was five yrs. Princ'l. of the Lawrence Acad., in Groton, Mass., during which time he studied Theol., and was sett. as an Orth'x. Cong. Min., at Walpole, N. H., in 1845, which place he left in 1851, and is now teacher of a Classical School, in Newton, Mass. He m. Eunice G., da. Rufus Clarke, Esq., of Bratt'o., Vt., in Aug., 1842, and has 1. Frances J., June 19, 1843, d. June 17, 1844. 2. Henry T., Mar. 10, d. Nov. 18, 1846. 3. Henry O., Nov. 15, 1847, d. Aug. 9, 1852. 4. Mary C., Sep. 18, 1849. 5. Sallie C., Sep. 2, 1851.

BASS, Rev. Benjamin, First Pastor of the First Church, in H., was s. of Joseph and Mary Bass, of Braintree, and a desc't. of Sam'l. Bass, of Rox'y., 1630. He was b. Dec. 19, 1694, grad. H. C., 1715, m. Mary, da. Rev. Jas. Gardner, of Mf'd., was sett. in H. in 1728, and d. May 23, 1756, and his wid. Feb. 25, 1772. See the chap. on Eccl. Hist. ch.: 1. Mary, Oct. 30, 1730, d. Mar. 21, 1802. 2. Elizabeth, Mar. 18, 1733—4, m. Edmund Sylvester, Jan. 30, 1752. 3. Benj.. Jnne 6,1741.

RESIDENCE OF MR. ELISHA BASS.

2. Benj., s. Rev. Benj., m. 1, Mercy Tolman, Oct. 28, 1765, who d. Ap. 4, 1792; and 2, Mary Eells, Mar. 3, 1793, who d. Jan. 8, 1808, and he Mar. 17, 1821. He was Dea. of thc Church for many years; Rep. in 1783, '95, '96–8, 1800, '01, '05, and '06; Town Clerk, from 1798—1807; and Selectman, from 1783—5. Lived first on Hanover st., in his father's house, where his ch. were born, and then on Broadway, where his son Elisha now resides. ch.: 1. Mercy, Sep. 14, 1766, m. Heman Holmes, of Kigs'n., Ap. 29, 1792, and d. June 9, 1794. Her son *George*, is proprietor of an extensive Furnace, in Prov., R. I. 2. Benj., June 26, 1768. 3. Cinderella, Dec. 30, 1770, d. Feb. 28, 1851. 4. Huldah,

May 16, 1773, m. Robt. Eells, Nov. 29, 1800. 5. Alden, Jan. 30, 1766, m. Rhoda Tyler, lived in Camden, Me., had ch., and d. Oct. 6, 1851. 6. Sarah, Dec. 14, 1778, m. Joseph Eells, Nov. 16, 1802. 7. Elisha, July 23, 1781. Lives on his father's place. Not m. 8. Mary G., Aug. 18, 1784. Lives with Elisha.

3. Benj., s. Benj. 2, m. Lucinda Sylvester, Dec. 4, 1794, and d. June 6, 1825, and his wid. May 10, 1840. Resided in his grandfather's house, on Broadway, the latter part of his life. ch.: 1. Benj., Oct. 8, 1795, d. at Brook'n., N. Y. 2. Mercy T., Mar. 29, 1797, m. Thos. Wright, Scit., Oct. 14, 1818 3. Michael, Mar. 21, 1799, d. at sea. 4. John, Nov. 15, 1800. Lives with Robt. Sylvester. 5. Christopher S., Dec. 15, 1802. Lives in S. Wey'h., m. Sophia Curtis, and has *Sarah J.*, m. John Blanchard, of Randolph; *Lucinda S.*; *Joseph H.*; and *George W.* 6. Bardin, Nov. 23, 1804. 7. Michal, Nov. 23, 1804, m. Geo'. Lovell, of Ab'n. 8. Ruth T., Feb. 12, 1807, m. Melzar Hatch, Mar. 25, 1828. 10. Robert S., Aug. 1808; lives in E. Ab'n., is a blacksmith, m. Lydia Loud, and has *Elisha*, *Alden*, *John Q.*, *Webster*, *Lucinda*, and *Robert.*

BATES FAMILY.

Arms: Sa. on a fesse ar. betw. 3 dexter hands couped bendways or., 5 mullets of the field.

BATES, or BATE, Clement, of Hertfordshire, Eng'd. ? a tailor, ae. 40, and Ann, his wife, of the same age, with their ch., James, ae. 14; Clement, ae. 12; Rachel, ae. 8; Joseph, ae, 5; and Benj., ae. 2; embarked at London, in the Elizabeth, William Stagg, Master, for N. Eng., Ap. 6, 1635, and sett. in H'm., Mass. In the same year, the father had land granted him, in Broad Cove meadows, and a house lot on the S. side of Town, now South st.

In 1637, he, with Nicholas Jacobs and others, had each lots of 2 acres granted them. He d. in H'm., Sep. 17, 1671, and his son Joseph, by w. Hester, was fa. of Joseph, who sett. in that part of Scit. now Hanover, ab. 1695, and was the ancestor of most of the families of Bates in H., and its vicinity.

2. Joseph, s. Joseph, and gr. s. Clement, of H'm., was in Scit., in 1695, but the name of his wife we have not learned. He prob. lived in that part of Scit. now Hanover, and on Centre st., near where Joshua Mann resides. He d. in H., July 9, 1740, and his wid. Aug. 15, 1742, being *very aged*. ch.: 1. Ruth, Ap. 9, 1695, m. Dea. Joseph Josselynn, Dec. 19, 1726. 2. Joseph, Jan. 25, 1697. 3. Mercy, Feb. 28, 1699. 4. Mary, Mar. 13, 1701. 5. Solomon, Dec. 25, 1702. 6. Amos, Nov. 25, 1705. 7. Clement, Dec. 27, 1707. 8. Rachel, Feb. 22, 1710, m. Stephen Torrey, Aug. 15, 1735.

3. Joseph, s Joseph 2, m. Mary Bowker, who d. a wid., July 30, 1759. Mr. B. prob. lived near his fa., and in the house afterwards occupied by his son Joseph, on Centre st., beyond Joshua Mann's, where part of his old orchard is standing. ch.: 1. Sarah, Dec. 27, 1730, m. Jacob Sylvester, Nov. 5, 1753. 2. Lucy, Oct. 14, 1732, m. Jeremiah Stetson, Jan. 3, 1753. 3. Joseph, July 7, 1734. 4. Ruth, Mar. 11, 1736, d. unm., Dec. 16, 1830. 5. Lemuel, July, 1738. 6. Benj., June 9, 1740. 7. Mercy, 1742? m. Joseph Ramsdell, Jan. 1, 1767.

4. Solomon, s. Joseph 2, m. Deborah Whiting, of H'm., May 1, 1730, and prob. d. Mar. 28, 1787. Lived on Broadway, and built the house afterwards occupied by his son Solomon. Of this house, which is a curiosity in its way, we find the following description in the Gospel Banner, of Me., from the pen of Rev. Geo. Bates, a descendant;—"It was substantially built, mostly of oak timber, and evidently by a ship carpenter. The walls were constructed of plank, grooved together, and treenailed to the sills and plates. The posts were all kneed, in the same manner that ships are kneed," ch. 1. Deborah, bap. Oct. 10, 1731, prob. d. Mar. 29, 1786. 2. Jerusha, Sep. 1734, m. Leonard Hill, of Pemb., Jan. 19, 1764. 3. Solomon, June 29, 1741. 4. Anne, 1745, d. July 25, 1799.

5. Amos, s. Joseph 2, m. Jemimah Caswell, Oct. 31, 1735, who was recom. to the Church, in Rochester, Mass., and moved there over a hundred years ago, being among the early settlers of that town. His ch. b. in H., were, 1. Amos, July 31, 1736, and 2. Jonathan, b. ab. 1741. After his removal to R., the fa. had 3. Elijah ; 4. Sylvester ; 5. Moses ; 6. David ; and perhaps some *daughters*, whose names we have not learned.

6. Clement, s. Joseph 2, m. Agatha Merritt, June 15, 1730, who d. Dec. 25, 1786, and he Mar. 14, 1788. ch. : 1. Clement, Nov. 17, 1730, d. June 11, 1753. 2. James, Nov. 10, 1732, went to N. Bedford, it is said, m., had ch., and d. there. 3. Seth, Aug., 1735. 4. Thos., bap. Jan. 17, d. Jan. 21, 1738. 5. Thos., bap. Ap., 1740. 6. Joshua, bap. Nov. 7, 1742, and it is said, d. at Rochester, Mass. 7. Gamaliel, Jan. 31, 1745. 8. Paul, bap. Oct. 4, 1747, d. Jan. 12, 1749. 9. Nabby, bap. Ap. 29, 1750, m. Jno. Chapman, and d. soon after. 10. Betsey, bap. May 12, 1751, d. Jan. 22, 1753. 11. Betsey, bap. Ap. 29 1753, d. Dec. 12, 1788. 12. Clement, bap. Sep. 21, 1755.

7. Joseph, s. Joseph 3, m. 1, Phebe Bowker, Oct. 28, 1762, who d. Dec. 2, 1772; and 2, wid. Tamsen Bowker, Dec. 23, 1773, who d. Feb. 7, 1791, and he Dec. 7, 1816. No ch. He lived on Centre st., in his father's house.

8. Lemuel, s. Joseph 3, m. Mercy Witherell, Oct. 16, 1766, who d. a wid. in Feb. 1825. It is said that he d. in Me., and that his descendants reside there. ch. : 1. Mercy, 1776, d. Dec. 25, 1848, in H. 2. Lemuel, went to Me., was m., and it is said, came to his death by the fall of a pile of wood upon him, in his barn. 3. An inf. son, d. Dec. 26, 1775. 4. Another ch., d. Dec. 3, 1776. Was there also another son, Joseph, who m. an Estes. ?

9. Benj., s. Joseph 3, m. Elizab. Crooker, of Pemb., Nov. 29, 1759, who d. Ap. 19, 1793. It is said, that he d. in Me. ch. : 1. Jabez R., bap. Nov. 16, 1760, m. Elizab. Barker, Ap. 11, 1785, and went to Me. 2. Benj., bap. Nov. 1, 1762. 3. Joseph, bap. May, 19, 1765, d. Mar. 17, 1766. 4. Molly, bap. Aug. 16, 1767, m. Abner Magoun, of Pemb., Dec. 16, 1796. 5. Betty,

bap. Aug. 5, 1770, m. Asa Pool, of S. Ab'n. 6. Lucy, bap. July 3, 1774, m. Thos. Bates. 7. Sarah, bap. Aug. 17, 1777, d. Nov. 3, 1802.

10. Solomon, s. Solomon 4, m. Aquilla, da. John Bates, of Scit., Nov. 20, 1769, lived first in his father's house, on Broadway, and thence moved to Me., in 1787, with all his ch. He was a shipwright by trade, and followed that business for several years after he went to Me., and built several vessels on the Kennebec. He owned, also, a farm in Greene, Me.; was ever regarded as an honest man, and a good citizen, and was "a stern and inflexible *republican.*" He d. in Fayette, ab. 1815, ae. 77. ch.: 1. Douty, bap. Jan. 20, 1766, an iron smith by trade; was out with his fa. in the Revolution, and his wid. drew a pension; m. Polly Perry, and had *Charles*, *Polly*, *Wm.*, *Jane*, and *Huldah*; all unm. but Chas., who has 4 or 5 ch. They live in Leeds, Me. The fa. d. Jan. 1, 1835, and was a man of excellent character. 2. Levi, bap. Mar. 30, 1766, m. Lydia Sylvester, Dec. 30, 1784, had *Harvey*, *Levi*, *Ezekiel*, *Betsey*, and *Lydia*, all m., and live in Leeds. The fa. was a ship carpenter, and d. 1825. 3. Solomon W., Aug. 27, 1765, bap. Mar. 30, 1766. (See No. 21.) 4. Abigail, m. Joseph Dunham, of Me. 5. Samuel, bap. Oct. 22, 1769, m. 1, Hannah Stetson, Mar. 27, 1791, and 2, Sarah Dagget; sett. in St. Albans, was a farmer, and had *John*, *Seth*, *Simeon*, and *Florentine*, and perhaps others. He d. ab. 1849. 6. Lucinda, m. 1, Prince Waterman, Feb. 3, 1791, and 2, Jabez Merritt, and is living. 7. Lydia, m. Abel Crooker. 8. John, bap. Oct. 9, 1774, m. Deborah Stetson, was a farmer, in Greene; had *Wheaton*, *Jason*, *Sibyl*,, *Sabrina*, and perhaps others; and d. ab. 1832. 9. Caleb, m. Betsey Herrick, was a farmer, in Greene; had *Thos. H.*, *Betsey*, *Amy*, *Sally*, *Caleb S.*, and *Henry H.*; who are all m. The fa. was one of the best of men, and d. in G., ab. 1846. 10. Alexander, m. a Robinson. 11. Sally, bap. Nov. 5, 1786. 12. Sylvia, m. Artemas Cushman. 13. Reuben, bap. Nov. 16, 1788, m. Susan Sprague, is a miller by occupation, and has one da., *Isabel*.

11. Jonathan, s. Amos 5, m. Ruth Stetson, Feb. 11, 1771, and lived and d. in Rochester, Mass. ch.: b. in R. I., 1. Nath'l.

living in R., ae. ab. 75. 2. Stetson, d. young. 3. Ruth, m. Barnabas Mendell, of R. 4. Rebecca, m. John Hall, of R. 5. Emily, m. John Bennett. 6. Julia A. 7. Jonathan, d. young.

12. Elijah, s. Amos 5, m. a Briggs, and lived and d. in Rochester. ch.: 1. Nathan, of New Bedford. 2. Roland, of Rochester. 3. Lydia. 4. Ephraim, of Rochester.

13. Sylvester, s. Amos 5, m. 1, a Landers, and 2. Sarah Sears, and lived and d. in Rochester. ch.: 1. Jemima, m. Wm. Handy, and moved to Me. (By 2d.) 2. Sylvester. 3 Lucinda, d. unm. 4. Paddock. 5. Polly, m. Owen Hines, of R.

14. Moses, s. Amos 5, m. Susan Mendell, and lived and d. in Rochester. ch.: 1. Lucy, m. Alden Wing. 2. Moses, d unm. 3. Sally, m. Philip Wing. 4. Noble E., 1791, m. Sarah Allen, in 1816, and lives in the new town of Marion. Has *Susanna*, Sep. 13, 1818, m. James Clark, and d. in 1849. *Charles T.*, 1817, d. 1820. *Charles T*, 1820, d. 1821, and *George S.*, Oct. 22, 1821, m. Sarah N. Blankenship, lives in Marion, and has *Marietta C.*, *James H.*, d. and *Sarah N.*

15. David, s. Amos 5, m., and had 1. Jared. 2. David, m. Hannah Harrington, lived in Me., and d. ab. 1812, having had *David*, and *Salome*. 3. Betsey, m. a Carr, of Westport, and d.

16. Col. Seth, s. Clement 6, m. Anne Neal, Dec. 21, 1757, who d. Dec. 12, 1810, and he, in Boston, Ap. 9, 1820. He was an officer in the Revolutionary War, and had the reputation of being brave and efficient. He built the house on Centre st., lately occupied by Enos Bates. ch.: 1. Seth. 2. Joseph N. 3. Paul. 4. Joshua. 5. Anna, m. Sam'l. B. Perry, Feb. 2, 1786. 6. Rebecca, Nov. 26, 1765, m. Cornelius White, Dec. 30, 1801. 7. Amos, Aug., 1769? 8. Michal, bap. and d. June 11, 1774. 9. Enos, b. 1772? 10. Ward, bap. Oct. 15, 1775. 11. Eli., bap. June 29, 1777, d. Jan, 12. 1778. 12. Michal, May 3, 1780, m. Capt. Thos. Stetson, Ap. 21, 1834, and d. 13. Celia, Ap. 15, 1783, m. Dryden Judd, from N. Y'k. State, Ap. 27, 1807. He d. in 1851, and she is yet living. 14. James, bap. July 14, 1785, d. Oct. 26, 1792.

17. Thos., s. Clement 6, m. Hannah Torrey, Jan. 29, 1767,

and d. Oct. 22, 1768, and his wid. m. Caleb Rogers, jr., Dec. 26, 1779. ch.: Thos. bap. June 3, 1770, prob. b. 1768.

18. Gamaliel Bates s. Clement 6, m. Mary Carver, of Pembroke, September 5, 1771, and d. Jan. 9, 1823, and his wid. June, 1836. Lived on Cross st., where his da. Lydia, lately resided, near Broadway, and was a mason by trade. ch.: 1. Lydia, Feb. 4, 1772. Living in H. Not m. 2. Gamaliel, Mar. 22, 1774. 3. Mary P., Jan. 19, 1776, d. unm. 4. Calvin, Oct. 29, 1777. 5. Hannah, Dec. 10, 1779, m. Levi Fish, Feb. 8, 1803, and is d. 6. James, Oct. 8, 1781. 7. John B., Aug. 20, 1783, m. the wid. of Jacob Taylor, and had one ch., who d., and he d. Mar. 7, 1831, in Plym'h. He was a master mason, and a man of note in P., and erected the court-house, and other public buildings. 8. Rebecca, Aug. 3, 1785, d. Oct. 11, 1786. 9. Deborah, Sep. 12, 1787, d. Mar. 22, 1788. 10. Deborah, Jan. 5, 1789, m. Jacob Capron, of Att'o., Jan. 1, 1809. 11. Reuben, Oct. 5, 1790, d. Jan. 31, 1829. A mason by trade. 12. Betsey, Aug. 5, 1792, d. Nov. 21, 1825. A school teacher for many years, and a woman of great intelligence. 13. Rufus, Mar. 16, 1794. 14. Ezekiel, Nov. 5, 1795. 15. Abigail, Sep. 10, d. Oct. 29, 1797.

19. Clement Bates Capt. Clement, s. Clem. 6, m. Rebecca Stetson, Dec. 25, 1785, who d. Sep. 29, 1813, and he Nov. 30, 1839. Lived on Cross st., where Hiram Studley now resides. He was a soldier in the Rev'n., and was at Dorchester heights, and elsewhere. See the chap. on the Rev'n. ch.: 1. Thos. M., Jan. 1787. 2. Clement. 3. Hira. 4. Joshua. 5. Lucy, m. Benj. Stetson, Sep. 10, 1820. 6. Nabby, m. Thos. Damon, Dec. 25, 1827, and d. in 1852. 7. Priscilla, m. Chas. Leach.

20. Benj., s. Benj. 9, m. Martha Stetson, Mar. 3, 1786, who d. Feb. 26, 1848. He still survives, and is a *revolutionary pensioner*, having served in R. I. ch.: 1. Abigail, m. David Her-

sey, of Ab'n. 2. Betsey, m. Wm. Bates, Mar. 4, 1812, and is living a wid., in So. Scit. 3. Lydia, m. Wm. Stoddard, of H'm., in June 1813. 4. Sally, d. unm. 5. Horatio. 6. Benj., m. Hannah Munroe, of Norton, and d. leaving ch., *Harriet*, *Amanda*, *George*, and another. 7. Oliver, d. unm. 8. John, is m. and lives in Roxbury.

21. Solomon W., s. Solomon 10, m. Mary Macomber, of Taunton, Mass., and is yet living, in Norridgewock, Me., ae. 88. He was a ship carpenter in early life, but after his removal to Me., devoted his time principally to farming and trading, and kept also a public house in Fayette. He was J. P., for ab. 30 yr's; Town Clerk of Fayette for 21 years; Rep. to the Gen'l. Court of Mass. for 10 years; and in the Senate 2 years. ch.: 1. James, Sep. 24, 1789. 2. Harriet, Ap. 10, 1791, m. John Hubbard, and d. in July 1828. 3. John, Mar. 4, 1794, d. unm. 4. Linda, June 2, 1796, m. Francis T. Haines. 5. George, Feb. 12, 1798. 6. Silas, Feb. 12, 1798, a lawyer by profession; d. in Havanna, in Nov. 1821. Not m. 7. Mary, Mar. 2, 1800, m. John Starbird. 8. Nircan, Nov. 27, 1801, is a physican, in Machias, Me., m. Charlotte Dennett, and has 2 or 3 ch. 9. Sophia, Dec. 8, 1803, m. Asa Clark. 10. Soloman W., Aug. 2, 1805, a merchant, in Gardiner, Me.: m. 1, Mary A. Neil, and 2, Elizab. Dennis, and has 5 ch. 11. Horatio, Sep. 22, 1807, is m., lives in N. York, and has 3 sons.

22. Sylvester, s. Sylvester 13, m. Melintha Clark, and lived in Rochester, where he d. ch.: 1. Albert, d. unm. 2. Sarah L., m. Stephen Luce, and lives in N. Y'k. 3. Charles, d. unm. 4. Thos. C., m. Rhoda Briggs, and lived and d. in Sippican, leaving ch., *Charles H.*, and *Elenor C.* 5. Polly, d. young. 6. Meletiah, d. young. 7. James, d. unm. 8. Orlando, m. Lucy Mendell, and lives in Princetown, Mass. No ch.

23. Paddock, s. Sylvester 13, m. Nancy Sturtevant, and lives in Marion, Mass. ch.: 1. John S., m. Hannah Hammett, lives near his fa., and has *Hannah*, *Nancy*, *Sauuel*, *Abby*, and *Roberta.* 2. Mary, m. Edwin Blankenship. He is d. 3. Thankful, m. Joseph S. Luce. She is d.

23. Jared, s. David 15, m. Eunice Allen, and moved to Me.,

where he d. ch.: 1. Jared, m. 1, Mary Clark, and 2, wid. Jemima Ellis, lives in Marion, is a shipwright, and has *Jared*, *Prince H.*, and *Salome E.* 2. Warren. 3. Eunice, d. 4. Adaline, d. 5. Betsey. 6. David. 7. Weston A., d. 8. Thos., d. 9. John, d. Others d. young.

24. Seth, s. Col. Seth 16, m. Irene Delano, of Dux'y., and lived in D. ch.: 1. Amasa D., Ap. 13, 1792. A shipmaster; d. in Halifax, N. S., ab. 1814. 2. Betsey, Oct. 31, 1794, m. a Patten, of Boston. 3. Nancy D., Feb. 9, 1798, m. Sam'l. Soule, of Dux'y. 4. Seth, Mar. 26, 1801, m. a Black, and lives in Boston. 5. Hannah C., Oct. 19, 1803, m. a Harwood, of Bath, Maine.

25. Joseph N., s. Col. Seth 16, m. Eunice Oldham, who d. Nov. 24, and he in May, 1828. He was a soldier in the Rev'n., and though young, did good service to his country. ch.: 1. Thos. O., July, 1786. 2. Joseph N., July, 1796, m. Ann Rainsford, is a shipwright, and lives in E. Bos'n. 3. Jane, May, 1797, d. unm. 4. Eunice O., May, 1797, m. Thos. Winslow, jr., Dec., 1820, and d. 5. James, Jan., 1800, m. Mary Reed, of Tyngsboro, and d. in Ap., 1850, and his wid. lives in Wey'h. His ch. were *James*, *George*, *Franklin*, *Jackson*, and *Lewis*.

NOTE,—Three ch. d. young in this family.

26. Paul, s. Col. Seth 16, m. Freelove Witherell, Ap. 8, 1795, and d. Feb. 2, 1826, and his wid. ab. 1837. Lived W. of Winter st., in a house standing back from the road. ch.: 1. Paul, Jan. 22, 1797, m. Temperance C. Tubbs, Mar. 13, 1825, and d. July 23, 1832, leaving ch., *Sophia M.*, Dec. 14, 1825; *Eliza P.*, Dec. 16, 1830; and *Maria A. H.*, Aug. 27, 1829, d. May 20, 1845. 2. Marshall, Dec. 30, 1798, m. Huldah Hall, of Mf'd., and has *Wm. M.*, Jan. 18, 1836; *Reuben S.*, Dec. 3; 1837, and perhaps others. Lives in Mf'd. 3. Henry, Oct. 22, 1803, m. Harriet W. Munroe, of Scit., May 5, 1835, is a tanner by trade, and lives in the old Nath'l Clark house. Has *Henry A.*, Oct. 5, 1843; *Adrian W.*, July 20, 1845; *Mary S.*, Aug. 21, 1847; and *Catherine F.*, Oct. 16, 1849, d. Sep. 6, 1850. 5. Judson, Dec. 22, 1806, m. Lydia P. Curtis, Aug. 11, 1830, is a black-

smith by trade; lives on Centre st.; and has *Judson C.*, June 29, 1831; *Paul*, Mar. 22, 1834; *Lydia P.*, July 12, 1836, d. Oct. 16, 1837; *George F.*, July 9, d. Aug. 29, 1838; *Lydia F.*, Dec, 28, 1839; and *Diana A.*, June 28, 1843. 6. Walter, June 24, 1810. A stone-cutter by trade. Not. m.

27. Joshua, s. Col. Seth 16, m. Bethia, da. Joseph Ames, of Bridg'r., in 1796, and d. in B., in 1839. In early life he went to Canada, and set up a large furnace, which he conducted with good success for many years. Subsequently he returned to Mass., and purchased a farm in Bridg'r., which is improved by his descendants, and which he occupied until the date of his decease. ch.: 1. Joshua C., 1797. A merchant, in Boston. Not m. 2. Zephaniah, 1803, d. unm. 3. George W., 1805, m. Hannah, da. Andrew Tucker, of Mid'o., in 1836, lives in Bridg'r., and has *Andrew*, *Ellen*, and *Sarah*. 4. Samuel W., 1808, m. Helen, da. Zenas Crooker, lives in Bridg'r., and has *Helen R.*, *Joshua*, *Corinna*, *Marcia P.*, and *Elizabeth A.* 5. Bethia W., 1813, m. Asa P. Keith of Bridg'r.

28. Amos, s. Col. Seth 16, m. 1, Sibyl Robbins, Nov. 25, 1802, who d. Mar. 27, 1816, and 2, Ruth Jenkins, Nov. 1, 1818, and built and occupied the house now occupied by B. B. Hall, on Centre-st. He d. May 8, 1833, and his wid., who survives, lives in the old Baldwin house. ch.: 1. Amos, Dec. 1, 1803, m. Deborah Hersey, lives in H'm. 2. Mary R., July 13, 1806, m. Nath'l. F. Chamberlin, June 11, 1837. 3. Phebe, June 14, 1809, m. N. F. Chamberlin, Nov. 10, 1832, and d. May 23, 1837. 4. Oren, June 14, 1812, m. Mary A. Martin, lives in Milton. 5. John P., June 12, 1814, m. Caroline Kimball, and lives in Milton. (By 2d.) 6. Ruth J., Oct. 17, 1819, m. Reuben Stetson, Ap. 26, 1846. 7. Sibyl R., Feb. 2, 1821. 8. Fanny, Nov. 16, 1822, m. John H. Carey, of H. 9. Betsey R., May 6, 1825, m. Benj. F. Studley, of H. 10. Rebecca W., Mar. 15, 1829. 11. Celia A. M., Sep. 4, 1831, m. Elisha Thayer, of Baintree, Ap. 20, 1851.

29. Lt. Enos, s. Col. Seth 16, m. Lydia Tilden, Oct. 5, 1809, and d. Feb. 10, 1814, and his wid. Feb. 5, 1852. Lived where his son Enos lately resided. ch.: 1. Enos, Mar. 10, 1810. Not

m. 2. Lydia, Dec. 26, 1812, m. Albert White, Esq., May 1, 1836.

30. Ward, s. Col. Seth 16, m. Ruth Stetson, in 1819, and lives on Centre st. He is a gunsmith by trade, and served as an artificer in the war of 1812, in the Co. of Capt. Alexander Parris. ch.: 1. Seth W., July 5, 1822, d. Jan. 7, 1848. 2. Adaline W., July 28, 1824, m. Geo. B. Perry, in May 1846, and d. in Aug. 1852.

31. Thos., son Thos. 17, m. 1, Lucy Bates, in Nov. 1792, and 2, Mary Ramsdell, and d. Mar. 13, 1817. Lived on Broadway, where Joshua Bates now resides. Old house gone. ch.: 1. Nathan, prob. d. at sea. 2. Jeremiah, d. on the Gurnet, Mar. 3, 1813. Four ch. by this w. d young. (By 2d.) 3. Mary, Ap. 1, d. Oct. 25, 1807. 4. Lucy, Jan. 27, 1809, m. Sylvanus Whiting, Nov. 20, 1828. 5. Cyrus, Mar. 7, 1811, m. Mary Alden, lives in S. Ab'n., is a carpenter, and has *Mary B.*, *Cyrus A.*, *Solon*, *Ezra T.*, *Julia A.*, d. ae. 6 mo's., *Abby A.*, *Charles O.*, and *Susan M.* 6. Hannah, Nov. 29, 1814, m. Francis Stoddard, of Scit. 7. Thos., Aug. 5, 1816, m. Lucy White, lives in S. Ab'n., and is a shoe cutter. No ch.

32. Gamaliel, s. Gamaliel 18, m. Elizabeth Coffin, of Boston, and there d. in May 1822. ch.: 1. Charles, m. 1. Eliza Packard, and 2, Miranda Balkom, and d. in Boston, in 1852, leaving a da., *Elizabeth A.* 2. Caroline, m. a Wyatt, of Medford, and d. 3. Mary A., is m. and lives in Pawtucket. 4. Eliza, m. a Gillespie, of Nantucket.

NOTE.—The son, Charles, was a member of the Ancient and Honorable Society of Freemasons, and belonged to Mt. Lebanon Lodge, Boston, and to St. Paul's Royal Arch Chapter; and on the occasion of his decease, both bodies passed resolutions highly commendatory of his character and abilities. Those of the former body state, that "for four successive years he presided over the interests of Mt. Lebanon Lodge, with unusual ability, filling the chair with great honor to himself, and benefit to the institution;" and by vote, the altar of the Lodge was clothed with mourning for three months. The resolutions of the latter body, of which he was presiding officer, state that, "in the death of Bro. Bates, we mourn the loss of an excellent, honest, true hearted man and mason:—one who has endeared himself to his brethren, by the urbanity of his manners, the uprightness of his deportment, and the benevolence of his heart." The altar of the chapter was also clothed with mourning; and we understand that a monument has been erected to the memory of Brother Bates, in the beautiful Cemetery at Mt. Auburn. Peace to his ashes!

33. Calvin, s. Gamaliel 18, m. Elizab. Stetson, Aug. 12, 1801, who d. Mar. 6, 1842. He lives on Winter st., is a man of enterprise; part owner of the Forge on King st.; and has been for many years engaged in the iron business ch.: 1. Eliza, Nov. 2, 1801, m. Albert Holbrook, June 23, 1836. 2. Olive, Aug. 10, 1803, m. George Bailey, of H'n., June 20, 1824. 3. Mary C., May 5, 1805, m. Ozias Perkins, May 21, 1832. 4. Lucinda, Mar. 1, 1807, m. Marcus Packard, Nov. 28, 1833. 5. Calvin, July 22, 1810, m. Jane T. Kingman, of N. Bridg'r., and d. there in 1843, leaving *Angeline L.*, and *Abby J. C.* 6. Merril, Aug. 21, 1812, m. Joseph Thomas, of H'n., Feb. 7, 1841. 7. Elmira, May 24, 1816, m. Wm. P. Russell, Ap. 2, 1837. 8. Angeline, Mar. 11, 1819, m. Lewis C. Church, of H. 9. Lydia. 10. Ruth.

NOTE.—We regret that we are unable to present a view of the residence of Mr. B., but the inclemency of the weather prevented its being taken with the others, during the artists stay in town.

34. James, s. Gamal. 18, m. Hannah Walker, of Pemb., May 21, 1807, and lives in P. ch.: 1. Wm. C., lives in Gardiner, Me. 2. James H., of Pemb. 3. Lydia, m. Capt. Allen Dawes, of Dux'y. 4. Emeline, m. Fred'k Eayres. He is d.

35. Rufus, s. Gamal. 18, m. Huldah, da. Eleazer Keith, of Bridg'r., and lives in H., on Broadway, in the house built by himself, ab. 1823. An upright and honorable member of Society. ch.: 1. George M., Ap. 13, 1823, m. Mary A., da. David Ramsdell, May 1852, and lives on Broadway. 2. Reuben, Ap. 10, 1830. 3. Wm. C., May 25, 1838.

36. Ezekiel, s. Gamal. 18, m. Lois Daggett, of Att'o., Dec 6, 1821; is a carpenter by trade; and was a master builder and contractor for many years, in Boston, of the firm of Bates and Kelsey. He has now retired from business, and resides in Att'o. A man of enterprise and integrity; of respectable standing and highly estemed. ch.: 1. Jesse D., July 31, 1823, m. Mary E. Fowle, July 9, 1845, and has *Lois D.*, Sep. 1, 1850. 2. John T., Nov. 25, 1831. 3. Mary A., Sep. 3, 1836.

37. Capt. Thos. M., s. Capt. Clement 19, m. Lydia, da. Bachelor Wing, July 12, 1807, and lives at the corner of Winter st., in

the house built by himself, in 1841, where the old Wing house stood. He was, for a time, Capt. of the Han. L. Inf. Co.; Selectman in 1840 and '41; Collector; constable, &c. ch.: 1. George, Jan. 3, 1808, m. Lucy, da. David Warren, of Plym'h., Oct. 25, 1832, and lives on Centre st., near Winter st., and has *George W.*, Mar. 16, 1834, d. ae. 2; *Wm. H.*, May 8, 1837; and *George W.*, Aug. 12, 1840. 2. Sylvia, Sep. 4, 1809, m. Stephen Bailey, Mar. 6, 1834. 3. Elizab. B., June 21, 1811, m. Cyrus Josselyn, Oct. 24, 1833. 4. Thos. M., Mar. 13, 1813, m. Bethia B. Cook, in 1836, had *Lorenzo T.*; his w. d., and he lives with his fa. 5. Melissa B., Ap. 29, 1816, m. John T. Tribou, Oct. 16, 1835. 6. Sylvanus W., Dec. 23, 1818, m. Rebecca C., da. Thorndike Felton, of N. Salem, N. H., lives in part of his father's house, and has *Lysander F.*, Mar. 8, 1843; and *Lucius W.*, Aug. 24, 1849. 7. Hannah B., Ap. 21, 1821. 8. Laura A., Feb. 21, 1824, d. Ap. 4, 1830. 9. Mercy T., Dec. 25, 1826, m. Wm. J. Vining, Mar. 5, 1849.

38. Clement, s. Capt. Clement 19, m. 1, Urania Burgess, and 2, Betsey Burgess, and lives in Plymouth. ch.: 1. Ozen. 2. Ruby, m. Geo. Drew, of P. 3. Hira. 4. Elizabeth, m. Sam'l. R. Winslow, Mar. 25, 1849.

39. Hira, s. Capt. Clement 19, m. Lucy Josselyn, Feb. 24, 1825, and lives on Broadway, in the house built by himself, ab. 1823. ch.: 1. Lucy C., Ap. 24, 1828, m. David W. Brown, of E. Bridg'r. 2. Hira W., Ap. 16, 1830. 3. Julia A., Ap. 5, 1832. 4. Ellen A., July 22, 1834. 5. Edwin J., Mar. 18, 1837.

40. Joshua, s. Capt. Clement 19, m. Mary S. Palmer, Feb. 3, 1830, who d. Aug. 3, 1849. He lives on Broadway, in the house fitted up by himself, and first built for a Tannery, which business he followed for a time. ch.: 1. Cordelia, Dec. 6. 1830, m. James Woodman. 2. Joshua E., Mar. 18, 1833. 3. Albert E., May 11, 1834. 4. Elizab. A., Mar. 27, 1838. 5. Julian, 1842.

41. Horatio, s. Benj. 20, m. Mary, da. John L. Munroe, and d. in Norton, Mass., leaving ch.: 1. Mary A., 1812, m. Richard H. Hall, of Norton, and has 6 ch. 2. Horatio, Feb. 3, 1819, m. Sarah H. Sweet, in Sep. 1838; lives in N., and has *Sarah J.*, Jan. 8, 1840, and *Savillion H.*, Feb. 23, 1842.

42. Dr. James, s. Solomon W. 21, m. Polly Jones, of Fayette, Me., and has 1, Lydia, is m. 2. Charles A., is m. 3. Emma C., is m. 4. James M., a physician by profession. The father stud. Med. with Dr. Ariel Mann, of Hallowell, and after spending 2 yrs. in the army, as a surgeon, he was in Company with Dr. M. for 6 yrs. He was Rep. to Cong., in 1831–'32, and is a gentleman of fine abilities, and correct deportment.

43. Rev George, s. Solo. W. 21, studied for the ministry under Rev. Hosea Ballou, of Bos'n, and commenced preaching in 1824. He was sett. 1st, in Livermore, Me., where he remained until 1830, and then in Turner, Me., until 1852. He now preaches in Hallowell. He m. 1, Hannah Haines, of Livermore, in 1821 ; and 2, Mrs. Lenora Prince; and has ch. 1. Laverna C., Mar. 17, 1822. 2. Salina M., Jan. 28, 1824. 3. Clarinda S., Feb. 17, 1826. 4. Harriet C., Jan. 29, 1829. 5. George S., May 21, 1833. 6. Silas E., Mar. 17, 1835. 7. Hannah L., Mar. 3, 1837. 8. Mary W., Mar. 18, 1839. 9. Adelia P., Feb. 23, 1841. 10. Julia A., June 22, 1843. 11. Solomon W., July 7, 1845. 12. Lucella J., Dec. 24, 1851. — Three of the das. are teachers in Georgia.

44. Thos. O., s. Joseph N. 25, m. Rebecca Bates, Oct. 11, 1809, is a brick-mason by trade, and lives on Silver St., in the old Simeon Curtis house. ch: 1. Thos. O., m. Mary, da. Anthony Sylvester, lives on Broadway, and has *Robert T.*, Aug. 2, 1848 ; and *Silas W.*, Aug., 1850. 2. Martin S., a machinist by trade, m. Olive Walker, lives on Silver St., and has had 2 ch., one only of whom is living. 3. Andrew H., Oct. 23, 1813, m. Abagail N. Cook, May 14, 1844, is a carpenter, lives in Hanson, and has *Gilman*, Mar. 20, d. Nov. 11, 1844 ; *Gilman*, Nov. 1846 ; *Zilpha A.*, Oct., 1849 ; and Silas W., Aug., 1850. 4. Silas G., 1818, m. Jane Briggs, and d. Sep. 22, 1848. 5. John G., m. Christiana Clapp, of Scit., Oct. 2, 1845, lives on Wash'n St., is a shoemaker, and had *John* G., July 28, d. Sep. 8, 1849. 6. James C.

45. Joseph S., s. Comfort, of Pemb., (and a descendant of *Caleb Bates*, of Hm.) m. Sarah, da. Col. John B. Barstow, Oct. 2, 1820, and lives on Broadway, E. of the Four Corners.

ch: 1. Henry S., Nov. 1821. 2. Sarah A., Nov. 1823. 3. John B., Feb. 17, 1826. Merchant at the Four Corners.

46. James, s. John, of Lynn, and gr. s. of John, m. Ann H., da. Joseph Damon, Aug. 16, 1838, and lives on Whiting st. Shoemaker. ch: 1. Lucy, Oct. 27, 1838. 2. Susan M., Oct. 24, 1840. 3. James A., Dec. 12, 1842, d. Sep. 20, 1851. 4. Joshua S., Nov. 25, 1844. 5. Emma R., Feb. 27, 1847. 6. Eliza E., Nov. 20, 1848. 7. Esther, Jan. 4, 1851.

BEAL, Zadoc, of Ab'n., s. Noah, (and prob. a desc't. of John, a shoemaker, who, with his wife, 5 sons, 3 das,. and 2 serv'ts. came from H'm., Eng. to H'm. Mass. in 1638.) was b. Feb. 10, 1788, and m. 1, Triphena, da. Homer Whiting, May 22, 1816, who d. Aug. 21, 1820 ; and 2, Rebecca, da. James Whiting, Nov. 30, 1837, and lives on Whiting st., in the house built by Asa Whiting. Farmer. He was one of the Selectmen in 1837. ch.: 1. Priscilla, Oct. 1, 1817, d. May 6, 1824. 2. an inf. son, d. Aug. 11, 1820.

BENNER, John H., s. Joseph, of Ab'n., m. Hannah S., da. Eleazer Josselyn, Jan. 1, 1835, and lives on Pleasant st, with his fa.-in-law, shoemaker. ch.: 1. Henry G., Jan. 1836. 2. Hannah M., Oct., 1839. 3. John 2., Aug. 30, 1842. 4. Joseph W., Nov. 23, 1848.

BINNEY, Spencer, of Hull, m. a da. of John Hatch, of Hanover, and his da. Ann, m. Rev. Aaron Josselyn, of Dux'y., and resides in D. His son Spencer, b. Sep. 24, 1828, lives in H., on Main st., with his fa.-in-law, m. Caroline F., da. Abisha Soule, and wid. of Martin S. Torrey. Sep., 1849, and has Mercy F., Ap. 23, 1850, and an inf., b. Ap. 27, 1852.

BLANCHARD, Ebenezer and Christopher C., sons of Ebenezer, of South Weymouth., came to H. in 1844, and commenced the shoe business, in which, and in trading, they are extensively engaged at their stores on Washington st., in the Northeasterly part of the town. They are both upright, enterprising, and valuable citizens, and have done much to build up the part of the town in which they reside.

BONNEY, Thomas, was of Dux., in 1643, and was the ancestor of most of that name in Plym'h Co. He was a shoemaker by trade, was of Sandwich, Eng'd., and came to N. Eng. in 1634, in the Hercules, John Witherley, master.

1. Josiah, s. Josiah, of Pemb., b. Nov. 30, 1794, a desc't. of Thos. of Dux'y., m. Mercy W., da. Timothy Rose, Ap. 2, 1820, and lives on Washington, corner of Union st., in the house built by Mr. Rose. Farmer. Was one of the Selectmen in 1842, 3, and 4. ch.: 1. Lucy J., Sep. 11, 1820, m. Robert H. Studley, of H. Oct. 23, 1844. 2. Josiah W., Sep. 17, 1828.

2. Allen F., s. Roland, of Hn., m. Mary R., da. John Estes, Nov. 1842, and lives on Circuit st. ch.: 1. Mary E., Nov. 21, 1844, d. young. 2. Virginia A., Sep. 26, 1846. 3. Everett, b. July, d. Sep. 21, 1849, ae. 3 mos.

3. Hiram B., s. Roland, of Hn., m. Elizabeth B., da. John Estes, and lives on Circuit st. ch.: 1. Elizabeth B., Nov. 27, 1842. 2. Ann M., Feb. 22, 1846. 3. Emma J., July 8, 1848.

BOWKER, Benjamin H., s. Richard, of Hn., is prob. a descendant of Richard, who was in H., in 1729, and resided on the gore, subsequently annexed to Pemb., and now part of Hn.; and Richard was a descendant of James, from Sweden, who was in Scit., in 1680, whose farm was laid out on the east of Burnt plain. (Deane.) Benjamin H. was b. Sep. 5, 1820, m. Lydia, da. Ephraim Whiting, of Ab'n., July 3, 1843, and lives on Main st. Shoemaker. No ch.

BRIGGS, Ezra, b. 1724. was s. Joseph, s. Lt. James, s. Walter, who was of Scit. 1651, and purchased a farm of Mr. Hatherly, on the North side of Farm Neck. The cove within the *glades* still bears the name of Briggs's harbor. (Deane.) Ezra d. in H., Oct. 22, 1804, and his wid. Nov. 26, 1805. He lived back of where his grandson, Joseph, now resides, East of Washington st., and was a soldier in the Revolution. ch.: 1. Ezra, 1758? 2. Enoch, d. unm. 3. Charles, d. unm. 4. Nathaniel, 1764, d. Dec. 31, 1817. 5. Lydia, d. May 14, 1766. 6. Lydia, bap. Oct. 5, 1777, m. Benj. D. Fillmore, and d. Jan. 12, 1848. 7. Moses, d. July 27, 1806. 8. Rachel, d. Feb. 21, 1777. 9. Sally, d. May 24, 1800, ae. 33. 10. Joseph, bap. Oct. 5, 1777.

2. Ezra Briggs Jun son of Ezra, married 1, Margaret, da. William Curtis, May 13, 1784, who d. Aug. 16, 1788. and 2, Lydia Southward, of Dux'y., May 1, 1789. He d. Nov. 2; 1815, and his wid. May 1, 1840, ae. 74. He was out in the Rev'n. It is said that he lived for a time on Main st., and that his house stood where stands that of Joseph Brooks, jr. ch.: 1. Martha, and 2. Rachel, bap. Oct. 22, 1786, both d. Aug. 13, 1792. 3. Ezra, bap. Sep. 21, 1788, d. Feb. 14, 1790. (By 2d.) 4. Hannah, Oct. 1789, d. Aug. 13, 1792. 5. Ezra, May 16. 1791, m. Elizabeth Ficket, lives in Braintree, Mass., and has several ch. 6. Joseph, Dec. 22, 1793. 7. Lydia, Sep. 6, 1795. 8. Hannah, Mar. 5, 1799, m. Dea. Ara Brooks, Feb. 20, 1823. 9. Thomas J., Aug. 20, 1801, d. May 5, 1808. 10. Sarah W., Sep. 3, 1893, m. Judson Vining, of H., Ap. 24, 1826. 11. Betsey, Ap. 19, 1805, m. Rev. J. M. Spear, of Boston, June 6, 1831, a distinguished philanthropist, and the "Prisoner's Friend." 12. Martha, Dec. 22, 1806, m. David Vining, of H., May 4, 1828. 13. Thomas J., Sep. 24, 1809, d. Aug. 20, 1813.

3. Joseph, s. Ezra 2, m. Jane Paine, of Newburyport, Ap. 23, 1817. Lived first on Main st. in the house occupied by Henry Curtis, built by Mr. B. ab. 1820, and now resides on Washiugton st., in the house built by himself in 1836. Farmer. ch.: 1. Jane, m. Silas G. Bates. He is d., and she lives with her father. 2. Joseph, Ap. 18, 1821, m. Mary T., da. Lemuel Dwelley, Nov. 24, 1842, lives at the corner of Union and Main sts., in her father's house, (who is deceased,) and has *Sarah F.*, Aug. 18, 1843, and *Joseph A.*, May 8, 1851. 3. John G., Oct. 11. 1823. 4, William S., Feb. 21, 1826. 5. Richard P., Oct. 21, 1828. 6. Maria A., July 4, 1831. 7. Margaret H., Sep. 29, 1833. 8. Charles B., Jan. 29, 1838. 9. Elbridge B,, June 13, 1840.

BROOKS or BROOKE, Samuel, was s. Gilbert, s. Nathaniel, s. William, ae. 20, who, with his bro. Gilbert, ae. 14, came to N. Eng. in 1635, in the Blessing, John Liecester, master. Wm. was in Scit. in 1644, and his farm was South of Till's, afterwards Dwelley's creek. Samuel lived on Walnut street, in a house built there before the present road was laid out, and to which the access was by a cart path through land of Capt. Elisha Barrell, near his house. By w. Elizabeth, da. Thomas Gray, of Dublin, he had 1. Betsey, m. Heman Stoddard. 2. Deborah, m. Cooms House, Ap. 4, 1796. 3. James, and 4. John, went to Me. Mr. B. d. in H., May 17, 1829, ae. 87, and his wid. Aug. 27, 1830, ae. 89, and it is said they lived together, in the married state, nearly 70 years!

2. *Joseph Brooks* bro. of Samuel, m. 1, Lydia, Stetson, 1769, who d. Aug. 17, 1792; and 2, Sarah, Dunbar, 1794. He lived on Curtis, now Main st., in the house owned by James Brooks, and built by Sam'l. Curtis, and there d. Dec. 20., 1820, ae. 74, and his wid. ab. 1840, ae. 93. ch.: 1. Curtis, Dec. 12, 1770. 2. Lydia, Mar. 26, 1773, d. May 30, 1849. 3. Sarah, Dec. 22, 1775, m. Zachariah Damon, of H., July 2, 1800, and d. Ap. 4, 1847. 4. Ellinor, May 4, 1778, m. Eells Damon, Jan. 1, 1810, and d. Nov. 12, 1846. 5. Joseph, Jan. 1, 1781. 6. Abi, Ap. 10, 1783., m. Albert Church, and lives in Bath, Me. 7. Hannah, Nov. 20, 1785, d. Aug. 6, 1792.

NOTE.—Mr. B., when but 5 yrs. old, went to live with Sam'l. Curtis, and remained with him until his death, and then occupied the house nntil his own death.

3. Curtis, s. Joseph 2, m. Anne Southward, of Dux'y., Feb. 10, 1793, was selectman in 1811 and '12, and d. Aug. 31, 1817. His wid. is still living with Mr. Samuel Brooks, on Main st., in the house built by her husband, and occupied by him until his death. ch: 1. Samuel, and 2. Thomas, June 7, 1794. 3. Anne, and 4. Ara, Mar. 17, 1796. Anne, m. 1, James Whiting, Oct. 25, 1817, and 2, Jesse Gray, and d. at Greene, Me., 1847. 5. Hannah, Ap. 7, 1799, m. Jeremiah Belcher, of Randolph, Dec. 22, 1820. 6. John, Sep. 3, 1802. 7. Ruth, Dec. 31, 1806. A pair of silver shirt buttons is preserved in this family, a present from Rev. John Mellen, to Mrs. B., on the birth of her first twins. He did not repeat the gift on the birth of the second!

4. Joseph, s. Joseph 2, m. 1, Mary Tower, of Scit., Jan. 16, 1803, who d. Mar. 21, 1847; and 2, wid. Hannah Serles, June 10, 1849. Lived in his father's house until his 2d marriage, and

now in the Charles Donnell house, and is part owner of the shingle and box-board mill, known as Brooks' upper mill. He was Selectman in 1837. ch.: 1. Mary, Feb. 1, 1804. 2. Lydia S., m. Silas Ripley, of Ab'n., and d. a wid. Jan. 12, 1847. 3. Lucy, Nov. 15, 1807, d. Dec. 23, 1825. 4. Deborah, Dec. 17, 1809, d. Jan 28, 1812. 5. Sarah D., Mar. 29, 1812, m. Piam C. Whiting, Sept. 15, 1831. 6. Joseph, July 2, 1814. 7. James, Mar. 20, 1817, not m. Lives on Main st. Has been Capt. of the Han. Artil. Co. 8. Betsey, Ap. 18, 1819, m. Lucius Ford of Ab'n. She is d. 9. Gilbert, July 18, 1821, m. Sibyl, da. Abisha Soule, lives on Main st., in the house built by himself ab. 1846, and has *Edward G.*, Oct. 3, 1842. and *Alfred S.*, Oct. 24, 1846. 10. Charles, Aug. 31, 1823, m. an Ames, of Ab'n. and went to California, and after he had left, his w. and only ch. d. (By 2d) 11. Lydia, Oct. 24, 1850.

5. Samuel, s. Curtis 3, m. Mehitable Larkum, of Beverly, and lives on Main st., in the house built by Curtis Brooks, ab. 1794. ch.: 1. Samuel, Mar. 19, 1819, m. Mary Morey, lives in Medford, and has ch. 2. Mehitable, Feb. 3. 1824. 3. Anne S., 1829, d. ae. 9 wks. 4. Anne S., Sep. 25, 1830, m. Rufus Crane, of Braintree, Sep. 24, 1850. 5. Elizabeth, 1835, d. ae. 4 wks.

6. Thomas, s. Curtis 3, m. 1, Mary Curtis, Feb. 28, 1816, and 2, Laura Almy, 1837. Was for ab. 12 yrs. Dea. of the Baptist Church, and moved to Tremont, Ill., where his w. d. in 1852. He is Dea. of the Bap. Church in Tremont. ch.: 1. Thomas, May 26, 1817, d. unm. 2. Wiiliam, June 27, 1819, m. Julietta Meriam, of Ill. and d. leaving no ch. 3. Clarissa, Jan. 24, 1822, m. Plummer Couch, of Ill. 4. Mary A., Aug. 2, 1825, m. Wm. P. Lazzell, of Ill. 5. Curtis, Dec. 6, 1827, d. young. 6. Charlotte ? m. Cushing Jones, of Ill.

7. Ara, s. Curtis 3, m. Hannah Briggs, Feb. 20, 1823, and lives in Bowdoinham, Me. He is Dea. of the Bap. Church in Richmond, Me. Has Lydia A.; Elizabeth; Hannah; Jane; Jonathan K.; Ara C.; and Luther S. Lost 2, d. young.

8. Dea. John, s. Curtis 3, m. Emma Mann, Dec. 4, 1823, and lives on Main st., in the house built by Levi Mann, ab. 1790, and which has been occupied by Mr. B. since 1832. He is a respec-

table and intelligent farmer, and is Dea. of the Baptist Church. ch.: 1. John S., Oct, 27, 1824, m. Nancy C. Binney, June 23, 1850, and lives on Main st., in the house built by himself, in 1851. 2. Levi C., Mar. 5, 1827, m. Angeline S. Curtis, lives on Main st., in the house with Melzar Hatch, and has *Ella*, Jan. 9, 1850. 3. Joseph W., Mar. 3, 1829. 4. Emma M., June 30, 1831, m. George W. Curtis, of H. 5. Sarah M., Dec. 12, 1832. 6. Ara, Ap. 28, 1835. 7. Mary E., Nov. 15, 1837. 8. Hannah E., Feb. 26, 1840. 9. Thomas D., June 23, 1843. 10. Elizabeth, Nov. 4, 1845. 11. George M., d. May 13, 1850, ae. 9 mos.

9. Joseph, s. Joseph 4, m. Emily T., da. Robert Gardner, of H'm., and lives on Main st., in the house built by himself ab. 1846, on the spot where stood the house of Ezra Briggs. Has been Town Clerk and Treasurer, since 1846. A shoemaker by trade. ch.: 1. Emily A., July 7, 1840. 2. Joseph L., Nov. 30, 1841. 3. Mary E., Ap. 16, 1846.

NOTE.—There was a Taylor Brooks in H., 1750, a *shipwright*, but left no ch. on record.

BURGESS, Benj. F., s. Loammi, of Harvard, Mass., b. Jan. 23, 1810, m. Matilda, da. Lemuel Jenkins, of Ab'n., and lives in H., on Washington st., in the old Belcher Sylvester house. A shoemaker by trade. ch.: 1. Sarah W., 1844. 2. Emory, 1847, 3. Harriet, Sep. 15, 1851. Has lost sev. ch. all of whom d. young.

CARY, John H., of E. Bridg'r., s. Francis, is a descendant of John, from Somersetshire, Eng'd., who settled in Dux'y. 1639, and who was an original proprietor of W. Bridg'r., and the first Town Clerk. John H. m. Fanny, da. Amos Bates, and lives on Circuit st. ch.; 1. Ann A., 1842, d. Dec. 18, 1849. 2. John F. 1845, d. Jan. 8, 1850. 3. Adelia F., Oct. 25, 1850.

CHADDOCK, Rev. Calvin, Fourth Pastor of the Church in H., was s. of Capt. Joseph, who d. in H., June, 1812, ae. 88, and perhaps a descendant of the *Chadwicks*, who were early in Wat. He grad. Dart. Coll., 1786, m. Melatiah Nye, of Oakham, and sett. first in Rochester, and then in H., in 1806, and d. in Va., in 1818? He was proprietor of an Academy, in Rochester, and founder of the Academy in H., and a man highly esteemed, and eminently useful. He was Rep. of the town in 1811. See the chapters on Education, and on Ecclesiastical History, for further particulars of his life. His wid. is still living in Boston, with her son Ebenezer N. ch.: 1. Ebenezer N., 1793, m. Hannah G. Fearing, of Wareham, kept store in H., for a time at the Four Corners, and now resides in Boston, his place of business being at Comey's Wharf. Has *Abby F.*, m. J. A. P. Allen, merchant, of N. Bedford; and *Sturgis*, m. Tirzah, da. Capt. William Savary, of Wareham, Aug. 1852, and is in Boston, with his fa. 2. Moses G., 1795, resides in N. Y., is m. but has no ch. 3. Roxa, m. Albert Smith, Esq., now a lawyer in Wash'n. D. C. 4. Mary S., bap. Aug. 23, 1807, m. Mason Campbell, Esq., Clerk in the Treas. Dep't. Washington, D. C. 5. Dulce, m. Jas. McFarland, of Va. 6. Nancy, July 10, 1807, m. Thomas Whittaker, of Charleston, Va. 7. John S. S., Oct. 14, 1810. In California. 8. Sarah S., of Portland, Me.

CHAMBERLIN, Henry, *Shoemaker*, according to Daniel Cushing's Record, with his wife, and mother, and 2 ch., came from Hm., Eng'd, and sett. in Hm., Mass., in 1638, in which year he was *freeman*, and a grant of 5 ac. of land was made to him "at the head of Nicholas Jacobs." In 1645, he had a grant of swamp land, "that is the Towns by the highway to Potkey ? hill;" and in both cases, he is called *the Smith*. He had a son Henry, and he a son Nathaniel, who was of Scit., and received grants of land in 1693, on the east of Dead Swamp, now called Chamberlin Plain. He also owned land in Duxbury, in 1710, according to Winsor. His son Freedom, was of Pemb., b. 1697, m. Mary Soule, Ap. 3, 1722, and had Nathaniel, Sep. 24, 1722, and ten others, several of whom sett. in Bridg'r, where their descendants still reside [1]

2. Nathaniel, s. Freedom, of Pemb., m. 1. Sarah Foster, Dec. 17, 1743, who d. 1765; and 2, Deliverance, da. Thomas Snell, of Bridg'r, 1767, and d. in 1814, ae. 91, and his w. the same year, ae. 86. He was in H. in 1747, and for a few years after. Most

[1] See Mitchell's Bridgewater, Deane's Scituate, and Lincoln's Bi-Centennial Address. My sketch of the family is a little different from Deane's and Mitchell's, and was obtained from the readers of Hm., Scit., and Pemb.

of his ch. sett. in Bridg'r, and their posterity still reside there. But one son sett. in H., viz., Josiah, who was b. Oct. 13, 1764.

3. Josiah, s. Nath'l. 2, was of H., and lived first in a house owned by Capt. Rob't L. Eells, which stood on Wash'n. st., near Wm. Curtis's, and then built on Spring st., where his son Josiah now resides. He m. 1, Lucy Pratt, Nov. 25, 1784, who d. Mar. 26, 1789; and 2, Abigail Crooker, of Pemb., Mar. 18, 1790, and d. Oct. 18, 1829, and his wid. Nov. 7, 1847, ae. 83. (She was b. Oct. 16, 1764.) ch.: 1. Lucy, Mar. 23, 1785, m. Ezra Phillips, of P., Sep. 25, 1814, and d. June 7, 1832. 2. Lydia, Aug. 21, 1788, d. Sep. 14, 1821. (By 2d.) 3. Nabby, Aug. 22, 1796, m. Cephas Perry, Oct. 7, 1838. 4. Josiah, Nov. 17, 1798. 5. Nathaniel F., Jan. 6, 1802. 6. A twin brother of the last, d. Feb. 15, 1802.

4. Josiah, s. Josiah 3, m. Sophia Taylor, of Scit., Aug. 26, 1821, and lives on his father's place. A shoemaker by trade. ch.: 1. Josiah W., Feb. 11, 1822. 2. Nathaniel P., Mar., 1824, m. Melatiah, da. Sam'l. Stetson, Aug. 20, 1848, and lives on Washington st., in part of Joseph Briggs's house. 3. William H., July 19, 1827. Not m. 4. Lucy, Sep., 1834. 5. George, and 6. Francis, b. Aug. 29, 1840.

5. Nathaniel F., s. Josiah 3, m. 1, Phebe Bates, Nov. 10, 1832; and 2, Mary R. Bates, June 11, 1837, and lives on Centre st., in the house built by Dan'l. Chapman, where stood the house built by Ezekiel Stetson, for his father, Seth. ch.: 1. Nath'l. M., Oct. 20, 1833. 2. John B., Mar. 18, d. Oct. 4, 1836. (By 2d.) 3. John B., Jan. 23, 1838. 4. Amos B., Aug. 24, 1839. 5. Myron T., Oct. 20, 1843. 6. Ida.

6. Josiah W., s. Josiah 4, m. 1, Melinda Coxe, of H'n., Sep. 12, 1841, who d. Dec. 21, 1845; and 2, Sarah T. Ewell, of Scit., Nov. 30, 1848, and lives on Broadway, in part of the Salmond house. Shoemaker. ch.: 1. Josiah W., Dec. 8, 1843. 2. Mary T., June 21, 1845. (By 2d.) 3. Sarah M., Jan. 6, 1850. 4. Alice G., Ap. 15, 1851.

7. Norman, s. of Alpheus, of Mansfield, Ct., b. May 19, 1819, m. Rebecca S., da. Thomas O. Bates, Oct. 4, 1841, and lives on Hanover st., in what was the Ephriam Palmer house, afterwards

occupied by Dr. Dwelley. He is a shoemaker by trade. ch.: 1. Leander E., Aug. 24, 1843. 2. Mira A., Ap. 6, 1847.

NOTE.—There are several distinct families of Chamberlin's in N. Eng., descendants of different persons who came early to the country. *Richard* was in Boston in 1642. *Thomas* was freeman, 1644. *Edmund* was in Chelmsford in 1665, and there was a family early in Ct. The name is found in England as early as 1069, and is on the famous Battle Abbey Roll.

CHANDLER, Henry D., s. Isaac, of Dux'y., b. July 14, 1825, came to H. in 1849, lives at the Four Corners, and is a carriage trimmer, and harness maker, which business he had previously carried on in Boston. Not m. See the chapter on Manufactures, &c.

CHAPMAN, Ralph, ae. 20, was of Southwark, Eng'd., and came to Am., in the Elizabeth, of London, Wm. Stagg, master, in 1635. He was of Dux'y., in 1640, a ship carpenter by trade, and afterwards of Mf'd. He m. Lydia Wills, Nov. 23, 1642, and d. ab. 1671, leaving sev. ch., of whom Ralph, had a son John, who was of Hanover. The name of Chapman is quite common in England.

2. John, s. Ralph, jr., m. Sarah, da. Abraham Booth, June, 1730, and was first of Newport, R. I., and then of H., where he d. Jan. 3, 1811, at the advanced age of 105! He is said to have retained, to a remarkable degree, his health and vigor to the last, and about "two years previous to his death, he rode on horseback a distance of nine miles, to visit his great grand daughter, that he might hold on his knees her two children, his descendants in the fifth generation. Going into the yard, he split a log of wood, mounted without assistance, and returned home."[1] He was of the Society of Friends. But one of his sons has descendants in H., viz: John, b. Ap. 5, 1741.

3. John, s. John 2, m. 1, Ruth Torrey, Mar. 13, 1766; 2. Abigail Bates, Mar. 22, 1786; and 3, Bethia Gardner, of Pemb., Dec. 14, 1790, and d. in H. May 20, 1809, and his wid. in Dec., 1841, ae. 83. The only one of his ch. residing in H., is Daniel, b. Jan. 27, 1800. The fa. lived for a time, on a small island, in

[1] Winsor's Dux'y., p. 244.

George's swamp, off the road, about one mile from Enos Bates', between his house and that of Thos. M. Bates.

4. Daniel, s. John 3, m. Clara Burbank, and lived first a short distance W. of the centre meeting house, where Nath'l. F. Chamberlin resides, and built that house. He now lives on Washington st., on what was formerly the Joshua Simmons' place, in the house built by himself, which stands where stood that of Mr. Simmons, which was torn down by Mr. C. ch.: 1. Clarissa, May 1, 1823, m. William F. Harris, of So. Scit., (b. Mar., 1822, s. Abiel, of Braintree,) and has *Wm. F.*, May 7, 1846; *Clara L.*, May 27, 1848, d. Aug. 18, 1850; *Charles W.*, Oct. 4, 1851 d. Aug. 8, 1852. 2. Harriet, Nov. 1, 1824, m. Laban Wilder, of So. Scit., July 9, 1844. 3. Ara, Oct. 14, 1827, m. Sally W., da. David Damon, had *Eugene L.*, and d., Sep. 1, 1852. 4. Timothy B., July 18, 1831. 5. Daniel L., Sep. 15, 1834. 6. Laura A., July 18, 1840.

CHURCH, Richard, b. 1608, s. Joseph, was freeman in Boston, 1630, and Plym'h., 1632, m. Elizabeth, da. Richard Warren, 1636, and was fa. of Col. Benja., the noted hero of the Indian Wars. In the life of Col. Church, drawn up by his son Thomas, it is said that Richard's fa. Joseph, "with two of his brethren, came early into New England, as refugees from the religious oppression of the parent state;" and Deane suggests, that *Richard*, who was early in H'm., may have been one of these "brethren," and hence uncle to the warrior; and this *Richard* had a son *Nathaniel*, probably the one who sett. in Scit., in 1666, whose farm was on the North River, South of Cornet Stetson's, including the *bald hills*, and his house stood near the river, and nearly opposite to Job's landing. From Nathaniel probably descended Timothy Church, of H.

2. Timothy s. Nath'l. ? and grandson of Nath'l., of Scit. ? m. Elizabeth Rose, Sep. 5, 1765, and lived E. of Washington st., near where Martin Church resides, and there d., Mar. 2, 1776, and his wid. Mar. 24, 1794. ch.: 1. Timothy, bap. May 29, 1768. 2. Hannah S., b. May 29, 1772, d. Ap. 17, 1795.

3. Timothy, s. Timothy 2, m. Rebecca, da. Samuel Stetson,

Nov. 27, 1796, and lived E. of Wash'n. st., where his wid. d., July 12, 1850, ae. 75. ch.: 1. Timothy, Sep. 20, 1797, drowned in N. River, May 2, 1815. 2. William, Dec. 19, 1799. 3. Samuel S., bap. July 4, 1802. 4. Martin, bap. 1805. 5. Elizabeth R., bap. Sep. 18, 1808. 6. Lucy, 1809, d. July 4, 1812. 7. Harvey, 1816, d. May 14, 1818. 8. An inf., d. Jan. 22, 1820.

4. William, s. Timothy 3. m. Lucy B., da. Robert Sylvester, July 29, 1821, and lives on Hanover st., on the place formerly owned by Rev. Mr. Bass, but in the house built by himself, in 1828. A tanner by trade. Was Selectman in 1849. ch.: 1. Lucy W., Nov. 21, 1824, m. Joseph B. Sylvester, Feb. 8, 1847. 2. Wm., Oct. 15, 1827. Lives with his fa., and is unm. 3. Eliza M., Feb. 1835. 4. Hannah, Nov., 1837. Two ch. d. young.

5. Samuel S., s. Timothy 3, m. Sarah E., da. Robert Sylvester, Dec. 14, 1828, who d. Dec. 28, 1850. He lives on Wash'n. st., in the house built by himself in 1828, on the spot where stood formerly the house of Jona. Pratt, which was torn down by Mr. C. ch.: 1. Samuel H., Sep. 15, 1830. Works in Curtis's Forge. 2. Timothy. Oct. 3, 1833. 3. Juletta. 4. Sarah. 5. Adeline. 6. Benjamin, Jan. 25, 1844. 7. Robert. 8. Alice R., Oct. 6, 1850, d. Mar. 10, 1851.

6. Martin, s. Timothy 3, m. Caroline, da. Edward Stetson, in May, 1832, and lives on Wash'n, st., opposite his brother's, in the house built by himself, where formerly stood that of Othniel Pratt. ch.: 1. Bradbury, Nov. 26, 1838. 2. Hannah M., Jan. 1, 1844.

7. Lewis C., s. David F., of Mf'd., b. Sep., 1816, m. Angeline, da. Calvin Bates, and lives on Winter st., in the house built by himself. Carpenter. ch.: 1. Lewis A., Mar. 29, 1839. 2. Amelia F., Jan. 25, 1841.

CLARK, Thos., came from Plym'h. to Scit., in 1674, and his farm was on the W. of Walnut tree hill, adjoining that of Cornet Buck. He m. Martha Curtis, 1676, and had Thomas and others.

Thomas Clark jr., succeeded to his father's house, and by w. Alice Rogers, whom he m. in 1705, had John, of Hanover, and others; and he and his w. moved to Rochester, in 1731. (Deane's Scit., 237.)

2. John, s. Thos. jr., m. Abigail Tolman, of Scit., who d. in H., a wid., Aug. 21, 1789, ae. 85. He lived in an ancient house, two stories high in front, sloping back nearly to the ground, which stood near the mansion of Mr. Samuel Salmond, on Wash'n. st., at the Four Corners. A shipwright by trade. ch.: 1. Hannah, d. in H., unm., Ap. 15, 1810, ae 88. 2. Ruth, m. James Blankenship, of Rochester, 1747. 3. Nath'l., 1731? 4. Ellrane, Rana, or Ellinor, d. unm., May 15, 1809, ae. 77. 5. John, was in the Rev'n. war, and d. near West Point, as it is said, by over drinking at a spring on a sultry day. He was m., and left ch., who moved to Rochester. 6. Benjamin. 7. Lydia, m. Joshua Barker, of Rochester, Aug. 3, 1760. 8. Belcher, of H. 9. Abigail, m. — Bolles, of Rochester? 10. Sage, m. Josiah Mann, jr., Scit., Mar. 2, 1769.

3. Nathaniel, s. John 2, lived on Washington st., where Henry Bates resides, and was a ship-carpenter by trade. He m. Alice Healy, Nov. 17, 1763, and d. in 1814, ae 73, and his wid. Jan. 11, 1818, ae. 75. See the chap. on Ship building. ch.: 1. John, m. a Roberts, and d. in Ply'h., leaving ch. 2. Nathaniel, a ship carpenter, lived first in Plymouth, and then in Rochester, where he has sons. 3. Benjamin H. 4. Alice, m. Levi Caswell, July 17, 1795, who d. in Me. 5. Chloe M., m. Jabez Studley, of H., Feb. 23, 1800.

4. Belcher, s. John 2, m. 1, Ann Wade, June 27, 1771, who d. ab. 1781; and 2, wid. Sarah Perry, da. Nath'l. Josselyn, of Pemb., Aug. 4, 1783, lived on Washington st., in a house which stood where stands that of Mr. Samuel Salmond, and was a ship-carpenter by trade. It is said that he was out in the Rev'n. ab. 8 mo's., at R. I., and elsewhere. He d. Oct. 17, 1826, ae. 84, and his wid. ab. 1831. ch.: 1. Silvia, d. Mar. 20, 1799, ae. 25, 2. Barnabas, d. unm., ae. 49. Shipwright. 3. Joseph W. 4. Zebulon, Aug. 4, 1780. (By 2d.) 5. Ruth, m. Alpha Tribou,

and d. in Ab'n., ab. 1846. 6. Sarah, bap. June 21, 1795, m. a Sampson. 7. Reuben, Feb. 1, 1795, d. unm. 8. Francis, living in Port'd., Me., is m. and has ch. 9. David, lives in Me. Mariner. Was on the Gurnet in the last war. He is m. and has ch.

5. Benjamin H., s. Nath'l. 3, m. Mary Neal, Oct. 10, 1802, and had in H., Thos. G., Feb. 21, 1804; and Benj. H., Mar. 28, 1805. The fa. moved to Mf'd., where he now resides, and has other ch., of whom a da., Mary, m. Nath'l. H. Whiting, of M. Mr. C. was a school teacher part of the time in H; and after his removal to Mf'd., was long in the employ of Mr. Jonathan Stetson.

6. Joseph W., s. Belcher 4, m. Beulah Bassett, of Kigs'n., who d. Oct. 19, 1847, ae. 67. Lives on Broadway. Followed the seas in his youth; but has lately given his attention to farming. ch.: 1. Ann W., Nov. 22, 1812, m. Joseph C. Stockbridge, and d. ae. 24. 2. Joseph, July 5, 1815, m. 1, Ann Caldwell, and 2, Jennet Crook, lives in Medford, and has *Julia A.*, *Elizab.*, and an *infant*. 3. Elizabeth W., May 1, 1818, m. Levi Sturtevant, May 20, 1849, and lives in Pemb. 4. Lydia, July 14, 1821, m. Gad J. Bailey, of H. 5. Andrew, Nov. 3, 1825. Works in Barker's Foundry, on King st. Not m. 6. Sophia B., July 1829. 7. Henry, Nov. 3, 1842. In E. Ab'n., learning the carpenter's trade.

7. Zebulon, s. Belcher 4, m. Christiana, da. Isaac Josselyn, 1812, and lives on Broadway, near the Four Corners. Blacksmith, shipwright, farmer, &c. ch.: 1. Almira, Dec. 20, 1813, m. Amander Alden, Oct. 7, 1838, and lives in Bridg'r. 2. Geo., Nov. 6, 1815, d. in Washington, N. C., ae. 27. 3. Samuel, Sep. 21, 1817, m. Lydia Eells, and lives in Medford. Has *Mary S.*, living. Has lost 2. 4. Charles, July 27, 1819, m. Sarah Cook, and lives in Pemb. Has *Sarah F.*, *Chas. C.*, *Lomira H.*, and *Eliza H.* Shoemaker by trade. 5. Lovisa, May 13, 1821, m. Alexander Alden, of Ab'n., June 9, 1850. 6. William, Nov. 23, 1823. Lives with Chas., in Pemb. 7. Priscilla, Jan. 10, 1826, m. George W. Eells, Nov. 16, 1845. 8. Mary A., Nov. 23, 1828.

CORTHELL, Levi, s. Robert, of Scit., b. June 20, 1742, m. Debo. Curtis, Oct. 12, 1769, and it is said, lived where Enos Curtis does, on Whiting st., the place being called Corthell's hill. He had several ch., and moved to Me. His son Calvin, b. Feb. 16, 1775, m. Patience Vinal, of Mf'd., was a blacksmith, lived nearly opposite Thos. M. Bates's, on Circuit st., and d. Aug. 16, 1839. His wid. is yet living. ch.: 1. Lucy L., Mar. 17, 1808, m. Francis B. Ellis, Jan. 9, 1826, who d., and she lives a wid. with her mo. 2. Calvin C., Aug. 4, 1813, d. May 23, 1814. 3. David, Mar. 16, 1816, m. Phebe S. Pratt, May 9, 1837, who d. Nov. 5, 1841, having had *Phoebe M.*, Dec. 7, 1838, and *Adaline*, May 29, 1841.

CROOKER, or CROCKER, Daniel, was in H., in 1736, m. Mary Ramsdell, Ap. 28, 1736, and had Daniel, b. June 5, 1740, who was father of Ensign, of E. Bridg'r., b. 1770, and gr. fa. of Ensign, of H. ?—also Tilden, b. 1755, who was of H., and others.

2. Tilden, s. Daniel, was a ship carpenter by trade, and kept tavern for a time, near the Four Corners, his house being now occupied by Rufus Farnum. He m. Priscilla Barker, of Pemb., and d. Sep. 8, 1818, ae. 63. ch.: 1. Capt. Tilden, June, 1782, m. wid. Dorothy Hillborn, Jan. 16, 1837, and lived in Boston. 2. Nathaniel, Mar. 12, 1784, m. Anne L. Smith, Mar. 9, 1806, and lived in Chas'n. 3. Priscilla, Jan. 21, 1787, m. George Langley, Esq., lawyer, of Boston. 4. Mary C., Feb. 19, 1790, m. Benjamin Stockbridge. Jan. 26, 1814, and d. Mar. 1, 1818. 5. Sarah B., Nov. 14, 1794, m. David Stockbridge, jr. 6. Silvia, Mar. 11, 1798, m. Charles F. Thacher, of Machias, Me., Feb. 1, 1820.

3. Ensign. s. Ensign, of E. Bridg'r., and gr. s. Dan'l., m. 1, Mary Bailey, Dec. 24, 1828, who d. May, 1841; and 2, Silvia Foster, Nov. 1841, and lives on Whiting st., in the house built by Caleb Whiting, jr., and Ezra Whiting. ch.: 1. Charles E., Ap. 28, 1830. 2. Henry W., Jan., 1832. 3. Mary E., 1835, d. Oct. 6, 1845. (By 2d.) 4. James F., Aug. 1, 1842. 5. John H., Feb. 20, 1847.

NOTE.—We think it prob. that Dan'l., of H., descended from Francis Crooker, who was in Scit., in 1748, and who m. Mary Gaunt, of Banstable, 1647. Deane says of him, that "he has posterity in H."

THE CURTIS FAMILY.

County of Kent.

Arms: Arg. a chev sa. betw. three bulls heads, cabossed, gu.

Crest: A Unicorn pass. or, betw. four trees ppr.

CURTIS, Corteis, &c., an ancient English Family, settled in the Counties of Kent, and Sussex. (See Berry's Genealogies.) Stephen Curtis, was of Appledore, Kent, ab. 1450, and several of his descendants were Mayors of Tenterden, a town from which some of the first settlers of Scituate came. The earlier desc'ts. of this pedigree, are taken from an original pedigree, in the possession of the family, under the hand and seal of office of Sir Wm. Segar, Garter King-of-Arms, transcribed by John Philpot, Blanch Lion, and entitled, "This descent of the auntient familie of the Curteises, in the Co. of Kent, *gents.*, faithfullie collected out of the office of Arms, the public records of the kingdom, private evidences of the familie, and other venerable monuments of antiquitie;" in which pedigree, and also in several old MSS., in the Harleian Coll., in the Brit. Mus., the arms of the family are given as annexed, without reference to any particular grant, but as borne by them in virtue of *ancient usage.*

William Curtis, came to N. Eng., in the Lion, in 1632, and was of Boston in that year, and afterwards of Rox'y., where his descendants still reside. He was the ancestor of Geo. T., and Benj. R., Esq'rs., of Boston.

Richard, William, and John Curtis, were of Scit., in 1643, and Thos., in 1649, who was of York, Me., and who returned there. John left no descendants on record. A few of the desc'ts. of Thos., are in Scit., and elsewhere; and more of the desc'ts. of Richard. The desc'ts. of Wm., are quite numerous, in Scit., Hanover, and other towns in Mass. These are here given.

1. William, bro. of Richard and John, was in Scit., in 1643, but the name of his wife is not given, nor have have we found the date of his death. His farm was on the North River, next South of the Wanton farm, (Deane,) and he was a member of the 2nd Church. His ch. were, 1. Joseph, May 1664. 2. Benj., Jan., 1667. 3. Wm., Jan., 1669. 4. Jno., Feb., 1671. 5. Miriam, Ap., 1673. 6. Mehitable, Dec., 1675. 7. Stephen, Sep., 1677. Left no desc'ts. on record. 8. Sarah, Aug., 1679, m. Wm. Cook, Aug. 30, 1705. 9. Sam'l., June, 1681.

2. Joseph, s. Wm. 1, by w. Rebecca, had 1. Joseph, Mar. 23, 1694. 2. Josiah, Ap. 5, 1697. 3. Rebecca, May 9, 1699. 4. Martha, Feb. 14, 1701, prob. m. Benj. Mann, Feb. 4, 1724. 5. Richard, Nov. 8, 1702, prob. d. unm., in H., April. 28, 1768 6. Elisha, Feb. 20, 1705. 7. Thankful, Jan. 17, 1708. 8. Jesse, Oct. 17, 1709. 9. Peleg, bap. Oct. 12, 1712. No desc'ts. are recorded.

3. Benj., s. Wm. 1, m. Mary Silvester, in 1689, and, it is said, built the Curtis mills, on the Third Herring Brook, now owned by T. J. Gardner, Esq. ch.: 1. Mary, Aug. 22, 1691, m. Meletiah Dillingham, Oct. 28, 1723. 2. Benj., Dec. 14, 1692. 3. Eben'r., Aug. 1, 1694. 4. Lydia, Feb. 27, 1695, m. Joseph House, jr., Dec. 13, 1716. 5. Sarah, Dec. 20, 1697, m. Sam'l. Clapp, jr., Jan. 7, 1725. 6. Ruth, Jan. 14, 1700. 7. Susanna, Mar. 23, 1702, d. Ap. 14, 1714. 8. Debo., Aug., 1704. 9. Wm., July, 1706, m. Martha Curtis, Nov. 3, 1738, lost 3 ch., d. young, and had *Anna*, May 19, 1748, m. Jno. Curtis. 10. David, June 26, 1708. 11. Peleg, Sep., 1710.

4. Wm., s. Wm. 1, was m., and prob. had 1. Mary, who m.

Joseph Benson, of Hull, May 17, 1727. 2. Rachel, who m. Neh'h. White, Ap. 25, 1737, and 3. a son Wm., b. ab. 1696. The records of this family are wanting.

5. John, s. Wm. 1, m. Experience Palmer, Mar. 4, 1708, and, according to Deane, settled near Hugh's Cross. We think it is prob. that his house stood where stands that of the late Lem'l. Curtis, on Washington, near Silver st. ch.: 1. John, Mar. 14, 1709. 2. Bezaleel, Sep. 9, 1711. 3. Susannah, bap. Oct. 16, 1714. 4. Elizabeth, bap. May 28, 1721.

6. Sam'l., s. Wm. 1, m. Anna Barstow, Sep. 11, 1707, and, according to Deane, settled on the paternal farm. He owned land in H., and was part owner of the first saw-mill erected on Main street. His ch. were, 1. Sam'l., June 24, 1708, m. Hannah Whiting, of H'm., Nov. 14, 1739, who d. Oct. 26, 1789, ae. 72, and he, Mar. 24, 1794, ae 86. No ch. Lived on Main st.; and Mr. Sam'l. Brooks, who was named from him, has in his possession a silver watch, and a pair of buckles, a legacy from Mr. C. 2. Anna, Ap. 14, 1711, d. Dec. 30, 1787, ae 77. 3. Martha, Aug. 3, 1713, m. Wm. Curtis, Nov. 23, 1738. 4. Miriam, Jan. 7, 1715–6. 5. Debo., Feb. 7, 1717–8. 6. Simeon, June 1, 1720. 7. Amos, July 15, 1722, m. Mary Faunce, of Kigs'n.. in 1744, lived in Scit., on the homestead, and d. in 1748, and his wid. m. Nath'l Church. He had ch., *Samuel*, Feb. 19, 1745, and *Amos*, Feb. 4, 1747, d. young. 8. Mehitable, Sep. 9, 1726.

7. Joseph Curtis s. Joseph 2, m. Mary Palmer, Septem. 27, 1727, who d. Ap. 9, 1750, and he, Dec. 31, 1753. Lived on Circuit st., it is said, and, with Joseph House, was proprietor of the mill, afterwards called Eliab's mill. He was known as *Governor* Curtis, and was a man of enterprise in his day. ch.: 1. Mary, Aug. 1, 1729, m. Wm. Gould, of Bridg'r., Dec. 25, 1751. 2. Joseph, Sep. 21, 1731, m. Abigail ——, and d. Aug. 14, 1759, having had *Joseph*, 1754, and *Seth*, 1757. 3. Joshua, Sep. 22, 1733. 4. Experience, July 28, 1735, d. June 25, 1738. 5. Stephen, bap. July 15, 1739, d. May 11, 1817? 6. Thankful, Ap. 2, 1742.

8. Josiah Curtis s. Joseph 2, m. Sarah Collamore, January 1, 1729, and d. in H., Feb. 26, 1777. Lived on Curtis, now Main st., and was an extensive land holder. ch.: 1. Abner, 1727.? 2. Rebecca, bap. Dec. 19, 1731, d. Mar. 10, 1732. 3. Seth, bap. Aug. 25, 1734, d. July 27, 1751. 4. Job, bap. Aug. 17, 1736, lived on Main st., and d. unm., Ap. 6, 1804. He was Selectman in 1781.

9. Elisha, s. Joseph 2., m. 1, Martha ——, and 2, Sarah Chittenden, Nov. 12, 1741, and seems to have lived on the lane now leading to T. J. Gardner's mill, in Scit. ch.: 1. Mehitable, bap. May 18, 1735, d. young. 2. Elisha, bap. Ap. 3, 1737. 3. Zechariah, bap. Nov. 25, 1739, m. Lydia Palmer, Jan. 21, 1762, and had *Zech.*, 1763, and *Lydia*, 1767. (By 2d.) 4. Mehitable, d. Aug. 10, 1744. 5. Martha, bap. June 2, 1745. 6. Calvin, bap. Sep. 27, 1747. 7. Luther, bap. Ap. 9, 1749. 8. Mehitabel, bap. Aug. 11, 1751.

10. Jesse, s. Joseph 2, m. Sarah Mann, Sep. 20, 1739, and d. in H., July 22, 1759, and his wid. Nov. 17, 1802, ae. 80. Lived on Curtis st. ch.: 1. Elijah, Ap. 16, 1740, d. Feb. 7, 1824. 2. Abel, Mar. 21, 1742, m. Ruth Turner, Feb. 12, 1776, and had *Abel*, 1777, *Gideon*, 1779, and *Ruth*, 1784. 3. Jesse, Mar. 27, 1744. 4. Debo., Ap. 17, 1746. 5. Gershom, Feb. 1, 1748, m. Mary Stetson, in 1780, and moved to Me. ch. b. in H.: *Briggs*, 1776; *Diana*, 1777; *Gershom*, 1781; *Turner*, 1785; and *Chas.*, 1787. 6. Sarah, Feb. 17, 1750, prob. d. Jan. 28, 1775. 7. Charles, July 10, 1752. Left no desc'ts. on record. 8. Amos, Oct. 31, 1759, d. Mar. 8, 1808. 9. Orpha, Oct. 16, 1759, m. Thos. Farrow, in 1807.

11. Benj., s. Benj. 3, m. Hannah Palmer, Dec. 13, 1716, and d. in H., Feb. 21, 1756. He was Selectman in 1727 and '28. ch.: 1. Benj., bap. Ap. 27, 1718, d. young. 2. Thos., bap. Sep. 4, 1720, m. 1, Sarah Utter, Aug. 20, 1741, who d. Dec. 28, 1753; and 2, Ruth Rose, Feb. 26, 1756, and had *Hannah*, 1742, d. 1749; *Debo.*, 1744, m. Levi Corthell, 1769; *Sarah*, 1746; *Thos.*, 1750; *Lydia*, b. and d. 1754; *Faith*, 1757; *Ruth*, 1759; and *Hannah*,

1762. 3. Luke, bap. Mar. 11, 1722. Left no desc'ts. on record. 4. Hannah, bap. Mar. 1, 1724. 5. Caleb, bap. May 8, 1726, prob. m. Mercy Low, of H'm., Oct. 30, 1752. 6. Nath'l., bap. Mar. 31, 1728, in Scit. Left no desc'ts. on rec. 7. Benj., bap. Oct. 4, 1730, in H. 8. Rachel, bap. Oct. 4, 1730, m. John Gould, Bridg'r., Oct. 26, 1749. 9. Mary, July 15, 1732, m. Marlboro' Turner, Nov. 26, 1753. 10. Relief, Oct. 1738.

NOTE.—There was a Benj., who m. Naomi Bailey, Mar. 9, 1741, and had *Ezra*, Sep. 10, 1741; *Stephen*, May 15, 1744; *Benj.*, Feb. 22, 1747; *Nath'l.*, Ap. 16, 1749; and *Jacob*, Mar. 22, 1753, A little obscurity hangs over these families, which we have found it difficult entirely to clear up.

12. Ebenezer, s. Benj. 3, from the best information I can gain m. Elizabeth Ramsdell, Feb. 2, 1749, and d. Mar. 6, 1753, and his wid. m. Joseph Bates, Jan. 3, 1761. He had ch.: 1. Elizab., May 18, 1750, prob. d. Dec. 9, 1810. 2. Wm., Oct. 14, 1751, m. Rebecca ——, and d. June 25, 1793, and his wid. m. Isaac Turner, Aug. 28, 1795. His ch. were *Wm. G.*, bap. June 25, 1775, stud. Law with Benj. Whitman, Esq., and d. June 25, 1795; *Rufus*, 1777, d. 1791; *Rebecca*, bap. May 23, 1779, m. Ozias Whiting, Mar. 2, 1797; *Saba*, bap. Sep. 16, 1787, m. Richard Estes, May 15, 1803; and *Samuel*, bap. July 4, 1790, d. Sep. 12, 1792.

13. David, s. Benj. 3, m. Bethia Sprague, of Dux'y., Dec. 14, 1732, and had in H., 1. Nehemiah, Jan. 3, 1733. 2. Ezekiel, Ap. 30, 1735. 3. Paul, May 29, 1737. 4. Michael, Ap. 30, 1739. 5. David, Aug. 23, 1741. 6. Ruth, July 31, 1743. After this date, the family disappears, and we find no farther trace of it. The father prob. moved from the town with his ch.,—and tradition says, to the Western part of Mass.

14 Peleg Curtis s. Benjamin 3, m. Experience Ford, ab. 1749, and lived in Scit., in the house afterwards occupied by his son Peleg, and now owned by his gr. s. Philip. He was quite a business man, a substantial farmer, and a man of industry and thrift. ch.: 1. Lucy, d. unm., ab. 1825. 2. Experience, m. Sam'l. Randall, of Scit. 3. Peleg. 4. Bethia, m. Jas. Gray, ab. 1785. 5. Thankful, m. Peleg Simmons, of Scit. 6. Leafy, d. young. 7. Joseph, Jan. 12, 1766,

15. William Curtis s. Wm. 4, m. Margaret Pratt, Jan. 29, 1718, and d. in H., Mar. 4, 1737. Prob. lived on Curtis st. ch: 1. Abel, Nov. 24, 1719. Left no desc'ts on record. 2. Jael, or *Joel?* Aug. 14, 1721. No desc'ts. are recorded. 3. Wm., Aug. 27, 1724, (m. Martha Mann, Nov. 13, 1747, and d. Jan. 11, 1759? leaving ch.: *Wm.*, Dec. 4, 1748, m. Debo. Curtis, Jan. 5, 1775, was Selectman in 1786, d. June 26, 1793, and his desc'ts. are in Me.; *Martha*, Dec. 11, 1750, m. John Barnes, jr., H'm., Feb. 16, 1772; *Abel*, Aug. 10, 1752; *Joel*, June 28, 1754; *Samuel*, May 24, 1756; and *Margaret*, June 28, 1758, m. Ezra Briggs, jr., May 13, 1784.) 4. Marg't., Nov. 6, 1726, m. Jno. Barnes, H'm., Dec. 24, 1746. 5. Reuben, Feb. 6, 1729. 6. Lemuel, Nov. 9, 1731. 7. Mehitable, Nov. 1, 1734, m. Elijah Waters, of H'm., Mar. 31, 1755.

NOTE.—Ebenezer, s. Wm., jr., m. Zintha Stetson, and had ch., of whom a da. Cynthia, m. Wm., Whiting, of H., and Mary H., m. Benj. Munroe. He had other ch., most of whom are m., and live in Me.

16. John, s. John 5, m. 1, Abigail Waters, of H'm., Sep. 23, 1738; 2, Sarah Franklin, of H'm., June 29, 1732; and 3, Mary Bryant, of Scit., Nov. 6, 1738, who d. June 2, 1797, ae. 86, and he Mar. 23, 1799, ae. 90. He had no ch. by his first w. By the 2d. w. he had, 1. Sarah, Mar. 16, 1733. 2. Miriam, Oct. 20, 1734. 3. John, May 6, 1737, d. young. (By 3d.) 4. Betty, Aug. 26, 1739, m. Solo. Bryant, of Plympton, May 1, 1766. 5. John, Jan. 2, 1741. 6. An infant d., Ap. 23, 1743.

17 Bezaleel Curtis s. John 5, m. Mary ——, who d. Mar. 8, 1792, ae. 73, and he, Ap. 26, of the same year. He built the house on the W. side of Washington st., a few rods S. of Hiram Gardner's, and there lived and d. ch.: 1. Susanna, June 8, 1744, m. Thos. Hatch, Jan. 12, 1769. 2. Eben'r., Sep. 28, 1745, (m. Mary Randall, of Scit., who d. in Oct., 1800, and he, Aug. 12, 1807. Lived where Hiram Gardner now resides, and had *Clarissa*, bap. Aug. 16, 1778, m. Nath'l. Winslow, jr., of Scit., Oct. 13, 1796; *Paul*, bap. June 13, 1779, d. unm.; and *Michal*, bap. June 16,

1786, m. Col. John Collamore, of Scit., and had 12 ch., of whom are John, Esq., dealer in glass and china ware, Boston, and Davis and Eben'r., of N. York.) 3. Mary, bap. Oct. 2, 1748, d. ae. 18. 4. Prince, bap. Ap. 1, 1750, d. Oct. 31, 1815. 5. Experience, bap. Jan. 6, d. Jan. 7, 1754. 6. Experience, bap. Ap. 13, 1755, d. Jan. 1842. 7. Elizabeth, bap. Oct. 1757, d. Dec. 9, 1810. 8. Paul, bap. Jan. 24, 1763, d. unm. 9. Nabby, bap. Sep. 9, 1764, d. Oct. 1, 1787.

18. *Simeon Curtis* (Capt. Simeon,) s. Samuel 6, m. 1. Asenath Sprague, of Duxbury, April 20, 1742, who d. September 14, 1757; and 2, wid. Lucy Macomber, and d. March 7, 1810. Lived in the house now occupied by Thomas O. Bates, W. of Silver st., and was a man of note in the town; highly intelligent, and useful in public affairs. ch.: 1. Simeon, July 4, 1743, d. Nov. 14, 1753. 2. Melzar, Ap. 17, 1745. 3. James, July 17, 1747. Moved to Freeport, Me., m., and had *James*, *Simeon*, &c. Was Rep. to the Mass. Leg., from Me. 4. Asenath, Nov. 21, 1749, d. Nov. 3, 1753. 5. Lusanna, Nov. 25, 1753, m. Elijah Stetson, Dec. 13, 1791. 6. Simeon, Oct. 11, 1756. (By 2d.) 7. Barker, bap. Nov. 18, d. Dec. 2, 1759. 8. Lucy, May 4, 1761, d. Dec. 17, 1793. 9. Asenath, bap. June 19, d. July 1, 1763. 10. Mary, July 30, 1767, m. Job Young? 11. Barker, Nov. 11, 1769, stud. Law with Benj. Whitman, and had an office for a time where Hiram Curtis now lives, but finally moved to Me., and m., but had no ch.

19. Joshua, s. Joseph 7, m. Abigail House, Dec. 17, 1761, and sett. in Ab'n., where both he and his w. d. ch.: 1. Joshua. 2. Abigail, m. Ebed Vining, of Ab'n. 3. Rufus. 4. Joseph, prob. lost at sea. 5. Marlboro'. 6. Leafy, m. Isaac Burrill. 7. Seth.

20. Abner, s. Josiah 8, m. 1, Debo. Mann, in 1749; (Scit. Rec.) 2. Sally Ford, July 3, 1766, who d. May 2, 1795, ae. 64; and 3, wid. Phebe Dunbar, formerly a Howard, Ap. 6, 1799, and d. in H., Sep. 18, 1799, ae 72 A curious document, containing the marriage contract between Mr. C., and his 3rd w., is in the possession of Dea. John Brooks, of H. Mr. C. lived on Curtis, now Main st., near the Baptist Church. ch.: 1. Abner, 1754?

2. Debo., m. Wm. Curtis, jr., Jan. 5, 1775. 3. Seth. 4. Huldah, m. Eells Damon, July 6, 1775. 5. Rebecca, m. Stephen Damon.

21. Elisha, s. Elisha 9, m. 1. Elizabeth Studley, Jan. 15, 1760, who d. July 10, 1776 ; 2, Elizabeth Church, July 20, 1777, who d. Nov. 15, 1795, ae 55 ; and 3, wid. Macomber, of Mf'd. Lived near Gardner's mill, also at the Tiffany place, and finally moved to N. Salem, N. H. ch. : 1. Reuben, m. Hannah Barker, of Pemb., and prob. d. Mar. 9, 1806, ae. 44. 2. Betty, bap. Ap. 15, 1764, m. Thos. Macomber, jr., Mf'd., Ap. 3, 1794. 3. Martha, bap. Oct. 19, 1766, d. unm. 4. Temperance, m. Nath'l. Stetson, Nov. 7, 1793. 5. Philip, bap. Aug. 12, 1776, d. same year. 6. Rebecca, m. Elisha Barker, of Pemb., Feb. 15, 1797. 7. Elisha, m. Hannah Curtis, and went to N. Salem, in 1802. 8. Lucinda, 1817, d. June 21, ae. 23.

22. Calvin Curtis (Captain Calvin,) s. Elisha 9, m. Martha Bryant, and lived on Mill st., where T. J. Gardner, Esq., now resides. His old house is gone. He was an officer in the Rev'n., and one whose name is often alluded to on the Rev'y. Rolls, and the records of the town. See chapter 8. ch. : 1. Calvin, Oct. 23, 1777, moved to Camden, Me., m. and d. there, leaving 3 sons. 2. Capt. Edward, Sep. 10, 1779, m. Desire Jacobs, Mar. 24, 1811, lived on his father's place, was a carpenter by trade, and a man much respected. He d. Nov. 12, 1845, leaving one da. *Elvira*, Ap. 2, 1814, m. T. J. Gardner, Esq., Nov. 29, 1832. 3. James, May 21, 1781, m. Prudence Bird, and lived and d. in Charlestown, Mass., leaving ch. 4. Lebbeus, May 10, 1783, lived in Chas'n., was m., and went into the Army, in the war of 1812. 5. Mary, Aug. 25, 1785, m. Joseph Tibbett, of Methuen. 6. Martha, Ap. 4, 1789, d. unm., Mar 25, 1847.

23. Jesse, s. Jesse 10, m. 1, Hannah Peterson, of Scit., July 27, 1768, who d. Aug. 5, 1791; and 2, wid. Lucy Morton, formerly a Leavitt, and d. Dec. 13, 1811, ae. 68. Lived on Main st., where the wid. Thomas now resides. ch. : 1. Hannah, m. Elisha Curtis, Nov. 29, 1787. 2. David, Jan. 22, 1781. 3. Jesse, Dec. 24, 1783. 4. Joseph, Feb. 12, 1786.

24. Peleg, s. Peleg 14, m. Ruth Bowker, lived in Scit., was a farmer, and d. in June, 1834, and his wid. Dec. 14, 1845, ae. 86. ch.: 1. Leafy, Mar., 1783, m. Stowers Clapp, and d. ab. 1803, leaving a son *Edward*, who is in Pawtucket. 2. Philip, June 5, 1786, a carpenter by trade, m. Sarah Everton, of Canton, and has *Leafy*, m. Wm. Ulman, of Boston; and *Sarah*, m. Samuel. Q. Cochran, of Boston. 3. Stephen, Feb. 1792.

25. Joseph, s. Peleg 14, m. Polly Bowker, Feb. 1, 1808, and lived in So. Scit., near the 3d Herring brook, where he d. Nov. 7, 1834. His wid. survives. ch.: 1. Leafy, Nov. 29, 1808, m. Joel Bowker, and lives in Bos'n. 2. Joseph, Aug. 10, 1810, d. Aug. 5, 1811. 3. Joseph, June 11, d. Nov. 14, 1812. 4. Joshua, July 21, 1814, m. Frances M., da. Seth Curtis, lives in Brighton, and has *Joshua F.*, July 1, 1848. 5. Peleg, Oct. 18, 1818, a carpenter by trade, m. Abby S., da. Seth Curtis, and has *Sophronia L.*, Sep., 1849, and an inf. s., b. 1852. 6. Joseph, Jan. 4, 1822. Merchant, of the firm of Curtis, Sampson, & Co., Kilby st., Boston. Not m.

26. Reuben, s. Wm. 15, m. Mary Randall, who d. Mar. 25, 1757, and he May 15, 1758, leaving one son, Snow, bap. Aug. 10, 1755.

Snow Curtis the son, was Selectman of H. for eighteen years, and possessed fine business talents. He m. Bathsheba Hatch, lived on his father's place, on Wash'n. st., where Wm. Curtis now resides, and there d. of a cancer, Dec. 31, 1823, and his wid. Nov. 2, 1831, ae 70. ch.: 1. Reuben, Ap. 26, 1784, d. Feb. 20, 1818. 2. Bela, Nov. 20, 1785, d. Ap. 17, 1803. 3. Capt. Levi, Oct. 29, 1787, m. Ruth Rogers, in 1814, lives on Elm st., was Selectman from 1821-1826; T. C., from 1815-18; and Capt. of the H. Artil. Co. No ch. 4. Bathshua, Oct. 2, 1789, d. Oct. 28, 1794. 5. Robert, Ap. 1., 1791, m. Katurah Studley, Ap. 16, 1826, lives on Wash'n. st., and has *Robert S.*, Feb. 12, 1827, Clerk with S. Josselyn. 6. Mary R., Ap. 28, 1793. 7. Barshua, July 31, 1798, m. Luther Curtis, Jan. 30, 1820. 8. Wm., Ap. 9, 1800, m. Sarah Winslow, Mar. 3, 1833, lives on his father's place, and has *Mary W.*, and *Sarah J.*

27 Lemuel Curtis s. William 15, m. Ruth Mann, Jan. 16, 1752, and d. Jan. 11, 1807, and his wid. July 29, 1808. He owned part of the Forge in H., now known as the Curtis Forge, and lived on Wash'n. st., where his grand-son John now resides. He was Selectman from 1773-'78. ch.: 1. Lemuel, Ap. 1753, d. June 27, 1767, being drowned. 2. Ruth, bap. Dec. 21, 1755, d. June 28, 1790. 3. Olive, bap. Ap. 8, 1759, d. July 14, 1798. 4. Lillis, bap. Mar. 22, 1761, d. Nov. 5., 1776. 5. Reuben Curtis (Reuben, Esq.,) bap. Ap. 24, 1763, m. Abigail Bailey, Nov. 23, 1801, who d. Dec. 24, 1841, and he Dec. 18, 1849. He was T. C. from 1807-'15; Rep. from 1815-'18, and from 1823-'25; lived where Capt. Thos. B. Donnell does, on Elm st.; was part owner of the Forge, and a trader. Left one da. *Ruth*, b. July 18, 1805, m. Capt. Thos. B. Donnell, in 1843, and d. Jan. 23, 1849. 6. Consider, 1765. 7. Sarah, bap. Ap. 30, 1769, d. Nov. 17, 1802. 8. Lydia, bap. Jan. 6, 1771, d. unm. ab. 1838. 9. Lemuel, June 6, 1772. 10. Nath'l., Sep. 14, 1777.

28. John, s. John 16, m. Anne Curtis, Mar. 28, 1765, who d. Jan. 14, 1823, ae. 75, and he Sep. 26, 1799. Lived on Curtis st., near where Joseph Dwelley now does. His house is gone.—He was Selectman in 1779. ch.: 1. Debo., d. unm. 2. Anne, bap. Dec. 14, 1766, d. Aug, 28, 1834. 3. Charlotte, bap. Jan. 3, 1768, d. Aug. 23, 1800. 4. John, 1770. 5. Wm., bap. Ap. 24, 1774, d. July 3, 1800. 6. Alathea, bap. Oct. 27, 1776, d. June 9, 1777. 7. Alathea, bap. Dec. 20, 1778, d. Ap. 16, 1801. 8. Sam'l., bap. July 25, 1784, d. Aug. 20, 1826. 9. Lucius, bap. May 29, 1791, moved to Me., m. and has ch. 10. Mary, bap. Oct. 6, 1799, m. Thomas Brooks, Feb. 28, 1816, moved to Me., and d. there. 11. Christopher, moved to Me., and there d. 12. Nath'l., went to Me., m. and had ch.

29. Melzar Curtis (Melzar Esq.,) s. Capt. Simeon, 18, m. Keziah, da. Dr. Jere. Hall, Ap. 25, 1771, and d. Nov. 8, 1801, and his wid. Mar. 9, 1816. Lived on Silver st., where the wid. of his son Melzar resides, in the house now owned by Martin S. Bates, built by Mr. C. and his bro. Jas. He was Selectman from 1783-'85; Rep. in 1784, and from 1790-'92; and T. C. from 1787-'93. ch.: 1. Keziah, Aug. 25, 1771, m. Joseph Cushing, Nov. 6, 1794, and moved to Me. 2. Jeremiah, Feb. 25, 1776, d. Dec. 1, 1798. 3. Joanna, July 15, 1784, m. Dr. David Bailey, of Scit., Nov. 7, 1801. 4. Lusannah, June 25, 1789, d. Ap. 16, 1790. 5. Melzar, Feb. 3, 1774, d. Jan. 25, 1777. 6. Melzar, Esq., bap. July 12, 1778, m. Sarah Collamore, sister of Col. John, of Scit., lived on Silver st., was Rep. in 1822 and '26; T. C. from 1818-'24; and Selectman for 11 years.—Left no ch. He d. in Jan., 1836. 7. Asenath, May 8, 1781, m. Geo. Bailey. 8. Laurentia, Feb. 4, 1787, d. May 4, 1790.—9. Luther, Ap. 20, 1791, a carpenter by trade; lived on Silver st.; m. Bathshua Curtis, Jan. 30, 1820, and d. Aug. 25, 1844, leaving *Bathshua*, Oct. 6, 1822, and *Wm. H.*, May 8, 1825, m. Susan M. Tower, of Braintree, Nov. 7, 1852, and lives in his father's house.

30. Capt. Simeon, s. Capt. Simeon 18, m. Bathsheba Sylvester, Dec. 13, 1791, and sett. in E. Bridg'r., where he d. in 1837, ae. 80. He was a soldier in the Rev'n. ch.: 1. Bathsheba, 1791, m. Capt. Isaac Keith, of Bridg'r., in 1815, and has *Quincy A.*, m. Priscilla Hathaway, has 3 ch., and lives in Ky.; *Robert C.*, m. Louisa Keith, and has 1 ch. living; *Bathsheba*, not m.; *Isaac*; and *Simeon C.* 2. Silvester, 1795, m. Heman Keith, of East Bridg'r. No ch. 3. Simeon, 1797, is unm., and lives on his father's place, in E. Bridg'r. 4. Robert, 1799, m. Abby M., da. Dan'l. Bryant.

31. Joshua, s. Josh. 19, was a shipmaster in early life, m. Nancy Ridyard, of Eng'd., and sett. in Ab'n., where he d. in Ap., 1825, ae. 62. ch.: 1. Joshua, 1791. 2. Rufus, m. a da. of Dea. Elijah Shaw, of Ab'n., lives in E. Randolph, and has ch. 3.

John, 1797, m. Eliza Holbrook, lives in E. Ab'n., is a shoemaker, and has *Eliza E.*, m. Jesse Reed, of Ab'n.; *Sarah H.*, m. Turner Reed; *Mary L.*, m. Wm. Fobes; *Ann*, d. 1851; and *John H.* 4. Nancy, m. Silas Lane, of Ab'n., and is d. 5. Joseph, is m., lives in Bos'n., and has *George*; and *Rebecca*, m. a Van Ambridge? 6. Thurza, m. Thos. Foster, of Ab'n. 7. Abigail, d. unm. 8. Marg't., d. ae. 21. 9. Salome, m. Reuben Burrill, and lives in N. Y'k. 10. Henry R., 1811, m. 1, Salome Studley, and 2, Elmira Studley, lives in E. Ab'n., is a shoemaker, and has *Mary F.*; *Henry S.*; and *Edward C.*

32. Rufus, s. Josh. 19, m. Diana Keen, of Dux'y., Nov. 29, 1802, and she is living a wid., in Scit. ch.: 1. Diana, m. 1, Colman Jenkins, and 2, Harvey Merritt. 2. Rufus, m. Rhoda Briggs, Feb., 1837, and has *Harriet A. B.*, July 1838; *Wm. F.*, Jan. 1846; and *Geo. H.*, Mar., 1851. 3. Thomas J., Nov. 17, 1808, lives at Scit. harbor, m. Jane T. Chubbuck, and has *Mary J.; Laura. A; Julia T.;* and *James H.* 4. Lydia P., July 27, 1809, m. Judson Bates, of H. 5. George, m. Debo. Lincoln, of H'm., who d., leaving ch.: *Emma S.; Geo. H.*; and *Lizzy M.*

33. Marlboro, s. Josh. 19, m. Lupira Bisbee, of Pemb., who was b. Dec. 7, 1784, and d. in H'm. ch.: 1. Abigail, m. Sam'l. Shaw, of E. Bridg'r. 2. Lupira, m. Eben'r. Joy, of S. Wey'h., 3. Joseph, m. Caroline Thomas, lives in S. Wey'h., and has *Joseph L.; Caroline F.*; *Edwin M.;* and *Prescott.* 4. Elbridge, m. 1. Eliza A., da. Jere. White, of Wey'h.; and 2, Matilda W., da. David Horton, of E. Bridg'r., lives in E. B., and has *Elbridge R.; Minot S.*; and *Edward B.* 5. John, m. Mary A. Torrey, of Wey'h., lives in S. Wey'h., and has *Anne F.* 6. Robert. 7 Mary A., m. Chas. Thompson, of E. Bridg'r., and has *Susan A.* and *Mary E.* Mr. T. is a painter by trade, and is s. of Cha's. of Hf'x.

34. Seth, s. Josh. 19, m. Sophia Pratt, of S. Wey'h., and had ch.: 1. Seth, Sep. 1806, not m. 2. Sophia, m. Christopher S. Bass, of S. Wey'h. 3. Sally, m. Noah Vining, shoe mf'r. of S. Wey'h. 4. Susan, m. Sam'l Wales, of N. Ab'n, 5, Maria, m. Wm. Tribou, of E. Bridg'r. 6. Freeman, m. Hannah Corthell, of H'm.,

lives in S. Wey'h, and has *Joseph*, and *Jane F.* 7. Joseph, m. Melinda Torrey, lived in S. Wey'h., and there d., leaving no ch. 8. Jane, d. ae. ab. 15.

35. Abner, s. Abner 20, m. Lydia Bowker, of Scit., and d. Feb. 2, 1838, ae. 84, and his wid. in 1852, ae. 94. ch.: 1, Davis, bap. Oct. 13, 1776, m. 1, Charlotte Lovice, of H'm.; 2, Mary Oliver, of Me.; and 3, Marg't. Standley; lives in Me., and has *Jas. M.; Jno. O.; Lydia*, m. a Gould, and d.; *Charlotte S.*, m. Benj. Carter; *Polly*, m. Nathan Barlow; *Charlotte*, m. Jno. Benner, and is d.; and *Hiram*, d. ae. 4. 2. Desire, Feb. 1, 1778, m. Thos. Farrow, of Townsend, Mass. 3. Job. 4. Sally L., m. Levi Nash. 5. Deborah, m. Isaac Wade, of H. 6. Mary, m. David Vining, of H. 7. Lydia, m. 1, Caleb Torrey, and 2, Dan'l. Bishop.

36. Seth, s. Abner 20, m. Persis Loring, and d. in June, 1812, and his wid. Oct. 1, 1825. Lived first where Benj. Mann, Esq., resides, and afterwards where Isaac Wade now lives, on Main st. ch.: 1. Lucy, Nov. 5, 1791, m. Dan'l. Dunbar, of H'm. 2. Rebecca, Feb. 16, 1773, m. Ephraim Stetson, of Ab'n., Feb. 1, 1819. 3. Seth, Ap. 16, 1794, m. Ruth Loring, of H'm., lives in So. Scit., is a farmer, and has *Charles A.*, Aug. 21, 1817; *Abby S.*, Jan. 6, 1820, m. Peleg Curtis; *Frances M.*, May 25, 1823, m. Joshua Curtis; and *Ruth A.*, Mar. 9, 1827. 4. Loring, Oct, 5, 1797, lives in H., near the Bap. Church, m. Merrill Mann, Jan. 23, 1823, and has *Nancy H.*, Jan. 26, 1825; *Mary H.*, Ap. 13, 1827; and *Sarah J.*, Feb. 23, 1829, m. Walter W. Wardrobe, Mar. 12, 1848. 5. Abner, Esq., June 11, 1800; resides in E. Ab'n.; is unm., and is one of the most extensive and enterprising shoe-manufacturers in Plym'h. Co.; giving employment to several hundred hands annually, and doing business to the amount of over $200,000, at his establishment in E. Ab'n., and at his extensive warehouse, on Pearl st., Boston. Mr. C. is distinguished as a liberal and public-spirited man; always ready to aid a good work; and for business talent, and decision of character, has few superiors. 6. Hannah, Mar. 15, 1802, m. Nath'l. Ficket, of Ab'n., Mar. 4, 1821. 7. Sophia, 1804, d. Feb. 12, 1808.

8. Enos, Jan. 31, 1807, m. Mary J. Burrill, of Ab'n., lives on Whiting st., and has *Sophia J.*, 1830, m. Wm. Studley, Dec. 17, 1851 ; *Lysander* ; and *Mary*. 9. Sarah, Ap. 11, 1809, m. Edmund Shaw, of Ab'n. 10. Peter, m. Clarissa Ripley, lives in E. Ab'n., and has *Persis*, and *Corinne*.

37. David, s. Jesse 23, m. Sarah, da. Paul, jr., and gr.-da. Paul Revere, of Bos'n., and d. in B. ab. 1841, and his wid. in 1843. ch.: 1. David, d. unm. ab. 1838. 2. Maria, d. ab. 1839. 3. Charles R., m. Lydia S. Barstow, lives in E. Ab'n., is a shoemaker, and has *Chas, H. ; David P.*, d. young; and *Geo. E.* 4. Wm. H., May 8, 1813, m. Jane M., da. Lem'l. Dwelley, and wid. of Geo. Merriam, in Sep., 1839, lives on Main st., and has *Edward R.*, Feb. 11, 1840 ; *Geo. M.*, Ap. 23, 1844 ; and *Ellen M.*, Aug. 12, 1849. 5. Caroline L., d. ab. 1838. 6. Geo. R., m. Hannah Hill, lives in Bos'n., and has *Mary R.*, and *Edwin*. 7. Edward A., Feb. 22, 1822, lives in Bos'n., is a Type Founder, m. Louisa M., da. Maj. Ephraim Andrews, of Lowell, in 1851, and has no ch. 8. Sarah A.

38. Jesse, s. Jesse 23, m. Sally Nash, and d. in Chas'n., and his wid. is living on Main st. in H., in her father's house. He was a shipwright by trade. ch.: 1. Ruth, m. Wm. Hayden, of Scit. 2. Roxa., m. Capt. Robinson. 3. Debo., not m. 4. Sophronia, m. Abner Loring, and d. in Bos'n. 5. Jesse, m. Alice Forbush, lives in Bos'n., and is a copper-smith. Has no ch.

39. Joseph, s. Jesse 23, m. Hannah Gardner, of H'm., and d. Dec. 28, 1841, ae. 56, and his w. Mar. 21, 1840, ae. 59. A ship carpenter by trade, and worked at the Navy Yard, Chas'n. ch.: 1. Hannah P., Ap. 5, 1806, m. Freeman Farrow, Nov. 21 1824, and is living in H. 2. Joseph, Dec. 5, 1808, m. Debo. Hayden, Nov. 26, 1829, and d. Nov. 22, 1844, and his wid. m. Thos. H. Gardner, Aug. 31, 1845. His ch. were : *Henry*, Feb. 23, 1833 ; *Geo. W.*, Feb. 22, 1841 ; and *Joseph H.*, Feb. 7, 1844. 3. Lucy C., Mar. 1811, m. Laban Wilder, Jr., July 15, 1832, and d. Ap. 21, 1843. 4. Capt. Benj. N., July 30, 1813, m. 1, Lydia S., da. Capt. Elisha Barrell, Dec. 25, 1836, who d. Mar. 24, 1840; and 2, Sarah, da. Calvin D. Wilder, May 12,

1844, lives on Walnut st., and had by 1st, *Lydia M.*, May 30, d. Oct. 8, 1838; and by 2d, *Frances A.*, Dec. 14, 1846.

40. Stephen, s. Peleg 24, m. 1, Lucinda Bailey, June 16, 1816; and 2, Mary S. Hitchcock, Dec. 3, 1818, and d. Mar. 6, 1831, and his wid. m. Eben'r. Simmons, Esq., and d. Ap. 30, 1837. ch.: 1. Lucinda, d. Aug. 18, 1817. (By 2d.) 2. Stephen, Sep., 1820, m. 1, Matilda, da. Hon. Sam'l. A. Turner, of Scit., in Aug., 1846, who d. Oct. 2, 1847, ae. 23; and 2, Eliza F., da. Sam'l. Payson, of Boston, and is clerk in the extensive jewelry establishment of Palmer & Batchelders. No ch. 3. Henry J., June 2, 1822, m. Abby, da. I. R. Jacobs, Esq., of Scit., Sep. 20, 1848, and is T. C. of So. Scit. No ch.

41. Consider, s. Lemuel 27, m. 1, Mary House, of Pemb., Nov. 10, 1806, who d. in 1809; and 2, Hannah Fuller, in 1811, who d. Ap. 24, 1832, and he in May, 1840, ae. 75. Was part owner of the Curtis Forge, &c. Had one son, George, b. Sep. 23, 1807, m. Nancy, da. Joel Bowker, of Salem, Nov. 11, 1834, lives on Elm st., and is the proprietor of the Curtis Forge. No ch.

RESIDENCE OF MR. GEORGE CURTIS.

42. Lemuel, s. Lemuel 27, m. Abigail Rose, lived on Wash'n. st., where his son John now resides, and was part owner of the Curtis Forge, &c. He is d., and his wid. survives. ch.: 1. Sally, Dec. 25, 1803, m. Michael Sylvester, of H. 2. Nabby, Aug., 1805, m. Josiah Winslow, of H. 3. Judith, Oct. 11, 1808,

m. Geo. Studley, Jan. 30, 1834. 4. Jno., Nov., 1812. Not m. 5. Lucinda, Oct., 1815. Not m.

43. Nath'l., s. Lemuel 27, m. Nancy Stoddard, of Scit., Mar. 3, 1805, who d. in Oct., 1842, and he Feb. 4, 1849. Lived where Charles Dyer does, on Water st., and was part owner of the works there. ch.: 1. Warren, Feb. 4, 1806, m. Harriet, da. Joseph Noyes, of Bos'n., May 2, 1829, lives in S. H'm., and has *Harriet*, Feb. 22, 1831; *Joseph W.*, d. ae. 11 mo's.; and *Sarah A.*, d. ae. 8. 2. Bethia, Jan. 27, 1808, m. Major Joshua Mann, of H., July 12, 1829. 3. Nath'l. H., July 6, 1812, a merchant, in N. Y'k. Not m. 4. Nancy N., Jan. 20, 1815, m. Benj. B. Hall, of H., Nov. 26, 1838.

44. John, s. John 28, m. Sally Mann, Nov. 1, 1798, and d. Dec. 5, 1851, ae. 80. Was Selectman in 1822. ch.: 1. Sally, Jan. 17, 1799, m. Ezra Whiting. 2. John, Aug. 3, 1801, d. Mar. 3, 1817. 3. Wm., Sep. 6, 1803. 4. Benj., Nov. 1, 1807, d. Aug. 28, 1833. 5. Martin, Feb. 6, 1810. 6. Alathea, July 12, 1812, m. Calvin Faxon, of Ab'n., Ap. 30, 1832, and d. June 29, 1845. 7. John, July 10, 1816, m. Marian A., da. Sam'l. N. Fuller, of Bos'n., in Oct., 1845, is a merchant, in Bos'n., and has *Alice B.*, Ap. 1847. 8. Lucinda, Aug. 16, 1819, m. Joseph H. Studley, Nov. 2, 1839.

45. Joshua, s. Joshua 31, m. 1, Nancy, da. Eliab Studley, Mar. 18, 1816; and 2, Marietta Gurney; lives in E. Ab'n.; is a shoe manufacturer; and has 1. Albert, d. ae. 25. 2. Leander, m. Maria L. Lane, lives in E. Ab'n., is a shoe mf'r., and has *Albert*, *Julia M.*, *Elvira L.*, and *Charles W.* 3. Elvira, m. Leonard Blanchard, and lives in Bos'n. 4. Joshua, May 31, 1825, m. Antoinette Atwell, of Lynn, lives in E. Ab'n., and has *Wendell R.*, and *Frederick M.*, d. Oct., 1851, ae. 2. 5. Mary E. 6. Marg't. K. 7. Sam'l. G. 8. George. 9. Ellen.

46. Job. s. Abner 35, m. Bethia, da. Abiel Farrow, lived in S. Scit., and there d., in Feb., 1843. His wid. survives. ch.: 1. Bethia, m. Hosea Whiting, of H'm., Oct. 24, 1827, and is d. 2. Job, m. Marilla Vining, Sep. 15, 1827, lives in E. Ab'n., is a shoemaker, and has *Edmund B.*, (m. Susan S. Cobbett, and has

Susan M., Oct., 1850); and *Catherine*, 1830, m. Benj. Burrill, of E. Ab'n. 3. Hiram, m. Lucinda Wilder, Nov. 27, 1834, lives in Snappet, and has *Lucinda E.*, Sep. 15, 1835; *Frederick H.*, Ap. 27, 1838; *Sarah W.*, July 5, 1843; and *Lucius W.*, Oct. 19, 1848. 4. Philip. 5. Harriet, m. 1, Jas. Doten, Dec. 9, 1832, and 2, Benj. Jacobs. 6. Nahum, m. Betsey Harlow, June, 1835, and has *Roxa A.*, Mar. 1, 1836; *Adaline M.*, July 1, 1839; *Bethia C.*, Ap., 1841; *Helen A.*, Feb. 29, 1843; and *Oscar H.*, Sep., 1851. 7. Abigail, m. Calvin Wilder. 8. Edwin, m. — Rogers, of Mf'd., and has ch. 9. Julia A., m. Henry A. Grose, July 11, 1847. 10. Adaline, m. Zenas Smith, of Ab'n.

47. Wm., s. Jno. 44, m. Cassandra Stetson, Dec. 3, 1826, lives on Union st., is a trader, and has 1. Geo. W., Sep. 12, 1827, m. Emma M. Brooks, lives on Main st., and has *Julia W.*, July 19, 1850. 2. Angeline, Jan., 1830. 3. Cassandra S., Jan. 23, d. Feb. 18, 1832. 4. Lucinda, 1834, d. 1836. 5. Lucinda, May, 1836. 6. Maria, Mar., 1838. 7. Benj., Sep., 1840. 8. John, May, 1842. 9. Avis L., May, 1844.

48. Martin, s. John 44, m. Debo. Stetson, in Feb., 1834, lived on Main st., in the house built by Wm. Curtis and Ezra Whiting, ab. 1827, and there d. Aug. 30, 1848, and his wid. improves his residence. ch.: 1. Helen M., Dec. 17, 1839. 2. Ann M., d. ae. 3 mo's. 3. Ann F., Ap. 17, 1844.

CUSHING, Matthew, with his wife Nazareth, his sons Daniel, Jeremiah, Matthew, and John, his daughter Deborah, and his wife's sister, Frances Ricroft, widow, sailed from Gravesend, Ap. 26, 1638, in the ship Diligent, John Martin, of Ipswich, master, and arrived at Boston, on the 10th of Aug. Matt., the fa., was b. in Eng'd., in 1588, and was s. of Peter, of Norfolk, whose gr. fa. had possessed large estates in Lombard st., London. He d. in H'm., Sep. 30, 1660, ae. 72, and his wid. in 1681, ae. 96. The Inventory of his estate may be seen in the Prob. Rec. Suff., vol. 3, pp. 219, 220. Date, Nov. 12, 1660. His four sons, and son-in-law Matthias Briggs, were the appraisers. *Deborah* and *Jeremiah*, left no children. The descendants of *Daniel*, and *Matthew*, are in H'm., and elsewhere. *John* settled in Scituate.

2. John, s. Matt., came to Scit., in 1662, according to Deane, and purchased the farm on "Belle house neck," of Capt. John, s. Wm. Vassal, to whom it was laid out in 1634. He m. Sarah, da. Nicholas Jacob, of H'm., 1656; was Dep. to the Col. Ct., many years, from 1674; Ass't. of the Col. Gov't., 1689–'91; and Rep. to the Gen. Ct., at Boston, after the union of the Colonies. His w. d. in 1678, ae. 38, and he in 1708. Of his ch.,

3. John, s. John 2, b. Ap. 28, 1662, m. 1, Debo. Loring, of Hull, May 20, 1687, who d. 1713; and 2, Sarah Holmes, 1714. He lived at "Belle house neck," was Chief Just. of the Inf'r. Ct., of Plym'h., from 1702–'10; Counc'r. of Mass, from 1710–'28; and Judge of the Sup'r. Ct., from 1728–37, of which, according to John Cotton, "he was the life and soul."[1] He d. in 1737. Of his ch.,

4. Elijah Cushing, s. John 3, b. Mar. 7, 1697–8, m. Elizabeth, wid. of Isaac Barker, of Newport, R. I., and daughter of Captain Joseph Barstow, in 1724, and resided on that part of the territory of Hanover, afterwards annexed to Pembroke, and near the spot where his grandson Elijah now resides, in Hanson. He is called Lt. and Capt., on the Rec. of H.; was for many years a Just. of the Peace; the first Rep. of the town, in 1737; and Selectman eleven years, from 1728–'39. He was one to whom much of the public business of the town was confided, and executed his trust with fidelity and success. Of his ch.

5. Jos. Cushing (Hon. Joseph,) s. Elijah 4, was b. Mar. 1, 1731–2, grad. at H. C., 1752, was one of the most valuable citizens of the town in his day. For a sketeh of his life, see p. 110. He was Selectman six years, from 1768–'74, and Representative from 1773–'75, and for '78–79, also Town Clerk from 1774–'78. He m. Ruth ——, and lived near the Four Corners, where he d. Dec. 19, 1791, and his

[1] Deane's Scit., p. 255.

wid. Feb. 12, 1822. ch.: 1. Ruth, m. David Stockbridge, jr., Dec. 23, 1779. 2. Charlotte, d. Aug. 24, 1825, ae. 60. 3. Elizabeth, m. Nathaniel Barstow, Aug. 31, 1786. 4. Joseph, m. Kezia Curtis, Nov. 6, 1794, and moved to Me., where his descendants still reside. He has a son *Benj.*, in Camden, Me. 5. Deborah, m. John Hathaway, of Camden, Me., Oct. 29, 1797. 6. Horatio.

THE JUDGE CUSHING HOUSE.

6. Horatio, Esq., s. Hon. Joseph 5, m. Ruth, da. John Bailey, and lived in his father's house near the Four Corners. He was Selectman nine years, for 1820, '23, '24, and from 1826–'32; also Rep. in 1831, and '33. ch.: 1. Mary B., Feb. 11, 1812, d. Sep. 1, 1815. 2. Horatio, June 13, 1813. 3. Henry W., Feb. 18, 1815. 4. Wm., Jan. 12, 1817. 5. Joseph, Dec. 6, 1818. 6. Edward, Ap. 26, 1820. 7. Mary E., June 12, 1821. 8. John H., July 8, 1822. 9. Frances, July 17, 1824. 10. Benjamin, June 20, 1825. 11. Anna O., July 17, 1826. 12. Charles S., May 22, d. Oct. 15, 1828. 13. Lucy E., May 18, 1829. 14. Charles S., Jan. 30, 1831.

NOTE.—Mrs. C., after her husband's decease, with her son Henry, built, it is said, the house now occupied by Capt. Nath'l. Barstow, near the Four Corners. She now resides in Hartford, Ct.

7. Dr. Ezekiel D. Cushing, a desc't. of Elijah 4, was in H., in

1827, and d. Ap. 5, 1828, ae. 38. See p. 100. By w. Delia, he had a son, Capt. Nath'l., who m. Elizabeth, da. Edward Barstow, and lived in H., near the Four Corners.

RESIDENCE OF REV. SAMUEL CUTLER.

CUTLER, Rev. Samuel, s. Sam'l., and w. Lydia (Prout,) was b. May 12, 1805, moved from Newburyport to Portland, Me., in 1826, and was there in business until 1834. In Feb. of that year, he moved to Bos'n., and was there in business until 1839. From 1836, to 1839, he spent his time in preparing for the ministry, under the Rev. Dr. Stone, and was settled in Hanover, Mass., in 1842. He m. 1, Julia A., da. Levi Cutter, of Portland, Me., Aug. 31, 1829, who d. Dec. 28, 1830, ae. 24; and 2, Elizabeth D., da. John Gardner, of Exeter. N. H., June 19, 1833. Has one son by her, Samuel G., b. Oct. 30, 1835. Mr. C. resides near the Four Corners, in the fine parsonage house, erected for him by his Society, in 1849, a view of which is annexed.

DAMON, Jno., and sis. Han'h., were in Scit. as minors, in 1633, under the guardianship of their uncle, Wm. Gillson. The desc'ts. are numerous, in Scit., H., and Mfd.

2. Eells, s. Zach., of Scit., and a desc't. of John, m. Huldah Curtis, May 1, 1777, lived on Whiting st., corner of North, was a

housewright, and d. Aug. 26, 1805, being drowned near Boon Island, Me., and his wid. d. Mar. 12, 1830. ch.: 1. Zach., Dec. 17, 1775. 2. Nath'l. E., Jan. 4, 1780, d. 1781. 3. Eells, June 15, 1783. 4. Job, Nov. 9, 1785, m. Ruth Cushing, went off, and has not been heard from for 20 years. 5. Sally, June 12, 1788, m. Eliph't. Belcher, Wey'h. 6. Rufus C., July 14, 1792, went to Ill's., and m. there. 7. Huldah, May 29, 1794, m. Alvah Wood, and died in Plym'h. 8. Abner, Ap. 19, 1797, d. Ap. 30, 1799. 9. Lenthea, Aug. 22, 1800, m. Sam'l. Turner, Randolph.

3. Zach., s. Eells, 2. m. Sarah Brooks, lived on Whiting st., was a carpenter by trade, and his w. d. Ap. 4, 1847. ch.: 1. Sarah B., Mar. 16, 1801, m. Chas. Thomas. 2. Thos., Oct. 20, 1804. 3. Joseph B., Nov. 13, 1809, edu. at Newton, m. wid. Martha Burbank, and is sett. as a Bap. min., in Lake Village, N. H. 4. Zach., Sep. 7, 1812, m. 1. Abig. Southward, Dux'y.; and 2. Ann Rogers, Wey'h., and lives in Philipston, Mass. 5. Debo. C., Oct. 3, 1815, m. Benj. Bowker, jr., Hn. 6. Franklin, Oct. 21, 1818, edu. at Newton, m. Han'h. Cushing, and is sett. as a Bap. min. in Brewster, Mass.

4. Eells, s. Eells 2, m. Eleanor Brooks, lived on Curtis st., was a housewright, and d. Feb. 25, 1831, and his wid. Nov. 12, 1846. ch.: 1. Elenor, Oct. 28, 1810, not m. 2. Eells, July 15, 1812, not m. 3. George, June 5, 1814, m. Sarah H. Crane, Dec., 1838, lives on Main st., and has *Sarah M.*, Sep. 29, 1839; *Geo. F.*, Aug. 6, 1841; *Lydia A.*, Feb. 15, 1844; and *Danl. W.*, Nov. 3, 1848. 4. Esther, Mar. 25, 1816, m. Wm. Orcutt, and d. May 24, 1845. 5. Lydia, May 21, 1818, d. Oct. 22, 1850. 6. Danl., Sep. 8, 1821, m. Lucy Crane, 1843, and lives on Main st., no ch.

5. Thos., s. Zach. 3, m. Nabby Bates, Dec. 25, 1827, who d. in 1852. He is a carpenter by trade, lives near the centre of the town, was Selectman in 1839, and has been Constable, Collector, &c. ch.: 1. Andrew T., Nov. 19, 1829, m. Fanny S. Perry, Ap. 22, 1851, and lives near the Cent. M. Ho. 2. Bernard, Aug. 17, 1831. 3. Nabby F., Oct. 15, 1838. 4. Rector, 1841.

6. Ezra, s. Joseph, of Ab'n., and a desc't. of Jno. of Scit., m. Anna Wilder, of Hm., and d. July, 1825, ae.71, and his wid. Sep. 23, 1831, ae. 75. ch.: 1. Anna, m. Jos. Jacobs, Oct. 4, 1801, and is d. 2. Elizab., m. 1. Wm. E. Smith, June 3, 1804, and 2. Jos. Jacobs. 3. Ezra, of Quincy, Mass., is m. and has ch. 4. Joseph. 5. Calvin, Ap., 1789. 6. Piam. 7. Mary, m. Jona. Arnold, Ab'n. 8. David, m. Lucy Wade, Aug. 8, 1821, and now lives in So. Scit. Has sev. ch. 9. Sarah, m. a Palmer, and lives in Hm. 10. Thos.

7. Joseph, s. Ezra 6, m. Lucy Tower, Sep. 6, 1812, lives on Whiting st., is a farmer, and has, 1. Lucy, July 29, 1813, m. Thos. Mann, and is d. 2. Jno., Dec. 3, 1816, m. Martha S. Chubbuck, who is d.. and he lives on Whiting st., and has sev. ch. 3. Alvira A., Jan. 3, 1819, m. Ezra Shaw, Abn. 4. Anne, July 3, 1821, m. Jas. Bates, Aug. 16, 1828. 5. Joseph, Nov. 26, 1823, m. Mary Gerrish, 1852, and lives with his fa. 6. Betsey, Sep. 15, 1825, m. Henry Shaw, Abn. 7. Debo. B., Jan. 12, 1827, d. 1847. 8. Esteria, Ap., 1828, d. Dec. 10, 1850. 9. Jas., July 3, 1821. 10. Mary A., Feb. 3, 1835.

8. Calvin, s. Ezra 6, took his mother's name, and is known as Calvin D. Wilder, lives in Snappet, and m. Sarah Barrell, Jan. 15, 1815, who died in 1845. He survives. His ch. are, 1. Lucinda, June 9, 1816, m. Hiram Curtis. 2. Calvin, Oct. 8, 1817, m. Abig. Curtis, and lives in So. Scit. No ch. 3. Wm., d. ae. 9 days. 4. Sarah, Sep. 13, 1829, m. Capt. Benj. N. Curtis. 5. Jno. B., Sep. 9, 1824, m. Lydia J. Randall, 1843, lives on Walnut st., and has *Ellen F.*, Dec. 9, 1845; *Geo. A.*, 1849; and *Mary C.*, Mar. 7, 1852.

9. Piam, s. Ezra 6, m. Olive Whiting, June 15, 1814, lives on Whiting st., is a shoemaker, and has, 1. Eliza E., Jan. 26, d. Feb. 21, 1817. 2. Martin W., May 23, 1818, m. Abig. S. Puffer, and now lives in Haverhill, Mass. 3. Ruth F., Nov. 7, 1820, m. Hosea Chubbuck, Dec. 22, 1839. 4. Jane T., May 6, 1823, m. Jno. Scott. 5. Elizab. E., Mar. 2, 1826. 6. Henry L., June 27, 1828, d. ae. 13. 7. Wm. W., Jan. 13, 1832.

10. Thos., s. Ezra 6, m. Almira Phillips, in 1828, and d. Ap. 6,

1852, leaving ch.: 1. Thos. W., Aug. 30, 1830. 2. Ann T., Feb., 1834. 3. Almira, May, 1836. 4. Piam, Aug., 1838. 5. Henry, Jan., 1842. 6. Wash'n., June, 1843. 7. Ezra, 1850.

DARLING, David, of Hull, b. July 1, 1793, s. Benj., of Pemb., m. Lydia Studley, Aug. 24, 1816, lives on Circuit st., and has, 1. Sally L., Oct. 8, 1818, m. David J. Davis, Dec., 1834. 2. Harriet L., Jan. 3, 1821, m. Seth H. Vinal, May, 1840. 3. Sophia S., July 11, 1826, m. Joseph Vinal, Ap., 1848.

DAVIS, David J., of N. Yk. State, s. Jona., m. Sally L. Darling, Dec., 1834, lives with her fa., and has, 1. Wm. F., Mar. 25, 1835. 2. Jno. T., Feb. 25, 1841. 3. Lydia A., May 14, 1843. 4. Horace L., May, 1846.

DAWES, Wm., b. 1790, s. Rev. Ebenr., of Scit., m. 1. Bathsheba, da. Wm. Torrey, of Pemb., Ap. 28, 1814; and 2. Amy, da. Jno. Bailey, and wid. of Edward Barstow, and lives on Wash'n. st., near the Corners. Had 2 ch., Wm. E., d. at sea, ae. 19, and Elizab. A., d. ae. 18 mos. Both by 1st w.

DELANO, James, b. Nov. 18, 1806, s. Geo., of Dux'y., and a lineal desc't. of Philip de la Noye, who came to Plym'h. in the Fortune, in 1621, lives on Centre st., with Geo. Bates, is a shoemaker, and unm.

DILL, Joseph, s. Lem., of Hm., m. Julia A., da. Joseph Vining, lived in H. for a time, and had Julia A., 1841, and Caroline, Jan. 25, 1843. He now lives in E. Abn., is a shoe mfr., and has Sariah, 1845, and Joseph W., June, 1847.

DOTEN, Jno., s. Edward, of Plym'h., b. Feb., 1823, and a lineal desct. of Edward, of Plym'h., 1623, m. Betsey Hughes, 1845, lives on Broadway, is a shoemaker, and has Geo. D., and Jno. T., twins, b. July 14, 1849.

DONNELL, Joseph, was in H. 1760, m. Sarah Palmer, and had, 1. Joseph, of Bristol, Me. 2. Thos., d. in the Rev'n. 3.

Patience S., m. Levi Mann, and d. Mar. 6, 1846, ae. 85. 4. Samuel. 5. Rebecca, m. Laban Wilder. 6. Charles, d. Sep. 14, 1832, ae. 62.

2. Samuel, s. Joseph, m. Jane D. Barstow, lived at the Corners, and d. June 5, 1807, and his wid. June 11, 1808. ch.: 1. Samuel, of Bath, Me., was m. and d. there. 2. Jane B., m. Calvin B. Bailey, of Bath, May 21, 1820. 3. Thos., d. Dec. 1, 1802, ae. 20 mos. 4. Jno., d. in S. Am'a. 5. Capt. Thos. B., Feb., 1804, a shipmaster for many years, now a farmer; lives on Elm st.; m. 1. Ruth, da. Reuben Curtis, in Oct., 1843, who d. Jan. 23, 1849, and 2. Sarah Bailey, Jan. 13, 1850. ch.: *Abby C.*, June 17, 1844; *Jane B.*, Aug. 5, 1845; (by 2d) *Reuben C.*, Nov. 23, 1850.

NOTE.—Hon. Saml. Donnell, b. 1645, one of the first Councillors of Mass., and J. P., &c., was of York, Me., where he d. in 1717, and his s. Nath. b. 1689, d. in York in 1780, ae. 90. Possibly Joseph, of H., was a desc't. of the Donnell's, of Me.

DUNBAR, Amos, of Hm., s. Amos, b. Sep. 1, 1786, a currier by trade, and for many years a respected citizen of H., but now of So. Scit., m. 1. Abig. Gray, who d. Feb. 12, 1830, and 2. Rebecca Gray, May 18, 1835, and has, 1. Debo., July 8, 1808, m. David Bailey, Ap. 24, 1833. 2. Amos, Aug. 23, 1811, m. Maria Lyon, and lives in Wey'h. 3. Abig., Sep. 25, 1814, m. Richmond Farrow, of So. Scit. 4. Lucinda, Mar. 22, 1817, m. Gilman Thompson, the enterprising expressman, of Wey'h. 5. Ruth R., Feb. 16, 1820, m. Rufus K. Trott, Wey'h. 6. Elizab. G., Jan. 24, 1825, m. Jere. Bailey, and is of Wey'h. 7. Emma F., Dec. 14, 1828, m. Alexr. Sherman, of Wey'h., Ap. 25, 1850. (By 2d.) 8. Jas. M., Mar. 26, 1837. 9. Harriet M., Jan. 5, d. Oct. 5, 1842.

DUNCAN, Rev. Abel G., b. in Chester, Vt., June 25, 1802, s. Jason, jr., and w. Lucy; gr. s. Jason, and w. Sarah (Gates), an early settler of Dummerston, Vt., memb. Leg., J. P., Judge, &c.; gr.-gr.-s. Simeon, and w. Bridget (Richardson); and gr. gr. gr. s. John, of Edinburgh, Scot'd., who m. Sarah Dutton, and lived and d. in Worcester, Mass. Rev. Abel G. m. Lucia Harlow, of

Harvard, Mass., Sep. 23, 1828, who d. Oct. 12, 1851, and has 1. Laura J., July 9, 1829. 2. Wm. P., Ap. 1, 1831, is at Amherst Coll. 3. Lucia A., Dec. 20, 1832. See Chap. on Eccl. Hist., and obit. of his w. in the Puritan Recorder for 1851.

DWELLEY, Richard, supposed by Deane to have been the same that was in Lancaster, 1654, and in H'm. a few yrs. after, was in Scit., 1665, and his farm was on the road leading from the 3d. Herring brook to the harbor, one mile north of the brook; and his house stood where stood, in 1831, that of Capt. Seth Foster, deces'd. He had meadow land at Tills, aft. Dwelley's creek; and in 1676, was a soldier in Philip's war, and received for his services a grant of land on what is now East st., in H. He d. May 27, 1692. We have not ascertained the place of his nativity, nor the year in which he came to N. Eng. The name is not common, and is rarely found in genealogical works. The name of his w. is not given, nor the dates of birth of his ch. We have only the bap. of Mary, in H'm., in 1664. There were sons Richard, and Jno.; and Sam'l., who d. 1690, in Phip's exped. to Canada. Richard jr., m. 1, Eamie, da. Roger Glass, Dux'y. Ap. 4, 1682; and 2, Elizab. Simmons, 1690, and d. Dec. 24, 1708, having had 1. Mary, 1684; 2. Richard, 1685, m. Grace Turner, Oct. 13, 1712, (who d. Feb. 16, 1715,) and had *Richard*, 1714, and *Grace*, 1716, m. 1, Jesse Turner, Dec. 18, 1734; and 2, Joseph Church? Aug. 2, 1742; 3. Elizab., 1687, m. Joseph White, Mf'd,, Dec. 21, 1710. 4. Joshua, 1689; 5. Ruth, 1691, m. Thos. Slack, Nov. 9, 1715; 6. Sam'l., 1693; 7. Lydia, 1695, m. Henry Burditt? Jan. 1, 1712; 8. Marg't, 1696, m. Henry Merritt, jr., Ap. 13, 1725.

2. John, s. Richard, sen'r., m. Rachel, da. Cornet Jno. Buck, Jan. 4, 1692-'3, and had 1. Jno., Jan. 15, 1693-'4, m. Judith Bryant, Dec. 20, 1721, and had *Jno.*, 1722, *Simeon*, 1725, *Ruth*, 1726, and *Benj.*, 1729. 2. Rachel, Sep. 27, 1695, m. Caleb Turner, Oct. 27, 1713. 3. Ichabod, Dec. 30, 1696. 4. Obadiah, Feb. 21, 1696-'7, d. Mar. 17, 1706. 5. Jedediah, Sep. 5, 1698. 6. Abner, Mar. 7, 1700. 7. Simeon, Dec. 22, 1701.— 8. Debo., July 25, 1703, m. Isaac Keen, Pemb., Feb. 17, 1724.

9. Joseph, bap. May 6, 1705. 10. Thankful, Dec. 12, 1706, m. Wm. Fobes, W. Bridg'r., Feb. 3, 1725. 11. Mary, May 18, 1708, d. young. 12. Benj., May 22, 1708. (T. Rec.) 13. Susannah, Dec. 19, 1711. 14. Mary, Sep. 24, 1714, m. Josh. Lincoln, Feb. 18, 1731. 15. Lemuel, June 25, 1717. Some of this family may have moved to Rhode Island, in which State the name is still extant.

3. Jedediah Dwelle s. Jno. 2, m. Elizabeth House, Oct. 7, 1726, and d. Ap. 16, 1738, having had, 1. Elizab., Ao. 27, 1726. 2. Debo., Sep. 22, 1728. 3. Lusannah, Mar. 20, 1730. 4. Abner, Mar. 6, 1733. 5. Josh., July 20, 1736. 6. Jededi., Mar. 15, 1737. 7. Lot, Ap. 6, 1740, bap. Mar. 16, 1741, being sick. His mo. then a wid. (Rec. 2 Ch., Scit.)

4. Abner, s. Jno. 2, m. Sarah Witherell, Oct. 12, 1721, lived on Elm st., near Col. Barstow's, where part of his orchard, known as the "Abner orchard," is still standing; and d. Sep. 1, 1732, as trad. says, by falling from a load of hay. He was Selectman in 1731 and '32. ch.: 1. Bradbury, July 17, 1722, d. 1728.—2. Wm., Ap. 13, 1724. 3. Jas. L., Jan. 5, 1726. 4. Sarah L., Dec. 2, 1728. 5. Luke L., Mar. 21, 1730.

5. Joseph, s. Jno. 2, m. Mary Ramsdell, Oct. 9, 1729, and d. ab. 1748. ch.: 1. Lusannah, bap. Nov. 8, 1730. 2. Mary, Jan. 15, 1731. 3. Drusilla, Dec. 11, 1733. 4. Bradbury, Nov. 26, 1735. 5. Joseph, Oct. 14, 1737, m. Mary Magoun, Pemb., Jan. 7, 1762, and was prob. fa. of Dr. Melzar, of H. 6. Lemuel, Aug. 10, 1741. 7. Ruth, Jan. 8, 1743. 8. Jno., bap. Ap. 9, 1749, his mo. being a wid.

6. Abner, s. Jeded. 3, m. 1, Sarah ——, and 2, Debo. House, ? Jan. 26, 1769, and had, 1. Abner, Jan. 10, 1758, prob. moved to the Western part of Mass., or to N. Y. State. 2. Jedediah, Oct. 5, 1760. 3. Elizabeth, Sep. 18, 1762. 4. Lucy, Sep. 9, 1766. 5. Debo., Nov. 13, 1768.

7. Joshua, s. Jeded. 3, m. Avis Ramsdell, Dec. 24, 1761, lived in H., and d. Mar. 15, 1787, and his wid. Mar. 19, 1831, ae. 90. He was a soldier in the Rev'n. ch.: 1. Debo., Oct. 18, 1762, m. Asa Whiting, Ap. 13, 1786. 2. Lemuel, Nov. 7, 1764.

3. Josh., Dec. 13, 1766. 4. Joseph, Nov. 2, 1772, moved to Me., and m. and d. there, leaving ch. 5. Lucy, Sep. 18, 1775, m. Seth Rose, Dec. 4, 1798, and d. Ap. 25, 1845. 6. Priscilla, May 20, 1780, m. Josh. Stetson, Oct. 20, 1804, and d. Nov. 27, 1845.

8. Jeded., s. Jeded. 3, was of Pemb., and m. Lydia Soule, Dux'y., Feb. 14, 1763, who d. Ap. 20, 1819, ae. 79. He was a soldier in the Fr. war. ch: 1. Chas., of Me. 2. Benj., m. Bradbury Stetson, Dec. 7, 1788, lived in P., and had *Frances*, Feb. 7, 1789; *Elizab.*, Nov. 13, 1792; *Bradbury*, Ap. 26, 1795, m. Lem'l. Grover, jr., Mfd., Jan. 2, 1823; *Sophia*, Nov. 1, 1797 d. unm.; *Mary*, July 22, 1799; *Benj.*, June 17, 1801, d. May 4, 1802; *Chas.*, Ap. 19, 1803; and *Julia*, Oct. 13, 1807. 3. Huldah, m. Christ'r. Thomas, Pemb. 4. Lucy, m. Chas. Josselyn, Pemb. 5. Nathan. 6. Aaron, lived and d. in Pelham, Mass. 7. George, m. Hope Cushing, Oct. 11, 1826, lives in P., and has *Geo.*, d. ae. 3; *Laura* A., Feb. 19, 1829, d. young; and *Huldah*, m. Henry Chapman, of P. 8. Lydia, m. Elisha K. Josselyn, of P., Mar. 12, 1797.

9. Lem'l. Dwelle s. Josh. 7, m. 1, Jane, da. Col David Cushing, H'm., who d. Dec. 1, 1816, ae. 44; and 2, Lucia Turner, Chas'n., Dec. 1818, lived at the corner of Union and Main sts., and d. Oct 29, 1846, ae. 84. ch: 1. Lem'l., June 18, 1798, m. Sarah J., da. Calvin Bailey, Ap. 1827, lives on Union st., was Selectman from 1827—'31, and from '42—'44; has *Geo. R.*, Dec. 5, 1829, at H. Coll.; *Edwin B.*, Jan. 2, 1831; *Jedediah*, Feb. 28, 1834; *Sarah B.*, Mar. 6, 1836; and *Chas. H.*, Oct. 7, 1843. 2. Jane R., Dec. 9, 1804, m. 1, Geo. Merriam, and 2, Wm. H. Curtis. 3. Geo. R., Sep. 27, 1807, d. Nov., 1827. 4. Jedediah, d. Mar. 26, 1834, at Middletown Coll., Ct. (By 2d,) 5. Joseph T., d. Oct., 1836. 6. Mary T., m. Joseph Briggs, jr.

10. Joshua, s. Josh. 7, m. Rachel Hatch, Mar. 16, 1797, who d. Dec. 11, 1831, and he Dec. 14, 1847. Lived in H. ch: 1. Josh., Aug 17, 1798, m. 1, Betsey, da. Chas. Bailey, Nov. 3, 1823, who d. Aug. 2, 1825; and 2, Keziah, da. Geo. Bailey, Jan. 16, 1827, and d. Jan. 30, 1842; had *Josh.*, d. Aug. 25, 1825; (by 2d,) *Josh.*, Jan 7, 1828, a carpenter; *Betsey B.*, Nov. 18,

1829, m. Josh. S. Whiting, June 20, 1847; *Laurentia C.*, Mar. 20, 1832; *Melzar*, Feb. 5, 1835; and *Geo. B.*, Aug. 7, d. Nov. 10, 1841. 2. Rachel, May 3, 1800, m. Benj. Bailey, of H., Ap. 14, 1822. 3. Jno., June 21, 1802, m. Mary Stockbridge, Ap. 1829, lives on Union st., and has *Almira*, Jan., 1833, d. May 3, 1839; *Jno. H.*, Feb. 18, 1835; *Hosea*, Dec. 10, 1836; *Joseph*, Feb. 14, 1839; and *Mary*, Dec. 31, 1843. 4. Almira, Aug. 14, 1806, d. Dec, 9, 1807. 5. Debo., Jan. 18, 1808, m. Jos. Stockbridge. 6. Joseph, Ap. 6, 1813, m. Sally Stockbridge, Feb. 3, 1836, lives on Main st., and has *Almira J.*, Aug. 3, 1840.

11. Nathan, s. Jeded. 8, m. 1, Elizab. Bonney, Sep. 26, 1793; and 2, Amy Bonney; and lived and d. in Pemb. ch: 1. Betsey, Aug. 21, 1794, d. Dec. 21, 1798. 2. Nathan, Feb. 19, 1797. 3. Mary D., Feb. 1, 1799, m. Melzar Sprague, Nov. 28, 1820. 4. Amy M. 5. Jas. H., m. Lois Josselyn, lives in Pemb., and has *Jas. H.*, *Geo.*, and *Mary E.* 6. Abner, Sep. 20, 1806, d. Nov. 2, 1811. 7. Chloe B., Sep. 12, 1808, m. 1, Septa Keith, Aug. 7, 1831, and 2, Thos. Perkins. 8. Hannah B., Oct. 29, d. Nov. 5, 1811. 9. Hannah, m. Silas Hollis, of H.

RESIDENCE OF CAPT. NATHAN DWELLEY.

12. Capt. Nathan, s. Nathan 11, m. Huldah B. Eells, Dec. 5, 1822, and lives at the Corners, in the Capt. Rob't. L. Eells house, a view of which is annexed. Mr. D. was, for a time, Capt. of the

H. Rifle Company. ch: 1. Elizab. E., Nov. 29, 1823, m. Waldo Bradford, Bridg'r., Nov. 28, 1847. 2. Rob't. E., Sep. 14, 1825, m. Mary Lyons, July 2, 1848, and had *Edwin B.*, Feb. 22, 1850, d. same yr. 3. Huldah B., June 8. 1830, d. young. 4. Nathan H., May 7, 1832. 5. Huldah B., July 2, 1834.

13. Dr. Melzar, s. Joseph, and gr. s. Joseph 5, with w. Sally, came to H. from Ashburnham, in 1797, and sett. on Hanover st. (see p. 20.) where he d. Nov. 25, 1828, ae. 57, and his wid. Feb. 10, 1841, ae. 65. ch: 1. Geo. W., Feb. 25, 1796, shipwright, of S. Boston. 2. Chas., Mar., 1798, m. 1, a Thayer, and 2, a Spear, and lives in S. Boston. 3. Sally S., Oct. 15, 1799, m. Asia Phillips, of Ashb'm., Dec. 25, 1820. 4. Harriet, Nov. 25, 1801, d. Dec. 14, 1818. 5. Jno. M., Nov. 17, 1803, living in H., unm. 6. Augustus, Feb. 7, 1806, of S. Boston. 7. Caroline, Aug. 23, 1808, m. Horatio N. Willard, Ashb'm., Nov. 30, 1831. 8. Abig. W., July 23, 1810, d. Oct. 1812. 9. Fred'k., July 16, 1812, of S. Boston. 10. Abig, W., Aug. 12, 1814, m. Leavitt L. Stockbridge, July 4, 1844. 11. Anne S., Nov. 1816, m. David Hatch, Mf'd. 12. Joseph, July 3, 1819, d. ae. 19.

RESIDENCE OF MR. CHARLES DYER.

DYER, Charles, s. Christ'r, of Ab'n., b. Jan. 12, 1796, m. 1, Cynthia Jenkins, of A., Nov., 1820, who d. Feb. 7, 1826; 2, Mary Ford, of Pemb., Sep. 10, 1826, who d. Nov. 17, 1831; and 3,

Sophronia Oldham, of P., Oct. 21, 1832; lives on Water st., and has been for some years engaged in the mfr. of Tacks. (See p. 141.) A view of his house is presented. ch: 1. Eliza, Sep. 27, 1821, m. Geo. M. Josselyn, Pemb. 2. Cynthia J., July 12, 1823. 3. Lucy S., Jan 12, 1825, m. Rob't. Hersey, of H. (By 2d,) 4. Charles, July 4, 1831. (By 3d,) 5. Theodore, Sep. 19, 1836.

EELLS, or EELES, John, was among the early settlers of Dorchester, and "dwelt at Fox-point." According to the History of Dorchester, now in the course of publication, and from which we quote, "it appears that he removed to Hingham;" and it is suggested, that "he may have been John the bee-hive maker, who finally settled in Newbury. He had a son *Samuel*, bap. in D., May 3, 1640."

s. of Jno., according to family doc'ts., sett. in Milford, Ct. He commanded a garrison at Dartm'h, Mass., in Philip's War, 1676; was J. P.; and Rep. from H'm., 1705–6; m. Anna, da. of Rev. Robt. Lenthal, of Wey'h.; and had 7 sons, and 1 da., the latter of whom m. on Long Island. The name of *Lenthal* was preserved in this family for a long time, and still exists in it. After the death of his 1st w., Mr. E. moved to H'm., Mass., taking with him his youngest son, Nath'l., and there m. 2, wid. Sarah North, formerly a Peck, (H'm. Rec.) She was prob. the wid. of Joseph Peck, of H'm., and her maiden name was North, she being a desc't. of the noble family of that name in England. The fa. d. in H'm., in 1709, and his wid. in Scit., in 1711. A son *John*, lived in Milford, Ct., and had 2 das., *Ann*, who m. Thos. Weldon, and Frances, who d. at her uncle Nathl's., in 1718.

NOTE.—We find the name of *John Eales*, among the freemen of Mass., in 1634, (N. E. Gen. Reg., Vol. 3, p. 92); and *Henry Eeles* was a Pass. for Va. in the Merchants' Hope, Hugh Weston, Master, in 1635. (Ib. vol. 4, p. 190.) It has been suggested, that the names of *Eells*, and *Ellis*, were formerly one; but of the correctness of this suggestion, we are not prepared to decide. *Similarity* does not always prove *identity*.

2. (Rev. Nath'l.,) s. of Capt. Saml., was b. in 1678, grad. at H. C. 1699, and sett. in Scit., over the 2d Church, in 1704. He was m. by his fa. to Hannah

North, of H'm., (aunt to Frederick, Lord North, afterwards Prime Minister of Geo. III.) Oct. 12, 1704, and d. in Scit., Aug, 25, 1750, ae. 72, and his wid., May 1, 1754. He is described, by Deane, as a man "of a stature rather above mediocrity, of broad chest and muscular proportions, remarkably erect, somewhat corpulent in his late years, of dark complexion, with black eyes and brows, and of general manners rather dignified and commanding, than sprightly and pleasing." He wrote a fair hand, as the Church Records show; and as a preacher, his discourses prove him to have been a man of great simplicity of style, and directness of argument. He prepared his own sons, and others, for College, and was a ripe scholar, naturally shrewd, and one eminently qualified for usefulness in the station he filled. ch.: 1. Sarah, Aug. 5, 1705, m. Benj. Turner, of Scit. 2. Samuel, Feb. 23, 1706–7. 3. Jno., Jan. 23, 1709, m. Abiah Waterman, of Scit., in 1730, and left desct's. 4. Nath'l., Feb. 4, 1710–11, grad. H. C. 1728, sett. at Stonington, Ct., in 1733, m. Mary, da. Hon. John Cushing, of Scit., Oct. 18, 1733, and has desct's. in Ct. 5. Edward, Jan. 4, 1712–13, grad. H. C. 1733, ord. at Middletown, Ct., 1737; was for some years Tutor at Yale Coll., where 3 of his sons grad., who sett. in Ct. The fa. d. in 1776. Concerning him, we find the following note, in the Stat. Acct. of Mid'x., Ct.: "In 1738, the Rev. Ed. Eells, s. of the Rev. Nath'l. Eells, of Scit., Mass., was ord. in the Upper Houses. Mr. E. acquired some celebrity by a pamphlet which he pub. in 1759, on the Walingford case. For several years he sustained the office of a trustee of Yale Coll., where 3 of his sons were educated, who were ministers in Eastbury, N. Bramford, and Barkhampstead, Ct." 6. Han'h., Jan. 30, 1714–15, m. Anth'y. Eames, of Mfd. 7. Mary, May 13, 1716, m. Seth Williams, of Taunton, 1738. 8. North, Sep. 28, 1718, m. Ruth Tilden, 1741, and left ch. 9. Anna L., Oct. 16, 1721, m. Zach. Damon, 1748.

3. Samuel, s. Rev. Nathl. 2, m. Hannah, gr. gr. da. Rev. Wm. Witherell, of Scit., Dec. 18, 1729, and sett. in H., his house standing where stands that of Joseph C. Stockbridge, on Broadway. He d. in 1741, (see p. 20,) and his wid. survived many years. ch.: 1. Wm. W., Dec. 14, 1730. 2. Robert L., Feb. 7, or 18, 1732.

3. Sarah, June 4, 1733, m. Bezal. Palmer, Ap. 8, 1752. 4. Samuel, Feb. 16, 1735. 5. Hannah N., Nov. 18, 1736, d. Sep. 2, 1737. 6. Hannah N., Jan. 22, 1738, m. George Bennett, of Ab'n., Ap. 5, 1759. 7. Mary, Dec. 26, 1739, m. Deacon Benj. Bass, Mar. 3, 1793. 8. Bradbury, Ap. 6, 1741, m. Benj. Stetson, Ap. 30, 1765.

4. Wm. W., s. Saml. 3, m. Sarah Pillsbury, and moved to Me., where his desct's. still reside. His w. d. Sep. 25, 1791? ae. 62. ch.: 1. Sarah, May 12, 1758, m. Hezek. Bosworth, and moved to Me. 2. Hannah W., bap. Sep. 11, 1763, m. Jacob White, of Ab'n., Mar. 12, 1778, and moved to Me. 3. Mary L., bap. Sep. 11, 1763, m. 1, Josh. Young, of Scit., Feb. 23, 1804; 2, a Ewell, of Mfd.; and 3, a Cobb, of Me. 4. Priscilla, bap. March 31, 1765, d. unm. 5. Lydia, bap. Ap. 26, 1767, m. Rev. Mr. Loring? 6. Wm. W., Dec. 4, 1768, lived in Me., was m., and had ch. 7. Rebecca, bap. Sep. 10, 1775, m. a Bartol, and, with her husband, d. in. N. York.

5. Robert Ll. Eells (Captain Robert L.,) s. Saml. 3, m. Ruth Copeland, of Scit., Dec. 1, 1757, and lived where Capt. N. Dwelley now resides, at the Four Corners. For a sketch of his life, &c., see p. 162. He was Rep. in 1776 and '77; Selectman from 1790–93; and d. June 19, 1800, and his wid. May 21, 1831, ae. 93. ch.: 1. Ruth, Oct. 31, 1758, m. Jno. Young, Feb. 2, 1797. No ch. 2. Betsey, Oct. 30, 1760, m. Col. J. B. Barstow, Feb. 7, 1788, and d. in 1851. 3. Huldah C., March 8, 1763, m. Wm. Wing, Nov. 26, 1789, and d. in N. York. 4. Anne L., July 18, 1765, m. Capt. Albert Smith, Aug. 23, 1787. 5. Robert, Nov. 29, 1767. 6. Nabby, Nov. 29, 1767, m. Josiah Smith, jr., Pemb., Mar. 13, 1794. 7. John, May 20, 1770, m. Lucy Thorndike, and went to Camden, Me., where he d. in 1848? leaving ch. 8. Nathl., Sep. 28, 1772, m. Mary Terry, moved to Belfast, Me., and there d. in 1840. 9. Joseph, June 5, 1774. 10. Lucy, Aug. 12, 1776, m. Dea. Elijah Barstow, Nov. 8, 1798. 11. Edward, Feb. 26,

1779. 12. Sarah, Aug. 2, d. Aug. 17, 1781. 13. Sam'l., Mar. 13, 1783.

6. Samuel, s. Samuel 3, m. Priscilla Palmer, lived on Elm st., where Josh. Stetson resides, and there his w. d., Nov. 27, 1763. ch.: Sam'l., Bezal., and Benj., all bap. Oct. 23, 1763. Sam'l. m. Lydia Josselyn, of Pemb., July 7, 1783, had *Benj.*, Aug. 7, 1784, and *Henry B.*, Dec. 10, 1786; lived in his father's house for a time, and thence moved to Me. Bezal. was a shipwright, and d. unm., in Me. Benj. m., and lived in Belfast, Me. The above is according to family tradition.

7. Robert, s. Capt. Robert L. 5, m. Huldah Bass, Nov. 27, 1800, who d. June 24, 1812, and he Oct. 5, 1844. He was P. M. for 39 years; Selectman from 1805–8; Rep. in 1819, '20, '27, '28 and '30; a blacksmith by trade, and occupied his father's house. ch.: 1. Huldah B., Feb. 21, 1802, m. Capt. Nathan Dwelley, Dec. 5, 1822, and occupies the homestead. 2. Robert, May 9, 1805, d. Aug. 29, 1808. 3. Elizab., Jan. 1, 1808, m. Jos. Ramsdell, jr., of Warren, Mass., Dec. 3, 1827.

8. Joseph, s. Capt. Rob't. L. 5, m. Sarah Bass, Nov. 25, 1802, and lived near the Four Corners, where his wid. still resides, in the old Dillingham house. He was a blacksmith by trade. ch.: 1. Sarah B., May 31, 1803, d. July 25, 1812. 2. Lucinda, Ap. 14, 1805, m. Isaac M. Wilder, Feb. 5, 1834. 3. Joseph, Ap. 7, 1807, m. Sarah B. Smith, Mar. 11, 1827, built the house in which Alex'r. Wood, Esq. now lives, and moved to Wisconsin. Has had 12 or 13 ch. in all, of whom were b. in H., *Sarah B.*, Aug. 1, 1828; *Ruth*, Nov. 5, 1829; *Albert S.*, Jan. 25, 1831; *Thos. D*; *Anne L.*; *Priscilla*; and *Lucinda*. 4. Ruth, Ap. 22, 1809, d. Dec 29, 1828. 5. Mercy B., Nov. 9, 1811. 6. Rob't., Ap. 5, 1813? m. Mary T. Stockbridge, Jan. 20, 1838, lives at the Corners, is a wheelwright, and had *Ellen A.*, Ap. 13, 1840, d. Sep. 12, 1847; *Rob't.*, Feb. 22, 1846, d. ae. 6 mos.; *Mary*, Ap. 7, d. Sep. 14, 1847; *Mary E.*, June 15, 1849, d. 1852; and two others, d. young. 7. Jas. G., Jan. 16, 1817, lives in Ct. 8. Geo. W., Nov. 5, 1819, m. Priscilla Clark, Nov. 16, 1845, lives on Broadway, and has *Priscilla C.*, Aug. 30, 1846; *Mary L.*, Nov. 2, 1848; and *Ella*, Nov. 29, 1850.

9. Edward, s. Capt. Rob't. L. 5, m. Sarah Stetson, and, it is said, d. in Medford, Mass. He was a shipwright by trade, and whilst in H., was Selectman in 1809 and '10. ch.: 1. Sarah C., Sep. 10, 1806, d. Mar. 23, 1812. 2. Rob't. L., Nov. 2, 1808, m. a Jones, of Boston, lives in Medford, and has 1 ch. living. 3. Edward, Sep. 2, 1810, m. Mary L. Smith, and d. in Arkansas, leaving a son *Josiah*, now in Niagara, N. Y. 4. Sarah. 5. Lusannah. 6. Lydia, m. Sam'l. Clark. 7. Alfred, m. a Parsons. 8. Ebenezer. 9. Alexander. 10. Micah, d.

10. Sam'l., s. Capt. Rob't. L. 5, m. Jerusha, or Rusha Tower, and lives near the Corners, on Broadway. He was Selectman in 1837, and '38. His w. d. Dec. 15, 1849, ae. 63. ch.: 1. Rusha P., July 19, 1806, m. Benj. Josselyn, of H'n. 2. Benj. H. T., Dec. 2, 1808, d. 1834. 3. Horace T., Jan. 27, 1811, prob. d. at Sea. 4. Henry B., Feb. 20, 1813, m., and lives on Staten Island, N. Y. 5. Wm. W., July 4, 1815, d. Oct. 4, 1833. 6. Nancy, Jan. 4, 1818, d. Dec. 4, 1835. 7. Elizab. J., Nov. 8, 1818. 8. John P., Aug. 12, 1822, m. Ann Mitchell, lives at the Corners, and has *Ann E.*, Nov. 3, 1849. 9. Helen M. T., Dec. 22, 1824. 10. Betsey F., 1828, d. young. Another ch. d. July 17, 1820.

ELLIS, John, was of Sandwich, in 1643, and from him descended the Ellises of H. He had a s. Mordecai, Mar. 24, 1650, prob. gr. fa. of Mordecai of H. We find records of the Ellis family in Eng'd., in 1559, at which date John was Dean of Hereford, (Willis's Cathedrals, pp. 536, and 591,) and there is a Coat of Arms in Berry's Gen. Kent, p. 64. There are several distinct families in N. Eng., some of which are quite extensive.

2. Mordecai Ellis, b. Jan. 4, 1718, a desc't. of Jno., of Sandwich, m. Sarah Otis, Sep. 1739, and lived on Circuit st., where Abner Magoun now resides, and there d. June, 1810, ae. 92, and his w. Ap. 22, 1796, ae. 77. He was for 13 yrs. Selectman, from 1750–'63. ch.: 1. Ruth, m. Jno. Bailey, and d. in 1786? 2. Rebecca, May 21, 1741, m. Geo. Bailey. 3. Sarah, Oct. 31. 1742, d. Mar.

13, 1803. 4. David, Aug. 1, 1744, m. 1, Ruth ——, who d. Jan. 10, 1773; and 2, Ann Jenkins. He d., and his wid. m. a Ford. His ch. were: *Jno.*, m. Nabby Sylvester, Ap. 23, 1801; *Ruth*, d. Oct. 15, 1802; and *Nancy*, m. David Gurney, of Ab'n. 5. Mordecai, Ap. 8, 1746. 6. Lucy, Aug. 16, 1748, m. Chas. Otis. 7. Priscilla, Nov. 12, 1750, m. Jno. Little, of Mf'd. 8. Elizab., July 1, 1752, m. Jos. Ramsdell, May 17, 1787. 9. Clark, Aug. 23, 1754. 10. Nath'l., Nov. 14, 1756. 11. Otis, Feb. 8, 1762, d. unm.

3. Mordecai, s. Mordecai 2, m. Priscilla Rogers, of Mf'd., Nov. 1777, was of the Soc. of Friends, lived where Otis Ellis now resides, and there d., and his wid. Sep. 8, 1850, ae. 96. ch.: 1. Huldah, Mar. 3, 1779, m. Nathan Studley, May 18, 1806. 2. Rebecca, Mar. 16, 1781, m. Wm. Gifford, of Falmouth, Mass. 3. Abig., Oct. 16, 1782, m. Jno. Sherman, of N. Y'k. 4. Mordecai, July 16, 1785, drowned in N. River, Jan. 25, 1796. 5. Priscilla, Ap. 30, 1787, m. Theoph. Gifford, of Falm'h. 6. David, June 19, 1789, m. Maria Loud, and lives in Lynn. 7. Sarah, Mar. 25, 1791, m. Sim., s. Jas. Hoxie, of Sandwich, in Aug. 1832, who d. in H., Jan. 28, 1851, ae. 79. No ch. She survives. 8. Otis, Nov. 4, 1795, m. Ruth Barker, of Dart'h., Mass., Ap. 12, 1827, lives on his father's place, and has *Rhoda B.*, May 10, 1830, and *Priscilla R.*, Ap. 26, 1835. 9. Elizab., July 4, 1797, m. Jona. Pratt, of Lynn, Dec. 2, 1817.

4. Clark, s. Mordecai 2, m. Ruth Spooner, of Ab'n., Sep. 26, 1782, and d. Ap. 27, 1836, and his wid. Sep. 19, 1846. Lived on Circuit st. ch.: 1. Lucy, Ap. 21, 1783, m. Barker Ramsdell, Aug. 31, 1810, who d. in Batavia, N. Y., and his wid. in Michi-, ab. 1845, leaving ch. 2. Spooner, Nov., 1787, living unm., on his father's place. 3. Thomas, Oct. 20, 1791, m. Marg't., da. Jona. Josselyn, of Pemb., Mar. 28, 1814, lives in Bridg'r., and has *Jona. W.*, Aug. 16, 1814, m. Meribah Tallman, and is a merchant, in N. Bed., no. ch.; *Jane*, Mar. 3, 1816, m. Capt. Jos. R. Tallman, of N. B., Oct. 29, 1838; *Lucy*, Mar. 3, 1816; *Wm.*, Ap. 25, 1820, d. ae. 21; *Eliza W.*, Jan. 1, 1823, m. Caleb Hobart, merchant, of Bridg'r.; *Thos. H.*, Ap., 1827, clerk in N. Bed.; and *Ruth S.*, Oct. 28, 1829.

6. Nath'l., s. Mordecai 2, m. Mary Ramsdell, July 20, 1787, and d. Feb. 5, 1817, and his wid., Jan. 22, 1848. Lived on his father's place. ch.: 1. Nath'l., Jan., 1790, m. Sally Josselyn, Dec. 21, 1813, lives in E. Bridg'r., and has *Sarah B.*, m. Sam'l. Hawes, Jan. 1, 1835; and *Waterman J.*, Nov., 1825, is m., lives in E. Bridg'r., and has ch. 2. Elizab. B., June, 1791, m. John Estes, Feb. 26, 1815. 3. Francis B., Oct., 1796, m. Lucy L. Corthell, Jan. 9, 1826, and d. Nov. 2, 1843, and his wid. lives with her mother, on Circuit st. ch.: *Lucy L.*, Feb. 13, 1828, d. May 26, 1830; *Francis B.*, Jan. 23, 1831; *Lucy H.*, Aug. 8, 1833, m. Frank Hutchins, and lives in Me.; *Lydia E.*, May 1, 1843, d. same year; and *Calvin C.*, Dec. 17, 1837. 4. Mary H., Jan. 1805, m. Abner Magoun, jr., Ap. 16, 1825. 5. Joseph, Ap. 1807, m. Mary, da. Benj. Bowker, of H'n., Oct. 1830, lives on Circuit st., is a shoemaker, and has *Benj. F.*, Jan. 8, 1831; *Nath'l. B.*, Feb. 18, 1834; and *Joseph T.*, Ap. 21, 1836.

ESTES, Matthew, according to an old Bible, in the possession of Wm. Estes, of H'n., was s. Rob't. and Dorothy E., and was b. in Dover, Eng'd., 3 mo. 28 d. 1645, and m. Philadelphia, da. Renald and Ann Jenkins, of Dover, N. Eng., 4 mo. 14 d., 1676. She d. 10 mo. 25 d. 1721, and he 6 mo. 9 d. 1723. Of their ch., Jno., b. 5 mo. 14 d. 1684, and Richard, b. 7 mo. 2 d. 1686, were of Lynn, in 1703, and signed the letter written by the Quakers of that town to Gov. Dudley. (N. Eng. Gen. Reg. vol. 2, p. 149.) Joseph, who was of Dover, 1719, who m., and whose desc'ts. are in Me., was another of the sons; also Matthew, jr., who d. in H., in 1774, ae. 85. The desc'ts. of the latter are here given, and in their possession is the old family Bible.

2. Matt., s. Matt., with w. Alice, appears in H. ab. 1726, lived on Plain st., where his desc'ts. yet reside, and there d., May 11, 1774, ae. 85, and his wid. Dec. 14, 1778, ae. 84. ch.: 1. Edward, b. ab. 1708, and with w. Patience, appear on the Recs. in 1731, and had ch., but none of his desc'ts. are in the town. Tradition says they removed to Bristol Co., where the name is extant, in the vicinity of Fall River, and N. Bed. 2. Wm., b. ab. 1710. 3. Matt., Dec. 19, 1826, drowned Sept. 24, 1747, in a rash attempt

to swim over N. River, with his clothes on. 4. Sarah, June 8, 1733, m. Thos. Sylvester. 5. Rob't., Jan. 12, 1736. Two ch. d. young.

3. Wm., s. Matt. 2, m. Elizab. Stetson, in 1736, and lived near his fa. ch.: 1. Susanna, June 29, 1737, m. Jno. Barker, ab. 1760. 2. Alice, June 29, 1737. 3. Wm., Feb. 11, 1739, moved to Wareham ? 4. Ruth, Nov. 9, 1741. 5. Richard, June 25, 1745. 6. Elizab., Aug. 10, 1747, d. May 31, 1750. 7. Zilpha, June 1, 1750, d. 1816. 8. Matt., Jan. 17, 1754, m., and left ch., and some of his desc'ts. are in Mf'd.

4. Rob't., s. Matt. 2, a saddler by trade, m. Beulah Wing, of Sandwich, lived on Plain st., and there d., Nov. 26, 1803, and his wid. Sep. 20, 1833, ae. 83. ch.: 1. Zaccheus, Dec. 20, 1760. 2. Rob't., Feb. 11, 1763, d. young. 3. Robert, Ap. 20, 1764, d. young. 4. Hannah, Aug. 7, 1765, m. Jos. Dillingham, of N. Y'k. State, Sep. 9, 1810 ? 5. Abig., d. young. 6. Joseph, m. Ruth Diliingham, and moved to N. Y'k. State, where he has desc'ts. 7. Alice, m. Steph. Rogers, Mf'd., and d. May, 1851; no ch. 8. Benj., m. Sarah Kirby, and d. in Wheatland, N. Y., leaving ch.

5. Richard, s. Wm. 3, m. Mercy Ramsdell, Nov. 4, 1778, and d. Mar. 11, 1797, and his wid. m. Josiah Ellis, of Sandwich, May 23, 1806. Lived on School st., where Josh. Gates now resides. ch.: 1. Betsey, m. 1, Benj. Stetson, Nov. 1, 1798, and 2, Josh. Gates, Sep. 1, 1828, and d. Sep. 8, 1851. No ch. 2. Richard, 1781. 3. Elijah, 1783, d. 1790. 4. Ruth, 1785, m. 1, Dan'l. Barstow, 2, Roland Sylvester, and 3, Joseph Sylvester, of Me. 5. Mercy, 1787, m. 1, Geo. Vaughn, of Middo'., Nov. 26, 1807, and 2, a Borden, of M., and d. Dec. 13, 1840. 6. Edward, Ap. 1790, went off 40 years since. 7. Wm., July 23, 1794.

6. Zaccheus, s. Rob't. 4, m. Elizab. Dillingham, who d. May 17, 1833, and he Feb. 19, 1846, ae. 85. Lived on Plain st., where his son Zaccheus now resides. ch.: 1. Robert, Oct. 20, 1788. 2. Zaccheus, June 14, 1790. 3. Jno., Ap. 28, 1792. 4. Sylvanus, Mar. 16, 1794, m. Ruth S. Ramsdell, Oct. 25, 1818, lives in Mich'n., and has ch. 5. Reuben, Mar 27, 1796, m. Mary B. Ramsdell, Mar. 18, 1819, and lives in N. Y'k. State. Has

ch. 6. Stephen, Ap. 10, 1798, m. Lydia Briggs, Feb. 28, 1819, lives in N. Y'k. State, and has ch. 7. Elijah, Jan. 14, 1800, m. Jerusha Wheeler, June 6, 1824, lives in Mich'n., and has ch. 8. Wm., Feb. 15, 1802, m. 1, Lucy E. Ramsdell, Mar. 14, 1825, who d. in N. Y'k. State; and he has since m. a 2d w., and lives in Baltimore, Md. 9. Rufus, Jan. 11, 1804, is m., and lives in Mich'n. 10. Clarissa, June 27, 1806, m. Nathan Wing, of Sandwich.

7. Richard, s. Rich'd. 5, m. Saba D. Curtis, who d. Nov. 22, 1831. He lives in E. Ab'n. ch: 1. Richard, July 26, 1805. 2. Saba D., m. Sam'l. Barstow, Oct. 28, 1830. 3. Betsey, m. Danl. Barstow, Dec. 30, 1830. 4. Priscilla L., Oct. 31, 1815, d. 1817. 5. Elijah, Jan. 17, 1818, d. same day. 6. Edward, Jan. 10, 1819, m. Betsey Stoddard, of Ab'n. 7. Elijah, May 30, 1824.

8. Wm., s. Rich'd. 5, m. Bethia Josselyn, Sep. 10, 1815, lives in H'n., is a blacksmith, and has, 1. Wm., Mar. 29, 1816, m. 1, Jane Lewis, of Pemb.; 2, Emeline Stetson; and 3, Lauretta Wing; lives in Sandwich, and has ch. 2. Lucy J., Dec. 15, 1817, m. Saml. H. Reed, of H. 3. Florin, Nov. 15, 1819, d. Aug. 28, 1820. 4. Florin, m. 1, Lydia Barker, of H'n.; and 2, Harriet, Barker; lives in H'n., and has *Betsey*, and *Florin*. 5. Mercy B., Dec. 3, 1824, m. Alvin Studley. 6. Calvin J., Mar. 8, 1827, m. Julia A. Sprague, lives in H'n., and has *Cary Lee*. 7. Helen, Mar. 8, 1831. 8. Dorothy J., Jan. 3, 1834. 9. Dan'l. B., Jan 22, 1839.

9. Rob't., s. Zaccheus 6., m. Experience Studley, lives in E. Ab'n., is a blacksmith and machinist, and has, 1. Elizab. D., Ap. 12, 1812, m. Josiah Torrey, of Ab'n., Jan. 5, 1830, and has sev. ch. 2. Rob't., July 4, 1815, m. Ann M. Morse, had *Rob't. W.*, and *Ellen M.*, and d. 1841. 3. Clarissa B., Oct. 27, 1818, m. Cyrus Pool, of Ab'n., Aug. 9, 1835, and d. Mar., 1843, leaving 1 ch., wh. d. soon after. 4. Nancy J., Aug. 9, 1820, m. Washington Jenkins, of Ab'n. 5. Beulah W., Oct. 3, 1823, d. May 27, 1835. 6. Rufus T., Sep. 20, 1826, m. 1, Sarah J. Tribou, who d. Dec. 29, 1850, and 2, Marg't. Binney; lives in E. Ab'n., and has *Alonzo C.*, Oct. 31, 1850. 7. Warren, Nov. 7, 1829, m Marietta Torrey, 1852. 8. Geo. H., Mar. 27, 1832.

10. Zaccheus, s. Zach. 6, m. Mary Dillingham, Nov. 2, 1818, lives on his father's place, and has, 1. Elizab., Aug. 3, 1819, m. Philander Studley, May 11, 1837. 2. Henry C., Jan. 29, 1822, m. Sarah A Torrey, of Wey'h., in May 1844, lives in W., and has *Mary E.*, July, 1849. 3. Mary A., Dec. 3, 1830.

11. Jno., s. Zach. 6, m. Elizab. B. Ellis, Nov. 26, 1815, lives on Pleasant st., and has, 1. Jno. W., Dec. 16, 1816, m. Polly Whiting, Dec. 30, 1841, and has, *Alonzo W.*, d.; and *Mary W.* 2. Elizab. B., Dec. 22, 1819, m. Hiram B. Bonney, of H. 3. Mary R., Aug. 19, 1821, m. Allen F. Bonney, of H. 4. Ruth D., m. Dan'l Willis, of H.

12. Joseph J., s. Joseph, and w. Rebecca, of Bethel, Me., and prob. a desc't. of Joseph, s. Matt. 1, m. Mary L., da. Josiah Torrey, of Ab'n., Mar. 27, 1851, lives in E. Ab'n., and is clerk in the store of Mr. Ellis. The mo. of Mr. E., m. Otis Perry, of H'n.

FARNHAM, or FARNUM, Rufus, of Hampton, Ct., s. Zebediah, b. Mar. 9, 1796, m. 1, Loisa C. Reed, of Ct., Sep. 2, 1798, who d. Feb. 17, 1805; 2, Mrs. Elizab. Kelley, da. Geo. Langley, Esq., of Boston, Sep. 2, 1811, who d. Jan. 29, 1814; and 3, Priscilla, wid. of Geo. Langley, jr., and da. of Capt. Tilden Crocker, June 12, 1815; was formerly a jeweller, in Boston, and now resides in H., near N. River bridge, in the old "builder Sylvester house," which was improved as a tavern for a time by Capt. Crooker. ch.: 1. Rufus, July 23, 1799, d. July 6, 1805. 2. Albert A., May 29, 1802, m. Eliza Wakefield, of Eng'd., and lives in N. York. (By 2d,) 3. Sarah W., Aug. 13, 1812, d. Sep. 25, 1813. (By 3d,) Loisa R., Jan. 13, 1823, m. Genl. Jas. D. Thompson, of N. Bed., Dec. 12, 1843.

Richd. Fitz Gerald the first schoolmaster in H., m. Marg't. Snowdon, of Scit., Ap. 1729, and d. Feb. 11, 1746, and his wid. Mar. 22, 1763. (See p. 87–8.) ch.: 1. Marg't., May 23, 1733, m. Hezekiah Bowker ? Ap. 7, 1765. 2. Catherine, Mar. 16, 1736, d. June 8, 1752.

FOSTER, Joseph, of Mason, N. H., s. Jona., m. Grace Turner, in 1809, lives on Cedar st., and has, 1. Reuben T., Feb. 16, 1810, d. 1812. 2. Louisa, Sep. 27, 1811, m. 1, Asa Harlow, and 2, Jno. Puffer, Aug. 15, 1831. 3. Reuben T., Jan. 20, 1814, m. Augusta J. Joice, and d. in 1848. No. ch. 4. And. J., Jan. 4, 1816, m. Rachel J. Lane, Dec. 6, 1838. No. ch. 5. Sylvia, Ap. 29, 1818, m. Ensign Crooker. 6. Josh., Nov. 23, 1820, m. Rosamond Scott, Nov. 23, 1846, and has *Anna*, *Emma*, and a da. b. 1852. 7. Mary, Dec. 16, 1824, m. Philander Lindsey. 8. Joseph E., June 29, 1827. 9. Harriet A., July 29, 1830, m. Jno. S. Tower, of Ab'n.

GARDNER, a name common in H'm., from which town most of the Gardners of Plym'h. Co. originated. It is found in N. Eng. as early as 1640, at which date Edmond, and Thomas, were made freemen. The name was anciently spelled *Garnet*.

2. Seth Gardner s. Joshua, of H'm., b. 1770, m. Susanna Hatch, of H., May 8, 1798, and d. in H., Nov. 25, 1852, ae. 82. His wid. survives. ch.: 1. Thomas J., Esq., Selectman in 1834, and '35, and Rep. in 1834, and '53, m. Elvira, da. Capt. Edward Curtis, lives on Mill st., is proprietor of the old Curtis Mills, and has one da., *Ellen*. Mr. G. is a man highly esteemed in the town, for his intelligence, and integrity. A view of his residence is given on the next page. 2. Hiram, Ap., 1803, a farmer, lives in the Ebenezer Curtis House, at the corner of Mill st., m. 1, Rebecca, da. Dr. David Bailey, June 5, 1831; and 2, Lucinda, da. Geo. Bailey; and has *Alfred*, Oct., 1831, d. Nov., 1848; *Anne R.*, Nov. 21, 1833, d. Dec. 17, 1842; *Seth*, Mar. 6, 1836; *Eben'r. P.*; (by 2d,) *Charlotte S.*, May 17, 1842; *Anne R.*, Feb. 8, 1844; *George*, Nov. 2, 1846; and *Curtis*, July 24, 1850, d. July 26, 1851? 3. Abigail, Oct. 25, 1804, m. Thos. Jones, of Scit., Nov. 13, 1831, and has one son, *Marcellus*. 4. Israel H., July 28, 1808, m. Harriet, da. Capt. Elisha Barrell, Nov. 15, 1830, lives with Capt. B., and has *John B.*, Sep. 25, 1831, and *Mary B.*, Ap. 29, 1836.

RESIDENCE OF T. J. GARDNER, ESQ.

3. Noah, s. Noah, of H'm., b. June 9, 1778, m. Patience, da. Jos. Damon, lives on Whiting st., is a shoemaker, and has one son, Henry W., Mar. 22, 1821, m. Hannah E. Ames, of Mf'd., Nov. 2, 1845, lives on Whiting st., and has *James H.*, Ap. 7, 1847; *Reuben N.*, Nov. 9, 1848, d. 1849; and *Sarah A.*, Feb. 10, 1851.

4. Minot T., s. Amos, of Ab'n., b. Feb. 24, 1826, m. Abigail W., da. Elias Pratt, of Scit., June 5, 1851, lives on Whiting st., in the house with Justus Whiting, and has one son, b. March 1, 1852.

5. Thomas H., b. Nov. 18, 1818, s. Alexander, of H'n., m. 1, Sally B., da. Thos. Chubbuck, and had 1. Mary A., June 30, 1837, d. Oct. 18, 1840; 2. Robert C., Jan. 23, 1839; 3. Henry C., Mar. 13, 1841; 4. Jno. D., Mar. 24, 1843; and 5. Lorenzo T., Mar. 30, 1845. His first w. d. May 23, 1845, and he m. 2, Debo., wid. of Joseph Curtis, Aug. 31, 1845, lives in South Scit., and has by her, 6. Mary A., July 23, 1846; and 7. Abby S., March 13, 1849.

GARRATT, Alfred C., M. D., s. Richard, of Brookhaven, L. I., was b. Oct. 3, 1813, received his preparatory education at Lenox Acad., and grad. at Columbia Coll., as A.B.; and as M.D., at the Coll. of Phys. and Surgs., N. Y., in 1835–6; studied med. with Duryee, a distinguished French physician, and received an additional degree of M. D., at the Berkshire Med. Coll. His health being feeble, he sett. for a time in Fulton Co., Ills., and was Surgeon to the U. S. Dragoons, at Fort Des Moines. Leaving the West, he travelled through the U. S, and the Brit. Prov's., and also visited the W. I. Islands, the Spanish Main, Venezuela, Hayti, &c., and was U. S. Vice Consul for two years, at Port au Prince. He m. 1, Harriet L., da. Geo. W. Taylor, Esq., of N. York, Oct. 13, 1836, and by her had Harriet L., Jan. 20, 1838, and Charles S., Oct. 23, 1843. His w. d. Jan. 5, 1847, and he m. 2, Elizabeth, only da. of Capt. Joshua Howe, of Ab'n., Jan. 19, 1848, and by her has Joshua H., Feb. 19, 1850, and Alfred, Jan 7, 1853. Dr. G. was sett. in Ab'n. for a few years, as a physician and apothecary, and now resides in H., near the Four Corners, in the fine mansion house, erected by Rev. J. G. Cooper, formerly Rector of St. Andrew's Church, and lately occupied by Dr. J. B. Fobes. A view of his residence is annexed.

RESIDENCE OF DR. ALFRED C. GARRATT.

GOODRICH, George W., m. Celia Chubbuck, of Ab'n., lives on Walnut st., and has George, William, Nathan, Celia, Joseph, Perez, Sewall, and Eliza.

GRAY, Thomas, of Dublin, with his w. Sarah, was in in Scit. 1730, and had ch.: 1. George, moved to Me. 2. William, m. 1, Abigail Perry, 1753, and 2, Sarah Hayden, 1765, and sett. in Boston. 3. Lucy, m. a Lane, of Cohassett. 4. Abigail, m. Dwelley Clapp, of Scit. 5. Elizabeth, Oct. 18, 1741, m. Samuel Brooks, of H. 6. Mary, Nov. 24, 1745. 7. Sarah. 8. James, 1755.

2. James, s. Thos., was a carpenter by trade, lived on the lane W. of Rocky Swamp, m. Bethia Curtis, in 1785, and had, 1. Abigail, June 3, 1787, m. Amos Dunbar. 2. Wm., prob. d. at sea. 3. Harrison, of the firm of Hilliard & Gray, publishers and booksellers, Boston; m. Clarissa Eastham, of Exeter, N. H., d., and his wid. returned to E. 4. Bethia, m. Capt. Thos. Simmons, of H. 5. Rebecca, June 1797, m. Amos Dunbar, now of South Scit. 6. Elizab., Aug. 22, 1802, d. Aug., 1824.

GROSE, GROCE, or GROSS, Edmond, was in Boston, in 1642, and there d. in 1655, the Inv. of his Est. being entered 5 d. 2 mo., 1655, on the Prob. Rec. Suff., Vol. 3, p. 21, in which he speaks of land at Muddy River, &c. His estate was appraised at £185, and Jere. Huckins, and Lt. Jas. Johnson, were appointed to administer in behalf of the wid. and ch. The estate was in debt to Matt. Grose, Mr. Cole, Clement Grose, Goodman Weeden, Mr. Starr, jr., Matt. Barnes, Mr. Starr, senr., Brother Burton, Goody Baker? Sister Davis, Mrs. Bowyer, Mr. Garret's fa. in Eng'd., for liquors, and to Barnard Squire. He left a s. Isaac? also a s. Simon? who m. Mary Bond, of Boston, in Oct., 1675, (N. E. Gen. Reg. 2, 254,) and sett. in H'm., where he was fa. of Simon, Aug. 11, 1676; Thomas, Nov. 4, 1678; Jno., Ap. 13, 1681; Josiah, Aug. 2, 1683; Micah, Feb. 20, 1685; Alice, Ap. 26, 1689; and Abigail, June 28, 1692. Most of these m. and left desc'ts. (See H'm. Rec.) Edmond Gross, a desc't. of Edmond, of Boston, was in H'm. in 1700, where he d. Mar. 18, 1727–8, and his w. Martha, Sep. 19, 1726. He had Elizab., Jan. 13, 1700; Anne, Feb. 22, 1701; Edmund, May 10, 1705; Obadiah, Mar. 28, 1708; and Martha, Mar. 29, 1711.

We incline to the opinion that there was also another son, Isaac b. ab. 1713, and not entered on the H'm. Rec. Edmond, son of Edmond, m. Olive Sylvester, in 1736, and sett. in Scit., where his desc'ts. yet reside, and was fa. of Elisha, whose sons John and Lewis, are still living in So. Scit.

2. Isaac, m. Ruth Sylvester, Oct. 27, 1740, and d. Oct. 17, 1773. His ch. were, 1. Mary, Mar. 21, 1742, m. Morris H. Clark, Ap. 2, 1789. 2. Sarah, Ap. 21, 1743, d. May 6, 1774. 3. Ruth, 1746, d, Sep. 6, 1820. 4. Thos., 1747, d. June 26, 1798. 5. Saml., 1749. 6. Jacob, a mariner, went off many years since. 7. Zilpha, 1752, d. Mar. 17, 1808. 8. Elizab., d. July 23, 1775. 9. Isaac, 1756, d. July 28, 1804.

3. Samuel, s. Isaac 2, m. 1, Elizab. Torrey, Feb. 24, 1780; and 2, Submit Gardner, of H'm., Mar. 3, 1791, who d. Sep. 15, 1816, ae. 45, and he Nov. 16, 1817. A soldier in the Rev'n. ch.: 1. Elizab. T., m. 1, Nathl. Pratt, Hfx., Nov. 29, 1803; and 2, Joseph Sylvester, of H. 2. Mary, m. David Turner, Aug. 3, 1800. 3. Ruth, m. Thos. Winslow, Feb. 20, 1800. (By 2d,) 4. Sarah S., m. Harris W. Totman, of Scit. He d. 1852. 5. Pamelia, m. Wm. Lucas, Plym'h. 6. Sylvia, m. Nathl. Bennet. 7. Nathl., drowned. 8. Melzar, Dec. 5, 1808, is m., lives in Cohas't., and has ch. 9. Ansel G., July 14, 1803. 10. Nathl., is m., and lives in E. Ab'n.

4. Ansel G., s. Saml. 3, m. Rebecca, da. Laban Wilder, Nov. 27, 1816, lives in So. Scit., and has, 1. Henry A., Mar. 12, 1826, m. Julia A. Curtis, July 11, 1847, lives in So. Scit., and has *Geo. H.*, Nov. 22, 1850. 2. Charles, June 15, 1828, m. Mary A. Hobart, July 11, 1847, lives in So. Scit., and has *Chas. W.*, Ap., 1849. 3. Dexter, June 9, 1830. 4. Nelson, Aug. 12, 1832. 5. Rebecca, Sep. 22, 1834. 6. Mary, Sep. 20, 1836, m. Perkins Clapp. 7. Helen M., Dec. 1, 1838, d. Oct. 1, 1840. 8. Jno., Dec. 1, 1840. 9. Geo. W., Jan. 14, 1844, d. Mar. 17, 1847. 10. Edward E., Sep. 14, 1845, d. Ap. 27, 1846. 11. Ellen, June 24, 1848. 12. Emma, Feb. 27, 1851.

GURNEY, Joseph W., s. Melvin, of Ab'n., and prob. a desc't. of Saml., of Ab'n., 1694, m. Iantha E. Studley, May 25, 1837, lives on Pleasant st., is a shoemaker, and has, 1. Warren S., June

5, 1839. 2. Matilda S., May 8, 1841. 3. Lysander F., June 8, 1843. 4. Ann E., Dec. 20, 1847.

2. Benoni, s. Benoni, of Ab'n., m. Eliza W. Delano, Oct. 14, 1846, lives on King st., and has, 1. Elenor J., Feb. 19, d. Sep. 18, 1847. 2. Willard A., Ap. 17, 1848. 3. Benoni H., Jan. 21, 1851.

HALL, Benj. B., s. Danforth, and w. Betsey (Trouant), of Mf'd., m. Nancy N., da. Nathl. Curtis, Nov. 26, 1838, lives on Centre st., in the Amos Bates house, and has, 1. Benj. E., Ap. 11, 1840. 2. Nancy A., Oct. 30, 1842. 3. Sarah C., Jan. 18, d. Feb. 11, 1846. 4. Helen, Oct. 31, 1847. 5. Francis A., Dec. 1, 1850.

HAMMOND, Henry, b. Feb. 3, 1825, and Joseph, b. 1834, sons Francis, of Pemb., with their mo., a wid., live on Wash'n. st., near East st.

HARDING, Seth W., s. Jno., of E. Bridg'r., and prob. a desc't. of Jno., of Braintree, 1707, m. Cynthia J. Tribou, lives on Centre st., is a shoemaker, and had Everett E., June 8, 1849, d. Oct. 27, 1851.

(William Hatch) a merchant, of Sandwich, England, with his w. Jane, five children, and servants, embarked in the Hercules, of Sandwich, John Witherley, master, for N. Eng., in 1634, with many others, who sett. in Scit.; and the same year we find him in Scit., living on Kent st. He was the first ruling elder of the 2d Church, in 1643, and was an active and useful man in the settlement of the town. His desc'ts., in Plym'h. Co., and elsewhere, are very numerous. Of these, Jeremiah bought the place of John Hanmer, ab. 1680, now occupied by Albert White, Esq., (see p. 24,) but of his desc'ts., none remain in Hanover. Israel Hatch, of Mf'd, had sons Jno., and Thos., who were of H., and some of their desct's. are still in the town.

2. John, b. May, 1739, s. Israel, of Mf'd., m. Barshaway Turner, 1760, and built the house on Main st., in which his son Jno. now lives. He was a Capt. in the Rev'n., and d. May 1, 1809. and his wid. in 1824. ch.: 1. Barshaway, May 30, 1761, m. Snow Curtis, of H. 2. Jno., July 28, 1762, d. Ap. 27, 1775, 3. Ezekiel T., June 14, 1764, m. Han'h. Bailey, May 8, 1788, and d. Feb. 1, 1797, leaving ch. 4. Melzar, May 8, 1766. 5. Ruth, Oct. 15, 1768, d. Mar. 7, 1775. 6. Sibyl, Sep. 7, 1770. Yet living, in H. 7. Lucy, Mar. 12, 1772, m. Ezra Beal, Pemb., Ap. 15, 1790. 8. Rachel, Mar. 1, 1774, m. Josh. Dwelley, Mar. 16, 1797. 9. Jno., Ap. 27, 1776, (m. Nancy Cleaves, of Beverly, who is d., and he lives on his father's place. Of his ch., *Lucy*, m. Wm. E. Smith, of H.; *Sibyl*, m. Danl. Dill, of Hull; John, is living in H., on Circuit st., m. Elizab. E. Stetson, Aug. 25, 1836, and has Ann E., Aug. 7, 1837; Sarah, Nov. 29, 1838; Alice J., Ap. 6, 1840; Benj. S., Sep. 22, 1842, d. Sep. 9, 1843; and Benj. S., Ap. 2, 1848; *Benj. C.*, lives in Taunton, and is m.; and the wid. of *Ezekiel T.*, is living in H., on Main st. There is also a da. *Ruth*, living with her fa.) 10. Gamaliel, Feb. 14, 1778, m. 1, Mary, da. Capt. Edward Wilder, of H'm., and sett. in Beverly; and, 2. Ann Bowker. He is d. Left sev. ch. 11. Ruth, Jan. 5, 1780, m. Stephen Bailey, Oct. 27, 1816.

3. Melzar, s. Jno. 2, m. Sally Barstow, Jan. 3, 1802, and d. Jan. 5, 1807, and his wid. Dec. 1, 1831, ae. 51. ch.: 1. Melzar, 1803, m. Ruth T., da. Benj. Bass, May 25, 1828, lives on Main st., in the house erected by himself, and has one son, Melzar, Oct. 2, 1832, m. Sarah E., da. Capt. James Farrow, and has a son *Walter*, b. 1852. 2. Sarah, 1805, m. Joshua Cushing. 3. Barshaway T., 1808, m. Jacob Sprague, Nov. 15, 1829.

HERSEY, David, b. Nov., 1785, s. Stephen, of E. Bridg'r., and a desc't. of Wm., of Ab'n., 1719, m. Jane, da. Col. J. B. Barstow, Nov. 12, 1816, who d. April 14, 1847. He lives on Broadway, in the old Bardin house. ch.: 1. Jacob, Dec. 31, 1816, is a ship-master; m. Frances G., da. Judge Kilborn Whitman, of Pemb., and lives in P.; no ch. 2. Jane B., March 8,

1820, d. March 1, 1847. 3. Robert, Ap. 10, 1824, m. Lucy S., da. Chas. Dyer, in 1848, lives with his fa., and has *Jane B.*, May 23, 1849. 4. Mary, Dec. 17, 1830.

HENDERSON, Wm., son Sam'l., b. Oct. 8, 1796, m. Mary Mann, Mar. 11, 1821, and d. in California, in 1828. His wid. lives on Main st. ch.: 1. Wm. L., May 18, 1823, m. Sarah Morse, Sept. 1, 1834, is in Cala., and has *Wm. F.*, *Jno. P.*, and *Charles C.* 2. Mary M., Sept. 27, 1830, m. Capt. Duncan T. Stoddard, Sept. 1851. 3. Sam'l. A., Aug. 5, 1833, m. Rebecca Spear, June 15, 1851. 4. Lloyd G., Jan. 1836. 5. Joseph M., June 22, 1840.

HOLLIS, Silas, s. Jno., m. Hannah B. Dwelley, lives on Broadway, is a carpenter, and has 1. Mary D., Aug. 1833, m. Chas. E. Thayer, of H. 2. Lydia A. S., Jan. 1836. 3. Hannah J., Feb. 1838. 4. Elizab. A., Mar. 9, 1844.

2. Abel, of Plym'h., m. Betsey Pratt, Nov. 1820, lives on Broadway, and has 1. Abigail, Feb. 27, 1826, m. Zenas Sturtevant. 2. Josh., May 16, 1828. 3. Betsey S., Sep. 9, 1833, d. 1834. 4. Betsey S., Jan. 4, 1836. 5. Sam'l., Dec. 8, 1841. 6. Lorenzo, Mar. 20, 1844, d. 1848.

HOLMES, Rev. Cyrus, s. Nath'l., of Hf'x., b. July 9, 1800, stud. at Phillips Acad., Exeter, N. H., grad. at Dart. Coll. 1828, and at And. 1831; was Princ. of the Acad. in Woburn, 1831-'35; Tutor of the Clas'l. Dep't of the High School, Northampton; after which he preached for a time, but ill health compelled him to abandon his profession, and in 1840, he came to H., and was Princ. of the Acad. till his death; and Rep. in 1848-'49. He d. Aug. 16, 1849, and his wid., Sophia A., da. Dr. Ant'y. Collamore, of Pemb., whom he m. June 17, 1832, survives, and lives in the Judge Cushing house. ch.: 1. Elizab., Ap. 24, 1833, d. Sep. 20, 1834. 2. Cyrus C., Oct. 2, 1836. 3. Luther W., Sep. 15, 1839. 4. Sophia A., Ap. 20, 1842. 5. Thos. B., May 14, 1844. 6. Eliza C., and 7. Nancy, Mar. 10, d. July, 1848.

HOUSE, Sam'l., was of Bos'n., prob. the same as Sam'l. of Scit., 1634; and Sam'l. of the 6th gen. from him, is now living in H., m. 1, Ruth Turner, and 2, Elizab. T. White, and has 1. Sam'l., May 15, 1823, m. Mary C. Josselyn, lives in H'n., and has ch. 2. Jas. W., May 17, 1827.

2. Julius, a desc't. of Sam'l. the first, m. Ruth Bailey, lives on King st., and has sons Julius and William.

HOWLAND, Alvin, s. Jona., of H'n., b. Nov. 20, 1808, m. Marcia Josselyn, Nov. 20, 1838, lives on Summer st., is a shoemaker, and has 1. Alonzo H., Aug. 4, 1839. 2. Charles A., June 1842.

JACOBS FAMILY.

Arms: A chev. gu., between three wolves heads, erased, ppr.

Crest: A wolf, pass. ppr.

JACOB, or JACOBS, an English family, probably of Jewish descent, settled in Berkshire, Middlesex, Suffolk, Warwickshire, and Wiltshire. William was among the gentry of Berkshire, in 1433; Nicholas was of Suffolk; Humphrey was of the gentry of Warwickshire, in 1433; and Thomas was of Wiltshire, and d. in 1646, ae. 73. (See Fuller's Worthies of Eng. passim.) The coats of arms of different branches, vary in some points, but agree in the main, tigers heads being occasionally substituted for wolves heads. (See Betham's Baronetage, and Burke's General Armory.)

Nicholas, the ancestor of a portion of the families in N. Eng., according to Dan'l. Cushing's record, "with his w., and 2 ch., and their cosen Thos. Lincoln, weaver, came from old H'm., and sett. in this H'm., in 1633."[1] He resided a short time at Wat.,[2] and was made freeman in 1635—6.

In June, 1635, there were granted to him 6 acs. of Planting ground, upon "weariall Hill." June 4, 1636, the first of the Great Lots next to Wey'h. river was assigned to him; and a lot of 6 acs. "at the head of the plain next to Edward Gillman, his bro. in law." He had also a house lot in Bachelor river, which he sold to Mr. Gillman. Mar. 23, 1637, he was one of the nine Selectmen. July 6, 1640, he was one of the 9 to divide Conohasset, where he had land. In 1648—49, he was Rep. to the Gen'l. Court. In 1655, he was one of the 3 Commissioners to be presented to the Court for the year ensuing. He d. June 5, 1657, leaving an estate of £393 8s. 6d., and a will, in which he gives legacies "to wife Mary, £30; to Joseph, Hannah, and Debo. Loring, £10 each; to son John, a double portion; to son Joseph, to da. Mary, w. of Jno. Otis, to da. Elizab., w. of Jno. Thaxter, to da. Sarah, w. of Jno. Cushing, and to das. Debo., and Han'h., equal shares." ch.: 1. John, b. in Eng. 2. Elizab., b. in Eng., m. Jno Thaxter, Dec., 1648. 3 Mary, b. in H'm., m. Jno. Otis, 1652—3. 4. Sarah, m. Jno. Cushing, 1653. 5. Hannah, bap. Feb. 23, 1640, m. Lt. Matt. Cushing? (See her brother's will.) 6. Josiah, bap. Nov. 6, 1642, d. young. 7. Debo. L., bap. Nov. 26, 1643, m. Cap. Nath'l Thomas, M'fd. Jan. 19, 1664, had 10 ch., and d. in 1696. 8. Joseph, bap. May 10, 1646.

NOTE: the wid. of Mr. J., m. Jno. Beal, of H'm., in 1659.

(Captain John,) son Nicholas, m. 1, Margery, da. of Anthony Eames, Oct. 20, 1653 who d. Ap. 7, 1659; and 2, Mary, da. Geo. Russell, Oct. 3, 1661; was of Glad Ti-

[1] Lincoln's Bi. Cent address, p. 42. [2] Ibid, p. 37.
[3] Deane's Scit. p. 292, and Prob. Rec. Suff.

dings Plain ; surveyor, 1658 ; one of the 13 who, in 1660, opposed Capt. Josh. Hobart's being freed from taxes "on acc't. of being Capt." In 1670, 10 shares in each of the 1, 2, 3, and 4, divsn's. of land were assigned him. In 1680, he was one of the 11 who voted against building the old meeting house, now Mr. Richardson's, where it at present stands. His quarterly tax this year was £3 4s. 6d. In 1682, he was Capt. of the Anc. and Hon. Artil'y. Co. ; and in 1685, he was one of Com'ee. of 8, to lay out highways in the Conohasset grant. He was much employed in town business ; and was a man of enterprise and shrewdness. He d. Sep. 18, 1693, leaving a will, in which he gives to his bro. Joseph, a piece of fresh meadow, then in his occupancy ; to his eldest son David, £50, over and above what he had already had ; —to Peter, and Sam'l., a saw mill and fulling mill, with the ponds and land adjoining, on both sides of the river, &c. ; and to Peter, £60, for his services since of age ; to John, house and land at Cohasset, at Cold Spring, occupied by Francis Howell, together with 70 shares in the 1st div. of lands, if he lives to have heirs, otherwise, 1-2 of the same to David's eldest son, and the other 1-2 to Peter, and Sam'l. ;—to da. Mary Bisbe, 12 acs., at G't. Plain, bought of Jno. Otis, and formerly owned by Thos. Turner, and £17, to be paid in six years ; to da. Sarah Hawkes, 4 lots at the Ware river and £20, to be paid in six years ;—to da. Jael Cushing, home land, bought of Jno. Magoone, and £10, in 6 years ;—to Elizab. Turner, 2 shares in the Major's purchase, and £50, in 6 years ;—to da. Hannah, £100, 1-2 in 1 year, and the rest in 6 years ;—to da. Debo., £100, 1-2 when of age, and the rest in 7 years ; to da. Lydia, 1-2 corn mill at Wey'h., and £20, when 18 years of age ; —and to da. Abigail, barn, upland, &c., at Cohasset, at a place called Beach Island,—the profits to be for her education till of age. He speaks of his gr. fa. Russell, for whom he makes provision in his old age ; also of his fa. Russell, and of his bros. in-law, Capt. Nath'l. Thomas, and Lt. Matt. Cushing ; and his estate was appraised at £1298 5s.[1] ch.: 1. John, Oct. 2, 1654, slain by the Indians, near his father's house, Ap. 19, 1676. 2. Mary,

[1] Prob. Rec. Suff. Aug. 1693, and the files.

March 30, 1657, called Mary Bisbe in her father's will; prob. m. Sam'l. Bisbe ? 3. Sarah, Sep. 20, 1657, m. Jas. Hawkes, July 9, 1678. (By 2d,) 4. Jael, Sep. 7, 1662, m. Matt. Cushing, 1684, and d. Dec. 23, 1708. 5. David, June 20, 1664. 6. Elizab., Ap. 11, 1666, m. Elisha Turner ? 7. Peter, Feb. 12, 1667. 8. Hannah, Dec. 26, 1669. 9. Sam'l., Nov. 30, 1671. 10. Debo., Aug. 15, 1674, d. Aug. 22, 1675. 11. Debo., May 8, 16 77, m. Jno. Cushing ? Dec. 27, 1694. 12. John, July 13, 1679, prob. m. Sarah, da. Dan'l. Cushing, Feb. 19, 1711, was of Cohasset, and Dea. of the Church, but left no ch. on record. 13. Lydia, Ap. 18, 1681, m. Jno. Gould, Hull, Jan. 17, 1699. 14. Abigail, Nov. 13, 1683, m. Nath'l Gill, Aug. 15. 1705.

3. Joseph Jacob son Nicholas, was freem., in H'm., and had lot of land near Great Hill, and 4 shares in the divis. of Lands in 1670. He was a carpenter by trade, and by wife Hannah, had 1. Joseph, Feb. 20, 1672, prob. d. young. 2. Joseph, Ap., 10, 1675. 3. Benj., Ap. 10, 1680. 4. Mary, Sep. 16, 1686, d. Mar. 22, 1695. This is all the record we have found of the family. He is named in the will of his bro. John.

4. David Jacob s. Capt. John 2, sett. in Scit., ab. 1688, when he purchased the lands of his uncle, Geo. Russell, on the south-east of Stockbridge's mill, anciently the Stedman place, and his house stood where stands that of the late Sam'l Hatch. He is called a "weaver" on the Prob. Rec. Suff., and was an active man in the town, of good education, Dea. of the church, and always employed in public affairs, and as a school-master. He m. 1, Sarah, da. Jno. Cushing, Esq., 1689, she being his cousin ; and 2, Mary Cushing. ch.: 1. David, Oct. 28, 1690, prob. d. young. 2. Mary, July 15, 1692, m. Josh. Barker. 3. Sarah, Sep. 15, 1694, m. Jededi. Lincoln. 4. Elisha, Oct. 30, 1696, d. young. 5. Debo., Ap. 22, 1698, m. Dr. Isaac Otis, Scit., the first regularly edu. phys. sett. in Scit., and a gent. of uncommon acccomplishments of

person and mind. He d. 1718.[1] 6. Lydia, Aug. 1, 1700. 7. Josh., Mar. 31, 1702. 8. Hannah, Ap. 27, 1704, m. Jno. Sparrowhawk, Plym'h., Dec. 2, 1715; and 2., Sam'l. Cushing. 9. Joseph, Aug. 16, 1707. 10. Benj., Ap. 10, 1709. 11. Elisha, Oct. 7, 1711. Left no desc'ts. on record.

5. Peter, s. Capt. Jno. 2, m. Hannah, da. Sam'l. Allen, of Barnstable, is called a "Fuller," on the Prob. Rec. Suff., and lived and d. in H'm. ch.: 1. Jno., Oct. 7, 1694, m. Mercy Farrow, 1724, was Rep. 1726, and had *Jno.*, 1724, *Mary*, 1726, and *Allyn*. 1728. 2. Hannah, July 22, 1695, m. Jacob Loring. 3. Mary, Sep. 19, 1698, m. Abel Cushing. 4. Elizab., Ap. 9, 1700, m. Thos. Andrews, H'm. 5. Peter, Oct. 25, 1701. 6. Jael, May 10, 1703, m. Benj. Loring, Dec. 24, 1728. 7. Lydia, Ap. 16, 1705, m. Rev. Ne'h. Hobart, Cohas't., Jan. 14, 1724, and d. Feb. 12, 1736. 8. Joseph, Aug. 11, 1706, d. young. 9. Joseph, Ap. 14. 1708, m. Ruth Wilson, and had *Mary*,, 1735, *Ruth*, 1737, and 1 da. d. young. 10. Abig., Dec. 3, 1709, m. Josh. Herrick, Beverly, Sep. 8. 1737. 11. Sarah, July 13, 1712, m. Jona. Lazell, Dec. 21 1743. 12. Debo., Aug. 28, 1714, m. Jas. Fearing, Nov. 22, 1733.

6. Sam'l. s. Jno. 2, m. Elizab. ——, is called a "husbandman," in the Prob. Rec. Suff., and d. intestate, Oct. 29. 1695, leaving one s., Sam'l., b. June 27, 1695, of whom his mo. was appointed guardian, and who sett. in Pemb., being called Lt. Sam'l., on the Pemb. Rec. By w. Susanna, he had, 1. Seth, m. Penelope Burton, Oct. 23, 1751, and had *Sam'l.*, (m. Mary Sprague, and had Jno. who m. Grace Larned,) Seth, Stephen, and Sam'l.; and 2. Burton.

7. Joshua, s. Capt. David 4, m. Mary James, Ap. 7, 1726, and lived in Scit., where I. R. Jacobs, Esq., now resides, having built that house. He was an early proprietor of the Jacobs Mills, with his bro. Dr. Joseph, and was an extensive landholder, and a man of industry, and active business habits. He d. Dec. 9, 1784, ae. 82, and his wid. July 22, 1803, ae. 99. ch..: 1. Sarah, Nov. 2, 1727, d. Aug. 13, 1753. 2. David, Jan. 16, 1729. 3.

[1] See the Otis' Geneology, in the N. E. Gen. Reg.

Mary, July 17, 1732, m. Col. Jno. Cushing, of Scit., and d., Ap. 27, 1814, ae. 82. 4. Jno., May 23, 1735. 5. Joshua, June 23, 1737. 6. Eunice, July 23, 1740, d. Dec. 4. 1784. 7. James, Mar. 6. 1742. 8. Lucy, Nov. 3, 1748, m. Nath'l. Jacobs, Jan. 6, 1780, and d. in 1812.

8. Dr. Joseph, s. Capt. David 4, m. Mary, da. Edward Foster, of Dorchester, in 1734, was sometime Deacon of the 2d. Church in Scituate, and lived where Col. Jno. Collamore now resides. He was a skilful physician, a man of good talents, successful in his practice, and of respectable standing. He was also part proprietor of the Jacobs Mills, and a large land holder, both in Scituate and Hanover. ch.: 1. Elisha, Aug. 29, 1735. 2. Relief, Jan. 16, 1737, m. David Jacobs. 3. Hannah, May 9, 1739, m. Jno. James. 4. Sarah, May 1741, m. Jno. Foster. 5. Lydia, May 30, 1743, m. Amasa Whiting. 6. Joseph, May 7, 1745, d. young. 7. Debo., May 12, 1747, d. unm. 8. Nath'l., Oct. 7, 1748, d. young. 9. Nath'l., Ap. 6, 1750. 10. Mary, Jan. 27, 1751, m. Jno. Foster,—his 2d w. 11. Abig., Dec. 1, 1753, m. Caleb Sylvester. 12. Joseph, July 12, 1755, d. young. 13. Joseph, May 5, 1757.

9. Benj., s. Capt. David 4, m. Mary Thomas, of Pemb., and lived and d. at his father's place, in Scit., since known as the Sam'l. Hatch place. ch.: 1. Anne, July 6, 1738, d. young. 2. Mary, Sep. 8, 1739, m. Sam'l. Hatch. 3. Anne, May 30, 1743, d. young. 4. Priscilla, Feb. 8, 1746, d. young. 5. Priscilla, d. unm. 6. Anne, Nov. 25, 1753, d. unm. 7. Sarah, Jan. 10, 1756, d. unm., Mar. 27, 1837.

10. Peter, s. Peter 5, m. Lydia, da. Jno. Lane, Ap. 5, 1731, and lived and d. in H'm., a respected and useful citizen. ch.: 1. Jno., Aug. 14, 1732. 2. Lydia, Aug. 3, 1734, m. Jno. Lincoln, Aug. 5, 1760. 3. Bethia, 1736. 4. Peter, Aug. 23, 1738. 5. Nicholas, Aug. 26, 1741. 6. Hannah, 1744, m. Isaac Sprague. 7. Mary, 1746. 8. David, 1747. m. Hannah Abbot?

11. David Jacob, s. Josh. 7, lived in H., m. 1, Hannah Richmond, June 2, 1759, who d. Mar. 17, 1776; and 2, Relief, da. Dr. Joseph Jacobs, Jan. 16, 1778; lived where

Rev. R. L. Killam now resides, in Snappet; and built that house, which he improved for many years as a Tavern. (See the view under Mr. Killam's name.) He was an extensive land holder, and surveyor; Selectman from 1776–'78; a member of the Com. of Safety in the Rev'n.; Rep. in 1780, 81, and 86; and d. Dec. 16, 1808, ae. 79, and his w. Jan. 6, 1805, ae. 68. ch.: 1. David, Ap. 20, 1763. 2. Perez, Oct. 29, 1765. 3. Richmond, Sep. 12, 1767, d. Feb. 4, 1775. 4. Hannah, May 29, 1769, m. Nath'l. Cushing, Scit.. 5. Eunice, Feb. 4, 1775, d. Feb. 27, 1850

12. Col. Jno., s. Josh. 7, m. Hannah Tolman, and lived in Scit., where Dr. Bailey's desc'ts. now reside. He was a mason by trade, a Col. in the Rev'n., and a man of great activity and ability. ch.: 1. Jno., Sep. 22, 1759, m. Mabel Litchfield, was a blacksmith by trade, and lived for a time in H., where Hiram Curtis now resides, whence he moved to Carlisle, Mass., where his desc'ts. still reside, and of which town his son *Jno.*, was Rep. to the Mass. Leg. in 1850. 2. Sam'l., or *Lem'l.*, June 10, 1761, m. Sarah Randall, was a shipwright by trade, lived in Scit., and had *Sarah*, m. Michael Ford.; *Lem'l.*, d. unm.; *Benj.*, now living in So. Scit., (m. Triphosa Sylvester, and has Sarah, Adeline, Warren and Tempe,) and *Nancy*. 3. Hannah, Ap. 4, 1763, m. Col. Chas. Turner, and is yet living, in So. Scit. 4. Sarah, Dec. 15, 1764, m. Calvin Bailey, of H. 5. Francis, Oct. 2, 1766. 6. Mary, July 20, 1768, m. Jas. Bourne. 7. Chas., May 26, 1770, m. Elizabeth Snelling, was a carpenter, lived in Bos'n., and had, *Elizab.*, m. a Peterson; *Nancy S.*; *Harriet*; and *Chas.* 8. Roland, Mar. 17, 1772, m Anna Eames, lives in Me., is a shipwright, and has *Roland*, m. a Young, and has ch.; *Warren*; *John*; *Mary*, m. a Bradford; *Ann*; and *Hannah*. 9. Walter, Dec. 27, 1774, m. Elizab. Turner, d. in Scit., and his wid. lives in Ab'n.; had *Walter*; *Mary A.*, (m. Milo Kellogg, and lives in E. Ab'n.); *Mariah*, (m. Marshal H. Litchfield,); *Roland*, (m. Emily Blanchard, and has Chas., Geo., Lyman, and Emily); *Chas.*; *Lyman*; *Ellinor*; and *Lydia*. 10. Fanny, Nov. 18, 1776, living in So. Scit. 11. Warren, Mar. 29, 1778, m. Rachel Clapp, was killed by falling from a building in Boston, and his wid. m. Stephen Hall, and is now a wid., in Medford. His ch. were *Warren*, (m. Tamsen Puffer, May 10,

1833, lives in So. H'm., and has Warren H., Jan. 10, '35, drowned in 1845; Mary C., Oct. 29, '38; Jno. 2., Jan. 23, '40; Andrew, Feb. 8, '43; and Warren H., June 4, 1850, d. May, 1851); *Rachel*, m. Dr. Milton Fuller, of Medford; and *Elizab.*, m. Stephen Coats, of Saugus. He is d.

13. Capt. Josh., s. Josh. 7, m. Elizab. Richmond, and lived where his son Loring's desc'ts. now reside. He was a cooper by trade; a Capt. in the Rev'n.; sometime Selectman of Scit.; and a man of sound sense, few words, and steady habits. He d. Aug. 9, 1808, ae. 71, and his w. Dec. 9, 1781, ae. 47. ch.: 1. Josh., Sep. 22, 1767. 2. Elizab., Oct. 24, 1769, d. unm. 3. Loring, May, 1771. 4. Lucy, Ap. 16, 1773, m. Josh. Hersey, H'm., Mar. 6, 1794. 5. Rhoda, Aug. 17, 1778, m. Jacob Beal, Mar. 14, 1798. 6. Mary, Aug. 26, 1780, m. Alex'r. Vining, and is living a wid., in So. Scit. 7. Sylvester, Sep. 1, 1782, lives in Groton, and has *Elizab.*; *Cynthia S.*, d. ae. ab. 28; *Sylvester*, d. ae. ab. 12; *Lucy*; *Amelia*; and *Charles*, now at H. Coll.

14. James Jacob s. Josh. 7, m. Debo. Richmond, Mar. 19, 1772, and lived where his son I. R. Jacobs, Esq., now resides, in So. Scit., where he d., Sep. 12, 1827, ae. 86, respected in life and lamented in death. ch.: 1. Jas., Jan. 3, 1773, d. at H. Coll., Sep. 16, 1793. 2. Ichabod R., June 27, 1774. 3. Debo., June 22, 1776, m. Capt. Chas. Cushing, H'm. 4. Thos. M., Sep, 22, 1777. 5. Nabby, June 19, 1780, m. Abiel Farrow, and is living, a wid., in So. Scit. 6. Michael, July 17, 1782, m. wid Huldah Bowker, lives in So. Scit., and has *Julia*, d., and *Edwin*. 7. Eunice, Feb. 3, 1783, m. Sam'l. Hatch, Scit., and d. Jan. 2, 1811.

15. Elisha Jacob s. Dr. Joseph, 8, m. Lusanna Randall, was a farmer and brickmaker, lived in Scit., where his son, Hon. E. F. Jacobs, now resides, (having built that house,) and d. Dec. 8, 1779, ae. 43, and his wid., May 4, 1821, ae. 82. ch.: 1. Elisha, Aug. 12, 1760,

m. in N. York, was Capt. of a corps of Artificers, in the Rev'n., and prob. d. at the South. 2. Saml., Mar. 4, 1762, a shipwright; sett. in Me.; m. 1, Marg't. Stinson; and 2, Marg't. McGlathery; was many yrs. Rep. to the Mass. Leg.; Justice of the Peace and Quorum; and d. Sep. 5, 1809, and his wid. in 1837, ae. 75; having had, by 2d w., *Samuel*, stud. law, but sett. as a merchant, and d. unm., in 1835, ae. 44; *Frederic*, m. Julia, da. Benj. Cushing, Esq., had Benj. C., Robt. W., Eliza, Adaline, Frederic, and Delia, and d. in 1834, ae. 39; *Robert*, d. unm., in 1829, ae. 31; *Bela*, d. unm., in 1849, ae. 52; and *Caroline*, m. Dr. Joseph H. Estabrooks, in 1823, and had 19 ch., of whom 12 are living. 3. Braddoc, May, 1764. 4. Benj., Sep. 29, 1766. 5. Lydia, Aug. 25, 1768, d. Sep. 24, 1785. 6. Bela, May 1, 1770, m. Polly Eaton, lived in Me., and d., leaving no ch. 7. Polycarpus, May 29, 1772, m. 1, a Clapp; and 2, Rebecca Coffin, Nantucket; sett. first in Me., as shipwright; and d. in Milton, Mass., in 1852; having had, *Melintha*, d.; *Susanna*, m. Lewis Tucker, Milton, and is d.; *Elizab. G.*, m. Rev. Gamal. C. Beman, Winchendon, Mass.; *Leah L.*, m. Henry Allen, of Me.; *Edwd. F.*, m. Lavina Ficket, and is d.; *Almena*, m. Nathl. Swift, Andover, Mass.; *Rachel*, m. Jno. Myers, Milton, Mass.; and *Benj. T.*, d. 8. Edward F., Oct. 23, 1774. 9. Lusanna, Nov. 20, 1777, m. Nathl. Tucker, and lives, in Dorch'r.

16. Nathaniel Jacob, s. Dr. Jos. 8, m. 1, Lucy Jacobs, Jan. 6, 1780, who d. Mar. 20, 1812; and 2, Charlotte Wade, Mar. 1, 1814; and d. Sep. 22, 1822, and his wid., Mar. 1, 1852. Lived in H., where the present Alms House stands; was a farmer, a man of good natural abilities, a kind father, and an industrious citizen. ch.: 1. Nathl., July 16, 1782. 2. Stephen, Mar. 6, 1786. 3. Wm., Oct. 6, 1788, a carpenter, d. at Canandaigua, N. Y., Aug. 25, 1814.

17. Joseph, s. Dr. Joseph 8, m. Hannah Eells, Dec. 3, 1780, was a schoolmaster, in H'm., for several years, and d. June 14, 1811, and his wid. Feb. 3, 1818. ch.: 1. Joseph, Nov. 6, 1781.

2. Hannah, Mar. 11, 1783, m. Smith Downing, of Lynn, and d. Aug. 7, 1837. 3. Ruth, Dec. 13, 1784, m. Job Damon, of H., and d. Sep., 1819. 4. Jas. H., Ap. 2, 1787, m. 1, Celenda Stetson, Nov. 24, 1811, who d. 1812; and 2, Lusanna Stetson, Nov. 26, 1812, and d. Mar. 4, 1825, and his wid. lives in South Scit., with her da. *Celenda*, b. Nov. 3, 1813. 5. Elisha, Oct. 11, 1790, is prob. d. 6. Clarissa, Oct. 28, 1792, m. 1, Elijah Downing; and 2, a Pool; and lives in Lynn. 7. George W., Dec. 3, 1797, d. Mar. 14, 1799. 8. David, Ap. 5, 1799, m. Olive Fly, of Me., lives in E. Ab'n., and has *Clarissa*, m. Gridley Wheeler; *David*, (m. Abigail Wheeler, lives in E. Ab'n., and has Wilbur R.); *Wm. F.; Olive M.; Jas. H.; Danl. W.; Mary A.*, d.; *Joseph*, d.; and *Walter R.* 9. Benj., Jan. 2, 1804, m. Harriet Doten, lives in So. Scit., and has *Geo. T.*; *Philip C.; Gustavus; Amasa*, d.; *Harriet S.;* and *Everett*, d.

18. Jno., s. Peter 11, m. Lydia Beal, Ap. 10, 1761, was a blacksmith by trade, lived in H'm., and d. Dec. 4, 1806, ae. 76, respected by the community, and lamented by his friends. ch.: 1. Jno., Sep. 5, 1762. 2. Lydia, July 26, 1764, m. Ezek'l. Cushing, and moved to Worthington. 3. Peter, Aug. 28, 1766. 4. Dan'l., July 18, 1768, m. Mary Jones, was a blacksmith, lived in S. H'm., and d. Ap. 15. 1806, having had *Sarah*, m. Piam Cushing, of H'm.; *Mary*, m. Leavitt Tower, of H'm.; and *Catherine*, m. Philip R. Bennett, and lives in Ills. 5. Hannah, Feb. 5, 1771, m. Isa. Tower, H'm. 6. Debo., July 6. 1773, m. Crocker Wilder, of H'm., and was mo. of *Crocker* and *Alden*, to whose Factory we have alluded on p. 34. 7. Jotham, Ap. 27. 1775.

19. David Jacob Jun s. David 11, m. Han. Hersey, H'm., and lived in H., in the house which stood where stands that of Perez Simmons, Esq., and there d. Aug. 2, and his wid. Aug. 28, 1799. Had his life been spared, we donbt not that the son, like the father, would have been a prominent man in the town, as his abilities were good, and his prospects flattering. ch.: 1. Hannah R., Oct. 13, 1782, living, unm. 2. Relief, Feb. 29, 1785, m. C. P. Sumner,

Esq., of Bos'n., and is mo. of *Hon. Charles Sumner, now in the U. S. Senate.* 3. David O., July 19, 1787, m. Lydia Blake, of Keene, N. H., is living in S. H'm., and had *Henry H.*, d. ae. 2; and *Caroline.* 4. Amanda, July 18, 1789, m. Capt. Galen James, Medford. 5. Matilda, Feb. 16, 1792, d. Aug. 25, 1799. 6. Hiram, Ap. 22, 1795, d. unm., in Bos'n. 7. Maria, Sep. 10, 1797, d. ab. 1825, being drowned, at the Navy Yard, Chas'n.

20. Peres Jacob, s. David 11, m. Relief Bowker, Scit.; lived in part of his father's house; and d. Mar. 8, 1828, ae. 62, and his wid. May, 1845, both leaving a good name for their children, as a valuable inheritance. ch.: 1. Desire, Sep. 25, 1788, m. Capt. Edward Curtis, and is living, a wid., in H. 2. Rebecca, Oct. 25, 1790, m. Jno. Bryant, of Chas'n. 3. Debo. R., August 9, 1795, d. May 17, 1796. 4. Debo. R., March 14, 1798, m. Snell Wade, May 11, 1819. 5. Eunice, December 12, 1799, m. 1, Joseph Mann, Dec. 5. 1822, and 2, Martin Stoddard, and lives in Mf'd. 6. Perez R., Oct. 22, 1806, m. Nancy Howe, Sep. 21, 1831, lives in Chas'n., is Dep. Sheriff, and has *George*, *Charles*, *Charlotte E.*, *Edward C.*, *Caroline M.*, and *Julia M.* 7. Theodosius, m. Sophronia Whittemore, and both are d; no ch.

21. Capt. Josh., s. Capt. Josh. 13, m. Hannah Cushing, May 30, 1796, lived in So. Scit., where his son Piam now resides, and d. May 3, 1840, and his w. Ap. 5, 1824, ae. 50. He was a man of sobriety, industry, intelligence, and virtue. ch.: 1. Hannah W., Feb. 24, 1798. 2. Mary J., Jan. 3, 1800, m. Benjamin Hersey, H'm. 3. Josh., Nov. 19, 1801, m. Ruth A. Davis, Feb. 1843, lives in Boston, is a stairbuilder, and has *Mary E. D.* 4. Theophilus, Dec. 15, 1803, d. Oct. 31, 1844, in Ohio. 5. Emma, Feb. 23, 1806, m. David Cushing, H'm. 6. Bela T., March 18, 1808, resided for some years in Valparaiso, but now in So. Scit.; a carpenter by trade; not m. 7. William C., Nov. 15, 1810, m. Louisa Dodge, is a stairbuilder, lives in Bos'n., and has *Hannah W.*, *Helen L.*, *Clara D.*, and *Martha*, living. 8. Piam, Jan. 5, 1813. 9. David R., July 24, 1817, lives in Salisbury, Ohio, is m., and has *Emma J.*, and *Hannah.*

22. Loring, s. Capt. Josh. 13, m. 1, Mary Simmons, May 30, 1802, who d. Aug. 23, 1805 ; 2, Rachel Wilder, Oct. 17, 1808, who d. Aug. 27, 1810 ; and 3, Meriall Wilder, June 12, 1811 ; and d. Dec. 6, 1846 ; his wid. survives. Mr. J. was a carpenter by trade, but the latter part of his life resided in So. Scit., as a farmer. An excellent citizen, and an honest and liberal minded man. ch.: 1. Franklin, March 21, 1803, fitted for Coll., but d. Sept. 5, 1833. (By 2d,) 2. Mary S., Ap. 19, d. Aug. 6, 1810. (By 3d,) 3. Loring, June 18, 1812, m. Mary E., da. Capt. Jno. M. Nichols, Plym'h., May 31, 1840, lives in So. Scit., was for some years a trader and shoe manufacturer; and was Selectman of So. Scit, from 1848–'51 ; no ch. 4. Andrew, July 29, 1813, m. Sophronia Litchfield, Ap. 1844, lives in So. Scit., and has *Andrew F.*, and *Lucy A.* 5. Mary A., Nov. 15, 1815, m. Dexter Bowker, Jan. 19, 1840, lives in Bos'n., and has ch. 6. Martha A., Sep. 28, 1817, unm. 7. Meriall, Oct. 18, 1822, m. Rev. H. P. Stevens, Sept. 13, 1846, and has one son. 8. Washington, Nov. 19, 1825, m. Harriet E. A. Keyes, lives in Bos'n., is a stairbuilder, and has *Josephine*, d. young ; *Washington I.* ; and *Ella M.*

23. Ichabod R., s. Jas. 14, m. Clarissa Richmond, of Little Compton, R.I., Oct. 16, 1805, who d. November 7, 1840, ae. 62 ; an amiable woman and an excellent mother. Mr. J. early learned the shoemaker's trade, but most of his life has been devoted to farming, and he has received a premium for the best cultivated farm in Plymouth County. He was Selectman of Scit., in 1840–41 ; has been for ten years a J. P., and is a gentleman of amiable manners and high moral worth. ch. : 1. Mary S., Sept. 24, 1806, m. Rev. Massena B., s. Rev. Hosea Ballou, Dec. 21, 1825, lives in Stoughton, and has three children living, *Massena H.*, (who is m.) ; *Clementina C.* ; and *Berthea R.* 2. Richmond, Oct. 4, 1808, d. Sept. 6, 1838, in N. Orl's, merch't. 3. Sarah, Feb. 18, 1810, m. Rev. Jno., s. Jno. Boyden, lives in Woonsocket, R. I., and has *Jno. R.* 4. Thos., July 8, 1812, m. Elizab. S. Ratley, March 9, 1847, lives in Shreeveport, La., and has *Benj. R.*, 1847. 5, Benj., Sept. 4, d. Oct. 21, 1814. 6. Benj., Sept. 17, 1815,

m. 1, Lydia M. P., da. Rev. R. L. Killam, May 26, 1839, who d. Sept. 7, 1846; and 2, Sarah J., da. Samuel Hatch, June 25, 1848; lives in part of the ancestral homestead, and has *Maria*, Feb. 7, 1841, and *Augustus*, July 24, 1843. 7. Clarissa, Mar. 19, 1818. 8. Abby S., Ap. 10, 1821, m. Henry J. Curtis, Sept. 20, 1848. 9. Barton R., June 23, 1823.

24. Thos. M., s. Jas. 14, m. Hannah, wid. Joseph Pocorny, and da. of Geo. W. Felton, of Petersham, Mass., March 22, 1815, and d. Nov. 4, 1845. He was a carpenter by trade, but resided, the latter part of his life, in So. Scit., opposite the Universalist Church, was a farmer, and by honest industry commended himself to the favorable notice of those who knew him best. ch.: 1. Eunice H., Jan. 5, 1816, d. Dec. 17, 1838. 2. James M., merchant tailor, Bos'n., of the enterprising firm of Jacobs & Deane, Court st.; m. Caroline E. Hendley, Sept. 9, 1849, who d. Mar. 28, 1852, ae. 28, leaving a da.. *Frances A.*, b. Nov. 25, 1851. 3. David H., a master mason and contractor, living in Bos'n.; m. Elizab. Ayres, Ap. 25, 1847, and has *Jas. A.*, October 15, 1848, and *Anna E.*, Jan. 14, 1852. 4. Aurelia F., June 22, 1823. 5. Thos. R., Nov. 24, 1825, clerk with his brother James.

25. Braddoc, s. Elisha 15, m. Sarah Hersey, H'm., in 1787, lived first in Scit., where the wid. of Thos. M. Jacobs resides; sett. in Littleton ab. 1807, and there d., April 5, 1847. His wid. survives. ch.: 1. Sarah, June 9, 1788, m. Moses Foster, ab. 1812, and d. Dec. 22, 1845, leaving *Sam'l. H.*, *Moses H.*, *Mary A.*, *Joseph V.*, *Francis E.*, and *Hannah A.* 2. Ancil, Dec. 20, 1789, d. Dec. 17, 1796. 3. Benj. H., Dec. 9, 1792, sett. in Lynn, 1810, m. Elizab. Downing, Oct. 4, 1818, and has *Lydia M.*, July 24, 1819; *Benj. H.*, Sept. 27, 1821, d. young; *Edwin S.*, Jan. 15, 1826; *Sophia E.*, Oct. 15, 1826; *Geo. H.*, Sept. 25, 1829; and *Joseph E.*, Sept. 23, 1832. 4. Lydia, Feb. 22, 1793, m. Nathan Johnson, Sept. 10, 1850, and he d. March 9, 1851. 5. Joann, May 28, 1797, m. 1, Oliver Locke, Lex'n., April 1, 1817, and had *Faustina M.*, d. 1850, and *Joann S.* Her 1st husb. d. Oct. 15, 1825, and she m. 2, Wm. Smith, Lex'n., 1832, and has *Mary E. B.* 6. Hannah, June 26, 1799, m. 1, Dan'l. Harring-

ton, Lex'n., Dec. 1824, who. d. 1826; and 2, Luther Brooks, Camb., June 1, 1830, who d. July 4, 1839, leaving her *Luther F.*, *Susanna J.*, *Chas. E.*, and *Everett W.* 7. Susanna, Aug. 7, 1801, m. James Wellington, Medford, Nov. 19, 1820, and has *Jas. E.*, d. 1826; *Angeline W.*; *Jas. E.*; and *Adria.* 8. Mary W., May 30, 1803, m. Isaac Wellington, Nov. 19, 1824, and has *Oliver L.*, *Isaac B.*, *Francena*, *Mary A.*, and *Luther B.* 9. Geo. H., Oct. 5, 1805, of Chas'n., m. Persis A. Teel, 1829, has been a successful merchant, and Alderman of C.; has *Geo. H.*, June 20, 1830; *Persis A.*, October 20, 1831, d. Feb. 27, 1832; *Angelia P.*, Dec. 1, 1834; and *Jas. W.*, May 12, 1839. 10. Sophia, Oct. 9, 1807, d. April 6, 1810. 11. Chas., April 27, 1810, of Medford, m. Octavia Burbank, Lex'n., Dec. 7, 1837, and has *Chas. S.*, Sept. 15, 1838; *Octavia A.*, Jan. 23, 1840; *Elizab. B.*, Dec. 16, 1842; *Henry B.*, April 1, 1845; *Sarah H.*, Jan. 8, d. June 20, 1848; and *Ed. F.*, Dec. 15, 1850.

26. Benj., s. Elisha 15, sett. in Dorch'r., Mass., in 1783, and m. 1, Sarah, da. Timo. Foster; and 2, Jemimah, da. Edward Foster; was a carpenter by trade; a man of successful enterprise, and honest industry; leaving to his children, at his decease, a valuable estate, and the legacy of a character, true in all the relations of life. ch.: 1. William, a cabinet maker, m. Eliza, da. Dea. Isaac Howe, Dorch'r., and has *Wm. T.*, (m. Ann, da. Wm. Holmes, and has Geo. H.;) *Sarah F.*; *Benj.*, (in Cala.); *Eliza A.*; *Caroline H.*; *Henry*; and *Elisha.* 2. Elisha, d. 3. Benj., merchant, of Bos'n; resides on his father's estate, in Dorchester, and is unmarried; a gentleman of character and standing in the community, well known to the business public. 4. Sarah, d. (By 2d,) 5. Sarah A. 6. Mary D., d. 7. Timothy, d. 8. Elisha, merchant, of Bos'n., m. Mary G., da. Nath'l. Coffin, Newburyport, and has *Benj. F.*; *Mary C.*; *Gertrude T.*; *Sarah A.*, d.; *Amelia G.*; and *Geo. C. S.*

27. Hon. Ed. F., s. Elisha 15, m. Priscilla, da. Wm. Clapp, Scit., Jan. 5, 1802, lives in So. Scit., was a shoemaker in early life, and afterwards a trader, and a manf'r. of brick, at his yard in S. A gentleman of great natural ability, who, even in high

party times, enjoyed the confidence of his townsmen, being often elected to offices of trust; acting for many years on the board of Selectmen; as Rep. to the State Leg.; and as a memb. of the Govr's. Council in 1836, and '37. ch.: 1. Edward, brick manuf'r., lives in So. Scit., m. Adaline, da. Perez Whiting, Ap. 16, 1826, and has *George E.*, Nov. 29, 1827, (a mason by trade, m. Esther C. Litchfield, Nov. 28, 1850, and has Alfred, Dec. 6, 1851); and *Howard B.*, a carpenter, b. June 14, 1833. 2. Lucy C., May 14, 1805, m. Perez Southard Whiting, and lives in N. Y'k. 3. Elisha, Mar. 12, 1808, merchant, Bos'n., m. Delia T., da. Luke Fay, Ap., 1842, and has *Elisha A.*, Mar. 28, 1843; *Delia M.*, Dec., 1844, d. Ap. 15, 1849; *Ed. F.*, Dec., 1848; and *Eveline W.*, Dec. 31, 1850. 4. Lydia S., Jan. 29, 1811, m. Rev. H. W. Morse, June, 1840, lives in N. Reading, and has ch. 5. Henry, Aug. 24, 1813, formerly an engraver, in N. Y'k., and Bos'n.; a gent. of fine natural abilities, and an excellent portrait painter; not m. 6. Frederick, Oct. 28, 1817, merchant, Bos'n.; m. Martha M. Fay, May 20, 1841, and has *Fred'k. F.*, Mar. 3, 1842; *Walter H.*, Nov., 1847; and *Alfred H.*, Oct., 1849. 7. Mary P., Oct. 26, 1820, d. Sep. 14, 1821.

28. Dr. Nathl., s. Nathl. 16, grad. H. C., 1806, stud. med. with Dr. Smith, of Hanover, N. H., sett. in Canandaigua, N. Y., where he taught an Acad. many years, and practised as a physician; m. Hannah Sanborn, and has 1. Chauncy O., d. ae. 2. 2. Elizab., m. Wm. Remington, Buffalo, N. Y. 3. Nathl. S., m. Freelove Watts, of Roch'r., N. Y., who d., leaving 2 ch., both of whom are decs'd. 4. Wm., m., lives at Black Rock, N. Y., and has *Lucinda*, and *Amelia*. 5. Caroline, m. Alex'r. Swartwout, Canandaigua. 6. Lavinia, not m. 7. Charles. 8. Mary A., d. ae. 14. 9. Leavitt, M., d. 10. Harriet P.

29. Stephen, s. Nath'l. 16, lives in H., on Wash'n. st., was Selectman in 1825, m. Rachel H. Otis, Dec. 31, 1812, is an intelligent and industrious farmer, and has 1. Lucy, May 17, 1814, d. June 23, 1816. 2. Wm., Ap. 23, 1816, d. Oct. 18, 1822. 3. Lucy, Oct. 1, 1818, m. Sam'l. Waters, Aug. 30, 1840, lives in So. Scit., and has *Jacob L.*; *Helen M.*; and *Lucy L.* 4.

Adaline M., Nov. 9, 1820, a school teacher, not m. 5. Wm., Mar. 7, 1825, of Randolph, wheelwright, m. Susan A. Loring, H'm., Oct. 1849, and has *Anna L.*, Sept. 28, 1851. 6. Stephen O., May 13, 1827, a mason by trade. 7. Charles, May 5, 1829, resides with his fa. 8. Albert, Oct. 18, 1831. 9. Franklin, June 24, 1835.

30. Joseph, s. Joseph 17, m. 1, Anne Damon, and 2, her sister Elizab., lived in So. Scit., where Col. Jno. Collamore now resides, and had, 1. Ann, prob. d. 2. Joseph, Mar. 10, 1804, manf'r. of edge tools, at his steam factory, H'm., m. Esther C., da. Jotham Jacobs, and has *Joseph*, Dec. 8, 1828, (m. Clarissa Cushing, Oct. 27, 1850, and has Clara A., July 19, 1852); *Esther C.*, June 2, d. Oct. 3, 1831; Grace A., Dec. 22, 1833; *Lucy M.*, Dec. 29, 1838; *Sarah C.*, Jan. 9, 1845; and *Fred'k. S.*, June 10, 1850.

31. Jno., s. Jno. 18, m. Tamar Cushing, Mar. 11, 1787, and d. June 7, 1847. Lived in H'm., and had, 1. Tamar, Jan. 19, 1788, d. May 20, 1805. 2. Mary, May 5, 1790, d. Mar. 10, 1791. 3. Mary, Jan. 10, 1792, d. unm. 4. Lydia B., Dec. 26, 1794, d. unm. 5. Jno., July 27, 1797, m. Martha Fearing, Jan. 10, 1833, is a blacksmith, lives in S. H'm., and has *Martha F.*, June 14, 1835, d. Jan., 1839; *Tamar C.*, May 26, 1837; *Martha*, Ap. 22, 1841; and *Mary C.*, Feb. 17, 1845. 6. Piam, Sept. 16, 1800, m. Clarissa Hathaway, Freetown, moved to Galena, Ills., and has *Mary; Geo. W.*, d.; and *Geo. P.* 7. Hannah, Nov. 19, 1803, m. Marshall Sherman, and lives in H'm.

32. Peter, s. Jno., 18, m. Amy Fearing, lived in H'm., and d. Oct. 13, 1810. ch.: 1. Amy, m. Fearing Burr, H'm., and is d. 2. Peter, m. a Hobart? and is d. 3. David, m. a Corthell, lives in H'm., and has ch. 4. Hawkes, of H'm. 5. Lincoln, of H'm.

33. Jotham, s. Jno. 18, m. Grace Tower, lived in H'm.; was a blacksmith by trade, and there both he and his w. d. ch.: 1. Lucy, m. Silas Chipman, and is living a wid., in Wey'h. 2. Laban, of Hm., manf'r. of edge tools, m. Caroline, da. Perez Whiting, Feb. 2, 1823, and has *Mary C.*, Sep., 1824, m. Wm. H. Lyon, of N. Y'k. State, and has ch.; *Wm. H.*, July, 1831;

Alfred, Jan., 1833; and *Adaline W.*, Jan. 4, 1838. Has lost 6 ch., d. young. 3. Joshua, d. young. 4. Debo., m. Peter Cushing, Wey'h., and has ch. 5. Esther, m. Joseph Jacobs, H'm. 6. Betsey, m. Robt. Gardner, H'm. 7. Cynthia, m. Theoph. Cushing, H'm. 8. Mary, m. Henry C. Wilder, H'm. 9. Joshua, m. 1, Emily Higgins, and 2, Lydia D., da. Capt. Seth Hersey, lives in H'm., and has *Joshua*.

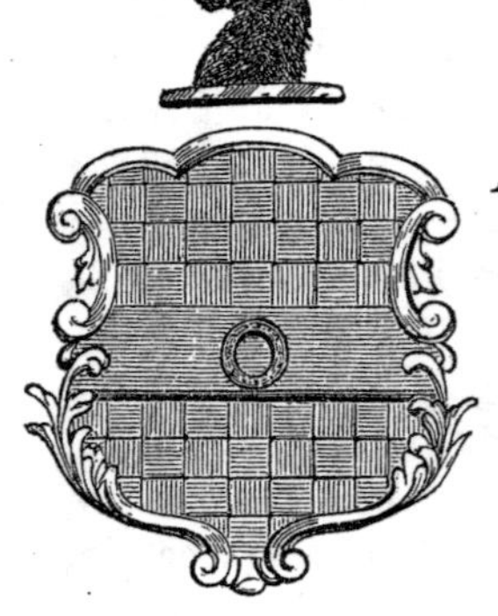

Arms: Chequy, gu. and az.; on a fesse of the first an annulet or.

Crest; A bear's head and neck sa., muzzled or.

JOSSELYN, JOSLIN, JOCELYN, &c., an old English family, dating back several hundred years, and sett. in Cornwall, Essex, Hertford, Kent, &c. The Earl of Roden, is of the Jocelyns; and Sir Ralph Josceline, of Hertfordshire, was Mayor of London, in 1474 and 1476, being made Knight of the Bath, by King Edward IV., in the former year. The coats of arms vary in different families, and there is one extant in H., different from that which we have presented above, and handed down by tradition. In America, Jno. Josselyn, gent., was in N. Eng. in 1638, and was the author, among other works, of one called "New-England's Rarities;" and Henry, his bro., (and son of Sir Thomas, of Kent,) was at Black Point, now Scarborough, Me., in 1634, being sent over, by Capt. Mason, to make "a more complete discovery," and examination of the advantages of the grant made to Capt. M. He was a memb. of the Gen. Court, at Saco, 1636;

[1] See Burke's Gen. Armory.

Councillor in 1639; Dep'y. Gov'r., 1645; a magistrate, and member of the gov't. of the province of Ligonia, 1650; and a commissioner and associate, under Massachusetts, 1658; and during the long period, from 1635 to 1676, he was one of the most active and influential men in the Prov., and during all the changes of proprietorship, and gov't., he held the most important offices.[1] He m. Marg't., wid. of Capt. Thos. Cammock, and it is said had one son, Henry. Family tradition, and other authorities, assert that this son sett. in Scit., Mass., in 1668, m. Abigail Stockbridge, 1676, and was the ancestor of the Josselyns of Plym'h. Co.[2]; but the correctness of this assertion, is somewhat doubtful.

According to the Mass. Hist. Coll., vol. 8, third series, "Thos. *Jestlin*, a husbandman, ae. 43; Rebecca, his w., of the same age; and their ch., Rebecca, ae. 18; Dorothy, ae. 11; Nath'l., ae. 8; Eliza, ae. 6; and Mary, ae. 1; with a maid-servant, Eliza Ward, ae. 38, came to N. Eng., in the Increase, of London, Robert Lea, master, in 1635"; and according to Lincoln's Hist. H'm., Thos., the fa., was in H'm. in 1637; and in 1654, he was in Lancaster, (Worcester Mag. 2, 280,) where he d. in 1660–1, (Midds'x. Rec.) his wid., Rebecca, being Exec'x. of his Est. She m. Wm. Kerley, 1664. *Abraham*, son of Thos., sen'r., was not with his fa., when he came to N. Eng., in 1635, but seems to have arrived afterward. He was in H'm., in 1647, but moved to Lanc'r. before 1663, and d. bef. 1670; and his wid., Beatrice, m. Serg't. Benja. Bosworth, of Hull.[3] The desc'ts, of Thos., the fa., and of Abraham, the son, still reside in Lanc'r., and the adjacent towns. The Josselyns of Scit., and H., are desc'ts from Abraham, *through his son Henry*.

2. Henry, s. Abraham, and gr. s. Thos. of London, sett. in Scit., 1669, was a blacksmith by trade, m. Abig., da. Chas. Stockbridge, Nov. 4, 1676; his house stood in the field, 50 rods east of Judge Wm. Cushing's farm-house, and he d. in H., Oct. 30, 1730, being

[1] Williamson's Hist. of Me., vol. 1, pp. 265, 278, 328, 392, 396, 439 & 682; also, N. E. Gen. Reg., vol 2, pp. 205—7.

[2] Deane's Hist. Scit., and the other works above quoted.

[3] See the elaborate communication of T. M. Harris, in N. E. Gen. Reg., vol. 2, p. 306, et seq.

called, on the Ch. Rec., "the oldest man in the town for years." His wid. d. July 15, 1743. ch.: 1. Abig., Ap. 1677, m. Benja. Hanmer, Dec. 15, 1715. 2. Abraham, Jan. 1678–9, left no ch. on record. 3. Anna, Feb. 1680–1, d. Nov. 17, 1683. 4. Chas., Mar., 1682–3, left no desc'ts on rec. 5. Mary, Jan. 1684, m. Benj. Munroe, of Swansey, Dec. 3, 1713. 6. Nath'l., Feb. 1686–7. 7. Rebecca, b. Mar., d. Ap., 1689. 8. Jabez, Feb. 1690–1, m. Sarah Turner, Jan. 3, 1722, and d. July 14, 1734, and his wid. Dec. 23, 1756, having had *Jabez*, 1723, (m. Mary Lindsey, July 20, 1742, and had Sam'l. 1742; Jabez, 1744; Keziah, 1746, d. 1750; and Lindsey, 1749); *Eliab*, Oct. 21, d. Nov. 9, 1724; *Sarah*, Dec. 29, 1725, d. Oct. 30, 1739; *Rebecca*, Jan. 14, d. Jan. 26, 1728. 9. Rebecca, May 1693, m. Jos. Perry, Ap. 24, 1728. 10. Jemima, Dec. 1695, d. Feb. 14, 1696. 11. Kezia, Dec. 1695. 12. Henry, Mar., 1697. 13. Joseph, Dec., 1699, m. 1, Ruth Bates, Dec, 19, 1726, who d. Jan. 6, 1742; and 2, Sylvester Barker, Pemb., Oct. 3, 1751; had no ch., and d. Ap. 30, 1787, ae. 88; and his wid., Mar. 5. 1801, ae. 91. He is called *Capt. Joseph*, on the H. Rec., and was a man of great enterprise, and an early prop'r. of the old Bardin Forge. He gave to the town the *bell* now hanging in the Centre Meet. Ho. 14. Thomas, Sep. 1702.

3. Nath'l, s. Henry 2, m. Frances Yellings, Dec. 27, 1711, who d. a wid. Aug. 26, 1755. She lived on what is now Spring st. ch.: 1. Mary, bap. in Scit., Mar. 29, 1713, d. Mar. 31, 1715. 2. Frances, bap. in Scit., May 29, 1715, m. Isaac Foster, Jan. 6. 1732. 3. Abraham, b. in Boston, 1717. 4. Mary, July 29, 1719. 5. Nath'l, July 6, 1722.

4. Henry, s. Henry 2, m. Hannah Oldham, and lived and d. in Pemb. ch.: 1. Hannah, Oct. 1, 1719, m. Henry Munroe, Swansey, Nov. 16, 1738. 2. Lydia, Aug. 25, 1722. 3. Mary, m. Shuble Munroe, Nov. 10, 1742. 4. Henry, June 11, 1727. 5. Marg't., Dec. 9, 1729, m. Seth Ford, Jan. 7, 1747–8. 6. Joseph, Jan. 2, 1731–2, d. young. 7. Joseph, June 22, 1734. 8. Chas., May 7, 1739. 9. Lucy, Oct. 5, 1741, m. Isaac Ford, Mf'd., Oct. 1, 1761. 10. Isaac, Nov. 4, 1743.

5 Thos: Josselyn s. Henry 2, m. Ann Stockbridge, June 1, 1732, was Dea. of the First Church in H., and gave the silver Communion Cups alluded to on p. 60. With his bro. Joseph, he was prop'r of the Bardin Forge; was Selectman in 1736, and from 1738–'44; and Rep. in 1738, '41, and '42. ch.: 1. Thomas, Sep. 26, 1733, m. Patience Barker, June 10, 1761, and d. in Pemb., Jan. 20, 1818, ae. 86, having had *Thos.*, Sep. 28, 1762, m. and d. in Me.; *Patience H.*, Feb. 28, 1765; *Bethiah T.*, Jan. 10, 1767, m. Barnab. Perry, 1789; *Joseph B.*, June 10, 1769; *Samuel W.*, Ap. 3, 1772, (m. Elizab. J. Coxe, May 20, 1798, and had Sam'l., 1799, Elizab., 1801, Debo.B., 1804, and Mehit., 1807); and *Anna S.*, 1776. 2. John, May 4, 1735, called *Ensign John*, on the Ch. Rec., m. Sage ——, and d. 1770, and his wid. 1775, having had *John R.*, 1764, m. Nabby Studley, Nov. 1, 1785, moved to Warren, Mass., and there d.; *Sage*, 1764, m. a Cookey, and moved to W.; *Cynthia*, 1766, m. 1, Oliver Bonney, Nov. 29, 1787, and 2, a Cookey?; and *Eunice*, 1769, m. Joseph Kingman, Bridg'r, Dec. 16, 1791. 3. Ann, or *Nancy*, Oct. 3, 1736, d. Ap. 21, 1801. 4. Stockbridge, Mar. 29, 1741. 5. Ruth, June 1743, m. a Lowden?, Plym'h. 6. Debo., bap. July 12, 1752. 7. Philip, bap. Jan. 27, 1754, d. unm., in Pemb. 8. Isaiah, d. unm., Ap. 3, 1804. 9. Seth, m. Priscilla Standish, Dec. 17, 1787, and moved to N. Salem, N. H.

6. Abraham, s. Nath'l. 3, m. Mary Soule, Dec. 16, 1741, and lived and d. in Pemb. ch.: 1. Mary, Feb. 8, 1742, m. Wm. Coxe, jr., Jan. 21, 1762. 2. Abraham, Jan. 14, 1744, m., lived in Woodstock, Vt., and left ch. 3. Elizab., Dec. 21, 1746, m Seth Coxe, Dec. 19, 1765. 4. Dorothy, Dec. 10, 1748, m. Reuben Clark, Dec. 23, 1768. 5. Abig., Sept. 26, 1755, m. Eleazer Ring, Worthington, Sep. 23, 1784. 6. Lydia, May 8, 1758. 7. Celia, July 25, 1760, m. Nathan Sprague, Mar. 31, 1785. 8. Eleazer, Sep. 14, 1762. 9. Tamar, May 1, 1765, m. Jas. Bourne, jr., Feb. 13, 1783. 10. Isaac, Aug. 15, 1768.

7. Nath'l., s. Nath'l 3, m. Sarah Low, and d. in H., May 2,

1790, ae. 68, and his wid. in Pemb., Aug. 18, 1802? ch.: 1. Ambrose L., Mar. 13, 1752, prob. d. young. 2. Sarah, Aug. 28, 1753, m. 1. Amos Perry, Sep. 7, 1777, and 2, Belcher Clark. 3. Nath'l., Aug. 24, 1755, moved to Freeport, Me. 4. Francis, May 27, 1757. 5. Chloe, July 23, 1759, m., and moved to Me. 6. Joshua, Aug. 30, 1761, m. Sarah Chapman, had *Judson*, 1789, *Ambrose L.*, 1791, *Ira L.*, 1791, and *Abraham*, 1793, and moved to Me. 7. Christiana, Nov. 10, 1763, d. Jan. 31, 1764. 8. Christiana, bap. July 28, 1765.

8. Henry Josselyn Jur s. Henry 4, m. Ann Palmer, and d. in Pemb., Mar. 1, 1818, ae. 91. ch.: 1. Hannah, Jan. 2, 1755, m. Seth Perry, of P., and is yet living, at the advanced age of 98! 2. Sylvester, Sep. 11, 1757, m. Jos. Sherman, July 26, 1780, and d. Mar. 4, 1801, and he moved to Me. 3. Nancy or *Anne*, Nov. 21, 1759, m. Pratt Allen, Mar. 17, 1796. 4. Henry, Oct. 12, 1761. 5. Huldah, Aug. 31, 1764, m. Jos. Dillingham, Feb. 29, 1793, and moved to Me. 6. Abigail, July 21, 1769, d. Mar. 5, 1806. 7. Charlotte, Feb. 17, 1772, m. Capt. Josh. Hall, Dux'y., July 12, 1792, and moved to Lunenburg. 8. Barzillai, Feb. 14, 1776, d. Dec. 24, 1792. 9. Harriet, Mar. 16, 1778, d. Aug. 23, 1796. 10. Joanna, Sep. 28, 1780, m. Levi Loring, Dux'y., Feb. 7, 1802.

9. Joseph, s. Henry 4, m. Mercy Waterman, of Hf'x., was an anchor-smith by trade, and lived in Pemb., where he d. ae. ab. 90. ch.: 1. Joseph, Mar. 12, 1757. 2. Waterman, Sep. 18, d. Dec. 14, 1758. 3. Jno., Mar. 30, 1761, m. Lucy Lowden, Nov. 25, 1784, and had *Jno.*, 1785; *Lucy*, 1787; *Mary W.*, 1791; *Edwin*, 1794; *Pamela*, 1796; and *Eliza*, 1798. 4. Priscilla, June 12, 1763, m. Freedom Chamberlin. 5. Jona., Ap. 8, 1767. 6. Marg't., June 9, 1770, m. Matt. Sylvester, Jan. 29, 1791. 7. Mercy, Jan. 19, 1774, m. Timo. Rose, June 9, 1795. 8. Freeman, Aug. 25, 1778, m. 1, Debo. Turner, and 2, Dolly Pushee, and moved to Lyme, N. H., where he has desc'ts. (See Turner Geneal. p. 37.)

10. Charles, s. Henry 4, m. Rebecca Keen, July 10, 1760, and lived in Pemb., where he d. Nov. 21, 1812. ch.: 1. Mary, Ap. 19, 1761, m. Lem'l. Keen, and moved to Me. 2. Lucy, Ap. 4. 1763, m. Josi. Bonney, Mar. 27, 1794. 3. Lydia, Jan. 13, 1765, m. Sam'l. Eells, July 7, 1783. 4. Charles, Jan. 9, 1767. 5. Jabez, Nov. 4, 1768. 6. Rebecca, Dec. 6, 1770, m. 1, Beza Ames, Bridg'r., Oct. 25, 1791, and 2, a Studley. 7. Elisha K., Sep. 28, 1772. 8. Jacob, Aug. 28, 1775. 9. Josiah, Aug. 21, 1778, m. Ruth Howard, and had *Josiah*, 1799, m. a Topliff, and lives in Bridg'r., Vt.; *Ruth H.,* 1801, d. 1802; *Jairus*, 1803, m., and lives in Bridg'r., Vt.; *Lewis*, Oct. 25, 1805, of Lynn, Ed. of the Bay State Democrat, and for 2 yrs. Clerk of the Mass. Ho. of Reps., is m., and has ch.; and *Robert*, 1810.

11. Isaac, s. Henry 4, m. Lois Ramsdell, Sep. 12, 1772, was engaged in the Forge, for many years; finally moved to Me., and there d. ch.: 1. Isaac, Jan. 3, 1774, m. Christiana Josselyn, Oct. 15, 1797, and d. Oct. 24, 1799, leaving 1 da., and 1 son, the last of whom was drowned at N. Bed. 2. Almorin, July 16, 1775, m. Chloe Whiting, July 28, 1801, and has *Eliza*, 1814, d. 1817; *Almorin*, of Batavia, N. Y., is m., and has ch.; *Houghton S.*, of Chelsea, Mass., is m., and has ch.; and *Caroline K.*, m. Warren A. Alley, of Lynn. 3. Lois, 1776, d. 1778. 4. Roland, May 3, 1778, m. Mary Church, lived in Me., and had ch. 5. Lois, Feb. 20, 1780, m. Jno. Woodworth, Nov. 26, 1801. 6. Hervey, Jan. 25, 1782, m., lived in Me., and had ch. 7. Hannah, b. and d. 1783. 8. Alden, May 20, 1784, m. a Paige, lived in Me., and had ch. 9. Ezra, Jan. 3, 1787, m., lived in Me., and had ch. 10. Sylvester, June 6, 1789, m. Simeon Prescott, and lived in Me. 11. Jno. D., June 4, 1791, m., lives in Me., and has ch. 12. Martin, 1793, d. unm. in Me.

12. Stockbridge, s. Thos. 5, m. Olive Standish, Nov. 24, 1768, who d. Sep. 10, 1803, and he May 10, 1817, ae. 76. ch.: 1. Olive, Nov. 10, 1769. 2. Stockbridge, Feb. 23, 1772. 3. Abigail, June 23, 1774, m., and went to R. I. 4. Lucy, Ap. 9, 1777, d. unm. 5. Ruth, Ap. 1, 1779, m. Capt. Dan'l. Hall, Dux'y., Nov. 27, 1798. 6. Seth, Dec. 6, 1782. 7. Jas., Nov. 15, 1785. 8. Christopher, May 2, 1788. 9. Amasa, Feb. 24, 1791.

13. Eleazer, s. Abraham, 6, m. 1, Bethia Bourne, Jan. 9, 1783, who d. Dec. 3, 1801; and 2, Alice W. Howland, Mar. 5, 1807; and lived and d. in Pemb. ch.: 1. Mary, Aug. 10, 1783, m. Jos. Munroe, Hf'x. 2. Lydia, Sep. 27, 1785, m. Jere. Stetson, H'n., Jan. 14, 1808. 3. Eleazer, Oct. 24, 1787. 4. Eph'm. A., Nov. 3, 1789. 5. Lyman, Nov. 9, 1791, m. 1, Betsey Delano; 2, wid. Bowditch; and 3, Sarah Holmes; lives in Dux'y.; no ch. 6. Nathan, Jan. 15, 1794, m. 1, a Lincoln; 2, a Lincoln; 3, a Lincoln; and 4, a Bronsden, and d. in Chas'n., leaving ch. 7. Bethia, Dec. 15, 1796, m. Wm. Estes, H'n., Sep. 10, 1815. 8. Priscilla, Mar. 10, 1789, m. Ezek'l. Turner. 9. Abraham, Jan. 20, 1801. 10. Calvin, May 7, 1803. 11. Lucy, Ap. 27, 1805, m. Job Luther, H'n. 12. Dorothy, Mar. 16, 1806, m. Benj. White, H'n. (By 2d,) 13. Debo. H., Dec. 12, 1807, m. Elb. Leach, N. Bridg'r. 14. Luther, Mar. 6, 1809, m. Jane G. Reed, E. Ab'n., in Jan., 1844, lives in H'n., and has *Luther A.*, and *Jane R.* 15. Elisha H., Jan. 24, 1811, m. Hannah Sawin, and lives in E. Bridg'r. 16. Julius, July 2, 1813, is m., and lives in H'n. 17. Jairus, Aug. 24, 1815, is m., and lives in Boston. 18. Issachar, Mar. 5, 1817, is m., and lives in Plymp'n. 19. Sophronia, m. Walter Reed, Ab'n. 20. Ezra, b. and d. 1819. 21. Ezra, d.

14. Isaac, s. Abraham 6, m. 1, Priscilla Bourne, Sep. 29, 1788; and 2, wid. Mary Boylston, and lived and d. in Pemb. ch.: 1. Abigail, Ap. 3, 1788, m. Reuben Shaw, S. Ab'n., Sep. 30, 1811. 2. Christiana, Feb. 12, 1790, m. Zebulon Clark, of H. 3. Priscilla, Ap. 21, 1791, m. Isaac Harkwell. 4. Sophia, Ap. 21, 1793, m. Josi. Cushing, Ab'n. 5. Isaac B., Jan. 17, 1797, moved to Albany, N. Y. (By 2d,) 6. Elenor, Ap. 25, 1799, m. Thos. H. Sampson, Pemb., Ap. 20, 1822. 7. Daniel, May 18, 1800, m. Debo. Damon, June 26, 1827, lives in Pemb., and has *Isaac*, Nov. 11, 1828; *Dan'l.*, 1831, d. 1834; *Marcus*, 1832, d. 1834; *Debo. M.*, June 14, 1835; *Jos. W.*, June 28, 1837; *Betsey J.*, June 22, 1839; and *Marcus M.*, July 23, 1841. 8. Celia, Jan. 24, 1802, m. 1, Jno. White, and 2, Noah Bonney. 9. Lois D., Dec. 15, 1803, m. Jas. H. Dwelley, Pemb.

10. Emily, Aug. 29, 1805, m. Elij. Damon, H'n. 11. Elizab. K., 1807, d. 1812. 12. Almira, July 11, 1809, m. Eben'r. B. K. Gurney, H'n.

15. Francis, s. Nathl. 7, m. Mary Hill, Feb. 17, 1782, and lived in that part of Pemb. now H'n., where he d. ch.: 1. Thos. H., b. and d. 1783. 2. Francis, Nov. 2, 1784. 3. Peter, Feb. 16, 1787. 4. Thos. H., 1789, d. 1792. 5. Jemima L., Oct. 4. 1791. 6. Mary, Feb. 24, 1794. 7. Sarah H., Jan. 25, 1798. 8. Alvah, Ap. 7, 1800. 9. Chloe, Oct. 7, 1802.

16. Henry, s. Henry 8, m. Lois Stetson, Ap. 15, 1793, and lived in Pemb. ch.: 1. Almy, Nov. 20, 1793, m. Eben'r. Mann, and moved to Me. 2. Wealthy, Dec. 25, 1795. 3. Charlotte, Nov. 12, 1797, m. Gad Soper, H'n., May 13, 1823. 4. Mary A., Aug. 13, 1799, m. Richard Bowker, H'n., Aug. 26, 1818. 5. Hannah, Mar. 14, 1801, m. Wm. Taylor, and d. in N. Bed. 6. Debo. S., Jan. 10, 1803, m. Josh. Stetson, Nov. 29, 1832. 7. Joanna L., Dec. 20, 1804, m. Elisha Mitchell, H'n. 8. Abigail, d. ae. 4. 9. Henry, May 1, 1807, m. Charlotte Stetson, June 11, 1833, lives in Pemb., and has *Joanna L.*, *Helen M.*, *Henry H.*, and *Charlotte E.*

17. Joseph, s. Joseph 9, m. Debo. Hatch, Aug. 23, 1784, lived in E. Bridg'r., and had, 1. Hercules H., Sep. 3, 1784, lived in Danvers, Mass., m., and had ch. 2. Demarcus, or Marcus F., June 7, 1786. 3. Joseph, Ap. 2, 1788, m., went to sea, and is prob. d. 4. Cyrus, July 6, 1790, m. Jane White, and moved to Plainfield. 5. Earle, July 11, 1792. 6. Debo. H., Jan. 15, 1795, m. Marcus Howe, Boston. 7. Branch, Dec. 3, 1797, m. wid. Lamson, and lives in Danvers. 8. Theron, Nov. 28, 1799, d. 9. Freeman, Nov. 28, 1799, m. wid. Hannah Morton, and lives in Me. 10. Eliza H., Sep. 22, 1802. 11. Jno. H., Sep. 22, 1805.

18. Jona., s. Joseph 9, m. 1, Sally Stetson, of Scit., and 2, Jenny Chase, and lived and d. in Pemb. ch.: 1. Waterman, Sep. 30, 1791, m. Melinda, da. Jona. Stetson, Scit., and d. leaving 2 das., one of whom is d. (By 2d,) 2. Marg't., May 18,

1794, m. Thos. Ellis, Mar. 28, 1814, and lives in E. Bridg'r. 3. Sally, Sept. 1, 1796, m. Nathl. Ellis, Dec. 21, 1813, and lives in Bridg'r. 4. Freeman M., Aug. 3, 1798, m. Priscilla L. Oldham, Dec. 11, 1820, lives in S. Boston, and has *George*, and *Freeman*. 6. Wm., Feb. 15, 1801, m. Abigail, da. Chas. Barstow, lives im Pemb., and has *Wm. B.*, Clerk in Boston, m. Hannah Barker, of Tiverton, R. I. 7. Jane, Jan. 1, 1803, m. Dan'l. Hall, jr., Dux'y., Nov. 20, 1823. 8. Eliza, Jan. 11. 1805, m. Jason Magoun, Nov. 30, 1826. 9. Hervey, Nov. 5, 1806, merchant, E. Bridg'r., m. Elizab. Tallman, and has *Sarah C.; Elizab.; Mary E.; Harriet;* and *Frank.* 10. Jas. M., May 12, 1809, m. 1, Lucy Josselyn, and 2, wid. Abby Delano, lives in Pemb., and has *Warren U.*, *Priscilla*, *Emma F.*, and *Amelia J.* Two ch. d. young. 11. Dorothy M., May 12, 1809, m. 1, Alex'r. Hillborn, Oct. 7, 1827, and 2, Tilden Crooker, Jan. 16, 1837.

19. *Charles Josselyn* s. Charles 10, m. Lucy Dwelley, Nov. 14, 1790, lived in H'n., and was for some years engaged in the Iron Business, at Sylvester's Forge, and on King st., and also in the Factory, in H'n. His w. d. in 1829, and he Nov. 2, 1846. ch.: 1. Lydia, Sep. 5, 1791, m. Benj. Mann, Esq., Mar. 10, 1810, and is d. 2. Oren, July 6, 1793. 3. Lucy D., Aug. 5, 1796, m. Hira Bates, Feb. 24, 1825. 4. Ozen, Mar. 29, 1798. 5. Mary, Aug. 21, 1800. 6. Chas., 1802, d. 1830. 7. Aaron, May 4, 1804, m. Amy, da. Spencer Binney, is a clergyman, of the Meth. denom., in Dux'y., and Rep. to the Mass. Leg. for the year 1853. ch.: *Joseph R.*, *Ed. S.*, *Albert S.*, *Charles G.*, *Martin B.*, and *Ann B.* Lost one. 8. Angeline, Feb. 26, 1806. 9. Marcia, July 8, 1808, m. Alvin Howland, Nov. 2, 1838. 10. Edwin, June 23, 1810, m. Nyreh Chandler, and lives in Chelmsford. 11. Julia A., Aug. 25, 1812, m. Dyer Robinson, Esq., S. Bridg'r. 12. Cyrus, Oct. 2, 1814, m. Elizab. B. Bates, Oct. 24, 1833, lives on King st., and has *Cyrus B.*, July 17, 1834; *Lewis*, Aug. 15, 1842; and *Angeline E.*, June 4, 1848. Lost 2, d. young. 13. Alonzo,

Jan. 23, 1818, m. Caroline A. Morse, Rox'y., lives in Boston, is an Iron Founder, and has *Charles D.*, 1848, and *Lucy M.*, d. 1851, ae. 1.

20. Jabez, s. Charles 10, m. Huldah Mann, Dec. 27, 1795, and had ch.: 1. Betsey, July 22, 1796, m. Calvin Barstow, Matt't., Aug. 7, 1814. 2. David, Nov. 25, 1798, m. Mary Bates, Dec. 15, 1822, lives in Pemb., and has *David A.*, Dec., 1823, m. Sophronia Keen, and lives in P.; *Benj. W.*, 1826, m. Lucy A. Brewster, and has Herbert A.; *Horatio*, 1828; *Caleb*, 1831; *Albert*, 1833; and *Jabez A.*, 1838. 3. Morrill, Dec. 4, 1801, m. Mary A. McIntosh, and lived and d. in Boston, leaving ch.: *Mary A.*, and *Sarah E.* 4. Jabez, Mar. 25, 1804, m. Eliza White, Feb. 6, 1827, and had 1 da., *Arabella W.*, m. Laban Rose, jr., of H. 5. Rebecca, Sep. 13, 1806, m. 1, Joseph Estes, of Me., and 2, Otis Perry, of H'n. 6. Isaiah, Feb. 17, 1809, m. Serena Bray, lives in S. Boston, is a Brass Founder, and has *Isaiah B.*, 1830; *George*, 1832; *Edwin*, 1834; *Mary A.*, d.; *Amelia A.*, 1839; and *Charles*, 1844. 7. Huldah, d. young. 8. Huldah, June 16, 1814. 9. Daniel, m. Lydia Wadleigh, lives in Me., and has *Edwin*, and *Herbert*. 10. Otis P., May, 1823, m. Abigail P. Delano, lives in Pemb., and has *Laura O.*, Dec., 1847. 11. Joshua, m. Mary Boylston, had 1 ch., who d.; his w. d.; and he went off in 1851, and has not been heard from since.

21. Elisha K., s. Chas. 10, m. Lydia Dwelley, Mar. 12, 1797, and is yet living in P. ch.: 1. Emily, Feb. 4, 1798, m. Isaac O. Stetson, May 5, 1821. 2. Caroline, Mar. 30, 1804, m. Seth Jones, of P. 3. George, May 8, 1803, m. Alice Walker, lives in Brookfield, Mass., and has ch. 4. Albert, 1805, d. ae. 24. 5. Lydia S., Mar. 6, 1808. 6. Elisha, Sep. 21, 1810, m. Abby Standish, Ap. 12, 1835, and has ch. 7. Almira, Feb. 13, 1814, m. 1, Thos. Baker, and 2, Jno. Mann, and lives in E. Bridg'r.

22. Jacob, s. Chas. 10, m. Abigail Ryder, of Plym'h., and lives in New Hampshire. ch.: 1. Wm., Aug. 19, 1796, sometime Capt. of the Han. R. Co., m. Ruth Rose, Oct. 8, 1820, and lived in H. on King st., where he d. in 1852, leaving ch.: *Abig. W.*, June

30, 1821, m. Ambrose Josselyn, and d. 1843; *Wm. E.*, Sep. 22, 1823, m. Lucy S. Littlefield, and lives in H'n.; *Eugene M.*, Sep. 2, 1826; *Mercy W.*, Dec. 31, 1831; *Priscilla*, July 10, 1834; and *Helen M.*, May 29, 1841. 2. Harriet, Feb. 13, 1798, m. Eli Stetson, of H'n., and is d. 3. Benj., May 10, 1802. 4. Elbridge, May 15, 1802, m. a Keith, lives in Lawrence, is sup't. of a foundry, and has ch. 5. Elijah, Ap. 2, 1804, m. Ednor Pike, and lives in S. Bos'n. 6. Leavitt R., Oct. 1, 1807, m. Hannah E. Hildreth, and lives in Chelmsford. 7. Algernon, Dec. 22, 1809, m. Mercy White, and lives in Lowell. 8. Edward, Aug. 20, 1812. 9. Maria E., Ap. 17, 1815, m. Caleb White, H'n. 10. Elizab. C., Mar. 14, 1818, m. Hezek. Reed, Ab'n.

23. Stockbridge, s. Stockbridge 12, m. Sarah Bell, Bos'n., Sep. 27, 1795, was for a time a merchant in B., and d. in Ab'n. ch.: 1. Henry E. G., Nov. 29, 1796. 2. Ralph A. S., Oct. 2, 1798, d. July 9, 1822. 3. Charlotte M. A., Feb. 4, 1801, d. Sep. 20, 1811. 4. Chas. O. W., Aug. 2, 1803. 5. Danl. S. S., May 27, 1805, m. a Hall, of Dux'y., and d. in N. Or's. 6. Frances S. S., Sep. 9, 1807. 7. Naomi O. R., Nov. 17, 1810, m. Silas Lane, E. Ab'n. 8. Austin M. C., Sep. 20, 1812, m. Elizab. J. Ware, Bos'n., 1841, and is proprietor of a Restorator in B. Noah. 9. Sarah C. A., Ap. 9, 1815, m. a Denton. 10. Mary A. B., b. and d. 1816.

24. Eleazer, s. Eleazer 13, m. Hannah Studley, Jan. 1, 1809, and lives in H., on Pleasant st. ch.: 1. Mary J., May 6, 1809, m. Ludov. Pool, E. Ab'n. 2. Stephen, Dec. 28, 1811, merchant and shoe manf'r., at the Four Corners; m. Eliza Studley, Nov. 16, 1834, and has *Eliza A.*, June 30, 1838, and *Geo. S.*, June 17, 1842. 3. Robert, Oct. 30, 1814, not m. 4. Hannah S., Aug., 1817? m. Jno. H. Benner, Jan. 1, 1835. 5. Eleazer, Feb. 14, 1823.

25. Abraham, s. Eleazer 13, m. Polly Cushing, Oct. 5, 1820, lives on Cross st., and is an anchor-smith by trade. ch.: 1. Wm. C., June 27, 1821, merchant tailor, late of Bos'n., m. 1, Thurza B. Shaw, and 2, Mary McDuffee, and has *Anna F.*, b. and d. 1845; and *Wm. A.*, Jan. 20, 1848. 2. Abraham A., May 18, 1823, d. Dec. 29, 1832. 3. Mary C., June 25, 1825, m. Geo. S. Newhall,

Dec. 21, 1843, and lives in E. Bridg'r. 4. Michal B., Oct. 9, 1827, m. Nathl. Pratt, and d. in Aug., 1848. 5. Bela C., Jan. 23, 1830, in Springf'd., Mass. 6. Sarah J., Sep. 15, 1833. 7. Henry C., Ap. 3, 1836. 8. Is'l. N., Jan. 31, 1839. 9. Geo. H., May 23, 1841. 10. Louisa C., May 23, 1844.

26. Francis, s. Francis 15, m. Debo. House, Jan. 15, 1810, and lived and d. in H'n., leaving ch.: 1. Hannah H., Ap. 12, 1810. 2. Mary, Ap. 29, 1811. 3. Ambrose, Dec. 17, 1812, m. Abig. W., da. Capt. Wm. Josselyn, and d. in H'n., leaving ch. 4. Ira, May 16, 1814, m. Sarah, da. Gad Bailey, lives on King st., and has *Sarah L.*, Dec. 4, 1842; *Anne A.*, July 18, 1845, d. Sep. 1849; and *Francis H.*, Aug. 14, 1851. 5. Thacher, May 18, 1816, d. Sep. 23, 1818.

27. Demarcus, or Marcus F., s. Joseph 17, m. Eunice Sawtell, and had ch.: 1. Marcus F. 2. Debo. H., m. Phineas Howard, of Canton. 3. Eunice S., m. Elijah Howard, of C. 4. Marcy W., m. Jas. M. Cook, Eng'r. Taun. & N. Bed. R. R. 5. Harriet N., m. Francis Farnsworth, and is in N. Y'k. 6. Eliza F., m. C. C. Williams, of Taunton, and d. in 1851. 7. Abigail, d. young. 8. Joseph H., May 13, 1820, stud. med. in the Pa. Univ., lives in Bos'n., m. Jane, da. David Kingman, Bridg'r., and has no ch. 9. Priscilla C., m. Francis A. Massey, Bos'n. 10. Lydia J., m. Chas. Howe, S. Ab'n., and has *Chas. W.*, *Emma L.*, *Edwy L.*, d., and *Joel J.* 11. Emily A., m. Jacob C. Young, of Bangor, and is in Cal'a. 12. Lucy F., not m. 13. Lucretia, m. Geo. H. Osborn, of S. Ab'n., and has *Amy C.* 14. Joel S., in Cal'a. 15. Benj. F.

28. Earl, s. Joseph 17, m. 1, Anne Brewster, and had 3 ch., all of whom d. He then m. 2, Sarah Hudson, of Bridg'r., and d. in Bangor, Me., Ap. 7, 1836, and his wid. m. Geo. W. Smith, of Bridg'r. ch.: 1. Earl P., May 16, 1822. 2. Asa H., Feb. 6, 1824, m. Harriet Hamilton, and lives in E. Bos'n. 3. Anna B., Oct. 6, 1825, m. Chas. Dyer, and lives in E. Wey'h. 4. Sarah J., Sep. 30, 1827, m. Galen Osborn, E. Bridg'r. 5. Caleb H., July 25, 1829, m. Harriet E. Fales, of Fox'o., and lives in W. Bridg'r. 6. Olive M., Oct., 1835, m. Thos. Lee, and d. July 15, 1851.

29. Oren, s. Chas. 19, m. Mary C. Mann, Feb. 14, 1816, lives on King st., and has been for many years connected with the foundry, in that part of H. He was Rep. from 1842–'44 ; T. Clk. in 1839, and '41 ; and from '43–'45 ; and Selectman in 1832, '33, '39, and from 1850–'53. ch. : 1. Oren C., Mar. 10, 1817, d. Ap. 6, 1819. 2. Mary C., Feb. 6, 1820. 3. Eli C., Mar. 13, 1822, m. 1, Hannah F. Robbins, Ap. 27, 1845, who d. July 14, 1846 ; and 2, Elener T. Ford, May 8, 1848 ; lives on School st., and has *Eli E.*, May, 1846, and *Florus*, Sep. 14, 1849. 4. Charles, Oct. 17, 1826, m. Rachael F. Winslow, May 16, 1850, lives on King st., and has *Clara*, Aug. 9, 1851. 5. Jane R., June 6, 1829, d. Jan. 2, 1830. 6. Geo. R., June 7, 1834.

30. Ozen, s. Chas. 19, m. Lucy, da. Elijah Barstow, who d. Nov. 26, 1842. Mr. J. lived for a time at the Four Corners, and kept the tavern there, but has lately been connected with the Custom House in Boston, as an Inspector. ch. : 1. Lucy B., Oct. 4, 1824, m. Caleb Packard, N. Bridg'r. 2. Ann E., May 2, 1826, m. Rob't. Barstow, Dec. 24, 1846. 3. Amelia W., Nov. 4, 1827, m. Henry A. Hall, Bos'n., Ap. 29, 1849. 4. Almira M., Jan. 24, 1829. 5. James O., Feb. 20, 1831, now living in H. 6. Maria C., June 14, 1834. 7. Mary, Dec. 1, 1836. 8. Melissa, June 22, 1839. 9. Helen, Nov. 1, 1841. 10. Robert, Oct. 9, 1842. 11. Saml., Oct. 9, 1842, d. Sep. 29, '44.

31. Henry E. G., s. Stockbridge 23, m. Minerva Gardner, lives in E. Ab'n., is a shoemaker, and has, 1. Henry W., m. Lydia A. Pool, lives in E. Ab'n., and has *Ann W.*, and *Miranda J.* 2. Charles S., m. Avis Ashley, and lives in E. Ab'n. No ch. 3. Harriet N., m. Jason Loud, of E. Ab'n., and has *Rosalina*. 4. Ann, d. ae. 15. Two other ch. d. young.

32. Marcus F., s. Marcus F. 27, m. Eliza Reed, and d. in Dec. 1846, having had, 1. Marcus F., Ap. 1828, m. Lucy Gurney, lives in S. Ab'n., and has *Walter W.*, July 28, 1850. 2. Wm. W., Feb., 1831, m. Amanda Fullerton, of Bridg'r., and has *Alice A.*, 1850, and *Ida W.*, 1852. 3. Eliza J. 4. Jas. W., d. 5. Jas. E. 6. Waldo E.

RESIDENCE OF REV. ROBERT L. KILLAM.

KILLAM, Rev. Robert L., b. June 29, 1790, s. of Asa, of Ipswich, and gr. s. of Isaac, (who descended from Austen Killam who was in Ipswich in 1637,) m. Phebe, da. Wm. Rice, of Marlb., Dec. 5, 1819; sett. in the ministry first in Marlbo'., from 1819–'21; then in Att'o., from 1821–'29; and since that period, has resided in H., on Wash'n. st., in the "Landlord Jacobs house," a view of which is annexed. He was pastor of the Univ. Soc. in Scit., from 1829–'37; has been one of the School Com'e. of H.; as a writer, has a logical mind, and a happy wit; and as a citizen, is universally esteemed, wherever he is known. ch.: 1. Lydia M. P., Oct. 27, 1820, m. Benj. Jacobs, May 26, 1839, and d. Sep. 7, 1846, leaving 2 ch. 2. Robert W., Mar. 22, 1823, m. Sophia B., da. Capt. Rufus Farrow, of Scit., May 7, 1848, and has *Lydia P.*, Jan. 13, 1849. 3. Charles H., Dec. 22, 1832.

LINDSEY, James, s. James of Pemb., m. Lovisa, da. Leonard Hill, June 26, 1808, who d. in May, 1842. He is yet living. ch.: 1. Mary, July 8, 1809, m. Geo. Beals, H'n. 2. Martin, June 19, 1811, m. Olive, da. Adam Perry, and d. July 21, 1843, leaving one son, *Martin A.*, Ap. 4, 1833. 3. Betsey B., Mar. 14, 1815, m. Wm. H. Joice, Sep. 19, 1839. 4. Philander, Aug.

29, 1817, m. Mary Foster, lives in Wey'h., and has ch. 5. Lovisa, July 14, 1819, m. Col. Jesse Reed, of Mf'd., for a sketch of whose life, see pp. 141–47. 6. James, Jan. 20, 1824, m. Jane A. Joice, and d. in Nov., 1843, leaving no ch.

LITCHFIELD, Lawrence, was of Barnstable, 1643, and bore arms. His son Josiah, b. 1647, m. Sarah, da. Rev. Nicholas Baker, and was the ancestor of Rev. Paul Litchfield, of Carlisle, Mass., and of Rev. Joseph, of York, Me., of whom we have spoken on p. 67. Frank Litchfield, of Scit., was also a desc't. of Lawrence, of Barnstable, and he was fa. of Lewis, of Hanover.

2. Lewis, s. Frank, of Scit., m. 1, Lucy Studley; 2, wid. Susan Wall; and 3, wid. Betsey Stetson formerly a Barstow; is a painter by trade; and has, 1. Marg't. L., June 22, 1808, m. Charles Winslow, 1827, sometime Selectman, of H. 2. Lewis, Sep. 23, 1811, m. Lucy L. Rogers, of Mf'd., Jan. 4, 1836, lives on Circuit st., is a shoemaker, and has *Lucy S.*, Sep. 26, 1837; *Delana*, Aug. 27, 1839; *Laura E.*, b. and d. 1841; *Emily*, Dec. 21, 1842; and *Lewis E.*, May 6, 1847. 3. Luther, Feb. 27, 1829.

LITTLE, John, s. Constant, of Mf'd., m. Abigail, da. Samuel Stetson, in Aug., 1835, who d. June 5, 1850, and he is living on Centre st.; a shoemaker by trade. ch.: 1. Mary F., b. 1837, d. 1838. 2. Abigail E., Aug. 13, 1839. 3. Jno. S., Jan. 24, 1843. 4. Zilpha A., b. and d. 1847.

2. Peabody, bro. of Jno., and s. Constant, of Mf'd., m. Olive, da. Benj. Stetson, in Dec., 1842, lives on Broadway, is a shoemaker, and has 1. Edward E., Sep. 25, 1843. 2. Augusta M., Nov. 17, 1845.

MAGOUN, Abner, of Pemb., is prob. a desc't of Jno. *Magoun*, or *McGoun*, who lived in the "Two Mile," now a part of Mf'd., in 1666, and who owned land in H. near Hugh's Cross. Abner m. Mary Bates, Dec. 16, 1796, and d. July 16, 1846, ae. 78, and his wid. Nov. 28, 1847, ae. 78. ch.: 1. Catherine, m. Jas. Bonney, of Pemb. 2. Abner, m. Mary H. Ellis, Ap. 1 1825, lives on Circuit st., is a shoemaker, and a man of respectable standing;—has *Horatio B.*, Nov. 20, 1826, m. Catherine B. Bonney, May, 1850, and lives near his fa.; *Mary H.*, Mar. 12, 1834; *Abner B.*, Feb. 17, 1836; and *Jane C.*, Dec. 30, 1839. 3. Mary S., m. Benoni Gurney, and is d. 4. Jason, m. Eliza Josselyn, and d., and his wid. and ch. are in S. Boston.

MANN, Richard, a "planter," was a youth in Elder Brewster's family, came to Plym'h. in the May-Flower, in 1620, was one on the Conihas. partners, in Scit., in 1646, and his farm was at the place known as "Mann hill." He died ab. 1655, and his wid. Rebecca, m. John Cowen, 1656. Of his ch., Thos., b. Aug. 15, 1650, was fa. of Benj., b. Feb. 19, 1697, who sett. in H. This is an old name in Eng'd., numerously represented there, the Earl of Cornwallis, being of the family, and Sir Horatio Mann, of Linton, Kent. There are other families in the U. S., besides the desc'ts. of Richard, who are sett. in Norfolk Co., and who are quite numerous in Randolph, and its vicinity. Samuel, was in Dedham, 1678; and Theodore, was in Wrentham, in 1700. The Manns of H. are desc'ts. of Richard, the planter.

2. Benj., s. Thos., and gr. s. Richard, m. Martha Curtis, Feb. 4, 1724, who d. Jan. 26, 1769, and he Mar. 2, 1770. He lived on Main st., it is said, in the ancient mansion, now occupied by Mr. Hanson, not far from the Bap. M. Ho., and was Selectman in 1745. ch.: 1. Martha, Jan. 6, 1725, m. William Curtis. 2. Benj., Aug. 4, 1727. 3. Rebecca, Aug. 13, 1729, m. Abner Curtis? 4. Sarah, Feb. 8, 1730, m. Robt. Gardner, H'm., June 5, 1760. 5. Ruth, May 12, 1735, m. Lem'l. Curtis, Jan. 16, 1752. 6. Mary, Aug. 13, 1737, m. Elij. Mann. Three ch. d. young.

3. Benj.a Mann s. Benj. 2, m. 1, Abigail Gill, Nov. 23, 1749; 2, the wid. of Charles Bailey, who d. in 1800; and 3, the wid. of Abner Curtis, and d. Jan. 27, 1816, ae. 89. He was Selectman in 1763 and '64, and erected the old grist mill, which formerly stood near the bridge, on North st. ch.: 1. Abigail, Sep. 9,

1751, m. Asa Turner, June 30, 1771, and d. in Me. 2. Benj , Mar. 3, 1753. 3. Olive, Ap. 18, 1754, m. Thos. Stetson, June 18, 1772. 4. Ezra, Dec. 11, 1755, d. in the Rev'n., Nov. 26, 1775. 5. Levi, Sep. 7, 1757. 6. Josh., July 14, 1759. 7. Bela, July 18, 1761, m. Ann Bryant, Scit., and moved to Lunenburg. 8. Sarah, Jan. 17, 1763, m. Jos. Neal, Cohas't., Dec. 6, 1791. 9. Susa G., Oct. 24, 1764, m. Caleb Whiting, Ap. 23, 1785. 10. Charles, Nov. 27, 1766, m. Abigail Gill, and d. in 1825, leaving *Abigail*, who m. Ithamar Whiting, of Ab'n., and *Merrill*, who m. Loring Curtis, of H., and others. 11. Perez, Nov. 7, 1768, m. Abigail Johnson, had ch., and d. in Beverly, Mass. 12. Sage, b. 1773, d. 1791. 13. Caleb, Sep. 13, 1775, m. Betsey Pratt, and d. Feb. 23, 1840, leaving a da. *Betsey*, who m. David Mann, of H.

4. Benj., s. Benj. 3, m. Hannah ——, and d. in H., Dec. 12, 1820, and his wid. May 21, 1827. ch.: 1. Hannah, m. 1, Thos. Whiting, and 2, Elisha Faxon. 2. Ruth, 1778? m. Isaac Wilder, Aug. 8, 1802. 3. Sarah, m. Jno. Curtis, Nov. 1, 1798.

5. Levi, s. Benj. 3, m. 1, wid. Anne Cooley, and 2, Patience Donnell, and d. Jan. 12, 1818, and his wid. Mar. 8, 1846. ch.: 1. Ezra, Ap. 21, 1780, m. Nabby Glover, of Beverly, and had ch. 2. Levi, Jan. 6, 1782, m. Marg't. Ames, of Boston, and had ch. 3. Alexander, Feb. 9, 1785, d. in S. Caro., ae. 28. 4. Jairus, Oct. 7, 1787, m. Desire Whiting, and lived in Chas'n. 5. Patience, May 1, 1791, m. 1, Eben'r. Arnold, 2, Joseph Cole, and 3, Job Pratt. 6. Anne K., Dec. 2, 1792, m. Henry Stoddard, of H. 7. John, Jan. 25, 1795. 8. Joseph, Oct. 12, 1797, m. Eunice Jacobs, and d. Dec. 2, 1835, and his wid. m. Martin Stoddard, of Mf'd. His ch. were *Jairus*, m. Emeline Runey, lives in Somerville, and has 3 ch.; and *Eunice*, m. William H. Smith, Chas'n. 7. Sarah, June 12, 1779, m. Wm. Henderson, Mar. 11, 1821. 10. Amy, Ap. 20, 1803, m. Dea. Jno. Brooks, Dec. 4, 1823.

6. Joshua Mann (Capt. Joshua,) s. Benj. 3' m. Mary Cushing, of H'm., Jan. 30, 1783, and d. Oct. 20, 1827, and his wid. July 1, 1849. He was Capt. of one of the Mil'y. Co's. of the town,

and Selectman from 1799 to 1802. Lived on Whiting st., where Albert Pool now resides. ch.: 1. Josh., 1784, d. 1792. 2. Molly, 1785, d. 1792. 3. Benj., 1788. 4. Mary C., 1794, m. Oren Josselyn, Feb. 14, 1816. 5. Josh., July 4, 1796. 6. David, Sep. 7, 1798.

7. John, s. Levi 5, m. Harriet Turner, his w. d., and he now lives in E. Ab'n. ch.: 1. Jno., Dec. 28, 1819, m. Sarah Chandler, lives in E. Ab'n., and has ch. 2. Josiah, Mar. 13, 1822. 3. Andrew, m. Abby O. Torrence, lives in E. Ab'n., and had 1 ch., which d. 4. Gustavus, Ap. 9, 1828, m. Elmira Vining, and lives in E. Ab'n. 5. Lucy T., 1829, m. Geo. Dunham, Oct. 16, 1850. 6. Harriet, m. Warren Lane, E. Ab'n. 7. Lydia, m. Lorenzo Foster, E. Ab'n. 8. Sarah. 9. Betsey.

8. Benj., Esq., s. Josh. 6, m. 1, Lydia Josselyn, and 2, Lydia C. Waterman, lives on Whiting st., was J. P. for many years, and a trader and farmer. ch.: 1. Benj. L., Ap. 19, 1812, d. in N. Orleans. 2. Albert G., 1813, d. 1817. 3. Lydia J., Feb. 25, 1815, m. Jno. Pool, jr., 1833, and d. 1852. 4. Almira, 1817, d. 1818. 5. Chas. F., Sep. 5, 1818. 6. Almira C., Jan. 11, 1820, m. Lysander Nash. 7. Henrietta M., 1822, d. 1838. 8. Newton, 1825, d. 1850. 9. Lucy A., Nov. 29, 1828. (By 2d,) 10. Marcus M., Nov. 22, 1840. 11. Albert G., July 17, 1843. 12. An inf., b. and d. 1846. 13. Everett N., June 24, 1847. 14. Abby J., May 13, 1851.

9. Maj. Josh., s. Josh. 6, m. Bethia Curtis, July 12, 1829, lives on Centre st., is a farmer, of respectable standing, and has, 1. Josh. W., Mar. 19, 1830, at the West. 2. Nancy J., Oct. 2, 1832, m. Martin T. Stetson, Oct. 6, 1850. 3. Rodney, Mar. 9, 1835. 4. Mary A., Nov. 10, 1839. 5. Horace, Nov. 12, 1842. 6. Geo. W., Mar. 12, 1845.

10. David, s. Josh. 6, m. Betsey, da. Chas. Mann, Ap. 4, 1821, lives at the corner of Main and North sts., and has, 1. David J., 1822, d. at sea, 1846. 2. Geo. H., Ap. 20, 1824, in Cal'a. 3. Mary J., Jan. 4, 1826. 4. Josh., Aug. 26, 1827. 5. Caleb, Ap. 3, 1829. 6. Sophronia, July 26, 1831, m. Jos. Hunt, Ab'n. 7. Russell C., July 30, 1836. 8. Albert G., June 26, 1838. 9. Howard F., Mar. 30, 1843. 10. Perez, d. ae. 18 mos.

McLAUTHLIN, Martin Parris, b. July 24, 1825, s. Martin, of E. Bridg'r., is the present worthy and accomplished Principal of the Academy, at the Four Corners; and is a gr. s. of Col. Jesse Reed, of Mf'd., of whom we have spoken on p. 141.

MORSE, Maj. Wm., of Newburyport, m. Marg't., da. David Prouty, Esq., the "plough maker," was Selectman for 9 years; Rep. 3 yrs.; often Moderator at Town meetings; and lived on Main st., until his removal to Lawrence, in 1847. ch.: 1. Lucy, Jan. 17, 1823, m. a Howard, of Hav'l. 2. Quincy, Dec. 14, 1824, m. wid. Elizab. M. Norton, Sep. 20, 1851, and lives on his father's place. 3. Sarah, Nov. 12, 1826, m. Wm. L. Henderson, Sep. 1, 1844. 4. Marcus, Dec. 12, 1828, m. Mary A. Leavitt, Scit., Nov. 16, 1849, lives on Main st., and has *Mary E.*, Oct. 27, 1849, and *Geo. R.*, Oct. 19, 1841. 5. Wm. M., Jan. 27, 1843.

MUNROE, Shuble, m. Mary Josselyn, Nov. 10, 1742, lived in a house which stood near Eben. Thayer's, on Centre st., and d. June 14, 1795, ae. 75, and his wid. Ap. 27, 1815, ae. 91. The hill near his house is still known as Shuble's Ridge. His son Shuble, b. Ap. 1, 1761, m. Abig. Stetson, Jan. 27, 1788, who d. June 5, 1812, and he Oct. 3, 1851, ae. 90. His ch. were, 1. Abig. S., m. Saml. Stetson, of H. 2. Jno., d., ae. 20. 3. Mary J., m. Eben. Thayer, of H. 4. Chas., of N. Y'k. 5. Isaiah, not m. Several ch. d. young.

NOTE. Tradition says that 5 bros. of the name of Munroe, came early to Am'a., and were the ancestors of the different families now existing in the U. S.; and from the N. E Gen. Reg. for 1847, p. 378, we learn that among the Scotch prisoners sent to N. Eng. in 1652, by order of the Eng. Gov't., were *Robert Monrow*, *John Monrow*, *Hugh Monrow*, and — *Monrow*. There were also 5 of the name of *Murrow*, viz.: *Jno.*, *Jno.*, *Neile*, *Jonas*, and *James*; and among the Settlers of Reading, Mass., were Henry, Jno., and Saml., *Merrow*, the former of whom d. in 1685. There was early a family of Munroes in R. I., and another in Va., from which President Munroe descended.

2. Benj., s. Benj., of Dorch'r., m. Mary H. Curtis, Nov. 11 1830, lives on Hanover st., and has, 1. Mary C., Aug. 28, 1831. 2. Benj. W., Ap. 22, 1833. 3. Lucinda T., Mar. 7, 1835. 4. Wm. H., Feb. 21, 1837. 5. David B., Oct. 14, 1839. 6. Geo. R., Ap. 26, 1843.

3. Hiram, s. Benj., of Dorch'r., b. 1811, m. Tempe. C. Stetson, May 6, 1832, lives on Spring st., is a shoemaker, and has, 1. Francis M., May 4, 1834. 2. Joanna S., Oct. 7, 1835. 3. Julia M., Dec. 22, 1838. 4. Lucy S., Mar. 23, 1841. 5. Eliza L., May 18, 1843. 6. Adaline T., June 15, 1846. 7. Sarah E., July 23, 1848.

NASH, Lysander B., s. Lewis, of Wey'h., b. Mar. 22, 1822, m. Almira C. Mann, and has Henrietta C., Ap. 15, 1846, and Lysander W., May 24, 1848.

PERCIVAL, Sylvanus, b. June 20, 1796, s. Benj. of Sandwich, m. Celia Ewer, of S., Nov. 14, 1816, and lives near N. River Bridge. ch.: 1. Jno. P. T., Oct. 19, 1818, m. Drusilla Snow, and lives in Cohas't. 2. Sylvanus, Mar. 8, 1820, m. Mary A. Stone, and lives in Dorch'r. 3. Celia E., Dec. 28, 1821. 4. Saml. W., Sep. 3, 1823, m. Lurana Cleal, and is in Cal'a. 5. Nancy W., Dec. 29, 1824. 6. Gustavus, Aug. 30, 1826, m. Josephine Josselyn, and lives in H'n. 7. Henry C., May 3, 1829, m. Maria, da. Abisha Soule, Feb. 11, 1851, and d. in 1852, leaving *Henry W.*, b. Nov. 12, 1851.

PERKINS, Ozias, b. June 9, 1804, s. Eben'r. of Bridg'r., (and a desc't. of David, of Beverly, who sett. in Bridg'r. bef. 1688, and was Rep., &c.) m. 1, Ann Wing, Nov. 13, 1828, who d. Sept. 25, 1831; and 2, Mary C. Bates, May 21, 1832; lives on Winter st.; is an anchor smith by trade, and a gent. of intelligence and respectability; has, 1. Ann W., Sep. 12, 1831. (By 2nd,) 2. Lorenzo, Oct. 12, 1836. 3. Lewis, May 15, 1839. 4. Mary C., Nov. 16, 1840.

PERRY, Richard, was one of the Mass. Co., in 1629, and his name often occurs on the annals of the Co. Jno. was freem. in Bos'n., 1632–3, was aft. of Rox'y., and d. in 1643; and the same year another Jno. Perry was freem. in Taunton. Isaac Perry was a freem. in Mass., in 1631–2. Thos. Perry, ae. 34, with his w. Dorothy, and s. Benj., were pass. for Va. in 1635; and we find a Thos. early in Ipswich, who may have been the same. Arthur Perry was freem, in Bos'n., 1639, and had Seth, Jno., Elishua, &c. Wm. Perry was freem. in Scit. in 1643, and some of his desct's. are still living in Scit. and Pemb., and elsewhere.

2. Thos. Perry, from Mass., according to Deane, was in Scit. bef. 1647, m. Sarah, da. Isaac Stedman, and had his farm on the S. part of Chamberlain plain. He may have been s. of Thos. of Ipswich. There is no record of births of his ch. in Scit.; but we are told that he had Thos., Wm., Henry, Joseph, and Jno. Of these, Wm. m. Elizab. Lobdell, 1681, and had Amos, who m. Ruth Turner, June 8, 1720, lived near the 3rd Herring brook, and was fa. of Dea. Isaac, the shipbuilder, of H., who was b. Sept. 5, 1736, m. Jemima Farrow, and d. Aug. 16, 1825, ae. 89, and his w. in Nov. 1824, ae. 78. His da. Priscilla, m. Elij. Packard, June 26, 1803; and his sons Timo., and Isaac, went to St. John's, N. B.; his da. Betsey, m. a Smith; and Ruth went to Me. Wm., s. Thos., Senr., had also another son, Benj., b. Dec. 31, 1688, who m. Ruth Bryant, Feb. 20, 1711, and had Saml., Nov. 28, 1712, and others. The desct's. of this son are here given, according to the best information we could obtain.

3. Saml., s. Benj.? s. Thos., lived in Pemb., and m. Eunice Witherell, Sep. 27, 1734, who d. a wid., Feb. 21, 1795. ch.: 1. Henry. 2. Mary, m. Howland Beal, Dec. 29, 1757. 3. Saml. 4. Noah, m. Jane Hobart, Oct. 1, 1772, and had *Hobart*? drowned, ae. 20; *Mary*, m. Jacob Ford, Oct. 11, 1792, and lived in Ab'n.; and *Danl.*, m. a Hobart, and lives in S. Ab'n. 5. Israel. 6. Betsey, m. Col. Amos Turner, Feb. 14, 1771. 7. Seth. 8. Adam.

4. Henry, s. Saml. 3, m. Bethia Baker, of Dux'y., Dec. 25, 1760, lived in Pemb. and d. March 23, 1815, ae. 80, and his wid. Jan. 20, 1822, ae. 89. ch.: 1. Saml. B. 2. Henry, Ap. 25, 1764. 3. Jno., m. Rhoda Barker, Jan. 27, 1793, and lived and d. in Plym'h., having had 4 ch., of whom 2 are living, viz.: *Lewis*, of Plym'h., and *Rhoda*, both bap. May 18, 1794. 4. James, d. unm. in Scit. John and James were twins.

5. Saml., s. Saml. 3, m. Alice Baker, lived in Pemb., and d. Sept. 5, 1816, ae. 76. ch.: 1. Chas., Oct. 2, 1771. 2. Elizab., Sep. 22, 1776, m. Caleb White. 3. Lucy, m. 1, Jabez Witherell, 2, a Crooker, and 3, a Harrob. 4. Saml., m. Lucy Oldham,

of Pemb., in 1807, and had *Otis*, Ap. 18, 1808, a carpenter by trade, m. wid. Rebecca Estes, Dec. 8, 1840, and lives in H'n., no ch.; *Almira*, Ap. 1, 1811, m. Thacher Perry, of Pemb.; and *Horatio*, May 4, 1814, living in Pemb., unm.

6 Israel Perry (Dea. Israel,) s. Saml. 3, m. 1, Abig. Baker, of Mf'd., who d. Dec. 14, 1807, ae. 61; and 2, wid. Relief Soper, Dec. 17, 1809; and d. Feb. 18, 1817, ae. 73, and his wid. Feb. 24, 1824, ae. 85. Lived back of Plain st., in the house known as the "Hanmer hook house," which has been torn down for many years. He was Selectman in 1797, and '98. ch.: 1. Israel, Ap. 28, 1771, of Newbyp't. 2. Thos., Aug. 30, 1772, m. wid. Sarah Ramsdell, June 11, 1810, and d. July 22, 1817, leaving no ch. 3. Hannah, June 18, 1775, m. Edward Stetson, Jan. 1, 1799, and is living in H. 4. Horatio, Oct. 3, 1784, sett. in Salem, Mass., and there d. 5. Paul, June 25, 1786, m. Chloe Bailey, Sep. 23, 1813, lives in Camden, Me., and has ch. 6. Oakes, sett. in Me., and there d. 7. Nabby B., Sep. 6, 1789, not m. 8. Hayti or *Ittai*, of Salem, Mass.

7. Seth, s. Saml. 3, m. Hannah Josselyn, July 2, 1782, and d. in Pemb. His wid. is living in P., with her son Josh., at the advanced age of 98, and retains to a remarkable degree, both her bodily and mental powers. ch.: 1. Elijah, Ap. 14, 1783, m. Chloe Stetson, July 6, 1806, lived in P., and d. Oct. 9, 1814, ae. 32, and his w. Dec. 27, 1812, ae. 26, leaving ch.; *Thacher*, 1807, d. 1811; *Isaiah S.*, Mar. 23, 1809, m. Julia A. Oldham, May 5, 1831, and lives in Me.; and *Edward Y.*, Oct. 4, 1812, m. Mary Oldham, July 8, 1834, lives in P., and is a manufacturer of tacks, in H., at what was formerly Dyer's works. (See p. 141.) 2. Joshua, Ap. 27, 1788, m. Mary, da. Capt. Ichabod Thomas, and lives in P. Has no ch.

8. Adam, s. Saml. 3, m. Elizab. House, Oct. 20, 1776, and lived in H., where he d. Aug. 23, 1830, ae. 78, and his wid. Feb. 12, 1845, ae. 89. ch.: 1. Elizab., Ap. 11, 1777, m. Moses

French, Bos'n. 2. Olive, b. 1779, d. 1783. 3. Adam, Dec. 28, 1780. 4. Calvin, b. and d. 1782. 5. Sage, 1783, d. 1799. 6. Calvin, June 19, 1785, m. Mary Litchfield, lived in Scit., and had ch. 7. Gideon, Mar. 23, 1787, m. Cath. Perry, Mar. 21, 1816, who d. June 3, 1822, he survives, and has *Catherine*, 1817, d. 1832; *Franklin*, May 17, 1821, living in H., not m.; and *Henry N.*, Ap. 17, 1828, lives in Medford. 8. Olive, Oct. 5, 1791, m. Martin Lindsey, and is living, a wid., in H. 9. Levi, Mar. 2, 1793, m. Sarah J. Colcord, Sep. 9, 1826, and had a son *Levi*, d. young. The fa. is living in H. 10. Lovisa, Sep. 1, 1797, m. Benj. D. Torrey, Mar. 30, 1818, and is living, a wid., in H.

9. Samuel B., s. Henry 4, m. Anne Bates, Feb. 2, 1786, lived in H., on Broadway, and had, 1. Wealthy, 1786, d. 1790. 2. Nancy, 1787, living, unm. 3. Levi, Jan. 20, 1789, m. Fanny Price, of H'm., and went to Ohio, many years ago. 4. Cephas, Sep. 3, 1790, m. 1, Anne Norris, Bos'n.; and 2, Nabby Chamberlain, Oct. 7, 1838, lives on Broadway, and has, 1. *Anne*, m. Levi Perry; *Lucy*, m. Wm. R. Skerry, Ap. 25, 1846; *Cephas*, Jan., 1828; and *Jerome*, Aug. 5, 1832. 5. Jno., Ap. 29, 1793, went to sea, and is prob. d. 6. Seth, Ap. 29, 1793, m. Melinda F. Cox, Feb. 5, 1828, and has *Jno. H.*, Jan. 19, 1831; *Caroline H.*, Oct. 20, 1832; and *Julia A.* 7. Bethia B., July 20, 1795, m. Dea. Isaac Cook, H'n. 8. Wealthy, Feb. 10, 1797, m. Albert Stetson, Nov. 29, 1830. 9. Saml., Jan. 24, 1799, m. Diana Brett, of E. Bridg'r., and had *Levi*, Nov. 9, 1820, (m. Anne Perry, and has Francena, Dec. 4, 1842; Alfred, Aug. 2, 1844; Albert S., June 1, 1847; Bradford, b. and d. 1848; and Florence, Oct. 19, 1849); *Kilborn R.*, Aug. 17, 1822, (m. Rebecca A. Gurney, Oct. 1845, lives on Centre st., is a shoemaker, and has Ellen A., Dec. 30, 1846; Sarah E., Jan. 11, 1849; and Emma W., May 13, 1851); *Anna*, m. Josh. S. Rose, of H.; and *Elizab. F.*, ae. ab. 12. 10. Alva, Dec. 15, 1800, d. unm. 11. Perez, May 24, 1803, m. Fanny Stetson, Nov. 2, 1828, lives on Broadway, and has *Perez E.*, 1829; and *Fanny S.*, 1831, m. Andrew T. Damon, Ap. 22, 1851. 12. Lydia N., Feb. 11, 1805, m. Stephen S. Bowers. 13. Jerome, Sep. 15, 1807, d. unm. in Ohio. 14. A da. d. young.

10. Henry, s. Henry 4, m. 1, Content Barker, Ap. 25, 1790, who d. Mar. 20, 1821; and 2, wid. Mary Ramsdell, and d. in P., Aug. 10, 1837, ae. 73. His wid. survives. ch.: 1. Nathl., Jan. 1, 1791, m. 1, an Edwards, and 2, the wid. of Jno. Perry, of Plym'h., and lived in N. Bed. 2. Catherine, May 15, 1794, m. Gideon Perry, Mar. 21, 1816, and d. Jan. 3, 1832. 3. Nabby B., Dec. 25, 1796. 4. Ethan, May 11, 1802. 5. Betsey, Oct. 27, 1805, m. a Dickerman, and d. Aug. 17, 1831. 6. Robert, Oct. 22, 1809, m. Betsey Macomber, lives in H'n., and has ch.

11. Chas., s. Saml. 5, m. Hannah Bisbee, Jan. 30, 1794, lived in Pemb., and had, 1, Chas. B. 2. Alice B., m. Levi C. Wright, E. Bridg'r., June 24, 1827. 3. Ruth. 4. Hannah, m. and lives in Bridg'r. 5. Jno. B., Oct. 4, 1806. 6. Priscilla, Jan. 27, 1809, m. Thos. Drake, Jan. 6, 1828. 7. Thacher, Jan. 7, 1812, m. Almira, da. Saml. Perry, Nov. 26, 1840, and lives in P. 8. Elijah, Oct. 13, 1815, of P. 9. Sherman, of Pemb.

12. Adam, s. Adam 8, m. Polly Field, lived in Dorch'r., and d. July 7, 1826, and his wid. Aug. 1, 1849. ch.: 1. Sage, d. 2. Josiah F., Sep. 17, 1808, m. Sarah Hildreth, Feb. 9, 1836, lives on Circuit st., and has *Sarah E.*, Jan. 25, 1837; *Josiah F.*, July 24, 1839; *James H.*, Mar. 5, 1844; and *Anna A.*, Oct. 25, 1850. 3. Eliza, d. 4. Levi, of Dorch'r. 5. Louisa. 6. Mary E. 7. Oliver, of D.

13. Ethan, s. Henry 10, m. Rosilla Ramsdell, July, 1823, lives at the corner of Main and Plain sts., is a farmer, and has, 1. Geo. B., Jan. 21, 1824, m. Adaline W. Bates, May, 1846, who d. in 1852, leaving *Francis*, Dec. 31, 1847, and *Seth W.*, Mar. 10, 1850. 2. Wm. G., Oct. 23, 1825, m. Charlotte Torrey, and has 1 ch. 3. Ethan T., Ap. 1829. 4. Elijah, Sep. 15, 1831. 5. Joseph, Aug. 1, 1833. 6. Rosilla C., 1836, d. 1839. 7. Rosilla J., Aug. 6, 1841. 8. Chas., Aug. 17, 1845.

PETERSON, Phineas P., b. Dec. 7, 1824, s. Benj., of Paris, Me., m. Avis H., da. Geo. W. Turner, July 4, 1848, is a shoemaker, lives on Whiting st., and has Geo. R., Jan. 9, 1851.

PHILIPS, Absalom, s. Chris'r., of H'n., m. Abigail Baker, and has ch.: 1. Gid. B., Jan., 1805. 2. Abig., Mar. 30, 1806, m. Chas. Lincoln, Bridg'r. 3. Almira, Dec. 29, 1808, m. Thomas Damon, and is living a wid. in H. 4. Jas., Feb., 1810. 5. Betsey, Oct. 9, 1811, m. Chas. Smith, of H. 6. Ann T., 1813, d. young. 7. Chas., 1815. 8. Thos. H., 1817. 9. William, Dec., 1820. 10. Nath'l., Feb. 4, 1822. 11. Zavan, Sep. 19, 1823. 12. Albert, Ap. 3, 1826.

2. Edmund, s. Edmund, of H'n., an anchor-smith, m. Joan Richmond, in Oct., 1845, lives on Winter st., and has 1. Allen, June 10, 1846. 2. Geo. L., Jan. 28, 1848. 3. Nancy B., 1850, 4. Mary M., Mar. 29, 1852.

POCORNY, Joseph, b. Dec. 16, 1809, s. Joseph, of Bos'n., m. Lydia Clapp, of Scit., May 20, 1832, and was the Landlord of the Tavern, at the Four Corners. ch.: 1. Joseph E., d. 1834. 2. Augustine P., Dec. 22, 1835, drowned, Aug. 29, 1850. 3. Cerena C., Jan. 3, 1828. 4. Eunice A., Aug. 8, 1841. 5. Joseph E., 1843, d. 1846. 6. Lydia A., Ap. 7, 1847.

POOL, Jno., b. Feb., 1812, s. Jno., of Ab'n., m. Lydia J., da. Benj. Mann, Esq., in Mar., 1833, lives on North st., is a shoemaker, and has, 1. Jno. S., Sep. 15, 1833. 2. Lydia M., May 18, 1836. 3. Benj. B., Jan. 6, 1841. 4. Marg't. A., July 11, 1849. 5. Alonzo N., Dec., 1851.

2. Joseph, s. Jno., of Ab'n., m. Debo., da. Ensign Crooker, lives on Whiting st., is a stone-mason by trade, and has, 1. Jos. W., Jan., 1839. 2. Debo. A., May, 1843.

PRATT, Jona., s. Sam'l., of Plym'h. ?, was in that part of Scit., now H., with his fa., in 1676, lived near where Martin Church does, on Wash'n. st., and d. June 28, 1729. He m. Marg't. Locke, or *Low*, Jan. 8, 1691–2, and had Othniel, Jan. 25, 1708, who m. Mary Prior, Dux'y., Ap. 2, 1737. She d. Mar. 12, 1758, and he June 23, 1758. His ch. were, 1. Jona., Oct. 15, 1740; 2. Othniel, Mar. 7, 1743, moved to Spencer; 3. Benj., Mar. 4, 1745; 4. Mary, 1750; and sev. ch. that d. young.

2. Jona., s. Othniel, m. 1, Lucy Church, Dec. 30, 1762, who d. Aug. 23, 1789; 2, Lydia Chamberlin, Ap. 15, 1790, who d. Nov. 23 of that year; and 3, Desire Palmer, Jan. 10, 1798; and d. Nov. 28, 1814. ch.: 1. Jabez, 1769, of Me., was m., and had ch. 2. Elisha, 1771, m. Rebecca Keen, and moved to Me. 3, Mary, 1773, d. in Me. 4. Lucy, m. Josi. Chamberlin, Nov. 25, 1784. 5. Jno., of Me. 6. Sarah, 1776, m. Cyrus Leavitt, of Me., June 1, 1794. 7. Joanna, 1779, m. Nath'l. Stetson, Mar. 7, 1811. 8. Church, 1789, of Me. 9. Debo., 1789, m. Luther Merrill, Me. (By 2d,) 10. Benj. C., Nov. 23, 1790.

3. Benj. C., s. Jona. 2, m. 1, Rebecca E. Sylvester, Dec. 5, 1819, who d. Dec. 3, 1847, and 2, wid. Marg't. Lane; lives on Elm st.; is a farmer, and nurseryman; and has, 1. Rebecca E., Jan. 27, 1821, m. Silas B. Jones. 2. Lydia C., d. ae. 10 ds. 3. Lucy B., Jan. 31, 1824. 4. Benj. F., Mar. 10, 1826, in Ab'n. 5. Geo., Aug. 27, 1828, works at the Curtis Forge. 6. Mary, Sep. 14, 1831. 7. Lydia C., Dec. 28, 1834. 8. Henry Mar. 11, 1839.

4. Jno. W., s. Isaac, and gr. s. Isaac, Wey'h., b. Dec. 9, 1829, lives in H., on Centre st. and is a shoemaker, and school teacher. Not m.

David Prouty

PROUTY, David, Esq., s. David, of Scit., b. May 18, 1778, m. Lydia, da. Hezek. Stoddard, lived in H. for some years, on Curtis st., being engaged in the plough business, (see the chap. on Mfr's.) and d. Mar. 31, 1846, ae. 68. ch.: 1. Marg't., Feb. 4, 1796, m. Maj. Wm. Morse, now of Lawrence, Mass. 2. Veniah, Ap. 9, 1811, kept the Half-way-House in Scit. for some yrs., (now occupied by his son, Jno.) and is at present in Framingham, Mass. 3. Lorenzo, May 3, 1806, of the firm of Prouty & Mears, Bos'n., m. Lucy W., da. Jno. Mears, and has *Lorenzo*, *Lucy C.*, and *Ellen*. 4. Lydia, July 19, 1807, m. Horatio Baker, Ab'n. 5. David O., June 7, 1818, m. Sarah A. Gray, lives in Philad., and has 3 ch.

PUFFER, Jno., s. Jno., of Ab'n., b. 1798, m. 1, Abig. S. Crooker, 1822, who d. Dec. 23, 1850 ; and 2, wid. Lovisa Harlow, Aug. 15, 1851 ; lives on Winter st. ; and is a shoemaker. ch. : 1. Abig., June 2, 1824, m. Martin W. Damon. 2. Tamar J., Oct. 31, 1827, m. Chas. Sampson, of H. 3. Mary M., 1830, m. Melzar Keen, Ab'n., Oct. 11, 1848.

RAMSDELL, or RAMSDEN, Joseph, was in Plym'h., in 1643, and Saml., one of his desct's., sett. in that part of Scit., now H., m. Martha Bowker, and had ch. Thos., prob. also a desc't. of Joseph, was of H., 1712, and had, by w. Sarah, 1. Gideon, Sep. 13, 1712. 2. Sarah, July 12, 1715. 3. Mercy, Nov. 5, 1717, m. Peleg Stetson, Mar. 9, 1738. 4. Lydia, Sep. 5, 1719. 5. Elizab. ? m. Eben'r. Curtis, 1747. 6. Grace, 1725, m. Adam Prouty, 1744. 7. Thos. ?

2. Joseph Ramsdell prob. another desc't. of Joseph, of Dux'y., m. 1, Mary Homer, Ap. 23, 1730, who d. June 1, 1754 ; and 2, Mercy Prior, Nov. 25, 1755, who d. July 20, 1766, and he, Aug. 22, 1787, ae. 86. ch. : 1. Mary, Jan. 6, 1731, m. Wm. Whiting, 1748. 2. Avis, July 14, 1732, d. Dec. 28, 1740. 3. Priscilla, bap. Sep. 8, 1734, m. Isaac Prouty, Dec. 25, 1755. 4. Nehemiah, Nov. 13, 1734, m. Rebecca Chamberlin ? Dec. 29, 1757, and moved to C't. 5. Thos., Oct. 3, 1736, d. March 13, 1757. 6. Joseph, Ap. 25, 1739, d. Ap. 6, 1740. 7. Avis, bap. Mar. 29, 1741, m. Josh. Dwelley, Dec. 24, 1761. 8. Joseph, July 3, 1843. 9. Japhet, Aug. 22, 1745, d. June 19, 1750. 10. Sarah, Ap. 19, 1749, m. Oliver Pool, Jan. 13, 1774. (By 2d,) 11. Mercy, Ap. 28, 1757, m. 1, Rich'd. Estes, Nov. 4, 1778, and 2, an Ellis, of Sandwich. 12. Lydia, bap. Aug. 26, 1759, m. Saml. Whitcomb, Nov. 6, 1791.

3. Joseph, s. Joseph 2, m. 1, Elizab. Barker, Feb. 1, 1770, who d. June 19, 1786 ; and 2, Elizab. Ellis, May 17, 1787, who d. Oct. 20, 1811, ae. 59, and he, Aug. 5, 1817. ch. : 1. Mary, July 29, 1771, m. Nathl. Ellis, July 20, 1789. 2. Priscilla, Mar.

18, 1773, d. July 24, 1774. 3. Joseph, Sep. 10, 1775. 4. Priscilla, July 1776, d. Oct. 17, 1777. 5. Barker, bap. June 13, 1779. 6. Homer.

4. Joseph, s. Joseph 3, m. Ruth Stockbridge, Feb. 3, 1800, and lives in Warren, Mass. ch.: 1. Joseph, Oct. 21, 1800, m. Elizab., da. Robt. Eells, Dec. 3, 1827, and has *Elizab. H.*, Ap. 25, 1830, m. Aaron King, of Palmer, Sep 1, 1852; *Adelaide*, Oct. 8, 1833; *Marg't. B.*, Oct. 6, 1841. 2. Mary, Oct. 16, 1803, d. Ap. 12, 1827. 3. Homer, Aug. 12, 1810, m. Francis E. L., da. Thos. Powell, Newburgh, N. Y'k., June 16, 1835, and has *Mary L. P.*, Mar. 23, 1836, d. July 29, 1841; *Frances J.*, May 31, 1838; *Thos. P.*, May 14, 1840; *Jas. A. P.*, Mar. 9, 1842; *Henry P.*, 1844; and *Homer S.*, 1852.

5. Barker, s. Joseph 3, m. Lucy Ellis, Aug. 31, 1800, and had, 1, Ruth S., Dec. 14, 1801, m. Sylvanus Estes, Oct. 25, 1818. 2. Mary B., m. Reuben Estes, Mar. 18, 1819. 3. Lucy E., Oct. 17, 1804, m. Wm. Estes, Mar. 14, 1825. 4. Homer, Ap. 12, 1807. 5. Tryphosa, Oct. 17, 1809. 6. Josiah B., May 15, 1812. 7. Joseph, Dec. 18, 1815.

6. Homer, s. Joseph 3, m. Betsy Stockbridge, Oct. 27, 1816, sett. in Warren, and d. Dec. 19, 1850, having had, 1. Wm. B., June, 1825. 2. Mary E., Sep. 25, 1829, m. Joseph K. Makepeace, Mar. 12, 1851, and has *Mary E.*, Feb., 1852.

7. Silas Ramsdell, of a different family from the above, is in H., with his son Jacob L., who is m., and has 1 da., Susanetta, b. Oct. 24, 1851. The fa., Silas, m. 1, Ann Lawrence, by whom he had Jacob L.; 2, Elenor Stetson; and 3, Lois Hammond. By the last 2, he has no ch.

RANDALL, William, was of Scit., 1640, and of his descendants, Gideon, and Elijah, resided in H. for a time. The latter, Elijah, was fa. of *Allen*, of H., who m. Betsey Jones, of Scit., and lives on Wash'n. st. His ch. are, 1. Elizabeth, m. Geo. Richardson, of Medford. 2. Allen, 1821, m. Eliza Kelly, Oct. 6, 1846, lives in S. Scit., and has ch. He is a shoemaker by trade, and a young man of respectable standing. 3. Lydia, m. John B. Wilder, of H.

REED, Capt. William, of Dux'y., m. Polly Glass, and lived for a time in H., on Centre st., where he d. May 9, 1851, ae. 65. His da. Wealthy, m. Lewis Hunt, of D.; and Hannah, m. Jared Alden, of S. Ab'n. His son, Saml. H., yet resides in Hanover; m. Lucy J. Estes, June 1835, and lives on Circuit st. ch.: 1. Wm. E., Sep. 24, 1836. 2. Bethia C., June 13, 1838. 3. Mary G., Dec. 26, 1839. 4. Lucy P., Feb. 10, 1842. 5. Celia J., June 28, 1844. 6. Eliza B., Mar. 8, 1846. 7. Augustine, Mar. 14, 1848. 8. A son, b. Mar. 3, 1850, d. young. 9. Jane L., June 31, 1851.

2. Col. Jesse, of Mf'd., b. 1778, is the one whose history we have given at large on p. 142. We present, above, a likeness of that gentleman, taken expressly for this work, as an accompaniment to our sketch.

RICE, Alvin, b. July 1, 1824, s. John, of Me., (and prob. a desct. of Edmond Rice, who was of Sudbury, 1640.) m. Charlotte Arnold, of Ab'n., d., lives on Whiting st., in the house built by Jared Whiting, and is a shoemaker. ch.: 1. Ann E., May 9, 1847. 2. Jno. W., Jan. 1852. Lost one ch., an infant.

RICHARDS, Dr. Jacob, s. Jacob, of Wey'h., grad. B. U., 1824; stud. med. with Dr. Jno. C. Warren, of Bos'n.; and sett, in H. from 1834 to 1836. He now resides in Braintree, Mass, He m. Elizabeth, da. Rev. Calvin Wolcott, formerly Rector of St. Andrew's Church, and she d. May 2, 1846. ch.: 1. Augustus Jacob, b. in H., Sep. 20, 1835. 2. George Calvin, b. in Br'e., Jan. 18, 1838. 3. Sarah Ann, Feb. 5, 1840. 4. Susanna Lincoln, Sep. 29, 1842. 5. Mary Gardner, Ap. 1, 1845.

RIPLEY, John, of Ab'n., lived on Whiting st., and d. Mar. 26, 1829, ae. 49, having had ch.: 1. John, d. unm. 2. Josiah, m. a Keen, and d. in Pemb. 3. David, d. unm. 4. Benjamin, d. unm. 5. Martin, m. a Lincoln, and lives in Cohasset. 6. Washington, Jan., 1826, lives on Main st., shoemaker. 7. William, d. young. 8. Seth, in Ab'n.

ROBBINS, Nicholas, was of Dux'y., 1638; and Thos. was of Dux'y., 1643. Richard was of Bos'n., 1643, and aft. of Camb., and had, *Saml.*, b. 1643. William, who was of H'm., 1665, m. Susanna, da. Geo. Lane, and had *Thos.*, 1665, is supposed to have been son of Richard, of Camb.; and Nathl., and Saml., who were of Camb., 1680, were doubtless of the same family; and tradition says, that the Robbins' of H., sprung from this stock.

2. Nathaniel, a desc't. of Richard ? m. Hannah, da. Saml. Witherell, May 15, 1740, and lived, not as Deane says, in Mf'd., but in Hanover, first in the "Beech woods country," and then at the corner of Grove st., where the cellar hole to his house is yet visible. He was killed in Mf'd., by the falling in of the stones of a well, on which he was at work; as the record says, Dec. 17, 1774, but as family tradition says, June 17, 1775,—the fall of the stones being occasioned by the jarring of the earth, induced by the

firing of the cannon at the battle of Bunker Hill. His wid. d. Jan. 7, 1807, ae. 86. ch.: 1. Nathaniel, Mar., 1741. 2. Timothy, Sep. 25, 1742. (Sep. 14, T. Rec.) 3. Hannah, 1744, d. Feb. 28, 1751. 4. Betsey, 1748. 5. Thomas, 1750. 6. Joseph, 1755, d. 1760. 7. Luther, 1757, m. Ann Barker, Sep. 16, 1779, and moved to Greene, Me., where his descendants reside. He was a soldier in the army, from Hanover, during the Revolution, and his name will be found in the lists we have given. 8. Joseph, m. a da. of Jas. Cushing, of Scituate, moved to Hebron, Me., where his descendants still reside. He was in the Rev'n. from H., in 1777, and went to R. I.

3. Timothy Robbins s. Nathaniel 2, m. Mary Tilden, Oct. 25, 1770, and lived on Centre st., near where his son Tim'y. resides. He was Dea. of the First Church; Town Clerk, from 1778–'87; a member of the Committee of Safety, in 1777; and altogether was a man of great usefulness in public affairs. He d. May 18, 1807, and his wid., Feb. 9, 1825, ae. 74. ch.: 1. Hannah, Oct. 14, 1771, m. Saml. Jenkins, of Scit., Nov. 30, 1797. 2. Mary, July 12, 1773, m. Elijah Sylvester, Dec. 19, 1793. 3. Bethia, Oct. 24, 1774, d. Oct. 16, 1801. 4. Elizab., Mar. 28, 1776, m. Joseph Elmes, of Scit., May 6, 1804, and d. Jan. 5, 1815. 5. Sibyl, Oct. 1, 1779, m. Amos Bates, Nov. 25, 1802, and d. May 26, 1816. 6. Timothy, Aug. 28, 1781. 7. Sarah, Dec. 17, 1783. 8. John, Dec. 9, 1785, d. Sep. 8, 1838.

4. Thomas, s. Nathl. 2, m. Sylvina Caswell, was a shipmaster, and was drowned in the harbor of Cohasset, Ap. 14, 1790, ae. 38, in the midst of his usefulness, and in the vigor of his life. He had 3 sons bap. in H., Sep. 19, 1790, viz.: 1. Walter; 2. Anson, Esq.; and 3. Thomas.

5. Timothy, s. Tim'y. 3, m. Hannah Wright, of Scit., in 1813, lives on Centre st., and is a worthy and respectable farmer. ch.: 1. Elenor, Sep. 25, 1813, d. Jan. 29, 1843. 2. Timothy, Jan. 1815, d. Aug. 14, 1850; much respected and greatly lamented. 3. Sibyl T., Feb. 22, 1817. 4. Hannah F., July 29, 1824, m. Eli C. Josselyn, Ap. 27, 1845, and d. July 15, 1846. Of these

4 ch., but one is left, a daughter, to solace her parents in their declining years.

6. Anson, Esq., of Scit., s. Thos. 4, m. Rachel, da. Thos. Sylvester, Aug. 28, 1803, and resides in So. Scit., near Mr. Stetson's Meeting House. He has long held the office of J. P.; and is a man of active business habits; of great diligence and perseverance; and one whose services have been much sought, not only in his own town, but in those adjacent. ch.: 1. George A., July 20, 1807, m. Almira Sylvester, lived in So. Scit., was a wheelwright by trade, had *Elizabeth T.*, and *George W.*, and d. in S. in Jan., 1853. 2. Walter, June 31, 1809, m. Mary O. Torrey, and lives in Charlestown, Mass. 3. Matilda, Feb. 16, 1811, d. Mar. 10, 1839. 4. Clarissa, June 16, 1813. 5. Horace, Ap. 20, 1816. 6. Charles, June 13, 1817, d. July 10, 1830. 7. Rachel S., Ap. 13, 1820, m. Dr. James Underwood, an intelligent and successful Physician, of E. Ab'n.

NOTE. The son, George, was a man of remarkable mechanical talent; ambitious, and enterprising; one whose career, at the date of his decease, seemed to be full of promise; and who was arrested, in the midst of his usefulness, by an affection of the brain, induced by over exertion, which caused his death. He was much respected in the community, and his loss is a severe blow to his family and friends.

ROGERS, John, of Wey'h., 1639, came to Scit. with Rev. Mr. Witherell, in 1644, but d. in Wey'h., in 1661, leaving a son John, and others. John, jr., was of Scit., and by w. Rhoda, da. Elder Thos. King, had also a son John, and others. John 3d., was fa. of Caleb, b. Ap. 14, 1718, who was of H.; and Caleb, by w. Mary Harlow, was fa. of Caleb, b. Dec. 16, 1747, and others. Caleb, jr., m. wid. Hannah Bates, and was fa. of Reuben, now of H., and of several daughters, of whom Ruth T., m. Cap't. Levi Curtis, of H.

2. Reuben, s. Caleb, m. Abigail Stoddard, of Scit., and lives on Water st., in the ho. built by himself, on the site of a former house, which was burnt. ch.: 1. Reuben H., m., and lives in Mich'n. 2. Zenas, m. Ruth Sumner, who is d. He lives in Braintree. 3. Edwin, not m. 4. Abigail J., m. Melvin Stoddard. 5. Bela T., d. ae. 4. 6. Harriet N., d. ae. 22. 7. Andrew, m. Mary A. Whiting, and lives in E. Ab'n. 8. Sophronia R., m. Henry Hobart, of H.

ROSE, Thomas, according to Deane, was in the "Two mile," in 1660, and had a son John, who was slain in the battle at Rehoboth, in 1676. By a 2d w., Alice, he had Jeremiah, who m. Elizab., da. Capt. Anthony Collamore, in 1698, and d. in 1699, leaving one son, Thomas, bap. June 27, 1708, who was of H. The wid. m. Timothy Symnes.

2. Thomas, s. Jeremiah, m. Faith Sylvester, Aug. 19, 1731, lived in H., was Dea. of the First Church, for a long time, and Selectman for 13 yrs., from 1750–'63. ch.: 1. Ruth, Sep. 13, 1732, m. Thos. Curtis, Feb. 26, 1756. 2. Desire, June 3, 1734, m. Amos Sylvester, Jan. 19, 1757. 3. Hannah, June 1736. 4. Thomas, July 25, 1738. 5. Elizab., Sep., 1740, m. Timo. Church, Sep. 5, 1765. 6. Timothy, Nov. 17, 1743.

3. Thos., s. Thos. 2, m. Rhoda Rogers, Nov. 12, 1761, and, it is said, moved to Me., with his family. ch.: 1. Deborah, 1762. 2. Thos., 1764, d. 1765. 3. Rhoda R., 1767. 4. Thos. 1768, d. 1772. 5. Jeremiah, 1772.

4. Timothy Rose (Capt. Timothy,) s. Thos. 2, m. Lydia Soper, Jan. 23, 1766, who d. Jan. 4, 1812, and he, Oct. 22, 1819. Lived where his grandson Seth now resides, on Hanover st. He was Selectman in 1789; an officer in the Rev'n.; a man of energy; active in his habits, and respected by his townsmen. ch.: 1. Timothy, Dec. 24, 1766. 2. Lydia, Mar. 19, 1769, m. Turner Stetson, Feb. 1, 1795, who was for over 20 yrs. Selectman of H. 3. Seth, Aug. 19, 1771. 4. Charles, 1774, d. 1778. 5. Lucy, Sep. 18, 1775. 6. Ruth, 1777, d. 1778.

5. Timothy, s. Capt. Timothy 4, m. Mercy Josselyn, June 9, 1795, who d. May 8, 1850. He built, and lived for about 15 yrs., in the house now occupied by Silas Hollis, on Broadway; and from thence moved to where Oren Josselyn lives, on King st., being interested in the iron works there. He finally settled where Josiah Bonney lives, on Wash'n. st., and there d. He was a millwright by trade. ch.: 1. Mercy W., Feb. 26, 1797, m.

Josiah Bonney, Ap. 2, 1820, and lives in H. 2. Ruth, m. Capt. William Josselyn, Oct. 8, 1820. 3. Maria, m. Horace Studley, Jan. 15, 1834.

6. Seth, s. Capt. Tim'y. 4, m. Lucy Dwelley, Dec. 4, 1798, who d. Ap. 25, 1845, and he, June 30, 1831. Lived on his father's place, and was a farmer. ch.: 1. Seth, Nov. 14, 1799, lives unm., on Hanover st., and is engaged in the Tanning business, with his brothers. 2. Lucy D., Oct. 31, 1801, d. Jan. 15, 1805. 3. Charles, Oct. 28, 1803, living, unm., at the old homestead. 4. Martin, July 5, 1806. Moved to N. Y'k. State, and lives in Batavia ; is m., and has ch. 5. Eliza D., Aug. 12, 1811, living with her brothers. 6. Mary H., July 25, 1814, d. June 6, 1815. 7. Edwin, June 8, 1816, m. Ann White, of Pemb., da. Capt. Caleb W., and lives on Hanover st.

7. Laban, s. Laban, of Scit., and a descendant of Thos. 1, m. Emily Young, Aug. 20, 1823, lives on Broadway, and is a shoemaker. ch.: 1. Joshua S., Mar. 17, 1824, m. Ann, da. Saml. Perry, and has *Ellen M.*, Oct. 12, 1846. Lives on Broadway. 2. Laban, Aug. 1826, m. Arabella, da. Jabez Josselyn, Jan. 1847, had *Jane M.*, May, 1847, and *Henry F.*, Oct., 1848, and d. Ap. 23, 1851. Lived on Broadway, in the house built by himself. 3. Henry, Oct., 1828. 4. Cordelia, Dec. 26, 1833. 5. Eliza, Dec. 14, 1838.

RUSSELL, William P., b. Oct. 15, 1814, m. Elmira Bates, Ap. 2, 1837, lives on King st., and is a shoemaker. ch.: 1. Lucius W., Mar. 3, 1838. 2. Lyman, Sep. 10, 1840. 3. Marcus P., July 18, 1842. 4. Elizab. S., Ap. 15, 1844. 5. Lydia C., Oct. 11, 1846. 6. George C., July 17, 1848. 7. Charles F., Jan. 9, 1851.

SALMOND, Robert, and his bro. Peter, were born in a small town in Scotland, lying between Edinburgh and Glasgow, within 8 miles, it is said, of the tree in which *William Wallace* hid, as is related in the Scottish Chiefs. Robert was born in 1749, and Peter in 1745. Previous to the opening of the Am. Rev'n., they came to this country, on a visit, and staid in Bridg'r., Mass., one year, from 1774 to 1775. Starting from thence to return to their native land, by the way of Halifax, N. S., they were there impressed into the British army, under Burgoyne; and when that officer was defeated, they left the ranks, and returned to Mr. Russell, their fellow countryman, at Bridg'r., with whom they had been tarrying. Soon they entered the employ of the Hon. Hugh Orr, also a native of Scotland,—who was a manufacturer of cannon, and other arms,—and with him they remained for four years, receiving, as their compensation, but $8 per month, and their board,—a sum which would now be considered small by most of our mechanics. From thence, both came to Hanover, and engaged in trade, in the humble capacity of *pedlers*. Peter, after remaining two years, moved to Pemb., and settled near the Rev. Morrill Allen's. He m. Eunice, da. Capt. Jonathan Bass, of E. Bridg'r., and widow of Seth Whitman, in 1785, and d. in Pemb., in Oct. 1828, ae. 83, leaving ch., of whom his son Peter, is still living in Pemb., on his father's place. Robert, the other brother, remained in H., and was, for about thirty years, engaged in the iron business at Sylvester's Forge,—28 years of the time with Nath'l. Cushing,—in manufacturing *Anchors*, and carrying on this business on an extensive scale. He lived first in the Baldwin House, so called, on Hanover St., and afterwards on Broadway, in what is now known as the "Salmond House." Both the brothers, were men of high moral worth, and one who knew them well, has said, that "if all were like them, we should need no penal laws." Both left behind a *good name* for their children,—a legacy far more valuable than gold or silver! The desc'ts of *Robert*, we give below.

2. Robert Salmond of Scotland, b. 1749, m. Mary, da. of Rev. Samuel Baldwin, of H., November 1, 1787, and d. in H., May 5, 1829, ae. 80, and his wid. September 5, 1847, ae. 79. ch.: 1. Robert, August 2, 1788, was in the service of the U. S., in the War Dep't., and d. unm. in Louisville, Ky., Ap. 9, 1822. 2. Samuel, twin to Robert, b. Aug. 2, 1788. 3. John, Aug. 1, 1700, was engaged, for several years, in the mfr. of Tacks, at his works, on the 3d Herring brook, and d. unm. Ap. 3, 1845. 4. William, Sep. 24,

1791, was in the Tack business with his bro. Jno., and also d. unm., Mar. 11, 1842. 5. Mary, Oct. 1, 1794, d. July 13, 1818. 6. Agnes, Oct. 4, 1776, m. Capt. Zephaniah Talbot, of Scit., July 20, 1826, and is living a wid., in Scit., her husband having been so unfortunately injured, by the bursting of a can of camphene, as to cause his death in a few days. 7. Peter R., bap. Aug. 1, 1802, d. at Baltimore, Md., May 18, 1828.

3. Samuel, s. Robert 2, m. Eliza, da. Hon. Albert Smith, of H., July 26, 1826, and lives on Wash'on. st., near the Four Corners. His life, like that of his father and uncle, has been eventful and instructive. At the age of 18, with his bro. Robert, he sett. in Bangor, Me., where, for 10 years, he was engaged in trade. In 1818, he left B., and journeyed to the South, tarrying there 4 years, until the death of his bro. Robert; and thence he went to Cuba, on which beautiful island he passed 7 winters. During a portion of this time, he was in the employ of the U. S. Gov't. In 1838, he sett. permanently in Hanover, and engaged in the Tack business, at the works previously occupied by his brothers, and at the spot where anciently stood the Stockbridge mill. Mr. S. is a man of modest and retiring manners, of unblemished integrity, never weary in well doing, and is respected most by those who know him best, and can best appreciate the excellencies of his character. ch: 1. Robert, Ap. 1827, d. Oct. 18, 1845. 2. Mary, Dec. 1832. 3. Eliza S., May 13, 1844. 4. Samuel, d. Aug. 14, 1850, ae. 11 wks.

SAMPSON, Otis, s. Stephen, of Pemb., b. Sep. 1805, m. Sarah, da. Anthony Sylvester, lives on Broadway, and is a carpenter. ch.: 1. Frances, Feb. 9, 1836. 2. Otis, Ap. 11, 1837. 3. Almira J., May 21, 1839. 4. Priscilla, May 1841. 5. Mary E., Aug. 27, 1843. 6. Lewis, July 22, 1846.

2. Charles, s. Chas., of Dux'y., m. Tamar J., da. Jno. Puffer, Dec. 9, 1847, lives on Centre st., is a shoemaker by trade, and has no ch.

NOTE. This name, on old records, is generally spelled *Samson;* and Henry, the ancestor of most of the Sampsons of Plymouth Co., arrived at Dux'y., in 1620, according to Winsor.

SIMMONS, Moses,—formerly written "*Moyses Symonson*,"—came to Plymouth in the Fortune, in 1621, and is usually reckoned as one of the *Pilgrims*, being among the early settlers of Plym'h. Winslow speaks of him as "a child of one that was in communion with the Dutch Church at Leyden," and as being "admitted into Church fellowship at Plym'h., in N. Eng'd., and his children also to baptism as well as our own." In the division of lands made in 1623, he, with Philip De la Noye, (now Delano,) received each one acre, "beyond the first brooke, to the wood westward;" and in 1628, Mar. 26, he, and Edward Bompass, sold each one acre of ground to Robert Hicks, "lying on the North side of the town,"—being probably the acre granted to him in 1623. In the division of cattle, made May 22, 1627, the first lot, consisting of the "four black heifers that came in the Jacob, and two she goats," fell to Francis Cooke, and his company, among whom was "Moses Simonson." He was in Dux'y., before 1637, and in that year, was one of a Jury of 12, "to set forth heigh wages about Plymouth, Ducksburrow, and the Eele River." In 1638–9, he received a grant of 40 acres of land in D. He is in the list of those able "to bear arms," in 1643; and in the list of freemen in D., in 1646. At about this period, he became one of the 54 original proprietors of Bridg'r., but soon after sold his share to Nicholas Byram. Under date of Mar. 7, 1652, he is spoken of, on the Col. Rec., as having one of the 34 shares, "of a tract extending 3 miles E. of the E. part of the river or bay called Acusshena, and soe alonge the sea side to the river called Coaksett, lying on the W. side of point prill (peril ?) &c., and extending 8 miles into the woods,"—said tract being land purchased of the Indians. He was a surveyor in Dux'y., in 1657; and in 1665, a *footway* was laid out through his land, and that of Sam'l. Chandler. In 1662, he was one of the proprietors of Midd'o., his lot being the 18th, and being "bounded with a red Oak and a Walnut tree marked." The name of his wife, we have not learned, nor the dates of birth of his children. We should infer, from Winslow's account, that some of them, at least, were born before he came to Am'a. Of his sons, we find recorded the names of *Moses* and *Thomas*. The family is prob. of English origin, and may be connected with the *Symonds*, or *Simonds*, of Devonshire, Dorset, Somerset, Gloucester, Norfolk, Hertford, &c. We find this family name sometimes spelled *Symons*, and *Simmons*, and the family itself, is numerous and respectable, and of quite ancient date.

2. Moses, s. Moses, sen'r., was of Dux'y., where he d. in 1689, (Winsor.) By w. Sarah, he had, 1. John, m. Mercy Pabodie, 1669, and had ch. 2. Aaron, was m., and had ch. 3. Mary, m. Joseph Alden. 4. Elizab., the 2d. w. of Richard Dwelley. 5. Sarah, m. Jas. Nash, Dux'y.

3. Thos., s. Moses, sen'r., was a householder in Scit. bef. 1647, and his house was on the Green field, between that of Sam'l. Nash, and Jno. Turner, jr. The name of his wife is not given, nor the dates of birth of his ch. We only learn that he had sons Moses and Aaron.

4. s. Thomas 3, m. Patience, da. Wm. Barstow, ab. 1664. ch.: 1. Moses, bap. June 10, 1666, d. in the Canada Expedition, 1690. 2. Jno. bap. Mar. 15, 1667–8. 3. Sarah, bap. July 31, 1670. 4. Aaron, bap. Aug. 4, 1672. 5. Job, bap. Oct. 4, 1674, owned land S. of "Old Pond," which he sold in part to Jona. Pratt, in 1696. 6. Patience, bap. Mar. 18, 1676, her mo. being then a wid.

5. Aaron, s. Thos. 3, m. Mary Woodworth, 1667, and, it is said, lived at the "Green field." (Deane.) ch.: 1. Rebecca, Dec. 12, 1679. 2. Moses, Feb. 24, 1681, m. Rachel Cudworth, 1711, and had *Moses*, 1718; *Aaron*, 1720; *Rachel*, 1723; and *Leah*, 1725. 3. Mary, Mar. 11, 1683. 4. Elizab., Aug. 27, 1686. 5. Ebenezer, Aug. 10, 1689. 6. Lydia, Mar. 27, 1693.

6. s. Aaron 5, m. Lydia Kent, 1714, and, it is said, lived where the widow of Charles Simmons now resides, in South Scituate. ch.: 1. Abigail, 1715. 2. Joshua, 1717. 3. Lydia, 1719. 4. Elizab., 1724. 5. Sam'l., 1725, moved to Ct.

6. Reuben, 1726, sett. at Nutter Hill, in H'm. 7. Peleg, 1728. 8. Ebenezer.?, lived on his father's place.

7. *Joshua Simmons* s. Ebenezer 6, m. Elizabeth Dillingham, November, 11, 1742, and lived in H., first in a house in the pasture back of where Dan'l. Chapman now resides, and then in a house which recently stood where stands that of Mr. C. His w. d. July 18, 1797, ae. 76, and he, Mar. 4, 1807, ae. 88. He was a memb. of the Com'e. of Safety in the Rev'n., and Selectman, in 1775, &c. ch.: 1. Joshua, Mar. 5, 1743, d. Mar. 6, 1819. 2. Elizab., Ap. 14, 1746, d. Sep. 11, 1824. 3. Lydia, Aug. 23, 1749. 4. Eben'r., Dec. 27, 1751, d. June 11, 1754. 5. Eben'r., Ap. 11, d. Oct. 7, 1754. 6. Mary, Sep. 26, 1755, m. Jno. H. Thacher, of Barnstab., Sep. 29, 1795, and d. Ap. 28, 1814, no ch. 7. Sam'l., Nov. 1, 1757, d. Sep. 17, 1762. 8. Elisha, June 16, 1759. 9. Lydia, July 14, 1763, m. Benj. Bailey, June 13, 1793, and d. Jan. 16, 1805. 10. Wm., Feb. 25, d. May 4, 1766.

8. *Elisha Simmons* s. Joshua 7, m. Martha Hersey, of H'm., and d. in H., Mar. 14, 1825, ae. 80. Lived in part of his father's house. ch.: 1. Hon. William., July, 9, 1782, grad. H. C., 1804, m. Lucia Hammett, of Plym'h., lived in Bos'n.; was Judge of the Police Court; and was fa. of *Wm.*, ed.; *Rev. Geo. F.; Chas. F.*, lawyer, Bos'n.; *Henry*, d.; and *Martha.* 2. Eben'r., Oct. 18, 1785. 3. Martha, Mar. 19, 1789, d. Feb. 1833. 4. Elisha, Dec. 1, 1790, d. Nov. 26, 1792. 5. Elisha, Nov. 19, 1793, was a merchant, and d. unm. in Bos'n. 6. Benj. H., Dec. 20, 1796, m., and d. in N. Or's., leaving 2 sons. 7. Geo. W., Feb. 20, 1800, merchant, in N. Y'k. Not m. 8. Elizab., Oct. 5, 1802, living in Boston. 9. Joanna, Oct. 5, 1802, m. Thos. Stevenson, of Bos'n., June 22, 1824. 10, Franklin, of Bos'n., not m.

9. *Eben'r. Simmons* (Eben'r., Esq.,) s. Elisha 8, m. 1, Sophia Richmond, of Prov., R. I.; and 2, Mary H., wid. of Step. Curtis, of Scit., Aug. 23, 1835, who d. Ap. 30, 1837, and he, in Nov. 1840. Lived on Wash'n. st., where his son Perez now resides, was a merchant; Selectman of the Town for 6 y'rs.; Rep. to the Gen'l. Ct. in 1835; and a man of enterprise and ability. ch.: 1. Perez, Esq., grad. B. U., 1833, and sett. as a lawyer, first in Prov., R. I., and then in H. in 1842. Has been Selectman of H. since 1849; was Rep. in 1852; one of the Comis's. of Insolvency, for Plym'h. Co.; is chosen as one of the Delegates, to the Convention to revise the Const'n. of Mass., which is to meet in Bos'n., in May, 1853;—m. Adaline, da. of Jno. Jones, of So. Scit., and has *Jno. F.*, June 26, 1851, and a da., b. Mar. 5, 1853. (By 2d w.) 2. Eben'r., Feb. 12, 1837.

10. Capt. Thos., s. Sam'l., of Scit., gr. s. Peleg, and gr. gr. s. of Eben'r. 6, m. Bethia Gray, Dec. 1, 1816, lives on Wash'n. st., in the N. E. part of the town; and was formerly a trader, and a man of successful enterprise. ch.: 1. Bethia, Nov. 14, 1817. 2. Thos., July 18, d. Nov. 21, 1819. 3. Warren, July 13, 1821. 4. Rebecca, Jan. 9, 1824.

SLASON, Rev. Wm. N., sometime Pastor of the Bap. Soc. of H., is s. Sylvanus and Mary Slason, of Vt., and was b. Feb. 26, 1809. He stud. for the ministry, under Rev. Dr. Barlow, and at the Newton Seminary, and has been sett. at Goffstown, N. H., Parsonsfield, Me., and elsewhere. He m. Hannah E. Jackson, of Camb., Mass., Jan. 7, 1833, and has, 1. Wm. T., Dec. 5, 1833; and 2. Francis W., June 11, 1836. Lives on Main st., in the house built by himself in 1852.

SMITH, Rev. Thos., of Pemb., b. Feb. 6, 1706, s. Joseph, of Yarmouth, Mass., grad. H. C. 1725, m. Judith, da. Josiah Miller, Aug. 28, 1734, and was sett. first in Yarmouth, and then in Pemb., where he d. ch.: 1, Mary, May 18, 1735, m. Rev. Isa. Dunster, of Harwich. 2. Josiah, Feb. 26, 1738. 3. Joseph, Nov.

22, 1740. 4. Thos., July 25, 1742, drowned in the river Elbe, in Europe, Dec. 19, 1767. 5. Josh., July 27, 1744, d. at sea, during the Rev'n. 6. Nathl., b. and d. 1746. 7. Judith, Nov. 4, 1747, m. Rev. Saml. Angier, E. Bridg'r.; no ch. 8. Thankful, Feb. 26, 1749, d. unm., Ap. 2, '98. 9. Nathl., Feb. 16, 1752, m. Elizab. Bass, of Bos'n., Ap. 27, 1806, and was fa. of *Nathl., Esq.*, T. C. of Pemb., and a scientific and tasteful agriculturist, as his beautiful residence in P. abundantly testifies; m. Susan S., da. Luther Briggs, and has *Moses B.*, and *Susan A.* 10. Edward, May 16, 1754, d. unm. 11. Catherine, Mar. 21, 1756, m. Isaac Thomas, Pemb., and had 2 ch. 12. Christ'r., Dec. 22, 1757, d. of the small pox, July 10, 1781, at Hfx., N. S.

2. Dea. Josiah, s. Rev. Thos., m. Mary Barker, of P., June 15, 1760, and d. Ap. 4, 1803, ae. 65, and his wid. who was b. May 2, 1740, d. Nov. 15, 1813, ae. 73. ch.: 1. Miller, June 22, 1761, d. Sep. 30, 1779. 2. Albert, Mar. 22, 1763. 3. Bowen, Aug. 27, 1764, sett. in Nova Scotia. 4. Josiah, Mar. 2, 1767. 5. Thos., May 31, 1769, d. May 30, 1774. 6. Elizab., May 9, 1771, m. Chas. Briggs, of P., and d. Nov. 16, 1798. 7. Ruth B., Ap. 12, 1773, m. Jno. Barker, of P. 8. Thos., Mar. 22, 1775, d. unm. in Nova Scotia. 9. Mary, Mar. 9, 1777, m. Bachelor Wing, Nov. 28, 1805. 10. Elisha, June 21, 1779, m. Mary Bass, of Bos'n., and had, *Mary*, m. a Cushing; *Joseph*, d. in France; *Elizab.*, m. Jno. Pillsbury, of Lowell; *Marg't.*, m. Josh. Loring, Cashier Blackstone Bank, Bos'n.; *Jane*, m. Jno. H. Batchelder, Dentist, Salem; *Cordelia*, m. Wm. R. Pearmain, Cashier Chelsea Bank; and *Sarah A.*, who m. a Lazell. 11. Miller, Feb. 9, 1782, m. Jane, da. Dav. Stockbridge, Esq., had *Jane S.*, m. Gen. A. W. Oldham, of Pemb.; and the fa. d. Dec. 23, 1818, being washed overboard at sea, near the "Three Sand Hills," on the coast of N. Carolina.

3. Capt. Joseph, s. Rev. Thos., m. 1, —Wadsworth, and 2, Bathsheba Torrey, and had, 1, Capt. Sylvanus, of Dux'y. 2. Joshua, d. unm. (By 2d,) 3. Lucia, living in H'n. 4. Bathsheba, m. Eleazer Carver, Bridg'r. 5. Christ'r., m. a da. of Maj. Wilder, and d. at sea, leaving no ch. 6. Judith, d. unm. 7.

Joseph, Ap. 12, 1791, not m. 8. Capt. Joshua, Aug. 23, 1793, for several years one of the Board of County Commis's. for Plym'h. Co., was m., lived in H'n., had ch., and d., and his desct's. are in H'n. 9. Dea. Thos., of H'n., May 31, 1795. 16. Thankful, Nov. 30, 1797, m. Elb. Keith, E. Bridg'r. 11. Catherine, d. unm.

4. Albert Smith (Hon. Albert,) s. Dea. Josiah 2, m. Anne L., da. Capt. Rob't. L. Eells, Aug. 23, 1787, and d. May 28, 1823, and his wid., May 7, 1835. (See p. 163.) ch.: 1. Anne L., Oct. 4, 1788, m. Nathl. Crooker, Mar. 9, 1808, who d. Jan. 20, 1847, and she, Dec. 12, 1846. 2. Joseph, Mar. 30, 1790, a Commodore, in the U. S. Navy, and Chief of the Bureau of Docks and Yards; lives in Wash'n., D. C., m. Harriet Bryant, of Me., and has ch. 3. Albert Esq., Jan. 3, 1793, grad. B. U., 1813, is an eminent lawyer, in Wash'n., D. C., m. Roxa, da. Rev. Calvin Chaddock, June 24, 1814, and has ch. 4. Mary, Oct. 21, 1795, m. Capt. David Whittier, of Belfast, Me., Sep. 27, 1815, and d. July 19, 1848, ae. 53, and her husb. Oct. 8, 1849, ae. 61. 5. John, Dec. 10, 1797, d. Sep. 5, 1813. 6. Thos. M., Aug. 15, 1799, d. Jan. 7, 1803. 7. Elizab., Mar. 20, 1801, m. Saml. Salmond, of H., July 26, 1826. 8. Sarah B., Nov. 25, 1802, d. same month. 9. Sarah B., Jan. 7, 1808, m. Joseph Eells, jr., Mar. 11, 1827.

5. Josiah, s. Dea. Josiah 2, m. 1, Nabby, da. Capt. Robert L. Eells, Mar. 13, 1794, who d. Aug. 3, 1812; and 2, Jane, da. Jere. Smith, and d. in H., Ap. 24, 1842, ae. 75, and his wid. in 1850. ch.: 1. Nabby E., Aug. 26, 1795, m. Theodore Whitney, of Niagara, N. Y. 2. Lucy W., Nov. 12, 1796, m. Dr. Wm. L. Loring, Dux'y. 3. Ruth C., Jan. 2, 1798. 4. Elizab. B., May 20, 1799, m. Ambrose Packard, Niagara, N. Y. 5. Mary L., Oct. 26, 1801, m. Edward E. Nash, of Medford, Mass., and d. in Arkansas. 6. Josiah M., Feb. 12, 1803, m. Frances Waterman, Scit., and lives in H., at the Corners, in the new house erected by himself. No ch.

6. Chas., s. Wm. E., m. Betsey Phillips, of H., and lives in H'n., on Walnut st., is a shoemaker by trade. ch.: 1. Betsey E.,

July 4, 1832. 2. Chas. W., May 30, 1834. 3. Jas. E., Feb. 9, 1838.

7. Wm. E., s. Wm. E., b. Feb. 27, 1801, m. Lucy, da. Jno. Hatch, Nov. 6, 1842, lives in H., on Main st., and is a shoemaker by trade. Has one son, John S., Aug. 24, 1843.

SOPER, Cap't. Joseph, s. Thos. of Scit., ? 1690, was b. 1703, m. Lydia Stockbridge, Nov. 20, 1729, and d. in H., May 1, 1790, ae. 87. No ch. are recorded, but he was prob. fa. of Capt. Joseph, b. 1737, who m. Ruth Curtis, 1760, lived on the hill, W. of Josiah Bonney's, was an Offi. in the Rev'n., and Selectman for 14 yrs. He d. Mar., 1804, ae. 67, and his w., Mar. 9, 1777. No ch.

SOULE, Abisha., s. Josiah, of Dux'y., (and a desc't. of George, who came to N. Eng. in 1620,) was b. July 13, 1805, m. Frances, da. Elij. Hobart, Esq., Ab'n., in Ap. 1825, lives on Main st., in the house which stands where stood the Jno. Bailey homestead, and has, 1. Sibyl H., Aug. 31, 1826, m. Gilbert Brooks, of H. 2. Caro. F., 1830, m. 1, Martin S. Torrey, May 3, 1846, and 2, Spencer Binney, Sep., 1849. 3. Maria E., Feb. 13, 1833, m. Henry C. Percival, Feb. 16, 1851, who d. in Cal'a., in 1852.

SPRAGUE, Melzar, s. Melzar, of Mf'd., and a desc't. of Francis, who arrived in N. Eng. in 1623, was b. in Mar. 1795, m. Mary D., da. Nathan Dwelley, Nov. 28, 1820, kept store for a time on Broadway, and now lives in Pemb. Had one son, Andrew J., July 14, 1823, d., ae. 18.

NOTE. Mr. S. is chosen as the delegate from Pemb., to the Conv'n., for revising the Const'n., which is to meet in Bos'n., in May, 1853.

STETSON, Cornet Robert, the ancestor of the Stetsons of the U. S., and a noted and valuable man in his day, prob. came from Yorkshire, Eng'd., from which county many of the first settlers of Scit. originated, and where, according to Rev. R. Breare, the name is still extant, being found in Richmond and other towns. Having already published a sketch of this family, entitled "Records of the Stetson Family," we do not deem it necessary to pursue its history at large here, and shall therefore confine this notice chiefly to those that settled in Hanover. We need only remark, that the Cornet had five sons, who left male issue, viz.: *Joseph, Benjamin, Thomas, Samuel and Robert.*

The descendants of the first of these—Joseph—settled principally in Scituate. A few resided in H., and these we shall give. More of the descendants of Benjamin and Samuel, and a few of those of Thomas, became residents of H.; but none of those of Robert. From the latter, however, descended Nahum Stetson, Esq., of whom we have spoken on p. 229.

2. Robert, s. Robert, and a desc't. of Cornet Robert through his eldest son Joseph, was b. Sep. 3, 1710, m. Hannah Tower, of Pemb., in 1738, and lived on what is now Centre st., in a house

lately torn down by Mr. Eben'r. Thayer. In 1746, he sold his first place to Wm. Stetson, and moved to where Albert Stetson resides. He had ch.; but his desct's are mostly in Me.

3. Capt. Joseph, s. Saml., and a desc't. of the Cornet through Joseph, was b. Mar. 25, 1724, m. Martha Gross, of Scit., in 1774, and lived, for a time, on Water st., where Chas. Dyer resides, and owned the mill and privilege where Perry's Tack works stand. He was a soldier in the French war, and was at Cape Breton, at the storming of the fort. He was a mariner for many years, and made voyages to Holland, and other countries of Europe. His da. Xoa, b. in May, 1779, is yet living in H.; also his son, Joseph, b. Aug. 27, 1787, who m. wid. Betsey Whitman, of Wey'h., May 12, 1839, lives on East st., and has *Joseph F.*, 1840, and *Martha E.*, 1841.

4. Joshua, s. Joshua, and a desc't. of the Cornet through Joseph, was b. Nov. 21, 1805, lives on Elm st., and is a shipwright by trade; m. Debo. Josselyn, of Pemb., and has, 1. Eliza A., May 8, 1834, d. Dec. 8, 1852. 2. Sarah J., July 25, 1836. 3. Debo. F., Mar. 28, 1839. 4. Lois A., July 27, 1842. 5. Joshua A., Dec. 2, 1845. 6. Andrew B., d. young.

5. Benj., s. Benj., and a desc't. of the Cornet through Capt. Benj., his 2d son, was b. July 1, 1696, m. Lillis Turner ? of H., in 1725, who d. June 1, 1755, ae. 84, and he, Aug. 31, 1758. He was Selectman from 1747–49. His da. Desire, m. Caleb Sylvester, in 1750, and Susanna, m. Abner Sylvester, in 1761. His son Job, m. Hannah Munroe, in 1762, and moved off. None of the desct's. now remain in H.

6. Benj., s. Matt., and a desc't. of the Cornet through Capt. Benj., was b. Ap. 7, 1740, m. 1, Bradbury Eells, Ap. 30, 1768, who d. Feb. 19, 1782; 2, Betsey Young, Nov. 8, 1784, who d. June 9, 1813; and 3, Betsey Stockbridge. He is said to have been a blacksmith by trade, and to have lived near the centre of the town. ch.: 1. Edward. 2. Bradbury, m. Benj. Dwelley, 1788. 3. Benj., m. Betsey Estes, Nov. 1, 1798, and d. Aug. 20, 1826, and his wid. m. Josh. Gates, Aug. 10, 1828, and is d. 4. Mary, m. Saml. Plyer, Nov. 21, 1819, and lived on Broadway. Four ch. d. young.

7. Edward, s. Benj. 6, m. Hannah, da. Dea. Israel Perry, Jan. 1, 1799, was a blacksmith by trade, lived on Broadway, and

d. in May, 1846. His wid. is still living. ch.: 1. Edward, Nov. 3, 1800, of New Bedford. 2. Mary E., Ap. 17, 1803, d. Aug. 15, 1839. 3. Bradbury E., Ap. 17, 1803, d. Oct. 1835. 4. Caroline, Nov. 25, 1805, m. Martin Church, in May, 1832. 5. Martin W., Nov. 16, 1807. 6. Eliza, m. Sumner Setson, July 6, 1829. 7. Horace, Ap. 22, 1817, d. Aug. 14, 1842. 8. Melissa, b. and d. 1815.

RESIDENCE OF MR. MARTIN STETSON.

8. Martin W., s. Edward 7, m. Ruth B., da. Lebbeus Stockbridge, in 1836, and lives on Broadway, in the house formerly owned by Hon. Albert Smith, and previously by Dea. Joseph Josselyn, a view of which is annexed. Mr. S. is a substantial and enterprising farmer, and mechanic, and an esteemed and respected citizen. ch.: 1. Ruth W., Jan. 27, 1838. 2. Mary T., Aug. 1840. 3. Betsey H., June, 1841. 4. Edward P., Ap. 14, 1844. 5. Hannah P., May, 1848. 6. George A., Feb., 1850.

9. John, s. Abijah, and a desc't. of the Cornet through Capt. Benj., was b. Ap. 17, 1731, and m. Thankful Curtis, Dec. 3, 1761, who d. Feb. 5, 1805, ae. 63, and he, Ap. 15, 1811, ae. 80. ch.: 1. Zilpha, m. Saml. Stetson. 2. Abig., 1765, m. Shuble Munroe, 1788, and d. 1812. 3. Thankful, 1768, d. 1826. 4. Joshua, Aug. 23, 1777. 5. Lebbeus, Ap. 27, 1783, sett. in Bos'n, and has desct's. there. Two other ch. d. young.

10. Josh., s. Jno. 9, m. Priscilla Dwelley, in 1804, was Selectman 7 yrs., from 1813–'20, and is yet living, on Union st., near Stetson's Brook. His wife is d. ch.: 1. Angeline, July 11, 1805, m. George Gray. 2. Cassandra, July 11, 1805, m. Wm. Curtis, Dec. 3, 1826. 3. Avis D., Nov. 2, 1808, m. Jno. Lane, of Ab'n., Dec. 22, 1831. 4. Dea. Jno., Aug. 26, 1811, a shipwright, in Medford. 5. James, July 3, 1817. Lives in Brighton.

11. Josh., s. Elijah, and a desc't. of Cornet Robert through Thos., his 3d son, was b. May 12, 1713, m. Lillis, da. Benj. Stetson, July 8, 1747, and lived in H. ch.: 1. Lillis, Ap., 1748, m. Saml. Stetson, of Pemb. 2. Lucinda, 1750. 3. Joshua, 1752, prob. d. 1754.

12. Nathl., s. Elij., and bro. of Josh. 11, m. Mary Dillis, Ap. 1, 1735, and she d. in H., Ap. 20, 1796, ae. 91. He had a son Nathl., who d. unm.; and a da. who m. a Jenkins.

13. Luke, s. Elij., and bro. of Josh. 11, m. Ruth Howland, of Dux'y., in 1762, who d. in 1764. He was a noted *schoolmaster* in H., and had but one ch., a da. Ruth, b. 1763, who m. Asa Soule, of Hf'x., Dec. 27, 1784.

14 Samuel Stetson s. Saml., 4th son of Cornet Robert, was b. in June, 1679, m. Rebecca Turner, May 12, 1719, and sett. in H., near the Cent. M. Ho., where his desct's. still reside. He is called "Drummer Stetson," on the Scit. Rec's., and was a somewhat noted man in his day, his house being a tavern stand, and a famous place of resort. He d. June 23, 1760, leaving 2 das., who d. unm., and a son Saml., b. ab. 1725.

15. Saml., s. Saml. 14, m. Alice Rogers, Dec. 14, 1766, lived on his father's place, and d. Feb. 5, 1791, and his wid. May 29, 1820, ae. 76. He was Selectman in 1779, and '80. ch.: 1. Turner, Sep. 8, 1767. 2. Reuben, 1769, d. 1778. 3. Saml., May, 1772. 4. Rebecca, Sep. 10, 1776, m. Timo. Church, Nov. 27, 1796. 5. Lydia, m. Ezek'l. Turner, Feb. 28, 1799, and d July 15, 1819.

16. Turner, s. Saml. 15, m. Lydia Rose, Feb. 1, 1795, and was Selectman for 27 years, and Rep. in 1812, and '13. He

lived at the corner of Plain and Circuit sts., where his w. d. Jan. 22, 1819, ae. 50, and he, Feb. 25, 1844. ch.: 1. Turner, June 22, 1795, living in Michigan. 2. Ruth, Sep. 24, 1797, living in H., unm. 3. Lydia R., b. and d. 1799. 4. Lydia, May 18, 1800, m. a Cobb, of Ab'n. 5. Aristides, Ap. 11, 1802, d. at the West, Oct. 16, 1839. 6. Saml., 1805, d. 1806. 7. Alice, Feb. 11, 1808, a school teacher for many years. 8. Eliza, Oct. 1, 1811, m. Jno. Hatch, jr., Aug. 25, 1836.

17. Saml., s. Saml. 15, m. 1, Zilpha Stetson, Jan. 29, 1798, who d. Jan. 5, 1807; and 2, Abig., da. Shuble Munroe, in 1808, and is yet living, on the old homestead. ch.: 1. Zilpha, b. 1799, d. 1800. 2. Albert, Esq., Aug. 8, 1802, Selectman in 1840 and '41; m. Wealthy Perry, Nov. 29, 1830, lives near the Cent. M. Ho., and had one da., *Zilpha*, b. 1832, d. 1843. 3. Fanny, July 22, 1805, m. Perez Perry, Nov. 2, 1828, and d. Mar. 19, 1831. (By 2d,) 4. Zilpha, Jan. 1, 1809, m. Zenas Rogers, Feb. 20, 1832. 5. Reuben, Oct. 31, 1810, m. Ruth J., da. Amos Bates, Ap. 26, 1846, lives in the *Baldwin House*, and has *Ruth E.*, June 1847. 6. Chas., b. and d. 1812. 7. Abigail, July 26, 1813, m. Jno. Little, Aug. 11, 1835, and d. June 5, 1850. 8. John, Jan. 15, 1815, m. Ann Hookway, of Syracuse, N. Y., July 20, 1843, and has *Henry M.*, Ap. 20, 1844; *Wm. H.*, May 14, 1847; *Saml. T.*, Jan. 28, 1850; and *Jno. E.*, Jan. 9, 1852. Lost 1 ch., d. young. 9. Mary, Sep. 27, 1816. Not m. 10. Saml., June 1, 1818, went to sea, and has not been heard from for several years. 11. Melatiah C., b. 1820, d. 1825. 12. Rebecca M., Jan. 18, 1822, m. Chas. Tower, and lives in H. 13. Josiah, b. and d. 1823. 14. Melatiah C., Feb. 28, 1825, m. Nathl. P. Chamberlin, of H. 15. Jeremiah, May 10, 1826. Not m. 16. Henry M., b. 1827, d. 1831. 17. Turner, Ap. 27, 1829. 18. Henry M., Dec. 29, 1832. 19. Lydia A., d. ae. 3 mos.

18. Seth, s. Saml., 4th son of Cornet Robert, was b. in June, 1698, m. Eliza Rose, Ap. 19, 1727, and his w. d. Sep. 4, 1787, ae. 83. ch.: 1. Elizab., 1732, d. unm. 2. Eli, d. 1734. 3. Seth, June 4, 1735. 4. Thos., b. 1737, d. 1739. 5. Jere., Aug. 8, 1740, lived in H'n., where his desct's. still reside. 6. Thos., July 23, 1741. 7. Saml., b. 1744, d. 1748.

19. Seth, s. Seth 18, m. Lucy Studley, Ap. 11, 1765, and lived in the house which stood where stands that of N. F. Chamberlin, on Centre st. ch.: 1. Rebecca, Dec. 17, 1765, m. Clement Bates, Dec. 25, 1788, and d. 1813. 2. Debo., Mar. 18, 1767, m. Jno. Bates, and moved to Me. 3. Hannah, Ap. 1, 1769, m. Saml. Bates, Mar. 27, 1791, and moved to Me. 4. Nathl., Jan. 6, 1771. 5. Seth, Mar. 4, 1773, of Boxford, Mass. 6. Saml., Mar. 22, 1775. 7. Lucy, Feb. 11, 1777, m. Joseph Tubbs, Aug. 18, 1797. 8. Thankful, June 7, 1779, m. Freeman Harden, Jan. 25, 1800. 9. Ezek'l., July 8, 1781, sett. in Me. 10. Reuben, 1784, d. 1793. 11. Martin, 1789, d. 1793.

20. Thos., s. Seth 18, m. Olive Mann, June 18, 1772, who d. July 20, 1819, and he Dec. 24, 1821. ch.: 1. Thos., Mar. 31, 1773, lives in H'n. 2. Olive, Mar. 20, 1775, m. Saml. Beals, May 7, 1796, and moved to Me. 3. Ruth, Mar. 10, 1777, m. David S. Whitman, Bridg'r., 1798. 4. Elizab., Jan. 30, 1780, m. Calvin Bates, Aug. 2, 1801, and is d. 5. Lucinda, 1783, m. Noah Mason, and is living a wid., in Ills. 6. Benj., 1786, d. young. 7. Benj., Sep. 28, 1790. 8. Eli, Oct. 13, 1794, a millwright by trade, is m., and lives in H'n., near his bro. Thomas.

21. Nathl., s. Seth 19, m. 1, Temperance Curtis, Nov. 7, 1793, who d. Nov. 6, 1808; and 2, Joanna Pratt, Mar. 7, 1811, and had ch.: 1. Nathl., Ap. 17, 1795, lives in Me. 2. Elisha C., May 3, 1797, m. Betsey Barstow, Jan. 14, 1816, and d. Jan. 21, 1845, and his wid. m. Lewis Litchfield, of H. 3. Saml., June 28, 1799, lives in Mf'd. 4. Seth, Sep. 18, 1802, m. Desire O. Palmer, Ap. 17, 1832, lives on Cross st., is a shoemaker, and has *Seth C.*, June 9, 1836; *Wm. W.*, Ap. 13, 1838; *Nathl. M.*, Mar. 1, 1843, d.; *Abby M.*, Aug. 25, 1844; *Mary E.*, Aug. 10, 1846; *Martha M.*, June 1849; and *Emeline O.*, Ap. 1852. 5. Harrison, a shoemaker, lives on Cross st., m. Olive L. Smith, of Catskill, N. Y., and has *Sarah C.*, Jan. 31, 1843; *Joanna P.*, May 2, 1845; *Hannah E.*, Ap. 5, 1847; *Theodore*, Ap. 29, 1850; and *Wm. L.*, Mar. 13, 1852. 6. Temperance C., m. Hiram Munroe, of H., May 6, 1832.

22. Benj., s. Thos. 20, m. Lucy Bates, Sep. 10, 1820, is a millwright by trade, and was Selectman in 1835, and '36; lives

on Centre st., and has ch.: 1. Olive, Jan. 30, 1821, m. Peabody Little. 2. Priscilla, Mar. 31, 1825, m. Wm. Whiting, and lives in H'n. 3. Benj. L., July 1, 1837.

23. Nathl., s. Saml., 4th s. of Cornet Robert, was b. in June, 1700, m. Rebecca Brisco, Feb. 13, 1738, and d. July 28, 1753, and his wid. m. David Cudworth, of Scit., in 1760. ch.: 1. Freelove, 1738, m. Theoph. Witherell, 1761, and d. 1824. 2. Rebecca, 1743, m. 1, Joseph Studley, 1765, who d. the same year; and 2, Elisha Witherell, Dec. 30, 1772, and moved to Chesterfield. 3. Ruth, 1746, m. Jona. Bates, of Rochester, 1771.

STOCKBRIDGE FAMILY.

Arms: Ar. on a chev. az. 3 crescents or. Crest: out of a cloud 2 dexter hands in armor conjoined, holding up a heart inflamed, all ppr.

1. John Stockbridge, a wheelwright by trade, came to N. Eng., in the Blessing, John Leicester, master, in June 1635, being then 27 years of age; and his wife Anne, ae. 21, and his son Charles, ae. 1. Several of the early settlers of Scit. came in the same vessel, among whom were elder Thos. King, Gilbert and Wm. Brooks, and Mr. Wm. Vassall. The fa. was in Scit. in 1638, at which date he took the oath of fidelity. His 1st. w. d. ab. 1642, and he m. 2, wid. Elizab. Soan, 1643, and 3, Mary ——. He was one of the Conihasset partners in 1646, and had a house near to John Hollet's, which is supposed to have been a few rods S. W. of the

late residence of Jesse Dunbar, Esq. He also owned a large, tract of land, purchased of Abraham Sutliffe, near "Stockbridge's mill-pond," so called, on the north and east. In 1656, he purchased half the mill privilege of George Russell, with the saw-mill, which Isaac Stedman had erected ten years before, and built a grist-mill, in partnership with Mr. Russell. In the same year, probably, he built the Stockbridge Mansion House, which was a garrison in Philip's War. This venerable building was torn down a few years since, and in some of its timbers, were found bullets, fired at the inmates by the Indians. The will of the fa. is dated at Boston, in 1657, and in it he gives, "To eldest son Chas., my water-mill, at Scit., house, ground, and orchard belonging to it, he paying to his sis. Elizab. £10, &c. To wife Mary, house and land at Bos'n., and the house in wh. Gilbert Brooks lives, at Scit., with the land adjoining; the same to be for her use through life, and then to belong to s. Jno., in case he survives his mo., he giving to his sis. Mary £10 ;—if he should not survive, the same to be equally divided among the rest of the ch. To da. Hester, the house in wh. Wm. Ticknor lives, at Scit., with the ground and orchard, and land at Brushy Hill, and at the 4th Cliff. To da. Han'h., w. of Wm. Ticknor, 40s. To da. Sarah, £10 at marriage, or at the age of 21, &c. To w. Mary, the household goods, and to s. Chas., the working tools." From the Bos'n. Rec's., we learn, that the fa. d. 13 d. 8 mo. 1657. The Inv'y of his Est. is on the Prob. Rec. Suff., vol. 3, p. 117. ch.: 1. Chas., b. in Eng'd., in 1634. 2. Hannah, 1636, m. Serg't. Wm. Ticknor, 1656. (By 2d,) 3. Elizab., 1644, m Thos. Hiland, Jan. 1, 1661. 4. Sarah, 1645, m. Jos. Woodworth, Jan. 6, 1669. 5. Hester, 1647. (By 3d,) 6. Abig., 1655. 7. Jno., b. in Bos'n., July 9, 1657, prob. d. young.

2. Chas., s. Jno., m. Abig. ——, and lived first in Bos'n., and Chas'n., but aft. in Scit., on his father's place. He is said to have built, by contract, the 2d water-mill in the Town of Plymouth, in 1676; also the corn-mill on the 3d Herring Brook, alluded to on p. 21. He d. 1683, and his wid. m. Amos Turner. ch.: 1. Chas., b. in Bos'n., Dec. 2, 1659, d. Feb. 1, 1659–60. 2. Abig., b. at Chas'n., Feb. 24, 1660–1, m. Henry Josselyn,

Nov. 4, 1676. 3. John, 1661 ? d. young. 4. Chas., Feb. 4, 1663. 5. Sarah, May 30, 1665, m. Is'l. Turner. 6. Thos., Ap. 6, 1667. 7. Elizab., Aug. 13, 1670, m. David Turner. 8. Jos., June 28, 1672. 9. Benj., Oct. 9, 1667. 10. Saml., July 9, 1679.

3. Chas., s. Chas. 2, inherited part of his father's mill, on the 3d Herring Brook, and lived in that vicinity. The name of his wife, we have not learned. He was Selectman in H., in 1727, and prob. d. Ap. 7, 1731. (H. Ch. Rec.) He left no son that survived, but had several da's. These were, 1. Rachel, Ap. 9, 1690. 2. Mary, Aug. 11, 1692. 3. Abig., Mar. 22, 1694–5, m. Gilbert Brooks ? Mar. 12, 1718. 4. Hannah, Jan. 30, 1697–8, prob. d. unm., Sep. 19, 1788, ae. 90 ? 5. Ruth, July 30, 1700, m. Hon. Jno. Cushing. 6. Experience, Jan. 1, 1703–4. 7. Judith, July 19, 1706. 8. Chas., Oct. 13, 1709, bap. Mar. 13, 1710, "being sick"; probably d.

4. Thos., s. Chas. 2, m. Sarah, da. Thos. Reed, of Wey'h., July 28, 1697, (H'm. Rec.,) and lived in Scit., where Eph'm. Stetson now resides. He is called *Ensign*, on the Rec. 2d Ch., in 1708. His wid. d. Sep. 7, 1758. ch.: 1. Sarah, Ap. 25, 1699. 2. Mary, Mar. 31, 1701. 3. Thos., Feb. 13, 1702–3. 4. Debo., June 21, 1705. 5. Anne, May 31, 1710. 6. Micah, Nov. 22, 1714, m. Mary Jones, Nov. 30, 1738, and had *Isaac*, b. and d. 1740; *Kezia*, bap. Jan. 10, 1742, being sick; and perhaps others. 7. Sarah, Oct. 26, 1718, m. Henchman Sylvester, 1747.

NOTE. Was there a da. Lydia, m. Joseph Soper, Nov. 20, 1729 ?

5. Joseph Stockbridge s. Chas. 2, m. Marg't., da. Jos. Turner, and lived first in H., and then in Pemb., where Capt. Haviland Torrey now resides. He was Dea. of the Ch. in H. for many years, and a man of activity, intelligence and usefulness. His w. d. Mar. 27, 1747, and he, Mar. 11, 1773, ae. 100! Whilst in H., he was Selectman, from 1731–35. ch.: 1. Joseph, Oct. 1, 1698. 2. Grace, 1700 ? m. Jno. Thaxter,

H'm., Jan. 15, 1719. (H'm. Rec.) 3. John, bap. July 2, 1704. 4. Barshua, bap. Dec. 1, 1706. 5. Marg't., bap. Oct. 31, 1708, m. Dea. Saml. Barstow, 1731. 6. Lusanna, bap. Nov. 25, 1711. 7. David, 1713 ?

NOTE. Was there another da., Abigail, who m. Jona. Turner, Nov. 15, 1738 ?

6. Benj., s. Chas. 2, m. Mary Tilden, 1701, succeeded to the Stockbridge mansion in Scit., and there lived and d. His son Benj., b. 1704, was the 2d regularly bred phys'n. sett. in Scit., being educated under Dr. Bulfinch, of Bos'n., and having a practice extending all over the Old Colony, and even to Worcester, and Ipswich. He also educated many in Med., from Bos'n., and other places, among whom was the distinguished Dr. Isaac Otis, who aft. m. his da. The w. of Dr. Benj., was Ruth, da. Job Otis ; and by her, he had but one s. that survived, Dr. Chas., b. 1734, also a phys'n. of high reputation, and a gent. of pleasing manners, and accomplished in literature. His s., Dr. Chas., b. 1790, d. early, at the outset of his professional career ; and with him, this branch of the family, in the male line, became extinct.

7. Saml., s. Chas. 2, m. Lydia, da. Wm. Barrell, 1703, and sett. at Mt. Blue, in Scit., in which vicinity some of his desct's. yet reside. He left a son Saml., who m. Sarah Tilden, Nov. 1, 1737, and who was fa. of James, Lydia, Sarah and others. The son Jas., d. in 1819, leaving ch.

8. *Thomas Stockbridge* s. Thos. 4, m. Hannah, ——, and lived on his father's place, by the 3d. Herring Brook. ch.: 1. Thos., bap. Aug. 6, 1725, d. unm. 2. Hannah, bap. Sep. 26, 1725. 3. Stephen, bap. Mar. 24, 1734, m., but had no ch., and d. in 1800.

9. *David Stockbridge* s. Joseph 5, m. 1, Deborah, da. Judge Jno. Cushing, Jan., 1736, who d. 1747; and 2, Jane Reed, and lived in H., where the new house of E. Q, Sylvester stands, near N. River

bridge, where he d. Dec. 13, 1788, ae. 75. He was Rep. from 1749–'56, and fr. 1760–62, and 72; T. C. from 1744–74; J. P. under king George for many years; and was an extensive land holder, a man of large estate, a valuable citizen, eminently useful, and thoroughly versed in everything pertaining to public affairs. His Justice Records are still in existence, and are in the possession of his gr. s., Lebbeus, of H. ch.: 1. Joseph, Aug. 20, 1737, grad. H. C., 1755, and d. at Falmouth, Me., Ap. 5, 1761, where he was established as a lawyer. He was also Reg. of Prob. for the Co. of Cumberland. 2. Betsey, Ap. 22, 1739, m. 1, Job Young, and 2, Benj. Stetson. 3. Jno., Dec. 7, 1741, killed in the woods by the fall of a tree. 4. Wm., Dec. 20, 1752. 5. David, 1755. 6. Debo., Aug. 18, 1761, m. Capt. Marlboro Turner, Jan. 7, 1790.

10 Wm. Stockbridge s. David 9, m. Ruth, da. Jno. Bailey, Oct. 9, 1774, who d. Dec. 10, 1839, and he Feb. 20, 1831. He lived first on Broadway, where Levi Perry now resides; then on King st., where Geo. Bailey lives; and finally sett. on Curtis, now Main st., and built the house occupied by his son Lebbeus. In 1798 he was the greatest landholder then in H.; and was a man of ready wit, lively and sociable in his habits, an agreeable companion, and an industrious and upright citizen. He was Selectman in 1812. ch.: 1. Joseph, Oct. 1, 1775, a merchant, d. unm. in N. Yarmouth, Me., Ap. 13, 1804. 2. Ruth, Nov. 8, 1777, m. Jos. Ramsdell, Feb. 3, 1800, and moved to Warren, Mass. 3. John. Ap. 18, 1780. 4. Wm. R., June 29, 1782. 5. Calvin, Sep. 19, 1784. 6. Lebbeus, Nov. 29, 1787. 7. Betsey, m. Homer Ramsdell, Oct. 27, 1816, and is living in Warren, with her son Wm. 8. Silvia B., Mar. 1, 1793, d. June 28, 1795. 9. Marcia, Ap. 7, 1795, m. Sam'l. G. Bowman, of Bath, Me., May 19, 1816, and had *Nath'l.*, July 28, 1817, a lawyer, d. at the South; *Sam'l. S.*, Aug. 27, 1818, m. Miss Hoover, and is in Louisiana; *Ruth E.*, Sep. 17, 1820, m. Lt. Jos. F. Green, U. S. N.; *Wm. S.*, Sep. 9, 1822, d. young; *Wm. H.*, Nov. 18, 1823, m. Helen L. Randall, of Bath, and lives at the South; *Marcia S.*, Feb. 9, 1826, m. Nath'l. C. A. Jenks, of N. Yar'h., Me.; *Sarah W.*, Feb. 10,

1828; *Francis J.*, May 9, 1830; *Orville R.*, Dec. 13, 1832; and *Howard D.*, Dec. 7, 1835, d. young. Mr. B., the fa., d. in Bath, Mar. 29, 1841, ae. 50. 10. Stephen, Ap. 3, 1797, d. May 14, 1818. 11. Luther, May 19, 1801, d. Mar. 26, 1802.

11. Hon. David, s. David 9, m. Ruth, da. Hon. Jos. Cushing, Dec. 23, 1779, who d. Ap. 14, 1833, and he Feb. 26, 1843. Lived on his father's place; was Selectman in 1782, '89, '99, and 1800; T. C. from 1793–98; Rep. 1794; in the Mass. Sen. 1818; and a gent. of fine talents, sociable habits, and correct deportment. ch.: 1. Jane R., Oct. 6, 1780, m. Miller Smith, Pemb., Sep. 15, 1803. 2. Benj., Nov. 7, 1781, m. Mary Crook er, Jan. 26, 1814, who d. Mar. 1, 1818, and he Oct. 16, 1847, having had *Mary B.*, d. Mar. 4, 1817; *Benj.*, d. young; and *Mary T.*, m. Rob't. Eells, Jan. 20, 1838. 3. David, Nov. 25, 1783, m. Sarah B. Crooker, July 28, 1811, and has *Caroline*, Sep. 13, 1812, m. Benj. White, Fairhaven, Feb. 15, 1833; *Maria T.*, Dec. 28, 1814, m. Capt. Jas. Gouch, Mar. 7, 1836, sett. in Ills., and d. in Oct., 1852; *Jno.*, Aug. 23, 1816, of N. Haven, Ct.; and *Geo. M.*, Dec. 6, 1821, in Cal'a. 4. Martin, Dec. 20, 1785, m. wid. Thurza Reed, who d., leaving him no ch., and he lives in Scit. 5. Horatio, Ap. 27, 1788. 6. Debo., Nov. 4, 1790, m. Thos. Turner, Pemb., May 10, 1811, and is living a wid., in H., with her son Thos. 7. Ruth, Mar. 23, 1793, m. Jas. Turner, and is living a wid., in H. 8. Joseph C., July 4, 1798, m. 1, Ann W. Clark, Dec. 29, 1833, who d. Jan. 26, 1837; and 2, Pamelia Ford, Dec. 13, 1838; lives at the Corners; was school teacher for sev. years; and has, 1. Ann E., Oct. 17, 1834. 2. Jos. C., Nov. 3, 1836. (By 2d,) 3. Pamelia F., Nov. 13, 1839, d. Oct. 5, 1841. 4. Amelia F., Feb. 18, 1843. 5. Emma B., Sep. 24, 1846.

12. Dr. John, s. Wm. 10, stud. Med. with Dr. Gad Hitchcock, of Pemb., Mass., and sett. in Topsham, Me., 1804, and moved to Bath, in 1805, where he d. May 3, 1849, ae. 69. He m. 1, Theodosia, da. Rev. Tristram Gilman, of N. Yar'h., Oct. 15, 1805, who d. Nov. 4, 1822, ae. 34; and 2, Eliza I., da. Hon. Jno. Russell, of Bos'n., (for many years ed. and prop. of the Bos'n. Com'l. Gaz.) Jan. 5, 1824. She survives. Mr. S. was

devoted to his profession, and in some of its branches became highly distinguished. He received the honorary degree of M. D., at Dart. Coll. in 1822, and was in practice 48 yrs. He was a scientific and successful practitioner, a consistent and devoted friend, and an honest and upright man. ch.: 1. Tristram G., Aug. 28, 1806, rec'd. the degree of M. D. at Bowd. Coll., 1827, is a distinguished surgeon and physician in Bath, and m. Mary R. P., da. Capt. Neh. Harding, of Bath. No ch. 2. Jno. W., Ap. 27, 1811, living in N. Orleans. 3. Marcia E., Mar. 25, 1815, d. Sep. 18, 1823. 4. Mary G., June 12, 1818, m. Capt. Wm. Drummond, of Bath, Oct. 30, 1848, and had 1 ch., b. 1849, d. 1851. 5. Theodosia, Sep. 20, 1819, living in Hanover, N. H. 6. Francis B., Dec. 27, 1821, d. Feb. 28, 1823. (By 2d.,) 7. Francis B., Ap. 9, 1826. 8. Cornelia R., Dec. 18, 1827. 9. Joseph H., Feb. 18, 1831. 10. Marcia E., Oct. 27, 1832. The last ch., with their mo., are living at the West.

13. Wm. R., s. Wm. 10, m. Olive True, of N. Yar'h., Me., and was one of the oldest and most eminent merchants in that town, with his bro. Calvin. He was also engaged in ship-building and navigation; and was a man of active habits, and highly esteemed by the community in which he lived. The following record of his ch. is from Mr. Wm. Dawes:— 1. Maria, m. Dr. Nelson H. Carey, of Me., a native of Bridg'r., Mass. 2. Marcia, m. Mr. Ring, Merchant, of Calais, Me. 3. Rev. Joseph, grad. Bowd. Coll., and stud. law, but is now a chaplain in the U. S. N., and resides with his family, at Bridgeport, Ct. He m. an Everett, of N. Yar'h. 4. Wm., grad. at the Waterville Inst., stud. Med., and is sett. as a Phys'n. at the West. Not m. 5. Olive, not m. 6. Sam'l., edu. as a merchant, but is now living, an invalid, in Me.

14. Calvin, s. Wm. 10, m. Rachel W. Rogers, of Mf'd., and was a merchant in N. Yarmouth., Me., and Dea. of the Baptist Church, and died in Me., in May, 1833. A man of warm religious feelings; influential in the denomination to which he belonged; of a benevolent heart, and upright and honest. ch.: 1. Wm. C., d. young. 2. Jno. C., ent. at Brunswick, but grad. at B. U., 1838; had charge of the female dept. of a seminary at War-

ren, R. I.; and sett. as a clergyman, first in Waterville, Me., in 1844, then in Woburn, Mass., 1847, and is now in Prov., R. I.; m. Mary T., da. Suchet Mauran, of Warren, R. I., and has *Mary S.*, and *Annie W.* 3. Wales R., Mar., 1821, auctioneer, Bos'n., of the firm of Holt & Stockbridge; m. Marg't. T. Southwick, of Vassalboro', Me., and has *Arthur B.*, Nov. 25, 1851. 4. Edward A., Sep. 1831, in Bos'n.

15. Lebbeus, s. Wm. 10, m. Lydia, da. Capt. Leavitt Lane, of H'm., in 1810, lives on his father's place on Main st., and is a farmer. ch.: 1. Wm., Nov. 5, 1812, m. Mary A. Damon, lives with his fa., and has *Fred'k. W.*, Aug. 7, 1842, d. Jan. 17, 1853; *Francis J.*, Oct. 3, 1844, d. Aug. 24, 1847; *Elizab. A.*, Mar. 8, 1847; *Frank*, June 30, 1849; and *Mary A.*, Aug. 11, 1852. 2. Leavitt L., May 5, 1815, a shipmaster; m. Abby W., da. Dr. Melzar Dwelley, July 4, 1844, and has *Geo. E.*, Dec. 13, 1845; *Ellen E.*, Feb. 18, 1848, d. Jan. 10, 1850; and *Chas. L.*, Ap. 3, d. Nov. 2, 1850. 3. Ruth B., Dec. 5, 1818, m. Martin W. Stetson, Dec. 1, 1836. 4. Lebbeus, Feb. 15, 1825, a mariner for the past 8 yrs., m. Mary T. Sylvester, June 24, 1849, lives on Broadway, and has *Edwin W.*, May 13, 1850. 5. Lydia L., Aug. 25, 1827. 6. Sarah L., Jan. 3, 1830, a school-teacher in Baltimore, Md.

16. Dr. Horatio, s. Hon. David, 11, at the age of 15, went to the Acad. at Bridg'r., under the charge of Mr. Zach. Eddy, and thence to the Acad. at Rochester, under the charge of Rev. Calvin Chaddock; and in 1804, ent. H. Coll., where he remained two yrs., after wh. he commenced the study of med., under Dr. Freeman Foster, of Scit., with whom he remained 2 yrs., and subsequently, was with the distinguished Dr. Jas. Mann, of Wrentham, one yr. Mr. S. was sett. first in Berwick, Me.; then in Medway; then in Blackstone Village, where he remained until 1833, at which date he moved to Woonsocket, R. I., where he has since resided, and where, for 18 yrs., he was engaged in the Druggist business, from which he withdrew, in 1851. In 1810, he m. Priscilla W., da. Saml. and Priscilla Faxon, of Fox'o., Mass., who proved a kind and aff. wife, and with whom he lived happily for 38 yrs., when she d. June 29, 1848, ae. 63. ch.: 1. Horatio, June 13,

1813, m. Data A. Kempton, of Mendon, Mass., Nov. 9, 1835, (she b. June 30, 1813,) and has, *Francis M.*, Ap. 20, 1837; *Harriet A.*, Aug. 26, 1839; *Horatio I.*, Dec. 27, 1841; *Lucia A.*, June 1, 1843; *Chas. E.*, Dec. 29, 1847; and *Walter S.*, Feb. 12, 1849. 2. Harriet A., Dec. 8, 1815, m. Elisha T. Read, Cashier of a Bank in W., May 16, 1834, and has *Jas. S.*, Sep. 9, 1835; *Harriet A.*, Oct. 2, 1839; *Geo. S.*, Sep. 22, 1842; and *Isabella*, July 20, 1850. Lost 2, d. young.

STODDARD, Henry, s. Laban, of H'm., m. 1, Polly Cudworth, and 2, Ann K. Mann; was a carpenter by trade; lived at the corner of Walnut and Main sts.; and d. June 30, 1848, ae. 64. ch.: 1. Henry, 1807, d. 1832. (By 2d,) 2. Ann C., Sep. 21, 1815, m. Edwin Packard, N. Bridg'r. 3. Mary C., Oct. 12, 1817, m. Thos. W. Gurney, Ab'n., Nov. 1, 1836. 4. Wm. B., Sep. 17, 1820. 5. Capt. Duncan T., Mar. 7, 1823, a carpenter, m. Mary M. Henderson, 1851, and has *Duncan T.*, 1852. 6. Abby S. H., 1825, d. 1844. 7. Isabella R., m. Henry Mann, June 13, 1850. 8. Jos. A., Mar. 24, 1830. 9. Henry A., Jan. 12, 1833. 10. Patience E., May 6, 1835. 11. Levi M., June 14, 1838.

2. Melvin, s. Hezek. of Scit., b. Oct., 1808, m. 1, Laura Young, 1832, who d. the same year; and 2, Abig. Rogers; lives on Broadway; is a shoemaker; and has, Martha A., Dec., 1843.

STUDLEY FAMILY.

Arms: Ar. on a fesse vert, betw. 3 stags' heads cabossed or.

Crest: A stag's head cabossed or, pierced through the scalp with an arrow in bend sinister, vert, feathered ar., headed sa.

STUDLEY, an old English name, found in the County of Kent, and also in Yorkshire,—the seat of the family, in the latter place, being at Studley Park, near which are the ruins of the celebrated *Fountains Abbey*, a famous place of resort for travellers, each one of whom is entitled, to "meat by measure, (a quarter of a yard of roast beef for dinner) and a great black jack of strong drink," on calling for the same.[1] We find two families in N. Eng. at an early date, one in Boston, and the other in Sandwich. A branch of each of these sett. in Scit., and have desct's. in H. We shall trace these separately.

I. Jno. Studley, and w. Elizab., were in Bos'n., in 1659, but when they came to the city, or how long they remained, we cannot say. Their s. Jno., was b. in Bos'n., Dec. 8, 1659; and their son Benj., was b. in B., May 23, 1661. This is all the notice we find on any of the records in B. The latter son, Benj., seems to have been in Scit., in 1683, m. Mary, da. Jno. Merritt, and sett. near Merritt's brook, a few rods S. E. of the bridge. ch.: 1. Jno., Dec. 11, 1684. 2. Benj., Dec. 7, 1687. 3. Jas., July 15. 1690, m. Sarah Farrow, of H'm., 1717, and had *Sarah*, 1718; *Jas.*, 1720; and *Elizab.*, 1725. 4. Jona., June, 19, 1693. 5. David, Jan. 19, 1696–7, m. Susanna Vinton, 1717, and left 1 da., and 3 sons, some of whose desc'ts. yet live in Scit. 6. Mary, Sep. 23, 1698. 7. Elizab., June 8, 1701. 8. Debo., Dec. 19, 1702—3. 9. Elizab., Sep. 10. 1706.

NOTE: We think it highly probable, that Benj. Studley, who was in H'm; in 1724, m. Susanna, da. Eben'r. Lane, Dec. 31, 1724, and had *Hannah*, 1725; *Sarah*, 1727; *Ruth*, 1729; *Lois* and *Eunice*, 1731; *Jona.*, 1734; d. young; *Rhoda*, 1735; *Irania*, 1737; and *Jona.*, 1728;—was a desc't. of Benj. of Scit., and prob. his *son*, as he is called "s. of Benj." We think it also probable, that most of this name, in H'm. and Cohas't., sprung from Jno. of Boston.

2. Eliab, s. Benj., and gr. s. Jno. I, m. Mary Briggs, of Scit., Ap. 10, 1729, and it is said, sett. in H., or what is now Pleas't. st., where David Studley resides. He was the first Studley owner of the mill long known as "Elihab's Mill," and was a noted Tavern keeper, his house being a favorite place of public resort. He d. December 13, 1785, and his wid. October 19, 1797, ae. 90. ch.: 1. Benjamin. 2. Martha, m. Jno. Shaw, of Ab'n., April 16,

[1] Gough's British Topography, pp. 416, 443, 461, and 474.

25

1752. 3. Elizab., m. Jno. Robinson, Plym'h., Feb. 12, 1754 4. Jas., lost at sea. 5. Thankful, m. 1, Michael Jackson, Ab'n., Feb. 15, 1759; and 2, Seth Keith, of Bridg'r., 1775. 6. Debo., m. an Erskine. 7. Lucy, m. Seth Stetson, Ap. 11, 1765. 8. Abig., m. Thos. Curtis, June 6, 1770. 9. Japhet, July 25, 1756. 10. Joseph, m. Rebecca Stetson, Jan. 10, 1765, was killed by lightning, June 16, of the same yr., and his w. had twin ch., Rebecca, and Lucy, who were bap. Ap. 2, 1768, and the mother m. Elisha Witherell, of Chestf'd., Dec. 30, 1772.

3. Benj., s. Eliab 2, m. Han'h. Litchfield, and was Selectman in H., from 1778–81, and in 1787, and '88. We find his ch. on the Ch. Recs. of H., as follows: 1. Elizab., bap. Oct. 13, 1754. 2. Benj., bap. June 5, 1757. 3. Abner, bap. June 5, 1757, prob. d. young. 4. Hannah, bap. June 1, 1760, m. Isaac Moore, of Warren, Mass., Mar. 18, 1782. 5. Mary, bap. Sep. 2, 1764. 6. Jas., bap. Sep. 2, 1764, d. Feb. 7, 1766. 7. Zenas, bap. Oct. 7, 1764, d. Ap. 11, 1771. 8. Nabby, bap. Aug. 3, 1776, m. Jno. R. Josselyn, Nov. 1, 1785. 9. Debo., m. Arad Woodworth, of Warren. 10. Zenas, m. and d. in Leicester, leaving ch. 11. Joseph, of Leicester.

4. Japheth Studley s. Eliab 2, m. Rachel Fearing, H'm., who d. Sept. 28, 1826, ae. 92, and he Jan. 2, 1842, ae. 85. ch.: 1. Rachel, May 5, 1781, m. Jesse Stoddard, Ab'n., Ap. 21, 1803. 2. David, Mar. 31, 1783. 3. Walter B., Mar. 7, 1786. 4. Lucy, Jan. 25, 1788, m. Lewis Litchfield, of H. 5. Lydia, Ap. 6, 1791, d. Mar. 11, 1793. 6. Luther, Jan. 26, 1793, m. a Cleaveland, and d. in N. Y. State, leaving a son *Eliphaz*. 7. Lydia, Sep. 25, 1796, m. David Darling, Aug, 24. 1816. 8. Japhet, Oct. 31, 1799, d. May 9, 1832.

5. Eliab, s. Benj. 3, m. Betsey, da. Peleg Stetson, Ab'n., and lived on Pleas't. st., in a house which stood a little N. of where Gridley Studley resides. He d. Aug. 14, 1826, and his wid. in

Jan., 1835, ae. 79. ch.: 1. Jas., Feb. 28, 1777. 2. Betsey, m. Capt. Thos. Stetson, Oct. 19, 1801. 3. Nathan. 4. Experience, m. Rob't. Estes. 5. Alvin, Jan. 1792, m. Nabby Stetson, who d. in 1844; he lives in E. Ab'n., is a shoemaker, and has 1 da., *Nancy*, not m. 6. Hannah, 1785, m. Eleazer Josselyn, Jan. 1, 1809. 7. Gridley. 8. Nancy, m. Josh. Curtis, Ab'n., Mar. 18, 1816, and is d.

6. Benj., s. Benj. 3, m. Silvester Bonney, of Pemb., Nov. 28, i1782, and, it is said, moved to Leicester, Mass. His ch., b. in P., were, 1. Abner, May 15, 1784. 2. Silvester, Oct. 24, 1786. 3. Silvia, Jan. 30, 1789. 4. Zenas, Ap. 25 1791. 5. Benj., May 3, 1793. 6. Wealthy, Aug. 8, 1795. 7. Sally, Sep. 24, 1797.

7. David, s. Japhet 4, learned the watchmaker's trade in H'm.; m. Hannah, da. Caleb Torrey, of Midd'o., and sett. on Pleas't st., where he yet resides. His w. d. May 19, 1850. Mr. S., is a man of natural mechanical ability, much esteemed as a citizen, and has raised a large and respectable family of sons and daughters. ch.: 1. Cephisa, Feb. 10, 1811, m. Ezekiel Reed, Ab'n. 2. David F., Oct. 6, 1812, a jeweller in N. Bridg'r., m. Martha J. Howard, and has *Martha J.* 3. Philander, Nov. 5, 1814, m. Elizab. Estes, May 11, 1837, lives on Circuit st., and has *Mary M.*, Oct. 5, 1839, d. Mar. 5, 1840; and *Amelia J.*, May 5, 1847. 4. Joseph H., Oct. 13, 1816, shoe mf'r., in H.; m. Lucinda Curtis, Nov. 2, 1838, lives on Main st., and has *Edwin H.*, June 9, 1839; *Maria*, Aug. 7, 1842; *Lucinda H.*, Oct. 19, 1846, d. Sep. 4, 1848; and *Ellen A.*, June 15, 1849. 5. Iantha E., Feb. 26, 1819, m. Jos. W. Gurney, May 25, 1839. 6. Luther, Dec. 28, 1820, jeweller, in N. Bridg'r.; not m. 7. Benj. F., Feb. 21, 1823, m. Betsey R., da. Amos Bates, lives on Circuit st., and has *Benj. W.*, Jan. 10, 1846; and *Betsey I.*, June 15, 1848. 8. Mary F., Mar. 5, 1825, d. Sep. 14, 1826. 9. Walter B., Jan. 10, 1827, a jeweller, in E. Ab'n., m. Susan Turner, Pemb., in Nov., 1848, and has *Susan L. B.*, and *Adelaide F.* 10. Henry C., June 3, 1829, of N. Bridg'r. 11. Han'h. M., June 28, 1834.

8. Walter B., s. Japhet 4, m. Matilda Crooker, Pemb., May 18, 1806, and moved to Hartford, Ct. Had one son b. in H., viz.: Danl., Aug. 25, 1806. We are informed that there were other ch., b. in Ct., but their names we have not learned.

9. Jas., s. Eliab 5, m. Mary D., da. Dr. Peter Hobart, in 1803, and lives near Hudson, N. Y. ch.: 1. Mary C., May 18, 1806, d. young. 2. Elizab. C., Mar. 3, 1808, m. Waldo Pool, E. Ab'n., and is d. 3. Marshall L., Mar. 23, 1809, m. Sarah E. Eells, Norwich, Ct., and d. in Demarara, leaving 1 ch., which d. 4. Elb. G., Sep. 1, 1810, m. Catherine Cole, lives in N. Y'k. State, and has ch. 5. Salome H., Jan. 30, 1812, m. Henry R. Curtis, E. Ab'n., and is d. 6. Elmira S., Jan. 28, 1814, m. Henry R. Curtis, E. Ab'n. 7. Lucy J., Sep. 27, 1817, m. Corn's. T. Stinkle, of N. Y'k. State.8. Jas. J., Dec. 18, 1821, m. Elizab. J. Boardman, lives in E. Ab'n., is a shoemaker, and has *David C.*

10. Nathan, s. Eliab 5, m. Huldah Ellis, May 18, 1806, and d. in 1849. ch.: 1. Wm., June 19, 1806, m. Elizab. J. Haskell, lives in E. Ab'n., and has *Wm. A.*, *Mary E.*, *Hannah M.*, *Nathan F.*, *Jno. A.*, *Adaline A.*, *Jacob N.*, and *Chas. E.* 2. Andrew, m. Mary, da. Zenas Jenkins, lives in E. Ab'n., is a dealer in provisions, and has *Mary A.*, *Austin*, *Jane B.*, *Andrew H.*, *Huldah E.*, *Sarah E.*, *Ferdinand and Isabella*, (the latter d.,) and *Elvira.* 3. Sophia, m. Jacob Nash, and is living a wid. in Ab'n. 4. Reuben, provision dealer, in E. Ab'n., m. Adaline Burgess, of Harvard, Mass., and has *Reuben W.*; *Geo. S.*; *Henry J.*, d.; *Horace W;* *Chas. H.*, d.; *Susan E.;* and *Emily M.* 5. Alvin, m. Mercy Estes, and lives in Natick, Mass. 6. Sylvia, m. Bela Smith, Ab'n. 7. Elizab., m. Stephen Standish, E. Ab'n., no ch. 8. Huldah, m. N. Porter Baker, of E. Ab'n., and has *Abby E.*, *Susan A.*, and *Andrew H.*

11. Gridley, s. Eliab 5, m. Rebecca Keen, of Pemb., July 11, 1820, and lives on Pleasant st. ch.: 1. Betsey, Nov. 23, 1820, m. Nathan S. Jenkins, E. Ab'n., and has *Albina*, and *Joseph H.* 2. Ruth M., Aug. 25, 1822, m. Jos. Hobart, N. Ab'n.; he is d. 3. Han'h. M., Dec. 15, 1824, m. Chas. Dunham, E. Ab'n., and d. leaving a da. *Ellen.* 4. Wm., Dec. 19, 1826, m.

Sophia J., da. Enos Curtis, and lives in E. Ab'n. 5. Gridley, Mar. 19, 1829. 6. Judson, June 3, 1831. 7. Lucy J., Nov. 4, 1833. 8. Rebecca A., May 6, 1836. 9. Mary K., Mar. 12, 1839.

SECOND BRANCH.

II. Benony Studly (Benoni), of Sandwich, Mass., was in that part of Scit., now Hanover, and his house, which was built in 1702, is the oldest now standing in the town, on Hanover st. He m. Abig., da. Jno. Stetson, of Scit., Dec. 22, 1701, and d. suddenly, Nov. 14, 1746, and his wid., Feb. 1, 1758–9, ae. 82. He left only a verbal will, drawn up, at his request, by Rev. Mr. Bass, and the same is now in the hands of some of his desc'ts. ch.: 1. Abig., Aug. 13, 1702, m. Joseph House, Dec. 14, 1732. 2. Jno., Feb. 25, 1704. 3. Josh., Aug. 1707. 4. Gideon, May 5, 1710, d. Aug. 3, 1734. 5. Sarah, Mar. 31, 1716. 6. Benoni, July 15, 1720, m., and had in H. a son *Benoni*, bap. May 10, 1741, and it is said that the fa. moved to Rehoboth.

2. Jno., s. Benoni II., m. Elizab. Doten, of Plym'h., who d. in H., Oct. 11, 1774, and he Sep. 23, 1787. Lived for a time in the Judge Cushing house, at the Corners, and finally built the house where his grandson Jabez now lives. ch.: 1. Sarah, July 2, 1731, m. Thos. Barstow. 2. Elizab., Oct. 30, 1734, m. Elisha Curtis, Jan. 15, 1760. 3. Gideon, Mar. 13, 1736, d. Aug. 5, 1737. 4. Jabez, bap. Aug. 17, 1738. 5. Rebecca, May 19, 1744, prob. d unm.

3. Josh., s. Benoni II., m. Lydia Pratt, of Pemb., Mar. 6, 1735, who d. July 9, 1759, and he July 15, 1760. Another rec. says she d. June 27, and he, July 9, 1759. ch.: 1. Gideon, May 15, 1738. 2. Lydia, Jan. 16, d. May 6, 1740. 3. Abig., bap. June 28, 1741, m. Danl. Crooker, Feb. 16, 1766, and d. in Sep. 1779. 4. Joshua, Sep. 26, 1742. 5. Joanna, Jan. 13, 1744, d. Ap. 16, 1779. 6. Ann, May 11, 1746, d. May 15, 1760. 7. Lydia, May 8, 1748, d. Sep. 27, 1826? 8. Jno., July 22, 1750, d. Jan. 17, 1751. 9. Rebecca, Mar. 8, 1752, d. May 16, 1754.

NOTE. It is said there were twins in this fam., who d. young.

4. Jabez Studley [signature], s. Jno. 2, m. Katurah Simmons, Mf'd., who d. June 21, 1790, and he Feb. 14, 1825, ae. 86. Lived on Wash'n. st., where his son Jabez now lives and was a soldier in the Rev'n. ch.: 1. Rebecca, bap. Jan. 2, 1774, m. Luther Sprague, Mf'd. 2. Jabez, bap. Sep. 22, 1776, m. Chloe M. Clark, Feb. 23, 1800, lives on his father's place, and has, 1. *Katurah*, Mar. 20, 1801, m. Rob't. Curtis, Ap. 16, 1826. 2. *Eliza*, July 10, 1803, m. Steph. Josselyn, Nov. 16, 1834. 3. *Jno.*, July 20, 1805, m. Eliza A. Herrick, Chas'n., is a shipwright, and has Jno., m. Mary F. Hammond, and lives in Chas'n.; Jas. W.; Edwin; Georgiana; and Chas. 4. *George*, Aug. 25, 1807, carpenter, m. Judith Curtis, Jan. 30, 1834, and lives near his father; no ch. 5. *Horace*, Jan. 6, 1810, m. Marcia Rose, Jan. 15, 1834, lives on Spring st., and has Horace C., Nov. 1834; Geo., Oct. 18, 1836; Marg't. S., Nov. 30, 1838; Timo. R., July 9, 1841; and Rebecca, Aug. 22, 1845. 6. *Hiram*, Ap. 28, 1812, m. 1, Sarah A. Brett, of Bridg'r., Mar. 27, 1836; and 2, Esther Hollis, May 4, 1845; lives on Cross st.; is a carpenter; and has Abby A.; Mary R., b. 1844, d. 1845; and Hiram A., b. 1848, d. 1849. 7. *Robert C.*, Oct. 31, 1815, d. Jan. 19, 1817. 8. *Robert H.*, Dec. 8, 1818, m. Lucy J., da. Josi. Bonney, and lives with his fa.; no ch.

5. Gideon, s. Josh. 3, m. Rosamond Church, Jan. 4, 1762, and d. Aug. 14, 1816, ae. 78, and his wid. Jan. 3, 1832, ae. 92. It is said that he was out in the Fr. War, in 1756, and we have seen old certificates of service, signed by Lieut. Jno. Bailey, and dated 1756, and '58. ch.: 1. Anna, Dec. 27, 1762, m. Homer Whiting, May 8, 1785. 2. Sarah, July 9, 1766, d. June 26, 1847. 3. Rosamond, June 9, 1768, m. Zattu Cushing, Ab'n., July 12, 1790. 4. Rebecca, Feb. 15, 1770, m. Benj. Tolman, Mf'd., Feb. 11, 1800. 5. Lucy, Oct. 12, 1773, living, unm., in H. 6. Gideon, July 19, 1776. 7. Abig., Oct. 19, 1778, m. David Pool, Ab'n., Sep. 15, 1801. 8. Dr. Joshua, Sep. 15, 1784, a physician in H. for 40 yrs.; T. C. from 1824–32; and an active and useful man. He d. unm., Feb. 28, 1848.

6. Josh., s. Josh. 3, moved to Sharon, Ct., was a carpenter by trade, and a man of successful enterprise; m. Ruth Allen, ? and had 1. Polly, m. a Coleman, and had *Fanny, Philena, Maria, and Polly.* 2. Amy, m. a Parsons, and had *Polly, Anna, Amy,* and *Caroline.* 3. Joshua, m. and had a da. *Maria,* and a son, who was drowned. 4. Ruby Ruth A., m. a Hatch, and had *Abig., Jno., Lydia A.,* and another. 5. Gideon, m. but had no ch. 6. Mary A., m. an Everett, and had a son *Josh.* She is d. 7. Lydia, m. an Everett, and had *Thos., Ichabod, Ruby R. A., Russell, Abig., Betsey, and Caroline.* 8. Ichabod, m. and had *Josh., Gideon A., Enoch, and Calvin.* 9. Abigail ? not m.

NOTE. The above is from papers left by Dr. Studley.

7. Gideon, s. Gideon 5, m. Sarah, da. Jno. and Grace Butler, of Oakham, Mass., Dec. 17, 1809, lived on Main, near Grove st., where his w. d. July 9, 1838, and he Jan. 10, 1850. ch.: 1. Ann, July 28, 1810, a school teacher for sev. yrs., m. Caleb Whiting, May 11, 1852. 2. Gideon, Oct. 19, 1811, a carpenter in Ab'n.; m. Priscilla B. Shaw, and has *Gideon,* d.; *Jas. B.; Sarah A.; Anna H.; Alice; and Gideon.* 3. Jno. B., June 27, 1813, living in H., not m. 4. Jas., Mar. 9, 1815, merchant, in Mobile, Ala. 5. Josh., Dec. 5, 1817, living in H., unm. 6. Sarah B., Dec. 23, 1819. 7. Geo., Nov. 11, 1822, m. Sarah, da. Croel Bonney, H'n., Nov. 28, 1850, and is a shoe m'fr, in E. Ab'n.

STURTEVANT, Rufus M., s. Geo. of Pemb., b. Feb. 17, 1830, m. Rebecca A. Woodman, Mar. 1, 1852, lives on Centre st., with Seth Harding, and is a shoemaker. No ch.

SYLVESTER FAMILY.

Arms: Ar. an oak tree, eradicated, vert.

Crest: A lion's head, erased, vert.

SYLVESTER, SILVESTER. This name appears to be of *French* origin, and in the French language, *sylvestre* signifies *a tree*, whence the coat of arms represents an *oak tree* in the shield, being a *parlant*, or *speaking* coat, descriptive of the name. We find the family sett. in Eng. not long after the Conquest, and the an cestor probably went over in the army of William, in 1069. *Stephen Silvestre*, is named by Fuller, among the gentry of Norfolk.[1] *Gabriel Sylvester*, D.D., was Prebend of Weeford, Litchf'd., in 1506;[2] and in 1538, *Robert*, was Archd'n. of Langtoft, York;[3] Preb. of York, 1541;[4] and Archd'n. of Nottingham, 1549.[5] The family is highly respectable in the old country, and is numerously represented in the U. States.

The first of the name in N. Eng., was Richard, who was of Wey'h., 1633, and of Scit., 1642, and sett. on the "Two Miles." The year in which he came over, and the name of the vessel in which he embarked, we have not been able to learn. Settlements were made at Wey'h., in 1619, 1624, and 1625. He prob. came in the company with Rev. Robert Lenthal, minister of Wey'h., and the cause of his coming to Scit., was on acc't. of difficulties, arising from his religious opinions.[6] He m. Naomi

[1] Worthies of Eng'd., vol. 2, p. 472. [2] Willis' Cathedrals, p. 471. [3] Ibid., 149. [4] Ibid., p. 180. [5] Ibid, p. 106. [6] Mather's Magnalia, vol. 1, p. 222.

Torrey, ab. 1632, and d. in Scit. in 1663. ch.: 1. Lydia, 1633, m. Nath'l. Rawlins, Sep. 4, 1652. 2. Jno., 1634, m., and had *Sarah*, 1671; *John.*, 1672; *Joseph*, 1674, who was of Marshfield, and left ch.; Samuel, 1676, also of Marshfield; m., and left ch.; *Lydia*, 1679. 3. Peter, 1637, d. 1642, being accidentally shot, on the Sabbath, by the discharge of a gun in his father's house. (See Winthrop's Journal, and Deane's Scit.) 4. Joseph, 1638. 5. Dinah, 1642, prob. d. unm. 6. Elizab., 1643, m. Jno. Lowell, Jan. 24, 1658, and d. soon after. 7. Richard, 1648, was of Milton, 1678, m. Hannah, da. "Old Jas. Leonard, of Taunton," and was prob. ancestor of the Sylvesters of Norfolk Co. 8. Naomi, 1649, m. Jno. Lowell, 1666. 9. Israel, 1651, had a house on the margin of the 2d Herring Brook, 1670, m., and had *Israel*, Sep. 23, 1675, who left desc'ts.; *Silence*, 1677; *Richard*, 1679, m. and left desc'ts.; *Lois*, 1680; *Martha*, 1682; *Mary*, 1683; *Elisha*, 1685; *Peter*, 1687, m. and left desc'ts., who are in Leicester, Mass., and in N. Hampshire; *Zebulon*, 1689, m. and left desc'ts.; *Barshua*, 1692; and *Debo.*, 1696. 10. Hester, 1653, prob. d. unm. 11. Benj., 1656, m. Lydia Standlake, 1684, and has desc'ts. in Mf'd.

2. Capt. Joseph, s. Rich'd., lived where Sam'l. Waterman's house stands, in So. Scit., near Church Hill, and improved the farm wh. he purchased of Jno. Whiston, 1664. We have given some sketch of his life on p. 22. As a reward for his services in the Indian wars, a grant of land was made to him and his company, by the Gen'l. Court, which was designed to have been in Maine, but which, when the line was run between the Provinces, proved to be in N. Hampshire; and on a repres'n. of these facts by Chas. Turner, and others, agents for the claimants, in 1765, a new grant was made in Me., on condition that 30 families and a minister should be sett., and a meeting-house built, within six y'rs.; and this is now known as the town of *Turner*, Me.[1] His ch., by w. Mary, were, 1. Joseph, Nov. 11, 1664. 2. Mary, Dec. 24, 1666, m. Benj. Curtis, 1689. 3. Naomi, Mar. 5, 1668. 4. Anna, May 5, 1669. 5. Benj., Dec. 11, 1680. 6. David, Ap. 20, 1683. 7. Amos, Nov. 15, 1685.

[1] Williamson's Hist. Me., vol. 2, p. 528–9.

3. Benj., s. Capt. Joseph 2, m. Jerusha Wheaton, Nov. 16, 1710, and had, 1. Benj., Nov. 15, 1711. 2. Ruth, bap. May 8, 1720. 3. Jas., bap. June 27, 1722, was m., and prob. lived on Wash'n., near East st., where remains of an old cellar are yet visible, and where his wid. *Sally*, resided some time after his decease. 4. Jacob, bap. Oct. 4, 1724, m. Mary Bates, Nov. 5, 1753, and d. July 25, 1806, and his wid. Dec. 24, 1811, ae. 86. No ch.

4. Amos, s. Capt. Joseph 2, m. Elizab. Henchman, Nov. 20, 1706, who d. Feb. 11, 1762, ae. 77, and he Oct. 23, 1753. His house stood on Wash'n. st., near where that of Rob't. Sylvester now stands, and was for many years a Tavern stand, kept by his widow after his decease. He was Selectman in 1743, and a blacksmith by trade, his shop standing near the house. When the old mansion was torn down, two chairs were preserved, one of wh. is in the possession of Rob't, and the other of Michael Sylvester. ch.: 1. Amos, Sep. 14, 1707. 2. Wm., Feb. 22, 1709. 3. Joseph, Jan. 9, 1711. 4. Henchman, Dec. 20, 1713, m. Sarah Stockbridge, Feb. 29, 1748, had no ch., d. Ap. 23, 1758, and his wid. m. Wm. Norton, bef. 1761. His house stood oppo. his father's. and is now occupied by B. F. Burgess. 5. Michael, Oct. 27, 1714 ? 7. Nath'l., Ap. 29, 1718. 8. Caleb, Dec. 14, 1719, m. Desire Stetson, Nov. 1, 1750, lived on what is now Main st., whence he moved to Townsend, Mass. His ch. were, *Desire*, 1752, d. 1754; *Caleb*, 1754, m. Abig., da. Dr. Jos. Jacobs, and moved to Me.; *Desire*, 1755; *Henchman*, 1758, a soldier in the Rev'n; *Lillis T.* and *Grace*, 1763; *Joseph*, 1764. 9. Edmund, June 20, 1721. 10. Mary, Oct. 19, 1723, d. Aug. 28, 1724. 11. Thos., Oct. 19, 1723, m. Sarah, da. Matt. Estes, who d. June 20, 1794, and he Oct. 1, 1760, leaving one son, *Matt.*, bap. Sep. 19, 1760, who m. a Josselyn, and d. in Pemb., leaving one da. Marg't., who m. Isaac Magoun, Pemb. The father's house stood where now stands that of Dr. Garratt. 12. Elizab., July 15, 1725.

5. Benj., s. Benj. 3, m. Abig. Buck, July 27, 1737, and d. Jan. 24, and his wid., July 29, 1796. Lived back of where Jno. Sylvester now resides, on a road long since discontinued. ch.: 1. Jerusha, Ap. 3, 1738, d. young. 2. Benj., Aug. 21, 1739, moved off. 3. Abig., bap. Ap. 8, 1742, m. 1, Abner House,

1758, and 2, an Alvord. 4. Sarah, bap. Dec. 18, 1743, m. Wm. Norton, Ab'n., 1759. 5. Jerusha, bap. Mar. 31, 1745, d. June 24, 1769. 6. Isaac, bap. Mar. 29, 1747. 7. Mary, bap. July 17, 1748, m. a Howland, Kgs'n. 8. Lydia, bap. Aug. 26, 1750, m. Jno. Oldham, Pemb. 9. Debo., bap. Dec. 31, 1752, m. Paul Webb, Scit., 1787. 10. Obadi., 1755, moved to Ohio, m., and it is said had 12 ch., who are in O. 11. Joel, bap. Aug. 14, 1757. 12. Cornelius, m. a Sprague, moved to N. Y'k. State, and had ch.

6. Amos Silvester Jun'r

s. Amos 4, m. Patience Palmer, February 7, 1732, and had, 1. Amos, 1734, m. Desire Rose, Jan. 19, 1757, and had *Amos*, 1758; *Thomas.*, 1760; *Jacob*, 1762, d. 1765; *John*, 1765; *Desire R.*, 1767; and *Hannah*, 1769. 2. Abner, Ap. 23, 1738, m. Susanna Stetson, Dec. 3, 1761, and prob. moved off. 3. Job, 1742, m. and had *Job*, m. Lydia Philips, 1790; *Roland*, of Durham, Me.; and *Joseph*, m. Ruth Estes, and is of Durham, Me.

7. William Silvester s. Amos 4, appears to have been a man of some note in his day, as we often find his name attached to deeds, and other instruments. By w. Mary, he had, 1. Wm., 1737. 2. Chas., 1739. 3. Mary, July 30, 1741. 4. Elijah, July 13, 1744. 5. Isaac June 27, 1746. 6. Hannah, Nov. 11, 1748. 7. Debo., 1751. After this date, the family disappears, and we find no further record of it.

8. Michel Sylvester s. Amos 4, m. 1, Mary, da. Captain Thos. Bardin, Nov. 12, 1741, who d. Oct. 29, 1755; and 2, Ruth Turner, Jan. 17, 1760; and d. Nov. 12, 1798, ae. 84, and his wid., Oct. 31, 1806, ae. 70. Lived on his father's place. ch.: 1. Bardin, d. Feb. 15, 1746. 2. Mary, bap. Mar. 12, 1745, d. Mar. 18, 1746. 3. Michal, bap. Nov. 9, 1755, m. Cornel. Turner, Dec. 8, 1768, and moved to Me. 4. Bardin, bap. Nov. 9,

1755. 5. Michael, bap. Nov. 9, 1755. 6. Mary, bap. Nov. 9, 1755, m. Chas. Tolman, May 19, 1774. (By 2d,) 7. Bathshua, bap. Feb. 13, 1761, d. June 4, 1768. 8. Robt., bap. Oct. 19, 1766, d. June 4, 1768. 9. Lucinda, bap. Ap. 10, 1768, m. Benj. Bass, Dec. 4, 1794. 10. Juliette, bap. Ap. 8, 1770, d. unm., Dec. 27, 1842. 11. Robert, bap. Aug. 9, 1772.

9. Nathaniel Sylvester s. Amos 4, known as "Builder Sylvester," a shipwright by trade, lived where Rufus Farnum now resides, m. 1, Sage, da. Capt. Thos. Bardin, Jan. 26, 1743, and 2d, Sarah Bates, who d. July 8, 1775, and he, Feb. 21, 1781. He was Selectman from 1765–67, and from 1772–74. ch.: 1. Nath'l., m. Sarah, da. Galen Clapp, was a shipbuilder; Selectman from 1794–96; and moved to Winchendon, Mass. His ch. were, *Polly*, *Lucy*, *Joanna*, *Patience*, *Ruth*, and *Bardin*. 2. Lydia, m. Thos. Barstow. 3. Sarah, m. a Hill, and d. Mar. 18, 1818? 4. Elijah, Nov. 24, 1767. 5. Sage, m. Prince Stetson.

10. Edmund, s. Amos 4, m. Elizab., da. Rev. Benj. Bass, Jan. 30, 1752, and d. Sep. 20, 1783, ae. 51, and his wid. Sep. 18, 1784, ae. 50. Lived for a time on Elm st., where Josh. Stetson resides, and afterwards in the house of his brother Henchman. ch.: 1. Edmund, 1753, d. June 16, 1757. 2. Elizab., 1755, d. March 10, 1840. 3. Olive, 1757, d. Dec. 16, 1782. 4. Molly G., 1758, d. June 12, 1784. 5. Bethiah, 1760, d. Jan. 12, 1792. 6. Edmund, 1763, d. unm. in Mar. 1829. 7. Belcher Silvester 1765, a cabinet-maker by trade, and d. unm. May 11, 1849. 8. Christopher., 1768, d. Nov. 13, 1789. 9. Lucy, 1771, d. Feb. 3, 1773. 10. Lucy, 1773, d. Oct. 9, 1786. No desc'ts. are left of this family, and the property passed into the hands of the desc'ts. of Michael.

11. Joel Silvester s. Benj. 5, m. Sarah Damon, who d. Sep. 10, 1820, and he in 1835. Lived in his father's house for a time, and finally built on Broadway, where

RESIDENCE OF MR. JOHN SYLVESTER.

his son Jno. now resides. A view of his house is here presented. ch.: 1. Benj., Aug. 19, 1789, a mariner; not m. 2. Joseph, Jan. 27, 1792, m. 1, Elizab. B. Silvester, and 2, Hannah M. Stetson; lives on Broadway, is a mf'r. of soap, and has *Joseph B.*, m. Lucy W., da. Wm. Church, Feb. 8, 1847, is an anchor-smith, and lives on Broadway. 3. Sarah, June 11, 1794, m. Turner Stetson, Mar. 3, 1822, and is in Mich'n. 4. Isaac, bap. Dec. 25, d. Dec. 30, 1797. 5. Jno., July 8, 1798, the present proprietor of Sylvester's Forge, and junior partner of the firm of Jno. Taggart and Co., Bos'n., importers and dealers in iron and steel; (see p. 140,) m. Lucy J. Bonney, in Nov. 1824, lives in the house built by his father, (see *view*,) and has *Sarah J.*, Sep. 27, 1830; *Benj. F.*, June 29, 1833; *Laura A.*, Mar. 16, 1835; *Jno. E.*, July 24, 1839; *Lucy A.*, Aug. 25, 1840; and *Amelia F.*, June 3, 1843.

12. Rob't., s. Michael 8, m. Lucy Bailey, Jan. 14, 1773, and built and occupied the house in wh. Wm. Dawes resides, until his father's decease, and then tore down the old family homestead, and built the house in wh. his son Rob't. now lives. He d. Aug. 17, 1807, and his wid. Oct. 7, 1840. ch.: 1. Lucy B., Sep. 1, 1797, m. Wm. Church, July 29, 1821. 2. Rebecca E., Nov. 27, 1799, m. Benj. C. Pratt, Dec. 5, 1819, and d. Dec. 1, 1847. 3. Michael, May 5, 1802. 4. Robert, Oct. 19, 1805. 5. Sarah E., Mar. 21, 1808, m. Sam'l. Church, Dec. 14, 1828, and d. Dec. 28, 1850.

13. Elijah, s. Nath'l. 9, m. 1, Elizab. Briggs, Oct. 13, 1791, who d. Jan. 23, 1792; and 2, Mary Robbins, Dec. 19, 1793; and d. Dec. 28, 1828, and his wid. June 26, 1829. He was a shipwright by trade, and owned a farm in H., which was conducted with neatness and skill. ch.: 1. Elijah, Nov. 22, 1794, m. Lucy Taylor, June 25, 1823, lived on Broadway, and d. in June, 1852, leaving ch.; *Mary T.*, Aug. 13, 1824, m. Lebbeus Stockbridge, jr., June 24, 1849; *Elijah W.*, Aug. 15, 1828, m. Christiana M. Bonney, Nov. 27, 1851; *Lucy P.*, Feb. 26, 1831, d. Oct. 14, 1833; *Elizab. B.*, Dec. 28, 1836; and *Geo. F.*, Oct. 24, 1839. 2. Elizab. B., May 2, 1798, m. Joseph Sylvester, Nov. 26, 1818, and d. July 16, 1840.

14. Michael, s. Rob't. 12, m. 1, Martha Reed, of Ab'n., Dec. 3, 1824, who d. Jan. 18, 1831; and 2, Sarah, da. Lem'l. Curtis, May 29, 1833, and lives on Wash'n. st., near his bro. Robert. A view of his residence is annexed. ch.: 1. Michael R., June 24, 1825, m. Emily S. Spear, of Bos'n., July 3, 1849, who d. Sep. 21, 1851, and an inf. with her. 2. Edmund Q., Ap. 29, 1827. Not m.,—the present owner of the David Stockbridge estate. (By 2d,) 3. Martha R., Dec. 20, 1839. 4. Lem'l. C., May 14, 1842. 5. Lydia, June 12, 1845.

RESIDENCE OF MICHAEL SYLVESTER.

15. Robert, s. Rob't. 12, m. Sarah, da. Loammi Burgess, of Harvard, Mass., Nov. 28, 1828, and lives on Wash'n. st., in the house built by his father, a view of which is annexed. ch.: 1. Loammi B., Mar. 18, 1832. 2. Susanna F., Ap. 5, 1834. 3. Belcher, May 26, 1837, d. July 21, 1838. 4. Elizab. B., July 5, 1839. 5. Sarah E., Sep. 1, 1843. 6. Juletta, Ap. 14, 1845. 7. Robert, June 20, 1847.

RESIDENCE OF MR. ROBERT SYLVESTER.

16. Jona., of Mf'd., a desc't. of Rich'd. of Scit., was m. and had, 1. Jona., m. 1, Rebecca Laphan, and 2, Ruth Jones, and had *Tabitha*; *Luther*, 1802; *Rebecca*, 1803, d. young. ?; *Rachel O.*, 1812. 2. Jas. 3. Deborah. 4. Molly. 5. Tabitha. 6. Eben'r., of Me. 7. Lydia, m. a Hall.

17. Jas., s. Jona. 16, m. Sarah Osborn, and was drowned in crossing N. River bar, with two others, Andrew Keen and Peter Rogers, in returning from a fishing voyage. The bodies were found, and int. in Mf'd. His wid. m. 2, Joseph D. Ramsdell, and 3, Thos. Perry, and d. Aug. 20, 1847, ae. 84. ch.: 1. Anthony, Oct. 27, 1787. 2. Joseph, Oct. 27, 1788, m. wid. Elizab. T. Pratt, Ap. 2, 1815, lives at the corner of East st., and has one son, Wm. T., Feb. 19, 1816, lives in So. Scit., m. Betsey Kendar, and has *Wm. K.* 3. Thos. O., m. Lucy Walker, of Mf'd., is a blacksmith by trade, lives in Quincy, and has *Roxana*, m. Hatch Carver, Mf'd.; *Debo.*, m. Geo. Hunt, baker, of H'm.; *Mary*; *Sarah*; and *Marcia*. 4. James, m. Betsey Young, and d. leaving ch.: *Jas.*, *Jno.*, *Francis*, and *Elizabeth*. 5. Wm., d. ae. 19.

18. Anthony, s. Jas. 17, m. Nancy Taylor, Jan. 1812, lived on Broadway, and d. in 1852, ae. 64. ch.: 1. Sarah, Feb. 1,

1813, m. Otis Sampson, Nov. 4, 1833. 2. Robert., Oct. 17, 1814, a shipwright by trade, m. 1, Hannah Sturgis, Sep. 11, 1836, and 2, Martha A. Coates, in 1852, lives in his father's house, and has *Geo. W.*, 1837, and *Helen M.*, 1839. 3. Almira J., Sep. 26, 1816, m. Jno. C. Damon, of Quincy, May 1, 1836. 4. Mary, July 1, 1818, m. Thos. O. Bates, jr., Dec. 11, 1836. 5. Horace, Sep. 16, 1820, m. Mary P. Holmes, Ap. 30, 1845, and is a mariner. 6. Jas., Dec. 27, 1822, in S. America. 7. Lydia A., Mar. 27, 1825, m. Austin Damon, July 11, 1841, who resides at the Corners, and is a blacksmith, with Mr. Warren Wright. 8. Nancy, June 18, 1827, m. Jno. Tower, Ap. 26, 1846. 9. Elizab. T., May 29, 1830, m. Thos. T. Lathrop, Jan. 31, 1847, and lives in Va. 10. Helen M., July 29, 1836, d. Feb. 9, 1837.

TAYLOR, Edwin P., s. Wm., of Pemb., b. June, 1826, a young man of fine promise, resides in H., and works at Mr. S. Josselyn's shoe mf'y. Not m.

THAYER, Eben'r., s. Barnabas, of Wey'h., and a desc't. of Richard, of Bos'n., 1640, and aft. of Braintree, m. Mary J., da. Shuble Munroe, Ap. 3, 1819, and lives on Centre st., near the site of the old Robert Stetson house. A shoemaker. ch.: 1. Martin C., Dec. 25, 1823. 2. Cha's. E., July 25, 1826, m. Mary D., da. Silas Hollis, Aug. 13, 1848, lives oppo. his fa., in the house built for him in 1851–2, and has *Cha's. W.*, Feb. 9, 1849; and *Mary A.*, Mar. 5, 1851.

THOMAS, Charles, of Georgetown, Mass., m. 1, Martha McFadden, and 2, Sarah B. Damon, lived on Main st., and d. Nov. 7, 1847, ae. 56. ch.: 1. Jas., is m., and lives in Me 2. Jno., d. at sea. 3. Mary, m. Isaac Packard. 4. Nancy, m. Sidney Everson, Kgs'n. He is d. 5. Cha's., Nov. 1821, m Mary Vining, lives on Main st., and has *Alonzo*, Nov. 1850. 6. David, m. Maria F. Eames, Mf'd., lives in E. Ab'n., and has *Izora F.*, 1850. (By 2d,) 7. Joseph. 8. Levi. 9. Martha. 10. Alpheus. 11. Ira, May, 1839. 12. Sarah, Mar. 16, 1842.

THOMPSON, Wm. E., s. Andrew, (and a desc't. of Jno., of Wales, who landed at Ply'h., 1622,) m. Eliza N. Gardner, Ap. 1841, lives on Whiting st., and has, 1. Mary E., Mar. 4, 1842. 2. Wm. F., Jan. 18, 1846. 3. Rufus D., Dec. 19, 1848. 4. Jas. F., Oct. 15, 1851.

2. Lyman, s. Francis, of Nelson, N. H., b. May 2, 1817, m. Barshaway, da. Luther Curtis, Jan. 1, 1853, and lives on Silver st., near his wife's mother.

3. Francis, bro. Lyman, b. June 28, 1823, m. Dorlisca Vinica, of Midd'o., Jan. 1, 1843, lives in the house built by his bro., on Silver street, and has, 1. Dorlisca A. 2. Elizab. R. 3. Francis G. 4. Eliza V.

1. Job Tilden Lieut. Job, a desc't. of Elder Nathl., of Scituate, m. Elizab. Vinal, and lived on Winter st., where, for many years, he kept a tavern. His bro. Jno., had previously occupied the same house, —part of which is still standing,—but on the marriage of Job, who had been fitted for Coll., and who m. against the wishes of his parents, at the early age of 17, he was sent to H., and Jno. returned to Scit. Job was a Lieut. in the Rev'n., and was a man of active habits, and good education. He d. Jan. 22, 1809, ae. 83, and his w. Mar. 2, 1799. ch.: 1. Sarah, 1746, d. 1751. 2. Betty, 1748, m. Dan'l. Barstow, July 4, 1771. 3. Nath'l., 1750, d. 1821. 4. Sarah, 1753, d. 1808. 5. Job, 1757.

2. Job, s. Job, m. Lydia Jackson, Scit., lived in his father's house, and there d. Sep. 27, 1820, and his wid., Aug. 23, 1848, ae. 88. He was out in the Rev'n., and his wid. drew a pension in her latter years. ch.: 1. Betty, 1786, m. John Gardner, Bridg'r., July 27, 1806. 2. Job, 1789, d. 1806. 3. Lydia, m. Enos Bates, and d. in 1852. 4. Polly, July 3, 1791, m. Jno. Tribou, Oct. 13, 1810. 5. Debo., Sep. 29, 1793, m. Elias Barrell, Bridg'r., Nov. 21, 1813, and has a da. *Debo.* living in H. 6. Sally, July 9, 1797, living unm. on her father's place. There was another son, Joseph, drowned at the age of 25.

TORREY, a name once common in H., but now extinct in the male line. The families sett. mostly on Winter st. Benj. D., s. Caleb, of Midd'o., b. November 16, 1796, m. Lovisa, da., Adam Perry, Mar. 30, 1818, was a watchmaker by trade, and lived on Circuit st., in the house built by himself, where he d. July 18, 1843, ae. 47. His wid. survives. ch.: 1. Lovisa P., May 25, 1818, m. Martin White, Mf'd. 2. Janet, Ap. 10, 1823, m. Wm. F. Tribou, of H. 3. Eliza M., April 16, 1825, m. Cyrus A. Willis. 4. Martin S., May 26, 1827, m. Caroline F. Soule, May 8, 1846, had *Caro. S.*, Mar. 22, 1847, and d. Mar. 24, 1848, and his wid. m. Spencer Binney. 5. Charlotte B., Oct. 3, 1827, m. W. G. Perry. 6. Marietta, Aug. 4, 1831, m. Warren Estes, 1852. 7. Sarah J., Dec. 14, 1833, m. Sylvanus Whiting, jr., 1852. 8. Wm. D., 1835. 9. Leander, Mar. 31, 1838.

TOWER, David, b. July 1786, s. Jas., (and a desc't. of Jno., of H'm., who m. Marg't. Ibrook, 1639,) m. Patience Palmer, Aug. 1811, lives on Spring st., is a shoemaker, and has, 1. Patience, 1812, d. 1817. 2. Jane, 1813, m. Jno. S. Tower, and d. Aug. 22, 1849. 3. Jno., July 1817, d. young. 4. David, Ap. 3, 1818. 5. Patience, June 29, 1821, m. Henry S. Hollis, Wey'h. 6. Jno., July 14, 1824, m. Nancy Sylvester, lives on Broadway, and has *Horace S.*, May 11, 1847; and *Jno. F.*, Nov. 15, 1849. Lost 2 ch., d. young. 7. Reuben, Ap. 17, 1828, of H'n. 8. Mahala, June 29, 1831, m. Francis Cobbin, Nov. 23, 1851, and lives in H.

John Tribou b. Feb. 26, 1788, s. Wm., and gr. s. Thos., of France, who sett. in Bridg'r., in 1745, m. Mary, da. Job Tilden, and lived at the corner of Centre street, and Broadway, where he d. Oct. 17, 1848. His wid. survives. ch.: 1. Mary A., Nov. 16, 1811, m. Sam'l. S. Turner, Oct. 28, 1832. 2. Jno. T., Feb. 3, 1814, m. Melissa B., da. Capt. Thos. M. Bates, Oct. 16, 1835, lives at the corner of Winter and Circuit sts., is a shoemaker, and has, *Andrew T.*, Sep. 27, 1837; *Mary J.*, Mar. 23, 1839; *Ann A.*, Oct. 24, 1844; and *Maria E.*, May 12.

1847. 3. Levi W., Mar. 22, 1816, m. Lucinda White, Dec. 1840, lives with his mo., and has *Corrissand W.*, Oct. 1841. 4. Wm. F., July 27, 1819, m. Jennet Torrey, Feb. 2, 1840, lives on Summer st., is a shoemaker, and has *Ellen M.*, Oct. 1842; *Wm. E.*, Nov. 16, 1846; *Walter S.*, July 29, 1848, d. Ap. 4, 1850; *Mary H.*, May 19, 1850, d. May 31, 1851; and *Laura J.*, Mar. 30, 1852. 5. Walter S., Jan. 8, 1822, went to sea, and is prob. d. 6. Emeline H., May 2, 1824, m. Seth Pratt, H'n. 7. Sarah J., June 7, 1827, m. Rufus T. Estes, of E. Ab'n., and d. Dec. 28, 1850. 8. Cynthia J., Sep. 21, 1829, m. Seth W. Harding, and lives in H.

TUBBS, Joseph, b. Ap. 14, 1770, s. Joseph, of Pemb., (and a desc't. of Wm., of Duxbury, 1637,) m. Lucy Stetson, Oct. 13, 1797, and lives on Winter st., in the old Torrey house. ch.: 1. Eunice W., Feb. 8, 1798. 2. Mary B., October. 22, 1800. 3. Harriet, Oct. 21, 1802, m. Cornelius White. 4. Lucy, Dec. 24, 1804, m. Seth Randall, Dux'y. 5. Temperance, Feb. 20, 1807, m. Paul Bates. 6. Joseph, May 9, 1809, living unm., with his fa. 7. Betsey C., July 1, 1811, m. Prescott Lathrop, E. Wey'h., and is d.

TURNER, an ancient family, of Norman French origin, which appears in Eng'd. as early as 1067, the date of the Norman Conquest, when "Le sire de Tourneur," accompanied King Wm. in his expedition. (N. E. Gen. Reg., vol. 2, p. 33.) There are various coats of arms, belonging to different branches, in most of which, the *mill-rind*, so called, is a distinguishing feature. Burke gives the names of 35 families, to whom coats of arms have been granted, and these have produced many eminent men, distinguished in historical, and literary annals. Several families appear early in N. Eng'd., among whom are, Humphrey, of Scit., the "tanner," who arrived with his family in Plym'h., in 1628, had a house lot assigned him in 1629; and erected a house, in which he prob. lived in 1633. (Deane.) He is the ancestor of most of the Turners in Plym'h. Co., though there have been some in H. descended from Thos., of H'm., 1637, whose son Thos. was in

Scit., 1680. As several sketches of the Turner family have already been published to the world, and the number who have sett. in H. is comparatively small, we do not deem it necessary to enter at large into its history here, and shall confine ourselves, therefore, principally to those that have sett. in H. We need only say, by way of introduction, that Humphrey, of Scit., had Jno., who was fa. of Amos, and Jona.; and Amos was fa. of Ezekiel, of H., and Jona. was fa. of Isaac, and he, of Wait and Jona., of H. Daniel, another son of Humphrey, had Amasa, and Abner; and Amasa was fa. of Amasa and Eliab, of H., and Abner was fa. of Abner, of H. Thos., of H'm., had Thos., of Scit., and he was fa. of Caleb, and he, of Caleb and Marlboro, of H. The descendants of these families are given in the following sketch:

2. Ezek'l., s. Amos, and gr. gr. s. I. Humphrey, m. 1, Bathsheba Stockbridge, who d. July 14, 1731; and 2, Ruth Randall, June 17, 1736; and d. Aug. 10, 1773, and his wid. May 25. 1805, ae. 86. He was Selectman from 1742–55, from 1762–67, and for 1772; and Rep. in 1761, and '67. ch.: 1. Mary, June 4, 1729, m. Wm. Torrey. 2. Debo., June 24, 1731, m. Freedom Chamberlain. 3. Ruth, Ap. 12, 1737, m. Michael Sylvester, Jan. 17, 1760. 4. Bathsheba, Ap. 9, 1739, m. Jno. Hatch, 1760. 5. Ezekiel, July 18, d. Oct. 18, 1740. 6. Amos, July 16, 1741. 7. Elizab., Mar. 30, 1743, m. Thos. Collamore, Scit., Jan. 23, 1766. 8. Abig., Ap. 9, 1744, m. Stephen Bailey.

3. Wait, or Waitstill, s. Isaac, and gr. gr. gr. s. Humphrey, lived near where the wid. of Thos. M. Jacobs resides, in Snappet, and m. Mary Staples, who d. July 15, 1768, and he Oct. 25, 1815, ae. 93. ch.; 1. Elisha, Mar. 15, 1762, prob. d. young. 2. Mary, bap. Oct. 6, 1764. 3. Hannah, July 23, 1765, d. young. 4. Hannah, bap. Dec. 14, 1766.

4. Jona., s. Isaac, and gr. gr. gr. s. Humphrey, m. Abig. Stockbridge, and, it is said, lived on Curtis, now Main st., where his w. d. May 13, 1756. We find no dates of birth of his ch. on the Recs. of H., but their names, as given in the Turner Genealogy, were, 1. Asa, Feb. 20, 1743, m. Abig. Mann, June 30. 1771, and moved to Me., where he d. Aug. 25, 1821, ae. 78. and his wid. Ap. 16, 1853, ae. 72. He has many desct's. in

Me., residing principally in Orland, and Norridgewock. 2. Reuben, a shipmaster, was m., but had no ch., and, it is said, was lost at sea. 3. Lydia. 4. Calvin, moved to Me., m., and d. there. 5. Isaac. 6. Susanna, m. a McGraw, and lived in Durham, Me. 7. Persis, m. a McGraw, his 2d w. 8. Ruth, m. Abel Curtis. 9. Luther, 1760. 10. Seth. 11. Philip.

5. Amasa, s. Amasa, and gr. gr.s. Humphrey, m. Elizab. ——, and was recom. to the Ch. in Lancaster, in 1748, whither he moved, with his family. ch.: 1. Elizab., June 4, 1729. 2. Hannah, Ap. 28, 1731. 3. Ichabod, Mar. 3, 1732–3. 4. Zilpha, Dec. 30, 1734. 5. Nathl., Jan. 31, 1736–7. 6. Lemuel, July 10, 1738. 7. Ezra, July 22, 1740. 8. Joseph, bap. July 31, 1743. 9. Lurana, bap. Sep. 6, 1747. 10. Amasa, bap. Sep. 6, 1749.

6. Eliab, s. Amasa, and gr. gr. s. Humphrey, m. Martha Barstow, May 12, 1731, and had, 1. David, Oct. 9, 1732. 2. A son, Feb. 3, 1735. 3. A ch., Jan. 12, 1738. 4. A ch., Mar. 4, 1740.

7. Abner, s. Abner, and gr. gr. s. Humphrey, m. Mary Munroe, Oct. 13, 1740, and had, 1. Naomi, Aug. 3, d. Aug. 22, 1741. 2. Abner, Oct. 14, 1742. 3. Mary, Mar. 1, 1744, m. Elij. Cushing, Pemb., Jan. 18, 1768.

8. Caleb, s. Caleb, and gr. gr. s. Thomas, of H'm., m. Ruth Barker, was a shipwright by trade, and d. Ap. 12, 1767, and his wid. Nov. 8, 1768. ch.: 1. Lucinda, Sep. 27, 1740. 2. Cornelius, May 5, 1742, m. 1, Michal Sylvester, Dec. 8, 1768; and 2d, a Soule. 3. Briggs, Feb. 9, 1744, m. Mary Gardner, of Gardiner, Me. 4. Caleb, Aug. 8, 1746, m. Peggy McCowan? of Me. 5. Ruth, Oct. 10, 1748, m. Atherton Wales, Ap. 5, 1768. 6. Alexander, Aug. 1, 1750, m. Sarah Soule, Waldoboro', Me. 7. Barker, Oct. 21, 1752, d. unm. 8. Robert, Feb. 1, 1756, m. a Rhodes, of Bristol, Me.

9. Capt. Marlboro, s. Caleb, and gr. gr. s. Thos., of H'm., m. 1, Mary Curtis, Nov. 26, 1753, who d. Oct. 3, 1776; and 2d, Abig. Curtis, Jan. 1, 1777; and was a Capt. in the Rev'n., and a valuable man in his day. ch.: 1. Marlboro, bap. July 30, 1757, m. Debo. Stockbridge, Jan. 7, 1790. 2. Nabby, bap.

July 30, 1757, m. Joseph Bicknell, jr., Ab'n., Nov. 8, 1775, and moved to Lunenburg. 3. Melzar, bap. Ap. 17, 1762, d. Ap. 20, 1763. 4. Joseph, bap. Sep. 1, 1765, moved to Lun'bg. 5. Lydia S., bap. Sep. 1, 1765. 6. Molly, Oct. 30, 1768, m. John Jones, Lun'bg., Feb. 9, 1792.

10. Col. Amos, s. Ezek'l. 2, m. 1, Betsey Perry, Feb. 14, 1771, who d. Dec. 30, 1815; and 2, Mary R. Stetson, Oct. 27, 1816, and d. Mar. 14, 1822, ae. 81. He was Selectman in 1775, and was an officer in the Rev'n. ch.: 1. Betsey, 1772, m. Dan'l. Keen, Pemb. 2. Ruth, 1774, d. 1775. 3. Ezek'l., 1776, m. Lydia Stetson, Feb. 28, 1799, who d. July 15, 1819, and had *Harriet*, 1800, m. Jno. Mann; *Wm.*, 1801, d. 1824, leaving one ch.; *Ezk'l.*, 1804, (m. 1, Priscilla Josselyn, 2, Nancy Turner? and 3, wid. Mary Bowen, and has Sarah R., 1821, Priscilla J., 1823, Cath. P., 1825, Ezek'l. T., 1833, Maria J., 1839, a ch. b. 1841, Chas. H., 1844, and Jno. A., 1848;) *Lydia S.*, 1807; and *Saml. S.*, (a housewright in H., m. Mary A. Tribou, Oct. 28, 1832, lives on Centre st., and has Saml. N., Aug. 16, 1834; Geo. G., Oct. 9, 1837, d. Oct. 8, 1838; Chas. E., May 23, 1839; Julia A., Oct. 25, 1842; Jane G., Sep. 22, 1844; and Walter, Ap. 27, 1847.) 4. Amos, m. Mary Reed, and had *Mary R.*, 1803; *Alice*, 1805; *Clarissa*, 1808; and *David R.*, 1811. 5. Ruth, 1784, m. Saml. House, and is d. 6. Seth, 1786, m. Priscilla Beal, and had *Seth*, 1811, of Bridg'r. m. Debo. House; *Nathan*, 1814; *Priscilla P.*, 1817, d. 1818. *Priscilla; Noah.* 7. Wm., bap. and d. 1787.

11. Isaac, s. Jona. 4, m. 1, Mary, da. Wm. Whiting, Dec. 10, 1778, who d. ab. 1795; 2, Rebecca, da. Wm. Curtis, Aug. 28, 1795; and 3, Esther Spaulding, of Townsend, and, it is said, d. in Vt., being killed by falling from a load of hay, and striking on a stake, which pierced his body. ch.: 1. Isaac, m. Abig. Whiting? 2. Priscilla, 1786, d. 1792. 3. Mary, Oct. 1794, m. Isaac Withington, Dorch'r., Dec. 15, 1799. 4. Avis, 17[illegible]2. 5. Betsey, 1784, m. Peter Hobart, Bos'n. 6. Sylvia, 1790, d. 1801. 7. Wm., m. Sally Gowen, and is d. 8. Saml., d.

12 Luther Turner s. Jona. 4, m. Grace, da. Wm. Whiting, was a baker by trade, and spent most of his life in mechanical employments; lived in H., and in Scit.; and d. in H., Oct. 14, 1839, ae. 80, and his wid. June 8, 1842. ch.: 1. Grace, Mar. 24, 1784, m. Joseph Foster, July, 1808. 2. Jane, 1791, m. David Hazen, of Vt., and is d. 3. Avis, 1793, m. Wm. Lapham, of Scit., and has one son, Wm. T., of Scit. 4. Luther, 1800, m. wid. Lucinda Whitney, and has *Geo.*, of Ab'n., m. Rachel Bennett, and has ch.: *Mary F.*, of Ab'n.; and *Luther*, of A., m. a Stoddard, and has ch. 5. Geo. W., Ap. 10, 1805, m. Avis, da. Wm. Whiting, Oct. 22, 1829, lives on Whiting st., and has *Avis H.*, Aug. 8, 1830, m. Phineas P. Peterson, July 4, 1848; and *Mary E.*, b. Mar. 8, d. Oct. 31, 1832.

VINAL, Joseph, s. Seth, of Scit., m. Sophia Darling, in April, 1848, lives on Pleasant st., and has Florence E., April 23, 1851. Mr. V. is a descendant of the widow Anna Vinal, who, with her sons, Stephen and John, and her daughter Martha, were in Scit. in 1636, and from whom, probably, most of the name of Vinal in New England are descended.

VINING, David, b. Dec. 27, 1797, s. Ebed, of Ab'n., and a desc't. of the Vinings, who were early of Wey'h., m. 1, Mary Curtis, Nov. 8, 1821, who d. Feb. 18, 1826, ae. 30; and 2, Martha Briggs, May 4, 1828; lives on Main st.; is a shoemaker; and has, 1. Mary S., July 29, 1822, m. Chas. Thomas. 2. David, Ap. 7, 1824, m. Cynthia Cobb, and lives in Midd'o. 3. Martha A., Feb. 23, 1829. 4. Israel L., Oct. 8, 1830, m. Nancy L. Matthews, Nov. 12, 1851. 5. Hannah B., Sep. 5, 1835. 6. Chas. C., Dec. 7, 1838. 7. Asaph D., Aug. 1, 1842.

2. Joseph, s. Ebed., of Ab'n., m. Hannah, da. Caleb Gardner, 1816, lives at the corner of North and Whiting sts., is a shoemaker, and has, 1. Hannah, Oct., 1817, m. Paul W. Hannam, E. Ab'n. 2. Abig., Nov. 1819, m. Caleb K. Gilman. 3. Julia A., Aug. 24, 1821, m. Joseph Dill, E. Ab'n. 4. Lucinda, Jan. 22,

1823, m. Isa. Gardner, of S. H'm. 5. Marietta, July 29, 1826, m. Harvey C. Burrill, E. Ab'n. 6. Joseph, Mar. 24, 1828. 7. Levi L., Nov. 17, 1832. 8. Wm. H., May 24, 1840.

3. Judson, s. Ebed, of Ab'n., b. Mar. 15, 1804, m. Sarah W. Briggs, Ap. 26, 1826, lives on Main st., is a shoemaker, and has, 1. Wm. J., Ap. 2, 1826, m. Mercy T., da. Capt. Thos. M. Bates, Mar. 15, 1849, lives on King street, and has *Georgiana*, July 15, 1850. 2. Sally B., Oct. 5, 1831. 3. Thos. J., June 10, 1828. 4. Lydia S., Oct. 22, 1834.

WADE, Isaac, s. Isaac, and w. Lucy (Harding, m. May 23, 1776,) lives in H., on Main st., is a farmer, m. Debo. Curtis, and has, 1. Lucy, Dec. 3, 1798, m. David Damon, Aug. 8, 1821, and lives in So. Scit. 2. Debo., Aug. 17, 1800, m. Jno. Damon, and d. July 3, 1849. 3. Louisa, Dec. 29, 1802, m. Andrew Gardner, H'm. 4. Maria, June 30, 1804, m. Thos. Wade, Bridg'r., 5. Sarah, Sep. 15, 1807, d. Ap. 15, 1827. 6. Matilda H., July 8, 1810, m. 1, Joseph Cushing, Ap. 10, 1835; and 2, Jno. C. Perkins. 7. Isaac, Ap. 15, 1813, m. Harriet Newell, Bos'n., had 1 ch., who d., and he has not been heard from for sev. years. 8. Mary, Oct. 4, 1816, m. Lewis Orcutt, Ab'n. 9. Dorcas, Jan. 31, 1820, m. Minot Wales, Ab'n., and d. ab. 1844. 10. Henry W., m. Maria Wilbur, lives in N. Bridg'r., and has 3 ch. 11. Sarah, June, 1830.

WARDROBE, Dan'l., b. in Ports'h., N. H., 1789, m. Orpha Morse, lived in H., on Main st., and had, 1. Dan'l., in Canada. 2. Walter W., Ap. 1822, m. Sarah J. Curtis, Mar. 12, 1848, lives on Main st., and has *Ella*, Jan. 9, 1849; and another ch., b. June 11. 1851. 3. Erastus H., m. Lydia Curtis, is now in Cal'a., and has *Herbert. E.*, June 25, 1849. 4. Reuben L., in Cal'a. 5. Sam'l. 6. Julia.

WHITE, Wm., with his w., and 5 ch., came to N. Eng. in the Mayflower, in 1620. Their s. Peregrine, was b. before the landing. The fa. d. the spring after, and his wid. Susannah, m. Edward Winslow, May 12, 1622, it being the first marriage solemnized in N. Eng. Peregrine, the son, lived in Mf'd., and there d., July 20, 1704, ae. 83. He m. Sarah, da. Wm. Bassett, of Dux'y., and she d. in 1711. ch.: 1. Dan'l. 2. Sylvanus. 3. Jonathan. 4. Peregrine. 5. Sarah. 6. Mercy, m. Wm. Sherman? Feb. 3, 1697. (Mf'd. Recs.)

2. Dan'l., s. Peregrine, m. Hannah Hunt, of Dux'y., Aug. 19, 1674. (Mf'd. Recs.) and had ch., 1. Jno., 1675, m. Susannah Sherman? Feb. 18, 1700. (Mf'd. Recs.) 2. Joseph, 1678. 3. Thos., 1680. 4. Cornelius, 1682. 5. Benj., 1684, m. Faith Oakman? Dec. 2, 1714. (Mf'd. Recs.) 6. Eleazer, 1686. 7. Eben'r., 1691, m. 1, Mary Doggett? Sep. 29, 1712, and 2, Hannah Doggett, ? Mar. 9, 1712–13. (Mf'd. Recs.)

3. Cornelius White s. Dan'l. 2, m. Hannah Randall, May 22, 1706, and in 1743, bought the Hatch place, on what is now Centre st., formerly part of the "Hanmer Hook," so called, which is still improved by his desc'ts. being occupied by Albert White, Esq. His ch. were, 1. Lemuel. 2. Cornelius, prob. m. Sarah Hewett, Bridg'r., 1747. 3. Paul, m. Elizab. Curtis, Feb. 24, 1737, and had in H., a son, b. Oct., 1737. This is all the notice of him on the H. Recs. 4. Joanna. 5. Dan'l. 6. Gideon. 7. Benj., 1721.

4. Benj., s. Cornelius 3, m. Hannah Decrow, and d. in H., Feb. 10, 1786, ae. 65, and his wid. Mar. 22, 1814, ae. 94. Lived on his father's place, on Centre st. ch.: 1. Penniah, Mar. 24, 1744, d. Aug. 9, 1763. 2. Robert, May 3, 1747. 3. Hannah, bap. Sep. 7, 1754., m. Dan'l. Crooker, Pemb., Dec. 19, 1776. 4. Benj., bap. Sep. 7, 1754. 5. Cornelius, July 9, 1755.

5. Robert, s. Benj. 4, m. 1, Mary Crooker, Ap. 25, 1771, who d. July, 1773; and 2, Anna House, Mar. 20, 1777, and d. at Thompson, Ct., ae. 88. ch.: 1. Penniah, bap. Aug. 8, 1773, d. Nov. 9, 1774. 2. David, bap. Sep. 9, d. Sep. 10, 1779. 3. Martin, of Ct. 4. Richmond, of Ct. 5. Charles, d. 6. Elijah., d.

6. Benj., s. Benj. 4, m. Mary Chamberlain, E. Bridg'r., 1780, and d. in H., July 12, 1839, ae. 88, and his wid. Mar. 27, 1841, ae. 86. ch.: 1. Lewis, Aug. 7, 1785, d. Ap. 3, 1813, being accidentally shot. 2. Cyrus, bap. Aug. 7, 1785. 3. Mary, bap.

Oct. 15, 1786, m. Reuben Peterson, jr., Dux'y., Ap. 26, 1812, and lives in Ply'h. 4. Sylvia, bap. Sep. 26, 1790, m. Ezek'l. Stetson, May 4, 1806, and moved to Me. 5. Benj., 1791, d. May 8 1793. 5. Benj., Nov. 27, 1795, m. Mary Hall, lives in Mr'd., and has *Geo.*, 1832; *Mary H.*, 1833, *Lewis E.*, 1835, *Benj. F.*, 1837, and *Harriet S.*, 1841.

7. Cornelius, s. Benj. 4, m. 1, Sarah L. Hill, of Pemb., May 21, 1787; and 2, Rebecca Bates, of H., Dec. 30, 1801, and d. Mar. 30, 1841, ae. 86, and his wid. Ap. 1, 1843, ae. 78. ch. 1. Cornelius, Jan. 26, 1788. (By 2d,) 2. Albert, Esq., Ap. 24, 1802, J. P.; T. C. from 1832–'39, and in 1840 and '42; Selectman 1842–48, '50–53; also a school teacher, and a useful and enterprising citizen; m. Lydia Bates, May 1, 1836, and lives on Centre st.; no ch.

8. Cyrus, s. Benj. 6, m. Ruth S. Keen, Pemb., Aug. 10, 1806, and went to Ohio, ab. 1817, since wh. time he has not been heard from. ch.: 1. Sylvia, m. Leonard Green, Sharon. 2. Lydia, d. ab. 1827, ae. 16. 3. Mary, Aug. 24, 1810, m. Algernon Josselyn, and lives in Lowell. 4. Cyrus, Nov. 2, 1811, m. Betsey H. Bonney, H'n., lives in S. Ab'n., and has *Levi; Wm.* d., ae. 1; *Cynthia A.*, d., ae. 1; and *Wm. Lloyd* and *Wendell Phillips*, b. Mar. 28, 1847. 5. Lewis, of Bridg'r., m. 1, Catherine Gardner, of Dux'y., who d. July 1847; and 2, wid. Anne Bell; and has *Laura A.; Catherine L.; Lucy T.; Algernon;* and *Sylvia G.* 6. Debo., d. Ap. 6, 1817, ae. 3. 7. Benj., Dec., 1816, m. Dolly Josselyn, lives in H'n., is a shoemaker, and has *Lousia*, d.; and *Ellen P.*

WHITWELL, Dr. Benj., s. Benj., Esq., of Bos'n., (a Lawyer, who grad. H. C., 1790, and m. Lucy Scollay,) was b. June 4, 1817, ent. at H. C., and grad. in the med. dep't., in 1848; stud. at the Tremont Med. School, under Drs. Bigelow, Storer, Jackson, &c.; and sett. first in Holyoke, Mass.; and in H., in 1850–1, under the auspices of Dr. J. B. Fobes. Lives at the Four Corners, and is unm.

WHITON, OR WHITING FAMILY.

Arms: Gyronny of four, az. and erm.; over all a Leopard's head, or; in chief 3 bezants.

Crest: A Lion rampant; beneath, a helmet, resting upon the shield.

WHITON, or WHITING, James, the ancestor of the families here recorded, appears in H'm., Mass., in 1647, Dec. 30th of which year, he m. Mary Beals. In his will, his name is spelled *Whiton*, and by a large number of families in H'm., it is still spelled in this way, though by others, it is spelled *Whiting*. The coat of arms handed down in the family, a copy of which is given above, agrees with that of the Whitings, as described by Burke, in his General Armory.

In 1657, land was granted to Jas. Whiton, and to Onesiphorus Marsh, in H'm.; and he owned large tracts in Scit., Ab'n., and Hanover. In Ap., 1676, his house, and "Jno. Jones's, Anthony Sprague's, Israel Hobart's, and Nathl. Chubbuck's," were burned by the Indians. His w. d. Feb. 12, 1696--7, and he Ap. 26, 1710, leaving a will, dated Sep. 29, 1708, in which he gives to his eldest s. Jas., land bo't. of Jos. Church; land bo't. of Wm. Ripley; land at Scit., bo't. of Rich'd. Dwelley, and "butting on the pattent line;" part of a lot bo't. of Humph'y. Johnson, at Great Plain; 3 shares of the com. land in H'm.; and one fourth of a lot in the "small shares," being in Ab'n. To s. Matt., he gives 5 shares in the eighth lot, 2nd div'n. of upland in Cohas't.; 12 acs. at Great Plain; a lot in the 4th div'n. of lands in H'm., and the meadow adjoining; the 2d part of his 3d division of Cohas't., upland; and one fourth of the "small share" lot. To Enoch, he gives one half of a lot of fresh meadow, bo't. of Rich'd. Dwelley, and Humph'y. Johnson, lying E. of the river, at Mast Bridge, H'm.; part of a lot in the 4th div'n. in H'm., bo't. of Jere. Beal; one fourth of the "small share" lot; two and a half shares of the com. land in H'm.; the front part of his 3d div'n. in Cohas't.; and the lands now in his possession, adjoining his dwelling house in H'm., &c. To the ch. of his s. Thos., decs'd., he gives his dwelling-house, barn, outhouses, and land on which they stand, with the orchard, of 25 acs., and all other lands and meadows that the said Thos. possessed while living; also one half the meadow at Mast Bridge; one fourth of the small shares; and two and a half shares of the com. land in H'm.; and the names of these ch. are given as Thos., Jona., Eleazer, Joanna, Jael, Leah, and Rachael. To his da. Mary Jordan, wid., he gives £36, to be paid out of what was left his 3 sons, and the ch. of Thos. The ch. of Jas., sen'r., were, 1. Jas., Ap. 10, 1649, d. Nov. 11, 1650. 2. Jas., bap. July 15, 1651. 3. Matt., Oct. 30, 1653. 4. Jno., bap. Dec. 2, 1655, d. young. 5. David, and 6. Jona, b. and d. 1657–8. 7. Enoch, Mar. 8, 1659. 8. Thos., May 18, 1662. 9. Mary, Ap. 29, 1664, m. 1, Isaac Wilder, Jan. 3, 1689, who d. Sep. 6, 1690, and 2, a Jordan.

2. Jas., s. Jas., lived in H'm., near his fa., and owned land on "Great Plain," and in Scit., and Ab'n. He d. Feb. 20, 1724–5, and his wid. Abig., May 4, 1740. In his will, which bears date Oct. 15, 1724, he gives, to w. Abig., his part of dwelling-house, and all his lands, and movable estate, and liberty to cart wood from his Scit. lot.; to son Benj., 10 acs. adjoining his house, &c.; to Jas. and Jno., of Plympton, Joseph, of Rehoboth, Saml. and Solo., of H'm., and das. Hannah King, of Plymouth, Judith White, and Rebecca Whiton, his Cedar lot in Ab'n., and that part of his Scit. lot not before given to Benj., to be equally divided between them. Appoints w. Abig., and friend

Jona. Farrow, Exec's. ch.: 1. Hannah, July 4, 1678, m. Jno. King, Plym'h., Jan. 13, 1704. 2. Jas., Feb. 17, 1679, m. Mary, da. Matt. Whiting, Dec. 26, 1704, had *Barsheba*, 1705, *Elisha*, 1706, and *Job*, 1708, and was of Plymp'n. bef. 1724. 3. Jno., Ap. 1, 1681, of Plymp'n. 4. Abig., Sep. 1, 1683, d. Dec. 10, 1695. 5. Saml., Nov. 12, 1685. 6. Joseph, Mar. 23, 1686–7, m. Martha Tower, Dec. 10, 1713, had *Elijah?* 1714, *Abig.*, 1716, and *Martha*, 1718, and sett. in Rehoboth before 1724. 7. Judith, May, 1689, m. Jas. White, Dec. 13, 1722. 8. Rebecca, Dec. 1691. 9. Benj., May 21, 1693. 10. Solo., June 10, 1695.

3. Matt., s. Jas., m. wid. Debo. Howard, Dec. 27, 1677, lived in H'm., and there d. intestate, July 22, 1725, and his wid. Sep. 19, 1729. Like the rest of his bros., he was a large landholder, and was early engaged in the business of *coopering*, or manufacturing the wooden buckets for which H'm. has been so long noted. ch.: 1. Mary, Sep. 25, 1678, m. Jas. Whiting, Dec. 26, 1704. 2. Jno., Jan. 10, 1680, m. Mary, da. Ibrook Tower, Feb. 3, 1704, and had *Jno.*, 1705, d. 1725; *Debo.*, Mar. 3, 1706, m. Solo. Bates, Scituate, May 1, 1730; *Margaret.*, Feb. 3, 1708, m. John Collamore, Scituate, April 27, 1732; *Josh.*, Ap. 15. 1710, sett. in Scit., was m., (w. Silence ——,) and had ch.; *Ann*, June 18, 1711, prob. d. unm., Sep. 13, 1799, ae. 88; and *Lydia*, May 26, 1714, d. Oct. 19, 1734. 3. David, June 5, 1681. 4. Matt., Nov. 28, 1682, prob. sett. in Pemb. 5. Elizab., Mar. 1684, m. Hezek. Tower, Jan. 13, 1704. 6. Susanna, Nov. 14, 1686, d. Aug. 22, 1750? 7. Lydia, Ap. 2, 1693, m. Saml. Tower? Nov. 26, 1719. 8. Isaac, Mar. 25, 1695.

4. Enoch, s. Jas., called "Sergeant Enoch" on the H'm. Recs., m. Mary Lincoln, Jan. 11, 1687, lived in H'm., and d. May 5, 1714, and his wid. Oct. 2, 1716. In his will, which is dated Dec. 30, 1713, he gives, to w. Mary, the improve't. of all his est., real and personal, except a few legacies, &c.; to das. Mary, Bethia, Abig., and Marg't., £50 ea.; and the rest to his s. Enoch. Est. appraised, £1021, 8*s*. ch.: 1. Sarah, Oct. 27, 1687, m. Caleb Marsh, Dec. 19, 1711. 2. Mary, Sep. 21, 1690, d. May 28, 1692. 3. Mary, Nov. 6, 1692, m. Jeded. Lincoln, Jan. 9, 1717, and d. Sep. 24, 1734. 4. Abig., Sep. 8, 1697,

m. Danl. Waters, Mar. 10, 1722. 5. Enoch, Sep. 25, 1699. 6. Marg't. Jan. 28, 1702.

5. Thos. s. Jas., m. Joanna Garnet, or *Gardner*, Jan. 26, 1689–90, lived in H'm., is called a "husbandman," on the Prob. Rec. Suff., and was also a cooper. Family tradition says, that he owned a large tract of cedar swamp in Ab'n., which he was accustomed to visit every winter, and from which trees of a very large size were cut, and split into clapboards for the Boston market; and that he came to his death near Cedar bridge, in Ab'n., Sep. 17, 1708, by the fall of a tree, a limb from which struck his head, and killed him instantly. His wid., who admin. on his est., aft. m. Nathan Farrow, Mar. 23, 1710. ch.: 1. Joanna, Jan. 27, 1691, m. Jona. Farrow, Oct. 27, 1714. 2. Jael, Feb. 12, 1693, m. a Hobart? 3. Leah, Ap. 4, 1695, m. Benj. Farrow, Dec. 14, 1715. 4. Thos., Feb. 10, 1697–8 m., and had *Thos.*, 1719. 5. Rachel, July 12, 1700, m. Sam'l. Riccard, or *Richards*, Oct. 19, 1721. 6. Jona., Mar. 5, 1702–3. 7. Eleazer, Nov. 15, 1706.

6. Sam'l., s. Jas. 2, m. 1, Marg't. ——, who d. Ap. 3, 1738; 2, Elizab. Williams, Oct. 4, 1738, who d. May 24, 1747; and 3, Rebecca Garnet, or *Gardner*, Nov. 12, 1747. He was commonly known as "King Whiting," lived near Accord Pond, and was a large landholder and farmer. ch.: 1. Sam'l., Mar. 8, 1712–13. 2. Dan'l., born and d. 1714. 3. Moses, Dec. 2, 1715, left no desct's. on rec. 4. Desire, Ap. 6, 1717, d. young. 5. Kezia, June 5, 1720, m. Stephen Dunbar, Dec. 13, 1739. 6. Dan'l., Nov. 15, 1722.

NOTE. It is said there was a da. Hannah in this family, who m. Sam'l. Curtis, of Hanover, Nov. 14, 1729, and d. Oct. 26, 1789, ae. 72; also a da. Abig., who m. Hezek. Stoddard, Nov. 22, 1743; and Marg't., who m. Obadiah Grose, Jan. 11, 1739. Authority of Mr. Joseph Whiting, H'm.

7. Benjamin Whiton s. Jas. 2, m. Sarah, da. Benja. Tower, H'm., Ap. 19, 1716, and sett. at "Queen Ann's Corners," his house standing in the field back of the shop of Mr. Sam'l. Waters. ch.: 1. Benj., Dec. 28, 1716. 2. Thos., Jan. 29, 1718–19. 3. Wm., Mar. 28, 1720. 4. Jacob, Aug. 10, 1723, m. Ann

Gibbs, Scit., had a da. Ann, who m. Caleb Beal, and the fa. moved to Plainfield, Mass. 5. Nath'l., b. and d. 1725. 6. Sarah, Oct. 22, 1726. 7. Lem'l., Aug. 7, 1729. 8. Abel, May 7, 1733. Left no desct's. on record.

8. Solo., s. Jas. 2, m. Jael, da. Jos. Dunbar, H'm., Oct. 19, 1721, and d. Dec. 18, 1745. ch.: 1. Jael, July 3, 1722. 2. Solo., Dec. 5, 1724. 3. Ruth, Sep. 22, 1726. 4. Debo., Oct. 7, 1728. 5. Mercy, Sep. 22, 1730. 6. Thankful, Oct. 26, 1732. 7. Silence, Nov. 23, 1734. 8. Comfort, Sep. 15, 1736. 9. Melea, Nov. 5, 1739, m. Jas. Chubbuck, Mar. 1, 1767. 10. Rebecca, Nov. 22, 1741.

9. (David) s. Matt. 3, m. Elizab. ——, and d. in H'm. May 24, 1747, being spoken of as "upright and industrious, and one who enjoyed the confidence and respect of his townsmen." ch.: 1. David, Ap. 12, 1716. 2. Elizab., Jan. 29, 1719, m. Jere. Sprague, jr., Dec. 19, 1739. 3. Sarah, Aug. 10, 1720, m. Jona. Hersey, Nov. 19, 1741. 4. Peter, Oct. 21, 1722, m. Ann Wilder, July 4, 1746, had *Rachael*, 1746, and *Anna*, 1748; the fa. d. Oct. 23, 1751, and the mo. Sep. 19, 1799. 5. Abijah, Ap. 2, 1729. 6. Lydia, July 9, 1732, d. May 30, 1737? 7. A ch., b. May 2, 1734?

10. Isaac, s. Matt. 3, m. Lydia Garnet, or *Gardner*, Mar. 17, 1720, who d. Jan. 26, 1756. The fa. lived in H'm., and had ch: 1. Isaac, Jan. 7, 1720–1, m. 1, Rachel Taylor, Jan. 7, 1745, who d. Ap. 10, 1746; and 2, Sarah Sears, Nov. 27, 1746; lived in H'm., near Hersey st.; had 3 ch., who d. young; he d. Nov. 4, 1797, ae. 90, and his wid. Sep. 15, 1804. 2. Stephen, Oct. 13, 1722. 3. Lydia, Nov. 27, 1724, d. Mar. 30, 1728. 4. Debo., Jan. 1, 1726–7, d. Jan. 24, 1756? 5. Lydia, b. and d., 1728. 6. Abraham, Mar. 18, 1730, m. Mary Ripley, Feb. 21, 1751, had *Mary*, 1752; *Abraham*, 1755; *Lydia*, 1758, m. Sherebiah Corthell; and *Rebecca*, 1762. 7. Jacob, Feb. 7, 1733. 8. Israel, Aug, 1734, d. Feb. 15, 1756? 9. Lydia, May 14, 1738.

11. Enoch Whiton s. Enoch 4, m. Leah, da. Benj. Stetson, of Scit., Nov. 16, 1732, lived on "Liberty Plain," near "Gardner's brook," and his w. d. Mar. 22, 1751. ch.: 1. Enoch, Aug. 29, 1733, d. young. 2. Enoch, 1734. 3. Leah, 1735, m. Eben'r. Simmons, Scit. 4. Elijah, June 8, 1737. 5. Mary, 1739, d. young. 6. Grace, 1741, m. Stephen Stoddard, Cohas't. 7. Elias, June 13, 1743.

12. Jona., s. Thos. 5, a "housewright," m. Hannah Dunbar, H'm., July 13, 1732, and d. in H'm., June 19, 1751, the inv'y. of his est. being dated July 24, 1751. (Prob. Rec. Suff.) His ch. were, 1. Hannah, Oct. 17, 1733, m. Benj. Barnes, H'm. 2. Jona., May 9, 1735, m. 1, Rhoda Rose, Jan. 5, 1763, and 2, a Gardner? and had *Jona.*, 1767; *Melzar*, d. at sea; *Rhoda*, m. Thos. Steel; and *Josh.*, who went off, and d. 3. Elisha, Nov. 3, 1737, m. Jael Dunbar, 1760, was a butcher, lived in H'm., had *Elisha*, Oct. 27, 1760, m. Chloe Wilder, Sep. 12, 1782, had Tamar, 1783, and the fa. went off; *Hannah*, Sep. 21, 1762, m. Elij. Lewis, May 16, 1784; *Grace*, June 21, 1765; *Rachael*, Aug. 23, 1767; *Emma*, Feb. 8, 1790, m. Martin Hersey, of Bos'n.; *Caleb*, b. 1772, d. 1773; and *Tamar*, b. and d., 1775. It is said there was another *Caleb*, who m. in Me., had 1 ch., and finally d. in Vt.

13. Eleazer, s. Thos. 5, a cooper by trade, m. Sarah Beal, H'm., Mar. 6, 1746, and sett. in Ab'n., where his w. d. Sep. 9, 1789, ae. 65, and he Jan. 17, 1795, ae. 98. He moved to A., at a time when the part of the town where he resided was comparatively uninhabited; built a log house first, which he occupied in the winter; and finally erected the frame house, now standing oppo. where his gr. s. Eleazer lives. ch.: 1. Jotham, Dec. 18, 1746. 2. Thos., Sep. 10, 1753, m. Jane Smith, lived where Melvin Gurney now does, had no ch., and d. Jan. 1, 1826, and his wid. July 13, 1838. 3. Barzillai, March 5, 1757. One ch., d. young.

14. Sam'l., s. Sam'l. 6, m. Mary Wing, of Hanover, and lived in H'm., where his wid. d. May 24, 1795. ch.: 1. Joanna, July 26, 1734, m. Enoch Whiting, Oct. 30, 1755. 2. Mary,

June 17, 1736, m. Lem'l. Whiting, Ap. 9, 1754. 3. Marg't., Aug. 4, 1738, m. David Prouty, Scituate, Nov. 27, 1777. 4. Thankful, Sep. 13, 1740. 5. Sam'l., Aug. 22, 1742. 6. Judith, 1744, m. Job Loring, H'm., Ap. 19, 1764.

15.

(Daniel Whiton,) s. Sam'l. 6, m. Jael Damon, Scit., who d. in H'm., Aug. 1, 1812, ae. 96. ch.: 1. Dan'l., Oct. 31, 1745. 2. Zach., Dec. 19, 1747. 3. Amasa, Aug. 24, 1749. 4. Martha, July 14, 1752. 5. Zenas, Oct. 1, 1754, m. 1, Sarah Loring, H'm., Sep. 17, 1778, and 2, Mary Loring, and had *Sarah*, Mar. 3, 1779, m. Peakes Grose; *Zenas L.*, July 3, 1780; *Harriet*, Aug. 2, 1782; *Sophia*, m. a Brownson?; and *Frances*. It is said that the fa. moved to Ct., and there m. a 3d w. He was a carpenter by trade, a man of superior mechanical ability, and, it is said, superintended the erection of the old Cambridge bridge, having previously superintended the erection of a bridge in Ireland. 6. Hosea, d. unm. in the Rev'n.

16. s. Benjamin 7, m. 1, Sarah Berry, H'm., Feb. 11, 1741, and 2, Jemima Stoddard, Nov. 7, 1783, lived in H'm., near Accord Pond, was an enterprising farmer, his w. d. Dec. 3, 1806, and he Dec. 5, 1808, ae. 92. ch.: 1. Benj., Jan. 1744. 2. Ezek'l., May 4, 1745. 3. Joseph, d. Aug. 1, 1776, in the Am'n. Army, at Ticonderoga. 4. Abel, 1757? 5. Nathaniel, m. Lydia Gardner, had *Lydia*, m. a Harrington, of Lunenburg; *Mary; Nath'l.*, m. an Adams; *Sarah;* and *Abig. W.;* the fa. moved to Lunenburg, in 1797, and his desct's. still live there. 6. Abig., not m. Two ch., Abel and Sarah, d. young.

17. s. Benjamin 7, m. Lydia Pratt, of Wey'h., and sett. in Hanover, on Whiting st., being one of the earliest residents in that neighborhood. His house stood where stands that of Caleb Whiting; he was an enterprising farmer, and d. Sep. 23, 1793, ae. 75, and his wid. Nov. 7, 1801, ae. 82. ch.: 1. Thos., June

3, 1743. 2. Lydia, May 22, 1745, d. Nov. 8, 1801. 3. Ozias, July 20, 1746, m. 1, a Vinal, and 2, a Fadden, had *Lucy*, *Lillis*, *Ozias*, and *Jacob*. Some of these ch. are m., and have desc'ts. 4. Lucy, Jan. 27, 1748, d. Nov. 28, 1789. 5. Sarah, Nov. 16, 1749, d. June 11, 1826. 6. Jas., July 26, 1751. 7. Elias, Feb. 8, 1753. 8. Asa, Ap. 2, 1755. 9. Priscilla, Mar. 14, 1757, m. Noah Beal, Ab'n., and d. in 1819. 10. Celia, June 8, 1759, d. unm. 11. Caleb, Aug. 9, 1761.

18. William Whiton s. Benj. 7, m. Mary Ramsdell, ab. 1748; lived on Whiting st., his house stood where stands that of his gr. s. Wm. ch.: 1. Wm., b. and d. 1752. 2. Abel, Oct. 12, 1752, m. Priscilla Peakes, Feb. 19, 1784, and d. Jan. 24, 1821, and his wid. Jan. 10, 1851, ae. 89; no ch. 3. Mary, Mar. 21, 1756, m. Isaac Turner, jr., Dec. 10, 1778. 4. Avis, May 14, 1758, d. Oct. 12, 1793. 5. Betty, May 4, 1760, m. Asa Whiting, Ap. 12, 1789. 6. Wm., May 23, 1762. 7. Grace, July 8, 1764, m. Luther Turner. 8. Homer, Aug. 24, 1766, m. 1, Anna Studley, May 8, 1785, who d. July 24, 1789; and 2, Tryphena Beal; and d, Oct. 11, 1793, and his wid. Oct. 31, 1851. His ch. were, *Homer*, bap. Sep. 14, 1788, m. Hannah White, and moved to Vt.; *Anna*, b. 1788, d. 1793; and *Tryphena*, bap. Oct. 21, 1792, m. Zadoc Beal, May 22, 1816, and lives in H.

19. Lem'l., s. Benj. 7, m. Mary Whiting, H'm., Ap. 9, 1754, and lived in H., on Whiting st., his house standing where stands that of Sylvanus Whiting. His wid. d. June 12, 1826, ae. 95. ch.: 1. Mary, Ap. 18, 1755, d. unm., at the house of Mr. Lebbeus Stockbridge, June 21, 1849. 2. Sam'l., June 4, 1757, m. Elizab. Gardner, Sep. 6, 1778, and moved to Lunenburg. 3. Thankful, Feb. 19, 1759, m. Jas. Whiting. 4. Lucinda, Mar. 8, 1761, d. July 19, 1771. 5. Marg't., Nov. 18, 1763. 6. Beulah, Mar. 17, 1766. 7. Lem'l., b. and d. 1769. 8. Bethana, Jan. 21, 1770. 9. Lem'l., b. and d. 1772. 10. Lem'l., Nov. 5, 1773. 11. Lucinda, Dec. 14, 1766. 12. Perez, Sep. 18, 1788. 13. Buchsa, Ap. 9, 1782.

20. Solo., s. Solo. 8, m. Mary Campbell, Aug. 12, 1746, liv-

ed in H'm., and d. Oct. 15, 1813, ae. 89. He was a blacksmith by trade, and his shop stood where stands the house of Chas. Cushing, Esq., on Great Plain. ch.: 1. Asa, Feb. 25, 1746–7. 2. Solo., Aug. 10, 1751. 3. Joseph, Ap. 19, 1754, m. Abig., da. Isaac Alden, 1778, and sett. in Bridg'r., (Mitchell's Bridg'r.) 4. Peleg, Nov. 1758. 5. Jael, m. Thos. Berry, Oct. 31, 1784. It is said there were other ch., Mary, Ruth, and Betsey, all of whom d. in H'm., unm.

21. Comfort, s. Solo. 8, m. Grace Fadden, and sett. in Dorchester? ch. 1. Joanna, Ap. 27, 1759. 2. Nath'l., Jan. 28, 1761, d. young. 3. Philip, Jan. 28, 1761. 4. Mary, Dec. 1, 1762. 5. Ruth, Nov. 6, 1764. 6. Rebecca, Mar. 6, 1767, m. Peter Billings, Canton, Dec. 2, 1784. 7. Nathl., Dec. 24, 1768. 8. Abig., Mar. 1, 1771. 9. Lem'l., 1773. 10. Grace, July, 1775. 11. Comfort, Mar. 1777.

22. David, s. David 9, m. Mary Gilbert, Oct. 29, 1739, and d in H'm., Oct. 12, 1751, and his w., (who was b. 1715,) d. Nov. 10, 1799, ae. 84. ch.: 1. Elizab., July 20, 1740, d. young. 2. Elijah, Feb. 5, 1741. 3. Ezra, Dec. 21, 1743. 4. Elizab., m. Elijah Lewis, Ap. 14, 1762. 5. David, Jan. 31, 1748, d. Oct. 11, 1751? 6. Moses, b. 1750, d. 1751. 7. Moses, Mar. 3, 1752.

23. Abijah, s. David 9, m. 1, Mary Gardner, and 2, Marian Gardner, ? Aug. 13, 1767, and had ch.: 1. Peter, Ap. 23, 1755. 2. Abigail, Oct. 11, 1756. 3. Lucy, Oct. 4, 1760. 4. Luther, June 21, 1764. 5. Mary, Oct. 22, 1765. (By 2d,) 6. Lucinda, June 8, 1768. 7. David, Nov. 10, 1769. 8. Elizab., Aug. 17, 1771. 9. Peggy, Dec. 17, 1772.

24. Stephen, s. Isaac 10, m. 1, Mercy Campbell, and 2, Sarah Stoddard, Dec. 20, 1755, and d. in H'm., June 14, 1812, and his wid. Sep. 30, 1823. Lived near Hersey st., and was a cooper by trade. ch.: 1. Debo., Feb. 5, 1756. 2. Israel, Sep., 1758. 3. Sarah, Nov. 8, 1759. (By 2d,) 4. Isaac, Oct. 21, 1778. 5. Dan'l., July, 1781.

25. Jacob, s. Isaac 10, m. Elizab. Marble, Nov. 10, 1756, lived in H'm., and was a cooper by trade. ch.: 1. Jacob, Sep. 10, 1757. 2. Betsey, Aug. 23, 1759, m. Josi. Sprague, Mar. 4,

1785, and d. soon after. 3. Laban, Nov. 18, 1761, d. at sea, unm. 4. Susa, Mar. 2, 1764, m. Josi. Sprague, Dec. 14, 1794. 5. Chloe, m. 1, Elij. Fearing, Nov. 9, 1788, and 2, Seth Lincoln ? 6. Lydia, m. Benj. Thomas, Aug. 19, 1798. 7. Debo., m. Amos Sprague, Oct. 21, 1796. 8. Reuben, d. unm.

26. Capt. Enoch, s. Enoch 11, m. Joanna Whiting, 1755, lived in H'm., on Liberty Plain, was a farmer by occupation, and d. June 21, 1778. ch.: 1. Joan, m. Thomas Chubbuck, June 11, 1787. 2. Chloe, m. Samuel Gardner, Aug. 23, 1789. 3. Bethia, m. David Loring, Oct. 8, 1780. 4. Enoch, Dec. 27, 1763. 5. Leah, Mar. 8, 1765, m. Jno. Abbott, Newark, N. J. 6. Laurena, Mar. 4, 1767, m. Dan'l. Parks, Lincoln, Nov. 11, 1805. 7. Dolly, Mar. 5, 1769, m. Lewis Squier, Newark, N. J. 8. Phœbe, Ap. 12, 1771, m. Daniel Whiting, jr., Brookfield, Jan. 11, 1798.

27. Elijah, s. Enoch 11, m. Mary Wilder, H'm., July 13, 1763, and d. in H'm., June 15, 1797, ae. 60, and his wid. in Jan. 1811? ch.: 1. Mary, Oct. 7, 1764, m. Enoch Dunbar, May 7, 1786. 2. Persis, Sep. 21, 1766, m. Jacob Sprague, June 1, 1794. 3. Elizab., Aug. 7, 1769. 4. Tamsen, Oct. 2, 1771, m. Chas. Simmons, Scit., Dec. 7, 1794. 5. Charlotte, Feb. 24, 1774, m. Nath'l. Bump, Midd'o., Nov. 26, 1803. 6. Merrill, July 3, 1776, m. Geo. B. Lapham, of Medford, ship-builder, of the firm of Lapham and Magoun. 7. Isaiah, Nov. 7, 1778, d. unm., Sep. 5, 1820. 8. Blossom, Ap. 30, 1781. 9. Walter, Nov. 28, 1783, a Major, in the U. S. A., was killed at the battle of Bridg'r., during the war of 1812.

28. Capt. Elias, s. Enoch 11, m. Sarah Blossom, June 22, 1769, lived in H'm., on Liberty Plain, and d. of the small pox, in 1778, and his w., who was b. in June, 1749, d. May 16, 1817, ae. 68. ch.: 1. Elias, Dec. 18, 1769, m. Mehit., da. Daniel Whiting, July 1, 1804, and d. in Brookf'd., Mass., having had *Elias*, d. on the coast of Africa; *Franklin*, of Ohio; *Nymphas*, and *Edward*, of N. Brookf'd.; *Sarah*, m. a Bailey, of Worcester ? and is d.; *Mehitab.*, m. Ed. Humphrey, and lives in Chas'n.; *Abig.*, d. unm.; and *Desire*. 2. Sarah, Oct. 18, 1771, m. 1,

Henry Cushing, H'm., Dec. 28, 1791, and 2, Seth Cushing, and is living, a wid., in H'm. 3. Priscilla, Dec. 21, 1773, m. Josiah Lane, jr., H'm., Dec. 28, 1801. 4. Martha, b. and d. 1775. 5. Martha, Oct. 10, 1776, m. Thos. Fearing, H'm., Dec. 25, 1808, and d. in 1852. 6. Marg't., Oct. 1778, m. Dimick Bowker, Scit., Feb. 10, 1798.

29. Jotham, s. Eleazer 13, m. Susanna Wilder, H'm., Jan. 1, 1771, a farmer by occupation, lived in E. Ab'n., where his w. d., Jan. 24, and he May 24, 1828. ch.: 1. Susanna, 1771, d. 1773. 2. Susanna, Mar. 9, 1774, m. Bela Cushing, H'm., 1803, and d. Aug. 27, 1818. 3. Mary, Oct. 9, 1775, m. Jos. Turner, H'm., 1796, and d. 1800. 4. Sarah, Mar. 6, 1778, m. Melzar Beal, Ab'n., July 15, 1797, and d. Jan. 31, 1850. 5. Lydia, Jan. 14, 1780, m. Jared Shaw, Ab'n., 1802, and d. Dec. 15, 1819. 6. Lucy, Ap. 10, 1782, m. Jos. Benner, Ab'n., 1803, and d. July 3, 1836. 7. Jerusha, Aug. 12, 1785, m. Wm. Wheeler, Quincy, 1806, and d. June 5, 1810. 8. Merrill, July 24, 1787, m. Samuel Colson, Ab'n, 1812, and d. Mar. 29, 1834. 9. Eph'm., Sep. 26, 1790. 10. Emma, Sep. 3, 1793, in Mich'n.

30. Barzillai Whiting s. Eleazer 13, m. Abig. Beal, H'm., who d. Ap. 22, 1844, ae. 84. ch.: 1. Abig., m. Isaac Turner, H'n., and d. Oct. 14, 1845. 2. Eleazer, Sep. 28, 1782. 3. Ithamar, 1786. 4. Joanna, Feb. 28, 1791. 5. Marilla, 1799, d. Jan. 25, 1802.

31. Daniel, s. Daniel 15, a farmer by occupation, m. Desire Stoddard, Scit., Ap. 7, 1768, who d. Feb. 28, 1820, and he ab. 1822. It is said that he lived first where Enoch Dunbar now resides, and in his latter days, at "High Hill," so called. ch.: 1. Martha, Nov. 25, 1767, m. Enoch Whiting, H'm. 2. Mehit., Ap. 23, 1770, d. young. 3. Dan'l., Ap. 23, 1772. 4. Galen, Feb. 1, 1774, m. Rachael Prouty, of Scit.? sett. in Brookfield, where he d. in Dec., 1849, having had ch.: *Galen*, d. at the West; *Leonard*, and *Charles*, sett. in Ill's.; *Andrew*, an invalid, unm.; *Wm.*, is m., and lives on his father's place; *Louisa*, unm.; and *Rachel*, m. Jere. Deming? and has ch. 5. Sylvanus, Dec.

7, 1776. 6. Hosea, June 24, 1778. 7. Mehit., Jan. 28, 1781, m. Elias Whiting, Brookf'd., July 1, 1804. 8. Josiah, Nov. 29, 1784, m. a Prouty, sett. in Brookf'd., and d. leaving ch.: *Osborn*, *Josiah*, *Julia A.*, *Elizab.*, *Merrill*, (d. young,) *Abig.*, *Martha*, and *Mary*; — all m., and have ch. but Elizab. 9. Abig., Mar. 1, 1788, d. Dec. 1795.

32. Zach., s. Daniel 15, m. Kezia Wilder, H'm., Dec. 12, 1770, and d. May 15, 1804? and his wid. in 1833. ch.: 1. Prudence, m. Enoch Lovell, Wey'h.; and d. in Me. 2. Chas., m. a Stoddard? and d. Feb. 7, 1849. 3. Theoph., Mar. 30, 1775. 4. Susan, m. Steph. Gardner, H'm., Dec. 29, 1796. 5. Sybil, Oct. 27, 1780, living unm. 6. Hosea, Sep. 11, 1782. 7. Polly, m. Joel Seymour, H'm. 8. Martha, m. Jotham Shaw, Wey'h., and d. in 1836? 9. Priscilla, m. Justin Rogers.

33 Amasa Whiton s. Dan'l. 15, m. Lydia Jacobs, Scit., and lived at "Queen's Ann's Corners," where he d. Nov. 5, 1818. He was a carpenter by trade, and lived in a house which stood where stands that now occupied by the wid. of his son Joseph J., and by his gr. s. Amasa. ch.: 1. Davis, Aug. 20, 1773, m. Abig. Bowker, Scit., and d. Ap. 12, 1833, having had ch., *Mary C.*, 1797, m. Leonard Cushing, H'm.; *Abig. B.*, January 4, 1799, m. Jas. W. Sivret, June 10, 1819, and lives in Dorch'r.; and *Davis*, Feb. 2, 1801, lost at sea, in May, 1828. 2. Perez, Ap. 3, 1775. 3. Jael, Mar. 18, 1777, d. Oct. 19, 1794. 4. Joseph J., Dec. 29, 1778. 5. Lydia, Oct. 25, 1780, m. Nath'l. Bump, Midd'o, June 15, 1807. 6. Abig., Sep. 30, 1783, m. Alex'r. Vining, Ab'n., Feb. 3, 1807, 7. Eunice, July 14, 1786, m. Neh. Ripley, jr., H'm., Feb. 4, 1807, and d. Oct. 1850. Was there another da. Jael? m. Harris Turner, Scit.? Oct. 19, 1794.

34. Benj., s. Benj. 16, m. Joanna Gardner, H'm., 1766, who d. June 14, 1807, and he Ap. 12, 1815. Lived in a house which stood where stands that of Eleazer Chubbuck, in H'm., was a farmer, and a man of great mechanical ingenuity, and industry. ch.: 1. Joanna, Jan. 11, 1767, d. July, 1782. 2. Asenath, Ap. 10, 1770, d. Feb. 11, 1840. 3. Benj., Jan. 22, 1773. 4. Joseph,

Jan, 9, 1777, lives in H'm., near Accord Pond, m. Lucy, da. Wm. Barrell, Scit., Dec. 22, 1812, and has ch.: *Jos. M.*, Nov. 6, 1813; *Lucy B.*, Jan. 17, 1815, m. Albert G. Mann, Oct. 19, 1834, and d. Jan. 3, 1837; *Ruth*, Jan. 26, 1818, d. Feb. 10, 1839; and *Salome*, Nov. 30, 1819. 5. Archelaus, Sep. 30, 1778, m. Elizabeth Gardner, H'm., May 4, 1799, who d. Oct., 1803, and in 1812, he enlisted from the frigate Constitution to go to the Lakes, and prob. d. there. He had 1 da., *Betsey*, Jan. 24, 1801, m. Eleazer Chubbuck, H'm., Jan. 13, 1838, and has 4 ch. 6. Luther, Mar. 16, 1781, m. 1, Cynthia E. Stetson, Dec. 31, 1815, who d. May 29, 1818; and 2, Lois Gardner, Dec. 27, 1818; and had, by 1st., ch.: *Cynthia S.*, Mar. 21, 1818, m. Benj. White, Dux'y., Feb. 1849; and *Sophia S.*, Mar. 21, 1818, m. Abner Loring, H'm., Mar. 22, 1840.

35. Ezek'l., s. Benj. 16, m. 1, Olive Stoddard, Scit., and 2, Mary Berry, Mar. 10, 1804, was a farmer, lived in H'm., and had ch.: 1. Sarah, m. Asa Souther, Cohas't., Nov. 29, 1795. 2. Lois, m. Jos. Hill, jr., Ab'n., Ap. 10, 1803. 3. Olive, m. Peleg Dunbar, H'm., Feb. 15, 1805. 4. Abig., m. Jno. Blake, or *Black*, Plym'h. 5. Judith, m. 1, Quincy Gardner, and 2, Nicholas Daniels. (By 2d,) 6. Ezek'l., Jan. 25. 1805.

36. Abel, s. Benj. 16, m. Grace, wid. Sam'l. Stoddard, Jan. 9, 1779, and moved to Worcester, where he d. ch.: 1. Abel, Dec. 4, 1779, m., lived in Blandford, Ct., and had ch. 2. Sarah, Mar. 19, 1782. 3. Sam'l., July, 1785, m., lived in N. Y'k. State, and has *Jas. W.*, and others. 4. Amos, July, 1788, m. Hannah Keith, Bridg'r., and had *Sidney*, and others. 5. Ezek'l., May 7, 1790, m. and had ch. 6. Ambrose, m. and had ch. 7. Laban. 8. Andrew, m. Lucy Briggs, lives in Waltham, and has ch.

37. Thomas Whiting s. Thos. 17, m. Rachael Peakes, Nov. 15, 1770, and d. in Hanover, Dec. 13, 1805, and his wid. Sep. 30, 1828, ae. 81. Lived on Whiting st., in the house now occupied by Piam Damon, and was Selectman from 1780–82, and in '89. ch.: 1. Wm. P., Ap. 28, 1771, m. Sally Wales, Randolph, and practiced law in Bos'n., where he d., leaving ch., *Mary W.*, m.

Levi H. Marsh, ? *Sarah A.*, d. ae. ab. 25; *Eph'm. W.*, was m., had 2 ch., and was lost at sea; and Ella S.? 2. Rachael, Oct. 14, 1773, d. May 7, 1849. 3. Thos., Aug. 16, 1776, m. Hannah Mann, June 8, 1797, lived on Whiting st., where he d. in 1806, leaving ch., *Marcia*, May, 1798; *Jairus*, moved to N. Y'k. State; *Oren*, (m. 1, Sarah C. Faxon, who d. Feb. 20, 1827, and 2, Mary Jones, May, 1831, lives on Whiting st., and has Lewis, Jan. 24, 1832; Oren T., Aug. 28, 1834; Lucius, Ap. 22, 1837; Abel H., 1841, d. 1842. Abel H., July, 1843; Albert, March 24, 1846; and Jno. B., Mar. 24, 1849,); *Lewis*, d.; and *Hannah M.*, m. Elisha Faxon, Ab'n. 4. Charles, bap. June 27, 1784, m. Betsey Pool, Ab'n., and had ch., *Albert*, Nov. 6, 1803; *Emily*, Dec. 7, 1806, m. David Pool, E. Ab'n.; *Nath'l. H.*, Nov. 24, 1808, m. Mary Clark, and lives in Mf'd., no ch.; *Wm.*, sometime a clergyman, of the Univ. denom., and now sett. in H'n., m. a da. of Benj. Stetson, of H., for his 2d w., and has ch.; and *Betsey*, m. Reuben Loud, E. Ab'n. 5. Olive, bap. July 22, 1787, m. Piam Damon, June 15, 1814. 6. Martin, bap. July 22, 1792, d. young.

38. Jas., s. Thos. 17, m. Thankful Whiting, lived in Hanover, and d. Sep. 26, 1812, ae. 65, and his wid. Aug. 3, 1832, ae. 73. Built and occupied the house in which Jno. W. Estes now lives. ch.: 1. Thankful, Nov. 6, 1781, d. Feb. 1, 1793. 2. Rebecca, May 28, 1784, d. Aug. 13, 1786. 3. Jas., Dec. 5, 1789, m. Ann Brooks, had no ch., d., and his wid. m. a Gray, of Me. 4. Mary, May 8, 1786, m. Uriah Lawrence, Lunenburg. 5. Horatio, Nov. 2, 1791, m. 1, Ruth Lovell, who d. Ap. 26, 1839, and 2, Lucy Lane, lives in Mf'd., and has ch., *Lucy*, Aug. 15, 1828, d. 1848? *Flora*, Ap. 24, 1830, d.; *Marcia*; and *Alden*. 6. Thankful, Dec. 1, 1794, d. unm. 7. Rufus, Aug. 7, 1797, d. Dec. 24, 1799. 8. Rebecca, Sep. 28, 1800, m. Zadoc Beal, Nov. 30, 1837.

39. Elias, s. Thos. 17, m. Debo. Jackson, and d. in H., May 20, 1790, and his wid. May 25, 1818, ae. 61. ch.: 1. Ruth, Jan. 30, 1779. 2. Justus, Sep. 14, 1780, m. Abig. Wilder, H'm., lives on Whiting st., and is a respectable farmer; no ch.

3. Benj., Ap. 23, 1782, is m., and lives in Me. 4. Sarah, Aug. 27, 1784, d. Mar. 4, 1804. 5. Amos, Aug. 9, 1786. 6. Edmund, b. and d. 1788. 7. Elias, b. 1789, d. 1793.

40. Asa, s. Thos. 17, m. 1, Debo. Dwelley, Ap. 13, 1786, who d. Jan. 8, 1787 ; and 2, Betty Whiting, Ap. 12, 1789 ; lived on Whiting st., and finally moved to Lunenburg, where he d. ch. by 2d w., 1. Asa, b. 1790, d. 1793. 2. Elijah, Aug. 22, 1792, a blacksmith, d. unm. ab. 1842. 3. Debo. D., Dec. 10, 1794, m. Nathan Beal, Ab'n., and d. Dec. 17, 1821, leaving a son *Nathan*. 4. Asa, Oct. 14, 1797, sett. in Lunenburg. 5. Betty, bap. Oct. 23, 1803, m. a Battles, and lives in Fitchburg.

41. Caleb Whiting s. Thos. 17, m. Susa G. Mann, Ap. 23, 1785, who d. Nov. 25, 1842, ae. 77, and he May 20, 1848, ae. 87. Lived in the house now occupied by Jas. Fish, on Whiting st. ch.: 1. Caleb, b. 1788, d. 1792. 2. Lucy, Jan. 17, 1791, d. June 15, 1840. 3. Susa G., Dec. 26, 1793, d. Oct. 11, 1794. 4. Caleb, Mar. 21, 1795, m. 1, Mary Whiting, June 9, 1823, who d. Sep. 2, 1850 ; and 2, Anne, da. Gideon Studley, May 11, 1852, lives on Whiting st., and had a da. *Mary W.*, b. Mar. 21, 1829, d. Sep. 25, 1843. 5. Sage, Ap. 20, 1797, m. David Nichols, Cohas't., Nov. 28, 1817. 6. Ezra, May 21, 1800, m. Sally Curtis, lived on Main st., and d. Oct. 3, 1831, having had ch., *Ezra*, Sep. 9, 1823, in Cohas't.; *Josh. S.*, Dec. 6, 1825, m. Betsey B. Dwelley, June 20, 1847, and has Elmira E., Aug. 10, 1850 ; *Lucius C.*, Mar. 20, 1828, in Cal'a.; and *Edwin*, Aug. 22, 1831, d. ae. 4. One other ch. d. young. 7. Jared, Ap. 15, 1804, m. Desire Loring, H'm., Jan. 1838, lives on Whiting st., and has *Caleb L.*, Jan. 4, 1839, and *Jared*, Aug. 15, 1842. 8. Lydia P., Sep. 26, 1806, m. Briggs Freeman, Ab'n., and d. Sep. 28, 1849.

42. William Whiting s. Wm. 18, m. Betsey Clapp, Scituate, was Selectman in 1803, and '04, lived on Whiting st., and d. Mar. 19, 1825, ae. 63, and his wid. Mar. 17, 1829, ae. 58. ch.: 1. Avis, Mar. 17, 1803, m. G. W. Turner,

Oct. 22, 1829. 2. Mary, Jan. 30, 1805, m. Caleb Whiting, June 9, 1823, and d. Sep. 2, 1850. 3. Silvanus, Feb. 9, 1808, m. Lucy Bates, Nov. 20, 1828, lives on Whiting st., is a farmer, and has ch., *Silvanus*, Nov. 24, 1829, m. Sarah J. Torrey, Jan. 14, 1852; *Betsey C.*, Oct. 7, 1831; *Nathan*, July 12, 1833; *Lucy M.*, July 5, 1835; *Laura A.*, July 28, 1837; *Adelaide*, Feb. 10, 1840; *Thos. H. B.*, Jan. 10, 1842; *Geo. D.*, Mar. 18, 1845; *Mary R.*, d.; and *Elmer*, Feb. 8, 1849. 4. Wm., Feb. 5, 1811, m. Cynthia Curtis, Nov. 20, 1831, lives on Whiting st., is a farmer, was Selectman in 1845, '47, '48, and '49; and has ch., *Triphena*, Dec. 13, 1832; *Cynthia*, Sep. 14, 1834; *Wm.*, May 19, 1836; *Simeon*, July 16, 1838, d. Mar. 4, 1839; *Betsey*, May 18, 1840; *Mary*, Ap. 1847; and *Walter*, Mar. 6, 1850.

43. Elijah, s. David 22, m. Lydia Lincoln, H'm., Jan. 7, 1768, was a farmer, lived on "Bull's Lane," so called, and d. Mar. 16, 1814. ch.: 1. Lydia, Aug. 29, 1768, m. Jno. Chadwick, Bos'n., Jan. 30, 1798. 2. Elij., b. 1770, d. 1778. 3. Peggy, 1771, d. 1773. 4. Peggy, June 17, 1775, m. Laban Beal, H'm., Oct. 2, 1796. 5. Olive, Dec. 3, 1777, m. a Felch, Boylston, Mass. 6. Elij., Dec. 29, 1779. 7. Bela, June 4, 1783, went South, m., and d. there.

44. Ezra, s. David 22, m. Martha Lincoln, Nov. 15, 1770, and d. in H'm., Oct. 25, 1773, and his wid. m. his bro. Moses. He had one son, Ezra, b. May 8, 1772, m. Emma, da. Thos. Jones, H'm., June 14, 1795, and d. in Mar. 1851, having had ch.: *Ezra J.*, Ap. 5, 1797, of Bos'n.; *Emma*, Ap. 17, 1800, m. Benj. Andrews, H'm.; *Ebed*, Sep. 18, 1802, m 1, Esther C. Richardson, and 2, Mary A. Howe, and lives in Bos'n; *Bela*, Oct. 18, 1804, m. Martha L. Whitney, and had a son, Geo. H., b. 1829, d. 1830; *Martha*, Sep. 16, 1807, m. a Wiggins, Bos'n.; *Susan C.*, Sep. 8, 1810, m. Zadoc Hersey, H'm.; *Thos. L.*, b. 1812, d. 1813; *Thos. L.*, Dec. 28, 1813; *Peter*; and *Hannah R.*, m. Bela H. Whiton.

45. Moses Whiton s. David 22, m. Martha, wid. of his brother Ezra W., and lived in H'm., where he d. June 9, 1823, and his w. Nov. 13, 1812. He was a merchant in H'm., on the Plain, and was a man of excellent character, and respectable standing. ch.: 1. David, Ap. 23, 1775. 2. Wilson, Sep. 26, 1777. 3. Mary, Aug. 26, 1780, m. Peter Sprague, Nov. 28, 1799. 4. Sarah, Jan. 11, 1783, m. Judge Abel Cushing, June 16, 1811, and lives in Dorch'r. 5. Moses, June 26, 1785. 6. Starks, June 26, 1785.

46. Israel, s. Stephen 24, m. Hannah Stowell, H'm., Jan. 14, 1781, and d. Aug. 2, 1840, ae. 82, and his w., who was b. Jan. 9, 1761, d. Ap. 11 ? 1827. ch.: 1. Israel, m. Rebecca Cleverly, Ap. 11 ? 1802, and d. Nov. 6, 1825 ; no ch. 2. Campbell, Feb. 19, 1784, known as *Kimball Whiting*, m. Desire Jordan, and had ch., *Henry ; Kimball ; Rebecca ; Harriet*, m. a Smith ; *Lydia A.*, m. a Watson ; *Mary A. ; Almira*, m. a Leavens ; *Ellen ;* and *George*. 3. Hannah, b. 1787, d. 1788. 4. Isaiah, Oct. 8, 1789, m. Martha Estabrooks, and had ch., *Martha D.*, Sep. 18, 1811 ; *Isa. G.*, May 5, 1813 ; *Chas. E.*, Feb. 22, 1815; *Susan A.*, May 24, 1817 ; *Debo. C.*, May 19, 1820 ; *Albert*, b. 1823, d. 1824 ; *Anna A.*, June 13, 1825 ; *Emily E.*, Oct. 11, 1827 ; *Albert*, Oct. 10, 1829 ; *Olive M.*, May 4, 1832 ; and *Wm. S.*, Oct. 28, 1834. 5. Royal, Feb. 2, 1792, m. Esther Cleverly, July 3, 1811, lives in Quincy, and has ch.: *Elizab. D.*, Ap. 9, 1812, m. Dr. T. L. Turner, Bos'n., Ap. 3, 1843 ; *Hannah S.*, Ap. 25, 1814, m. Jairus Beal, Nov. 29, 1838 ; *Cath. C. A.*, b. 1816, d. 1818 ; *Cath. C. A.*, b. 1818, d. 1838 ; *Royal*, July 26, 1820, m. Rebecca A. Lothrop, Nov. 1, 1843 ; *Hiram*, Mar. 22, 1823 ; *Jas.*, b. 1825, d. 1826 ; *Hannah J.* ? b. 1829, d. 1848 ; *Rebecca E.*, b. 1830, d. 1832. 6. Job S., Jan. 23, 1797, m. Lucy Fadden, of Ct., and had ch.: *Lucy*, Sep. 26, 1822 ; *Lydia E.* ? b. 1825, d. 1845 ; *Josi. W.*, Dec. 4, 1827 ; *Lyman B. ;* and *Mehit. S.*

47. Enoch, s. Capt. Enoch 26, m. Martha Whiting, Sep. 14, 1786, and d. in H'm., Dec. 30, 1811. ch.: 1. Desire, Ap. 15, 1787, m. Jairus Mann, June 9, 1811.? 2. Enoch, b. 1789, d. 1790. 3. Enoch, b. 1791, d. 1792. 4. Joanna, May 30, 1793, m. Ed. Humphrey.? 5. Martha, Feb. 27, 1795. 6. Sam'l., Ap. 7, 1797. 7. Mary W., Ap. 5, 1799, m. Jona. D. Pratt, Nov. 17, 1823. 8. Enoch, Oct. 12, 1801, m. Sarah, da. Col. John Collamore, Scit., lived in H'm., and d. ab. 1837, leaving ch.: *Sarah A.;* and *Mary C.*, m. Henry W. Clark, of Boston, April 17, 1851, and lives in Woburn. 9. Bethia, July 27, 1803. 10. Christopher, Dec. 8, 1806. 11. Leah S., Mar. 21, 1808, m. Cushing Barnes, H'm., Dec. 16, 1830.

48. Elij., s. Elij. 27, m. Charity, da. Job Loring, H'm., May 20, 1798, was a carpenter by trade, and a farmer, and d. in H'm., in Mar. 1837. ch.: 1. Elijah, Mar. 6, 1799, m. Lydia, da. Crocker Wilder, H'm., Sep. 18, 1822, and has ch., *Chas.*, Nov. 9, 1824, (m. Sarah J., da. Capt. Seth Hersey, and has 2 ch., Sarah J., 1848, and Chas., Mar. 27, 1850;) and George, Oct. 12, 1828. 2. Loring, Oct. 29, 1801, a skilful carpenter, was m., and is prob. d. He had ch., *George*, who is one of the community of Shakers, at Harvard, Mass.; *Stephen*, a mariner, drowned on a voyage to Smyrna, 1852; and *Caroline*, who is m., and lives in Bos'n. 3. Lavinia, February 2, 1804, m. Jacob Tirrell, Wey'h., and has 5 ch. 4. Elizab., 1806, unm. 5. Charlotte, b. 1808, d. 1813. 6. Alvan, Sep. 23, 1811, living unm., in H'm.

Note. The son Elijah, is a man of rare mechanical ability, and has been the successful inventor of various machines, several of which have been patented, and have been found highly useful. His latest invention, a machine for sawing volutes and cylinders, is now in operation, in H'm., and promises to work quite a revolution in the bucket business. Did our limits premit, we might fill a long chapter with a sketch of the life of Mr. W., whose varied incidents would be instructive and encouraging to the young. He has been somewhat in political life, and is a man of great energy of character, persevering in whatever he undertakes, and carrying it on to a successful issue.

49. Blossom, s. Elijah, 27, m. Sarah Lincoln, and lived in Chas'n., where he d. ch.: 1. Blossom L. 2. Jas. 3. Albert. 4. Walter. 5. Henry. 6. Sarah. 7. Mary, m. Mark Warren.

50. Ephraim, s. Jotham, 29, m. Mehit. Hobart, Ab'n., in 1810, and d. Ap. 14, 1842. Lived in Ab'n., and was a shoemaker by trade. He was also a trader for a time in Bos'n. ch.: 1. Eph'm. W., Mar. 16, 1811, of Bos'n., m. Sarah Morton, Dux'y., and has *Helen E.*, *Adelaide L.*, and *Walter B.* 2. Geo. L., Mar. 24, 1813, m. Maria Peterson, Dux'y., and has *Sasan M.*, July 4, 1835. 3. Alden, May 9, 1816, m. Sophronia Huntington, Ct., and has *Amelia S.*, and *Lydia.* 4. Henry, Feb. 23, 1819, m. Almedia? Watson, and lives in Dux'y. 5. Polly, Nov. 15, 1821, m. Jno. W. Estes, of Hanover. 6. Peter W., Dec. 3, 1825, d. Oct. 1, 1847. 7. Lydia, Dec. 3, 1825, m. Benj. H. Bowker, of Hanover. 8. Merrill, Sep. 25, 1835.

51. Eleazer, s. Barzillai 30, m. 1, Reverence Nash, Ab'n., 1810, who d. Feb. 19, 1816; and 2, Nancy Hobart, Nov. 18, 1821, lives in E. Ab'n., and has ch: 1. Clarissa, Jan. 27, 1811, m. Vincent Blanchard, N. Ab'n. (By 2d,) 2. Elbridge, Aug. 1, 1822, surveyor; a young man of fine talents, and great promise, now engaged on one of the railroads in Ill's. 3. Leonard, May 8, 1824, m. Elizab. Hobart, Dorch'r., lives in E. Ab'n., and has *Harriet E.*, July 25, 1847; *Leonard A.*, Jan. 1849; and *Henry*, 1850. 4. Jacob, Dec. 28, 1825, lives in Milford. 5. Marilla, May 26, 1828, m. Jos. W. Davis, E. Ab'n., and has *Willard W.*, and *Geo. H.* 6. Rowena, b. 1831, d. 1832. 7. Roxa A., July 13, 1833. Joanna E., Jan. 3, 1838.

52. Ithamar, s. Barzillai 30, m. Abig. Mann, and lived in E. Ab'n., where he d. July 31, 1820, ae. 34. ch.: 1. Lydia G., Dec. 28, 1811, m. Gideon B. Phillips, and lives in E. Ab'n. 2. Abig., Ap. 24, 1813, m. John H. Marsh, Worcester. 3. Stephen, Ap. 13, 1819, m. 1, Mary Prouty, who d. Ap. 10, 1844; and 2, Judith A. Baker, Midd'o., lives in E. Ab'n., and has *Stephen W.*, b. 1843, d. 1844; (by 2d,) *Simeon D.*, June 15, 1847; and *Herbert J.*, Aug. 6, 1849. 4. Rowena, May 11, 1814, d. ae. 3.

53. Daniel, s. Daniel 31, m. Phœbe, da. Capt. Enoch Whiting, and sett. in N. Brookf'd., in 1810, where he d. in Feb. 1850. ch.: 1. Lewis, is m., and has *Caroline*, *Rebecca*, *Phœbe*, and *Frances.* 2. Nelson, m. Cath., da. Sam'l. Gardner, H'm., and

had 1 son, *Gardner*, d. ae. 11. 3. Daniel. 4. Rev. Lyman, of Reading, Mass. 5. Eliza, m. Parker Johnson, of N. Brookfield.

NOTE.— The anniversary of the fiftieth wedding day of Mr. Daniel W., and his wife, was celebrated by appropriate festivities, on which occasion, the following odes were sung:—

THE GOLDEN MARRIAGE,

OR THE

FIFTIETH MARRIAGE ANNIVERSARY

OF

MR. DANIEL AND MRS. PHŒBE WHITING.

[Jan. 11, 1798.] [Jan. 11, 1848.]

HYMN.

Our Father God, before Thee now,
Together we, thy children bow,
And joyful, willing songs of praise
From lip and heart, to Thee we raise.

We 're gathered on the cherished spot,
Where thou in wisdom cast the lot
Of parents; who, before Thee stand
With children, these, a filial band.

Back half a century's rolling years,
This night; with love, and hopes and fears,
Their bridal vows, they made in youth;—
Since kept with holy faith and truth.

Through life's bright prime; through wiser days,
Together toiled their blended ways,
And now Age smites, they kiss the rod,
And patient wait their call to God.

Now, sons and daughters, come to bless
Their kind parental faithfulness,
And childrens' children, join and sing—
While orphan hearts thank-offerings bring.

Departed ones, who shared this love.
Raise holier songs in homes above!
Help us, O God! to join THEIR song
And in thy praise their strains prolong. S.

ADDRESS. PLACING THE RING.

HYMN.

Father, and Mother! Husband, Wife!
Names in which dwell earth's holiest charms,
We hail this length of wedded life,—
Of aged vows—of trembling palms.

Dim eyes, gray locks, were bright the day
These bridal vows, ye *youthful* took,
Tho' dimmed the eye, the locks turned gray,
Their bonds, not loosened, nor forsook.

Since that far day, how sore the strife
In household toil, ye two have borne
Daughters and Sons—life from your life
Have drawn; 'till yours' is waste and worn.

We *children* greet you on this day,
Father and Mother, take our song,—
While "little longer" you may stay,
We would in peace your hours prolong.

Now old, fond love, drop gladsome tears,
These children hands, shall 'fend from need,
'Till *we all* end our mortal years,
Then Jesus, count us "holy seed." L.

54. Sylvanus, s. Dan'l. 31, m. Hannah Stoddard, H'm., Feb. 26, 1800, and lives in H'm. ch.: 1. Sylvanus, m. Sibyl Gardner, H'm., Jan. 1, 1828, and has *Adaline O.* 2. Nathan, m. Tempe. Bicknell, Wey'h., and has *Tempe.*, *Susan A.*, and *George.* 3. Nahum, m. Meribel Orcutt, lives in E. Wey'h., and has *Mary A.*, and *Anna L.* 4. Silas, m. 1, Mary Dyer, Braintree, and 2, Anne Newcomb, Wey'h., lives in W., and has *Mary L.*, *Susan M.*, and *Emma J.* 5. Hannah, m. Chas. Gardner, jr. 6. Lydia, m. Chas. Whiting. 7. Mary, m. Jas. Matthewson, Wey'h.

55. Theoph., s. Zach. 32, m. Hannah Collamore, Scit., who d. Sep. 25, 1824, and he May 4, 1831. ch.: 1. Hannah C., Dec. 14, 1798, m. David Cushing, E. Ab'n., and has *Wm. S.*, *Davis*, *Brainerd*, *Urban W.*, *Sarah C.*, *Andrew J.*, *Fanny W.*, and *Henry J.* 2. Lusanna, Dec. 21, 1800, m. Silas Ripley, Ab'n., 1821, and d. Feb. 15, 1830. 3. Theoph. W., Dec. 7, 1802, m. Mary Paine, Rdl'ph, and had *Nancy A.*, b. and d. 1833, and *Leonard W.*, d. 1840. 4. Zenas L., Oct. 3, 1804, m. Mary Lane, Ab'n., 1825, and has *Hiram L.*, Nov. 1825; *Mary A.*, Sep. 26, 1827, m. Andrew Rogers, Hanover; *Edwin W.*, Dec. 9, 1830; *Albert L.*, b. and d. 1834; *Henry L.*; *Emily L.*; *Albert F.*; *Josephine M.*; and *Wm. L.*, Jan. 26, 1849. 5. Maria, July 28, 1807, m. Peter W. Beal, E. Ab'n. 6. Gilman C., Feb. 16, 1809, m. Diantha Stoddard, Abington; lives in H., on Main street, has been constable, &c.; and has ch.: Diantha S., September 27, 1830; *Mary W.*, August 22, 1831; *Nathan G.*, April 15, 1833; Hannah M., June 10, 1835, d. September 27, 1852; *Soranus W.*, October 1836, d. July, 1839; *Anson V.*, Aug. 1838; and *Lusanna M.*, April 14, 1842. 7. Piam C., June 27, 1811. m. Sarah D. Brooks, September 15, 1831, and died Aug. 12, 1845, leaving ch., *Piam* W., b. 1832, d. 1833; *Edwin W.*, Dec. 2, 1833; *Angeline S.*, Aug. 9, 1836; *Piam A.*, Ap. 1838; and *Lucy M.*, Feb. 28, 1843. 8. Edwin, July 19, 1813, m. Mary Battles, N. Bridg'r., and d. Jan. 2, 1844, and his wid., in 1851, leaving no ch. 9. Hiram, Jan. 28, 1818, d. Feb. 6, 1823.

56. Hosea, s. Zach. 32, m. 1, Anne Stoddard, H'm., Nov. 11, 1804, who d. June 16, 1844; and 2, Alice Turner;—lives in H'm., and is a farmer. ch.: 1, Hosea, Jan. 12, 1806, m. 1, Bethia Curtis, Oct. 24, 1827, who d. July 13, 1831; 2, Maria A. Hawes, 1831, who d. Sep. 1841; and 3, Mary E. Stone, June 10, 1843; lives in H'm., is a shoemaker, and has ch., *Geo. B.*, Oct. 19, 1828, (m. Mary Damon, Mf'd., Jan. 1, 1851, and lives in Wey'h.); *Alfred B.*, June 27, 1832; and *Florinda C.*, Oct. 22, 1839. 2. Ann, Mar. 6, 1808, m. Spencer Shaw, Ap. 1, 1838. 3. Chas., March 30, 1811, m. Lydia Whiting. April 1, 1838, lives in Wey'h., and has *Rowena C.*, and *Chas. D.* 4.

Jane, May 26, 1813, m. Chas. Shaw, Cummington. 5. Persis, January 2, 1815, m. John Haynes, Charlestown. 6. Ruth, m. May 10, 1817, m. Jno. W. Penniman, H'm., Feb. 26, 1837. 7. Harriet, June 27, 1819, m. Dexter M. Wolcott, Jan. 8, 1843. 8. Dexter, Jan. 5, 1824, m. Ann Tisdale, Oct. 20, 1847, and lives in H'm.; no ch. (By 2d,) 9. Alice R., June 6, 1846.

57. Perez, s. Amasa 33, a carpenter by trade, m. 1, Mary Bowker, Scit., Nov. 13, 1799, who d. Ap. 4, 1823, and 2, Sarah Simmons, Dux'y.; and lives in So. H'm. His 2d w. is also d. ch.: 1. Perez S., Oct. 19, 1800, m. Lucy C., da. Hon. E. F. Jacobs, and lives in N. Y'k. 2. Mary, Feb. 6, 1802, m. Rev. Calvin Gardner, Waterville, Me., Dec., 26, 1825. 3. Adaline, Feb. 2, 1804, m. Ed. Jacobs, Scit., Ap. 16, 1826. 4. Caroline, Feb. 2, 1804, m. Laban Jacobs, H'm., Feb. 2, 1823. 5. Geo., Mar. 1, 1806, d. Ap. 7, 1823. 6. Chas., May 29, 1808, m. Anna C. Fearing, H'm., Jan. 10,, 1830, is a mf'r. of edge tools, in H'm., near Accord Pond, and has *Chas. D.*, Mar., 1831, d. June, 1848; *Cath. B.*, 1835; and *Geo. F.* 7. Albert, Feb. 23, 1810, a master mason, and contractor, m. Sarah G. Fearing, H'm., and has *Albert T.*, Sep. 30, 1833, clerk with J. J. Whiting & Co., Boston; *Geo. F.*; and *Sarah H.*, Mar. 21, 1849. 8. Winslow L., Ap. 1, 1813, m. Ann E. Ripley, of H'm., lives in Newark, and has ch. 9. Benj. S., Mar. 22, 1815, m. Olive Fearing, H'm., who d. ab. 1849, and he is living in Ab'n. Has *Webster A.*, Sep. 27, 1840; *Shurtleff;* and *Olive A.* 10. Davis J., Nov. 15, 1816, unm. 11. Julia A., Feb. 7, 1820, m. Wm. Brown, shoe manf'r., Ab'n.

58 Joseph Jacob Whiting

(Capt. Joseph J.) s. Amasa 33, a house carpenter by trade, and for many years a highly respectable master mechanic in Bos'n., m. 1, Anna E. Crane, and 2, Cath. Bowker; lived latterly in S. H'm., where his son Amasa now resides, where he d. in Oct. 1838. A view of his residence is given in the Frontispiece. ch.: 1. Joseph J., b. in Bos'n., June 25, 1818, and now an extensive merchant in B., of the firm of Whiting, Kehoe & Galloupe, dealers in clothing, &c., on Federal st. Not m. 2. Amasa, Oct. 15, 1821, m. Hannah L. Fearing, H'm., lives on his father's place, and has ch., *Mary L.*, June 21, 1845, and *Amasa J.*, Ap. 2, 1849. 3. Catherine, Jan. 24, 1823 ? d. Oct. 9, 1826.

59. Benj., s. Benj., 34, m. Lydia Stoddard, Dec. 10, 1797, and lives in H'm., near Accord Pond. A blacksmith by trade. ch.: 1. Jared, May 26, 1798, d. Dec. 1817. 2. Richard, Ap. 19, 1800, m. Mary Stoddard, lives in H'm., and is a shoemaker; no ch. 3. Lydia, Jan. 3, 1803. 4. Maria, Dec. 7, 1804, m. Freeman House, H'm. 5. Joanna, Mar., 1807, m. Freeman French, H'm., Dec. 28, 1826. 6. Joel, May, 1809, m. Eunice Ide, of Seekonk, lives in Ab'n., is a shoemaker, and has *Benj. S.*, d. young; and *Eunice I.* 7. Pamela, Oct. 6, 1814, m. Benj. Mann, Hanover. 8. Jared, Mar. 31, 1819, not m. 9. Elizab., Oct. 1821, m. Jas. M. Burrill, H'm.

60. Elijah, s. Elijah 43, m. 1, Susan Beal, who d. Aug. 1, 1812; and 2, Mary Lincoln, Wey'h; lived in H'm., was a packet man, of the line running from Bos'n. to H'm., and d. in H'm., June 17, 1841, ae. 61. ch.: 1. Susan L., Dec. 27, 1809, m. Eben'r. Pratt, Bos'n. (By 2d,) 2. Elijah L., Jan. 15, 1814, m. Rachael C. Lincoln, H'm., Jan. 1, 1840, lives in H'm., is a hatter, and has ch., *Dexter B.*, 1842; *Charlotte L.*, 1844; and *Mary L.*, Aug., 1848. 3. Bela H., Feb. 14, 1816, wheelwright, lives in H'n., m. Hannah, da. Ezra Whiting, Feb. 22, 1844, and has *Frances H.*, Jan. 30, 1846, and *Elenor R.*, Jan. 24, 1848. 4. Fred'k., May 4, 1818, hatter, of Bos'n., m. Sarah Waters, and has *Sarah W.*, and *Susan.* 5. Mary L., Ap. 17, 1820, m. Sidney Sprague, H'm. 6. Lucy, Oct. 9, 1822, m. Luther Sprague, H'm. 7. Erastus, Jan. 11, 1826, m. Priscilla Burr, in Jan. 1853, and lives in H'm. 8. Jno. C., Aug. 21, 1828, of Bos'n.; not m.

61. David, s. Moses 45, m. Nabby Fearing, H'm., Jan. 16, 1803, and was for many years a diligent and successful merchant in H'm., in the grain and flour business. He d. Aug. 14, 1843. ae. 68. ch.: 1. Merriall, Dec. 3, 1803. 2. Nabby F., Sep. 6, 1805, m. Morris Fearing, H'm. 3. Mary R., Sep. 28, 1806, d. Jan. 2, 1808. 4. Mary R., June 18, 1808. 5. David, Oct. 9,

1809, m. 1, Lucy P. Dorr, Bos'n., Nov. 3, 1842, who d. Sep. 4, 1843; and 2, Ellen L. Kelloran, of Portland, Me., and is of the well known firm of Whiton, Train & Co., Bos'n.: no ch. 6. Wm., Nov. 3, 1811, m. Abig. Ripley, of H'm., Jan. 31, 1849, is of the firm of Whiton, Train & Co., and has ch., *Abby H.*, Jan., 20, 1840, d. ae. 2; *Wm. T.*, d. ae. 3; *Chas F.*, Aug. 20, 1844; *Lucy D.; Abby R.;* and *Laura* and *Fanny*, twins, b. Mar. 23, 1851. 7. Harriet, Jan. 9, 1814. 8. Lydia R., Feb. 11, 1816. 9 Thos. F., Ap. 14, 1821, merchant, Bos'n.

62. Wilson, s. Moses 45, m. Chloe White, Wey'h., Oct. 21, 1804, and for many years kept the well known packet station, at the head of Long Wharf, Bos'n. He is yet living, in H'm. ch.: 1. Wilson, Feb. 1, 1805. 2. Jane T., Mar. 31, 1807. 3. Thos. J., Mar. 7, 1809, of Bangor, Me., is m., and has 2 ch. 4. Jno. P., June 13, ? 1811, m. 1, Maria E. Orne, Camb., Feb. 5, 1838, who d. May 5, 1844; and 2, Lydia B. Bancroft, of Danvers, in June, 1846; is a merchant in Bos'n.; and has ch., *Jno. W.*; *Chas. H.*; (By 2d,) *Maria L.*; lost one son, d. young. 5. Henry, Aug. 14, 1812, ? of Bos'n.; not m. 6. Adaline, Sep. 16, ? 1816. 7. Elizab. H., Mar. 2, 1820. 8. Sarah C., Ap. 5, 1822, d. Sep. 29, 1823.

63. Moses, s. Moses 45, m. Ann Stoddard, H'm., Jan. 7, 1810, lives in H'm., and is a grain dealer, at the Cove. ch.: 1. Moses L., May 1, 1814, m. Sophia M. Parker, Bos'n., Jan., 1837, lives in Somerville, and has ch., *Mary A.*, d. ae. 4; *Geo. H.*, 1840; *Sophia*, 1842; *Caroline E.*, d. ae. 4; and *Rachael P.*, June, 1848. 2. Mary A., June 8, 1816, m. Jno. W. Pierce, carpenter, Feb. 11, 1841. 3. Stark, of Bos'n.; not m. Some ch. d. young.

64. Starks, s. Moses 45, m. Hannah, da. Capt. Benj. Dyer, Wey'h., and was a merchant, in W. ch.: 1. Joseph, of Camb. 2. Lydia, m. Jno. P. Lovell, Wey'h. 3. Benj., d. unm. 4. Lucinda? 5. Hannah? m. a Reed, and lives in Bangor. The records of this family are wanting.

WILDER, Isaac, of H'm., s. Isaac, m. Ruth Mann, and lived in Hanover, on Main st., where he d. Mar. 30, 1818, ae. 41. His wid. survives. ch.: 1. Ruth, Ap., 1803, m. Vaniah Prouty, Sep. 11, 1822. 2. Isaac M., June 19, 1805, a trader at the Four Corners, m. Lucinda Eells, Feb. 5, 1834, and has ch., *Isaac*, Nov. 15, 1834; *Joseph E.*, Ap. 24, 1839; and *Lucinda*, July, 1841. 3. Hannah, Sep., 1807, d. Nov. 12, 1829. 4. Jno., 1809, m. Mary Tolman, and lives in Bridg'r. 5. David, 1812, of Bridg'r. 6. Caleb, d. May 22, 1818, ae. 16 mos.

2. Laban, bro. Isaac, and s. Isaac, of H'm., m. Rebecca Donnell, and d. in H., Mar. 6, 1848, ae. 63, and his w. ae. ab. 60. Lived on Main st., in the Chas. Donnell house. ch.: 1. Rebecca, m. Ansel G. Grose, of So. Scit., Nov. 27, 1826. 2. Jane, m. Ezek'l. T. Hatch, Oct. 16, 1833. 3. Laban, m. 1, Lucy C., da. Joseph Curtis, July 15, 1832, who d. Ap. 21, 1843, and 2, Harriet, da. Daniel Chapman, July 9, 1844, is a shoemaker, lives in So. Scit., and has sev. ch. 4. Chas., Dec., 1811, m. Mary A. Hayden, lives in So. Scit., is a shoemaker, and has also sev. ch. Another da. m. a Ford.

3. Joseph C., s. Joseph, jr., of H'm., b. June 13, 1815, m. Priscilla, da. Geo. W. Bailey, lives on King st., with his fa.-in-law, is a shoemaker by trade, and has ch.

WINSLOW. Five brothers of this name, ch. of Edward Winslow, of Droitwich, in Worcestershire, Eng'd., came early to New Eng'd., and from these have sprung most of that name now in the U. S. Edward, the first, known as Gov. Winslow, with his w. Elizab., came in the Mayflower, 1620; and his w. dying the spring after, he m. 2, Susanna, wid. of Wm. White, 1622, lived in Mf'd., at his seat called Caresrull, and there d. Gilbert, the 2d, arrived in the same vessel, but soon after left the colony, and it is said went to Portsmouth, and d. before 1660, without issue. Jno., the 3d, came in the Fortune, in 1621, and m. Mary Chilton, the adventurous maiden, who was the first to step on the memorable *rock* of Plymouth. Some of his dec'ts. live in Bos'n. Kenelm, the 4th, arrived at Plymouth, in 1629, m. Elenor, wid. of John Adams, 1631, and sett. in Mf'd. He had sons Kenelm, Nath'l., and Job, and d. in 1672. From the son Nath'l., descended Maj. Nath'l., of Scit., the ancestor of Josiah Winslow, now living in H. Josiah, the 5th brother, came with Kenelm, in 1629, was in Scit. in 1637, and in Mf'd., after 1643, and d. in 1674, ae. 69, leaving ch. As but few of the descendants are now living in H., we do not deem it necessary to extend our sketch further than to show the connexion between them and the original settlers.

2. Nath'l., s. Kenelm, m. Faith Miller, 1664, was of Mf'd., and his oldest son,. Nath'l., b. 1667, m. Lydia Snow, 1692, and had *Oliver*, 1702, who was of Scit., m. 1, Agatha Bryant, and 2, Bethia Prior, 1749, and lived near the 3d Herring Brook, where his descendants still reside. His ch., bap. in Hanover, were 1. Oliver, killed in the French war, in 1758, leaving a son *Oliver*, a Rev'n. pensioner, in Scit., now d. 2. Ruth, July 22, 1739. 3. Nath'l., Oct. 11, 1741. 4. John, Feb. 5, 1743, moved to Nobleboro', Me. (By 2nd,) 5. Bethiah, Sep. 29, 1751. 6. Joseph, 1753, d. early.

3. Nath'l., s. Oliver, s. Nath'l. 2, early espoused the Am. cause, in the Rev'n. War, entered the Army in 1776, rose to the rank of *Major*, and acquitted himself with honor in the southern expeditions. He m. Sarah Hatch, 1766, and was fa. of Nath'l., b. 1767, who m. Clarissa, da. Ebn'r. Curtis, of H., Oct. 13, 1796, and had *Josiah*, now of H., who m. Abigail, da. Lemuel Curtis, and lives on Washington st., ab. one mile N. of the Four Corners. No children.

4. Thomas, s. Thos., of Plym'h., m. 1, Ruth Grose, Feb. 20, 1810, who d. Feb. 13, 1828, ae. 45; and 2, Harriet Delano, of Dux'y. A carpenter by trade. ch.: 1. Thos. G., July 20, 1800, m. 1, Susan, W. Gardner, of H'm., Oct. 28, 1822; and 2, a Pollard, of Me., lived in Boston, and d. ab. 1846. 2. Joshua, May 12, 1801. 3. Charles, May 16, 1803. 4. Richmond, July 30, 1804. 5. Pelham, Nov. 17, 1805. 6. Lucy T., Sep. 26, 1808, m. Geo. Hildreth, of Dorch'r., May 24, 1830. 7. Henry, Nov., 1810. 8. Wm., Feb. 10, 1812. 9. Ruth G., July 24, 1814. 10. Elizab., b. Feb. 9, d. June 23, 1816. 11. Elenor J., Dec. 28, 1816, m. Isaiah Jenkins, and d. 1848. 12. Samuel, Oct. 14, 1818, d. Oct. 14, 1820. 13. Mary, Nov. 22, 1819, m. David Freeman, of Dux'y. 14. Priscilla B., Dec. 28, 1821. 15. Samuel. L. F., Nov. 18, d. Dec. 27, 1825.

5. Charles, s. Thos. 4, m. Margaret L. Litchfield, in 1827, lives on Circuit st., and is a shoemaker by trade. Was Selectman

from 1846–48. ch.: 1. Charles L., Mar. 3, 1828. 2. Rachel F., June 16, 1832, m. Chas. Josselyn, May 16, 1850. 3. Helen, Feb. 9, 1838.

6. Richmond, s. Thos. 4, m. Harriet Howard, of Dux'y., Jan. 10, 1828, lives on Circuit st., and is an anchor smith by trade. ch.: 1. Samuel R., Mar. 14, 1829, m. Elizab. Bates, Mar. 22, 1849, and lives in Plym'h. 2. James B., Oct. 22, 1830. 3. Rebecca H., Sep. 22, 1832. 4. Erastus B., July 14, 1834. 5. John A., Mar. 2, 1837. 6. Joshua S., July 15, 1840. 7. Daniel W., Dec. 15, 1842. 8. Frederick R., Ap. 2. 1848.

7. Henry, s. Thos. 4, m. Harriet, da. Nath'l. Pratt, June 15, 1835, lives on Summer st., and is a shoemaker. ch.: 1. Harriet F., Feb. 10, 1841.

WOLCOTT, Rev. Calvin, a desc't. of the noted family of Wolcotts, of Ct., m. Sarah, da. Col. Saml. Gardner, of Danvers, Mass., collat. desc't. of Gen. Putnam, of Ct., and was sett. in H., as Rector of St. Andrew's Church, from 1818 to 1834, and is now colleague with Rev. Dr. Tyng, of N. York. ch.: 1. Elizab. G., b. in Marblehead, Dec. 30, 1812, m. Dr. Jacob Richards, of Braintree, and is d. 2. Augustus C., b. at Danvers, Oct. 15, 1814, d. at Havana, in 1832. 3. Sarah A., b. at Marblehead, Mar. 27, 1817. Not m. 4. Samuel G., b. in Hanover, Jan. 2, 1820, grad. Wash. Coll., Hartford, Ct., and is sett. as a Physician in Utica, N. Y. 5. Henrietta B., b. in Hanover, May 15, 1823, m. Edwin A., s. Hon. Joseph Richards, of Braintree, and lives in B. 6. Asa G., b. in Hanover, Ap. 25, 1825, grad. Wash. Coll., and is sett. in N. Y. city, as a Teacher of Languages. 7. George C., b. in H., July 15, 1827, grad. B. U., 1848, and d. Oct. 24, 1851. Principal of the Acad. in H. for one term.

WOOD, Alexander, Esq., s. Ichabod, of Midd'o., b. Nov. 5, 1796, m. Louisa Bourne, of M., Oct. 1824, lives near the Four Corners, was formerly a lawyer. Is P. M., and has been engaged in trade for many years. ch.: 1. Louisa B., Mar. 21, 1826. 2. Wm. B., Oct. 27, 1831. 3. Ed. F., Sep. 28, 1834. 4. Henry A., Oct. 22, 1836. 5. Ellen P., Dec. 25, 1838. 6. Lucy P., Jan. 16, 1843, d. Feb. 15, 1850.

2. Abner, s. Ezra, of Midd'o., m. 1, Marg't. Bessey, and 2, Mary Bessey, and lives on Centre st. ch.: 1. Abner A., July 1, 1827. 2. Marg't. B., Mar. 1, 1831. 3. Ezra, Nov. 11, 1833. 4. Mary B., July 19, 1835. (By 2d,) 5. Charles R., May 12, 1848.

WOODMAN, James, s. Barney, of Scit., m. Mary C. Bates, Nov. 24, 1850, lives on Centre street, and is a carpenter by trade. ch.: Mary V., Mar. 15, 1851.

WRIGHT, Warren, s. Levi, of Plymp'n., m. Ruth J. Haskins, of Scit., May 29, 1839, and lives near the Four Corners, in the house built by himself. A blacksmith by trade. ch.: Warren J., Feb. 26, 1846. 2. Frances J., June 12, 1848.

APPENDIX.

Barstow Family. Since this work went to press, we have obtained the following additional particulars relative to the Barstow family. The *original* name seems to have been *Burstow;* and we find this name in Sussex Co., in the reign of Edward II., A. D., 1308, at which date grants were made to *Roberto de Burstowe.* See "Documents Illustrative of English History, in the 13th and 14th Centuries," in the N. E. Gen. Soc. Lib.; and Rymer's Foedera, vol. 3. In the reign of Henry III., A. D., 1271, we find in Suffolk Co., *Will. de Burstowe,* and *Christiana, his wife.* See "Excerpta Rotulis," &c., vol. 3, in the N. E. Gen. Soc. Lib. In the "History of Surrey and Sussex," pub. in London, in 1829, vol. 2, p. 273, we find the parish of *Burstow* described, which is "situate in the weald of Surrey, and is not mentioned in Domesday Book. It adjoins Horne on the east, Horley on the west, Blechingley and Nutfield on the north, and Worth, in Sussex, on the south. In 1821, there were 915 inhabitants, and 106 houses in this parish. The manors of *Burstow Court lodge, Burstow, Burstow lodge,* and Red hall, are situate in this parish, and principally belong to M. Sanders and T. Dickson, Esqrs. The benefice is a rectory, in the deanery of Ewell. It is rated in the valor of Ed. I. at 12 marks, in the king's book at £15 13*s.* 4*d.* It is a peculiar of the Archbishop of Canterbury, and is in the patronage of the king. The church, dedicated to St. Bartholomew, consists of a nave and south aisle, a chancel, and a wooden turret and steeple at the west end. The interior is particularly neat. On Smallfield Common, in this parish, is the remaining part of a mansion-house, built of stone, which belonged to the family of *De Burstow*, and passed from them to that of Byshe, long settled there. It was formerly called Cruttings, and was given by Bartholomew, (Lord Burgherst,) to John de Burstow, as an acknowledgment for assistance received from him when thrown from his horse in an engagement with the French. The house, of which part is now standing, is supposed to have been erected by Edward Byshe. He was a bencher of Lincoln's Inn, and a great practitioner in the Court of Wards, where he amassed his fortune, and used jokingly to say, that he "built his house with woodcocks' heads."

We think it probable, that branches of this family,—the Burstows,—settled in Yorkshire; and from the latter, sprung the Barstows who emigrated to America.

www.ingramcontent.com/pod-product-compliance
Lightning Source LLC
LaVergne TN
LVHW020933110826
845150LV00004B/847

* 9 7 8 1 4 2 5 5 5 2 7 8 7 *